Y0-DYV-645

DONALD MARQUAND DOZER

Are We Good Neighbors?

Three decades of
Inter-American relations
1930-1960

University of Florida Press

Gainesville-1959

1960

OCT

64222

To My Father With Gratitude

A University of Florida Press Book

COPYRIGHT, 1959, BY THE BOARD OF
COMMISSIONERS OF STATE INSTITUTIONS OF FLORIDA
ALL RIGHTS RESERVED
LIBRARY OF CONGRESS CATALOGUE CARD No. 59-13537
PRINTED BY H. & W. B. DREW COMPANY, JACKSONVILLE, FLORIDA

Are We Good Neighbors?

Three decades of
Inter-American relations
1930-1960

2⁴⁷

Other Inter-American Titles

BARTOLOME DE LAS CASAS—HISTORIAN by Lewis Hanke

DIFFERENTIAL FERTILITY IN BRAZIL by J. V. D. Saunders

THE EMERGENCE OF THE REPUBLIC OF BOLIVIA
by Charles W. Arnade

THE "FUERO MILITAR" IN NEW SPAIN, 1764-1800
by Lyle N. McAlister

GRINGO LAWYER by Thomas W. Palmer

LAND REFORM AND DEMOCRACY by Clarence Senior

MAN AND LAND IN PERU by Thomas R. Ford

MIRANDA: WORLD CITIZEN by Joseph F. Thorning

PEASANT SOCIETY IN THE COLOMBIAN ANDES
by Orlando Fals-Borda

SANTA CRUZ OF THE ETLA HILLS by Helen Miller Bailey

SEARCH FOR A LATIN AMERICAN POLICY by Thomas W. Palmer, Jr.

A WORKING BIBLIOGRAPHY OF BRAZILIAN LITERATURE
by José Manual Topete

Foreword

SCHOLARS ENGAGED in Latin American studies and
not a few members of Congress have viewed with
favor and appreciation the change in attitude in the United States
toward the Latin peoples of the Western Hemisphere that characterized the years following 1929. This has been especially true of the
policies of the Franklin D. Roosevelt administration, which have
been described as the policies of the Good Neighbor.

But while scholars and congressmen have been fairly familiar
with the suspicion, fear, and even hostility of the leaders of Latin
America during much of the nineteenth century and the early decades of the twentieth and had gained the general impression that
these unpleasant sentiments had tended later to disappear, they have
lacked the documentary evidence warranting this general impression.
The amazing industry and acumen of Professor Donald M. Dozer
have at last enabled him to set forth the factual basis for this general
belief. No other volume has dealt so fully and carefully with this
record, and both Professor Dozer and the University of Florida Press
merit the thanks of all those who are interested in this important
phase of inter-American relations.

Many have now begun to feel that these relations have deterio-
rated since the departure of the second Roosevelt, Cordell Hull, and
Sumner Welles from their dominant positions in American diplomacy.
I have discussed inter-American relations before many audiences in
recent years and have often been questioned about this deterioration.
I have not felt justified in positively stating that no adverse modifi-

v

cation has occurred. I have limited my response to the assertion
that our neighbors have felt neglected, have suffered from disappointment, and that, in view of the crises confronted in the rest of
the world, this was probably inevitable. On some occasions, however,
I have added that diplomats of succeeding administrations may have
"lacked the Roosevelt tact" and that such change of sentiment as
had occurred among our Latin neighbors might be attributed in
part to this deficiency, in part to their failure properly to assess the
magnitude of the Soviet menace, in part to Marxist propaganda, in
part to the possibility that Latin mistrust had never entirely disappeared, and in part to inadequate information regarding the extent
of assistance that they have received from the United States, directly
and indirectly, officially and from private sources.

Professor Dozer has dealt with inter-American relations since 1930
as a background to an understanding of the present relations between
Latin America and the United States. What he has done in a superb
manner is this: for the years 1933 through 1945 he has set up a
model and has laid a firm foundation for all studies of both subsequent and previous periods. For the period since 1945 he has presented abundant evidence to explain the deterioration which has
occurred in inter-American relations and has analyzed it convincingly. I must confess that his account of inter-American relations
during the period 1933 through 1945 has been most helpful to me
in the preparation of my small volume entitled *Globe and Hemisphere*,
in which I have tried to present the postwar relations of the United
States and Latin America in their world setting. Indeed, I must
further confess that I have not had access to the resources required
for a survey of Latin American opinion with Professor Dozer's patient
thoroughness. His is a significant book which deserves to be carefully
read by all who are concerned with this very vital subject, and that
should mean every literate citizen of both the United States and
Latin America.

J. FRED RIPPY

Preface

*7*HIS IS A BOOK about the two Americas—the United
States and Latin America—and their interaction
upon each other during the past three decades. What were the reactions of the Latin Americans to the Good Neighbor Policy of the
United States and to World War II? How have they been affected
by the cold war between the United States and Soviet Russia? How
solid are the relations of the United States with the Latin American
nations today? In a future hot war can the United States count upon
the support of the peoples to the south?

These are some of the questions that this book seeks to answer. It
presents the record of inter-American relationships since 1930 and
deals with those relationships as a background to present problems. It
is intended to contribute to a better understanding between the two
Americas. It therefore offers suggestions as to what can be done to
create among all the nations of the Western Hemisphere a durable
conviction of a common Pan-American destiny.

The United States and the twenty Latin American nations together
comprise almost one-fifth of the land mass of the world and more
than one-seventh of its population. The area south of the United
States must be considered as many separate geographical and population entities. Generalizations that treat Latin America as a unit,
therefore, must be made with caution. The same must be said for
generalizations that treat of this area only in terms of the ruling
classes. For Latin America is people—about 175 million of them—
and not just twenty governments.

When this book presents Latin American viewpoints it seeks to give a comprehensive coverage of all viewpoints, often in the language of the Latin Americans themselves. In those sections of the book I have therefore conceived it to be my role to serve chiefly as compiler, showing not what is necessarily true in inter-American relations but what Latin Americans consider to be true. An author obviously cannot accept or identify himself with all these viewpoints, many of which are mutually contradictory. Without attempting to analyze all the problems in inter-American relations I have sought to get beneath the surface to the Latin American mind and to interpret inter-American relations not in the routine formulas of the diplomats but in terms of the feelings of the peoples.

The United States has a large stake in Latin America. Not only does our national life depend upon the products of that area, but we could not permanently endure in a hemisphere of unfriendly peoples. In times of stress we may find sullen, bitter neighbors in the Western Hemisphere almost as disagreeable as armed enemies. The Latin American countries, though individually weak in comparison with the United States, taken together constitute a powerful bloc whose friendship or enmity may be a decisive factor in our very survival.

Efforts by the people of the United States and Latin America to know each other better are investments in goodwill which draw compound interest. They are money in the bank to be drawn upon in future emergencies. If there is indeed no such thing as love between nations there is nevertheless the possibility of something just as adequate—understanding between peoples. Merely knowing one's neighbors creates a bond of sympathy with them. In both the Americas one finds people who are well disposed toward the other. The indispensable thing is to strengthen the mystic cords which bind together these men and women of goodwill. In this process they must move to meet each other. Together they can constitute a force of almost limitless possibilities in the future world. Nothing should be allowed to obscure or weaken the basic unity of interest which is so essential to relations of good neighborliness among the peoples of the Western Hemisphere.

This book has grown out of my personal experiences as an official in several United States government agencies concerned with Latin America from 1941 to 1956 and a study of a wide selection of source materials, including newspaper and magazine articles, reported interviews and official statements, books of comment and opinion, radio commentaries, public-opinion polls, travelers' descriptions, and scientific studies and reports. In preparing it I have found the staffs of the Library of Congress, the Pan American Union, the International Cooperation Administration, the Records Service Center of the State Department, and the United Nations Information Center in Washington unfailingly helpful. Acknowledgment is also made here to the following friends and associates who have given more than generously of their time and advice: Professor Roland Dennis Hussey, Mrs. Mary Ellen Milar, Mrs. Daisy Biggs, Miss Ann Peyton, Mr. Belisario Contreras, Dr. Alexandre de Seabra, Miss Alyce Jacobs, Mr. William Sanders, and Dr. George Wythe. Special thanks are due to Professor J. Fred Rippy of the University of Chicago for much helpful guidance and to many Latin American friends, particularly Dr. Carlos Urrutia Aparicio, Dr. Abelardo Patiño, Dr. José María Cháves, Dr. Rafael Heliodoro Valle, and Mr. Enrique Sylto. To these partners in interest goes the credit if I have been able to write, as was my hope, without "leaving anything at the bottom of the inkwell," in Sancho Panza's phrase. But they must be acquitted of responsibility for errors of fact and interpretation that, despite an author's best efforts, sometimes intrude. For the efficiency and cooperation of Dr. Lewis Haines and his associates at the University of Florida Press, especially Mr. Henry W. Limper, I express my thanks. My wife has furnished immeasurable help to me at every stage of the prolonged work on this book. To all these benefactors I owe obligations which were as pleasant to incur as they are impossible to repay.

D. M. D.

University of California
Santa Barbara
September, 1959

Contents

FOREWORD.. v

PREFACE.. vii

I. CALIBAN TRANSFIGURED.................................... 1

II. HEMISPHERIC ISOLATION.................................... 38

III. ON THE BRINK OF WAR.................................... 70

IV. PARTNERS IN WARTIME.................................... 109

V. "YANQUI" TRAITS.................................... 152

VI. WEAKENING PARTNERSHIP.................................... 188

VII. ILLUSION AND DISILLUSION.................................... 226

VIII. NEW DIRECTIONS IN LATIN AMERICA.................................... 274

IX. REACTION TO THE COLD WAR.................................... 310

X. CHARTING THE FUTURE.................................... 355

BIBLIOGRAPHY.................................... 415

INDEX.................................... 447

Chapter 1

CALIBAN TRANSFIGURED

Ariel, genius of the air, represents, in the symbolism of Shakespeare's work, the noble winged element of the spirit . . . transforming . . . the tenacious vestiges of Caliban, symbol of sensuality and baseness.
—José Enrique Rodó, *Ariel*, 1900

*T*HE UNITED STATES, by reason of both its real and its imagined thrusts toward its southern neighbors in the Western Hemisphere during the nineteenth century, came to be viewed by Latin Americans as an aggressive, imperialistic, expanding, and ruthless Yankee nation. Because of its concern for Cuba, manifested as early as the Jefferson and Madison administrations, it was characterized by a Cuban writer in 1811 as "a colossus which has been constructed of all castes and languages and which threatens to swallow up, if not all our America, at least the northern portion of it."[1] This characterization seemed to Latin Americans to be fearfully realized near the middle of the century when the United States occupied Mexico's capital city and imposed a treaty upon that country which transferred more than one-third of its territory to the government at Washington. The territorial appetite of the United States seemed insatiable as jingoists there talked about carrying the national boundaries southward to the Isthmus of Panama and bringing all of Mexico and all the Central American and Caribbean nations into the Union.

The United States thus became a source of apprehension and

1. Francisco Arango y Parreño, quoted in Carlos M. Trelles, *Estudio de la Bibliografía Cubana sobre la Doctrina de Monroe* (Havana, 1922), 219.

1

anxiety to Latin America. "That immense nation," commented a Mexico City newspaper in September, 1854, "like everything big frightens us, like everything strong seduces us, like everything rich arouses our envy and makes us forget the clay feet of the Anglo-American colossus to focus our attention upon its head of gold." Like the Russia of Czar Nicholas I, that newspaper continued, the United States "has physical greatness, a heterogeneous population, diversity of customs and institutions, the insolence peculiar to an absolute government, and that spirit of aggression, that thirst for conquest which, like the cistern of the Danaides, can never be satiated."[2] As Latin Americans saw this image more clearly delineated before their eyes by such episodes in the 1850's as William Walker's filibustering activities in Central America and the Ostend Manifesto, they tended in their own interest to emphasize the Bolivarian ideal of Hispanic-American unity and to seek to perfect a strength and culture of their own.

The interest of the United States in Latin America flagged after the 1860's, not to revive again for two decades. With the launching of the modern Pan-American movement in 1889 the United States began to expand its commercial activities in that area. Its growing trade interests in Latin America, combined with its domestic policy of protectionism, aroused new apprehensions among Latin American patriots. The United States was beginning "to bring into the open its latent spirit of aggression," warned José Martí, who was soon to give his life in the cause of Cuban independence.[3] Near the close of the nineteenth century the United States signalized its new interest in Latin America by waging a war against Spain which left it in occupation of Cuba and in possession of Puerto Rico. These martial victories in the Caribbean, so humiliating to the parent country of Spanish America, restored the old stereotype of the United States as a bullying, imperialist nation and tended to confirm Latin Americans in their conviction that they belonged to a race of higher spirituality.

Their later attitude was persuasively set forth by the Uruguayan Hispanicist José Enrique Rodó, whose Ariel, first published in 1900, established the Caliban-Ariel concepts respectively for the United States and Latin America. Rodó considered that the United States, with all its emphasis upon liberty, work, public education, ingenuity,

2. *Correo de España,* Mexico City, September 27, 1854.
3. Quoted in José de Onís, *The United States as Seen by Spanish American Writers (1776-1890)* (New York, 1952), 198.

piety, optimism, and will, nevertheless gave "a singular impression of insufficiency and emptiness. . . . Orphaned of the basic traditions which set the course of its life, that people," he wrote, "has not known how to replace the inspiring idealism of its past with any high unselfish conception of the future. It lives only for the immediate, for the present, and it subordinates all its activity self-centeredly to its personal and collective well-being." The United States, he charged, follows a "pagan cult of health, dexterity, and strength" and makes even religion a prop to utility. Writing under the shock of the recent victory of the United States over Spain, Rodó concluded that Latin America's neighbors to the north "openly aspire to the position of leadership in world culture, to the direction of its ideas, and they consider themselves the creators of a type of civilization which will prevail. . . . It would be useless to try to convince them that the work done by . . . Aryan Europe during the past three thousand years on the shores of the Mediterranean, . . . a civilizing and glorious work which is still being carried on and in whose traditions and teachings we [Latin Americans] live, makes a sum which cannot be equaled by any equation of Washington plus Edison."[4]

For more than a generation Rodó was the plumed champion of Latin American cultural nationalism, racialism, traditionalism, and resistance to Yankee influences, which increased as the United States assumed its role as a world power after 1900. Its new concern for an interoceanic canal through the isthmus of Central America involved it in a sometimes interventionist canal diplomacy, and its government frequently abandoned its traditional nineteenth-century policy of diplomatic *laissez-faire* to take sides for or against established Latin American regimes. Its private capital penetrated into new areas of Latin America in search of profitable fields of investment. Its officials took over customs receiverships in several Caribbean and Central American countries, and its naval vessels and marines were used to employ *force majeure* in the implementation of government policy of policing disorderly and bankrupt nations. All these actions lent color to the Latin American image of the United States as an imperialist power, bent upon overwhelming Latin American nationality and culture.

4. *Ariel* (Barcelona, 1930), 80, 83-94. Propagandists of Spain and Spanish America exaggerated Rodó's disdain for the pattern of values in the United States; he admired some of the ideals and traits of its people. For a judicious appraisal of Rodó's thought see William Rex Crawford, *A Century of Latin-American Thought* (Cambridge, 1944), [79]-90.

Rodó's disciples have been legion. Through the writings and actions of Rubén Darío of Nicaragua, Antonio Prado of Brazil, Rufino Blanco-Fombona of Venezuela, Manuel Ugarte of Argentina, José Vasconcelos and Carlos Pereyra of Mexico, Francisco García Calderón and José Carlos Mariátegui of Peru, and a host of less important figures, this formidable and repellent image of the United States became established. The Yankees were commonly thought of in Latin America, as Jesús Semprúm expressed it in 1918, as "rough and obtuse Calibans, swollen by brutal appetites, the enemies of all idealisms, furiously enamored of the dollar, insatiable gulpers of whiskey and sausages—swift, overwhelming, fierce, clownish."[5] Referring to the role of the United States in "the dismemberment of Colombia" in 1903 and its "armed intervention in Nicaragua" after 1909, one of the lesser figures in this movement, Salvador R. Merlos, writing from San José, Costa Rica, in 1914, described the Yankees as "the eagles of the North, thirsting for blood and conquests."[6] The purpose of the United States in promoting the Pan-American movement, according to the Argentine statesman Roque Sáenz Peña, was "to make of America a market, and of sovereign states, tributaries."[7] Writing in 1925, an Argentine Under Secretary of Foreign Relations, Lucio M. Moreno Quintana, charged that the United States was pushing for "an advantageous commercial field by the absorption of the whole of Iberian America."[8] This absorption was being hastened by the money power of the United States of which the dollar was the symbol. "Every dollar that crosses our frontiers," protested the Mexican nationalist Isidro Fabela in 1926, "not only has stamped on its obverse the North American eagle but carries also in its hard soul the flag of the stars and stripes, which is today the most imperialistic in the world."[9] Yankee policy, complained a distinguished Liberal leader of Nicaragua to a representative of Rotary International in 1930, seemed designed to establish and maintain an "imperialistic hegemony" in Latin America.[10] In certain acts of all the administrations in Washington after 1900, Latin Ameri-

5. "El Norte y el Sur," *Cultura Venezolana*, Caracas, I (November and December, 1918), 132.
6. *América Latina ante el Peligro* (San José, Costa Rica, 1914), 6.
7. *Escritos y Discursos* (Buenos Aires, 1914), I, 163.
8. "Pan Americanism and the Pan American Conferences," *Inter America*, VIII (June, 1925), 434.
9. *Excelsior*, Mexico City, 1927, reprinted in *Cuadernos Americanos*, LXXIX (January-February, 1955), 56-60.
10. Francisco J. Medina, Managua, Nicaragua, May 1, 1930, "Memoran-

cans saw threats to their national, cultural, and sometimes even territorial integrity. How then could there be any real community of ideals and action between them and the United States?

The reaction in Latin America was to strengthen the idea of Hispanic solidarity as a counterweight to Anglo-Saxon hegemony in the New World. A pamphlet published in Havana in 1897 by José F. Gómez called for the formation "of a Latin Confederation on this continent against the Saxon preponderance represented by this Anglo-American Colossus which we have opposite us."[11] Such a confederation would enable Latin Americans to develop their own authentic racial and national tradition and to build up their own indigenous strength, undiluted and unhybridized by pressures from their non-Hispanic neighbor to the north. The Argentine Pan-Hispanist Manuel Ugarte wrote in 1910 that the only hope for the Latin American nations was to be found in a Pan-Latin movement from which the United States would be excluded.[12] In further defense against the Yankee peril an Argentine, Francisco V. Silva, writing in 1918, called for an aggressive Pan-Hispanic program of action for the "liberation" of Puerto Rico, the Falkland Islands, and the Panama Canal from control by non-Hispanic nations, for a Pan-Hispanic guaranty of "the integrity of Mexico," and for a concerted movement to counteract Yankee influence in the Dominican Republic, Cuba, and Central America.[13] Such sentiments were widely voiced by intellectual and political leaders in many parts of Latin America who, because of the illiteracy and inarticulateness of the great majority of the people of their countries, exerted an influence much greater than their numbers warranted. As a result, fear and resentment grew apace as the United States expanded its interests and pursued its policy of intervention in that area.

In the writings and speeches of the Argentine intellectual José Ingenieros this movement took the form of an eloquent *grito* of Latin American independence. Speaking in Buenos Aires in 1922 he

dum on Present Conditions in Nicaragua," enclosure in I. B. Sutton, Chairman, Finance Committee, Rotary International, to Secretary of State, August 24, 1930, Department of State Archives, Washington.

11. *La Solidaridad Latina en América* (Havana, 1897), pamphlet, 22 pages, cited in J. Fred Rippy, *Latin America in World Politics: An Outline Survey* (New York, 1928), 204.

12. *The Destiny of a Continent* (English translation, New York, 1925), 3-14.

13. *Reparto de América Española y Pan-Hispanismo* (Madrid, [1918]), 471.

characterized the United States as "the powerful neighbor and officious friend whose ruling class had converted the government into an instrument of imperialism and who had no other objectives than to gain sources of wealth and to speculate in the labor of human beings already enslaved by an iron-willed clique of unpatriotic and immoral bankers." The Monroe Doctrine had been converted into an instrument of this policy. "If," declared Ingenieros, "the Monroe Doctrine appeared during the past century to be a guaranty for the 'principle of nationalities' against the 'right of intervention' today we perceive that this doctrine, in its present interpretation, expresses the 'right of intervention' of the United States against the 'principle of Latin American nationalities.' A hypothetical guaranty has been converted into a present danger." This danger in its first phase consisted of the gradual mortgaging of the independence of the Latin American nations to United States capital through loans which were destructive of the sovereignty of the recipients. "Let us make sure," he enjoined, "that the cooperation of powerful friends does not take the form of a protectorate which may become a bridge to slavery." To prevent this result he urged the formation of a moral union of Latin Americans against foreign imperialistic capitalism, which would take the form of political, ideological, and social regeneration in each country, a new Latin American consciousness of racial and cultural solidarity, and perhaps eventually a political confederation.[14]

Here was revealed a deep-seated apprehension that the wealth of the United States and its "brooding omnipresence" boded little good to the Latin American countries. When the United States refused to join the League of Nations, the Latin American countries welcomed the League as a counterweight to the United States, and all of them, at one time or another, became members of the League.[15] Within the inter-American organization their efforts were directed toward the

14. "Por la Unión Latina Americana," *Nosotros,* Buenos Aires, XLII (October, 1922), [145]-158. For studies of these Latin American attitudes toward the United States see J. Fred Rippy, "Literary Yankeephobia in Hispanic America," *Journal of International Relations,* XII (January, April, 1922), 350-371, 524-538; and Clarence H. Haring, *South America Looks at the United States* (New York, 1929). See also Víctor Raúl Haya de la Torre, *Impresiones de la Inglaterra Imperialista y la Rusia Soviética* (Buenos Aires, 1932), 92; *El Antimperialismo y el APRA* (Santiago de Chile, 2d ed., 1936), 35-36, 152, and *¿A Donde Va Indo-américa?* (Santiago de Chile, 1935), 44. See also Crawford, *op. cit.,* 116-142.

15. John A. Houston, *Latin America in the United Nations* (New York, 1956), 4.

erection of juridical barriers against continued interventions by the United States. At the Sixth International Conference of American States at Havana in 1928 a resolution was introduced denouncing all forms of intervention, diplomatic as well as armed, permanent as well as temporary. It was strongly supported by Argentina, Peru, Mexico, Colombia, El Salvador, Honduras, and other Latin American delegations. The refusal of the United States delegation to accept this resolution was interpreted to mean that intervention would remain an essential part of its Latin American policy.[16]

By reason of its use of this "immense sanction" outside its borders the United States was characterized in 1931 by Dr. Carlos Saavedra Lamas of Argentina as the *gendarme fabuloso* or "fabulous policeman."[17] Possessed of incomparable economic power, it "is a colossus whose financial might has no equal in history," declared an editorial writer in *El Diario Ilustrado* of Santiago, Chile (June 26, 1930). The aim of the United States seemed to be "America for the Americans— of the North." Upon the assumption that such was the aim of the United States, Latin American delegations at the meetings of the Assembly of the League of Nations at Geneva in 1930 confidentially discussed a plan to form a union of the Latin American nations members of the League which would possibly supplant the Pan American Union.[18]

Moreover, the orgiastic 1920's laid bare many of the gaudy, meretricious aspects of life in the United States and introduced into the Latin American countries hordes of pelf-hungry speculators and thrill-greedy tourists from the north. To the Mexican José Juan Tablada, writing in 1931, the United States was the epitome of "material and moral bankruptcy, polarized around Wall Street . . . and having for its equator the girdle of the Venus of Hollywood, that citadel of sex appeal."[19]

The odious aspects of life in the United States were graphically depicted in murals painted on the interiors of buildings from California to New York by two of Mexico's outstanding artists, Diego Rivera and José Clemente Orozco, between 1930 and 1934. These muralists represented their host country as a soulless phantasmagoria wracked by

16. República de Cuba, *Diario de la Sexta Conferencia Internacional Americana* (Havana, 1928), 486-505.

17. *La Nación*, Buenos Aires, June 1, 1931.

18. Memorandum from Dr. Leo S. Rowe, Pan American Union, to the Secretary of State, June 12, 1930, Department of State Archives.

19. *El Universal*, Mexico City, August 20, 1931.

strikes, dominated by the machine, and spiritually regimented.[20] It was small wonder that the intellectual and articulate classes in those countries took refuge in the conceit that Anglo-American civilization was a Caliban bent upon brutalizing and enslaving their Ariel-like culture! Their attitude of "contemptuous superiority" as befitting those who belong "to a race of higher spirituality" was sometimes expressed in the folk question "Did you ever see a pig look at the sky?"[21]

Particularly vocal and effective was the campaign of the *APRA* (*Alianza Popular Revolucionaria Americana*) of Víctor Raúl Haya de la Torre against "Yanqui" imperialism during the 1920's and early 1930's. As the young Haya de la Torre steamed out of New York City, Europe-bound, in 1924 he looked back at the statue supposed to be symbolic of liberty and surrounded by Wall Street. It no longer seemed such a symbol to him.[22] Later, as the movement which he inspired organized national centers in Cuba, Peru, Mexico, Puerto Rico, Argentina, Chile, and even Paris, the United States appeared rather as a sinister giant, using its economic power for the political subjugation of Panama, Nicaragua, Cuba, the Dominican Republic, Haiti, and other formerly independent countries and converting them into "true Yankee colonies or protectorates."[23]

To Haya de la Torre, North American imperialism had become "a gigantic monopolizer, the most perfect, complicated, and dangerous of the world's imperialisms."[24] It was particularly dangerous to Indo-America because of its proximity. North American businessmen, as they wrung concessions from Latin American governments, were only spreading "vices, corruption, false horizons of life and progress."[25] Even when the United States appeared in the role of arbitrator in disputes between Latin American states, he charged, it always contrived deliberately to "leave the apple of discord" among them.[26] Its intervention even for good appeared always to produce baneful effects.

* * *

20. Laurence E. Schmeckebier, *Modern Mexican Art* (Minneapolis, 1939), 93-95, 146-153; Lewis Mumford, "Orozco in New England," *New Republic,* LXXX (October 10, 1934), 231-235; Bertram D. Wolfe, *Diego Rivera: His Life and Times* (New York, 1939), 330-376; and Diego Rivera, *Portrait of America* (New York, 1934), *passim.*
21. Jorge Fernández, *El Comercio,* Quito, May 4, 1944.
22. *Impresiones,* 92.   23. *El Antimperialismo,* 25-36.
24. *Ibid.,* 152.   25. *¿A Donde Va Indo-américa?,* 44.
26. *El Antimperialismo,* 36.

In the late 1920's both the people and the government of the United States made it an object of high concern to improve Latin America's attitudes toward them. Antipathy to the United States south of the Rio Grande had reached an unprecedented degree of bitterness. "Never before in our history have we had fewer friends in the Western Hemisphere than we have today," wrote the governor of New York, Franklin D. Roosevelt, without exaggeration in *Foreign Affairs* in July, 1928. With large material interests in Latin America the United States could not afford to be confronted with a hostile public opinion there. By 1925 its trade with Latin America was considerably greater than the combined total of that of Britain, France, and Germany.[27] At the end of 1929 the book value of United States direct investments in Latin America was $3,518,739,000, which was much more than twice the value of its investments in any other geographical area of the world.[28] Might not the economic stake of the United States in Latin America and its supposedly large possibilities for future trade and investment there be blighted by a continuation of existing Latin American resentments?

In an effort to improve relations between the United States and Latin America, the Coolidge administration sent Dwight L. Morrow to Mexico to establish new bases of understanding with that country, and President-elect Herbert Hoover made a good-will tour through Central and South America, during the course of which he repudiated the "big brother" concept of relations between the United States and the Latin American countries and abjured both the principle and practice of intervention.[29] The Hoover administration encouraged presidents and presidents-elect of several Latin American nations to visit Washington and issued a "Memorandum on the Monroe Doctrine," prepared by Under Secretary of State J. Reuben Clark, which by assuring the Latin American nations that the Monroe Doctrine was "not an instrument of violence and oppression" attempted to dissociate that doctrine from the so-called Roosevelt Corollary to it. As more concrete evidence of the change of spirit in the United States the Hoover administration declined to undertake new military interven-

27. Rippy, *Latin America in World Politics,* 243.
28. Department of Commerce, *American Direct Investments in Foreign Countries* (Washington, 1930), 18.
29. Alexander De Conde, *Herbert Hoover's Latin American Policy* (Stanford, 1951), 21-22. See also Samuel F. Bemis, *The Latin American Policy of the United States: An Historical Interpretation* (New York, 1943), 202-225.

tions in Panama, Honduras, and El Salvador and made plans for an
early liquidation of intervention in Nicaragua, the Dominican Republic, and Haiti.[30] The policy of intervention, in particular, which the
United States had pursued—fairly consistently since 1895, except for
brief intervals—was subjected to much critical examination by the
administration.[31]

The effects of the interventionist policy upon the United States in
dollars and cents are difficult to appraise, for they are complicated by
such imponderable factors as the trade dislocations caused by World
War I and the economic depression after 1929. During the period
from 1910 to 1929, for example, when the United States almost continuously intervened in Nicaragua, its trade with that country steadily
increased from an annual average of $3.8 million in 1910-1914 to
$12.7 million in 1929. The subsequent decline in this trade to only
$8.4 million in 1930, $5.8 million in 1931, and $3.9 million in 1932
need not be attributed to a reaction against United States intervention
but can be explained by the world-wide economic depression of those
years. But the curve of United States trade with Nicaragua during the
period of its intervention there—1910-1933—quite faithfully followed
the curve of its general trade with the rest of Latin America during
the same period, from which conclusion it might be argued that United
States intervention did not produce any benefits for United States
commerce which would not have been obtained without intervention.
These benefits were even less apparent in the case of Haiti, whose annual average trade with the United States after the intervention of
Yankee troops there in 1915 did not show the same increase as did the
trade of Latin America generally with the United States, rising only
from $6.5 million in 1910-1914 to $10.2 million in 1929. The effects of
the ensuing economic depression upon Haiti's trade with the United
States were the same as those suffered by Latin American trade gen-

30. De Conde, *op. cit.,* 60-63, 80-89; and Department of State, *The
United States and Nicaragua: A Survey of the Relations from 1909 to 1932*
(Washington, 1932), *passim.*

31. Some of the books published in the United States criticizing this policy
toward Latin America were Scott Nearing and Joseph Freeman, *Dollar Diplo-
macy, a Study in American Imperialism* (New York, 1925); J. Fred Rippy,
The Capitalists and Colombia (New York, 1931); Emily Greene Balch (ed.),
Occupied Haiti (New York, 1927); Melvin M. Knight, *The Americans in
Santo Domingo* (New York, 1928); Harold N. Denny, *Dollars for Bullets, the
Story of American Rule in Nicaragua* (New York, 1929); and Margaret A.
Marsh, *The Bankers in Bolivia: A Study in American Foreign Investment*
(New York, 1928).

erally despite the continuance of the United States intervention in Haiti until 1934. That trade declined to $8.2 million in 1930, to $5.5 million in 1931, to $4.6 million in 1932, and on down to $4.4 million in 1933.[32]

Paucity of data makes it difficult to determine the effects of the interventionist policy of the United States upon the direct private investment of its citizens in Latin Amercia. Such investments in South American countries, in which the United States did not follow an overt interventionist policy in the 1920's, increased much more rapidly during those years than did similar investments in the Central American and Caribbean countries in some of which the United States maintained a marine occupation or operated customs receiverships.[33] Though such investment in the Central American and Caribbean countries showed some increases during the periods of intervention, adequate returns to the investors were made possible in many cases only through the landing of United States marines, the establishment of customs receiverships, and other interventionist procedures. Direct investment capital of United States citizens in Nicaragua, for example, increased from approximately $5 million in 1926 to $12 million in 1927, and $13 million in 1929; but some of this new capital was required to finance the elections held under United States supervision and to support the new *Guardia Nacional* organized by United States officers. In the more usual investment channels, contributing directly to the economic development of the country, investment proceeded slowly because of the adverse climate of opinion . "The intervention of the U.S. Government in the internal affairs of Nicaragua has proved a calamity for the American coffee planters doing business in this Republic," wrote one of these planters from Nicaragua to Secretary of State Henry L. Stimson. "Today we are hated and despised. . . . This feeling has been created by employing the American marines to hunt down and kill Nicaraguans in their own country."[34]

Not only did this policy appear to be injurious to United States capital investment, but it imposed an additional burden upon taxpayers in the United States. In 1931 the quartermaster general re-

32. Department of Commerce, *Statistical Abstract of the United States, 1934* (Washington, 1934), 424-425.
33. Department of Commerce, *American Direct Investments,* 23, and Cleona Lewis, *America's Stake in International Investments* (Washington, 1938), 606.
34. W. J. Hawkins, Matagalpa, Nicaragua, to Secretary of State Henry L. Stimson, June 10, 1931, Department of State Archives.

ported to the House Appropriations Committee that the cost to the
United States of maintaining its marines in the occupation of Nicaragua, the Dominican Republic, and Haiti up to that time had been
$8,941,816 over and above the cost of maintaining them at home.[35]
As a result of all these factors, the policy of subverting established
governments in Latin America and of maintaining unpopular regimes
in office by force came to be considered unprofitable in terms of dollars
and cents. The United States convinced itself that many years of experience of political intervention in certain Latin American countries
had not brought benefits either to it or to them. Secretary of State
Stimson acknowledged in a radio address delivered on May 9, 1931,
that "former differences with Mexico" and the marine occupations of
Haiti and Nicaragua "have damaged our good name, our credit, and
our trade" with Latin America.[36] "The policy of the *big stick*," observed *La Nación* of Buenos Aires (June 9, 1931), "has yielded bitter
fruits."

Quite apart from these "bitter fruits," however, the diminishing
trade of the United States with Latin America and its shrinking financial investment there resulting from the economic depression after
1930 counseled abandonment of the policy of intervention. The
reduced stakes of the United States made that policy appear inde-
fensible if not even a little ridiculous as an economic procedure in a
depression era—a policy incompatible with a contracting domestic
economy.

The overt abandonment of intervention by the Hoover administration and its other acts of repentance and goodwill began to soften the
attitudes of Latin Americans toward the United States. They hailed
this new "Hoover Doctrine," as it was called, as inaugurating "a new
era in the relations between the two sections of the Continent." "Once
this cause of ill-feeling is removed," declared *El Impulso* of Caracas
(April 21, 1931), "all the nations of the Continent are prepared to
cooperate with the best of will in drawing tighter the ties which bind
them." According to *Mundo al Día* of Bogotá "the whole South
American press commented favorably" on this policy and "expressed
the hope that it will serve as a basis for a policy of mutual understanding founded on respect for every right." The Clark memorandum, in particular, was interpreted enthusiastically as indicating that

35. *New York Herald Tribune*, February 10, 1931, reporting testimony
before the House Appropriations Committee on February 9, 1931.
36. Department of State, *Press Releases*, III (May 9, 1931).

the Monroe Doctrine had now become only "a historical relic" and an "irritating anachronism," that intervention by the United States in Latin America would be abandoned, and that fuller inter-American cooperation would become possible.[37] President Hoover's policy, declared *La Prensa* of Buenos Aires on May 3, 1931, "constitutes a decisive step toward bettering the relations between the United States and Central America and toward the consolidation of continental confidence."[38]

The United States was beginning to undergo a transformation that would soon delight the eyes of the Latin Americans. The Chilean ambassador to the United States, Carlos G. Dávila, told his countrymen in July, 1930, that there was "no vestige" of imperialism left in the United States. "American public opinion," he declared, "does not want to hear of political penetration nor even of any difficulties whatsoever with any of the countries of this hemisphere."[39] A sympathetic writer in *El Mercurio* of Santiago, Chile, observed in January, 1930, that "the so-called Yankee imperialism is nothing more than the power of money, which is and always will be required, just as the fields need rain."[40] Even this "power of money" was now being transmuted into an inoffensive kind of imperialism. The "new North American imperialism," an editorial in the same Chilean newspaper declared on July 8, 1930, was "that of commercial, technical, scientific, cultural and moral penetration. . . . That imperialism gathers its strength of penetration from the spirit of enterprise of the North

37. *El Tiempo,* Guatemala, March 29, 1930; *El Tiempo,* Bogotá, March 6, 1930; *El Espectador,* Bogotá, March 5, 1930; *Diario del Plata,* Montevideo, March 9, 1930; *La Mañana,* Montevideo, March 6, 1930; *La Prensa,* Buenos Aires, March 6, 1930; *El Orden,* Buenos Aires, March 12, 1930; *La Nación,* Buenos Aires, March 8, 1930; *El País,* Havana, March 29, 1930; *O Jornal,* Rio de Janeiro, March 7, 1930; *La Nueva Prensa,* San José, Costa Rica, April 4, 1930; *El Cronista,* Tegucigalpa, April 6, 1930; *Diario Moderno,* Tegucigalpa, May 5, 1930; *El Espectador,* San Salvador, May 10, 1930; *La Opinión,* Santo Domingo, May 23, 1930; and *El Mercurio,* Santiago, August 17, 1930.
38. Editorials of the same tenor appeared in *Heraldo de Cuba,* Havana, May 12, 1931; *Diario de la Marina,* Havana, May 14, 1931; *El Comercio,* Lima, May 11, 1931; *La Prensa,* Buenos Aires, April 25 and July 6, 1931; *La Nación,* Buenos Aires, July 3, 1931; *El Nuevo Tiempo,* Bogotá, July 6, 1931; *Excelsior,* Mexico, August 24, 1931; C. Bauer Aviles in *Nuestro Diario,* Guatemala, April 22 and May 24, 1932; and *El Telégrafo,* Guayaquil, July 4, 1932.
39. Address delivered in Santiago, Chile, July 6, 1930, and reprinted in English under the title *North American Imperialism* (New York, 1930), 10.
40. Emilio Tagle Rodríguez, "Yankee Imperialism in South America," *El Mercurio,* Santiago, Chile, January 5, 1930.

American, from the excellence of all his technical organization in the field of free competition and from the economic power of a people who have the capacity to try all possibilities." According to this writer, Carlos Silva Vildósola, one of the ablest newspaper men in Chile, the extension into foreign countries of the great forces of production and distribution developed by the United States constituted "a new form of legitimate imperialism: that of cooperation," which presented no danger to Latin America.[41]

The power and objectives of the United States, however, were not so generously interpreted elsewhere in the region. Haiti's delegate to the League of Nations complained in an address before the League in September, 1930, that Latin Americans were afraid of United States "imperialism," of "the shadow of a dreadnought behind each Yankee dollar."[42] A writer in *El Diario* of La Paz, Bolivia, attributed the plight of Latin America to "the capitalistic pressure of Yankee imperialism" which "was feudalizing their nations to North American gold and assassinating their liberties."[43] The center of this pressure seemed to be New York City. José Vasconcelos, writing from that city to *La Prensa* of Buenos Aires (May 24, 1931), explained that "the banana plantations of Honduras, the mines of Mexico, petroleum from Venezuela, wheat from the West and cotton from the South bring their unnecessary tribute here, thus supporting this nonsensical mercenary city with the harvest of a continent." To this Mexican nationalist philosopher, New York seemed the fitting symbol of the *Gigantasia* which was the United States. It would be better for Latin America, he wrote "if the blast of a cataclysm should sweep away the skyscrapers and the Island were to return to the ploughing of its smiling meadows in the period of the Dutch engravings." In this nation of "rackets," alleged a Colombian journalist, a giant "racket" had been organized in New York City for the diabolical purpose of acquiring a monopoly of all electric power, telephone systems, petroleum, banana and banking enterprises, mining concerns, and railroads in Latin America.[44] In fact, bitterly disgruntled voices were raised against "the Barbarians of the North," "enormously cruel and selfish," who

41. An appreciative estimate of Carlos Silva Vildósola as a leader of Chilean journalism was given by the Chilean poetess Gabriela Mistral in *El Mercurio,* Santiago, November 10, 1940.

42. *New York Times* editorial, September 14, 1930.

43. Abraham Váldez, "La Ciudadanía Continental," *El Diario,* La Paz, July 27, 1930.

44. Bernardo Angel, *El Heraldo,* Caracas, June 17, 1931.

were controlled by "a few rogues of Wall Street" and did not "lose a single moment in insulting and belittling us."[45]

The bitterness of the Latin Americans toward the United States obviously had not been erased; the chasm of hostility and misunderstanding between them had not been effectively bridged. Critics were quick to point out that the professions of good neighborliness and nonintervention by the Hoover administration were not immediately or consistently carried into practice. Its promises fell short of performance. For the Hoover administration to show, as it did by publishing the Clark memorandum in 1930, that the policy of intervention was not justified by the Monroe Doctrine was not enough, for it was the policy and fact of intervention itself that was considered objectionable. As long as intervention continued to be practiced by an Anglo-American nation derogating from the sovereignty of Spanish-American nations, the intervening nation would be disliked throughout Latin America. The Hoover administration's professions of a change of policy while it continued the practice of intervention only aggravated Latin America's grievance by making those professions seem hypocritical.[46] As late as November, 1932, the United States was still supervising presidential elections in Nicaragua, and it did not finally withdraw its marines, numbering more than 1,000, from that country until January, 1933. At the same time in Haiti the United States remained in control of the finances of the country and the *Garde Nationale*. In the Dominican Republic it continued to operate a customs receivership.[47] Latin American resentment at these delays in the liquidation of the interventionist policy of the United States was compounded by the Smoot-Hawley Act of 1930 which by heightening the tariff wall around the United States, stirred up talk of trade reprisals against it, notably in Argentina.[48]

As the economic depression swept over the United States after 1929, the former complaint that the "United States is too rich to be loved" lost much of its force in Latin America. Moreover, the accumulating mass unemployment in the United States after 1929 seemed to belie the vaunted perfection of its industrial system. This unemploy-

45. Vicente Romo Lamurro, "Before the Barbarians of the North," *El Noroeste,* Nogales, Sonora, Mexico, June 24, 1931.

46. Ambassador Robert Woods Bliss to Stimson, Despatch 1168, Buenos Aires, April 16, 1931. See also editorials in *La Prensa,* Buenos Aires, May 3, 11, and 13, 1931.

47. Dana G. Munro, *The United States and the Caribbean Area* (Boston, 1934), 141-142, 190-193.   48. De Conde, *op. cit.,* 75-77.

ment was attributed by an editorial writer in the official *La Opinión* of Santo Domingo in the Dominican Republic (December 4, 1930) to "the regime of trusts and the maladjustment which exists between the system of human labor and the progress of machines. . . . Over the people of the United States is the plutocracy of the United States, which is the highest inspiration of all American policies, both domestic and foreign." Some of these criticisms were believed in the United States to be Communist-inspired. Regardless of their source it was plain at the close of the Hoover administration that the United States still had a long way to go before winning the friendship and support of Latin America.

* * *

A nation blighted as was the United States after 1929 by a devastating economic depression unparalleled in its history was deemed in Latin America to be ready for a change in its political leadership. It was thought to have largely created its own plight by raising ever higher barriers against the importation of foreign products and at the same time endeavoring to find wider outlets for the products of its own vast industrial machine. The presidential election of 1932, conducted in time of national crisis and resulting in a victory for the Democratic candidate, Franklin D. Roosevelt, was acclaimed in Latin America as a "beautiful episode" in democracy,[49] and the triumph of his party was generally interpreted as evidence that the United States was bent upon "a policy of democratic and liberal action."[50] The Republicans, observed *O Jornal* of Rio de Janeiro, Brazil (November 11, 1932), "are always inclined to accentuate national aspects and to lean toward isolation, which forms a part of the traditional psychology of the Nation." Hoover's campaign, explained *La República* of La Paz (November 16, 1932), had been "supported by the great capitalist forces." The Democrats, on the other hand, observed *Excelsior* of Mexico City (November 10, 1932), "have always represented themselves in the political and social fields as the champions of the oppressed, of the immigrants, of the disabled, and, in general, of those dissatisfied with conditions. Their tendencies toward the betterment of the lower classes, however, have not a revolutionary origin but are mainly con-

49. *El Universal*, Mexico City, November 10, 1932.
50. *Jornal do Comércio*, Rio de Janeiro, November 11, 1932; and *La Prensa*, Buenos Aires, November 10, 1932.

servative." This same newspaper (November 9, 1932) regarded it as quite significant that although the United States had seven or eight million persons out of work "the good sense of the American public" rejected Communist and Socialist candidates, thus "maintaining itself faithful to its traditional good judgment, moderation, and devotion to the established order."[51] "It is probable that Mr. Roosevelt will be a great president," predicted *La Razón* of La Paz, Bolivia (November 11, 1932), a few days after his election.

But some apprehension was expressed that the new President might follow the same course toward Latin America as had his Democratic predecessor, Woodrow Wilson, whose interventionist actions had created bitter resentment south of the border. Had not Roosevelt admitted, even boasted, that while Assistant Secretary of the Navy he had written the new constitution for Haiti in 1918? Latin America's forebodings were allayed, however, by the new President's inaugural address on March 4, 1933, which was interpreted as showing that a profound transformation had taken place in the outlook and policy of the United States. "The weak nations now have no reason to fear the gigantic Republic of the North," exulted *El Orden,* an independent newspaper of Asunción, Paraguay (May 31, 1933). "This same nation," it added, "is abandoning its unsociable seclusion in order to constitute itself into an immense force at the service of humanity and of the peace and welfare of the world."

In particular, the international policy which Roosevelt announced in his first inaugural address seemed to augur new cooperative attitudes toward the peoples and governments of Latin America. This policy had been foreshadowed in the Democratic platform of 1932, which had called for "no interference in the internal affairs of other nations" and for "cooperation with nations of the Western Hemisphere to maintain the spirit of the Monroe Doctrine." The methods by which this might be worked out for Latin America had been embodied in a memorandum of suggestions to the president-elect from Sumner Welles. In that memorandum this intimate friend of Roosevelt, who was soon to become Assistant Secretary of State in charge of relations with Latin America, had proposed that "the creation and maintenance of the most cordial and intimate friendship between the United States and the other republics of the American Continent must be regarded as a keystone of our foreign policy." To establish this relationship the

51. *Excelsior,* Mexico City, November 9, 1932.

United States must abolish the impression that its policies involved "a threat to the sovereignty or to the national well-being of any republic of the Western Hemisphere." In particular the application of these policies "should never again result in armed intervention by the United States in a sister republic." In addition Welles went on to suggest the improvement of the procedure and machinery of consultation among all the American nations and the abolition of the "barriers and restrictions which now hamper the healthy flow of commerce between their respective nations."[52]

This policy, it is easy to recall, was set forth by Roosevelt in his inaugural address as the "policy of the good neighbor—the neighbor who resolutely respects himself and, because he does so, respects the rights of others—the neighbor who respects his agreements in and with a world of neighbors." A similar policy had been announced repeatedly by many of Roosevelt's predecessors and their associates in government but had been seldom followed. Secretary of State Henry Clay had characterized his policy toward Latin America with this phrase over a century before.[53] Secretary of State John Forsyth had referred to "the obligations of good neighborhood" in discussing the relations of his government with Latin America in 1835.[54] President Tyler in his message to Congress on December 7, 1841, had declared it to be "the ardent desire of the United States . . . to fulfill all the duties of good neighborhood toward those who possess territories adjoining their own." The treaty of Guadalupe Hidalgo of 1848 ending the war between the United States and Mexico mentioned "the spirit of . . . good neighborship" (Article XX). President Abraham Lincoln had advocated a policy of "strengthening our ties of goodwill and good neighborhood" with the republics of this hemisphere in a message to the Senate on May 30, 1862. Senator Charles Sumner of Massachusetts, in his "Naboth's Vineyard" speech in the Senate on December 21, 1870, urged that the United States follow a policy of "good neighborhood" toward the independent countries of the Carib-

52. Charles C. Griffin (ed.), "Welles to Roosevelt: A Memorandum on Inter-American Relations, 1933," *Hispanic American Historical Review,* XXXIV (May, 1954), [190]-192. This memorandum had been foreshadowed by Sumner Welles in the last chapter of his *Naboth's Vineyard: The Dominican Republic, 1844-1924* (New York, 1928), II, 913-937.

53. Samuel Flagg Bemis, *John Quincy Adams and the Foundations of American Foreign Policy* (New York, 1949), 557.

54. Forsyth to John G. A. Williamson, United States chargé d'affaires at Caracas, April 15, 1835, William R. Manning (ed.), *Diplomatic Correspondence of the United States,* XII, Document 5977.

bean Sea.[55] The phrase was also used by Secretary of State Thomas F. Bayard in the late 1880's.[56] It had formed the basis for policy and pronouncements on Latin American affairs by at least two later secretaries of state, James G. Blaine and Elihu Root, the latter having used the phrase "good neighborhood" in describing the relationship of the United States with Santo Domingo in 1907.[57] And President-elect Hoover on his goodwill tour through Latin America in 1928-1929 repeatedly characterized both his own attitude and the future policy of his administration toward Latin America as that of the "good neighbor."[58]

If now this policy of "live and let live," as President Roosevelt described it in his speech at Cartagena, Colombia, in July, 1934, could be properly implemented it might conceivably transform Caliban into an angel of light. Roosevelt himself disarmingly admitted in a speech at the Woodrow Wilson Foundation on December 28, 1933, that if he had been engaged in a political campaign as a citizen of some other American republic he might have been strongly tempted to play upon the fears of his compatriots "by charging the United States of North America with some form of imperialistic desire for selfish aggrandizement. As a citizen of some other republic," he said, "I might have found it difficult to believe fully in the altruism of the richest American republic. . . . I might have found it hard to approve of the occupation of the territory of other republics, even as a temporary measure." He explicitly pledged that "the definite policy of the United States from now on is one opposed to armed intervention" and thus recognized the primary responsibility of each nation for "the maintenance of law and the orderly processes of government in this hemisphere." In that same month Secretary of State Cordell Hull signed an inter-American pledge to this effect at the Seventh International Conference of American States at Montevideo, declaring unequivocally that "No state has the right to intervene in the internal or external affairs of another."[59]

55. *Congressional Globe,* 41st Cong., 3d Sess., 228.
56. Charles C. Tansill, *The Foreign Policy of Thomas F. Bayard, 1885-1897* (New York, 1940).
57. Philip C. Jessup, *Elihu Root* (New York, 1938), I, 541, 563.
58. De Conde, *op. cit.,* 18-23.
59. For Hull's account of this conference see *The Memoirs of Cordell Hull* (New York, 1948), I, 308-341. See also Department of State, *Report of the Delegates of the United States of America to the Seventh International Conference of American States, Montevideo, Uruguay, December 3-26, 1933* (Washington, 1934), 109.

Such heart-warming sentiments as these, particularly when confirmed by actions, gave Latin America a new conception of the United States. Here was a nation transformed into an altruistic, anti-imperialist, peace-loving neighbor, whom the Latin Americans could admire and love. As the Good Neighbor Policy was put into execution by the Roosevelt administration through the repudiation of unilateral armed intervention, the abrogation of the Platt Amendment with Cuba, the final withdrawal of United States troops from Haiti and the Dominican Republic, the negotiation of a new canal treaty favorable to Panama, the abandonment by the United States of earlier rights of free transit across the Isthmus of Tehuantepec in Mexico, and the signing of many bilateral trade agreements, Latin Americans were persuaded to soften their harsh attitudes toward the United States and to accept their powerful neighbor as a winsome and trustworthy friend. As a result of such acts as these implementing the Good Neighbor Policy, jubilated *La Nación* of Buenos Aires (July 12, 1934), "a current of frank and sincere friendship is bringing together Anglo-Saxons and Latin Americans," and the previous "colonial policy" of the United States toward Latin America was being transformed into the policy of the "good neighbor." "The policy of the 'Big Stick' and the later 'policy of the Dollar' have passed into history," it concluded.[60] "There is in the White House," declared José Manuel Puig Casauranc, Mexican delegate to the Montevideo Conference in 1933, "an admirable, noble, and good man—a courageous man who knows the errors of the past but who feels that the errors really belong to the past."[61]

The changed attitude toward the United States was reflected generally in the Latin American press. On December 15, 1934, *El Cronista,* a leading newspaper of Tegucigalpa, Honduras, observed: "Mr. Roosevelt, and with him the powerful party that supports his decisions, does not limit himself to making effective his declaration of 'good neighbor' but besides, with broad judgment and devotion to the highest principles, is making amends for the offences and damages that some of his predecessors inflicted on other nations, obtaining in this manner, for himself and his great nation, gratitude and sincere sympathy, and at the same time the admiration of the world." According to *El Mercurio* of Santiago (March 10, 1934), "confidence and trust in the

60. See also *La Prensa,* Buenos Aires, July 13, 1934; *La Razón,* Buenos Aires, July 18, 1934; and *Listín Diario,* Santo Domingo, December 21, 1935.
61. Seventh International Conference of American States, Montevideo, Uruguay, *Minutes of the Second Committee, Problems of International Law, Minutes of the Fifth Session* (December 19, 1933), 109.

United States" had replaced "the profound animosity which existed when Mr. Roosevelt became President." No longer, declared *Jornal do Brasil* (August 21, 1935), did Latin America "see in the United States a superior power, terrifying and arrogant, always disposed to impose its will by force when methods of persuasion have failed." To the newspaper *El Uruguay* of Montevideo it seemed that the "horrible specter" of Yankee imperialism which had been "hovering over the peace and sovereignty of our peoples and which loomed above all our frontiers in the shape of the despotic capitalism of Wall Street, backed by the gigantic shadow of its naval squadrons," was now almost entirely dissipated. The Good Neighbor Policy was proving itself to be, in the words of *El Diario* of Montevideo (July 15, 1934), a policy of "continental fraternity." This change in Latin America's attitude toward the United States was largely due, as Sumner Welles later observed, to the Roosevelt administration's pledge and policy of nonintervention, to its demonstrated lack of aggressive designs against its weaker neighbors.[62]

A few commentators south of the border continued, however, to view with jaundiced eyes this relatively sudden conversion of the United States into a good neighbor of the Latin American peoples. They insisted that its policy of good neighborliness was dictated mainly by considerations of self-interest. To the Roman Catholic newspaper *La Palabra* of Mexico City (February 26, 1935) the Good Neighbor Policy was the new method which the United States had chosen for making its economic, political, and cultural influence felt in Latin America. According to *La Opinión* of Ciudad Trujillo (March 30, 1936), "the ruling classes" in the United States had "come to recognize after many years that it is more profitable for them to have friendly and satisfied peoples south of the Rio Grande than people who are discontented and full of old rancors and whose sentiments might possibly take a dangerous form in some emergency in which the United States might find itself involved in the future." United States offenses against Nicaragua were recapitulated in a pamphlet of diatribe entitled *La Garra Yanqui (The Yankee Claw)* written by Agenor Argüello and published in El Salvador in late 1934. So persistent was the fear of a revival of the interventionist spirit that in 1935 there was a general feeling in Nicaragua, as reported by the United States minister there, that the next president of that country would be chosen by the United

62. *The Time for Decision* (New York, 1944), 200.

States.[63] *Listín Diario* of Santo Domingo (June 2, 1933) cynically suggested that the United States had withdrawn its troops from Nicaragua only in order to be in a better position "to formulate accusations against the imperialistic policy of Japan in the Far East." According to an influential Guatemalan journalist, Carlos Bauer Aviles, the primary reason for the efforts of the Roosevelt administration to develop more cordial relations with Latin America was to relieve the economic depression in the United States by increasing its export trade to Latin America and also to further Pan-American solidarity as a measure of security to the United States in readiness for possible conflicts in the Far East.[64] He cautioned that Roosevelt's promises of nonintervention committed only his administration and did not completely renounce intervention since they left open the possibility of resort to it in cases of absolute necessity.[65]

This possibility seemed to present itself when Roosevelt declared in an address at Chautauqua, New York, in August, 1936, that "if there are any distant nations which do not wish us well . . . we shall protect ourselves and we shall protect our neighbors." The independent *Ultimas Noticias* of Mexico City (August 15, 1936) spurned this pronouncement in an editorial entitled "Don't Protect Us, Old Chap!" Here was evidence, it felt, that "under the allurements of the good neighbor and despite its solicitude and flattery, the imperialism of the United States though transformed still persists." As late as 1936, Haya de la Torre was writing that the Good Neighbor Policy was only "transitory and precarious," and that "what it boils down to is a political maneuver." He expected that the United States, under the compulsion of inexorable economic laws, eventually would resume its policy of loans, interventions, and political domination.[66] In the event of "war between the United States and any other rival power," predicted Haya de la Torre, "the imperialist pressure on the governments of our countries . . . would attempt to involve us in the conflict to profit by our blood and our resources. . . . It would invoke, also in this case, as a dominant principle 'the defense of the interests of North American citizens' and in its name would give an honest appearance to the excesses of power of the stronger."[67]

63. Arthur Bliss Lane to Hull, March 15, 1935, Department of State, *Foreign Relations of the United States, 1935,* IV, 845.
64. *Nuestro Diario,* Guatemala, July 9, 1934.
65. *Ibid.,* April 17, 1934, and January 22, 1935.
66. *El Antimperialismo,* 27
67. *Ibid.,* 103.

Complementary to, and perhaps equally influential with, the Good Neighbor Policy in creating a favorable conception of the United States in Latin America was the New Deal. To "liberal" elements the policies of a "controlled economy" were particularly appealing, since they proclaimed, in the words of *El Diario* of Montevideo (November 9, 1934), "the predominance of the community over the individual, collective welfare over personal prerogative." Roosevelt's New Deal was characterized by *El Nacional* of Mexico City (August 25, 1935) as "one of the greatest efforts ever made to establish a system of social justice within the procedures of a reformist system." And Latin Americans early perceived that the "internal policy" of the New Deal was sister to the "continental policy" of the Good Neighbor. Only when "the more democratic sentiment of that great republic began to overcome the mammon power of the millionaire trusts," observed *El Uruguay* of Montevideo (June 7, 1936), did "the imperialism of the Dollar and the tyranny of Wall Street" fade into the background and allow a more enlightened policy to be followed toward Latin America. The most "redoubtable" hindrance to "the free flow of confidence among all the nations of the continent" was removed, the Mexican political leader Ezequiel Padilla later wrote, when "the trusts and monopolies—as an all-powerful force controlling international and domestic policies"—were brought under the power of the people of the United States by means of the New Deal program.[68] Plutocracy beaten at home was also forced to desist from its exploitation abroad. Latin America felt that Roosevelt's "policy of moderate radicalism," as a writer in *El Hombre Libre* of Mexico City (June 11, 1936) called it, was directed not only at promoting recovery in the United States but also at stimulating commercial interchange between his nation and the rest of the world.[69] That increased interchange meant economic advantage for the peoples of Latin America.

* * *

68. *Free Men of America* (Chicago and New York, 1943), 47. For additional newspaper comment on Latin American attitudes toward the New Deal see *El Diario*, Buenos Aires, November 4, 1936; *Diario de la Marina*, Havana, November 5, 1936; *El Mundo*, Havana, November 5, 1936; *El Universal*, Mexico City, November 5, 1936; *Avance*, Havana, November 4, 1936; *Noticias Gráficas*, Buenos Aires, November 3, 1936; *El Uruguay*, Montevideo, November 7, 1936; and *El Diario de Hoy*, San Salvador, November 2, 1936.
69. Diego Arenas Guzmán.

The Latin American policy of the United States, as set forth by Secretary Hull in a radio address on February 28, 1936, was "(1) to promote better understanding among our sister republics of this hemisphere; (2) to lend every assistance for the maintenance of peace and the perfection of peace machinery on this continent; and (3) to eliminate excessive artificial barriers to inter-American trade." The assumption underlying the policy and conduct of the Roosevelt administration toward Latin America was that the general welfare of the United States was linked with that of the other American nations. For this reason it behooved the people and government of the United States to have well-disposed neighbors in the Western Hemisphere, who would develop with them a mutually advantageous commerce and who would support them in international affairs. The object of the United States was declared to be "the maintenance of relations of complete trust and friendship among the American Republics." If the previous use of force as a method of extending the influence of the United States in the Western Hemisphere had been self-defeating, perhaps sincere words, acts of friendship, and increased commercial interchange would be effective.

The execution of this policy was deemed to call for more frequent inter-American consultation and collaboration. With the active concurrence of the United States all the American nations, as noted above, repudiated the practice of unilateral armed intervention by one state in the affairs of another at the Seventh International Conference of American States at Montevideo in 1933. At subsequent conferences held at Buenos Aires in 1936 and Lima in 1938 plans for closer economic cooperation and for mutual exchange in the fields of science, technology, literature, and the arts among all the peoples of the Americas were worked out. Under the leadership of the United States the American nations subscribed to certain high principles of conduct including the recognition of the juridical equality of states, the proscription of territorial conquest, respect for international law and treaty obligations, racial and religious tolerance, and the settlement of all international differences by peaceful means, which they consecrated in the "Declaration of American Principles" signed at Lima in 1938. In all this the American nations, under the inspiration of the United States and with its full cooperation, emphasized the essentially moral basis of the revitalized inter-American system of interdependence and cooperation.

At the same time an important catalytic agent in changing Latin

America's unfavorable opinion of the United States after 1933 was the trade policy of the Roosevelt administration. In the year before Roosevelt's inauguration the value of United States trade with Latin America sank to less than $575 million, its lowest point in twenty-three years.[70] The new administration, therefore, undertook as one of its prime objects the task of correcting this situation which was so obviously unprofitable to both the United States and Latin America. At the Montevideo conference in 1933 Secretary Hull secured the adoption of a resolution that the American nations would promptly undertake "to reduce high trade barriers through the negotiation of comprehensive bilateral reciprocity treaties based upon mutual concessions," a resolution which was reaffirmed at the Buenos Aires conference in 1936 and the Lima conference in 1938. In accordance with this principle of liberalized trade relations the United States between 1934 and 1938 concluded trade agreements with ten Latin American nations—Cuba (1934), Brazil (1935), Haiti (1935), Colombia (1935), Honduras (1935), Nicaragua (1936), Guatemala (1936), Costa Rica (1936), El Salvador (1937), and Ecuador (1938).

The gradual drying up of Latin American markets in Europe under the system of economic nationalism rampant there made Latin Americans particularly receptive to overtures which promised them enlarged outlets for their products in the Western Hemisphere. Their esteem for the United States heightened after 1933 generally in proportion to the increase in the prices received and the expansion of their markets in the United States for Cuban sugar, Uruguayan meat, Chilean wines, and other products of their countries. In this trade program, declared Agustín Edwards, proprietor of *El Mercurio* of Santiago, Chile (March 4, 1935), the North American nation, "which is essentially practical, is not seeking to impose itself politically or militarily but rather it is seeking economic understandings of reciprocal benefit." The people of the United States were motivated by the simple purpose, as it seemed to him, "of procuring the products which they do not have in sufficient quantity and of sending us in return the material resulting from their fertile and inexhaustible mechanical genius." Partly as a result, Latin America came to assume a much more important place in the commercial relations of the United States than ever before. The trade benefits to the United States, so desperately needed in the depression

70. Department of Commerce, *Historical Statistics of the United States: A Supplement to the Statistical Abstract of the United States* (Washington, 1949), 250-251.

era and so skillfully worked out by the reciprocal trade agreements program, were immediate and considerable. Between 1933 and 1937 United States imports from Latin America jumped from $329.4 million to $705 million, or over 114 per cent; during the same period its exports to Latin America increased from $240.4 million to over $639.4 million, or more than 166 per cent. At the same time, by way of contrast, its imports from Europe increased by only 82 per cent and its exports to Europe by only 60 per cent. In other words, by 1937 the general trade relationship of the United States with Latin America, expressed in terms of foreign trade statistics, was 236 per cent better than it had been in 1933, whereas its general trade relationship with Europe had improved by only 167 per cent. To cite specific examples of these economic gains in Latin America, United States trade with Chile, Cuba, Mexico, and Peru doubled between 1934 and 1937, and with certain other countries it even trebled in either exports or imports. Trade with Argentina, in particular, showed a phenomenal gain increasing from $72.1 million to $233.1 million, or 223 per cent, during that period.[71] Whereas between 1929 and 1932 the United States had accounted for 35 per cent of the total foreign trade of Latin America as a whole, by 1938 it was responsible for 45 per cent of the total foreign trade of that area. During the years before the outbreak of the European war the Good Neighbor Policy paid off in dollars and cents, as it was later to pay off in strategic materials furnished and lives saved from the holocaust of war. As early as 1934 this policy was characterized by *La Prensa* of Buenos Aires (June 17, 1934) as a policy of "practical Americanism."

To Latin Americans, the contrasts and stresses in the United States were sharply accentuated as the presidential election of 1936 approached. Since Woodrow Wilson's administration they had had a predilection for the Democratic Party in the United States as being less directly involved in a policy of intervention in their affairs than the Republican Party, as the more Roman Catholic of the two major parties, and as being generally opposed to the raising of high tariff barriers against their products. In 1936 the Republican Party, declared *La Nación* of Buenos Aires (June 13, 1936), was contending for a "policy of economic isolation which, six years ago, brought about the most prejudicial effects of the world crisis; it has taken no warning whatever from the terrible catastrophe that has befallen trade since the

71. Department of Commerce, *Foreign Commerce and Navigation of the United States for the Calendar Year 1937* (Washington, 1939), 785-786.

erection of the Chinese wall of protectionist duties, dividing the world into watertight reservoirs and compelling other nations to protect themselves by similar means in order not to be absorbed by the formidable financial power of a nation which buys nothing and wants to sell everything." Moreover, as *El Cronista* of Tegucigalpa (January 16, 1936) explained, Latin America considered that former "Republican rulers" of the United States had undertaken "to oppress various countries of the South, to impose on them standards of living, to set at naught the determination of their sovereignty, to seize their sources of production for the profit of North American capitalism." Since all these hateful operations might be re-enacted "with the ascent to power of the Republican Party and of a chief with imperial tendencies," many Latin American newspapers frankly advocated President Roosevelt's re-election.

By reason of both the Good Neighbor and the New Deal policies, President Roosevelt had already become to Latin America a symbol of high achievement and of roseate hope for the future. On his visit to Cartagena, Colombia, in July, 1934, the first visit of a President of the United States to a South American country, he was effusively praised by Latin American as "the courageous initiator of the new era of understanding and of mutual support which has to be the basis of continental progress."[72] According to the official report of his visit by the United States minister to Colombia, "the President's personality made a splendid effect on all who saw him" and "will have a beneficial effect on our relations with Colombia."[73]

Evidence of Roosevelt's popularity throughout Latin America was overwhelming. *El Panamá-América* of Panama (April 20, 1936) considered him " a real democrat" because of the New Deal, which served the interests of labor, and the Good Neighbor Policy. Asked to name the president among "those rulers who have occupied the White House in Washington whose policy has been most beneficial for Hispano-American countries," its "categorical answer" was "Franklin Delano Roosevelt." Under Roosevelt's leadership, declared the editor of a Guatemalan newspaper, *Diario de Centro-América* (September 8, 1936), "the former threatening shadow of the White House has been

72. *El Tiempo,* Bogotá, July 12, 1934. See also *El Diario,* Montevideo, July 15, 1934; *La Nación,* Buenos Aires, July 12, 1934; *La Prensa,* Buenos Aires, July 13, 1934; *La Razón,* Buenos Aires, July 18, 1934; and *El Espectador,* Bogotá, July 11, 1934.
73. Sheldon Whitehouse to Hull, Despatch 249, Bogotá, July 16, 1934, Department of State Archives.

changed into the friendly beam of a lighthouse which points out not only to the United States but also to the other countries of America and of the world the directions of new policy." The conservative *Diario de la Marina* of Havana (January 22, 1936) was impressed with the admirable results of Roosevelt's program including "the policy of farsighted intervention in agriculture and industry, the policy of interchange, that of the 'New Deal,' that of the relations of good neighbor with the American countries and of reciprocity with as many of them as possible." "Mr. Roosevelt governs a Democracy," declared *La Nación* of Buenos Aires (August 16 and 20, 1936), and "personifies its ideals of welfare and tranquillity, which are the ideals of the whole of America." His vigorous personality exuding the quality of confident leadership appealed to Latin Americans. "An admirable example of the great men of North America," generalized *Diario de la Marina* (January 22, 1936), "in him are combined both idealism and the faculty of action." To *La Epoca* of Tegucigalpa (June 26, 1936) it appeared that "All the America of Columbus renders him its homage of admiration."

Whether Roosevelt won re-election or not, however, Latin Americans hoped that his policy toward Latin America would, in the words of *Listín Diario* of Ciudad Trujillo (March 25, 1936), "be declared a national policy, without being subject to changes of interpretation by the Democrats or Republicans that alternate in power." *La Opinión* (March 30, 1936) of the same capital explained that "it is only fair to recognize that this policy had Presidents Coolidge and Hoover as its precursors," that "it was President Coolidge who, through his instructions to Secretary of State Charles Evans Hughes, ordered the cessation of intervention in our country," and that "it was President Hoover who arranged for the evacuation of Nicaragua by American forces and took the first steps (Forbes Commission) toward the evacuation of the Republic of Haiti." Mindful of the mutually beneficial effects of the Good Neighbor Policy, *El Imparcial* of Santiago, Chile (November 7, 1936), forecast that even in the event of a Republican victory the government at Washington could not and would not abandon that policy.

The United States which re-elected Roosevelt by a greater majority than any of his predecessors was a nation that seemed to Latin America to have vindicated democracy. According to *Diario Latino* of San Salvador (November 7, 1936), the "GREAT DEMOCRACY" had re-elected the "GREAT DEMOCRAT." His victory, said *El*

País of Montevideo (November 4, 1936), represented a triumph for "the ideal of democracy, of liberty, and of peace." In an extraordinary action the Cuban Senate voted unanimously to send a message of congratulations to the United States Senate on his re-election.[74] "Here," enthusiastically declared *Noticias Gráficas* of Buenos Aires (November 3, 1936), "is the United States giving the world the example of its extraordinary civic faith and its devotion to order and respect for the law."[75] The North Americans, observed *Diario de la Marina* of Havana (November 5, 1936), "possess in high degree the virtue which Salvador de Madariaga described with the English expression 'fairplay.' . . . For the citizens of North America elections are much the same as a sporting event. Before the 'match' factions are irreconcilable and they fight bravely using all the instruments which the law allows. After the 'match' both teams shake hands and even give each other enthusiastic 'cheers.' The loser is the first to recognize the legitimate triumph of his opponent. The winner, on the other hand, applauds the courage and the decorum with which his adversary has fought." Not only the fair play but also the orderliness of the election of 1936 appeared to give the lie to the criticisms of democracy which were being increasingly spread by Nazi-Fascist propagandists. Latin Americans considered it especially significant that neither the Socialist nor Communist parties nor the Constitutional Union Party led by Congressman William Lemke attained any measure of success. "Under the Democratic regime," observed *Avance* of Havana (November 4, 1936), "the Union does not appear to be threatened by the dangers which are rising in other nations of the world. The red phantom is not in the house of Uncle Sam, as in European lands, a sinister specter which haunts the dream of those who are fond of the present system."

For this situation Latin Americans gave considerable credit to Roosevelt's New Deal. That program, representing "the solution of social problems by normal and legitimate means," made Roosevelt, according to *El Diario* of Buenos Aires (November 4, 1936), "the greatest obstacle to local Fascism and . . . as well the sure preventive against Communism because of his careful, serene, and unprejudiced consideration of social ills." His New Deal, said *Diario de la Marina* of Havana (November 5, 1936), "has revealed to the New Continent

74. Despatch 7585, Havana, November 6, 1936, Department of State Archives.
75. Similar views were expressed by *El Heraldo,* Caracas, November 4, 1936; *Diario de Costa Rica,* San José, November 4, 1936; *El Universal,* Mexico City, November 5, 1936; and *El País,* Montevideo, November 11, 1936.

an interesting formula by which it is possible to cure completely the frantic 'isms,' not by abandoning democratic procedure but by making it more flexible and by adjusting it to the times." In this way, Senator José Manuel Casanova of Cuba declared, "the great American people openly identifies itself with the work of social renovation, oriented toward the improvement of the conditions of the poorer classes and directed toward the attainment of a more equitable and useful distribution of wealth."[76] The result was that in this election "all the power of the strongest plutocracy of our times and of history," as *El Universal* of Mexico City (November 5, 1936) declared, "was obliged to surrender, to yield to the irresistible will of the people. All the apparatus of economic royalty, the crushing weight of its money, the eighty-five per cent of the press which served as its mouthpiece, Wall Street and Heart [Hearst] . . . were swept away by the largest torrent of votes that has ever been seen in the United States." It was, according to *Avance* of Havana (November 4, 1936), this "frank and sincere policy" of achieving "a better standard of living for the man who works and fights—a thing which is equivalent in these troubled times to guaranteeing internal peace—which is the reason for the greatness of the great northern people."

Here was a nation which, to the delight of Latin America, had purged itself of its offensive habits and was now practicing "democracy" at home and good neighborliness in its international relations. It had made itself, as *Noticias Gráficas* of Buenos Aires (November 3, 1936) declared, "a model for the other nations of the continent." It had become, said *El Uruguay* of Montevideo (November 7, 1936), "as it was in the eighteenth century, the victorious emblem around which may rally the multitudes thirsting for social justice and human fraternity." In particular, Roosevelt's victory meant for Latin America "the consecration of the 'Good Neighbor' policy."[77] Under Roosevelt's leadership the North American people had, in the words of *El País* of Montevideo (November 2, 1936), "demonstrated, by a sustained action over a period of four years, their purpose to become good neighbors in fact, to act in a democratic spirit and on a basis of equal footing." Their government had abandoned "dollar diplomacy" and was no longer acting as "the agent of the bankers of Wall Street." To *Diario de Hoy* of San Salvador Roosevelt represented "the tendency to con-

76. *El Mundo,* Havana, November 5, 1936.
77. Senator José Manuel Casanova quoted in *El Mundo,* Havana, November 5, 1936.

ciliation in the American family."[78] This was especially demonstrated when at his suggestion representatives of all the American nations assembled at Buenos Aires in December, 1936, "to determine how the maintenance of peace among the American republics may best be safeguarded." At that conference a greater degree of unanimity among the American republics was manifested than at any previous conference for many years back.

Roosevelt himself attended the Buenos Aires conference and took advantage of his trip to pay brief visits also to Rio de Janeiro and Montevideo. At Rio de Janeiro the day of his visit was declared a national holiday. As he disembarked from his ship he was greeted by thousands of school children, who waved red, white, and blue banners and sang the national anthem of the United States. He then made a triumphal tour of the city with President Getúlio Vargas. For his visit Vargas' Itamaraty Palace was lavishly decorated with orchids, some of which had been furnished by generous citizens who stripped their own plants of blossoms for this occasion, and others had been supplied by florists at a total cost of approximately $2,100, an extraordinary expense in a country where orchids were cheap.

During his visit Roosevelt addressed a special joint session of the Brazilian Congress and Supreme Court. After his address he was hailed by the spokesman of the Brazilian Congress, amidst applause, as "the *Man*—the fearless and generous man who is accomplishing and living the most thrilling political experience of modern times."[79] "The President completely captivated the officials of the Brazilian Government, as well as the press and people," reported the United States embassy in Rio de Janeiro. "His tremendous personal charm and great dignity were commented [on] widely and there has not been a single discordant note in the voluminous editorial and news comment which filled the Brazilian press during the days immediately preceding and succeeding the President's visit. . . . The newspapers, many of which had special commemorative editions on the day of his arrival, termed him the outstanding world figure in public life today."[80]

78. Manuel Barba Salinas in *Diario de Hoy,* San Salvador, November 7, 1936. Similar views were expressed by *La Estrella de Panamá,* Panama, November 6, 1936.
79. Speech by Raul Fernandes, *Jornal do Comércio,* Rio de Janeiro, November 28, 1936.
80. R. M. Scotten, chargé d'affaires ad interim, to the Secretary of State, Despatch 1217, Rio de Janeiro, December 9, 1936, Department of State Archives.

The same outpourings of popular acclamation occurred when
Roosevelt reached Buenos Aires. Again the day of his arrival was declared a national holiday. "The charm of his manners and his personality completely captured the Latin mentality and imagination of his
hosts," reported the United States ambassador in Buenos Aires.[81]
Again in Montevideo, where Roosevelt stopped briefly after leaving
Buenos Aires to return to the United States, he received tremendous
acclaim. "No word of anything but friendliness toward him appeared
in any section of the press," reported the United States minister in
Montevideo.[82] Even the normally anti-"Yanqui" *El Debate* (December 3, 1936) welcomed him as a "worthy successor of President
Monroe!"

The sentiments in favor of peace and democracy which Roosevelt
expressed in his speech opening the Buenos Aires conference were applauded by Latin American public opinion.[83] Now, jubilantly proclaimed *Diario de Costa Rica* of San José (December 24, 1936), the
Monroe Doctrine was being given a "continental character." According to *Diario de Hoy* of San Salvador (December 1, 1936), the Latin
American countries "will not have to fight against the strategy of
Nordic imperialism but will be able to devote all their strength to enthusiastic and loyal collaboration with the United States for the maintenance of continental peace." Roosevelt's warm reception in Rio de
Janeiro could perhaps have been expected by reason of long United
States-Brazilian amity, but his complete acceptance in Argentina, where
antipathy to the United States was traditional, impressed Latin Americans as something of a phenomenon.[84] There, as also in Uruguay, the
emphasis which Roosevelt placed upon democracy was seized upon by
the opposition as a weapon with which to belabor the existing govern-

81. Ambassador Alexander W. Weddell to the Secretary of State, Despatch
1425, Buenos Aires, December 11, 1936, Department of State Archives. For
newspaper comment on Roosevelt's visit see *La Nación* and *La Prensa,* Buenos
Aires, December 2, 1936. See also Despatch 1456, Buenos Aires, January 7,
1937, and *The Cruise of President Franklin D. Roosevelt to South America*
(Log of the U.S.S. "Indianapolis," November 18 to December 15, 1936)
(Washington, 1937).

82. Minister Julius G. Lay to the Secretary of State, Despatch 410, Montevideo, December 10, 1936, Department of State Archives. For examples of
newspaper comment, see the following Montevideo newspapers for December 3,
1936: *El Plata, La Mañana, El Día, La Tribuna Popular, El Pueblo,* and *El
Diario.*

83. *El Espectador,* Bogotá, December 2, 1936; *El Tiempo,* Bogotá, December 1, 1936; and *La Razón,* Bogotá, December 2, 1936.

84. *Diario Comercial,* San Pedro Sula, Honduras, December 14, 1936.

ments of their own countries, that of President Agustín P. Justo of Argentina and President Gabriel Terra of Uruguay, as antidemocratic.[85] In both countries attention was called to the need for the United States to follow up Roosevelt's visit by relaxing its tariff barriers and its sanitary restrictions against their products.[86]

The new attitudes of the United States toward Latin America and the affinity of the Good Neighbor Policy with the New Deal were clearly demonstrated in the reaction of the Roosevelt administration to the expropriation policy of the Lázaro Cárdenas government in Mexico in 1938. When that government, in pursuance of its program of recovery of the resources of the Mexican nation and the distribution of land to the landless, expropriated agricultural and petroleum lands, some of which were owned by citizens of the United States, the Roosevelt government did not resort to intervention or threats of intervention. Instead, Secretary of State Hull assured Mexico that the United States did not question the right of that government "in the exercise of its sovereign power to expropriate properties within its jurisdiction." The Roosevelt government, Hull informed the Mexican ambassador, "has frequently asserted the right of all countries freely to determine their own social, agrarian and industrial problems. This right includes the sovereign right of any government to expropriate private property within its borders in furtherance of public purposes." Hull adverted to the fact that "The Government of the United States has itself been very actively pursuing a program of social betterment . . . in short, it is carrying out the most far-reaching program for the improvement of the general standard of living that this country has ever seen. Under this program it has expropriated from foreigners as well as its own citizens properties of various kinds, such as submarginal and eroded lands to be retired from farming, slums to be cleared for housing projects, land for power dams, lands containing resources to be preserved for government use." The United States therefore obviously could not complain against the policy of the Mexican government so similar to its own. But Hull insisted that, in accordance with international law, the owners of these expropriated properties must receive prompt, adequate, and effective compensation.[87] In the ensuing negotiations the

85. *El Plata,* Montevideo, December 4, 1936; and *El Día,* Montevideo, December 4, 1936.

86. Julius G. Lay to the Secretary of State, Despatch 410, Montevideo, December 10, 1936, Department of State Archives.

87. Hull to the Mexican Ambassador Francisco Castillo Nájera, July 21, 1938, Department of State, *Press Releases,* XIX (July 23, 1938), 50.

United States concerned itself, therefore, not with the Mexican government's policy of expropriation as such but only, in general, with the amount of compensation and the arrangements for its satisfactory payment.[88]

This self-restraint toward Mexico was hailed by President Cárdenas in a message to the United States ambassador in Mexico City on March 31, 1938, as a new "proof of friendship" which the Mexican people would carry in their hearts. He paid tribute to the United States which "through its President continues to support the policy of friendship and respect of each nation, a policy which is winning for your country the affection of many peoples of the world."[89]

Not only in Mexico but in other Latin American countries as well public opinion responded favorably to the position taken in Washington. Peruvian newspapers expressed praise for "the admirable calmness of the Secretary of State."[90] El Telégrafo of Guayaquil declared that the United States was quite right in its attitude, "which could not be more moderate and conciliatory." Other newspapers, including El Relator of Cali, Colombia, and El Sur of Concepción, Chile, warmly commended the temperate action of the United States.

Under Roosevelt's Good Neighbor Policy, then, the United States had frankly laid the Big Stick on the shelf and was relying upon the development of a community of interests in the Western Hemisphere to produce common attitudes and unity of action. It had withdrawn its forces of occupation from Latin American countries, had renounced the use of armed force in its future dealings with them, had assumed treaty obligations not to intervene in their affairs, and had reversed its restrictive trade policy to their advantage. Roosevelt even assured Argentina during his visit to Buenos Aires in 1936 that he would work for the removal of restrictions upon the importation of Argentine meat into the United States. As a result, little by little the distrust of the United States, built up in Latin America by previous pressures, had abated and confidence had been slowly re-established. Chile and Argentina invited the United States in April, 1935, to join them in the mediation of the Chaco War between Paraguay and Bolivia—a medi-

88. Bemis, *The Latin American Policy*, 345-350, and Frank Tannenbaum, *Mexico: The Struggle for Peace and Bread* (New York, 1950), 278-280. Resentment against the claims of the United States oil companies in these negotiations was expressed editorially in *El Universal*, Mexico City, June 5, 1940.
89. Department of State, *Press Releases*, XVIII (April 2, 1938), 435-436.
90. Despatch 353, Lima, March 28, 1938, Department of State Archives.

ation which resulted in the establishment of peace in that troubled area three years later.

This changed inter-American relationship—largely the result of the United States policy of self-restraint, international decency, and cooperation—was reflected in the Latin American press. The United States through President Roosevelt, concluded *La Nación* of Santiago, Chile (October 7, 1937), was "directing its expressions of goodwill toward the American nations, with whom it feels itself logically bound by the closest bonds of mutual understanding and interest." Roosevelt and his Secretary of State, Cordell Hull, said *O Jornal* of Rio de Janeiro (March 19, 1938), "have given to American relations the practical character of good neighborliness, which consists in the defense of common interests and in the solidarity of all, in safeguarding the integrity and independence of the nations of this continent, in augmenting commercial interchange, and in the harmony of the republics of this hemisphere." President Roosevelt's Good Neighbor Policy, concluded *El Liberal Progresista* of Guatemala City (May 10, 1937), "has already brought about a complete change in the relations between the United States and the American countries and a flourishing intercourse in matters relating to continental commerce." This powerful northern nation, according to *La Crónica* of Lima (March 8, 1938), was no longer "the big brother, the tutor, and the caretaker of the patrimony of all America, through the development of an imperialistic policy." A radical change had taken place in its policy and attitudes. As *El Liberal* of Bogotá (October 14, 1938) generalized, "From the 'Big Stick' to the 'Good Neighbor' policy was not only an evolution but a revolution. The people presided over by the second Roosevelt has really been a good neighbor to Latin Americans." The distrust and fear of the United States formerly so prevalent in Latin America, declared *La Prensa* of Buenos Aires (November 17, 1940), "have been dissipated and replaced by an atmosphere of friendship." In this new atmosphere "an unlimited horizon" opened up, said *La Nación* of Santiago (October 7, 1937), "for the hopes of the people of America for a near future built upon solidarity, cooperation and unity of outlook for the countries of the continent."[91]

For "this new atmosphere," this changed orientation of the United States, Latin Americans were inclined to give credit to the leadership of the Democratic Party and President Roosevelt. In a formal resolu-

91. See also *El País*, Montevideo, November 10, 1938.

tion unanimously adopted by the Colombian Senate "the figure of the North American statesman" was declared to be "one of the greatest and most noble of our epoch. . . . With respect to the American republics," the Senate resolution continued, "the policy called that of the good neighbor, which President Roosevelt preaches and practices with firm loyalty as the application of democratic principles internationally, has completely eliminated the justifiable resentments produced by the opposite policy."[92] The idea grew up, and was encouraged by the Roosevelt administration, that the United States, under previous Republican administrations, had been committed, in the words of *El País* of Montevideo (October 7, 1937), to a "policy of intervention, protectionism *à outrance,* and economic imperialism" and that a return to these policies would make "impossible the march toward a true solidarity of the two Americas in defense of their liberty and their peace." Only the Democratic Party favored *rapprochement* with Latin America and fair treatment of its peoples, it was said. According to *Ahora* of Caracas (November 10, 1938), the Good Neighbor Policy was entirely a policy of the Democratic Party and the replacement of that party by the Republicans would mean an "intensification and extension of the imperialism that would swallow up countries in Central and South America."

To others it seemed that this unhappy result was to be anticipated not only from the Republicans but also from other administrations in Washington of whatever political complexion. The Mexican nationalist José Vasconcelos repeatedly argued that there was a basic incompatibility between "Bolivarism" and "Monroism" which rendered a durable good neighbor policy impossible.[93] The Good Neighbor Policy could not be accepted at its face value, argued the Chilean government newspaper, *La Nación* (May 20, 1939), because it might be altered by Roosevelt's successors in the White House and also because strong nations can always evade their obligations to weaker countries.

But in general it was said in Latin America that greater progress had been made toward the attainment of inter-American harmony in this brief period of Roosevelt's Good Neighbor Policy than during the entire previous century of inter-American relations. International tensions which had embittered the feelings of the American peoples had been relieved. Official relations which had often been character-

92. Resolution transmitted to Department of State in Telegram 73, Bogotá, November 18, 1938, Department of State Archives.
93. *Hoy,* Mexico City, June 4, 1938.

ized only by formal amity had become genuinely cordial. New techniques of inter-American cooperation had been applied in a system of joint consultation and multilateral action based upon mutual trust and respect for agreements. The Pan-Hispanic movement had been largely disarmed and the cause of Pan-Americanism saved. Even if some of the Latin American paeans of praise for the Roosevelt administration are discounted as mere flattery or only characteristic Latin American effusiveness, it was clear at the beginning of his second term as President that responsible opinion in Latin America had been largely won over to the United States and was disposed to cooperate with him in the programs of his administration. His strong personal leadership, his aggressive use of the national powers of the presidency, and his left-of-center domestic program coincided generally with the ideas and expectations of Latin Americans in the 1930's.

Many obstacles to full inter-American cooperation remained. "Three years of a changed policy," commented *Avance* of Havana (March 2, 1936), "have not been enough to destroy the mountains of fears which other governments raised under the sign of the dollar." A real and durable *acercamiento* between Latin America and Anglo-America which would subdue old suspicions, alter traditional patterns of trade, and produce new ideological affinities would manifestly be a long and slow process. But it was highly important that this new orientation should have been begun and that it should have been initiated with intelligence, eloquence, and high purpose by the Roosevelt administration. Moreover, it had been brought about fortuitously just at a time when new bases for inter-American solidarity appeared to be needed for a common defense against outside forces of aggression which might threaten the independence and way of life of the nations of the Americas. Whether the improved relations between the United States and Latin America would withstand the shocks which might come as the glowering storms of war gathered in Europe and the Far East remained to be seen.

Chapter 3

HEMISPHERIC ISOLATION

The Meeting of the Foreign Ministers of the American Republics
resolves to reaffirm the status of general neutrality of the American
republics.

—Resolution V of the First Meeting of
the Foreign Ministers of the American
Republics at Panama, October 3, 1939.

*7*HE ISSUES of the approaching conflict between the
Axis powers and the United Nations shaped up sharp-
ly in Latin America, as they did in the United States, in the late 1930's,
altering traditional attitudes and creating new political alignments.
The leadership of the United States had been enhanced by its repudiation of unilateral action in its policy toward its neighbors in the Western Hemisphere, but Latin American reactions to this leadership varied
from subservience on the one hand to hostility or indifference on the
other. Old suspicions and fears of the United States in Latin America,
economic considerations of both a domestic and an international character, reservations as to the alleged evil designs of the Axis powers
against the American nations, and the strength of political nationalism
—all these tended to retard the attainment of the hemispheric solidarity which the United States sought. And the development of that
solidarity was also hampered by the conflict in the United States between the proponents and the opponents of involvement in European
and Far Eastern imbroglios.

The Good Neighbor Policy was enunciated originally by President
Roosevelt as a world policy for the United States but was not—perhaps could not be—followed in its dealings with certain governments

38

in Europe and Asia and accordingly was narrowed down to the Latin American area. Roosevelt in his first Pan-American Day address in April, 1933, specifically applied it to the relations of the United States with the nations of Latin America. Toward those nations the policy of the Roosevelt administration took on gradually more and more of the character of a security policy designed to protect not only the United States but also all the American nations from attack from outside the hemisphere. Pan-American policy now occupied first place in the foreign relations of the United States. Welles had suggested in his memorandum to Roosevelt in early 1933 that as the Monroe Doctrine was a doctrine of self-defense for the United States it could also be considered a doctrine of "continental self-defense," and that its principles "are as vitally important to every other republic of this Hemisphere as they are to the United States itself." He therefore urged that they should be adopted by all the American nations.

The Roosevelt administration, alarmed by the growing Axis threat, undertook to establish the bases of a continental security policy. At the Inter-American Conference for the Maintenance of Peace, which assembled on Roosevelt's initiative in Buenos Aires in December, 1936, official representatives of all the American nations agreed that whenever their peace should be threatened they would consult together for the purpose of finding and adopting collective methods of averting a common danger to the American continent. At the Eighth International Conference of American States at Lima two years later, Secretary Hull explained in his opening address to the delegates that the policy of the United States in relation to the Latin American nations was directed toward strengthening the inter-American system of consultation and common action in order to enable them to resist "the invasion of their hemisphere by the armed forces of any power or possible combination of powers" and to destroy the forces which would prevent their unity of action. The object was to defend and preserve the peace of the American hemisphere. To this end all the American governments affirmed in the Declaration of the Principles of the Solidarity of America, the so-called "Declaration of Lima," their "continental solidarity" and their determination to defend the basic principles of their common life "against all foreign intervention or activity that may threaten them." The appearance or development of a danger to any American state was declared to be a matter of concern to all and to justify the initiation of the procedure of consultation. Thus was evolved at the inter-American conferences in 1936 and 1938 the beginnings of an inter-American security system to meet the threat of possible aggression.[1] The United States and the Latin American nations concluded that they had a shared interest in the defense of their own peace and independence. This hemisphere, as it was becoming an oasis of peace in a world that seemed tragically heading toward World War II, was preparing the bases for that unity of action which it would need when the European war came.

The dominant feeling among the peoples of America both North and South was one of prideful difference from Europe. "Here we have new countries," complacently observed *La Nación* of Buenos Aires (February 20, 1936), "without any tradition of national hatreds, of rivalries dating from centuries back." In this "contrast between two worlds" *La Nación* found "the spiritual basis of Pan Americanism"; in it the United States and Latin America had a common stake. The very neutrality legislation of the United States furnished evidence that it was bound to the Western Hemisphere in a special relationship. This conviction of the separateness of America from Europe was reinforced by the Good Neighbor Policy of the United States. Together they were producing a north-south orientation in foreign affairs, building an American Axis. To an America thus strengthened as "the hemisphere of peace, of respect for the rights of others," concluded *El Diario de Hoy* of San Salvador (December 1, 1936), would inevitably fall the responsibility of taking over "the scepter of civilization from the decrepit hands of old Europe."[2]

A more serious challenge to this generally accepted American doctrine of the two spheres could scarcely have occurred than was presented in 1936 by the outbreak of civil strife in Spain, the mother country of eighteen Latin American nations. To the heirs of Spanish culture in the New World the effusion of Spanish blood in this civil conflict was shocking, and the attempt by General Francisco Franco, assisted by the forces of both Mussolini and Hitler, to overthrow the constitutional government of Spain was deemed to call for positive action by the American nations. In general, leftist groups and labor organizations in Latin America hoped for the success of

1. Department of State, *Report of the Delegation of the United States of America to the Inter-American Conference for the Maintenance of Peace, Buenos Aires, Argentina, December 1-23, 1936* (Washington, 1937), 116-124; and Pan American Union, *Eighth International Conference of American States, Lima, Peru, December 9-27, 1938, Report on the Results of the Conference* (Washington, 1939), 92-93.
2. See also *La Prensa*, Buenos Aires, December 2, 1936.

the existing Spanish government, and clerical groups, large landowners, propertied classes, and other conservative elements of the population supported the Franco revolution. The latter were partly motivated
by their aversion to the strong Communist influences in the Spanish
government and their apprehension that the triumph of that government would encourage the spread of Communism in the Spanish-
speaking nations of Latin America.[3] Implicit in the movement for
action by the American nations either for or against the so-called
Republican government in Spain was a denial of the policy of noninterference by the New World in the affairs of the Old World.

From the beginning of the Franco rebellion the United States
followed a policy of hands-off in relation to the civil conflict there.
"In conformity with its well-established policy of noninterference with
internal affairs in other countries," the Department of State instructed
its representatives in Spain on August 7, 1936, "this Government will,
of course, scrupulously refrain from any interference whatsoever in the
unfortunate Spanish situation."[4] But soon afterward the Uruguayan
government invited all the American states to join in a mediation of
the Spanish situation. This proposal, which would obviously benefit
the revolutionary forces, constituting, as it would, a virtual recognition
of their belligerency, was accepted without reservations by eleven Latin
American states including Venezuela, Colombia, El Salvador, Ecuador,
Guatemala, Haiti, Honduras, Nicaragua, the Dominican Republic,
Bolivia, and Paraguay, several of which, observed a principal opposition newspaper of Montevideo, *El Día* (August 27, 1936), were nations
"with a marked dictatorial organization." But the Uruguayan proposal was promptly rejected by the United States, which explained that
it was committed to the principle of noninterference in the internal
affairs of other countries.[5] Supporting the position of the United
States were three of the greater Latin American nations: Argentina,
Brazil, and Mexico.[6] Uruguay postponed further action.[7]

3. See, for example, "The Frightfulness of Communism," *El Cronista,*
Tegucigalpa, September 23, 1936.

4. William Phillips, Acting Secretary, to all consulates in Spain, August
7, 1936, *Foreign Relations of the United States, 1936,* II, 471.

5. Lay to Hull, Telegram 32, Montevideo, August 17, 1936, and Phillips
to Lay, August 20, 1936, Department of State Archives.

6. The Uruguayan proposal was also opposed by Panama, and was accepted
with reservations by Cuba, Chile, and Peru. *El Pueblo,* Montevideo, September
3, 1936.

7. José Espalter, Uruguayan Minister of Foreign Affairs, to Don Alberto
Mañé, Uruguayan envoy extraordinary and minister plenipotentiary to France,
Montevideo, August 28, 1936, *El Pueblo,* Montevideo, September 5, 1936.

But Uruguay continued to spearhead the demand for intervention by the American nations in Spain. In September, 1936, it withdrew its diplomatic representatives from Spain in protest against the failure of the Spanish government to protect Uruguayan citizens. In November, 1936, both Guatemala and El Salvador extended recognition to the Franco faction in Spain, and Nicaragua soon also established official relations with it.[8]

"The sentiment in Latin America regarding the Spanish situation is highly combustible," Secretary Hull reported from Buenos Aires in December, 1936.[9] But the United States reaffirmed its neutral position when Congress early in 1937 approved a joint resolution prohibiting the exportation of arms, ammunition, and implements of war from the United States to Spain.[10] As the previous action on behalf of the Spanish rebels had been taken by Uruguay, so counteracting action on behalf of the legal government of Spain was now taken by Mexico. As early as August, 1936, Mexico began to export arms to the beleaguered Spanish government.[11] Early in the following year it sought to gain Latin American support and to persuade the United States to abandon its policy of nonintervention in order to help the legitimate government of Spain.[12] The Mexican President, Lázaro Cárdenas, himself, "being deeply impressed by the acts of unheard-of violence recently committed by the Spanish rebels against open cities and their civilian population," pressed Roosevelt to offer mediation.[13] But contrary action which would help the Franco forces in Spain was urged upon the United States by several other Latin American governments. Such was the intended effect of Uruguay's new proposal in August, 1937, for example, of a joint recognition of the belligerency of the opposing forces in Spain by all the American governments.[14] This proposal was promptly endorsed by Venezuela, but was, in effect, rejected

8. Telegram 52, San Salvador, November 8, 1936, Telegram 76, Guatemala, November 9, 1936, *Foreign Relations of the United States, 1936,* II, 553, 576; and Telegram 235, Managua, November 27, 1936, Telegram 4, Managua, January 9, 1937, and Telegram 25, Managua, April 9, 1937, Department of State Archives.

9. Telegram 37, Buenos Aires, December 7, 1936, Department of State Archives.

10. Senate Joint Resolution 3.

11. *El Nacional,* Mexico City, August 29, 1936.

12. F. Castillo Nájera, Mexican Ambassador, to Hull, April 6, 1937, *Foreign Relations of the United States, 1937,* I, 274-275.

13. Nájera to Hull, June 24, 1937, *ibid.,* I, 337-338.

14. *Ibid.,* I, 380.

by all the other American governments, including the United States, which in its reply referred to the policy of noninterference "which it has consistently maintained since the beginning of the Spanish conflict."[15] When Cuba soon afterward proposed a joint offer of good offices to the warring factions in Spain by all the countries of America, the United States gave the same negative reply, based, as Acting Secretary of State Welles explained, upon its "policy of noninterference in the internal affairs of another country."[16] The Cuban proposal was rejected by several other American governments for the same reason.[17] It should be noted that the same policy of nonintervention was being followed by the so-called International Committee for the Application of the Agreement Regarding Non-Intervention in Spain, composed of representatives of twenty-seven nations and sitting in London.

The Cuban proposal, like the earlier Uruguayan and Mexican proposals, disclosed wide disagreement in the hemisphere as to the wisdom of the doctrine of the two spheres. According to the Cuban Secretary of State eleven American governments supported Cuba's proposal, but six refused to associate themselves with it because of their policy of nonintervention.[18] The successive Uruguayan, Mexican, and Cuban proposals during 1936-1937, whether intended to benefit one or the other faction in the civil conflict in Spain, all implied a certain skepticism as to the wisdom of continued adherence to the policy of neutrality. Americans, both North and South, were torn between their desire to avoid involvement in war and their concern to terminate the bloody civil conflict in Spain.

The increased participation of German and Italian troops in the Spanish civil war on the side of General Franco, and particularly the shelling of Almeria by a German squadron in May, 1937, produced grave apprehensions in Latin America as to the imminence of World War II and strengthened the general determination of the American

15. *Ibid.*, I, 385-386, and 390-391; see also *ibid.*, 276-277, 318-320, 323-324, 348, and 383-385.

16. Despatch 235, Havana, October 22, 1937, Department of State Archives; and *Foreign Relations of the United States, 1937*, I, 440-441.

17. For the texts of the replies respectively of Bolivia and Panama see *La Razón*, La Paz, October 30, 1937; and *La Estrella de Panamá*, Panama, November 19, 1937. For the replies of Ecuador and Nicaragua see Despatch 954, Quito, November 10, 1937; and Despatch 718, Managua, November 16, 1937. For a newspaper summary of the replies see Despatch 374, Havana, December 20, 1937, *Foreign Relations of the United States, 1937*, I, 466-467.

18. Telegram 2, Havana, January 5, 1938; and Despatch 412, Havana, January 5, 1938, Confidential.

nations to adhere to a policy of neutrality.[19] "It was considered advisable," declared *La Prensa* of Buenos Aires (August 1, 1937), "for the New World to keep aloof from the Old." As with the assistance of Hitler's and Mussolini's forces General Franco was able by November, 1937, to extend his control over approximately 59 per cent of the area and 56 per cent of the population of Spain the pressure in Latin America, particularly in Argentina, for recognition of the Franco government mounted.[20]

By November, 1938, Roosevelt himself was willing to consider plans for securing a Spanish armistice, but it seemed desirable to secure the advance support of some South American countries, and if possible make it a unanimous act of the forthcoming Lima conference.[21] Cuban and Argentine proposals to deal with the Spanish situation were discussed in committee at the Lima conference but were not submitted for debate at the conference because of their anticipated controversial nature.[22] As a result the Lima conference took no action on the Spanish situation.

Soon after the adjournment of the Lima conference Uruguay extended recognition to the Franco government and, after Franco's capture of Madrid in March, other American governments also recognized his government. Mexico, however, continued to support the defeated Spanish government and branded the neutrality of the American nations in the conflict as a crime since it was, in the words of the Mexican Undersecretary of State Ramón Beteta, "tantamount to aiding the strong against the weak."[23]

The Spanish Civil War, then, which produced varying reactions among the American nations, tended to disrupt the newly forming unity of the hemisphere. In the judgment of some Latin Americans the United States, by reason of its too scrupulous neutrality toward

19. *La Nación, La Prensa, El Mundo, El Diario,* and *La Razón,* Buenos Aires, June 1, 1937; *El Día,* Montevideo, June 4, 1937; and *La Nación,* Santiago, June 2, 1937.

20. Geopress, Geneva, November 1937, "The two Spains," typewritten copy in Department of State Archives, showing percentage of the area and population of Spain in possession of the two adversaries in the Spanish civil war. See also Telegram 216, Buenos Aires, November 10, 1937, *Foreign Relations of the United States, 1937,* I, 444-445; and Despatch 543, Montevideo, February 28, 1939, Department of State Archives.

21. Assistant Secretary of State Adolf Berle to President Roosevelt, November 19, 1938, *Foreign Relations of the United States, 1938,* I, 255. See also *ibid.,* 258, 260, 261.

22. Telegram 44, Lima, December 19, 1938, Department of State Archives.

23. Speech by Ramón Beteta, *Excelsior,* Mexico City, December 10, 1937.

that conflict, was not moving fast enough to save humanity from the threat of totalitarianism. Though the United States professed to be championing international law and order at a time when the totalitarian powers were insisting that force was the only reality worthy of consideration, the North Americans seemed to be too insistent upon maintaining their "liberty of action."[24] They seemed to be unwilling "to submit themselves to the discipline and to the obligations of every collective action" designed to strengthen international law.[25]

For this reason President Roosevelt's call, in his address at Chicago in October, 1937, for the quarantine of international aggressors, pointedly directed at the totalitarian powers of Europe and Asia, may have been better received by Latin Americans than by his own countrymen. Telegrams of congratulation were sent to him by the presidents of Argentina and Cuba, and editorial comment on the speech throughout Latin America was generally favorable.[26] It was hailed by several journalists as evidencing the virile democracy of the United States and as foreshadowing the abandonment of the policy of isolation which that country had been following since 1918. "All the democracies of the world," declared *Ultima Hora* of La Paz (October 7, 1937), "threatened as they are directly or indirectly by Fascist madness, will find a firm moral support in the great North American nation." According to *El Día* of Montevideo (October 7, 1937), "the gallant American Executive" now stood revealed as "the herald and standard-bearer of the cause of civilization." Another newspaper of Montevideo, *La Mañana,* an organ of the Riverista Party, observed that "the idealistic voice of 'Ariel' now comes from the north."[27] The new Ariel was challenging the Nazi-Fascist powers in defense of the sanctity of treaties and morality in international life.[28] Roosevelt's warning was, said *El Tiempo* of Bogotá, a "quiet and clean affirmation of right" in a world almost overwhelmed by the avalanche of Fascism. But it alone might not be sufficient to stop the advance of Fascism. "Unless his

24. *Diário da Noite,* Rio de Janeiro, July 29, 1937. See also *El Liberal Progresista,* Guatemala, August 2, 1937; Dr. José Espalter in *El Pueblo,* Montevideo, March 11, 1939; and *El Imparcial,* Guatemala, August 3, 1937.
25. Carlos Bauer-Aviles in *Nuestro Diario,* Guatemala, August 5, 1937. The United States established diplomatic relations with Franco on April 1, 1939, *Foreign Relations of the United States, 1939,* II, 771.
26. Telegrams, Havana, October 5, and Buenos Aires, October 7, 1937, Department of State Archives.
27. Despatch 38, Montevideo, October 8, 1937, Department of State Archives.
28. León Angel in *La Razón,* Bogotá, October 7, 1937.

words are backed by United States machine guns and he is prepared to use them," cautioned the *Panama American* (October 7, 1937), "his will be just another voice crying in the diplomatic wilderness."[29]

Germany's occupation of Austria in March, 1938, and of the Sudeten areas of Czechoslovakia in the following October quickened the apprehension of Latin Americans as to the menace of European dictatorship and strengthened their feeling of reliance upon the United States as a physical and moral bulwark against that menace. They began to realize that, as the Paraguayan Minister of Foreign Affairs confidentially informed the United States ambassador in Asunción, all the Latin American countries existed by virtue of the protection of the United States. Unless they could now assure themselves of the support of their powerful northern neighbor they might suffer the same fate as the small nations of Europe.[30]

Monroe's warning of 1823 against any attempt on the part of European powers "to extend their system to any portion of this hemisphere" now seemed to take on a new and urgent pertinency. Long considered a threat to the countries south of the United States, it became, as the totalitarian powers grew more threatening, a shield, behind which Latin Americans could seek shelter.[31] It should no longer be considered, said *La Crónica* of Lima (March 8, 1938), "a perturbing element to upset the peoples of America . . . but a generous instrument of peace for the defense of the integrity of the whole American continent." Latin Americans concluded that the Monroe Doctrine had beneficent possibilities for them and might, particularly if given Pan-American approval, serve as a collective guaranty of the territorial inviolability of all the American nations. They were willing to admit "the broad fraternal meaning of this doctrine," testified *La Nación* of Santiago, Chile (April 22, 1938).[32] Indeed they insisted that the essential principle of that doctrine, the defense of the New World, had historically originated with Francisco de Miranda, Juan Egaña, Bernardo O'Higgins, Simón Bolívar, and other early Latin American patriots.

29. October 7, 1937. For additional newspaper comment on Roosevelt's "quarantine speech" see *El Nacional,* Mexico City, October 8, 1937; *Star and Herald,* Panama, October 7, 1937; and *Nuestro Diario,* Guatemala, October 6, 1937.

30. Despatch 566, Asunción, March 19, 1938, Confidential.

31. *La Prensa,* San Salvador, February 7, 1938; and *La Nación,* Santiago, April 22, 1938.

32. April 22, 1938. See also *La Crónica,* Lima, March 8, 1938; *Universal,* Lima, October 7, 1937; *Diário Latino* and *O Jornal,* Rio de Janeiro, August 20, 1938; and *Star and Herald,* Panama, April 21, 1938.

Confronted with new rising dangers in Europe, they began to advocate the continentalization of the Monroe Doctrine in order to convert it into a Pan-American obligation for the defense of the hemisphere.

As early as 1936 President Alfonso López of Colombia had proposed that the Monroe Doctrine be replaced with a multilateral treaty.[33] As plans were laid for the Eighth Conference of American States at Lima in 1938, this same suggestion was made with increasing frequency in Latin America. If "an alliance for mutual defense among the American nations" could be formed, argued the *Star and Herald* of Panama (April 21, 1938), "the United States could engage to assist the poorer nations of Latin America to create air bases and naval bases as a part of a vast system of Continental defense against aggression." The Latin American nations would then become "real and effective partners with the United States in the defense of the political and territorial integrity of the New World, rather than weak dependants [*sic*] on the will or convenience of the United States for the defense of the Monroe Doctrine." On the eve of the Lima conference the presidents of both Guatemala and El Salvador proposed to the United States ministers in their capitals that the Monroe Doctrine be transformed into a multilateral concept to counter the threat of Japanese imperialism, Italian Fascism, and German Naziism.[34] By making it a genuinely "American Doctrine" all the nations of America would give warning to the world that an act of aggression against any American nation would be considered as an act of aggression against all American nations.[35]

But should the Latin American nations link themselves with the United States for peace or for war? As the Good Neighbor Policy had convinced them that the United States, under Roosevelt's leadership, was a nonaggressive nation, so Roosevelt's country came to be looked upon by them as the champion and hope of peace. To the extent that they believed the United States to be pursuing a peace policy they were impelled to unite their fortunes with it. They moved toward increased unity and joint action with the United States because of their longing for peace, neutrality, and security in a world which seemed to be heading toward debacle. Hemispheric isolationism, however, was the dominant theme of inter-American cooperation. The

33. Despatch 1005, Bogotá, September 29, 1936.
34. Despatch 539, Guatemala, March 17, 1938; and Despatch 696, Guatemala, September 24, 1938.
35. Despatch 539, Guatemala, March 17, 1938.

Americas were to remain a hemisphere of peace in a warring world. Their pacific and fraternal ideals contrasted sharply with "the clash of imperialism found in Europe."[36] They would remain aloof from "the lunacies of Europe."[37] The history of intervention by the United States in their affairs convinced them of the dangers both for the United States and for themselves of intervention in Europe and Asia against the Axis powers.

In fact, in the judgment of many Latin Americans Roosevelt had already gone too far in implicating them in the European melee. The growing physical and moral power of the United States and its preoccupation with the protection of the entire American hemisphere against aggression from outside powers seemed ominous. The military preparedness program of the United States in particular was viewed with misgivings. Since it seemed not to be fully justified as a strategic necessity its apparent aim, according to some commentators, was an increase in offensive power. The Latin American nations would be unwise, advised El Diario of Montevideo (March 14, 1939), organ of the Colorado Riverista Party, to burden their budgets similarly with military expenditures against "imaginary perils." According to Ultimas Noticias of Mexico City (March 2, 1939), the Roosevelt administration was inviting involvement in extracontinental matters only as a means of consolidating its political position both at home and throughout the American hemisphere. It was "putting forth its greatest disguised efforts" to provoke a war because a war would "solve at one blow all the present acute problems, and Uncle Sam would again swim in the abundance and prosperity which he enjoyed from 1917 to 1929, when the inevitable crash came." The acidulous Herrerista newspaper of Montevideo, El Debate (March 17, 1939), charged Roosevelt with seeking to communicate his "war spirit" to the peaceful Latin American countries and to alarm them with talk of a possible Nazi invasion. These unfriendly critics as well as others less unfriendly therefore insisted that in the approaching conflict Latin America should adhere to a policy of strict neutrality.

Latin America's insistence upon a policy of peace for the American continents was reinforced by economic considerations. Despite the considerable improvement in trade relations between the United States and Latin America which had resulted from Roosevelt's policy of com-

36. El País, Montevideo, November 11, 1936.
37. Manuel Barba Salinas in Diario de Hoy, San Salvador, November 7, 1936.

mercial reciprocity and the inevitable cyclical upswing of the economies of the Latin American countries from their depression lows, Latin America's total trade with the United States for the year 1936, amounting to $958,000,000, was still valued at less than half the 1929 figure of $2,079,000,000. The United States had to face the old circumstance that some of the South American countries had rival rather than complementary economies with its own. Their economic as well as their cultural ties were with Europe rather than with the United States. When Germany lost her colonies after World War I Latin Americans considered her to be no longer an imperialistic nation like the United States and Great Britain and used her therefore to counterbalance both United States and British influence. Between the periods 1929-1932 and 1935-1937 the trade of the Latin American countries with the Axis countries, stimulated by the incentives of bilateral barter agreements, the Aski-mark system, and roseate trade offers, increased by $88,146,-000 a year in terms of annual average values between the periods 1929-1932 and 1935-1937. By 1938 Latin America's total trade with the Axis nations was valued at $517,844,000, as compared with their total trade with the United States of $1,051,824,000. By that time the United States program of reciprocal trade with the Latin American nations had come to a virtual standstill. Nations with which the United States wished to conclude reciprocal trade agreements were unable, because of prior commitments, to assure the most-favored-nation treatment upon which Secretary Hull insisted. In particular, negotiations with Argentina and Uruguay were held up because of their discriminatory practices in connection with official exchange control.

The considerable stake of Latin America in the trade of the Axis nations counseled a policy of moderation if not appeasement, particularly in the southern countries of the hemisphere. The Argentine Foreign Minister, Dr. José María Cantilo, threw out the chilling reminder, in an interview with Duncan Aikman of the *New York Post* in September, 1938, that relations between his country and Roosevelt's country could not be close because "the trade currents of Argentina and the United States are not coincident" and Argentina's "cultural affinities are greater with Europe than with the United States," though he hastened to deny that Argentina's "intellectual and aesthetic inclinations" were with "new European ideologies of the totalitarian nations or of Communist Russia."[38] Argentina thus manifested a standoffishness which was ominous for the future.

38. *La Nación,* Buenos Aires, September 17, 1938.

In the capital of Uruguay *El Debate* (November 23, 1938), supporting the Terra dictatorship in that country, argued that no true understanding could be reached between the United States and the twenty Latin American countries because "The United States . . . is our commercial enemy, . . . *our competitor.*" It was seeking to exercise a so-called protective function over Latin America only because it was *"on bad terms with Europe and especially with the strong and well-armed nations, Italy and Germany, and it is on worse terms with Asia, particularly with Japan, which is . . . dislodging it from all its positions."* Therefore the United States was really seeking the protection of Latin America.[39] This explanation was echoed by the official *El Universal* of Caracas (December 14, 1938), which said that "our older brother and neighbor of the North is the one who most needs continental defense at the moment and cannot assure a defense without the immediate cooperation of the other American countries." In Chile publicists charged that the United States had become concerned about the advance of the antidemocratic nations because its trade was being adversely affected by those nations.[40] And Felipe Barreda Laos, the distinguished ambassador of Peru to Argentina and Uruguay, wrote that what the United States was really contending for was "the freedom of the seas, under British-North American control."[41] Meanwhile Panama took advantage of the neutrality legislation of the United States, which banned United States trade with the belligerents, to permit foreign neutral merchant vessels to register under the Panamanian flag and thus to carry on a lucrative commerce with both sides in the war.

The prodemocratic pretensions of the Roosevelt administration also were viewed suspiciously by some of the liberals and radicals. Since few of the Latin American governments could justly be called "democratic," what did Roosevelt's invocations of a union to defend the democratic systems of the continent really signify?[42] If opposition to totalitarianism was his real object, why did he oppose the dictators of the Axis countries while seeking closer relations with American dictators? *APRA* leader Haya de la Torre, writing in *El Mundo* of Havana (February 20, 1938), regretted that Roosevelt did not "condemn more explicitly, in the name of the peoples who suffer, the Latin autocrats

39. Italics in original.
40. Carlos Gaedechens, "Chile y la Conferencia Pan Americana," *Economía y Finanzas,* Santiago, February 1939, 5-6.
41. *¿Hispano América en Guerra?* (Buenos Aires, 1941), 68.
42. *Ibid.,* 65-67.

who consider Mr. Roosevelt their 'great and good friend.' " When the Roosevelt government welcomed President Anastasio Somoza of Nicaragua to Washington in early 1939 and concluded certain agreements with him *El Universal* of Mexico City charged that "the Good Neighbor doctrine . . . is transforming itself into a league of 'mestizo' dictators, with the United States destined to guarantee the slavery of Latin American peoples."[43] Sergio Carbó, a strongly pro-United States columnist of *El Crisol* of Havana (June 21, 1940), also felt that "Washington should put an end to its mistaken policy of protecting petty dictators." The democratic and "liberal" professions of the New Deal administration seemed to such Latin Americans to require logically, therefore, that the United States dissociate itself from, or even crusade against, undemocratic and illiberal regimes everywhere. Hemisphere defense against totalitarian aggression, they felt, was not strengthened by collaboration with Latin American despots.

Nor was it strengthened by Roosevelt's policy of collaboration with Russia, which was deeply repugnant to conservative and oligarchic groups in Latin America. Such groups considered it abhorrent that the United States should seek a *rapprochement* with "that other people whom all the South American countries have placed outside the law."[44] To these groups the apparent similarities between Roosevelt's New Deal and the state-directed systems of Soviet Russia and National Socialist Germany made his collaboration with the former and his antagonism to the latter perplexing.

These ideological paradoxes in the policy of the administration in Washington heightened Latin American fears as to the real objectives of the United States. The United States had become concerned about the advance of the antidemocratic nations, alleged the official *Universal* of Lima (August 18, 1938), only when its trade with the Far East and its political position in the Philippine Islands was threatened. Might it be the purpose of the United States now to use the Axis threat as a pretext for establishing its own control over the Latin American countries? Behind the "diplomatic statements and great oratorical phrases," charged *El Universal* of Mexico City (November 18, 1938), raged "a struggle for economic realities and not for political or social theories." Latin Americans must determine not to be exploited or subjugated by any foreign imperialism, including that of

43. Despatch 270, Ciudad Juárez, May 25, 1939, Department of State Archives.
44. Gerardo Uzátegui, *El Comercio,* Lima, October 18, 1937.

the United States. When Roosevelt emphasized in a press conference in the following year that the United States would not permit a non-American power to extend its possessions in the American hemisphere, *Ultimas Noticias* of Mexico (September 13, 1939) pointed out that his statement left the door "maliciously wide open for the United States itself to acquire lands and bases in the New World if it needs them." At the same time the rightist *La Hora* of Santiago, Chile (October 30, 1939), though giving full credit to the sincerity of the Good Neighbor Policy, warned in addition that "imperialistic penetration—not official, not imparted or accepted perhaps by Washington—exists and exists very powerfully in all South American countries: it is an economic and financial penetration by the magnates of Wall Street, who, from their luxurious offices, pull mysterious wires to produce the most unexpected political, economic, and social phenomena in our small and modest republics." Old injuries to Latin America by the United States were alarmingly recapitulated—including "the injuries to Texas, Arizona, New Mexico and California in 1847, to Puerto Rico and Santo Domingo, to Panama, to Veracruz in 1914, and that of the Pershing Punitive Expedition in 1915 [1916], not to mention many others,"[45] and evidences of new imperialistic designs against Latin America were cited.

Some of these anxieties seemed justified by the policy counsel occasionally voiced in the press and Congress of the United States as the activities of Axis sympathizers and agents in Latin America were intensified. Latin Americans were dismayed at the occasional suggestion in the United States press that, in order to checkmate Germany and Japan, the United States ought to march into Mexico, assume the role of trustee of that country until the European war was over, and similarly take over the Central American countries in order to protect the Panama Canal. They noted with disapproval a proposal of an Arizona congressman in November, 1936, that the United States negotiate with Mexico for territory in Sonora near the outlet of the Colorado River to provide a seaport on the Gulf of Lower California.[46] Both *Ultimas Noticias* and *Excelsior* of Mexico City (April 1, 1938) denounced as "idiotic" and "absurd" a later proposal by a Los Angeles colonel that the United States purchase Lower California from

---

45. Querido Moheno, Jr., in *Todo*, Mexico City, May 4, 1939. For similar views see *Ultimas Noticias*, Mexico City, August 17, 1938.
46. *El Universal Gráfico*, Mexico City, November 25, 1936; and *Ultimas Noticias*, Mexico City, December 1, 1936.

Mexico. A similar suggestion by a California congressman was indignantly resisted by *El Mundo* of Tampico (October 30, 1939) as "a symptom of a tendency which is growing among the people on the other side of the Río Bravo." These expressions of territorial covetousness tended to throw shadows of doubt over the noninterventionist professions of the Roosevelt administration. "In spite of all the good intentions of the Democratic Party," concluded *El Bien Público* (June 23, 1939), a Roman Catholic publication in Uruguay, "the great masses of Yankees have not ceased to be imperialists."

Considerations such as these help to explain why at the Lima conference in 1938 the Latin Americans rejected the United States' program for a hemisphere front against possible aggression from the totalitarian nations in favor of a simple declaration of common principles and good intentions. The policy of the United States in relation to the Latin American nations, as expressed by Secretary Hull in his opening address to the representatives of all the American governments at that conference, was to strengthen the inter-American system of consultation and common action in order to enable them to resist "the invasion of their hemisphere by the armed forces of any power or possible combination of powers" and to destroy the forces which would prevent their unity of action. With this objective in view the United States wanted all the American republics to bind themselves by treaty to resist collectively any threat to their peace, security, or territorial integrity from a non-American source. Aroused to the threat from Germany, it desired to create a permanent committee of the foreign ministers of the twenty-one American governments and to issue a collective warning against Nazi intrigue. But Argentina, backed by Bolivia, Chile, Paraguay, and Uruguay, refused to join in any hostile reference to Germany and pointedly sought to broaden the United States proposal to favor consultation in the event of threats from either a "continental or extracontinental power." "When a nation from the outside really threatens us," declared the Argentine Foreign Minister José María Cantilo, "then is the time we are to take decisive and united action to defend ourselves." The Argentines, he said, were unwilling to offend the European nations which "give lifeblood to our nation and buy our products."[47] They and their allies refused, therefore, to sign any pact which might entangle them in future non-American conflicts. All that the conference finally could agree upon was a declaration that any threat to one of the American

47. Interview with Dr. Samuel Guy Inman, December 12, 1938.

nations from any source was of concern to all and should give rise to "the procedure of consultation," without derogating, however, from their right to "act independently in their individual capacity, recognizing fully their juridical equality as sovereign states."[48]

In an effort to counteract this indifference and to encourage cooperation for defense, friends of the United States in Latin America, distressed by the rising Axis threat, took pains to deny that the United States was hatching imperialist designs against its southern neighbors. It was absurd, declared *Ahora* of Caracas (November 24, 1938), to suppose that President Roosevelt's initiative in favor of continental defense meant that the United States was trying to secure hegemony over Latin America.[49] Anti-Axis newspapers in Latin America reported with approval the growing strength of the interventionist movement in the United States headed by Roosevelt.[50] They professed to believe that all the nations of America appreciated, as *La Nación* of Santiago, Chile (June 17, 1939) expressed it, that "the fate of democracy is in the balance."[51] But in fact the American hemisphere was still sharply divided. The outbreak of the European conflict in the following year and the resulting severance of Latin America's trade with Europe were required to drive these nations into a closer solidarity with the United States at Panama in September, 1939.

* * *

With the beginning of war in Europe in 1939 almost every tongue in the Western Hemisphere began to ask, "How can the American nations stay out of the conflict? How can we keep war away from our New World and immunize our hemisphere from its electric shocks? In the face of international chaos abroad how can we maintain our American way of peace?"

The war had scarcely begun when its shocks were felt by the American nations. Indeed the naval phases of the war started in the

48. Department of State, *Report of the Delegation of the United States of America to the Eighth International Conference of American States, Lima, Peru, December 9-27, 1938* (Washington, 1941), 190; Cordell Hull, *Memoirs,* I, 601-611; William L. Langer and S. Everett Gleason, *The Challenge to Isolation, 1937-1940* (New York, 1952), 41; and O. Edmund Smith, Jr., *Yankee Diplomacy: U.S. Intervention in Argentina* (Dallas, 1953), 37-46.
    49. See also *Diario de la Marina,* Havana, February 5, 1939.
    50. *El Día,* Montevideo, March 22, 1938.
    51. See also *El País,* Montevideo, November 10, 1938.

Western Hemisphere. Only four hours after Great Britain declared war on Germany in September, 1939, the British cruiser "Ajax" sank the German freighter "Olinda" in South Atlantic waters approximately 600 miles off the coast of Uruguay and sent the German survivors into Montevideo. Immediately the United States and all the Latin American nations issued declarations of neutrality in accordance with the traditional international codes of neutral conduct, specifically the Hague Conventions of 1907, the Declaration of London of 1909, and the Convention on Maritime Neutrality signed at the Sixth Inter-American Conference in 1928.[52] But they did not stop with these measures to maintain their individual neutrality; they also prepared for collective action toward the same end. On the very day of Germany's invasion of Poland, President Eduardo Santos of Colombia addressed a message to all the American governments suggesting that they take cooperative action on the basis of the principles of solidarity proclaimed in the Pan-American conferences, and these governments promptly made plans to hold a consultative meeting of their foreign ministers.

All the delegations at this first meeting of the foreign ministers which began in Panama City on September 23, 1939, agreed upon the necessity of keeping their countries free from the horrors of war. Their primary purpose was to defend and preserve the peace of the American hemisphere, or, as stated by Sumner Welles, United States Under Secretary of State, "to keep war away from this continent."[53] To this end, recalling "their unanimous intention not to become involved in the European conflict," they reaffirmed "the status of general neutrality of the American Republics." In general they agreed also upon methods of preserving the neutrality of the Americas. As in their national neutrality enactments they now collectively announced that they would deny the use of their territories as bases of belligerent operations, would prevent the recruiting of troops within their jurisdictions, would compel belligerent warships to leave their waters after twenty-four hours, and in general would seek to make uniform the enforcement of their neutrality in accordance with the accepted prin-

52. For examples of Latin American declarations of neutrality see República del Ecuador, *Registro Oficial* (Quito, September 4 and 5, 1939), 1146; and República de Colombia, *Diario Oficial* (Bogotá, September 7, 1939), Decree No. 1776 of 1939. The neutrality declaration by the United States is printed in *Department of State Bulletin*, I (September 9, 1939), 203-211.

53. Statement of September 15, 1939, *Department of State Bulletin*, I (September 16, 1939), 252.

ciples of international law. In pursuance of these objects they established for the duration of the war an Inter-American Neutrality
Committee, composed of seven experts in international law, to present
from time to time recommendations on the problems of neutrality
arising out of the changing circumstances of the war.

But the most far-reaching and controversial decision of this meeting of foreign ministers was the Declaration of Panama, which was
reminiscent of a proposal offered as a means of maintaining the neutrality of the nations of the American hemisphere during the period
of their neutrality in World War I. As early as August, 1914, Peru
had proposed that all the American nations declare that their commerce on the American continents and in the waters extending to a
line equidistant from Europe on the one hand and Asia on the other
should not be "subject to the contingencies of the present European
war." At the same time Brazil had also suggested that a neutral zone
be drawn around the continent of South America from which all
warships would be barred. Substantially this same proposal was conceived by President Roosevelt in September, 1939, and was accepted
at Panama. Making the assumption that the interests of belligerents
must not be allowed to prevail over the rights of neutrals, the Declaration of Panama proclaimed "as a measure of continental self-protection" on behalf of all the American nations that the belligerent
nations must refrain from the commission of hostile acts within a
defined "zone of security" extending from 300 to 600 miles to sea
around the American continents excepting only "the territorial waters
of Canada and of the undisputed colonies and possessions of European countries within these limits." The American governments
further agreed to ask the belligerents through joint representation to
respect the declaration, and they announced that if necessary they
would consult together to secure its observance. In addition they
said that they might undertake to establish a patrol in this neutralized
zone.

The Declaration of Panama was based upon the unexceptionable
right of self-protection which all nations possess, in the words of the
Declaration itself, "as of inherent right." It was intended to provide
neutral security for the Americas against the incursions of an increasingly totalitarian war. But almost immediately this "zone of security"
became a zone of insecurity. As the American nations altogether
could furnish not more than seventy vessels to patrol the zone, comprising more than five million square miles of water, its sanctity could

obviously be broken by the belligerents almost with impunity. It was variously criticized as being unenforceable, as constituting a departure from accepted rules of international law on freedom of the seas, and as tending to embroil the Americas in war. Either the zone of neutrality would be unenforced, declared the conservative *El Siglo* of Bogotá (December 27, 1939), or "it will lead to war." This "chastity belt" around the Americas could not be enforced, declared *Ultimas Noticias* of Mexico City (October 5, 1939), since none of the Latin American nations "possesses a fleet which could effectively patrol such an extensive zone" and the United States navy was inadequate "to protect its own coasts along with the vast coasts of all America." The venerable pro-British *Mercurio* of Santiago, Chile (February 19, 1940), called it "the greatest mistake of Pan-Americanism" and repeatedly ridiculed "the juridical nonsense, the impracticability and the inconvenience of the visionary zone." Some officials and publicists, on the other hand, objected to the Declaration as a too limited version of the rights of neutrals and demanded instead that the American nations as a bloc insist that the flags and the cargoes of neutrals be protected and their rights respected everywhere, not simply in the waters of the American hemisphere. To them it represented an abandonment of the traditional neutral right to freedom of the seas. *Ultimas Noticias* of Mexico City (October 5, 1939) even charged that the United States had sponsored this maritime belt around the American continents in order to gain control for itself over the maritime commerce of the western world.

Despite the Declaration of Panama the European war again invaded the American hemisphere in December, 1939, when the German pocket battleship "Graf von Spee," appropriately named for the German admiral whose squadron had been destroyed by a British fleet off the Falkland Islands in 1914, fought a naval battle with the three British cruisers "Exeter," "Ajax," and "Achilles" within the territorial waters of Uruguay. In this naval encounter a French merchant vessel "Formose" was also involved. Badly crippled, the "Spee" made its way into the Montevideo shipyards where it received repairs but was required to depart at the expiration of the time limit prescribed by international law. Faced with certain destruction by the British cruisers lying in wait, Captain Hans Langsdorff of the "Spee" scuttled his vessel inside Uruguayan territorial waters, after first arranging to have the officers and crew transported to Buenos Aires. After they arrived there the German captain committed suicide and more than one thousand members of the crew were interned in the interior of Argentina.[54]

This violation of the peace of the hemisphere evoked prompt remonstrances from the Americas. Uruguay complained officially to both the British and German governments against this "violation of its national sovereignty." The Argentine government was moved to issue warnings that radio information must not be sent from Argentine territory to belligerent war vessels at sea. At the suggestion of the United States, all the American governments joined in addressing a protest on December 23, 1939, to Great Britain, France, and Germany against naval engagements fought in "American waters" as defined in the Declaration of Panama. In this protest they impartially complained against the detention and sinking of vessels by both the British and the Germans within the American security zone. Referring to sanctions mentioned in the Hague Convention on Maritime Neutrality of 1907 they informed the belligerents that in order to implement their neutrality they proposed "to prevent belligerent vessels from supplying themselves and repairing damages in American ports when the said vessels have committed warlike acts within the zone of security established in the Declaration of Panama."[55] In other words, they threatened to deny the use of their ports to vessels violating the neutrality of the zone.

These joint representations and the sanctity of the neutrality zone upon which they were predicated were rejected by all three of the principal European belligerents.[56] But their refusal to respect the maritime rights of the neutral American nations did not deter those nations from continuing to insist upon respect for their status as neutrals. Nor did it persuade them to abandon the security zone of the Declaration of Panama. President Roosevelt disclosed on April 25, 1941, that the Pan-American neutrality patrol had been operating as far as 1,000 miles to sea off certain parts of the American continents. At that time he announced that the United States was extending this patrol still farther out into the Atlantic not only for the purpose of gathering information but also "for the defense of the American hemisphere." Because, as he said, the danger to the Western Hemisphere was growing greater, the patrol was operating farther

54. República Oriental del Uruguay, Ministerio de Relaciones Exteriores, *Antecedentes Relativos al Hundimiento del Acorazado "Admiral Graf Spee" y a la Internación del Barco Mercante "Tacoma"* (Montevideo, 1940).
55. *Department of State Bulletin*, I (December 23, 1939), 723.
56. *Ibid.*, II (February 24, 1940), 199-205.

at sea and would operate still farther as need to do so developed.[57] It continued to be one means by which the American nations, largely through the enforcement action of the United States, undertook to maintain their status as neutrals. As it was thus enforced it demonstrated to the Latin Americans that their combined relative weaknesses could be transformed into a union of strength when joined to the power of the United States.

But the neutrality policy of the American nations became increasingly fictional as the juggernaut of the totalitarian nations rolled with gathering momentum over most of western Europe, swallowing up successively Poland, Norway, Denmark, Belgium, Luxemburg, the Netherlands, and France. Germany's occupation of Denmark and Norway in April, 1940, showed that small neutral nations could no longer rely upon international law for protection and that neutral rights would not be allowed to stand in the way of action deemed militarily necessary by the belligerents. Latin Americans expected this German action to have also the adverse effect of curtailing or perhaps entirely terminating the operations of the Danish and Norwegian merchant marine, which had been of great assistance in moving Latin America's waterborne commerce. The foreign ministers of Chile and Argentina announced that their governments would not recognize the German conquest of Denmark and Norway. The Peruvian Chamber of Deputies adopted a motion deploring "that the action of the war in Europe should have been carried into the Scandinavian countries violating their rights as sovereign nations."[58] Similar declarations were issued by other American governments. *La Esfera* of Caracas painted a gloomy picture of the results for the entire American hemisphere of further German victories in Europe. These results, it predicted, would include the transfer to Germany of all the English, French, and probably also Dutch possessions in America, the partitioning of Brazil, the establishment of a German protectorate over Central America, the application of "direct influence upon Mexico, and Nazi intrusions on the rest of the continent." In Europe, concluded *La Esfera* (April 15, 1940), was being decided "the future destiny of all the American countries, from North to South. . . . What is happening in Europe to small countries is proof of what can happen

57. President Roosevelt, press conference, April 25, 1941, Samuel I. Rosenman (comp.), *The Public Papers and Addresses of Franklin D. Roosevelt*, X (New York, 1938-1950), 132-136.
58. Despatch 14, Lima, April 12, 1940, Department of State Archives.

to American nations, all incapable of defending themselves without the United States."

Further "proof" was provided by Germany's occupation of Belgium, Luxemburg, and the Netherlands in May, 1940, which produced a reaction of indignation in the Americas. The Foreign Minister of Ecuador considered this act "so serious an outrage of the rules of international law and of the basic principles of our civilization" that he addressed a note (May 10, 1940) to the conquered governments expressing sympathy with them as victims of "unjustifiable aggression." Similar messages were sent soon afterward by other Latin American governments, and a joint protest, suggested by Uruguay, was issued by all the American governments against "the ruthless violation by Germany of the neutrality and sovereignty of Belgium, Holland and Luxemburg."[59] President Roosevelt's denunciation of this invasion in his radio address of May 10 was widely approved in Latin America. In Buenos Aires even the ardently nationalist *La Fronda* (May 13, 1940) criticized "the brutal German invasion" and praised the protest against it presented by Argentine President Roberto M. Ortiz. No longer, concluded *El Tiempo* of Bogotá (May 16, 1940), could Latin Americans rely upon having their rights scrupulously respected simply because "we are peaceful, honorable, and law-abiding and do not threaten anyone and because it is not physically possible to organize an attack at a distance so great as that which separates us from the Old World."

These aggressions against neutral countries created a generally unfavorable public opinion for Germany in Latin America, even among those who had formerly held that Germany was being strangled by the western powers. Latin American organs of opinion, which had previously shown a studied impartiality, such as *La Nación* of Ciudad Trujillo, now condemned the action of Germany, which, as that newspaper declared, "unveils its mad thirst for power."[60] Against this public feeling of indignation and outrage the German information and propaganda agencies in Latin America henceforth waged a losing struggle.

But the horror inspired by these German acts of "barbarism," as they were characterized by many Latin American newspapers, also strengthened the pacific inclinations of Latin Americans and increased

59. Department of State, *Press Release* No. 239 (May 18, 1940).
60. Telegram 74, Ciudad Trujillo, May 11, 1940, Department of State Archives.

their desire to remain aloof from the holocaust. Moreover, the easy successes of the German military machine counseled moderation among those Latin Americans who concluded that Germany would be victorious and who did not want to prejudice their trade with Germany after the war. In Argentina influential groups in the government were reported by the United States ambassador to be willing to declare for inter-American solidarity and cooperation but were not willing to make any military or economic commitments or to take any defense measures that might offend Germany and Italy.[61] There was a strong disposition among Latin Americans, including high officials, to seek the best possible bargain they could get from the victors, whoever they might be. Indeed it was suggested that a German-dominated Europe might even benefit Latin Americans by providing them with a rival to the United States for their commerce and other favors. The countries conquered by Germany, some Latin Americans pointed out, would continue as before to need the products of Latin America.[62] *El Siglo* (June 23, 1940), the organ of the Conservative Party of Colombia, even argued that the defense of the Panama Canal was of concern only to the United States. It contemplated with equanimity the possibility that "tomorrow, in a division of spoils among the conquerors the [Panama Canal] Zone of which we were despoiled should pass under the domination of England, Japan or even Germany."

Moreover, Nazi victories stimulated Latin American admiration for Germany as a successful nation and raised doubts as to whether the United States could effectively defend the Western Hemisphere. In particular, they made a generally favorable impression upon armed forces in the Latin American countries, many of whom had been trained in German war methods by German military missions. The German army seemed to be invincible. Hitler, it was widely believed, would win the war, and if he did so he might take reprisals against those who had opposed him. Italy's entry into the conflict as an ally of Germany inspired President Getúlio Vargas of Brazil to deliver an address in which he praised "the strong and virile peoples who are pursuing their purposes instead of wasting their time in idle contem-

61. Despatch 1015, Buenos Aires, July 26, 1940, Department of State Archives.
62. Statement to the Associated Press by Dr. Carlos L. Torriani, Director of the Section of Economic and Consular Affairs of the Foreign Office in the Argentine Ministry of Foreign Affairs, reported in Despatch 848, Buenos Aires, June 27, 1940.

plation of that which is corrupted and worthless."[63] Italy, by her act of joining the Nazis, gave pause to her Roman Catholic coreligionists in Latin America who had been critical of the Nazis. *El Mercurio* of Lima suggested mildly that European totalitarianism might possibly be found to contain principles that would contribute to the progress and welfare of the American nations; and reacting against President Roosevelt's denunciations of these totalitarian actions, *La Noche* of the same capital insisted upon a policy of absolute neutrality as being in the best interests of Latin America, independently adding that the ideas of President Roosevelt could not be expected to suit all the twenty-one American nations.[64] During this period of the Hitler-Stalin pact Communists also urged a policy of strict neutrality. "The Yankee imperialists," declared the Communist *Hoy* of Havana (June 12, 1940), "are working like demons by means of propaganda and economic pressure, influencing the politicians of our countries, to consolidate their dominion in our America so that they will be the only masters and force us to play the part which they wish us to play in this new partition of the world." But Communist opposition to Roosevelt's policy helped to win support among Latin American conservatives for his opposition to the totalitarian powers.

These pragmatic arguments for continued Latin American neutrality in the war were reinforced by the obvious division of public opinion in the United States regarding the policy to be pursued toward the European conflict. The long debate over the repeal of the Neutrality Act, the apparently substantial opposition to the policy of aiding Britain, the continuing unwillingness of a considerable segment of the public to renounce isolation, the prevalence of strikes and other dissension in the United States, and the failure of this greatest industrial nation in the world to swing swiftly into quantity production of planes and armaments gave Latin Americans a picture of a divided country which might not support indefinitely Roosevelt's strong policy toward the Axis aggressors. If the people of the United States were not united in opposing those aggressors, might they not perhaps succumb to a policy of compromise or even surrender in dealing with the Axis nations? Their rejection of such a course of defeatism would be revealed only if they began an all-out defense effort encompassing the entire American hemisphere and at the same

63. Telegram 267, Rio de Janeiro, June 11, 1940, Department of State Archives.
64. Despatch 156, Lima, June 13, 1940, Department of State Archives.

time undertook to save the languishing economies of the Latin American nations, perhaps by purchasing all their essential exports.

In the face of Germany's expanding European conquests cooperation among all the American nations seemed imperative as a means of safeguarding their common interests. "Americanism," declared *Avance* of Havana (May 13, 1940), "which, up to now, had for its inspiration and guide the strengthening of intercontinental relations in the political and economic fields must assume an even more responsible mission: the safeguarding of the actual structure of the American nations." The big question was "Will the United States enter the war?" If Germany should overrun all of Europe and proceed to threaten the nations of America, "what then," asked *La Esfera* of Caracas (April 15, 1940), "would the United States do, the elder and powerful brother isolated before a triumphant invader?" The attitude and actions of the United States might be decisive in respect to the American nations to the south of it. If it should become involved in war the continued neutrality of considerable parts if not all of Latin America would cease to be a possibility. But happily, declared the conservative *Alerta* of Havana (May 10, 1940), "for the present at least, our powerful neighbors have no desire to fight with any enemy. Public opinion in the United States repudiates all armed intervention in the present European conflict." The people of the United States, according to *Hoy* of Mexico City (June 29, 1940), were "irreconcilable enemies of war." Their policy was, according to *Diario de la Marina* of Havana (February 5, 1939), "isolation and armed defense: two solid bases of wise action and a well-thought-out plan toward internal and external peace."

At the same time Latin Americans wanted to be sure that if war invaded the Western Hemisphere they could depend upon protection from the strong right arm of the United States, which, as Roosevelt's giant rearmament program finally got under way, seemed to be putting itself in a posture to defend not only itself but all of America. The hard fact was that, as *Diario de la Marina* of Havana (June 9, 1940) pointed out, "In the whole of America south of the Rio Grande there does not exist a single factory capable of constructing a tank, an airplane, or an anti-aircraft gun. Under such conditions the Latin American countries have to depend exclusively upon the aid of the United States for their defense against the aggression of a great power." If, as some of the southern countries of South America feared, they did not wholeheartedly support the policies being followed by the Roosevelt administration perhaps the United States would not defend them. It might decide to concentrate its protection only in the Caribbean area and in northern South America.[65] Indeed, it was well known in Latin America that the United States was considering a plan of only "quarter-sphere" defense, stopping at the bulge of Brazil and leaving all of South America below the bulge undefended. As the Nazi successes continued, even those Latin Americans who were critical of inter-American solidarity as it was being promoted by Roosevelt seemed to be not only willing but even eager that the United States should assume the responsibility of protecting the entire American hemisphere. They welcomed the gradual weakening of the isolationist position in the United States as strengthening its protective attitude toward Latin America and as enabling it more effectively, in the words of *El Día* of Montevideo (March 22, 1938), "to coordinate its international action with that of other governments which have the same ideals and character."

The official policy of the Latin American governments and the dominant feeling of their peoples continued to favor abstinence from participation in the war. Neutrality as defined in their own national proclamations and their collective declaration at Panama was their criterion of official action. But neutrality for the nations of America in the terms of the Declaration of Panama was now seen to be increasingly unrealistic if not impossible of continuance. Perhaps it was a luxury that could only be maintained at the cost of danger to the very existence of nations which desired it.

As Latin Americans became more and more convinced that the European conflict was a struggle between two hostile systems, the one dedicated to liberty and the other to authoritarianism, and that their own independence was menaced by the aggressive policies of the Axis nations, their predilection for a policy of mere defensive neutrality began to weaken. The longer the war continued, observed *La Plata* of Montevideo (April 15, 1940), the greater was the possibility that the nations of America would turn from a policy of neutrality to one of open alignment with the Allies. Neutrality, *La Razón* of Bogotá (May 16, 1940) warned, seemed to offer the prospect of "immense dangers" to those who clung to it. The conservative *Diario de la Marina* of Havana (May 12, 1940) predicted that "within a very short time the war will become literally world-wide" and that "it will be very difficult for any people in the world to remain at peace."

65. *El País*, Montevideo, May 2 and 5, 1941.

Avance of Havana (May 13, 1940) fatalistically concluded that neutrality "is only a waiting room in which passengers wait for the tragic train."

Some Latin Americans were unwilling to wait passively for war to come to them and began, instead, to advocate open alignment with Britain and France in their struggle against Nazi militarism. Continued neutrality appeared to constitute "a direct service in favor of the German military command," said *El Pueblo* of Montevideo (May 11, 1940). At the same time the New York correspondent of *La Nación* of Buenos Aires criticized the United States for not defending the rights of neutrals with sufficient vigor.[66] Concern began to be felt, too, over a possible German "fifth column" lodged in Latin America to commit acts of sabotage and possibly to deliver certain countries into the hands of the Nazis, as the Norwegian quislings had done. At the behest of the United States, efforts were begun to remove Germans from their positions as pilots and officials of German air lines, particularly SCADTA in Colombia. These efforts were largely dependent, as the United States realized, upon its own aggressive assistance and would not be carried through without it. With Italy's attack upon France, characterized by President Roosevelt as a dagger stabbed "into the back of its neighbor," the large Italian colonies in Latin America, particularly in Brazil and Argentina, came to be viewed with suspicion as possible centers of "fifth columnist" action. In Costa Rica a crowd of more than a thousand people immediately surrounded the home of President Rafael Angel Calderón Guardia shouting "Viva Roosevelt!" and were satisfied only when Calderón addressed them and pledged his government to help defend the democracies.

The fall of France before the German invaders in June, 1940, and the occupation of Paris, the spiritual home of cultured Latin Americans, further accentuated the feeling of insecurity in the Western Hemisphere. It was probably more responsible than any other event for convincing Latin American nationalists of imminent danger from the Axis powers. It demonstrated that cooperation with both the United States and Great Britain was necessary for the survival of their own countries.[67] The governments and peoples of the Americas expressed genuine alarm that the Axis nations in Europe might now move against them by way of Dakar and the bulge of Brazil, that

66. Alberto Caprile in *La Nación*, Buenos Aires, April 10 and 13, 1940.
67. Manuel Seoane, *Nuestra América y la Guerra* (Santiago de Chile, 1940).

they might inspire, finance, and direct rebellions in the Americas, or that they might try to take over the colonial territories of the vanquished French in the Caribbean area and even on the South American mainland.[68] The sea-borne commerce of the American nations was now exposed more than ever before to their predatory submarine operations. Furthermore, Latin Americans were apprehensive that if the British government should be forced to move to Canada the neutrality of the Western Hemisphere would be directly compromised. Would the United States be able, under those conditions, to defend all the Americas? "A shiver has run along the spinal column of the entire continent," reported *El Dictamen* of Veracruz, Mexico (June 27, 1940). "What would we do if America were invaded . . . ? This nightmarish vision has made us all nervous." The only alternatives which were possible to Latin America, said *Hoy* of Mexico City (June 29, 1940), were to be "IN FAVOR OF OR AGAINST THE UNITED STATES." Facing this dilemma it concluded that a century and a quarter of experience with their "formidable neighbor" had shown that Mexico's foreign policy "must harmonize and not clash with that of the United States." For realistic reasons, therefore, Mexico must "forget the injuries of the past" and resolve to be "WITH THE UNITED STATES."[69] In this crisis President Alfredo Baldomir of Uruguay called for "a meeting of Ministers of War and Chiefs of General Staffs of all the American nations to examine the matter of common defense from the viewpoint of strategy."[70]

In the now accelerated military preparedness program of the United States, Latin Americans found cause for admiration and comfort. Such a program appeared to be plainly justified by the need for national as well as continental defense.[71] By the "gigantic efforts of the United States to increase its moderate military power," observed *Diario de la Marina* of Havana (October 26, 1940), it was preparing itself "to repel victoriously any attack, whether by one or more nations, not only against its territory or its possessions but also against the territory or the possessions of any of the other American republics or of Canada."[72] In these efforts the commandant of the Cuban army, after visiting military establishments in the United States in late 1940,

68. *El Nacional* and *El Universal,* Mexico City, November 7, 1940.
69. Italics and capitals in original.
70. Interview published in *Noticias Gráficas,* Buenos Aires, June 19, 1940.
71. See *El Liberal Progresista,* Guatemala, June 14 and 15, 1940.
72. See also the issues of May 30 and June 19, 1940.

saw the means for "the necessary protection of the integrity of the democratic ideals which are so precious to those of us who live in the Western Hemisphere." The arsenals, fortifications, training camps, aviation fields, and other examples of the growing military might of the United States convinced Latin Americans of the need for a strengthened American brotherhood—*una hermandad americana*—for if the storm should unfortunately break over their heads all of America must be closely united in order to resist it victoriously.[73] "Only inter-American cooperation," declared *Crítica* of Buenos Aires (January 16, 1941), "will safeguard the peace and independence of the continent." The influential *La Nación* of the same capital began in November, 1940, to prepare Argentine public opinion for fuller cooperation with the United States on all questions of continental defense, even being willing that Argentine bases should be made available to the United States and to other countries of the hemisphere for purposes of defense. To the feelings of "romantic continentalism" which had formerly been appealed to as a means of reconciling the Anglo-American and the Latin American peoples of the hemisphere was now added a compelling urge for collective Pan-American security. This feeling of "togetherness" in danger produced a new *rapprochement* among them.

In an effort to prevent the transfer of France's possessions in the Americas to a victorious Germany, the United States decided to reaffirm its traditional "no-transfer principle," which had been announced originally in 1811 in President Madison's administration and later incorporated in the Monroe Doctrine by President Grant. Mindful specifically of the French territories in the Americas the United States now notified Germany that "in accordance with its traditional policy relating to the Western Hemisphere," it "would not recognize any transfer, and would not acquiesce in any attempt to transfer any geographic region of the Western Hemisphere from one non-American power to another non-American power."[74] Since Pan-American support of this principle seemed desirable, Cuba recommended that all the American governments unite in establishing a joint trusteeship or guardianship over the colonial possessions of the European belligerents in the American hemisphere. This action was a prelude to the adoption by the foreign ministers of the American nations, in their Second Meeting at Havana in July, 1940, of the Act

73. *Diario de la Marina*, Havana, October 26, 1940.
74. *Department of State Bulletin*, II (June 22, 1940), 681, 682.

of Havana in which they arranged to establish a provisional administration over such colonial possessions if they should be threatened or attacked by a European belligerent. This act was supplemented by a convention which, subject to ratification by the signatory governments, declared that the American nations would refuse to recognize the transfer of these possessions to any other non-American nation and which set up a permanent Inter-American Commission on Territorial Administration to supervise their administration. Thus the official representatives of all the American nations for the first time gave collective confirmation to the no-transfer principle and arranged to enforce it through collaborative action. Also for the first time they explicitly agreed, in a declaration of "Reciprocal Assistance and Cooperation for the Defense of the Nations of the Americas," that any attempt by a non-American nation against the territory, sovereignty, or political independence of an American nation "shall be considered as an act of aggression" against all the American nations. Resistance to foreign intervention in the American hemisphere, which had been a cardinal element in the Monroe Doctrine, was virtually recognized as a common responsibility of all the nations of the hemisphere rather than the unilateral obligation of one. In order to implement this declaration they agreed to hold future consultative meetings and to conclude pacts of mutual assistance.[75]

Germany's occupation of France, completing its conquest of western Europe, had been required to convince Latin Americans of the urgent need of measures of collective defense. Both *El Mundo,* and *Información,* leading newspapers of Havana, declared that the Monroe Doctrine, extended to represent the attitude of the entire hemisphere, was now the principal defense of the American republics against European aggression.[76] All the elements of the Monroe Doctrine had come to be accepted, in fact if not in name, as a collective responsibility of all the American nations for safeguarding the security of the hemisphere. Those nations had made plain their united opposition; first, to European interference with their political system, defined by the foreign ministers at Panama and Havana as "the common inter-American democratic ideal"; second, to European territorial expansion in America; and third, to the transfer of European colonies in Amer-

75. Department of State, *Second Meeting of the Ministers of Foreign Affairs of the American Republics, Havana, July 21-30, 1940, Report of the Secretary of State* (Washington, 1941).
76. Editorials in *El Mundo* and *Información,* Havana, June 21, 1940.

ica from one European nation to another European nation. The threats from abroad were producing a stronger Pan-Americanism than had ever before existed. "Never," declared *Correio da Manhã* of Rio de Janeiro in July, 1940, "has the sentiment of continental solidarity been so strong nor the links which bind us together so close as today."[77] Pan-Americanism, which previously had scrupulously sought to avoid political questions, had now been converted into a predominantly political movement. Although the objective of this new and strengthened Pan-Americanism was the maintenance of peace and the defense of the American hemisphere, not involvement in the war, the efforts of all the American nations to guarantee and maintain their collective neutrality were preparing the way for the kind of concerted action which would be required when the United States itself became a belligerent.

77. Despatch 3304, Rio de Janeiro, July 20, 1940, Department of State Archives.

Chapter 3

ON THE BRINK OF WAR

I am 100 per cent for the Monroe Doctrine—America for the Americans. Any time the United States disappears as a free and powerful country our fate will be to become a colony of a European or Asiatic nation.
—PRESIDENT ANASTASIO SOMOZA of Nicaragua

HE EUROPEAN WAR had a progressively adverse effect upon the economies of the Latin American nations. By mid-1940 Hitler's engulfment of most of western Europe in his "Continental system" had produced a serious deterioration in their economic condition. After the fall of France in June, 1940, and the subsequent British blockade of the European Continent, surplus export commodities began to pile up on the wharves of Latin American ports and to confront their governments with the prospect of economic collapse. Italy's entry into the war had the effect of depriving Chile, for example, of markets for about 12 per cent of her total exports, largely copper and nitrate. Argentine furnaces began to burn locally produced corn instead of imported coal and fuel oil. Haiti's foreign trade, which had amounted to an annual average of $17,700,000 for the ten years preceding the war, declined to only $13,339,000 by 1940. The prospect of an unopposed German control of the entire European Continent boded ill for America. As "the slave labor of Europe would ruinously compete with American labor," predicted *Excelsior* of Mexico City (May 29, 1941), "it would pave the way for the ultimate domination" of all America by Hitler. The Latin American governments accordingly looked to the United States for relief. *El Mercurio* of Santiago, Chile (November 15, 1940), for example, which was friend-

70

ly to the United States, pointed out in November, 1940, that expansion of commerce, "the blood of nations," was necessary in order to make Western Hemisphere unity something more than a mere rhetorical phrase.[1]

Anticipating this situation, President Roosevelt pledged as early as April, 1939, in his Pan-American Day address that if the method of economic pressure was resorted to by European belligerents, the United States would "give economic support" to the Latin American nations "so that no American nation need surrender any fraction of its sovereign freedom to maintain its economic welfare." Accordingly, after the outbreak of the European war Under Secretary of State Sumner Welles announced at the Panama meeting of foreign ministers in September, 1939, that the United States, in order to prevent the dislocation of inter-American commerce as a result of the war, would expand the facilities of its shipping lines serving the other American nations and would assist them financially to develop new fields of production. The delegates of the American nations at that meeting agreed to set up an Inter-American Financial and Economic Advisory Committee in Washington, composed of an economic expert from each of the American countries, to suggest methods by which the American nations could overcome the financial and economic dislocations caused by the war. The committee was authorized to provide for the interchange of information among the American nations on financial and commercial problems and to make recommendations on such subjects as the establishment of a customs truce, the creation of an inter-American institution for financial cooperation between the treasuries and the Central Banks of the American governments, and the organization of an Inter-American Commercial Institute for the promotion of trade.[2] Thus the American nations sought to solve their common economic problems which were caused by the harassments of the raging European conflict.

So swiftly did the economic condition of the Latin American nations degenerate that in mid-June of 1940 Roosevelt sent a memorandum to some of his top advisers in Washington calling attention to the economic inroads that the Axis powers were making in Latin America and to the psychological appeal of their doctrines to peoples

1. See also similar editorials in *El Mercurio*, November 7 and 10, 1940.

2. Department of State, *Report of the Delegate of the United States of America to the Meeting of the Foreign Ministers of the American Republics Held at Panama, September 23-October 3, 1939* (Washington, 1940).

whose national economies were confronted with breakdown. Because of this threat the memorandum recommended that "emergency measures should be taken to absorb surplus agricultural and mineral products affecting the prosperity of the countries of the hemisphere" and that "the freest possible flow of trade should be established" between the United States and those countries. Such measures not only would provide the United States with materials needed for its defense program but also would maintain employment and prosperity in Latin America at levels which would counteract the allurements of Nazi propaganda.[3] Two months later, in August, 1940, the Office for Coordination of Commercial and Cultural Relations between the American Republics, later the Office of the Coordinator of Inter-American Affairs (CIAA), headed by Nelson A. Rockefeller, was set up in Washington, under the direct responsibility of the President, to promote "hemisphere defense, with particular reference to the commercial and cultural aspects of the problem."[4] It was the determined hope of the United States that, as Secretary of State Cordell Hull explained to the Second Meeting of Foreign Ministers at Havana in July, 1940, "the American nations can build a system of economic defense that will enable each of them to safeguard itself from the dangers of economic subordination from abroad and the dangers of economic distress at home."[5]

On the eve of this meeting at Havana plans were broached in Washington for the establishment of a Pan-American trade cartel under the leadership of the United States which would serve as a central planning and action agency to control the trade of all the Western Hemisphere nations with the outside world. These plans seemed to represent the next logical economic step to be taken under the policy of neutrality and continental isolationism, and they aroused the enthusiasm of many Latin Americans, who felt that the formation of an enormous hemispheric cooperative purchasing and marketing arrangement covering all raw materials would relieve their economies of the stresses caused by the war. This proposed arrangement was strongly endorsed by the important *Diario de la Marina* of Havana, by the six leading daily newspapers of Buenos Aires including *La Nación, La*

3. President Roosevelt to the Secretaries of State, Commerce, Treasury, and Agriculture, June 15, 1940, printed in Coordinator of Inter-American Affairs, *History of the Office of the Coordinator of Inter-American Affairs* (Washington, 1947), 279-280.

4. *Ibid.*, 7, 280-282.

5. *Department of State Bulletin*, III (July 27, 1940), 43.

Prensa, El Mundo, Crítica, Noticias Gráficas, and *La Razón,* and by both the *Jornal do Brasil* and the *Correio da Manhã* of Rio de Janeiro.[6] But it was not given warm support in the United States. Despite considerable pressure from the Latin American nations, the United States was not willing to contemplate the concept of inter-American self-sufficiency, that is, the establishment of the Americas as a tight economic unit. While such a plan would immeasurably strengthen Latin America's economy and would free the United States from dependence upon the products of the Far East and Europe, it would require the expenditure of hundreds of millions of dollars in utilizing the tropical and semitropical products of Latin America as substitutes for the rubber, oil, fibers, and other commodities customarily imported from outside the hemisphere. It was also opposed by Argentina on the ground that the United States, which possessed the bulk of the world's supply of gold, intended to use the cartel plan as a means of supporting the value of this metal.[7] It was criticized by some Latin Americans as likely to subordinate their countries completely to the United States.

The foreign ministers at Havana therefore did not endorse this proposal for a Pan-American trade cartel, but they instructed the Inter-American Financial and Economic Advisory Committee to suggest ways of increasing domestic consumption and mutual interchange among the American nations of commodities formerly sent abroad and to establish agencies for storing, financing, and marketing these commodities. They also authorized the committee to recommend methods for improving the standard of living of the American peoples, for distributing a part of their surplus products in humanitarian and social relief work, and for evolving "a broader system of inter-American cooperative organization in trade and industrial matters."[8]

The United States well realized that a German victory in Europe might mean the loss of important Latin American markets. German commercial houses in Latin America were continuing, despite the effective British blockade, to conclude contracts which included "penalty clauses" calling for 10 to 20 per cent payment for nondelivery by

6. *Diario de la Marina,* Havana, June 21, 1940; and Despatch 848, Buenos Aires, June 27, 1940, Department of State Archives.

7. Statement to the Associated Press by Dr. Carlos L. Torriani, Director of the Section of Economic and Consular Affairs of the Foreign Office in the Argentine Ministry of Foreign Affairs, reported in Despatch 848, Buenos Aires, June 27, 1940.

8. Department of State, *Second Meeting . . . , Havana, July 21-30, 1940.*

certain specified times.[9] In 1941 they still maintained intact their commercial organizations and continued in effect their contracts with Latin American business houses, scrupulously paying claims for nonperformance of contracts by means of Aski-mark credits. If while sustaining this commercial structure Germany could successfully establish itself in control of all Europe, including Britain, it might, it was feared, displace the United States in the trade and commerce of Latin America. The position of the United States with respect to the trade of the Latin American nations would then become disastrously inferior to that of Germany.

The economic control of Latin America seemed to be at issue here. The United States realized that the trade of Germany with Latin America, if based upon the industrial machinery of the entire European continent, would have a complementarity which its own trade with the predominantly agricultural and raw-materials countries of Latin America lacked. When officials in Washington added together the prewar trade of Germany, Italy, France, Britain, and the small European countries with Latin America, its total exceeded the normal share of United States trade with Latin America, amounting to approximately 30 per cent of exports and approximately 34 per cent of imports by value. German terms of trade, customarily more favorable than those of the United States, could be expected to be conducted upon a barter basis which would be independent of United States exchange. A victorious Germany, if it should follow up its commercial pre-eminence in Latin America by securing the best mining and public utilities concessions, might obtain control over the economies of the Latin American countries and thus shatter the Pan-American system with all it implied for the security and defense of the United States.[10]

With these efforts of the Axis powers the foreign nationality groups of Axis origin in Latin America would assuredly cooperate. In southern Brazil lived more than a half-million Germans speaking their native language, maintaining their Lutheran religion, and dedicated to the "Vaterland." The Italian population in Brazil, numbered over 1.5 million. In Argentina the German and Italian nationality groups were still larger, and their close identification with the economic and politi-

9. Despatch 1015, Buenos Aires, July 26, 1940, Department of State Archives.

10. Memorandum, "The Menace to the United States through the Other American Republics of a German Victory," Division of the American Republics, Department of State, January 24, 1941, Department of State Archives.

cal life of their adopted country made them seem to the Roosevelt administration especially dangerous to the peace and security of the hemisphere. The Argentine population of Italian ancestry was estimated at 4.5 million, or one-third the total population of the country. Of this number 1.3 million remained citizens of Italy. Italian influence was second only to the Spanish and permeated every phase of Argentine life. In south-central Chile German enclaves of settlement had long existed and were regarded in Washington as outposts of Hitlerism. In Brazil Japanese immigrants numbering more than 200,-000 had established themselves in the coffee-growing areas of São Paulo and the rubber region around Pará. In Peru considerable Japanese colonies of agriculturists and fishermen were found. All these were regarded by officials in Washington not only as means of economic leverage by the Axis powers in the Western Hemisphere but also as centers of Axis intelligence and espionage operations.

In the interests of both the Good Neighbor program and the defense of the hemisphere the efforts of the United States to woo the Latin American peoples were therefore redoubled. "Good Neighbors help each other mutually, each according to his capacities," declared *El Panamá-América* (June 3, 1941). In early 1939 President Roosevelt, on his own initiative and to the astonishment of his advisors, secretly promised President Somoza of Nicaragua that the United States would construct with defense funds a highway—the so-called Rama Road—more than 150 miles long to connect the eastern and western portions of Nicaragua, passing incidentally by one of Somoza's own *fincas*, in an effort to enlist his cooperation with the United States.[11] Already ambitious plans had been drawn up for the construction by the United States of an all-weather inter-American highway extending through the length of the American continents, and construction work on it in Central America began in April, 1940. On the plea that this work would bring economic and political stability to the Central American countries, would enable them to develop their material resources, and would be of great military benefit to the United States, Congress authorized in 1941 the expenditure of $20 million to be spent under the supervision of the Department of State and the Bureau of Public Roads.[12] In the previous September Roosevelt pro-

11. J. Fred Rippy, "State Department Operations: The Rama Road," *Inter-American Economic Affairs*, IX (Summer, 1955), 17-32.
12. Rippy, "The Inter-American Highway," *Pacific Historical Review*, XXIV (August, 1955), 293.

posed that surplus coffee stocks in Latin American coffee-producing countries be distributed for use in Stamp Plan communities in the United States. Before the end of 1941 the United States government, assisted by many private organizations, was trying to help the Latin Americans to dispose of other exportable surpluses, to secure essential commodities formerly imported from outside the hemisphere and now unobtainable, to develop new sources of national income, to increase their purchasing power, to stabilize their economies, and, through both financial and technical assistance from the United States, to improve their agriculture, health, and transportation. The lending authority of the Export-Import Bank was increased from $200 million to $700 million to enable it "to assist in the development of the resources, the stabilization of the economies, and the orderly marketing of the products of the countries of the Western Hemisphere."[13] A loan of $50 million advanced by the United States to Argentina in December, 1940, was soon followed by a loan of $60 million to the same country and of $7.5 million to Uruguay to aid them in making purchases in the United States. In all, between early 1939 and the autumn of 1941 the Export-Import Bank offered credits exceeding $130 million to twelve Latin American governments for the purchase of industrial and agricultural equipment and other purposes. The United States also undertook in August, 1941, a broad program of collaboration with Bolivia, offering to assist highway construction in that country, to encourage expansion and diversification of its agricultural production, to stimulate the output of small companies mining tin, tungsten, and other minerals, to extend financial and technical assistance for these purposes, and to aid in stabilizing Bolivian currency in relation to the dollar.[14] In order to process the Bolivian tin needed to assure a continued supply as sources outside the hemisphere were cut off, the United States began to construct the largest tin smelter in the Western Hemisphere at Texas City, Texas, at an eventual cost of $13 million.

As a result of all these efforts, during the first twelve months after the outbreak of the European war in 1939 the export trade of the United States with Latin America increased by 50 per cent and its imports from Latin America by 31 per cent. By the end of 1941 the

13. Export-Import Bank of Washington, *Annual Report for 1942*, typewritten.
14. Department of State, Memorandum, dated August 1, 1941, published in República de Bolivia, *Boletín Oficial del Ministerio de Relaciones Exteriores*, May-August, 1941, 105-106.

trade of the Latin American countries with the United States had again reached its 1929 level, their exports to this country in that year amounting to approximately $1 billion and their imports from it showing a correspondingly high figure. "The United States has already demonstrated," *El Panamá-América* concluded on June 3, 1941, "that this ideal of good neighborliness should be accompanied by a sincere and effective economic collaboration."

The inauguration by the United States of the procedures of stockpiling strategic minerals and of preclusive buying for the purpose of keeping such materials out of the hands of the Axis powers also redounded to Latin America's economic advantage. In September, 1940, President Roosevelt requested United States government agencies to give priority to Latin American products when purchasing strategic and critical materials in foreign markets. Under this policy the United States began to conclude purchase agreements with several Latin American governments for strategic materials, including rubber, lead, bauxite, industrial diamonds, manganese ore, quartz crystals, mica, nickel, chromite, beryl ore, and others, thus committing itself unilaterally to provide adequate markets for these export products. In November, 1940, for example, it signed a tin-purchase agreement with Bolivia and in the following May contracted for the purchase of the entire Bolivian tungsten production.[15] Moreover, the principal copper producers in Latin America were offered markets for their production of copper in compensation for their agreement to cease selling to Japan. Early in 1941 this program was greatly expanded as the economic competition between the United States and the Axis powers was intensified.[16]

These concrete measures of assistance to Latin America were reinforced by the prospect, offered by the United States, of continued close economic collaboration after the war. Secretary of State Hull in an address on May 18, 1941, called for a postwar system of freer commercial intercourse as a requisite for permanent peace; and Latin Americans, convinced that such a system would benefit their economies, responded enthusiastically. *La Prensa* of Buenos Aires (May 20, 1941) agreed that "if peace is to be made secure" it would be necessary "to prevent nationalism from expressing itself again in forms of excessive commercial restrictions, to open up trade to all countries without dangerous discriminations, to facilitate the access to all countries of

15. República de Bolivia, *op. cit.,* 148-159.
16. Charles B. Henderson, *Report on Activities of Metals Reserve Company from June 28, 1940, to November 1, 1944,* 6.

the sources of raw materials, to conclude agreements for the furnishing of articles of prime necessity taking into consideration the interests of the consumers, and to eliminate the obstacles to payments in the international sphere." Such a postwar program held out glowing allurements to the raw-materials nations of Latin America. If these ideas could be put into practice, declared Dr. Honorio Pueyrredón, a former foreign minister of Argentina, "we can hope for better days for America and for the world."[17]

Economic measures of the United States designed to win the support of Latin America and to strengthen its own defense were supplemented by measures of military collaboration. By June, 1940, military officers from this country were carrying on detailed staff conversations with military authorities of several of the Latin American governments. These conversations, carried on with Cuba, Ecuador, Brazil, the Dominican Republic, Uruguay, Costa Rica, Chile, Haiti, Nicaragua, Panama, Peru, Honduras, Guatemala, El Salvador, Paraguay, and Bolivia, were conducted under heavy censorship and with frequent press denials, both in Washington and in Latin American capitals, that they were being carried on. They looked toward the use of naval, land, and air bases in the territories of these countries by United States forces, the liberalization of transit rights through their air spaces for the benefit of United States aircraft, and the supplying of their military needs. The United States also tried to ascertain in these conversations whether Latin American governments, in case they should receive aid from it, would place at its disposal their means of communication, their airdromes, and their ports and port facilities, would authorize its naval and air forces to patrol their coasts in search of foreign merchant vessels, war materials, and enemy personnel, and would replace the German military missions operating in their countries with United States military missions. When the secrecy of these negotiations could no longer be preserved, the explanation was given that the various air and naval bases were being placed at the service of all the American governments for the common defense of the hemisphere. In a further effort to keep those governments "sweet," Roosevelt decided to "let them have a few tiny driblets" of arms.[18] These efforts at hemisphere defense were supplemented by the establishment of a Mexican-United States Joint Defense Commission in De-

17. *Crítica,* Buenos Aires, May 20, 1941.
18. Secret memorandum from Roosevelt to Marshall, June 24, 1940, "National Latin American Arms Policy," Department of State Archives.

cember, 1940. In the following July plans were laid for setting u
Brazilian-United States Joint Defense Board, and in November, 19
a Joint Military Board for the Northeast was set up to plan construction and base facilities required for hemisphere defense on the bulge
of Brazil.

The subversive activities of Axis agents and sympathizers in Latin
America were also deemed to require positive action by the United
States. Beginning in September, 1940, representatives of the Federal
Bureau of Investigation in Washington were supplied to certain Latin
American governments to assist them in ferreting out subversive agents
in their countries. In the name of national defense the Roosevelt administration began in mid-1940 to make plans for the improvement
of aviation facilities in the countries of the Caribbean area and along
the east coast of South America and to eliminate German control over
certain national aviation services in South America, particularly
SCADTA in Colombia, SEDTA in Ecuador, LUFTHANSA in Peru,
the Lloyd Aéreo Boliviano in Bolivia, and Condor in Brazil. Using Pan
American Airways as a cover, the administration negotiated with Brazil in 1940 for the use and development of air bases in that country.[19]
Conversations were held in August, 1941, between the United States
ambassador in Buenos Aires and Argentine authorities looking toward
military staff cooperation between those two countries.

Responding to these efforts several Latin American governments
initiated programs of collaboration with the United States. They saw
clearly that their aid in the preparation of the United States for its
own defense was, in the words of El Comercio of Lima (March 10,
1941), "a guarantee also of continental security." Brazil began to take
economic, political, and military action against the Axis powers, including the suppression of subversive Axis activities, the control of
Axis funds and export of strategic materials to the Axis powers, the
elimination of Axis-controlled air lines, and the granting of preferential economic and military rights to the United States. Cuba agreed
in September, 1940, to the free use of its ports, territory, and air not
only for the defense of itself and of the United States but also for the
defense of the rest of Latin America. A special code for communications between the United States naval forces and those of Peru and

19. Wesley Frank Craven and James Lee Cate (eds.), Air Historical Group,
United States Air Force, The Army Air Forces in World War II (Chicago,
1949) II, 4-5; and General H. H. Arnold, Global Mission (New York, 1949),
204.

Brazil was prepared. In April, 1941, Mexico agreed by treaty to give United States military airplanes right of way over its territory with landing and servicing facilities. In the summer of 1941 Ecuador authorized the armed forces of the United States to use the airports of that country and its dependencies for their military airplanes, to fly and land on Ecuadoran territory, and to let their uniformed crews travel freely inside the country. It also authorized airships and maritime vessels of the United States which were patrolling the Pacific Ocean to enter freely into the Galápagos Islands and other Ecuadoran ports. The military agreements concluded with some of the Latin American governments included guaranties of mutual assistance in the event of attack. In pursuance of the no-transfer principle, which was given Pan-American sanction at the Havana meeting of foreign ministers, the United States, in cooperation with Brazil, occupied Dutch Guiana in November, 1941.

These efforts on behalf of the defense of the hemisphere struck a snag in Panama. There President Arnulfo Arias was loath to comply with the request of the United States, first presented in October, 1940, for cooperation in defending the canal and for the lease of some seventy-one defense sites outside the Canal Zone for that purpose. The Panamanian government sought to limit the size of United States garrisons permitted in these defense sites, to stipulate for prompt termination of their occupation at the close of the European war, and to fix an annual rate of rental at $4,000 per hectare for the occupied areas—a rate which would have made the annual cost of the Río Hato area alone amount to $30 million! Not until after President Arias was overthrown and replaced by Ricardo Adolfo de la Guardia on October 1, 1941, was the United States able to secure the kind of defense sites agreement with Panama which it considered necessary.[20]

The Lend-Lease program of the United States, inaugurated in March, 1941, contemplated the arming of the Latin American nations to resist aggression. Under it the United States undertook to transfer military, naval, and other defense materials to cooperating Latin American governments and opened up negotiations for this purpose almost immediately with several of them. In July, 1941, for example, it initiated such negotiations with Brazil and in the following month

20. Almon R. Wright, "Defense Sites Negotiations Between the United States and Panama, 1936-1948," *Department of State Bulletin,* XXVII (August 11, 1952), 212-217; and William L. Langer and S. Everett Gleason, *The Undeclared War, 1940-1941* (New York, 1953), 610-615.

with Argentina. Immediately after the passage of the act, Roosevelt approved a proposal recommended to him by the Secretaries of State, War, and Navy on April 22, 1941, to deliver $400 million of war matériel to Latin American nations over a period of several years, $101 million worth to be delivered in the first year of the agreements. Of the funds appropriated by Congress on October 28, 1941, in the Defense Aid Supplemental Appropriation Act, $150 million were set aside for military and naval equipment for the Latin American nations. By the time of Pearl Harbor the United States had negotiated Lend-Lease agreements with seven Latin American governments— Bolivia, Brazil, Cuba, the Dominican Republic, Haiti, Nicaragua, and Paraguay—and had begun to furnish them with equipment and supplies. At that time also special United States military missions were at work in eight Latin American countries, naval missions in six, and military aviation missions in five.

In addition the United States assiduously cultivated the Latin American peoples by means of an extensive information and cultural program. When investigation disconcertingly revealed that all the libraries in a large Brazilian city, São Paulo, contained only ten books on United States history, the Library of Congress in Washington prepared a list of six thousand books which best depicted life and thought in the United States, and the State Department's Division of Cultural Relations undertook to send copies of these books to the Latin American countries. In the summer of 1939 thirty-two publishing companies in the United States exhibited their books in Buenos Aires, Montevideo, and Rio de Janeiro and at the close of the exhibitions presented them to local organizations in a gesture which was widely acclaimed in those three southern capitals as contributing to improved inter-American relations. Rockefeller's Office for Coordination of Commercial and Cultural Relations between the American Republics dispatched to Latin America archaeological expeditions, art exhibitions, college glee clubs, a ballet caravan, and several outstanding movie stars; it financed the publication of guide books to the Latin American countries and supplied them with newsreels; it facilitated the exchange of "creative workers," medical internes, and journalists; it brought the Chilean ski team to the United States; and it gathered fashion-promotion material for distribution to newspaper syndicates and magazines in an effort to stimulate the interest of Latin Americans in New York as a style center and the interest of New York fashion designers in Latin American motifs. As a part of this cultural *rapprochement* exhibitions of Latin American arts and crafts were featured in many cities in the United States, orchestras "discovered" the music of Brazil's Heitor Vila-Lobos, Latin American beauties were invited to compete in Atlantic City's beauty contests, and Fifth Avenue stores offered their customers South American brooches, called *topos,* and "turbans twisted in the flirtatious manner of the Bahianas." Even the National Automobile Show in New York celebrated a Pan-American Day. Educational institutions in the United States turned their attention to Latin America with unprecedented enthusiasm. By 1939 courses in Latin American studies in colleges and universities numbered 981 serving more than 18,000 students. The American Association of University Women made its 1940 program revolve around the theme of Pan-Americanism.[21] In these and countless other ways the idea of a common feeling and a common interest among all the peoples of the Americas was deliberately and generously encouraged.[22]

"Your businessmen," complained a Brazilian visitor in the United States to an official of the Roosevelt administration in Washington, "always consider us Brazilians and South Americans in general as only customers, buyers of radios, refrigerators, automobiles, and other high-priced articles." "We have committed many errors," humbly replied the official. "I hope it is not too late to make reparation."[23] The similarities of historical experience and the cultural affinities of the peoples of the American hemisphere were now stressed as factors making for unity in the inexorably approaching struggle against the Axis powers. This propaganda build-up called attention particularly to their common origins as colonies of western European powers, their similar struggles for independence from those powers, the influence of the constitutional system of the United States upon Latin America, and the persistence of Spanish culture and the Roman Catholic tradition in California, Florida, Texas, New Mexico, and other parts of the United States. As a part of this campaign of emphasis upon the cultural homogeneities of the Americas, all the American peoples, it was alleged, unlike those of Europe, shared a common aspiration for democracy. Even the undemocratic regimes in Latin America were

21. William Rex Crawford, "Cultural Relations in 1941," in Arthur P. Whitaker (ed.), *Inter-American Affairs, 1941* (New York, 1942), [115]-150.
22. Donald M. Dozer, "The New Social Pan-Americanism," *The Catholic World,* CLIII (July, 1941), [449]-453. See also Bemis, *The Latin American Policy,* 326-330.
23. Erico Verissimo, *Gato Preto en Campo de Neve* (Porto Alegre, 1941), 80.

apologetically represented as merely provisional, and in any case *El Caudillo* in Latin America was declared not to be the same as *Der Führer* in Nazi Germany or *Il Duce* in Fascist Italy. "The American dictatorships have never been imperialistic or totalitarian," explained President Juan Arosemena of Panama to the foreign ministers meeting in Panama. "They have been the expression of an incipient patriarchal state or the logical product of the incapacity of the governing classes to handle skillfully the delicate machinery of democracy. . . . Thus it is that the American dictatorships always have been a local phenomenon, without international ramifications. They have followed no special ideology and have attempted to spread none. Thus the peoples who have supported dictatorships have been able to emerge from them untainted spiritually."[24]

Even, then, in the matter of a common acceptance of democratic ideology there was, it was argued, an American self-consciousness, a traditional feeling of American continentalism, with distinctive excellences over that of warring and degenerate Europe. This almost mystic "Western Hemisphere idea," which had been prevalent in the eighteenth and early nineteenth centuries and which formed the ideological premise of the Monroe Doctrine, was now forcefully revived by the felt need for mutual protection against danger from overseas. The new accent upon the existence of an American society, deriving from a common historical and cultural pattern, stimulated new hopes for growth in spiritual unity among the Americas and for the elimination of the remaining barriers to understanding among them. Together they could work out better than ever before a new way of life and manner of living, an American civilization, a "history with a tomorrow."[25]

* * *

24. *Discurso pronunciado por el Presidente de la República de Panamá, Dr. Juan Demostenes Arosemena, en la Sesión Inaugural de la Reunión Consultativa de los Ministros de Relaciones Exteriores de las Repúblicas Americanas* (Panamá, 1939); also printed in *Memoria que el Secretario de Estado en el Despacho de Relaciones Exteriores y Comunicaciones Presenta a la Asemblea Nacional en sus Sesiones Ordinarias de 1940* (Panamá, 1942), Part I, [417]-420.

25. The "unities" of the Americas had been lovingly preached for more than a generation by the intellectual high priest of this "Greater America" cult among historians, Professor Herbert E. Bolton. They were set forth succinctly in his address as president of the American Historical Association at its meeting in Toronto in December, 1932, subsequently printed under the title "The Epic of America" in the *American Historical Review*, XXXVIII

How did Latin Americans view the people of the United States, with whom they were now cooperating for their common security? Was there still any truth in the conclusions of Latin American writers of Rodó's school as to the character of the United States and the characteristics of its people? What impressions did Latin American visitors to the United States form as they traveled over this nation, which was tottering on the brink of war?

One of the most discerning and articulate Latin American visitors was the Brazilian novelist Erico Verissimo, who made a three-months' tour of the United States as a guest of the Roosevelt government in early 1941. Wherever he traveled from New York to Hollywood, he found a general curiosity about Latin America combined with a sometimes ludicrous ignorance. The guests at a New York cocktail party who crowded around him made clear "with charming simplicity" that they believed that the Brazilians spoke Spanish and lived constantly under the threat of Indian uprisings. "Do you have your own literature?" they asked. "Do you like North Americans? Are there many Germans in your country? What do you think of Roosevelt?" In Nashville he was asked, "Is Brazil a British possession?" At the same city he had to explain that Brazil is located in South America. The capital of his country was often assumed by North Americans to be Buenos Aires instead of Rio de Janeiro.

To Verissimo the United States appeared as a machine civilization, dynamic and powerful. It was "full of material things whose spontaneous symbol is the skyscraper, a machine for living." The inhabitants of the large cities were obsessed with the word "time." *"Time is money, to save time, to have a good time* are expressions which one constantly hears. They live, therefore, according to formulas which save time. They have formulas for everything: for eating, for dressing, for reading, for resting, for being courteous, for writing, and even for believing. . . . They eat fast, they read fast, they speak fast, they write fast, and even worship fast." In the cafeterias of the large cities where each customer served himself and women wearing mink coats seated themselves at tables alongside shop girls, Verissimo saw an institution which he considered very representative of the North American ideals

(April, 1933), 448-474. See also Pan American Union, "Is America a Continent? A Round Table Discussion," *Points of View,* Number 2, October, 1941, 1-24; Edmundo O'Gorman, "Do the Americas Have a Common History?" *Points of View,* Number 3, December, 1941, 4-10; Jorge Basadre, "¿Tienen las Américas una Historia Común?" *Excelsior,* Lima, June-July, 1942, 7-9.

of "mind your own business," "cash and carry," and "live and let live." In the nation's capital he was shocked at the violent contrast in living conditions of the Negroes and the whites and at the drawing of the color line even in churches in the southern states.

And yet the diversity of life in the United States which resulted from the racial and religious mixtures was counteracted by certain forces making for national unity. Among these, Verissimo concluded, were a common religious life based upon the precepts of the Bible, the advertising and standardization of certain products from coast to coast, the emphasis upon the common ideals of liberty, equality, and fraternity, which, he said, underlay the Declaration of Independence and the Constitution of the United States, and the admirable facilities for transportation and communication which bound the nation together and shortened the distances between its various parts. These made it "one vast neighborhood" in which "all citizens loved liberty and practiced mutual respect." The people of the United States, he concluded, had developed their own characteristic society, their own American type. He noted particularly their addiction to the daily bath and to physical exercises, their aversion to morbid themes, their disposition to form and join clubs of all sorts, their respect for women and children, their fondness for humor, their dedication to hobbies, their passion for cleanliness and comfort in their homes, their practice of the cult of hospitality, their thirst for information and for discussion, their delight in inventing things of a practical nature, and their passion for bright colors. In short, the North Americans were a combination of the infantile and the adult. They seemed to him like children in their love for the dance, for jokes, for colors, for adventure stories, for mechanical toys, and for fast music. But though they danced the "swing" and at times acted like clowns they showed an adult courage in the presence of danger and a spirit of sacrifice which few other peoples possessed. The great majority of them, he concluded, were normal, industrious, and cheerful, but they did not allow their cheerfulness to interfere with their work. But their "mania for standardization," he concluded, was giving this naturally spontaneous people an artificial mode of life. This was the result of industrialization which had "a tendency to dehumanize workers, converting them into cogs in a gigantic machine."

In the United States, Verissimo observed, there were differences in wealth between John D. Rockefeller, Jr., and the beggar in the street, but there were no classes in a political, sociological, and philosophical sense. Different economic levels had not produced a class mentality, and even rich men were proud to say that they had begun their careers as manual workers. Existing economic differences were being equalized by President Roosevelt who had imposed heavy tax burdens and other restrictions upon the millionaires. The laws of the United States recognized no privileged class and made no distinction among citizens on the basis of social position. Wherever Verissimo traveled in the United States, he noted that the "little man" showed a natural gentility and a spirit of goodwill which were very touching.

Underlying all developments, social events, and discussions, and disquietingly ominous—Verissimo reported in January, 1941, as he traveled through the United States—was "the idea of war, the possibility of armed intervention by the United States in the conflict. The newspapers conduct polls. Should we aid England? How much? In what way? Even at the risk of involving ourselves directly in the struggle?" But the European war, he reported, had not yet altered the "rhythm of life" in the United States. Everything appeared to be "running in the grooves of normality." But "we must not forget," he added, "that the Americans are quixotic. . . . They were accustoming themselves to standardization, but they have a great feeling for the life of their fellow men and they fill themselves with enthusiasm for noble crusades."[26]

To Latin Americans, President Roosevelt symbolized the ideal *caudillo*. His political magnetism, his captivating oratory, his personal charm and superlative self-confidence, his conception of a government of action, his concern for the underprivileged were qualities which Latin Americans associated with their most successful chieftains. He was the people's champion, the hero of the underprivileged, a political Don Quixote. His methods of direct action, his scorn of traditional and even long-venerated constitutional procedures, his poised cocksureness fitted well the Latin American pattern of personal leadership. To believers in *personalismo* these methods were not only intelligible but appealing. In addition, Roosevelt's previous experience of suffering and his continuing infirmity struck with them a common chord of sympathy and pity.

By 1940 Roosevelt's leadership was deemed in Latin America to have produced a profound improvement in the attitudes of the United States toward its hemisphere neighbors and at the same time to have put it at the forefront of the democratic forces of the world. His bid

26. *Op. cit., passim.*

for an unprecedented third term in the presidency in 1940 therefore evoked general support among Latin Americans. They harbored the fear, encouraged by the Roosevelt administration, that a return of the Republican Party to power would signalize a revival of the old policies of the Big Stick and dollar diplomacy associated with Theodore Roosevelt and Philander C. Knox. A Republican victory might bring a new wave of interventionism, protectionism, and economic imperialism to prevent the consummation of a true solidarity of the two Americas.[27] Never, declared *El Cronista* of Tegucigalpa (August 7, 1939), had Latin America "felt so sure in respect to its liberty and to its interests as during the administration of Mr. Roosevelt, and it naturally desires the continuance of this regime which has maintained so successfully the policy of the Good Neighbor." *El Panamá-América* (July 19, 1940) felt that "No other leader of the United States possesses his liking for Latin America; no other is so well qualified as he to strengthen the goodwill of the continent, to consolidate the plan of defense of the Americas."[28] Dozens of other newspapers praised Roosevelt as "the greatest champion of democracy in modern times,"[29] "the man whom humanity needs,"[30] "the greatest citizen of the present world,"[31] even the representative of a heavenly order speaking with "messianic grandeur."[32]

Roosevelt's victory at the polls was therefore applauded in Latin America as a victory for the whole hemisphere. Newspapers gave over most of their front pages to the news of his re-election. The *Diario de la Marina* of Havana (November 7, 1940) jubilated that " 'our' candidate has triumphed in the United States." His victory, declared *La Prensa Gráfica* of San Salvador (November 7, 1940), "is a triumph for all of America."[33] President Jorge Ubico of Guatemala telegraphed to Roosevelt, "I congratulate you and we congratulate ourselves."[34] Similar messages were sent to him by the

27. *El País,* Montevideo, October 7, 1937; and *Ahora,* Caracas, November 10, 1938.
28. See also *Panama Tribune,* Panama, July 18, 1940.
29. *La Estrella de Panamá,* July 19, 1940.
30. Leo Pardo, *ibid.*
31. *Diário de Notícias,* Rio de Janeiro, July 20, 1940.
32. *Noticias Gráficas,* Buenos Aires, July 17, 1940. See also *La Mañana,* Montevideo, November 7, 1940.
33. Similar views were expressed by *El Gran Diario,* San Salvador, November 9, 1940. See also *La Época,* Tegucigalpa, November 6, 1940; and *La Prensa,* Buenos Aires, November 17, 1940.
34. Despatch 1565, Guatemala, November 7, 1940, Department of State Archives.

Minister of Foreign Affairs, the National Legislative Assembly, and the Convention of Mayors of El Salvador, the National Assembly of Panama, and the Senate of Ecuador. Both Houses of the Peruvian Congress adopted resolutions expressing their satisfaction with his re-election "as a guaranty of the security of America and of continental solidarity."[35] The Rotary Club of Tegucigalpa passed a resolution congratulating him.[36] After his third inauguration the title of "Eminent Citizen of America" was conferred upon him by a unanimously approved resolution of the Cuban Senate "by reason of his defense of democratic principles and his lofty spirit of inter-American fraternity," and his portrait was unveiled in the Gallery of Honor of the Cuban Senate in a ceremony in which the United States ambassador participated.[37] Soon afterward, he was unanimously elected an honorary member of the Brazilian Bar Association (Instituto de Ordem dos Advogados Brasileiros).[38] "Oh, Roosevelt!" exclaimed a writer in *El Diario Latino* of San Salvador (November 8, 1940), "the destiny of democracy and of liberty are today in your hands."[39] Roosevelt could not have received higher acclaim if he had been elected president of the American hemisphere.

Perhaps the primary significance to Latin Americans of Roosevelt's third electoral triumph was its vindication of his Good Neighbor Policy and its assurance of continued concern by his government for their welfare and safety.[40] It also was interpreted to mean a continuation of the social reforms of his New Deal. To Latin Americans who favored state intervention to promote the general welfare and to level out inequalities of wealth, Roosevelt's program made a particularly strong appeal.[41] His purpose, said the Brazilian writer

35. *El Comercio,* Lima, November 7, 8, 1940.
36. Despatch 1160, Tegucigalpa, November 8, 1940, Department of State Archives.
37. *Diario de la Marina,* April 15, 1941. See also George Messersmith, Ambassador to Cuba, to Philip M. Bonsal, Havana, April 18, 1941, Department of State Archives.
38. Despatch 4633, Rio de Janeiro, May 19, 1941; Despatch 4690, Rio de Janeiro, May 29, 1941; Despatch 4971, Rio de Janeiro, July 10, 1941; and Despatch 5070, Rio de Janeiro, July 26, 1941, Department of State Archives.
39. See also *El Norte,* San Pedro Sula, Honduras, November 6, 1940.
40. *La Prensa,* Buenos Aires, November 7, 1940; *La Nación,* Buenos Aires, November 7, 1940; *La Prensa Gráfica,* San Salvador, November 7, 1940; *La Crítica,* Santiago, November 9, 1940; *Crítica,* Caracas, November 6, 1940; and *La Noche,* Lima, January 22, 1941.
41. See *El Nacional,* Mexico City, November 6 and 7, 1940; and *El País,* Montevideo, November 9, 1940.

José María Belo in a lecture in Rio de Janeiro as early as 1939, was "reform of a democracy which is no longer content with political liberty and equality but seeks a form of better social and economic equality."[42] His third election to the presidency, President Anastasio Somoza of Nicaragua told a crowd of celebrants in Managua, meant that Roosevelt had "triumphed over capitalism."[43] It represented, according to a correspondent of *El Mercurio* of Santiago, Chile (November 15, 1940), "the triumph of Christianity in the United States." Roosevelt's call in his address of January 6, 1941, for the establishment of the four freedoms—freedom of thought, freedom of worship, freedom from want, and freedom from fear—everywhere in the world seemed to be an attempt to universalize his New Deal and emphasized to Latin America the "humane principles" which underlay his program.[44]

But by 1940 the example and future prospects of the New Deal were much less interesting to Latin America, at least to governments and spokesmen of the governing classes, than were the future international policies of the United States. Its new program would involve, not so much continued internal social readjustment as, in the words of *El Panamá-América* (November 8, 1940), an intensification of "the struggle for the democratic ideal, for the defense of the inalienable rights, the liberty, and the dignity of man, . . . the consolidation and increase of the defense forces of the continent, greater unity in continental thought, the extirpation of Fifth Columns," and a closer union of the forces of liberty against totalitarian persecution. Since Roosevelt was "the candidate of international democracy," as *La Mañana* of Montevideo (November 7, 1940) described him, his triumph took on "universal importance."[45] He was now free to act, said *El Mundo* of Buenos Aires (November 7, 1940), "in every place where democracy may be in danger and needs help."[46] A great messianic future, a crusading mission opened up brilliantly before Roose-

42. Lecture "The United States and Brazil" arranged by the Committee on Intellectual Cooperation in the Brazilian Department of Foreign Affairs, copy sent by José María Belo Filho to President Franklin D. Roosevelt, September 16, 1939, Department of State Archives.

43. *Novedades,* Managua, quoted in Despatch 1288, Managua, November 12, 1940, Department of State Archives.

44. *La República,* San Salvador, January 10, 1941.

45. Similar views were expressed by *El Universal,* Mexico City, November 7, 1940; *La Nación,* Buenos Aires, January 20, 22, 1941; and *La Prensa,* Buenos Aires, January 20, 1941.

46. See also *La Crónica,* Lima, January 22, 1941.

velt's country. This America under the leadership of the United States seemed to be the new hope of the world.

As, under Roosevelt's leadership, the United States abandoned the hope of maintaining "a solid iron wall" around the territory of the Americas, an effort was made to convert its Western Hemisphere neighbors to the futility of continuing a "continental" policy. The commitments of the United States and the pressures of both official and public opinion in many of the Latin American countries for the defeat of the Axis were clearly rendering the policy of peace and neutrality no longer practicable for the Americas. The inadequacy of that policy became increasingly apparent as leaders of both the United States and the Latin American nations convinced themselves that Nazi Germany and its militant allies directly threatened the peace and security of their nations. By 1940 the second-in-command of the *APRA* movement, Manuel Seoane, was advocating an alliance between the Latin American nations and the United States in common resistance to totalitarianism.[47] An ex-president of Cuba, Dr. Ramón Grau San Martín, who had bitterly blamed "Washington" for his fall from power in 1934, now explained in an address given in Havana in September, 1940, that the United States, in its new policy of inter-American cooperation for the defense of democracy, deserved to be supported by a united and well-prepared hemisphere.[48] President Somoza of Nicaragua told a newspaper correspondent of the *Chattanooga Times* in October, 1940, "Any time the United States disappears as a free and powerful country, our fate will be to become a colony of a European or Asiatic nation."[49] In January, 1941, the Cuban Prime Minister, Dr. Carlos Saladrigas Zayas, announced that if war came "Cuba, as an American nation, will be on the side of the United States in the defense of liberty, democracy and justice."[50] This announcement was reinforced by the distinguished Cuban elder statesman, ex-Foreign Minister Cosme de la Torriente, who warned his countrymen in an address in May, 1941, that unless they joined the United States in the forthcoming

47. *Nuestra América y la Guerra,* 142; and Arthur P. Whitaker (ed.), *Inter-American Affairs, 1941,* 46.
48. *Luz,* Havana, September 3, 1940.
49. Interview with Albert E. Carter of the *Chattanooga Times,* Chattanooga, Tennessee, reported in Despatch 1275, Managua, November 2, 1940, Department of State Archives.
50. Statement of January 11, 1941 in *The Havana Post,* Havana, January 12, 1941.

war they would find themselves in a very serious situation in the event of Britain's defeat.[51]

At the same time responsible officials of other Latin American nations, including Haiti, the Dominican Republic, Ecuador, Costa Rica, Guatemala, Colombia, Panama, Honduras, and Nicaragua, assured the United States, some confidentially, some publicly, that if it became involved in the war their countries would march at its side "in defense of democratic principles and of the continent itself."[52] "Brazil will maintain a policy of complete collaboration and absolute solidarity with the United States," declared *Diário Carioca* of Rio de Janeiro (April 1, 1941). The Foreign Minister of Mexico, Ezequiel Padilla, also reaffirmed his government's support "of full continental solidarity in defense of democratic principles."[53] To the United States as a world power was falling the lot of protecting the smaller nations in its part of the world against abuses by the strong nations.

Latin Americans watched with more than a detached interest the decline of neutralism in the United States and the progress of Roosevelt's preparedness program. In effect the United States was already poised for war. According to the hostile *Boletín de Unidad* of Mexico City (November 7, 1940), Roosevelt's election to a third term as president was equivalent to "an announcement of the entry of the United States into the war in the not too distant future." "This attitude of prebelligerency," as *El Cronista* of Tegucigalpa (January 20, 1941) called it, "in which the United States has now placed itself and the acts which must necessarily follow sooner or later foreshadow the possibility that, as in 1917, the armies of the United States will go to fight on the fields of Europe or of the Far East." The assistant director of *Diario de la Marina* of Havana, Dr. Raúl Maestri, reported from San Francisco to his newspaper on May 23, 1941, that in his travels through the United States he observed everywhere a "unanimous conviction that a Hitler triumph would be equivalent . . . to an American defeat, or, at least, to a manifest

51. *El Mundo*, Havana, May 28, 1941.
52. Despatch 163, Port-au-Prince, June 13, 1941; Despatch 2247, Havana, June 26, 1941; Telegram 12, Ciudad Trujillo, January 20, 1941; Telegram 13, Quito, January 18, 1941; Telegram 17, San José, January 20, 1941; Telegram 15, Guatemala City, January 23, 1941; Despatch 890, Panama, January 18, 1941; Telegram 5, Tegucigalpa, February 3, 1941; Telegram 197, Montevideo, May 19, 1941, Department of State Archives.
53. Despatch 12070, Mexico, January 20, 1941, Department of State Archives.

compromise of America's position in the world." The people of the
United States had long since become economically, ideologically, and
politically tied to the anti-Axis nations and were bound to insure
their victory. They had been taking part in the war, reported a distinguished Peruvian visitor to the United States, Dr. Alberto Ulloa,
in *La Prensa* of Lima (April 15, 1941), "from the moment in which
they abandoned their initial position as neutrals to express officially
their ideological affiliation with and their political inclination toward
one of the warring sides, to convert themselves into limitless pro-
viders of material indispensable to the resistance of the British, and
to declare officially and unequivocally their desire for the destruction
of totalitarian regimes." Meanwhile the United States, as Dr. Ulloa
observed, was spending "immense" sums on its defense program
"which includes not only the diversion to this purpose of plant production formerly devoted to other uses but also the construction of
plants entirely new and the enlargement and perfecting of those
which already exist." In all this it was gaining time to prepare itself
both physically and psychologically for possible direct participation
in the war.

As a result of these efforts the United States was steadily growing
in strength as a world power. In relation to the Latin American
nations it was making itself supreme, reported the Washington correspondent of the *Diario de la Marina* (August 25, 1940), Dr. Ramiro Guerra. But, he continued, "in its Latin American policy, it
has repudiated the use of force" and instead "consults all the other
countries of this hemisphere, pays careful attention to their opinions,
patiently discusses differences with them, and concludes agreements
satisfactory to all." These methods, contrasting sharply "with the
methods of brutal violence which other powers use" and showing
rather "respect for the rights and susceptibilities of others," were being
employed to advance the interests of the entire Western Hemisphere.
The reality of its growing supremacy in the hemisphere "may not
be pleasing to the nationalist sentiment and the fiercely independent
spirit" of the Latin American peoples, but who could deny it? asked
Dr. Guerra. Fortunately, antagonizing incidents had been avoided,
Latin American goodwill was being deliberately cultivated by the
United States, and the beginnings of a mutual security system had
been laid, multilateralizing the Monroe Doctrine in order to enable
the hemisphere to meet unitedly the threats to its safety.

As President Roosevelt increasingly and eloquently championed the cause of Britain confronted by a hostile Europe, his leadership was enthusiastically praised in Latin America. His voice became, as *La Razón* of Bogotá (December 30, 1940) characterized it, "the voice of America, of a free America which believes in its liberty and is opposed to tyranny and despotism." His fireside chats and other radio addresses were printed in full in dozens of Latin American newspapers. *La Epoca* of Tegucigalpa (December 30, 1940) called Roosevelt "the mighty defender of the rights of man." Dr. Honorio Pueyrredón of Argentina described him as "the greatest citizen of the civilized democratic world."[54] An Argentine Socialist leader called him "the living voice of free men of America who aspire to preserve liberty and right."[55] Said the *Jornal do Comércio* of Rio de Janeiro (May 29, 1941), "If there is anyone authorized to speak for the highest principles of justice among nations, of democracy and of liberty, it is without doubt President Roosevelt, who represents a great power predestined to prevent tyranny and destruction from spreading throughout the world." To the *Diário Carioca* (May 29, 1941) of the same capital Roosevelt spoke in the name of the entire New World. He was the spokesman "of American intervention for the defense of the Christian civilization of the world." He was defining, said *Crítica* of Caracas (December 31, 1940), "in a clear and final manner the position which the peoples of this hemisphere must take in the face of the European conflict."[56]

The Lend-Lease Act of March 11, 1941, irrevocably committing the United States to the defense of the nations under attack by the Axis, was widely acclaimed in Latin America. The kind of preventive action which the United States was taking reminded sympathetic Latin Americans of the Spanish proverb: "When there is a fire in the neighborhood, it is not at all helpful to pour water on your own home, but it is better to run to the fire and throw water on your neighbor's house which is burning."[57] This policy would benefit the whole

54. *Buenos Aires Herald,* Buenos Aires, May 28, 1941.
55. *Ibid.,* May 28, 1941.
56. See also *La Esfera,* Caracas, December 31, 1940; *La Noche,* La Paz, December 30, 1940; *La Razón,* La Paz, December 31, 1940; *Panama American,* Panama, December 30, 1940; *Star and Herald,* Panama, December 31, 1940; *La Crónica,* Lima, December 31, 1940, and March 18, 1941; *El Comercio* Quito, December 31, 1940; *Diario de la Marina,* Havana, December 31, 1940, and January 3, 1941; *Avance,* Havana, December 31, 1940: Rafael Suárez Solis in *Información,* Havana, January 1, 1941; *Montevideo,* Montevideo, January 2, 1941; and *Listín Diario,* Ciudad Trujillo, March 18, 1941.
57. Telegram 17, San José, January 20, 1941, Department of State Archives.

of America. In the opinion of *El Comercio* of Lima (March 10, 1941), "the aid of the United States to the democracies and the preparation of its own defense is a guaranty also of continental security." In Santiago, Chile, the important Roman Catholic newspaper *Diario Ilustrado* (May 29, 1941), which had been previously unfriendly to the United States, began to advocate cooperation of the American nations with the United States in the common defense of their sovereignty and independence. Now, declared *La Noche* of La Paz (May 28, 1941), "the defense of each one of us is the defense of all." For this reason the Costa Rican Congress, acting upon the direct instigation of President Rafael Angel Calderón Guardia, passed an extraordinary resolution by a vote of 38 to 1 expressing its approbation of the passage by the Congress in Washington of the Lend-Lease bill "prompted in the defense of the continent and the democracies."[58] The Cuban Senate likewise voted unanimously to send "its most sincere congratulations to the Congress of the United States of America" upon the passage of this act for aid to Great Britain and the "defense of democratic institutions."[59] Two months later President Fulgencio Batista of Cuba announced his government's "moral identification with the peoples of the American continent and the pronouncements of President Roosevelt regarding the defense of the Americas and their democratic principles as a high human duty of loyalty and solidarity with such principles and with the United States to whose destiny our own is intimately bound."[60]

But there was also a realization in Latin America that Roosevelt's policy of aiding the beleaguered British Isles actually put the United States directly into the war and might encourage Axis reprisals against the entire hemisphere. "The American help to Great Britain," *La Nación* of Buenos Aires (November 7, 1940) prophetically warned, "may create difficulties." An incident might occur anywhere —in Dakar, the Canary Islands, the Portuguese possessions in the Atlantic, the Netherlands Indies, the Philippines—which would bring war to the Western Hemisphere.[61] Latin Americans thus began to express uneasiness as to possible military and naval action against

58. Telegram 43, San José, March 14, 1941; and Despatch 2989, San José, March 17, 1941.

59. *Avance,* Havana, March 13 and 24, 1941; Despatch 1806, Havana, March 31, 1941; and Despatch 1833, Havana, April 3, 1941.

60. *Diario de la Marina,* Havana, May 29, 1941.

61. For later similar newspaper views see *El Tiempo,* Bogotá, December 31, 1940; and *La Opinión,* Santiago, March 16, 1941.

them by Germany and Japan. They began to feel that they were being committed to a policy which was more aggressive and dangerous than they had previously realized and that in the formulation of it there had not been full opportunity for inter-American consultation.[62] As late as March 26, 1941, Mexican newspapers headlined a declaration by Foreign Minister Ezequiel Padilla that Mexico had not assumed any obligation to become involved in an extracontinental war nor to send a single man into such a war.[63] In short, the policy of the United States was now seen clearly to be one of belligerency and not of neutrality. Its military preparedness program was no longer preparation merely for defense but for participation in the hostilities on the antitotalitarian side.

This gradual change of posture by the United States provoked new heart-searchings among Latin Americans who still clung to a policy of peace and neutrality for the hemisphere and who at the same time found it difficult to wipe from their minds the recollection of past oppressions by their great neighbor to the north. Despite Roosevelt's great personal popularity throughout Latin America, distrust of the methods and intentions of the United States persisted. When the Roosevelt administration negotiated for military, naval, and air bases in mid-1940, several Latin American nations expressed fear that the United States if granted these bases might not be willing later to leave them. To quiet their fears it became necessary for Under Secretary Welles to assure the Cuban Ambassador in Washington that any necessary arrangements for the defense of this hemisphere would be made with a sovereign Cuba.[64]

Latin American distrust of the United States was fully exploited by pro-Nazi journalists in Latin America. For example, *El Pampero* of Buenos Aires (December 1, 1941), edited by the Argentine Naziphile Enrique P. Oses and reporting a daily circulation of 100,000, bitterly accused the people of the United States of being impelled by an "insane kind of geographical fever . . . to extend as far as they can (and as far as others will let them) the endless tentacles of their all-absorbing imperialism. . . . Yankee imperialism is like a stain of oil. It runs and spreads implacably once it has been made to fall on a place chosen for expansion." After extravagantly reciting the history of this imperialism from the early subjugation of the In-

62. Telegram 83, Lima, March 17, 1941, Department of State Archives.
63. *Excelsior,* Mexico City, March 26, 1941.
64. Despatch 335, Havana, May 27, 1940, Department of State Archives.

dians by the "unscrupulous 'Puritans' of Massachusetts" in 1620 to the occupation of the bauxite country of Dutch Guiana by Yankee troops after Hitler's conquest of the Netherlands, *El Pampero* concluded: "Justice and legality do not appear in any phase of the chronicle of the successive acts of Yankee expansionism, either in the past or in the present. . . . Now the Yankees talk about 'continental security,' 'Pan-American solidarity,' 'liberty,' 'human dignity,' 'collective aid,' et cetera. But the result is always the same: the oil stain of Yankee expansionism spreads unceasingly, like a sinister shadow, over the continent." In this hue and cry of Latin American Nazis against the United States during this period of the Hitler-Stalin pact the Communists in Latin America joined, repeatedly charging that the United States was trying to drag Latin America into an imperialistic war.

Fear of a possible renewal of an imperialistic policy by the United States seemed to be particularly acute in Mexico. "Mexico is a friend of the people and Government of the United States, but never of international imperialism," read a banner carried in a procession of almost a hundred thousand labor union members and government employees before President Cárdenas in Mexico City on April 11, 1940.[65] It is not surprising that during the period of the Soviet-Nazi pact the Marxist head of the Confederación de Trabajadores de América Latina, Vicente Lombardo Toledano, charged repeatedly that the capitalistic forces of the United States were creating a war psychosis among the peoples of both the United States and Latin America.[66] But writers of less extreme affiliations also expressed alarm. The conservative *Ultimas Noticias* of Mexico City (October 5, 1939) spoke scornfully of the self-assumed role of the United States as "patriarch of American democracy." United States oil companies, it was alleged, were campaigning against the Mexican government in reprisal for its previous expropriation of their properties, and as long as they continued to do so it would be very difficult for Mexicans to feel themselves united by a community of interests with the people of the United States.[67] The weekly Mexican magazine *Hoy* (June 29, 1940) presented a long list of previous acts of aggression by Mexico's

65. Telegram 126, Mexico City, April 11, 1940, Department of State Archives.
66. For example, see his speech before the Consejo Extraordinario del Sindicato de Trabajadores de la Enseñanza de la República Mexicana on June 4, 1940, *El Popular*, June 5, 1940.
67. *El Universal*, Mexico City, June 5, 1940.

northern neighbor and sorrowfully concluded, "Poor Mexico! So far
from God, and so close to the United States!"

In 1940 there was a widespread belief in Mexico during the presidential campaign there that "the White House at Washington will
determine who will be the next president of Mexico."[68] Early in the
following year the newspaper *El Dictamen* of Veracruz (February 4,
1941) warned that the cession of military bases to the United States
might "turn out to be like the hospitality of the elephant, which asked
permission to place its trunk in the cave to protect it from the storm
and ended by entering completely into the cave and making himself
its master." Even as late as October 3, 1941, *El Universal* of Mexico
City was apprehensive that the strengthened ties between Latin
America and the United States "might be converted into instruments
of political subjection, into channels of undue penetration into the
national public life, into new chains of financial bondage which at
any time could be tightened by military and naval power." So serious
were strictures of this nature that Senator Dennis Chavez of New
Mexico felt it necessary, only a little less than two and a half months
before the Japanese attacked Pearl Harbor, to assure an audience of
distinguished Mexican officials that the United States had no intention of taking additional territory in America, especially from Mexico, or "of using its power to dominate any nation."[69]

Nor were such forebodings confined to Mexico. In Cuba a newspaperman named Evelio Alvarez del Real, soon to become Minister
of Justice, charged that the aim of the United States was to maintain
its "system of exploitation which extends its tentacles from Wall
Street to Patagonia."[70] The vitriolically hostile *El Debate* of Montevideo (July 5 and 9, 1940) accused the United States of exaggerating
"imaginary perils with the inward intention of setting foot in and
taking possession of the territory of others" in Latin America. The
only aim of the "plutocracy of the North," it asserted, was "to swallow up all competitors and to become the possessor of the universal
market." During the defense negotiations which the United States
carried on with Uruguay, the opposition Herreristas in the Uruguayan Senate made strong public protests against all treaties or conventions with the United States for the establishment of naval bases that

68. Ambassador Josephus Daniels to Hull, Despatch 11469, Mexico, D. F.,
September 19, 1940, Department of State Archives.
69. *Excelsior,* Mexico City, September 21, 1941.
70. *Tiempo,* Havana, December 18, 1940.

would "imply a servitude" or "diminution of national sovereignty."[71] When a Washington senator declared in hearings before the Committee on Foreign Relations in February, 1941, that if a country "such as Argentina" refused its cooperation in the defense of the continent, the United States should obtain bases there by force if necessary, using the navy, the usually friendly *La Nación* of Buenos Aires (February 5, 1941) pointed out that his declaration contradicted the Good Neighbor Policy. "What would remain of the Good Neighbor Policy," it pointedly asked, "if cooperation were imposed?"[72] The unfriendly *El Siglo* of Bogotá (June 23, 1940) bluntly characterized the Good Neighbor Policy as the policy of the Big Stick in disguise. As work on the eleven United States air bases in Brazil proceeded, younger officers in the Brazilian Air Corps showed increasing uneasiness, comparing it to the German penetration of Rumania. The distribution of military equipment by the United States to certain Latin American countries under the Lend-Lease program was particularly criticized as upsetting the normal peacetime military equilibrium in Latin America, as amounting to intervention in their affairs, and as ignoring the processes of inter-American consultation. These complaints were made in a book published in November, 1941, by Peru's ambassador to Argentina, Dr. Felipe Barreda Laos.[73]

The purport of these criticisms was that the Roosevelt administration was motivated by ulterior purposes which threatened the welfare and interests of the Latin American peoples. They tended to strengthen the sentiment in Latin America for continued neutrality and pacifism in the contest between the Anglo-American and the Nazi-Fascist nations. After all, as even the pro-United States *La Nación* of Buenos Aires (December 15, 1940) pointed out, the defense problems of the American nations south of the equator were different from those of nations to the north. Those nations were not only farther away from European and Asiatic attack but their economic interests were not so closely connected with those of the United States. Barreda bitterly inveighed against Roosevelt's deceptive and unilateral involvement of the Latin American nations in his own war policies and urged that the Latin Americans, instead of acting merely like colonies of the belligerent nations, should present a united neu-

71. Despatch 681, Montevideo, November 27, 1940, Department of State Archives.
72. See also *El Pampero*, Buenos Aires, February 4, 1941.
73. *¿Hispano América en Guerra?*, 71-75, 91-93.

tral front against the prevailing war madness, adhering to the resolutions to that effect which they had adopted at the Panama and Havana meetings of foreign ministers. Barreda Laos went even further and suggested that in this crisis the nations of Latin America had a high duty to restore peace to the world—a peace of reconciliation and harmony, to be brought about by a concerted Hispanic-American neutralist movement. This he proposed as a necessary work of "human redemption" to which Latin America was summoned.[74] In the tense debates on this question the Mexican philosopher Alfonso Reyes also urged that Latin America assume a mediating role in the world conflict.[75]

* * *

But such a role became increasingly impracticable for Latin Americans as the grinding importunities of the world situation impelled them to overcome some of their scruples about cooperation with the United States. However bitter their memories of past altercations with their big neighbor, the possibility of invasion by totalitarian troops from outside the hemisphere seemed to confront them with even greater dangers. The European blitzkriegs were crumbling old antagonisms. When, immediately after President Roosevelt's speech of May 27, 1941, proclaiming an unlimited national emergency and calling for hemispheric cooperation and solidarity, German diplomats approached the governments of Bolivia, Brazil, Colombia, Chile, Cuba, Guatemala, Panama, and Uruguay asking for their reactions to the President's speech, these inquiries were rebuffed by all the governments approached. Some governments went so far as to express their full support of hemisphere solidarity under the leadership of the United States. In addition, the foreign ministers of Costa Rica, the Dominican Republic, Nicaragua, and Paraguay, when apprised of the action of the German diplomats, assured the United States either of their solidarity with the President's statements or of their disapproval of the action of the German representatives.[76]

74. *Ibid.*   75. *Ultima Tule* (Mexico, 1942).
76. Memorandum June 9, 1941, Department of State Archives. For newspaper comments on Roosevelt's speech of May 27, 1941, see *El Imparcial,* Santiago, May 28, 1941; *La Nación, El Mercurio, La Hora, El Diario Ilustrado, La Opinión,* and *El Siglo,* all of Santiago, May 29, 1941; *Panama Tribune,* Panama, May 28, and June 1, 1941; *El Dictamen,* Veracruz, June 1, 1941; and *Universal,* Lima, May 31, 1941. See also Despatch 939, Caracas, June 4, 1941, Department of State Archives.

It was clear now that all America stood on the brink of war. President Roosevelt had unequivocally taken his stand against the Axis threat, and other American governments were being faced with the stern necessity of making a choice. No longer, said *La Nación* of Buenos Aires (May 28, 1941), did the United States "pretend to be neutral."[77] *El Mundo* (May 29, 1941) of the same capital urged full acceptance of the offer made by President Roosevelt to collaborate in continental defense and to fulfill the hope expressed by him that the twenty-one American republics would know how to understand the significance and the permanent value of internal solidarity against any enemy who might attempt to alter it through violence or treason. Presidents of several Central American countries sent official messages of support and approval to President Roosevelt.

If responsibility for the security of the Americas in war devolved upon the United States, President Roosevelt aggressively exercised that responsibility. Early in 1941 his government intensified its efforts to prevent the extension of Axis-controlled air lines in Latin America and to deny supplies to them, using the promise of priorities on equipment to cooperating companies and, later, the threat of black-list action against any company in Latin America which furnished supplies to Axis lines. The object was to secure the removal of Axis influence and control over aviation, particularly over those lines which operated near the Panama Canal and other strategic sites, by encouraging Latin American governments either to nationalize these air lines or to supplant Axis air-line companies with United States companies. The Roosevelt administration later extended its pressures to other types of transportation and communication which were subject to Axis influence.

As a further means of combatting the power of Axis nationals and agents in Latin America, President Roosevelt authorized on July 17, 1941, the promulgation of "The Proclaimed List of Certain Blocked Nationals" who were deemed to be serving Axis interests and with whom further trade was forbidden. The stated purpose of this so-called "Black List" was to deny the benefits of inter-American trade to individuals and companies who were "undermining the peace and independence of the Western Hemisphere" and to transfer that trade to persons who were "committed to the solidarity of the

77. See also *Información*, Havana, March 19, 1941; *El Norte*, San Pedro Sula, Honduras, March 18, 1941; and *Correio da Manhã*, Rio de Janeiro, April 27, 1941.

Americas in the face of threats from abroad." Firms and individuals which served as "cloaks" to carry on disguised operations on behalf of firms on the Proclaimed List would themselves be put on the list. The first list included the names of more than 1,800 persons and business institutions, and from time to time other names were added to it.[78] When the Roosevelt administration froze all the Japanese assets in the United States by executive order on July 26, 1941, it pressed the Latin American governments to do the same.

In June, 1941, the Hitler-Stalin pact was abruptly terminated and Germany invaded the Soviet Union. This diversion of Germany's armies eastward was interpreted reassuringly in Latin America as postponing the day of American involvement in the war. It seemed to offer a new possibility of peace, at least for the Western Hemisphere. In Chile public opinion generally hoped that neither of the new antagonists would be victorious, but that both of them would exhaust themselves in the struggle.[79] In Cuba the conservative *Acción* (June 25, 1941) rejoiced that now the two great forces opposed to democracy were in conflict with each other. In Guatemala the semiofficial *Nuestro Diario* (July 5, 1941) expressed the hope that both Naziism and Communism would fall as a result of the conflict. In fact, a great many Latin Americans, especially those who belonged to ruling groups, found it difficult to accept the sudden new decision of the Roosevelt administration to support Soviet Russia, and if they accepted it at all they accepted it only as tactically necessary, insisting that the Soviet regime was as hostile to democracy as was the Nazi regime and that in any case the Communist parties in America must now be required to abandon their sabotage and other subversive activities.[80] On the other hand, Communists in the Americas now began to call for unlimited American aid to the Soviet Union and suddenly abandoned their campaigns of vilification and denunciation of the United States. Their press, formerly bitter enemies of "Yanqui imperialism," now became more favorable to Roosevelt's policies than any other newspaper bloc.[81] The middle-of-

78. *Department of State Bulletin,* V (July 19, 1941), 41-43; (August 2, 1941), 98-99; (December 6, 1941), 452; (December 13, 1941), 520-521; (December 27, 1941), 590.

79. Despatch 1858, Santiago, September 25, 1941.

80. *Diario de la Marina,* Havana, June 21, 1941; Sergio Carbó in *Prensa Libre,* Havana, June 23 and 24, 1941; *El Mexicano,* Ciudad Juárez, Mexico, June 30, 1941; and Barreda Laos, *op. cit.,* 66-67.

81. *Hoy,* Havana, June 22 and 26, 1941.

the-road and the liberal press also swung around—but more slowly than the Communists—to support of the Soviet Union as an ally against the greater threat of Nazi totalitarianism, and exiled Spanish Republicans in Latin America likewise intensified their campaigns of support for the United States and the defeat of the Axis.

As the Soviet forces fell back before Hitler's invading armies and as the governments of Roosevelt and Churchill rushed aid to Hitler's new victims, the hope of a respite for the American nations from the threat of war became more illusory. In the propaganda appeal of the Atlantic Charter, proclaimed by Roosevelt and Churchill on August 14, 1941, Latin Americans perceived a new stage in the "ideological warfare against the Axis nations," as *El Mercurio* of Santiago, Chile (August 16, 1941) expressed it. "Never before have liberal concepts reached such vast proportions," declared *Diario de la Marina* of Havana (August 15, 1941), "since they range all the way from respect for the sovereignty of both large and small nations to the right of the individual to lead a better life."[82] The Ecuadoran Congress officially endorsed the charter, thus reaffirming, as it declared, "its faith in democracy and its condemnation of regimes of force and oppression."[83] But those principles in the charter which Latin Americans most resoundingly acclaimed were those which they themselves had often stressed in their controversies with the United States. The Foreign Minister of Mexico, Ezequiel Padilla, interpreted the charter to mean "no territorial conquests, nor economic hegemonies, nor interventions—visible or invisible—in the internal organization of each country, nor financial dictatorships, nor material or spiritual tyrannies."[84] President Arnulfo Arias of Panama, whose overthrow was still several weeks in the future, expressed his great satisfaction that the Roosevelt-Churchill declaration extolled "the sacred principles of territorial integrity and of the political independence of all nations," but pointedly added that he was especially pleased that it recognized "the right of all people to adopt that government which is most in accord with their idiosyncrasies and their

82. See also *Avance,* Havana, August 14, 1941; *Hoy,* Havana, August 15, 1941; *Prensa Libre,* Havana, August 15, 1941; and *El Crisol,* Havana, August 15, 1941. "Reports on the Reactions in the Other American Republics to the Meeting of President Roosevelt and Prime Minister Churchill" were summarized in a memorandum prepared in the Division of American Republics, Department of State, August 20, 1941.

83. Telegram 258, Quito, August 23, 1941; and Despatch 2056, Quito, September 16, 1941.

84. *Excelsior,* Mexico City, August 15, 1941.

needs, and with the desire of their own people."[85] Latin Americans, on the whole, now seemed to be glad to be "bound geographically and by ties of friendship, economies, and a spirit of liberty to one of the great nations which is joining in the gigantic but indispensable task of reconstructing national and international societies."[86] The United States was making itself, as *La Nación* of Santiago, Chile (September 13, 1941), declared, "a voluntary defender of the weak regardless of what the cost may be."[87] Stated in these terms, the issue could be resolved in only one way. Latin America must throw its weight on the side of the United States. If the postwar world was to be reconstructed and directed along the lines of the Atlantic Charter, Latin Americans wanted to help in establishing more just and humane conditions both for themselves and for the rest of mankind. To their growing sense of need of cooperation with the United States for the sake of their own security and to their chivalric desire to combat the evil which seemed to be incarnate in the Nazi system was now added the roseate prospect of Latin American participation in the creation of a postwar Utopia.

Meanwhile the United States as the arsenal of democracy was engaged in a prodigious effort at production not only for its fighting allies but also in preparation for its own obviously imminent involvement in the war. In this effort it undertook to meet the essential commodity requirements of the twenty Latin American countries. Under Secretary Welles promised the Latin Americans in an address on August 25, 1941, that "insofar as concerns the type of goods of which the United States is the principal or sole supplier they will be made available on an equal basis to the people of the other American republics as liberally as they are to the people of this country."[88] The United States thus accepted the obligation to replace, insofar as its own facilities permitted, the former overseas suppliers of Latin America, who were now engaged in a death struggle, and to balance

85. *Panama Tribune,* Panama, August 22, 1941. For the official views of President Rafael A. Calderón Guardia of Costa Rica see *La Tribuna,* San José, August 22, 1941; and of President Anastasio Somoza of Nicaragua see *Novedades,* Managua, August 15, 1941.

86. *Excelsior,* Mexico City, August 15, 1941.

87. For additional editorial comment on the Atlantic Charter see *Universal,* Lima, August 16, 1941; *La Crónica,* Lima, August 16, and September 13, 1941; and *La Nación,* Ciudad Trujillo, August 23, 1941. For comment from Buenos Aires see Telegram 844, Buenos Aires, August 16, 1941, Department of State Archives.

88. Department of State, *Press Release* No. 415, August 25, 1941.

the stated requirements of one Latin American government off against those of another in relation to its own production and needs.

But in Washington security considerations were recognized as the decisive factors in relations with Latin America. Neither economic concessions nor cultural efforts nor even eloquent political appeals would be as effective as the shared consciousness among Latin Americans of a common danger to the safety of the entire hemisphere. In a speech on September 11, 1941, Roosevelt charged that secret Nazi air-landing fields were being maintained in Colombia within easy range of the Panama Canal. The resulting Colombian reaction of dismay at this disclosure was to align that nation with the United States more firmly than before.[89] The zeal of Latin Americans for resistance to the Axis was further whipped up by President Roosevelt's disclosure in his Navy Day address on October 27, 1941, that he had in his possession a secret map which showed Hitler's plan for division of South America into five vassal states. German ministers in Latin America, on instructions from their government, hastened to deliver notes to the governments to which they were accredited denying the existence of the map.[90] But Roosevelt's horrendous revelation was headlined in the press of Latin America, and it intensified the belief that the safety of the entire hemisphere could only be preserved by the destruction of Germany.[91] Henceforth self-interest alone seemed to demand that Latin America support the United States in its opposition to Hitler.[92] *Diário Carioca* of Rio de Janeiro (October

89. *El Tiempo,* Bogotá, September 13, 1941.

90. Telegram 206, Port-au-Prince, November 5, 1941; Telegram 230, Managua, November 6, 1941; Telegram 534, Bogotá, November 7, 1941; Telegram 608, Mexico City, November 7, 1941; Telegram 325, San José, November 8, 1941; Telegram 211, Ciudad Trujillo, November 8, 1941; Telegram 1641, Tegucigalpa, November 4, 1941; Despatch 2131, Lima, November 7, 1941; Despatch 173, Managua, November 8, 1941; Despatch 536, Port-au-Prince, November 6, 1941; Despatch 2244, Quito, November 8, 1941; Despatch 284, Montevideo, November 7, 1941; Despatch 14187, Mexico City, November 7, 1941; Despatch 1307, La Paz, November 10, 1941; Despatch 2226, Lima, November 21, 1941, all in the Department of State Archives.

91. For reactions to Roosevelt's Navy Day disclosure in various Latin American capitals see Telegram 166, Havana, October 29, 1949; Despatch 2027, Santiago, October 30, 1941; Despatch 2064, Lima, October 30, 1941; and Despatch 54, San José, November 7, 1941. See also *Listín Diario,* Ciudad Trujillo, October 30, 1941.

92. The map referred to by Roosevelt has not been found in the Roosevelt Papers, Mr. Herman Kahn, Director of the Franklin D. Roosevelt Library, Hyde Park, New York, to the author, August 17, 1954. See also Langer and Gleason, *The Undeclared War,* 595.

29, 1941) declared that the President's words constituted "a last warning."[93] *Excelsior* of Mexico (October 29, 1941) now concluded: "We must cooperate with those who have assumed the task of defending the territorial integrity of America in case of aggression. . . . The close collaboration of each and every one of the American countries cannot be put off any longer under the present circumstances." Roosevelt's emphasis in the same address upon Hitler's challenge to freedom of conscience and religion also strengthened the support of the Roman Catholic press in Latin America for the course which the United States was pursuing.[94]

As the year 1941 entered upon its last fateful months, the attention of Latin Americans was focused closely upon the United States. They were deeply involved, whether they fully realized it or not, in the diplomatic impasse in which their ever more powerful northern neighbor found itself in relation to the Axis nations, Germany, Italy, and Japan. The objectives for which it was struggling had become, or would soon become, their objectives, and the outcome of that struggle would settle their fate as nations. President Roosevelt, by means of his Good Neighbor Policy, had created a community of interest and ideology between his nation and the Latin American nations, with the result that they now found themselves implicated in policy decisions made in Washington.

The people of the United States, as Latin Americans viewed them, had been disinclined to participate in another world war. "All circumstances," reported *Hoy* of Mexico City (June 29, 1940), "cause them to love peace above all things: their traditions, their customs, their constitutional life, and especially the bitter harvest they reaped from the last world war." But as they condemned war they also condemned aggression, as committed by both Germany and Japan, and they developed an aversion toward those nations, which Roosevelt skillfully encouraged. "All the outrages and all the excesses of Naziism were needed," reported Fernando Ortiz Echagüe, the Washington correspondent of *La Nación* of Buenos Aires (November 2, 1941, and March 11, 1944), to draw the United States out of its isolationism. But finally it scrapped its neutrality and "placed all its resources at the service of the defeat of the Axis; its arms went to war before its men did." By mid-November, 1941, it was clear to

93. See also *O Jornal*, Rio de Janeiro, October 29, 1941.
94. *La Nación*, Ciudad Trujillo, October 29, 1941; and *El Bien Público*, Montevideo, October 29, 1941.

this acute Argentine observer in Washington that "the course of the nation has been fixed." That course was one of potential if not actual belligerency.

In the oncoming struggle between the Axis powers and the Anglo-American coalition, Latin Americans gradually aligned themselves with the latter. When, following the Nazi attack upon the United States destroyer "Greer" in September, 1941, President Roosevelt made plain that the United States was still insisting upon the full freedom of the seas within the defense zone adopted in the Declaration of Panama, his resolute determination thus to combat Axis aggressions on the high seas with the United States navy was construed in Latin America as evidence that "real war between the United States and the Axis has commenced."[95] He was leading the world into a "war against Nazi piracy," said El Liberal of Bogotá (September 12, 1941) approvingly. His leadership in defense of the principles of freedom of the seas, which had long been a principle proclaimed by all the American nations, emphasized, as it seemed to the Foreign Minister of Mexico, Ezequiel Padilla, in a statement issued on September 13, 1941, not only "the growing nearness of war" but also the need for America to prepare "as rapidly as possible a united economy and an efficient hemisphere defense."[96] Since the United States was already in effect engaged in hostilities, asserted El País of Montevideo, President Roosevelt should issue a clear declaration of war.[97] Meanwhile, however, the gigantic war production of the United States was making it, as La Nación of Buenos Aires (September 3, 1941) expressed it, "the arbiter of the destinies of the world." To increasingly desperate Latin Americans Roosevelt now appeared as "the Savior of Christian civilization."[98]

For reasons of self-preservation, if for no other, Latin Americans could hardly refrain from becoming identified with the United States in its opposition to the Axis powers. The main compulsion to inter-

---

95. La Nación, Ciudad Trujillo, September 13, 1941.
96. Excelsior, Mexico City, September 13, 1941.
97. Reported in Telegram 393, Montevideo, September 13, 1941, Department of State Archives. For additional newspaper comment on the "Greer" incident and Roosevelt's policy see Listín Diario, Ciudad Trujillo, September 9, 13, 1941; La Nación, Ciudad Trujillo, September 13, 1941; La Nación, El Mundo, and La Prensa, all of Buenos Aires, September 13, 1941; and El Mercurio, La Nación, El Imparcial, and El Siglo, all of Santiago, September 13, 1941.
98. La Nación, Santiago, reported in Despatch 1797, Santiago, September 3, 1941.

American unity was now the apprehension as to Axis designs for the subjugation of the Western Hemisphere and the fear that a divided hemisphere would open the way to invasion. There was, explained *Listín Diario* of Ciudad Trujillo in the Dominican Republic (November 15, 1941), a "large threatening cloud rising in Europe which might, unless something was done about it, soon darken our sky, the sky of all Americans, of every man who works and dreams in this continent." Economically, psychologically, and politically, Latin Americans were constrained to swing into the foreign-policy orbit of the United States. To Latin American exponents of closer collaboration with the United States it seemed clear that an American Axis must be formed to meet the threat presented by the German-Japanese-Italian Axis. The inter-American system, formed to advance the peace-time collaboration of the twenty-one nations of the Western Hemisphere, must now be transformed into a war-making system for their common defense. In it the United States, by reason of its power and prescience, could be expected to exert a strong leadership, which would be tempered, however, in relation to Latin America, by the noble professions of the Good Neighbor Policy.

Between 1939 and 1941 the issues which would determine the attitudes of all the American peoples toward the totalitarian and aggressive nations of Europe and Asia were penetratingly analyzed. Upon the outcome of this debate in Latin America the United States exerted a dominating influence through its antitotalitarian propaganda, its moral leadership, its positive campaign for inter-American cooperation, its increasing importance as a source of necessary supplies, and the magnitude of its preparedness program for defense or war. But the debate between those who favored and those who opposed an active campaign against the Axis powers stirred public opinion throughout the Americas. The pressure for a united front or for solidary hemispheric resistance to the Axis threat did not go unchallenged. Opposing it were the forces of Latin American nationalism, regionalism, and neutralism, all of which were deeply rooted in the tradition of the Hispanic-American peoples. Even into late 1941 many Latin American officials and organs of opinion still either refrained from commenting on the international situation or maintained a studiously neutral position in relation to it. Sentiment favorable to the United States appeared to be strongest in the Caribbean and Central American countries, countries which would inevitably share the military consequences of United States policy. But skepticism as to the wisdom of that policy was strong in Mexico and in those South American countries which were located beyond the Caribbean orbit of the United States.

The continental lineup behind the United States was far from complete. As late as September, 1941, the United States ambassador to Brazil reported, with considerable concern, that "the Brazilians have very little interest in hemisphere defense as such: for the most part they are doing what we ask them to do because we ask them to do it." They were "definitely apprehensive," he added, over the military operations which the United States, in the interest of hemisphere defense, was carrying on in their country and which looked to them like "penetration. . . . They are sorely disappointed that after so many years of so much talk and so many promises we have done nothing for them in the way of air materials and only what our War Department calls a 'token shipment' for the Brazilian military. Their lack of confidence in us is growing daily."[99]

Antagonism to the United States and its policies was even stronger in the countries south of Brazil. According to a Brazilian official who made a visit to the southern countries in November, 1941, "all classes of Chileans" were "very critical of the United States" and in Argentina "he found active hostility in all classes against us." A common remark directed against the United States in both countries, he reported, was that what the United States calls "an American interest is merely a United States interest."[100] Argentina's uncooperativeness was accentuated by the confused domestic political situation in that country, where by reason of the illness of President Roberto Ortiz political power was devolving upon his Vice President Ramón S. Castillo and Foreign Minister Enrique Ruiz Guiñazú, both of whom were highly susceptible to Argentine nationalist pressures.

The disagreements on high policy between the so-called "interventionists" and "isolationists" were not confined to the United States. They had their counterparts in every country of the Western Hemisphere, and they were resolved only when the Japanese came to the aid of the interventionists by attacking Pearl Harbor on December 7, 1941.

99. Jefferson Caffery to Hull, Despatch 5437, Rio de Janeiro, September 24, 1941, Department of State Archives.
100. Caffery to Hull, Despatch 5922, Rio de Janeiro, November 28, 1941, Department of State Archives.

Chapter 4

PARTNERS IN WARTIME

Horizons must be broadened with the sincerity and nobility of peoples who are constructing a bridge of understanding over their hatreds.

—José C. Valadés

ROOSEVELT'S GOOD NEIGHBOR POLICY, like the Monroe Doctrine, was a unilateral declaration. The United States agreed to stop misbehaving. It decided to begin minding its own business. It chose to abandon strong-arm, coercive methods, to make just and overdue concessions, and to redress long-standing Latin American grievances in order to accomplish the larger objective of winning the goodwill of the Latin Americans. As Laurence Duggan, a State Department official, once wrote: "The other American republics came to see that Uncle Sam was not going to bash them over the head when he became annoyed or when he wanted something they were not prepared to give." The essence of the Good Neighbor Policy, as originally enunciated and practiced by the Roosevelt administration, was nonintervention by the United States in the internal affairs of the Latin American states. The United States thus recognized the right of a Latin American government to commit errors and even stupidities if it wished to do so, provided that it did not molest the United States or threaten its vital interests. This was a policy of mutual respect for the sovereignty of other states and the acts of their governments. It repudiated the guardian-ward relationship and assumed that each nation of the hemisphere would play a responsible, mature role in the inter-American community. It was simply, as the

Aprista leader Manuel Seoane defined it, "a doctrine of 'good manners.' "[1]

Only once during the period from 1933 to 1940 did the Roosevelt administration overtly deviate from this course. In 1933-1934 it refused to recognize the government of Dr. Ramón Grau San Martín in Cuba and maintained warships in Cuban waters during his brief regime—with unfortunate results throughout Latin America.[2] But for this act President Roosevelt virtually apologized in 1944 when he welcomed to Washington Grau San Martín, then president of Cuba for a second time;[3] and in other cases the principle of nonintervention was faithfully adhered to as the basic element in the Good Neighbor Policy. When a political crisis broke out in Nicaragua in March, 1936, Secretary Hull reminded the United States minister in Nicaragua, Arthur Bliss Lane, that "our relations with Nicaragua today are on exactly the same basis as our relations with other countries, that is, on a basis of full friendship and scrupulous respect of sovereignty. To continue this relationship, we must refrain from interference in Nicaragua's internal affairs."[4] The principle of nonintervention was even interpreted to inhibit diplomatic officers of the United States from offering advice to Latin American governments on any domestic question, even when such advice was requested from them. For example, in May, 1936, the United States, responding to a request from El Salvador, declined "to express any opinion with regard to the policy which the Government of Salvador may determine to pursue in its relations with the Nicaraguan Government. What that policy shall be is a matter solely for the determination of the Government of Salvador."[5] As late as April, 1940, Under Secretary Welles firmly denied in an instruction to the United States minister in Nicaragua, Meredith Nicholson, that "there was any slightest desire on the part of this Government to intervene directly or indirectly in the internal affairs of Nicaragua."[6]

1. "Where Do We Go from Here?" *The Inter-American,* V (March, 1946), 23-24.
2. Edward O. Guerrant, *Roosevelt's Good Neighbor Policy* (Albuquerque, 1950), 5-7; Sumner Welles, *The Time for Decision,* 194-200; and Bemis, *The Latin American Policy,* 280-281.
3. The warmth of President Roosevelt's treatment of President Grau in 1944 was indicated in the United Press story that Roosevelt received him at the White House with a broad smile and said: "And to think that I did not recognize you eleven years ago." *New York Times,* September 4, 1944, 22.
4. Hull to Lane, March 28, 1936, Department of State, *Foreign Relations, 1936,* V, 817.
5. Hull to Boaz Long, Minister to Nicaragua, May 9, 1936, *ibid.,* 821.
6. Welles to Nicholson, April 16, 1940, Department of State Archives.

The Good Neighbor Policy was thus construed to mean that the United States would not assume to dictate courses of action, either internal or external, to the Latin Americans. Negotiations with them would be based upon continuous respect for their sovereign status. The policy of not tolerating hostile governments in Latin America was, as Welles affirmed, "as dead as the dinosaur."[7] In an address to the Pan American Union on April 15, 1940, Roosevelt declared that the Good Neighbor Policy required "self-restraint and the acceptance of the equal rights of our neighbors." Continuing, he said, "We have agreed, as neighbors should, to mind our own business. We have renounced, each and all of us, any right to interfere in each other's domestic affairs, recognizing that free and independent nations must shape their own destinies and find their own ways of life."[8] In pursuance of this principle the Roosevelt administration added another to its long series of self-denying acts in the following September when, to the delight of Latin America, it concluded a new agreement with the Dominican Republic finally allowing that government to resume collection of its own customs revenues, which under a treaty of 1924 had been collected by an official appointed by the President of the United States.[9] Underlying the Good Neighbor Policy was the dominating assumption that, as a Mexican journalist-politician, José C. Valadés, observed, "horizons must be broadened with the sincerity and nobility of peoples who are constructing a bridge of understanding over their hatreds."[10] In pursuit of that purpose the Good Neighbor Policy reversed the traditional policy of force, or rather sought to sublimate the power of the United States into a moral force. As a result it established, in the words of *El Tiempo* of Bogotá (April 14, 1945), "a new spiritual relationship between the republics south of the Rio Grande and the United States."[11]

But to the original element of "live and let live" in the Good Neighbor Policy was added the element of "help live" after the outbreak of

7. *Post,* Mexico City, November 2, 1940.

8. Rosenman (comp.), *The Public Papers and Addresses of Franklin D. Roosevelt,* IX, 160.

9. For typically favorable comments on this agreement in the Latin American press see *Correio da Manhã,* Rio de Janeiro, October 15, 1940; and *El País,* Montevideo, November 4 and 5, 1940.

10. Syndicated article distributed by ANTA, a Mexican news agency, in November, 1942, published in *Hoy,* Mexico City, November 7, 1942; *Acción,* Nogales, Sonora, November 12, 1942; and other Mexican journals.

11. Similar sentiments had been expressed editorially in *La Prensa,* Buenos Aires, November 17, 1940.

World War II. The cooperation of the United States "with all the Americas in defending the entire Western Hemisphere," Roosevelt declared in an address on February 27, 1941, was "a natural outgrowth of our own good neighbor policy in our relations with the other American Republics."[12] He did not identify or equate this cooperation with the Good Neighbor Policy but called it only an "outgrowth" of that policy. It was now modified into a new policy of Pan-Americanism. The determination of the United States to respect the rights of the Latin Americans "in and with a world of neighbors" was transformed after 1940, and particularly after the Japanese attack upon Pearl Harbor, into a determination to seek the active partnership of the Latin American nations in the war. The primary purpose of the United States in relation to Latin America became the attainment of hemispheric solidarity against the Axis nations in the interest of the security, if not indeed the survival, of all the nations of the Americas. This new policy was based upon a conviction of a common identity of interest and a fear of a common enemy, eloquently set forth by President Roosevelt and increasingly shared by nearly all the Latin American governments and their peoples.

As first enunciated by President Roosevelt, the Good Neighbor Policy had not required to be implemented by money appropriations, but in the late 1930's it began to be thought of in terms of dollar programs. When World War II broke out in Europe, the United States began to back its diplomacy in Latin America with an abundance of dollars. It assumed realistically in this serious crisis that the friendship and cooperation of the Latin Americans, living in geographical propinquity in a common neighborhood, could be won only by paying a price. They not only must be convinced of the exigency of a common cause; they must be offered material inducements to support it. The original passive policy, merely implying repentance for past misdeeds and promising respect for the rights of others in the future, became, under wartime pressures, an outgiving, positive policy used for the purpose of consolidating the entire hemisphere, first in a defensive neutrality, and later in a joint war effort. At first a policy of nonintervention in political matters, it came to be thought of during the war as a policy requiring vigorous action by the United States in both economic and social matters. Roosevelt, in an address on December 8, 1942, suggested the term "the Policy of the

12. President Roosevelt, address to Annual Awards Dinner of Academy of Motion Picture Arts and Sciences, Rosenman, *op. cit.*, X, 41.

Good Partner" as describing this enlarged or altered policy toward Latin America. "In other words," he added, "all of these Republics of ours are not just neighbors. We are partners for the common good —all of us. We are recognizing more and more that the word 'partner' means that any country—on either hemisphere—cannot be happy and prosperous until all the hemisphere is happy and prosperous."[13] As Roosevelt suggested, the original policy of "live and let live" had been converted by the United States and Latin America into a policy of "one for all and all for one."

Fortunately for the United States, its entry into World War II was not preceded, as had been its entry into World War I, by incidents that antagonized Latin America, such as the shelling of Veracruz, the Pershing expedition against Villa, intervention in Nicaragua, and marine occupations of the Dominican Republic and Haiti. "If dollar diplomacy or the Big Stick or any of the formulas which gave graphic expression to the imperialistic policy had been in force when Japan attacked Pearl Harbor," El Tiempo of Bogotá (January 15, 1946) concluded, "certainly the United States could not have counted upon the enthusiastic adherence of these republics." But the United States had predisposed Latin Americans to support it by pursuing a hands-off policy toward them and by deliberately cultivating their friendship, a policy which had created an overflowing reservoir of goodwill and respect for the United States among them. In particular, as coupled with the New Deal program for the redistribution of wealth, it had won the support of Latin American labor.[14] The Good Neighbor Policy, concluded the foreign ministers of the American republics in their Third Consultative Meeting at Rio de Janeiro in January, 1942, "has been one of the elements contributing to the present solidarity of the Americas and their joint cooperation in the solution of outstanding problems of the Continent."[15]

The United States now passed from a good neighbor into the protector of Latin America. The lightning assault on Pearl Harbor suggested to Latin Americans that the United States had become the hemisphere's "first line of defense," that its defeat would open the way to the hostile invasion of the hemisphere, and that distance and

13. President Roosevelt, Toast at the State Dinner for the President of Cuba, Rosenman, op. cit., XI, 531.

14. Vicente Sáenz in El Popular, Mexico City, October 30, 1942.

15. Department of State, Final Act of the Third Meeting of Ministers of Foreign Affairs of the American Republics, Rio de Janeiro, January 28, 1942, Press Release No. 47, February 1, 1942, Resolution XXII.

ocean could no longer be considered as guaranties against attack.[16] Moreover, the Japanese assault on the Philippines, simultaneous with their assault on Pearl Harbor, provided a racial motivation for Latin American support of the United States. Former critics of North American imperialism in Latin America now saw a greater danger in Japanese imperialism, which proffered, as José Vasconcelos wrote, "fourteen hours of work and three rations of rice a day with a little bit of hot liquid, and the obligation to pray to the Mikado."[17] The power of the United States in the Pacific must be maintained, declared *La Prensa* of Lima (December 9, 1941), two days after Pearl Harbor, as a guaranty of the defense of the entire West Coast of America. Newspapers in Ecuador suggested that their government assist the United States by turning over the Galápagos Islands to it as naval bases and fueling stations.[18] "We are and will be with the United States," promised *El Tiempo* of Bogotá (December 19, 1941). The Latin American countries, declared *El Comercio* of Lima (December 8, 1941), "must take their places at the side of the United States . . . which is now defending the destiny of America." In the first excitement after Pearl Harbor *Diário de Noticias* of Rio de Janeiro (December 10, 1941) was confident that the United States would "have at its side an entire America undivided, indivisible."

The official response of many Latin American governments to Pearl Harbor was based upon Resolution XV of the Havana meeting of foreign ministers in 1940 which declared that any attempt by a non-American state against the integrity, the territorial inviolability, the sovereignty or political independence of an American state would be considered as an act of aggression against all the signatory states. Within five days after the Japanese attack El Salvador, Guatemala, Haiti, Honduras, Cuba, Nicaragua, Costa Rica, the Dominican Republic, and Panama had declared war on Japan, and before the middle of December all of them had similarly declared war against Germany and Italy. These same nine nations joined the United States, Great Britain, and their other allies in signing the Declaration of the United Nations on January 1, 1942, agreeing to employ their full resources against their Axis enemies and not to make a separate armistice or peace with them. In addition Colombia and Mexico severed diplomatic relations

16. Statement by the Argentine Socialist deputy Américo Ghioldi, *Noticias Gráficas* and *Crítica*, Buenos Aires, December 25, 1941.

17. *Todo*, Mexico City, February 19, 1942.

18. See, for example, *El Universo*, Guayaquil, December 9 and 11, 1941; and *El Telégrafo*, Guayaquil, December 8 and 10, 1941.

with the Axis nations; Ecuador, Paraguay, Peru, and Brazil declared their solidarity with the United States; and Uruguay, Argentina, Chile, Bolivia, and Venezuela offered to deal with the United States as a nonbelligerent, exempting it from the limitations which would otherwise be imposed upon it within their territories by their international obligations of neutrality. Under Secretary Welles told the foreign ministers of the American republics at their third meeting at Rio de Janeiro on January 15, 1942, that "the shibboleth of classic neutrality in its narrow sense can, in this tragic modern world, no longer be the ideal of any freedom-loving people of the Americas." In pursuance of conclusions to this same effect jointly arrived at by these foreign ministers at that meeting, all the rest of the Latin American governments except Argentina and Chile severed diplomatic relations with Germany and its allies before the end of that month.[19]

The bombing of Pearl Harbor by the Japanese mightily intensified the interest of the United States in gaining the support of Latin America, its "second line of defense." Its own advantage, if nothing else, persuaded it to strengthen its cultural, military, political, and economic ties with the Latin Americans. Its object was to organize a partnership of twenty-one nations in the Western Hemisphere for concerted action in the war. To that end it actively interceded with Ecuador and Peru to settle their acrimonious boundary controversy which was troubling the peace of the hemisphere. The nation which called itself the Good Neighbor now eagerly sought to become a Good Partner to the rest of the American nations and to enlist them also as partners in a common cause. "Inter-Americanism has moved to the field of positive action," President Roosevelt told President Getúlio Vargas of Brazil in a telegram sent on the day after Pearl Harbor.[20]

Immediately the United States expanded its public relations program in Latin America. During 1942 three Latin American heads of state and one president-elect were brought to the United States and lavishly feted. Cultural cooperation with the Latin American peoples was broadened to unprecedented proportions. The Office of the Coordinator of Inter-American Affairs (CIAA) increased the number of copies of its "slick" publication *En Guardia*, distributed gratis

19. *Department of State Bulletin*, V (December 13, 1941), 485-504; (December 20, 1941), 545-561; (December 27, 1941), 583-584; VI (January 3, 1942), 6; and (January 31, 1942), 89-90. See also Pan American Union, *Report on the Third Meeting of the Ministers of Foreign Affairs of the American Republics, Rio de Janeiro, January 15-28, 1942* (Washington, 1942), 7-8.
20. *Department of State Bulletin*, V (December 13, 1941), 489.

in Latin America, from 75,000 to 200,000 and correspondingly stepped up its radio broadcasting and motion picture programs. It contracted over a half million dollars to Walt Disney Productions, Inc., for a Latin American research unit and the production of motion picture cartoons dealing with Latin America. Films depicting such diverse topics as life in old New Orleans, baseball, and victory gardens in the United States were widely distributed there. The Yale University Glee Club was sent on a Latin American tour. New emphasis was given to all means of cultural and psychological *rapprochement*.[21]

At the same time the health and sanitation work of the United States in Latin America was expanded for the avowed purpose, among others, of demonstrating "by deeds as well as words the tangible benefits of democracy in action and to win active support of civilian populations." In September, 1942, for example, the United States government, acting through the CIAA, began to assist the Bolivian government in meeting its public health needs. With the aid of $1 million from the Coordinator's Office and further funds from Bolivia, there was set up the Servicio Cooperativo Interamericano de Salud Pública operating with the Bolivian Ministry of Labor, Public Health, and Social Welfare. Its program included the building of hospitals and dispensaries, the granting of scholarships for training doctors, technicians, and nurses both in the United States and in Bolivia, and the establishment of a complete diagnostic laboratory and a leprosarium. Under the auspices of this Servicio an intensive campaign was launched against malaria, hookworm, and other endemic diseases in Bolivia.[22] Altogether between the fiscal years 1941 and 1943 the obligations and commitments of the CIAA in all its manifold activities in Latin America, including basic economy, information, education, economic development, and transportation, increased from slightly more than $2.5 million to over $30 million.[23] This sum represented a phenomenally large investment in goodwill. The United States undertook to do, in the words of the *Panama American* (September 6, 1944), "a 'total' selling job" in Latin America.

Not long after Pearl Harbor, Axis submarines began to invade the Western Hemisphere. On a single day in February, 1942, they sank seven tankers carrying Venezuelan oil.[24] During this time of crisis in

21. CIAA files, The National Archives, Washington.
22. International Labour Office, *Labour Problems in Bolivia, Report of the Joint Bolivian-United States Labour Commission* (Montreal, 1943), 36.
23. Coordinator of Inter-American Affairs, *History,* 265.
24. Milton S. Eisenhower, "United States-Latin American Relations: Report

the Caribbean, it was later revealed, only one out of every two ships bound for the Caribbean area was reaching its destination safely.[25] As a result the Caribbean area was declared a military zone and was closed to unconvoyed merchant shipping. The resulting isolation of the peoples of the Caribbean islands became a matter of acute concern to the United States, for these peoples, by reason of their traditional preoccupation with the production of a few exportable money crops, such as sugar and cotton, were largely dependent upon imported food-stuffs, including rice from Burma, salt fish from Newfoundland, meat from Argentina, and canned goods from the United States, which were now shut off by the exigencies of war.

The food problem in the independent Caribbean nations—Cuba, Haiti, and the Dominican Republic—did not reach emergency pro-portions. The progress which Cuba had made prior to the outbreak of World War II in diversifying its industry and agriculture provided the Cuban people with certain food surpluses in addition to their tra-ditional sugar and molasses, including dairy products, coffee, corn, bananas, pineapples, grapefruit, avocados, oranges, and fresh vege-tables, especially tomatoes. Early in 1942 the Cuban government, in an effort to meet anticipated shortages, issued a decree law providing for obligatory planting of certain areas in food crops. With respect to Haiti and the Dominican Republic, normally more dependent upon imports than Cuba, an important factor in the food situation was the scarcity of automobile tires and gasoline which took many auto-mobiles and trucks out of food distribution. By 1941-1942 the volume of Haiti's imports reached an all-time low—only 49,000 metric tons. This decline consisted largely of imports of foodstuffs—fish, flour, lard, and cooking oils—which were essential to the well-being and the sta-bility of the country.

Bad as these conditions were, the situation in the remaining Carib-bean islands was much worse. Lying farther from the mainland, Puerto Rico and the Virgin Islands, belonging to the United States, had been traditionally more dependent upon imported foodstuffs than had the three independent nations of the Caribbean. Before the war only 20 per cent of Puerto Rico's cropland had been utilized as subsistence crop farms. To meet the total food requirements of the Puerto Rican

to the President, November 18, 1953," *Department of State Bulletin,* XXIX (November 23, 1953), 698.
25. Charles W. Taussig, "Regionalism in the Caribbean: Six Years of Prog-ress," *Department of State Bulletin,* XVIII (May 30, 1948), 691.

population the island was normally obliged to import one-third of its requirements by bulk and two-thirds by nutritive or water-free value. In the Virgin Islands less than 9 per cent of the harvested crop acreage was devoted to food crops before the war, and the islands were required to import probably as much as 85 per cent of their basic supply, calculated on a nutritional or water-free basis. Within less than a year after Pearl Harbor, Puerto Rico's food imports amounted to less than 20 per cent of what they were before the war. Lack of raw materials and of export facilities also forced practically all factories to close and created grave problems of unemployment.

In their isolation the island governments turned to developing their own domestic food resources. Barbados, which had raised only 5 per cent of its own food before the war, now required every plantation to devote 25 per cent of its arable land to subsistence crops. Other Caribbean governments enacted similar measures. But the islands could not locally meet the food requirements of their dense populations. The Virgin Islands could at best produce, it was estimated, only 25 per cent of their own food supplies. The Bahamas did not have sufficient arable land to feed their populations. At least 40 per cent of the cane lands of Trinidad were unsuitable for food production. If all the arable lands in Barbados and Puerto Rico could be cultivated they would not provide adequately for local needs. The emergency attempts of the Caribbean governments, therefore, to develop self-sufficient economies proved inadequate to relieve their immediate distress.

In late 1942 the situation in the European colonies in the Caribbean appeared to the United States to be critical and to call urgently for the initiation of social, economic, and political measures. These were intended to relieve current unemployment, principally through the inauguration of public works. Constitutional changes in these colonies were also deemed by the United States to be necessary. In particular it was felt that the constitution of Jamaica ought to be changed to broaden the franchise and to curtail the governor's reserve powers and that the constitutions of Bermuda, Barbados, and the Bahamas should be similarly changed. The interest of the United States in these problems sprang perhaps primarily from the military or strategic importance of the Caribbean to its own security but also from its concern over the economic plight and possible political instability of the European West Indies for which, under the strangulating effects of the war, it felt a responsibility. Upon it, under these circumstances, devolved the task of maintaining the economic life of this area and of stabilizing its political situation. Social and political unrest there might have unpleasant consequences for the United States. Its interests, traditionally associated with those of the British, French, and Dutch, now seemed to be dominant over those of the European colonial powers.

The United States accordingly moved to relieve the plight of the Caribbean peoples. The Office of the Coordinator of Inter-American Affairs and the Department of State in Washington undertook a survey of the fishery resources of the Caribbean area as a new source of wartime food supplies. In addition the United States took the lead in organizing the Anglo-American Caribbean Commission composed of three members from each country headed by cochairmen Sir Frank Stockdale, Controller for Development and Welfare in the British West Indies, and Charles W. Taussig, president of the American Molasses Company. This commission was authorized to study and make recommendations to the two governments on "matters pertaining to labor, agriculture, housing, health, education, social welfare, finance, economics, and related subjects" in the Caribbean region. In dealing with the problem of emergency supplies the commission recommended at its meetings on March 26-31, 1942, that "immediate steps should be taken to build up reserves of imported food supplies" on the American and British islands and that "the local administrations should immediately study the possibilities of developing a system of inter-island distribution of supplies by schooners and small local steamers from a few central depots to be fed by supplies imported by ocean steamers." They also recommended an increase in "local production of all kinds of foodstuffs in substitution for imported supplies during the war emergency."[26]

As the food situation in the islands further deteriorated under the impact of the German submarine warfare in 1943 the independent nations of the Caribbean—Cuba, Haiti, and the Dominican Republic —were drawn into this cooperative arrangement. Priority was given to the problem of food supplies as a measure of survival for the beleaguered populations. Supply caches or stock piles of food and drugs were built up in Cuba and transferred from there to other Caribbean islands by means of the schooner pool. Haiti and the Dominican Republic agreed to cooperate in developing an overland route for

26. *Report of the Anglo-American Caribbean Commission to the Governments of the United States and Great Britain for the Years 1942-1943* (Washington, 1943), 39-40.

shipment of these supplies through their territories, the United States agreeing to pay all the expenses involved in any improvement work undertaken. The United States also made available limited quantities of critical materials needed to augment food supplies, including agricultural implements, irrigation equipment, poultry wire and fencing, cold storage facilities, and fishing tackle. The facilities of the caches and of the interisland schooner pool were made available not only to Puerto Rico and the Virgin Islands but also to the British islands in the Caribbean for relieving their food and drug shortages.

When the German submarines were driven from the Caribbean in mid-1943, the economic plight of these islands became still worse as the United States terminated the construction work on its bases, particularly those in Jamaica, St. Lucia, and Trinidad. In order to relieve the food plight of Trinidad, lying in close proximity to the South American mainland, the United States now made arrangements for an army bomber to fly fresh meat to the island from British Guiana for the use of the United States bases. For the relief of the civilian population arrangements were made for the bauxite vessels plying between Surinam and United States ports to carry foodstuffs to the island on their return trip from the United States. As a result of these emergency efforts of the United States, cooperating with the home governments, the lives of thousands if not tens of thousands of people on the Caribbean islands were preserved and the stability of the area was assured.[27]

* * *

In order to cushion the shock of the war upon Latin America the United States announced less than three weeks after Pearl Harbor that it would aid "the economic stability of the other American Republics by recognizing and providing for their essential civilian needs on the basis of equal and proportionate consideration with our own." In

27. The above paragraphs are based on United States Section of the Anglo-American Caribbean Commission, *Sugar and the Caribbean Problem for 1942-43-44: A Report to the President of the United States* (Washington, 1942), *passim;* Department of State, *The Caribbean Islands and the War: A Record of Progress in Facing Stern Realities* (Washington, 1943), *passim;* Anglo-American Caribbean Commission, *Report of the Anglo-American Caribbean Commission, passim;* and Anglo-American Caribbean Commission, Meeting at Charlotte Amalie, St. Thomas, Virgin Islands of the United States, August 17-21, 1943, *Nutrition, Agriculture, Fisheries and Forestry*, 14. See also Bernard L. Poole, *The Caribbean Commission: Background of Cooperation in the West Indies* (Columbia, South Carolina, 1951), 180-206.

pursuance of this policy decision it undertook, in its allocation of both scarce civilian materials and transportation facilities, not to discriminate in favor of its own civilian economy against that of the Latin American nations. This policy became extremely difficult to carry out as the United States found itself more and more deeply involved in war operations around the world, but it was nevertheless adhered to as a policy. The imposition of "ceiling prices" on United States commodities exported to the southern countries, though not rigidly enforced because of such variable factors as war risk insurance and maritime freight, was intended to prevent United States industrialists and exporters from taking advantage of a monopoly market to make exorbitant profits at Latin America's expense. Francisco de Assis Chateaubriand, publisher of the Associated Dailies of Brazil, writing in *O Jornal* of Rio de Janeiro (September 14, 1943), praised this as "a generous system of commercial aid to the Latin American countries"— a system with a "humane and social orientation," exemplifying "the beautiful American attitude toward our poverty."

The United States now became almost entirely dependent upon Latin America for certain strategic materials, including natural rubber, tin, cinchona bark for quinine, sisal, abacá, antimony, tuna oil, and menthol, as Asiatic sources of supply were cut off by the war. It also increased its takings from Latin America of certain other products which were thrown into short supply, including asbestos, beryllium, manganese, balsa, kapok, nitrate, quartz crystal, chromite, cobalt, industrial diamonds, platinum, silver, vanadium, zinc, bauxite, copper, rotenone, babassú kernels, henequen, flax, wool, sugar, coffee, cacao, fats and oils, and many others. It accordingly undertook to secure increased production of many of these materials in Latin America and their exclusive sale to its own purchasers at prices agreed upon by the governments concerned. In March, 1942, for example, it agreed to take all of Haiti's carry-over of cotton from the 1940-1941 crop, all the surplus of the crop of 1942, and to buy all cotton subsequently produced in Haiti during the war, thus underwriting all of Haiti's cotton crops for the duration of hostilities.[28] By contracts it stimulated the gathering of rubber in Brazil and cinchona in Ecuador and Peru, the collecting òf oil-bearing nuts in Brazil, the mining of ores in Chile and Bolivia, the production of hemp in Mexico and the Central American countries, and the expansion of sugar cultivation

28. Harry N. Stark, "War Bolsters Haiti's Economy," *Foreign Commerce Weekly* (December 12, 1942), 8.

in Cuba, Haiti, and the Dominican Republic. In 1943 the United States government purchased the entire sugar crop of these last-named countries.

At the same time, in order to increase the interest of United States businessmen and investors in Latin America, the United States added the Western Hemisphere Trade Corporations clause to the Internal Revenue Code, granting lower tax rates to United States companies which derived all their income from countries in the Western Hemisphere other than the United States. Under this legislation maximum encouragement was given to a company which would undertake to carry on its total enterprise in Latin America, as, for example, by running a railroad or air line, by operating a utilities system, or by manufacturing and selling its products there. The incentives offered by this legislation had the effect mainly of opening the way for the expansion of Latin American markets for United States goods and the development of the natural resources of Latin America.[29] The United States also sought to equalize the allocation of shipping in order to maintain the essential flow of Latin American exports to its own ports and at the same time to secure an equitable distribution among the Latin American nations of the rapidly decreasing quantity of manufactures which could be made available to meet the requirements of their local economies.

Military collaboration with Latin America also became an objective of United States policy, as already suggested. To this end the Roosevelt government made use of the newly created Inter-American Defense Board, which was located in Washington, and of a special Mexican-United States Defense Board, set up to deal with the special problems of military cooperation with its next-door neighbor to the south. In addition it expanded the personnel and scope of its military missions which had been operating in several Latin American countries before Pearl Harbor and sent new missions to the Dominican Republic, Ecuador, Panama, Paraguay, and Venezuela. In pursuance of understandings arrived at before Pearl Harbor the United States established air bases in Cuba, Colombia, Haiti, Panama, and the Galápagos Islands of Ecuador, and made military installations in Chile, Peru, Uruguay, and Venezuela. Before the war ended, it was maintaining as many as 165,000 troops in Brazil. The northeast-

29. United Nations, Economic and Social Council, *Taxation in Capital-Exporting and Capital-Importing Countries of Foreign Private Investment in Latin America,* 11, 25-26, 49.

ern corner or bulge of that country became an indispensable supply base and point of transshipment for the United States in its land operations in North Africa in 1942, and one of its essential links with the fighting fronts all over the world. Through this "Corridor of Victory" in 1942 a total of 1,238 aircraft flew the South Atlantic route to and from the war theaters. In 1944 the military traffic through this air corridor was greater than that through all the other military air routes in the world combined. To facilitate these military operations after Pearl Harbor the United States negotiated Lend-Lease agreements with all the Latin American governments with which it had not already concluded agreements, except Argentina and Panama. To some of these countries it sent considerable quantities of military supplies at about 30 per cent of army list prices. In order to improve the military defense of the Western Hemisphere and to lessen its vulnerability to Axis forces the United States also sought, through cooperative action whenever possible, to eliminate Axis agents and sympathizers from positions of economic and political influence in Latin America. For this purpose and in order also to gather information about the pro-Axis proclivities of certain Latin American governments it intensified its intelligence activities in that area and tapped telephone conversations of Latin American ambassadors in Washington.

Operations were carried on by the United States in almost every corner of Latin America. By the end of 1942 it had constructed or enlarged airports in fifteen places in Brazil, had established naval and seaplane bases, warehouses, observer posts, hospitals, and radio transmitters in that country, had acquired radio and bunkering facilities in Uruguay, was building the Pioneer Highway in Central America to connect the Panama Canal with the Mexican Government Railway System, and had established the land-sea highway by way of Cuba, Haiti, and the Dominican Republic to Puerto Rico for the transport of defense and civilian materials to all the Caribbean islands. By the end of 1943 the total purchases by the United States in Latin America were computed at $1,361,151,000, consisting mainly of purchases by the Commodity Credit Corporation and the Reconstruction Finance Corporation but including also certain developmental expenses such as advances for factory construction, payments for capital costs of certain mines, and development of rubber-producing areas. Of a total $13,045 million which the United States spent between July 1, 1940, and June 30, 1945, for both military and nonmilitary purposes in foreign countries, $3,326 million, or over 25 per cent, were spent in Latin

America, the largest amounts going to Cuba, Chile, Brazil, and Mexico in that order.[30] Of this amount $53 million went to support work in health and sanitation, coordination committees and programs in food supply, transportation, and education.

The largest, by far, of the programs of financial aid by the United States government to Latin America during the war was the Lend-Lease program. Aid furnished to Latin America under this program, consisting of either direct military or military end-use equipment, accounted for $475 million distributed as follows in thousands of dollars:

Bolivia	$ 5,026	Guatemala	$ 1,735
Brazil	347,944	Haiti	1,362
Chile	22,038	Honduras	368
Colombia	8,277	Mexico	38,620
Costa Rica	156	Nicaragua	885
Cuba	6,154	Paraguay	1,952
Dominican Republic	1,457	Peru	18,000
Ecuador	7,208	Uruguay	6,941
El Salvador	877	Venezuela	4,480

The major recipients of this Lend-Lease assistance were Brazil, Mexico, Chile, and Peru, but all the Latin American countries except Argentina and Panama received some wartime aid under Lend-Lease. If to this Lend-Lease aid are added the grants extended to Latin American countries through other United States government agencies, including the Reconstruction Finance Corporation, the Institute of Inter-American Affairs, and technical assistance organizations, the total dollar aid furnished to Latin America during World War II in the form of government grants will be seen to have been $742 million. These wartime government grants were extended to all the Latin American countries, but the bulk of them went to the countries that received preference under Lend-Lease; namely, Brazil, Mexico, Chile, and Peru.[31]

The attention which the United States thus lavished upon its wartime partners in the American hemisphere was very gratifying to them. From this shared relationship in a common effort they derived a new buoyancy of attitude and outlook. "The United States is

30. Department of Commerce Press Release, November 26, 1945.
31. Department of Commerce, Bureau of Foreign and Domestic Commerce, *Foreign Transactions of the U.S. Government (Basic Data through June 30, 1950)* (Washington, September, 1950), Tables 3 and 7.

granting us loans on favorable terms and is giving us money," enthusiastically declared a former president of Costa Rica, Julio Acosta García, in an interview published in *La Tribuna* of San José (October 20, 1942). "The United States is sending its agricultural, industrial, and livestock experts to aid us in our production plans. . . . The United States is making a real effort of great significance to demonstrate to us with facts—not with words only—how great is their esteem for us and also to show us clearly and objectively that the policy of the 'Good Neighbor' is an accomplished fact and neither an abstraction nor a subterfuge. . . . The United States wants to know us better; it is interested in our books, our intellectual movement, our writers, poets, journalists, painters, and experts. They maintain toward us and we maintain toward them a position of absolute equality." From this new relationship Latin America was deriving many practical benefits. Assurances of guaranteed markets and anticipation of future financial help from the new partner in the north created great expectations of a new prosperity which would continue into the years beyond the war. Cooperation on a fully shared basis would be the new watchword of inter-American relations. "If the sacrifices and efforts to win the war have been shared," declared *Excelsior* of Mexico City on December 8, 1943, "the benefits of the peace also must be shared, since it would not be fair if only some profited from that which all contributed toward gaining." *Excelsior* insisted that after the war the allied peoples "must begin to practice the Christian principles of love for others and, with this, equality of treatment; racial prejudices will end, and each one will be judged only by his works." Not only practical considerations, therefore, but also idealistic expectations of a new type of world to be created after the war persistently inspired Latin Americans to unprecedented efforts for the winning of the war.

The Latin American allies of the United States furnished it with highly constructive cooperation for victory. The military and economic strengths of several of those countries were closely integrated with those of the United States. Brazil developed with the United States its air defense facilities, which made possible the successful Allied land operations in North Africa in late 1942 and which throughout the war provided points of air transshipment to all the fighting fronts of the world. Brazil also supplied a fighter aircraft squadron which operated under the strategic direction of the United States Twelfth Air Force in Italy, an infantry division which was placed under the command of the United States Fifth Army in Italy, and a considerable naval contingent which functioned in South Atlantic waters under Admiral Jonas Ingram, commander of the United States South Atlantic Fleet. By 1944 this naval unit was given responsibility for the antisubmarine patrol in South Atlantic waters. Early in 1943 Mexican Foreign Minister Padilla suggested to Under Secretary Welles that elements of the Mexican armed forces be allowed to participate in armed combat on the fighting fronts. Accordingly arrangements were made for a Mexican air squadron to serve under General Douglas MacArthur in the Philippine Islands.

The drawing power of the enriched Good Neighbor Policy or the Policy of the Good Partner, as well as the example of the New Deal, was also responsible in large part, as already intimated, for bringing Latin American labor to the support of the United States in the war. Manual workers in the cane fields, tin mines, rubber development projects, nitrate areas, and shipping services received increased wages because of generous supply contracts negotiated and paid for in Washington. In addition, by 1945 more than 100,000 Mexican laborers and an almost equal number of British West Indians had been brought into the United States to work on farms and on railroads, generally at wage rates prevailing in the United States. But most important of all, the Latin Americans provided vitally needed war materials through government-to-government supply agreements generally at prewar prices, thus denying themselves opportunities to secure large profits. Under the policy of the Metals Reserve Company, which was the purchasing agent of the United States government, the prices paid for copper, lead, and zinc, all prime products of Latin America, were not increased during the war. By contrast, in World War I the prices of these metals increased by about 100 per cent. Many other mineral products of Latin America, including tungsten, manganese, aluminum, vanadium, nickel, and antimony, were purchased throughout World War II at prices no higher than those which prevailed before the war began.[32] Cuba sold its entire sugar crop to the United States below world market prices throughout the war. During the entire war period 1941-1945 Latin America furnished almost 40 per cent of all the imports of the United States as compared with only 24 per cent in the immediate prewar period 1936-1940. Secretary of State Cordell Hull accurately summarized Latin America's contribution to the war effort in December, 1943, as follows: "At the blackest moment of the war, during the meeting of

32. Charles B. Henderson, *op. cit.*, 6.

Foreign Ministers at Rio de Janeiro, our sister republics raised their banners alongside ours. They opened their ports to our ships. They welcomed and quartered our troops on their soil. They devoted their mines, their forests, and their fields to the intensive production of strategic war materials. They rounded up Axis spies and saboteurs, and they shut off trade of benefit to the Axis. They cooperated in the defense of the Panama Canal and in the suppression of the submarine menace. All this and much more they did as their contribution to victory."[33] In other words, in time of war these little friends proved to be great friends.

* * *

The war disrupted the normal trade channels of Latin America, made ocean transport increasingly difficult and expensive, threw unusual burdens upon even normally inadequate systems of internal transportation, imposed restrictions upon imports, and caused acute shortages of tools and machinery replacement parts. On the other hand, the food-purchasing and food-production programs of the United States caused vast new areas of land in Latin America to be brought under cultivation. Shortages of imported civilian supplies and higher prices also tended to stimulate local production. The war raised the cost of living, but without correspondingly elevating wages and levels of living. As European markets were lost, both imports and exports sharply declined and crop surpluses piled up. A gradual shift took place from European to American markets, while the production of commodities which were determined not to be essential to victory in the war was almost entirely stopped, and in the case of some commodities, as for example bananas, the means of future production were either neglected or in some cases destroyed. Other commodities were either stored, awaiting the day when the shipping blockade would be lifted, or were thrown away. Haiti, for example, was forced to dump 894,000 gallons of blackstrap into the sea. In Argentina when imports of foreign coal declined, local industries were forced to burn large quantities of corn and linseed oil as fuel. As the shipping situation improved after 1943 the Latin American countries were enabled once more to move their exports to the United States, but they continued to be troubled by unavailabilities of consumer supplies.

33. *Department of State Bulletin,* IX (December 18, 1943), 430-431.

In summary, the economies of the Latin American countries came to revolve more and more exclusively around the United States during the war, depending upon the demand situation there for their raw materials and the availability of its manufactures, transport facilities, and capital for their wartime economic activities and industrial development. The commercial dependence of those countries upon Europe was lost, and the United States moved into first place as both their supplier and customer. Whereas in 1938 nearly 55 per cent of Latin America's exports had gone to Europe and nearly 44 per cent of Latin America's imports had come from Europe, in 1944 only 20 per cent of its exports were going to Europe and only 7 per cent of its imports were coming from Europe. On the other hand, from 1941 to the end of the war the Latin American countries sent over 50 per cent of their exports to the United States and received back from it between 54 and 62 per cent of their imports.[34] But their wartime needs could not be met by their imports from the United States, nor could they use up in purchases abroad the large dollar credits which they were able to accumulate from their own exports, largely raw materials, to the United States during the war. In the first eleven months of 1944, for example, these exports to the United States, valued at about $1,500 million, totaled more than half again the value of their imports from the United States. Not only did the disparity between their export and their import trade with the United States widen but their share of the export trade of the United States tapered off to their disadvantage. During the years 1941-1945 it dwindled to only 12 per cent of the total of United States exports as compared with an average of 17 per cent during the prewar decade 1931-1940. In other words, though trade with their northern ally showed an extraordinarily favorable balance, they could not "cash in" on it during the war, at least to the full extent that they wished. Economically they seemed to be losing much more to the United States than they were giving. Their prosperity appeared only as a ledger advantage in the form of unexpendable dollar credits.

The wartime aid from the United States was both wanted and unwanted in Latin America. It was criticized as, on the one hand, too little and, on the other, too much. The amount of financial grants and credits supplied by the United States was considered disappoint-

34. Amos E. Taylor, "The Impact of European Recovery on Inter-American Trade," in *Political, Economic, and Social Problems of the Latin American Nations of Southern South America,* University of Texas (Austin, 1949), [7].

ing when compared with the amount furnished by the United States to its other allies in the war. Prior to the war, or strictly speaking, prior to June 30, 1940, Latin American governments received gross commitments from the Export-Import Bank of over $217 million, or half the total amount, $436 million, of the gross commitments of the United States to all nations of the world. But from that date to June 30, 1945, the share of both direct and indirect aid which they received from the United States, amounting to $433 million, was only 0.9 per cent of the total of such aid to all world areas, $47,281 million. Similarly their share of the Lend-Lease aid distributed by the United States among its allies was only 1.1 per cent, amounting to $475 million out of a total disbursement of $42,021 million. With this assistance, which they regarded as too limited, they were obliged to try to meet dire war shortages, to satisfy accumulating consumer demands, and to raise the living levels of their peoples in this war for "freedom from fear and want." Moreover, they objected that the financial aid from the United States was not expended in ways most advantageous to them, specifically in the diversification and industrialization of their economies. President Juan Antonio Ríos of Chile, for example, was quoted in the newspaper *Hoy* of Santiago in October, 1942, as complaining that "In Chile, with copper and iron, we are like the 'work horse' who carries an abundance of fresh hay but is not allowed to eat it. . . . It is absurd that millions of tons of iron ore should be taken from Chile to the United States and that in order to produce nails we should have to resort to a thousand expedients to persuade them to grant us a little wire." Similarly, he explained, "There are many Chilean industries which require copper, whether in ingots, in sheets, or in other forms. Nevertheless, as in the case of the 'work horse,' though we produce copper we cannot use it except in driblets. . . . That is not right. We need to revise our understanding of the 'good neighbor.' "[35]

But there were some Latin Americans who feared the North Americans "bearing gifts." Even before Pearl Harbor, in early 1941, when the Washington government proposed to give some $200,000 for the relief of earthquake victims at Colima in Mexico on the ground that "the Mexican Government has shown its desire to cooperate with us in matters relative to national defense," the proposal was resisted in Mexico as constituting a "tip" offered "in exchange

35. Interview with President Juan Antonio Ríos by Ismael Edwards Matta, October 29, 1942.

for naval bases, aviation fields, military highways for transporting American troops, the official strengthening of Pan-American Day, as well as the official neglect of our Hispanity." The Mexican government declined the gift.[36] The United States, it seemed, though it had repudiated "dollar diplomacy," was still using the dollar to promote its Good Neighbor Policy, but its dollars now were more dangerous than the dollars of previous years because they were being advanced by the government itself and so had political importance.

Against this new type of dollar penetration Latin American nationalists spoke out strongly. A prominent leader of the opposition party in Bolivia, Alberto Mendoza López, published a book in 1942 in which he charged that Pan-Americanism was "in practice the extension of the imperialism of the United States which has imposed its weight of crushing slavery on the Indo-American peoples by bribery and force of arms." To counteract it he advocated the creation of a regional South American or Latin American union.[37] Early in the following year Dr. Oscar Gans y Martínez, Cuban minister to several Central American nations, enjoined Latin Americans "not to expect everything from Washington as if Washington were Destiny," but rather "to make an effort of their own to defend their economic interests energetically. . . . We must learn to stand proudly on our own feet," he declared, "to regain our position as allies, and to defend the patrimony of our peoples."[38] Latin American manufacturers were urged by the Chilean poetess Gabriela Mistral to "help us conquer or at least to restrain the deadly invasion . . . from blond America, which wishes to monopolize our markets and to overwhelm our farms and cities with its machinery and textiles."[39] Dr. Clodomiro Picado, famous for bacteriological research, complained in *Diario de Costa Rica* of San José (January 5, 1943): "We are surrendering everything, pride, sovereignty, the feeling of race in order to continue living on our own soil on the alms which the agents of penetration wish to give us. . . . Our saviours, the North Americans, greatly love democracy and the liberty of the world, but they will take everything we own. . . . We give all, and we receive nothing in exchange." All the wartime aid by the United States, cynically

36. Erasmo Lozano Rocha, "Yankee Charity," *La Reacción,* Mexico City, May 12, 1941.
37. *La Soberanía de Bolivia Estrangulada* (La Paz, 1942), 160-171.
38. *Diario de Costa Rica,* San José, January 6, 1943.
39. "El Grito," *Boletín de la Sociedad Geográfica "Sucre,"* XXXVIII (August, 1943), 174.

concluded the Panama *Star and Herald* (July 10, 1945), as the war neared its end, was not given "as a means of building Latin American goodwill. We are pretty sure that every dollar spent was in response to some strategic need and the need of developing areas the use of which was necessary for the protection of the United States. . . ."

That Latin Americans gave more than they received was the predominant theme of an anonymous three-page pamphlet, published in Lima on March 14, 1942, which was a potpourri of charges against the United States and may well have had a Nazi origin. For Peru, it bitterly complained, "the affectionate and close solidarity with the United States up to the present time has produced the following results: a tremendous increase in the cost of living; insecurity for the future; limitations on business activity; the closing of commercial establishments because of the stopping of sale of certain articles; unemployment and misery in general; lack of shipping facilities; maintenance of prohibitive quotas for Peruvian cotton; maintenance of high tariffs through the Panama Canal; lack of drugs and medicines; monopolizing of foodstuffs in order to export them to the United States; the imposition of high duties in order to compensate for the deficits in importations; etc., etc." The newspaper organ of the Workmen's Revolutionary Party, which was the Chilean Section of the Fourth International or Trotskyite Communist organization, charged in January, 1944, that the activities of United States companies in Chile were making that country "a Yankee colony" to fill "the pockets of a few great North American monopolistic dukes." In the foreign policy of the United States, it alleged, "a trend is apparent which repudiates the policy of the 'Good Neighbor' and augurs an attitude of 'the mailed fist.' "[40] An anonymous chain letter leveling some of the same criticisms at the United States and circulated in Brazil in late 1944 charged that the United States was using export subsidies and the navicert system to give a "death blow" to Brazil's trade in cotton, was taking Brazil's rubber "at miserable prices," was furnishing it with "synthetic rubber at exorbitant prices," and was using its wartime powers to divert Brazil's exports to its own use. All this, alleged the circular, was the policy, not of the "Good Neighbor" but rather of "Friend Bear."[41]

40. *El Militante,* Santiago, reported in Despatch 8594, Santiago, January 13, 1944, Department of State Archives.
41. Chain letter in Portuguese entitled "The Friendship of the United States for Brazil: The Good Neighbor Policy," dated São Paulo, November 15, 1944.

If Latin America was suffering material losses at the hands of the United States, much more serious, in the opinion of critics of the wartime Policy of the Good Partner, was its loss of "spiritual integrity" before the "cultural aggression" from the north. Though "the North American people and government offer us an enthusiastic, ardent, admiring friendship," declared the magazine *Así* of Mexico City (September 18, 1943), at the same time "they seek to substitute —we might say supplant—our thinking with Yankee thinking, our concept of culture, of history, of art, of philosophy by the North American concept of these same expressions of ideas and spirit." *Así* considered "this friendly invasion of our Fatherland much more dangerous in final results than a military aggression achieved by real enemies, for if they realize their ambitions Mexico will become a country without Mexicans." As a result of the manifold influences from the north in the form of magazines, newspapers, motion pictures, and radio broadcasts, reported *Así*, "Mexican thought is adapting itself little by little, unconsciously, to a mentality which is strictly North American, and all the problems of the world and of humanity are envisaged not from the point of view of our life nor from the angle of Mexican convenience but rather from the point of view and angle of interest of a citizen of the United States." Eventually, it anticipated, the Mexican mind would be exactly like "that of an inhabitant of San Francisco, Chicago, or New York" and "the existence of a frontier between countries which differ in nothing will be considered useless. Friendship, directed thus, will have devoured us forever, and we will cease to be a distinctive people in the world and in history." *Así* warned that "the friendly people of the north should respect our idiosyncrasies, our natural characteristics, and our physical and moral personality," and called upon the Mexican people to repel "with a virile sentiment" any threat to their "Mexicanism."

The Roman Catholic, conservative *Novedades* of Mexico City (September 8, 1944) also gave an editorial warning that "Mexico and the other Latin countries will defend, above everything else, the peculiar elements which give to each one of our peoples a definite personality, with which they are content." These elements "and these values," it added, "are what Hispano-America can and wishes to offer as friendship to the North Americans." Dr. Toribio Esquivel Obregón, writing in the same *Novedades* (May 16, 1945), pointed to the historical submersion of old Mexican culture and customs in California and Texas as evidence of what could be expected if Mexico made further concessions to the United States. To Latin Americans who cherished their traditional national and racial values this threat of an imposed acculturation by the United States seemed formidable. The Colombian publicist Eduardo Caballero Calderón expressed the fear, in a series of polished essays published in 1943 and in addresses to university students in Bogotá, Popayán, and Medellín in the following year, that the downfall of Latin civilization would result from the increasing power and influence of the United States.[42]

As was natural, some of the methods by which the United States carried on its wartime cultural program in Latin America were criticized. The binational cultural centers, maintained in several of the Latin American countries to promote understanding of the United States, and the various agencies of the CIAA were characterized as instruments of cultural penetration. A Bolivian newspaper found fault with the efforts of "John Rockefeller's grandson, the young and dynamic Nelson," to exchange "intellectuals" with Latin America by sending "the dynamic Douglas Fairbanks" to Buenos Aires and by bringing Latin Americans to the United States to be "thunderstruck" by the hugeness of New York and to acquire "a taste for the great avenues and the painted girls of the night clubs."[43] Caballero Calderón also criticized the United States for attempting to "buy goodwill," for paying subsidies to the Latin American press, and for taking their public men and journalists on grand tours of the United States.[44] According to a disgruntled columnist for *Diario de la Costa* of Cartagena (March 4, 1945), Ramón Manrique, the Colombians selected by the Coordinator's "Society of Mutual Flatterers" in Bogotá for visits to the United States were "expendable little writers" who, when they wrote their impressions of the United States in the Bogotá newspapers, "said pretty things about Marlene Dietrich's legs, about Betty Grable's curves, about the taste of spaghetti in the Latin Quarter, about the smile of the women of Broadway, about the family secrets and love entanglements of Hollywood, that is to say, about nonsense."

Underlying all this criticism was the belief, as expressed by Assis Chateaubriand, in 1945, that "though unexcelled in commercial propaganda . . . Americans were mediocre in intellectual or political propaganda." In the past, he observed, North Americans had shown "incapacity in dealing with Latin Americans and in sensing

42. *Latinoamérica: Un Mundo por Hacer* (Bogotá, 1944).
43. *La República,* La Paz, June 24, 1942.   44. *Op. cit.,* 105.

their reactions."[45] The biggest mistake of the United States, wrote a Bogotá journalist in the same year, was its egotism, its desire that Latin America think as it does. "Wherever Americans go they are always Americans," he declared. "Coordination committees, institutes, boards and other groups ignore almost completely the native element, launch programs, make plans that are one hundred per cent North American. . . . Numerous are the diplomats whom we have known, and few of them have tried to understand the Latin way of thinking."[46] These methods were reprehended as being not so much sinister as inept. What these critics wanted was understanding by the United States of the wartime problems of Latin America, appreciation of its distinctive culture and nationality, and patient cooperation in working out common problems. They felt that the intense concentration of the North Americans upon the attainment of victory in the war, unexceptionable as that objective was, had nevertheless blunted their sensibilities toward Latin Americans. North Americans were wooing their southern allies too impetuously and too extravagantly and were, in this process, weakening their will and diluting their Latin American nationality.[47]

These common failures of understanding between the United States and Latin America were aggravated by occasional overt gestures made in Washington against the southern countries. To those countries the occupation by the United States of air and naval bases in their territories was a particularly sensitive matter, even involving their sovereignty. Rumblings from the United States of an intention to retain the bases after the war were therefore disquieting. These intimations were made explicit in the so-called Merritt Report by the Aviation Subcommittee of the House Military Affairs Committee, which recommended in 1943 that the United States extend its use of Latin American air bases into the postwar period and stressed particularly the importance of "continued utilization by this country of its Galápagos base after the war in the interest of hemisphere defense."[48] Public opinion in Ecuador concluded in dismay in late 1943

45. *O Jornal*, Rio de Janeiro, September 3, 1945.

46. Carlos Puyo Delgado, *El Correo,* Medellín, Colombia, February 1, 1945.

47. Manuel Seoane, "If I Were Nelson Rockefeller," *Harper's Magazine,* CLXXXVI (February, 1943), [312]-318; and Benjamin Subercaseaux, "The Cloying Good Neighbor," *The Nation,* CLVII (September 11, 1943), 293-295.

48. Arthur P. Whitaker (ed.), *Inter-American Affairs, 1943,* III, 42-43; and 78th Congress, 1st Session, House Report No. 950.

that "the prevailing attitude in the United States" toward its bases on the Galápagos Islands as expressed by friends and partisans of Roosevelt was "frankly imperialistic."[49] *O Jornal* of Rio de Janeiro (April 30, 1944) expressed the hope that "as soon as the war is over the Americans will leave the Brazilian bases which they occupy at present" and assured the United States that they would be made available to them again "if times similar to those through which we are now living should occur again in the world." Only "the ingenuous and the ignorant" in the United States, it said, would now advocate the retention of the bases, and it hinted at armed resistance in Latin America against such retention. "The occupation of Nicaragua is an episode too recent to be lost sight of," it concluded. Even the strongly pro-United States newspaper, *Diário de Pernambuco* (September 24, 1943), felt it necessary to explain that Brazil was not to be considered "as anybody's satellite."

Anxiety over United States policy on the question of the bases was widespread in Latin America. When the Brazilian professor Hernane Tavares de Sá, after spending more than two years in the United States, returned to his native country in mid-1944, he was asked everywhere, "What will *os ianquis* do about the bases?"[50] *Así* (April 1, 1944) of Mexico City was disturbed also at the same time by a specific resolution of Senator Styles Bridges of New Hampshire proposing that the United States assure itself the control and ownership of all the air and naval bases constructed abroad with United States funds, by a later proposal of Senator Robert Reynolds of North Carolina that the United States negotiate with Mexico for the acquisition of Lower California, and by similar proposals by two California congressmen. But *Así* was confident that these aberrations by "a small minority of fools" would not "upset a sensible people." Against them, it advised, "Mexico has one defense—North American public opinion itself, its innate sense of justice. . . . Happily there is in the United States at present a spirit desirous of comprehension, of cooperation, of friendship."

Again in the same year, 1944, a proposal that the United States acquire the Galápagos Islands aroused alarm in Ecuador. "Only in the imperialistic mentality of an orthodox element of the Republican Party of the United States," declared *El Telégrafo* of Guayaquil

49. *La Patria,* Quito, December 10, 1943.
50. "Camouflage of Harmony," *The Inter-American,* III (August, 1944), 10.

(March 16, 1944), "can such an aim find sympathy; it is an objective which will not merit the slightest attention from the noble North American people." This "maneuver," as it (August 19, 1944) called it, "of the Republican groups still under the influence of capitalistic domination which inspired the 'dollar policy' . . . will break American unity and distort the respect of territorial rights which is preached by the 'Good Neighbor Policy' and which is one of the principles of the Atlantic Charter." When Democratic Senator Kenneth McKellar of Tennessee later espoused this move, the popular tabloid *Pica-Pica* of Quito (August 20, 1944) somewhat hysterically pronounced it the authentic voice of "Yankee Land," "the voice of conquest," "the Monroe Doctrine above the Doctrine of the Good Neighbor," "the Democracy of North America clamoring for conquest and speaking of plunder." It exhorted Ecuadorans to defend "the true democracy of the small rather than yield to the dominating and enslaving democracy of the powerful, which they impose with gold or guns." According to the more restrained *El Universo* of Guayaquil (August 19, 1944), this McKellar proposal revealed "only a very superficial idea of Latin American nationalism," "a somewhat primitive psychology," and a "complete lack of knowledge of Latin American realities, of the Latin soul, of the patriotic spirit of these countries." So violent was the reaction against the McKellar proposal in Ecuador that both the Ecuadoran Assembly and President José María Velasco Ibarra issued ringing declarations that Ecuador would neither sell nor lease any part of its territory. The Ecuadoran president cautioned in a newspaper interview that Senator McKellar's was only an "isolated opinion" not to be confused "with positive action by the American authorities in full consciousness of their authority and their responsibility."[51]

* * *

From incidents such as these Latin Americans conjured up new bogies of Yankee imperialism, bogies that became especially fearful as the United States expressed its displeasure, in both tangible and intangible ways, with the failure of certain Latin American governments to extend the kind of cooperation in the war effort which the Roosevelt administration deemed necessary. As early as March, 1942,

51. *El Comercio,* Quito, August 19, 1944. See also *El Panamá-América,* Panama, September 4, 1944; and *La Nación,* Buenos Aires, March 4, 1945.

the Board of Economic Warfare in Washington refused licenses to United States exporters to sell electrical equipment, chemicals, and other items to Argentina; and an Argentine military and naval mission which visited Washington at that time to arrange for the purchase of war supplies was sent home empty-handed.[52] Sponsors of official cocktail parties in Washington were advised by the State Department not to include Argentine representatives as guests. In the following October Under Secretary Welles, speaking in Boston, bluntly denounced both Argentina and Chile for allowing "their brothers and neighbors of the Americas, engaged as they are in a life-and-death struggle to preserve the liberties and integrity of the New World, to be stabbed in the back by Axis emissaries."[53] Additional political and economic pressures were applied to both governments. The result was that Chile broke diplomatic relations with the Axis nations on January 20, 1943, but these pressures proved unavailing against Argentina. The ensuing diplomatic offensive of the Roosevelt administration against that government became a principal source of criticism of the United States during the remainder of the war.

The policy of the State Department toward Argentina was based on information that Axis agents were operating in that country with the knowledge and positive aid of the Argentine government. As long as they thus operated, it was felt, that government was violating its inter-American obligations and could not be allowed to obtain supplies which would increase its war potential. Secretary Hull believed that the majority of the Argentine people favored the Allied cause and disapproved the neutral or pro-Axis attitude of their government. He convinced himself that pressure, therefore, must be applied against that government by both the United States and the inter-American regional organization through majority action in order to force it to interpret better the will of its own people. A recalcitrant nation was to be disciplined in the interest of the security of the American hemisphere and in the name of the Good Neighbor Policy.[54] One means of doing this was to withhold Lend-Lease supplies from Argentina

52. *New York Times* and *New York Herald Tribune,* March 25, 28, and April 1, 1942.
53. *New York Times,* October 9, 1942.
54. Cordell Hull, *Memoirs,* II, 1379-80, 1144-46. The evidence for Argentina's alleged violations of its inter-American obligations was presented in several memoranda prepared by the Emergency Advisory Committee for Political Defense, Montevideo, and summarized in its annual reports. See especially its *Second Annual Report . . . July 15, 1943-October 15, 1944, . . .* (Montevideo, 1944).

while supplying them to those Latin American governments, notably
Brazil, which were cooperating with the United States in the war,
thus strengthening their military position and correspondingly weakening that of Argentina.[55]

The Argentine Foreign Minister, Vice Admiral Segundo Storni,
undertook to redress this situation. Writing to Secretary Hull on
August 5, 1943, he denied as "absolutely false" the assumptions that
the Argentine government professed "a markedly totalitarian ideology" or looked "upon the Axis powers with great sympathy." He
called Argentina's attitude one of "benevolent" neutrality toward the
United States and its allies in the war and argued that his government could not suddenly break relations with the Axis without afford-
ing "grounds to believe action is being taken under the pressure or
threat of foreign agents and this would not be tolerated by either the
people or the armed forces of the country." To Storni's representations Hull responded with a rebuke that caused Storni's resignation.[56]

Soon thereafter the United States decided to apply the principle
of nonrecognition to the new regime of Major Gualberto Villarroel
which came to power in Bolivia by revolution in December, 1943, and
which seemed to the United States to be "the first of a series designed
to break down the existing anti-Axis front in South America." Following a recommendation of the Emergency Advisory Committee for
Political Defense, located at Montevideo, all the American governments excepting only Argentina agreed, after consulting with one
another, not to recognize the new Bolivian regime. Secretary Hull
gave as his reason for withholding both diplomatic recognition and
economic assistance from it that it was not adequately contributing
to "the security of the hemisphere . . . and the war effort of the
United Nations." Here was an act of collective intervention by the
American states using nonrecognition as a method of coercion. The
government of Uruguay pointed out at the time that this act could
not be approved except as an emergency war measure and that if its
scope was extended it would be open to criticism as a violation of
the principle of nonintervention. As under this pressure the Villarroel
regime modified its policy, the United States recognized it on June
23, 1944.[57]

55. Smith, *op. cit.,* 68.
56. *Department of State Bulletin,* IX (September 11, 1943), 159-166.
57. Emergency Advisory Committee for Political Defense, *op. cit.,* 16, 79-
92, 97; and *Department of State Bulletin,* X (June 24, 1944), 584.

Under both political and economic pressure from the United States the Argentine government finally broke relations with Germany and Japan on January 26, 1944, but the reaction to this move in Argentina was so violently unfavorable as to cause the downfall of the government. The newspaper *La Fronda* of Buenos Aires (July 26, 1944), financed by the Argentine nationalist Manuel Fresco, declared that Argentina had succumbed to the efforts to form "a continental superstate under the effective tutelage of the United States." Two days later *La Fronda* was put on the United States Proclaimed List. Allegations, believed in Washington to be Nazi-inspired and financed, that the people of the United States "want to exercise over us an absolute economic, spiritual, political and military domination" circulated in Argentina. A circular, distributed in July, 1944, and signed "Agrupación D.A.S." of whose character, membership, and purpose nothing has been disclosed, bitterly asked "Is this an example of democracy, Pan-Americanism, and good neighborliness?" The Nazi-subsidized *El Federal* of Buenos Aires (May 22, 1944) declared that the purpose of the Roosevelt administration was "to 'set' one South American republic after another in the imperialistic necklace of Uncle Sam."[58] Argentine nationalists castigated the "insolent nation in the north" for its "policy of imperialism and absorption."[59] To *El Debate* (August 10, 1944), the newspaper organ of the Herrerista political faction in Uruguay, the United States had become the odious "boss" of the hemisphere and "when someone who has his own ideas does not perform his work to the satisfaction of him who 'gives the orders' . . . the lightning bursts over his head and 'the squeezing hand' begins to operate." This "enslaving technique" was "unbearable." The United States was a "master who is artificial, cold, foreign, and arbitrary acting only in his own interest and through his brutal strength."[60] The simple explanation offered by *Marcha* of Montevideo (July 28, 1944) was that "Argentina is in America, and in America the United States cannot tolerate disagreements."

When the new regime in Argentina, headed by General Edelmiro Farrell and controlled by Juan Domingo Perón, showed the same indisposition as its predecessor to favor inter-American union and

58. See also column by David Paredes in *Cabildo,* Buenos Aires, July 21, 1944.
59. *El Municipio,* Almirante Brown, Argentina, August 3, 1944.
60. See also *El Debate,* Montevideo, July 29, 1944.

common action against the Axis nations, the Roosevelt administration applied further economic pressures against it. Exports to the Argentine armed forces and armaments industry were prohibited, no shipments of railway locomotives or rolling stock or automotive vehicles to Argentina were permitted, and other restrictions were imposed upon the trade of that country with the United States. In order to check Argentina's suspected imperialistic designs upon neighboring countries, the United States gave secret assurances to Uruguay of military assistance and virtually guaranteed its territorial integrity against Argentine aggression. It sought to dissuade the British from concluding a long-term purchase contract for Argentine meat and itself stopped all army purchases of Argentine canned beef through the British Ministry of Food. As long as Argentina was controlled by a regime which was considered to be pro-Nazi and anti-United Nations, the United States sought to weaken it by limiting its commercial operations and by persuading other countries to do the same. It also withheld recognition from the Farrell regime and tried to apply again, as it had earlier in the case of the Villarroel regime in Bolivia, the principle of collective nonrecognition on the grounds that the Farrell regime "(1) has deliberately violated the pledge taken jointly with its sister republics to cooperate in support of the war against the Axis Powers . . . , and (2) has openly and notoriously been giving affirmative assistance to the declared enemies of the United Nations."[61] This stand was supported by the Caribbean and Central American nations, Brazil, and Peru. In most of South America, however, it was strongly criticized, and Chile, Paraguay, and Bolivia, challenging Hull's policy, immediately established diplomatic relations with Argentina.[62]

61. Department of State, *Press Release* 27, January 26, 1944.
62. Telegram 1434, La Paz, July 26, 1944; Telegram 1435, La Paz, July 26, 1944; Telegram 1271, Santiago, July 27, 1944; Telegram 530, Guatemala, July 27, 1944; Telegram 334, Panama, July 27, 1944; Despatch 124, Panama, July 27, 1944; Telegram 234, Tegucigalpa, July 27, 1944; Telegram 255, Guayaquil, July 28, 1944; Despatch 19032, Mexico, July 28, 1944; Despatch 130, Panama, July 28, 1944; Despatch 119, Port-au-Prince, July 28, 1944; Telegram 486, Managua, July 28, 1944; Telegram 245, Port-au-Prince, July 28, 1944; Airgram 2675, Mexico, July 28, 1944; Despatch 131, Panama, July 28, 1944; Telegram 252, San Salvador, July 28, 1944; Despatch 2438, Managua, July 28, 1944; Telegram 416, San José, July 28, 1944; Despatch 4630, Montevideo, July 28, 1944; Airgram 643, Caracas, July 28, 1944; Telegram 2704, Rio de Janeiro, July 28, 1944; Despatch 2049, Tegucigalpa, July 28, 1944; Despatch 4100, La Paz, July 28, 1944; Telegram 2719, Rio de Janeiro, July 29, 1944; Despatch 869, Guayaquil, July 29, 1944; Despatch 2320. Asun-

Pressure for a tight, exigent wartime inter-American solidarity thus produced schism in the hemisphere. Members of this new "Austral bloc" could no longer look upon the United States as a good neighbor. The Good Neighbor, who had taken the pledge to refrain from meddling in the 1930's and who had essayed the role of Good Partner with them when confronted with the Axis threat, now appeared to have become the Bad Neighbor or the Bad Partner. The "hands-off" policy had become a "hands-on" policy. The principle of nonintervention had been transformed into a principle of intervention, which was now openly acknowledged to be such but was justified as "Pan-American intervention" because it was carried out in the name of the inter-American community. But when Latin Americans scrutinized this community closely many of them saw only the colossal figure of the United States.

In late 1944 an elaborately reasoned defense of Argentina's policy was made by Castillo's Minister of Foreign Affairs, Enrique Ruiz-Guiñazú, in his book *La Política Argentina y el Futuro de América* published in Buenos Aires. Refuting the contention that Argentina had not fulfilled its international obligations Ruiz-Guiñazú argued that the resolutions adopted by the consultative meetings of foreign ministers had no obligatory character but were only suggestions and proposals to be complied with by a state when, in conformity with its own legislation, it saw fit to do so. The purpose of the consultative procedure, as developed at the conference in Buenos Aires in 1936, was "to determine the proper time and manner in which the signatory states, if they so desire, may eventually cooperate in some action tending to preserve the peace of the American continent." The Argentine formula which was unanimously adopted by all twenty-one of the American states at the Third Meeting of the Ministers of Foreign Affairs at Rio de Janeiro six weeks after Pearl Harbor had merely "recommended" the breaking of diplomatic relations with Japan, Germany, and Italy and made even this recommendation subject to "the position and circumstances obtaining in each country in the existing continental conflict." Accordingly Argentina, acting

ción, July 29, 1944; Telegram 1452, La Paz, July 29, 1944; Telegram 1287, Santiago, July 29, 1944; Telegram 766, Caracas, July 30, 1944; Despatch 1897, Quito, July 31, 1944; Despatch 4640, Montevideo, July 31, 1944; Despatch 6263, Caracas, July 31, 1944; Despatch 4152, Bogotá, July 31, 1944; Despatch 4106, La Paz, July 31, 1944; Despatch 4641, Montevideo, July 31, 1944; Despatch 19059, Mexico, July 31, 1944; and Despatch 17138, Rio de Janeiro, July 31, 1944.

in compliance with its national interests and traditions, had quite properly refrained from carrying out this recommendation.

Pan-American unity, argued Ruiz-Guiñazú, had been disrupted by the international ambitions of the United States and by the resulting cleavage between those American nations which had succumbed to pressure from it and those which had resisted this pressure in defense of national sovereignty and the right of self-determination. The high regional ideals of union, solidarity, and "defensive" cooperation had given way before the objectives of a Cyclopean power, the United States, which executed its policies in all lands and seas, in all directions, and despite all criticism. The true and traditional Pan-American policy was one of neutrality, and Argentina had cooperated with the United States in maintaining that policy through the Havana meeting of foreign ministers and well into the year 1941. It had subsequently attempted to resist the alteration of this policy by the United States and the resulting perversion of Pan-Americanism. When the United States finally declared war and sought to involve the entire hemisphere in that war, it did so as a result of an event— the attack on Pearl Harbor—which was wholly different from anything that had preceded it in inter-American negotiations and which occurred in the Pacific Ocean as a sequel to ten years of friction arising out of the nonrecognition by the United States of Japan's occupation of Manchuria in 1931. The Hawaiian Islands, Ruiz-Guiñazú noted, were located beyond the maritime neutrality belt which had been proclaimed by the foreign ministers of the American nations at Panama in 1939. Nevertheless Argentina had decided to extend nonbelligerency status to the United States, thus favoring it with the elimination of the restrictions which a declaration of neutrality would have imposed.

The unwillingness of the United States to work within the traditional American system, to supply Argentina with Lend-Lease equipment, and to recognize the importance of Argentina's contributions to hemisphere defense were responsible, Ruiz-Guiñazú charged, for the current impasse between the two countries. Moreover, Argentina resented the "Black Lists" which had been issued by the United States, he said, without any consultation with his government and which produced business uncertainty, unemployment, and diminution in Argentina's productive capacity. The failure of the United States to allow the other American nations to participate in the formulation of the "Black Lists" was incompatible with the Pan-American spirit of equality and mutual respect for other sovereign nations. He deplored that as a result of the war the ideological pressure of the United States was already extending to "the politics of the entire hemisphere." Only if Argentina understood that this force must be resisted would it win the right to survive, to reaffirm its national existence as well as to defend its traditional foreign policy. The hemisphere was being subjected to "a new form of Yankee imperialism, cloaked under the shibboleth of 'continental solidarity.' " The only counterweight to the "Great Republic of the North," he concluded, was the theory of equality of states based upon the free exercise of sovereignty.

The suspicion became rather widespread in Latin America that the United States in its handling of the Argentine problem was not giving adequate consideration to the views of the Latin American governments and that it was using methods of coercion which were contrary to the Good Neighbor Policy and the fraternal principles of the inter-American system. The United States steadily resisted suggestions that a Pan-American conference be held to discuss political questions and instead was employing a procedure of consultation which was carried on only through diplomatic channels and in which Washington seemed to be, in Professor Whitaker's phrase, "both clearing house and umpire."[63] The results achieved by this method, as demonstrated in the case of Argentina, were far from satisfactory. Dr. Assis Chateaubriand, after a visit to Chile, reported in his *O Jornal* of Rio de Janeiro in November, 1944, that "Chilean political circles are as impassioned over the Argentine case as if it embraced the cause of civil and political liberties of the continent and . . . as if it involved a problem of sovereignty." A staunch defender of the policies of the United States in the war, he deplored "the anti-American or only slightly friendly attitude toward the United States" which he found throughout Latin America.

Schism in the hemisphere was seen to be disadvantageous to all the American nations, not only because it derogated from the complete Pan-American solidarity which seemed necessary for effective prosecution of the war against the Axis, but also because it might limit the possibilities of united international action in the peace settlement at the end of the war. As early as mid-1943 when the United Nations were beginning to win military victories and to formulate their plans for postwar reconstruction, Latin Americans started to give consider-

63. Arthur P. Whitaker, "Pan America in Politics and Diplomacy" in Arthur P. Whitaker (ed.), *Inter-American Affairs, 1944,* 57.

ation to practical methods by which they might participate effectively in the postwar peace conferences. But the Latin American nations were not all on the same footing with respect to the war. At that time only twelve of them had declared war—the original nine plus Mexico, Brazil, and Bolivia—seven others had merely severed diplomatic relations with one or more of the Axis nations; and one, Argentina, remained in a neutral status. After Bolivia declared war against the Axis in April, 1943, President Enrique Peñaranda of that country visited several Latin American countries which had not yet declared war and undertook to convince them of the desirability of doing so. In the newspaper publicity given to the action of Bolivia and its president, the suggestion was made that nations which had merely severed relations with the Axis might be denied the same measure of participation in the postwar settlement as would be accorded to nations which had entered into belligerent status.

Soon afterward the Colombian government, under President Alfonso López, took the lead in attempting to organize the seven remaining "nonbelligerent" South American nations—Chile, Colombia, Ecuador, Peru, Paraguay, Uruguay, and Venezuela, but not including Argentina—into a bloc for united action as associated nations in the war effort. According to the Colombian proposal, their purpose should be to ascertain and define with the governments of the United Nations the bases of their collaboration in the negotiations looking toward postwar settlements. In order to strengthen their positions in relation to those governments, they might also wish to assume belligerent status by adhering to the Declaration of the United Nations of January 1, 1942. Colombia's proposal, which was submitted to these nations on August 2, 1943, contained at least the implication that the twenty non-English-speaking countries of America might strengthen their representation in the postwar planning councils if they took advantage of their common ideological and economic interrelationships to speak with a single voice.

After the nine Central American and Caribbean governments declared war against Japan and Germany immediately following Pearl Harbor, the United States decided neither to require nor to encourage further Latin American declarations of war. At the meeting of foreign ministers in Rio de Janeiro in early 1942, therefore, it pressed the remaining Latin American governments only to sever relations with Japan and Germany. The United States was apprehensive that if the South American governments should go further and declare war it might have difficulty in defending their coasts. It was satisfied, therefore, that these nations should remain in a quasi-neutral legal status in relation to Japan and Germany. Their agreements to elimi- nate Axis influences in their countries and to supply the United States with the materials of war were deemed sufficient to ensure their maximum posible contribution to the war effort. Actual declarations of war presumably would not increase their assistance to the United States and its allies. Nevertheless, declarations of war against both Germany and Japan were issued by three more Latin American na- tions during 1942 and 1943: by Mexico on May 22, 1942, by Brazil on August 22, 1942, and by Bolivia on April 7, 1943.[64]

The United States, then, was not inclined to recognize or draw any distinction between Latin American governments which, though not at war with the Axis nations, fulfilled their inter-American com- mitments and those which had declared war. Continuing to adhere to this view, it looked askance upon the Colombian proposal, particu- larly since it appeared to contain the implication of united South American bloc action. The only tangible result of this proposal was that Colombia itself adhered to the Declaration of the United Nations and allied itself with the United States in the war against Germany on November 26, 1943. But among the governments to which the Colombian proposal was broached it stimulated interest in inter- American consultation on postwar problems and organization.

By early 1945, as the armies of the United Nations were unmis- takably triumphing and the plans for a postwar international collec- tive security organization began to take shape, the United States swung around to an advocacy of declarations of war by the Latin American nonbelligerents. To this decision it was pressed by the pained outcry of the Latin American nations at the noninclusion of their representatives, as well as the representatives of other small nations of the world, in the Dumbarton Oaks meetings in October, 1944, to plan the postwar world order.[65] The Roosevelt administra- tion was now embarrassed by its previous policy of not encouraging declarations of war. The six South American nonbelligerents, exclud- ing Argentina, insisted that even though they had not declared war, they should be brought into the planning councils for the postwar

64. Katherine E. Crane, "Status of Countries in Relation to the War, April 22, 1944," *Department of State Bulletin,* X (April 22, 1944), 373-379.
65. For Latin American reaction to the Dumbarton Oaks proposals see Whitaker (ed.), *Inter-American Affairs, 1944,* 67-70.

United Nations organization because they had simply been following the advice of the United States in not issuing declarations of war. Accordingly in January, 1945, President Roosevelt informed the presidents of those six nations that if they wished to attend the Conference of the United Nations they must issue declarations of war. The previous policy, Roosevelt concluded, had been a mistake.[66] As a result four of the remaining nonbelligerent Latin American governments— Paraguay, Peru, Uruguay, and Venezuela—declared war against both Germany and Japan in February, 1945, and the other two—Chile and Ecuador—declared war against Japan during the same month.

United Pan-American action was now planned to elicit a declaration of war from Argentina. If Argentina proved recalcitrant, the United States prepared to give military and economic guaranties to each of Argentina's neighbors, to seek to isolate Argentina in the hemisphere, and to determine upon an economic and financial policy toward Argentina in cooperation with the British and the other American governments which would give maximum support to the war effort and the attainment of its own political objectives.[67] At the Mexico City Conference on Problems of War and Peace in February, 1945, in which Argentina was not included, an effort was made by the representatives of all the other twenty American governments to agree upon conditions under which Argentina might qualify for readmission to the American family of nations. This formula was reached in Resolution LIX which expressed the hope that Argentina "will cooperate with the other American Nations, identifying itself with the common policy these nations are pursuing" and adhering to the Declaration of the United Nations. Soon afterward, on March 27, Argentina accepted these conditions and declared war against Germany and Japan. Thus the breach which had opened up in the inter-American system was apparently closed, and all twenty-one American nations put themselves in a position to participate in the San Francisco Conference of the United Nations in June, 1945.[68]

* * *

66. James F. Byrnes, *Speaking Frankly* (New York, 1947), 38.

67. Department of State, Memorandum for the President, January 2, 1945, Subject: United States Policy toward Argentina (Unclassified). This memorandum was initialed "OK. FDR." Department of State Archives.

68. The Argentine government sought to demonstrate the "absolute identity of its tradition and principles" in international relations with those of the Act of Chapultepec, the Declaration of Mexico, the United Nations Declaration,

During World War II the New World attained the high point of solidarity which had been envisioned for it by Henry Clay a century and a quarter earlier. When Pan-Americanism began to take practical form in the 1880's, it had been conceived almost exclusively in terms of expanded commercial interchange among the nations of America, but during World War II it was broadened out again to match Clay's conception. It now came to include not only expanded trade relations but also financial, military, political, and particularly moral cooperation. Inspired by the Good Neighbor Policy of the United States in the 1930's, sustained by the threats to the security of the American nations from abroad, guided by the moral leadership of the United States, and nourished by its generous largess, Pan-Americanism became a new, enriched, and vivid reality for the peoples of America in the war against the Axis nations of Europe and Asia.[69]

For the tangible benefits which flowed from their unprecedented closeness with the United States, most articulate Latin Americans seemed grateful. They saw neither sinister purpose nor baneful result in the "new dollar diplomacy." "Thanks to the power of the United States," rejoiced President Juan Jóse Arévalo of Guatemala in his inaugural address in March, 1945, "the war is being kept far away from our soil."[70] The "new Yankee gospel of hygiene" and the feats of sanitation which the United States accomplished during the war among the indigenous peoples of South America were especially commended.[71] "What," asked Ramón Manrique, "have the Yankees asked . . . in exchange for the millions spent in the war against malaria, in the campaigns against yellow fever, or in the merciless attack on uncinariasis, carried on by the Rockefeller Mission? Nothing. . . . What have they left? The sanitation of our fields and the health of our farmers."[72] In the wartime cooperation of the United States with Latin America, declared *El Telégrafo* of Guayaquil (December 7, 1944), that nation had performed a "magnificent job of Americanism." It had exercised a proper leadership over the nations of America in a righteous cause and had shown laudable self-restraint in the application of

---

and the Atlantic Charter in a 990-page volume, primarily documentary, prepared by Carlos Alberto Silva and published in early 1946. Carlos Alberto Silva, *La Política Internacional de la Nación Argentina* (Buenos Aires, 1946).

69. *Star and Herald*, Panama, November 9, 1942.

70. *Discursos en la Presidencia, 1945-1948* (Guatemala, 1948), 9. For similar sentiments see *Vanguardia*, Lima, June 28, 1946.

71. *La Prensa*, Lima, July 4, 1945.

72. *Diario de la Costa*, Cartagena, Colombia, March 4, 1945.

its economic and military strength. Its moral force had been commensurate with its physical force. President José María Velasco Ibarra of Ecuador pointed out in *El Comercio* of Quito (August 19, 1944) that "if the United States had been real imperialists and annexers in the manner of the imperialisms of the so-called Old Continent, we would now be enslaved and would be unable to protest against imperialism."[73]

This transformation was generally attributed by Latin Americans to the Good Neighbor Policy, which was now broadly construed to include all the wartime phases of relationship between the United States and Latin America. As the exponent of that policy, President Roosevelt became the object of a cult of admiration, even adoration among Latin Americans. In their opinion no praise of him was too extravagant, no tribute undeserved. He was exalted as a *ciudadano continental*, a citizen of the entire continent, a representative and leader of the American hemisphere, a symbol of Pan-Americanism. As a champion of justice and liberty he was associated with such great American figures as Benjamin Franklin, George Washington, Thomas Jefferson, Simón Bolívar, Benito Juárez, and Abraham Lincoln. To the Peruvian Manuel Seoane, Roosevelt was the "Magician who had performed miracles"; with his New Deal and his international policy of democracy he had made "Tomorrow become Today."[74]

This Latin American reverence for Roosevelt was one of the most important reasons for the extraordinary *entente cordiale* between the peoples of the hemisphere that was achieved during his administration. The leftist *La Tribuna* of San Salvador (March 8, 1945) considered that "both oppressed Yankees and oppressed Latin Americans were favored" by Roosevelt's "democratic policies."[75] He was the symbol of friendship between the people of the United States and the people of Latin America. His Good Neighbor Policy had established itself as a shibboleth, a magic formula ensuring good relations between them. It had become all things to all men. When it was sharply criticized by Republican Senator Hugh Butler of Nebraska in November, 1943, on the ground that it was serving as only a cover for extravagant "boondoggling" in Latin America and was bringing the United States into

---

73. See also *El País,* Montevideo, June 7, 1944; *Hoy,* Mexico City, December 30, 1944; and *Jornal do Brasil,* Rio de Janeiro, November 25, 1945.

74. *El Gran Vecino: América en la Encrucijada* (Santiago, 1942), 145.

75. See also *Flecha,* Managua, Nicaragua, editorial by the director Hernán Robleto, September 23, 1943; and *Star and Herald,* Panama, August 20, 1944.

contempt there, his strictures provoked strong protests in Latin America.[76]

But would this happy relationship survive Roosevelt's administration? This question became particularly interesting to Latin Americans in the presidential campaign of 1944 between President Roosevelt and Governor Thomas E. Dewey of New York. "The thing which is still to be determined precisely and which causes some disquiet to our spirits," observed Dr. Pío Jaramillo Alvarado, a highly respected Ecuadoran university professor and former Minister of Government, "is whether the Good Neighbor Policy between the North Americans and the Indo-Americans is a permanent international relationship . . . or whether it is simply a circumstantial relationship . . . sustained by the mutual interest in defense under the threatening compulsion of the present war."[77] *Novedades* of Mexico City (May 9, 1944) felt that "the Good Neighbor Policy requires more solid and permanent guaranties than the undoubted goodwill of President Roosevelt. While he is in power . . . we do not have to fear a change in policy, but we cannot affirm that the doctrine will outlive his administration." Such assurances seemed to be supplied, however, by Republican endorsements of the Good Neighbor Policy which followed Senator Butler's criticism of it. President Isaías Medina Angarita of Venezuela, after returning from a visit to the United States in January, 1944, reported that "even the members of the Republican Party, with whom I had occasion to speak at length, comprehended the benefits that are being derived from the policy initiated by President Roosevelt with such great success."[78] *Diário de Notícias* of Rio de Janeiro (December 12, 1943) hailed a declaration, as it said, of "many outstanding leaders of the Republican Party in the United States . . . to the United Press that the Good Neighbor Policy is a national policy of that great nation, which is above all partisan politics and which all political groups completely and firmly support."[79]

Although the Good Neighbor Policy, then, could not be considered an issue in the campaign of 1944, Latin Americans were nevertheless gratified by the victory of the architect of that policy, to whom they had already accorded their highest accolade "Man of America." It

76. 78th Congress, 1st Session, Senate Document No. 132; and *New York Times*, November 27, 28, 29, 1943.
77. *El Comercio*, Quito, March 26, 1944.
78. *El Heraldo*, Caracas, February 19, 1944.
79. See also *The Panama American*, Panama, September 8, 1944.

had demonstrated its effectiveness both as a medium of ideological *rapprochement* and as a means to the achievement of common practical benefits in hemispheric relations. The purpose of the original Good Neighbor Policy—the policy of "live and let live"—was to win the cooperation and friendship of Latin America through a frank recognition and acceptance of national differences. Those differences were not to be permitted to justify a patronizing, paternalistic, or exploitative attitude. The success of that policy clearly demonstrated the possibility of the *convivencia* of dissimilar peoples in the Western Hemisphere. Moreover, through the slow operation of the forces engendered by the principles of mutual respect and nonintervention upon which the Good Neighbor Policy was based, the everywhere latent democratic elements in Latin America steadily gained ground. As the Good Neighbor Policy forged a method of combat-unity to unseat the overseas dictators, so it strengthened the movement for popular government in Latin America by allowing it to develop under its own proper conditions and in its own national milieus. This was the democratic significance of the Good Neighbor Policy for Latin America. As wartime inter-American problems proved to be of broader scope than the original Good Neighbor Policy, that policy was stretched to cover them. It proved to be the most successful formula that had been developed for the conduct of the relations of the United States with Latin America.

With this policy Roosevelt's name was inseparably identified. The news of his death in April, 1945, just when the world struggle was about to end in victory for the United States and its allies, came as a shocking experience to Latin Americans. They melted in sorrow over his passing. "We have wept for Roosevelt in Peru as though he had been a great Peruvian," reported the Communist *Vanguardia* of Lima (June 28, 1946). Latin Americans, wrote Germán Arciniegas, still had to rub their eyes to believe that the United States which had produced the filibuster William Walker, the "insolent" Theodore Roosevelt who boasted that he "took Panama," and other advocates of the Manifest Destiny of the United States to extend its influence throughout all America should have produced also this man "who loved liberty and justice."[80] The United States had worn a "Christian countenance," said *Le Soir* of Port-au-Prince (July 4, 1945), during the twelve years when it had been governed by Roosevelt. Fernando Ortiz Echagüe, Washington correspondent of Argentina's *La Nación* (April 24, 1945), fulsomely described him as "a cosmic personality, a human universe, com-

80. *El Tiempo,* Bogotá, April 17, 1945.

bining in his own generous self the Man of America and the Man of Europe." To the Paraguayan Dr. Juan Boggino, Roosevelt "seemed to elevate the whole moral stature of the species."[81] No leader of the United States has ever attained in Latin America the stature and prestige that Roosevelt enjoyed during his lifetime. In him, even after his death, Latin Americans felt they still had a friend and champion.[82] Because of the continental enthusiasm for his Good Neighbor Policy one of the early acts of the new President, Harry S. Truman, which most commended him to Latin America was his declaration, on the day of Roosevelt's death, that "to the Good Neighbor Policy of which he was the author I wholeheartedly subscribe."[83]

81. Address to the Rotary Club of Asunción, July 4, 1945, *El País,* Asunción, July 5, 1945.

82. For similar comments see *El Tiempo,* Bogotá, April 12 and July 4, 1945; *El Día,* Montevideo, April 13, 1945; *La Tribuna Popular,* Montevideo, April 16, 1945; *La Tribuna,* San Salvador, April 20, 1945; *La Nación,* Santiago, April 17, 1945; Pedro Julio García, *Nuestro Diario,* Guatemala City, April 19, 1945; "Rumiñahui," *El Universo,* Guayaquil, July 4, 1945; "Ulises" (Eduardo Zalcmca Borda), *El Espectador,* Bogotá, August 10, 1945; *La Tribuna,* Asunción, April 12, 1946; *Relator,* Cali, Colombia, April 12, 1949; and *El País,* Montevideo, April 12, 1949.

83. Message from President Truman to the Governing Board of the Pan American Union, April 14, 1945, *Department of State Bulletin,* XII (April 15, 1945), 669.

Chapter 5

"YANQUI" TRAITS

Nobody can deny this fact: There is a North American civilization which possesses a strong personality of its own, a content and a form which easily identify it. All the elements of its civilization are fresh, recent, as young as the spirit of its people; its tradition does not go back for centuries and it has a capacity for ridding itself of the past which enables it to continue in a state of constant renewal.

—JORGE FERNÁNDEZ

HE TRAITS of the "Yanquis," their "manner of living," and the underlying bases of their civilization were given close scrutiny by Latin Americans as the Good Neighbor Policy unfolded, particularly after the outbreak of World War II, which by curtailing their traditional contacts with Europe focused their attention immediately and intensively upon the United States. Under the Good Neighbor Policy the Latin Americans were more assiduously cultivated by their northern neighbor and were afforded more opportunities for analyzing and appraising the "Yanqui" way of life than ever before. Between Roosevelt's enunciation of the Good Neighbor Policy in 1933 and the end of World War II in 1945, seventeen Latin American presidents and presidents-elect were welcomed to Washington and given state receptions. Numerous "leaders," including not only heads of state but also journalists, physicians, professors, musicians, chiefs of police, businessmen, and many others from all the Latin American countries were brought to the United States on "goodwill" missions or for technical training. At the same time Latin Americans became acquainted with swarms of United States officials who visited

152

or worked in their countries during the war and with many men
and women in the United States armed forces stationed at defense installations there. From all these contacts they formed their own conclusions about the behavior and the culture of this people whom they
observed at first hand. Many Latin Americans, particularly those who
possessed professional articulateness, undertook to interpret the United
States to their fellow Latin Americans.

As Latin Americans witnessed the metamorphosis of life in the
"embattled democracy" of the north after Pearl Harbor, they were particularly impressed with its stupendous material production for war.
To Alejandro Carillo, a Mexican deputy and director of *El Popular,*
who visited this country in early 1942, it seemed "like a giant who is
shaking itself to enter a fight."[1] At the same time Manuel Seoane
noted that 50 per cent of the factories in the United States were wholly
given over to war production.[2] "The entire territory of the Union,"
reported *El Liberal Progresista* of Guatemala City (April 17, 1942),
"vibrates with the hum of the manufacture of machinery and implements of war in unheard-of quantities, which are possible only because
of the richness and the young and warlike energy of that nation. Every
factory, every shop, every laboratory, which could be transformed into
a war arsenal has been so transformed with the marvelous activity and
the admirable spirit of cooperation which appear to be the secret of
that great republic." Instead of automobiles, these people were now
producing tanks; instead of typewriters and radios, they were turning
out "frightening quantities of shells, airplanes, cannons, and machine
guns." They were using these materials of war not only to defend their
own territory but also "to reinforce the peoples and armies who are
fighting against the aggressors from China to Russia, from England
to Turkey, wherever they are needed in the service of humanity." This
industrial transformation seemed "miraculous" and "astonishing."[3]

In the fierce energy of this industrial effort the sustained and unified
patriotism of Uncle Sam's workers aroused the admiration of Latin
Americans. In the United States, commented *Excelsior* of Mexico
City (December 8, 1943), "it is the workers, men and women, winning
the 'battle of production,' who are determining the victory." *O Radical*

1. Reported in Despatch 946, Mexico, April 16, 1942, Department of State
Archives.
2. *El Gran Vecino,* 234.
3. Professor Francisco Frola of the National University of Mexico, *El Diario
de Hoy,* San Salvador, June 7, 1943; and statement by President Isaías Medina
Angarita of Venezuela on February 19, 1944.

(February 1, 1944), a leading newspaper of Rio de Janeiro, noted that after the employees of the Brooklyn Navy Yard had completed the construction of the great battleship "Missouri," they donated to the Red Cross "approximately fifteen thousand liters of blood." To *O Radical* this contribution was "an eloquent demonstration of the attitude and conscientiousness of the working classes of the United States . . . today coordinated and united for the purpose of reaching its objective: the survival of democracy." According to another newspaper of Rio de Janeiro, *Correio da Manhã* (December 1, 1946), "The entire world owes an enormous debt to the American workers." When "they armed Russia and their own country" they performed an "industrial miracle." "The American Negroes," too, reported Raymundo Magalhães Júnior, in *A Noite* of Rio de Janeiro (April 5, 1944), "are working for victory in the war plants and in the shipyards. . . . Today the Negroes have their generals and colonels; they have their battalions and regiments in action. . . . The Negroes are sincerely fighting for the United States and for the North American cause."

Less comprehensible and also less admirable to Latin Americans was the participation of women in this prodigious war enterprise, for their conception of the role of women in society did not include service in either industry or the armed forces. To the brilliant Enrique Santos, author under the pseudonym "Caliban" of one of Latin America's most trenchant newspaper columns, this war work, combined with the system of coeducation prevalent in the United States, had a brutalizing or a defeminizing effect upon North American women. Traveling to Europe in mid-1945 in company with seven other Latin American journalists on "L'Ile de France," a troopship loaded to the gunwales with United States troops, he particularly observed the WACs, "girls who have enlisted for various reasons, among which one of the most important is to have a good time," and he concluded: "These lassies would be very agreeable friends for a fleeting moment; but they have no heart. They have no feelings; they have no emotion. . . . The kind of mother who hovers for weeks over the cradle of her sick child, who tells him a thousand nonsensical words of affection, who would defend him like a lioness; the kind of sweetheart who is capable of all madness and all sacrifices; the kind of wife with whom it will be pleasant to grow old . . . ; the kind of inseparable companion whether in happiness or in disgrace—this kind we do not find among these WACs nor among the women who deserted their homes to work in factories." He foresaw that "the most serious problem that peace will bring to the peoples of Europe and of the United States will be the problem of returning women to the home."[4]

A regimen of austerity prevailed in wartime United States, as "that rich, peaceful, creative, and luxury-loving people," in the words of *El Liberal Progresista* of Guatemala City (April 17, 1942), "put on the tight belt of sacrifice." Their self-discipline was noted particularly in the systems of rationing and price ceilings. Roberto Chacón, president of the Cuban National Association of Commission Merchants in Foreign Trade, told the Lions Club of Havana that on a sixteen-days' visit to Washington he and the other members of a Cuban foodstuff commission "ate meat only once and butter twice." He hastened to add that "the production of these articles is not curtailed; on the contrary, they [the United States] are now producing these commodities in fantastic quantities, but they omit them from their diet in order to furnish them . . . to countries which their armies are daily freeing from barbaric ignominy."[5] A discerning Ecuadoran journalist, Jorge Fernández, also noted that in wartime United States "all the best goes to the armed forces; the best in food, the best in materials for making equipment and arms; the most nutritious in quality goes to the combatants."[6] "One has to recognize and admire the spirit of self-abnegation which those people have," concluded President Isaías Medina Angarita of Venezuela after a visit to the United States in 1944. "That spirit of self-denial has driven them to sacrifice." They were constrained by their indomitable will for victory to forego the comforts and advantages to which their tremendous production would, in time of peace, have entitled them.[7] In this they showed a kind of spiritual quality or, at least a lack of obsession with material wealth, which was surprising to Latin Americans trained in the clichés of Rodó.

That in these circumstances the abundant and free circulation of money in the United States did not produce either war profiteering or inflation was difficult for Latin Americans to explain, unaccustomed as they were to the same measure of social discipline. An intelligent Brazilian visitor to the United States in the latter part of 1944, Professor Moacir Alvaro of the São Paulo School of Medicine, told a

4. *El Tiempo*, Bogotá, July 16, 1945.
5. Speech of Roberto Chacón, president of the Asociación Nacional de Comisionistas del Comercio Exterior, as reported in the *Boletín Oficial* of the Asociación, April, 1945.
6. "Aspects of North American Life," *El Comercio*, Quito, May 5, 1944.
7. Article by Dr. Ruiz Paz Castillo, editor of *El Heraldo*, Caracas, in that newspaper on February 19, 1944, reporting an interview with President Medina.

Brazilian news agency that "the wealth flowing from the feverish activity in the 'war effort' is distributed equitably, as it should be, in accordance with the economic-social standards of the American Union," that the situation had become more favorable to those who performed manual work than to those who had fixed incomes, and that the "great abundance of money in the hands of persons anxious to spend, combined with the relative shortages of things to buy," did not cause higher prices because the ceiling system was enforced.[8] Another Brazilian visitor, Father Roberto Saboia de Medeiros, who was president of Social Action of São Paulo, considered "it a miracle comparable only to the war effort itself that the United States has not succumbed to inflation." He attributed this "miracle" to "rationing which has been rigidly carried out" and to "the fact . . . that the public was well informed and understood that inflation would bring serious consequences to themselves."[9] For this effort the people of the United States were psychologically conditioned by a gigantic propaganda campaign. "In the streets, shops, clubs, public offices, trains, everywhere," reported Jorge Fernández, "the impact of the war on the country is shown by the propaganda appeals to conserve material, to keep silence on matters which concern the national security and to contribute to the Red Cross, to buy bonds and war stamps."[10] It seemed noteworthy to Latin Americans that these objectives did not have to be secured by coercive methods. The government's propaganda was not imposed upon the people but, appealing to their sense of common cause, was accepted as a common obligation. Only a voluntary acceptance of restrictions imposed for the acknowledged good of all could explain the effectiveness of their total mobilization for war.

This mobilization for war was not deemed to require an abridgment of the essential human freedoms, though it necessitated certain regulations of them. The people of the United States, noted Fernández, "remain vigilant for the security of the inalienable rights of citizenship," and political speakers often mentioned "the duty of the people to reclaim on the day following the proclamation of peace the rights which they have temporarily lost."[11] Civil rights were as precious to these people in war as in peace. An Argentine visitor, Nicolás Repetto, while talking with an outstanding leader of the American Federation of Labor, was impressed to learn that labor union locals could meet with-

8. *Diário de Noite,* Rio de Janeiro, December 26, 1944.
9. *O Jornal,* Rio de Janeiro, October 4, 1944.
10. *El Comercio,* Quito, May 5, 1944.   11. *Ibid.*

out securing permission from police and municipal officials and that their speakers could freely criticize the government.[12] The editor of *El Tiempo* of Bogotá, Roberto García Peña, after spending eleven months in the United States in 1943 and 1944, reported in his newspaper that censorship was applied only "to military matters" which might adversely affect "strategic plans or the morale of the fighting men and civilians. But as regards the liberty of analyzing, criticizing, dissenting, there has been no limitation. The commentator analyzes the facts and official acts as he pleases; the newspapers censure or praise without being subjected to any state regulation, law, or instruction from the government, and even the people themselves . . . unreservedly comment on matters pertaining to the war, foreign policy, and the daily war news."[13]

In this mobilization effort the institutions of higher learning were also involved. These "militarized universities" of the United States, as Professor Hernane Tavares de Sá of the University of São Paulo observed after a visit to some seventy-five such institutions in 1942, were taking in "hundreds—sometimes thousands—of military students for intensive courses of the most diverse types." The military influence on the teaching curriculum, he said, could be considered on the one hand "a dangerous influence since it gives great prominence to the teaching of applied sciences and to discipline of a utilitarian character, to the detriment of the arts, of pure science, of disinterested research. . . . On the other hand . . . intellectual discipline and intensive work have returned to the important place to which they were entitled and from which they had been driven by activities of a social, or to express it better, of a worldly character." The postwar demobilization of the ten million men under arms would undoubtedly produce serious problems for the universities, particularly since public opinion seemed to favor encouraging these men to take up university training. "Perhaps," he said, "we shall see the socializing of the universities."[14]

The equalitarian and cooperative relationship between social classes in the United States under wartime conditions impressed Latin Americans tremendously. Society, particularly under the equalizing influences of the war, appeared strikingly homogeneous. "Under the American way of life," reported the Panama *Star and Herald* (May 27,

12. *Impresiones de los Estados Unidos* (Buenos Aires, 1943), XV.
13. Interview published in *El Tiempo*, Bogotá, May 10, 1944. The interview was conducted by Gerardo Valencia, director of Radio Nacional, and was originally broadcast over that station on May 8, 1944.
14. *O Diário*, Belo Horizonte, Brazil, March 11, 1944.

1945), "there are no privileged castes entitled to rule by right of birth, or ancestry or inheritance." Brazil's ex-President Washington Luis Pereira de Souza, who spent the years of World War II in the United States, reported that he saw "no castes there, no aristocracy and no masses."[15] In wartime civilian life, observed Rómulo Betancourt, a leader of the Venezuelan political party *Acción Democrática*, after a four-weeks' visit in the United States, "all from the wife of a taxi driver to the upper-class wife of a Boston senator take their place unquestioningly in the queues that form in front of the butcher shops to get their share of the food quotas which are rationed equally because of war needs. . . . It is not unusual to see side by side in a cafeteria, hurriedly partaking of the Spartan meal of a sandwich and a cup of coffee which constitutes the normal luncheon, the head of a great business pressed to get back to his office, his modest clerk, and a workman in overalls." Here was exemplified what he called "the leveling instinct of democracy." All here, said Betancourt, except those whose skin is "pigmented by Negroid elements," had "a calm assurance that their rights would be respected." Even the rich knew that "the privilege of having wealth brings with it no special prerogatives under the law."[16]

To Dr. José M. Baldomir, a Uruguayan physician who had observed life in the United States while studying at the University Hospital of the University of Michigan and at the Massachusetts General Hospital, the explanation of this absence of class stratification seemed to be that "the North American drinks in this spirit of equality and justice from the home, where in his earliest days the child is considered a being whose rights are respected, and from the school where he learns to venerate the leaders of democracy." He considered that the example of North American democracy reaches "its high point in its respect for women: the woman is as free as man, not only before the law but also in the sentiments of every citizen."[17] To Latin American eyes, however, this arrangement had its disadvantages, for, as a correspondent of *El Diario de Hoy* of San Salvador wrote from San Francisco, California, "Here where women have equal rights with men, they have equal vices; women are often seen on the streets and in saloons in a drunken condition."[18]

15. Address published in *A Noite*, Rio de Janeiro, September 19, 1947.
16. *El País*, Caracas, August 7, 1945.
17. *La Mañana*, Montevideo, March 19, 1945.
18. Marco Tulio Canjura, *El Diario de Hoy*, San Salvador, October 8, 1945.

Latin Americans noted that the cooperative spirit was also conspicuously displayed among the diverse religious groups. Father Roberto Saboia de Medeiros told representatives of a Brazilian news agency after his return to São Paulo in 1944 that Roman Catholics, Protestants, and Jews in the United States, though they differed in doctrine, "collaborate in many ways. They write books jointly and debate social problems."[19] From the absence of bickering among them Washington Luis concluded that "in this country of respect for liberty of conscience, there has developed a people profoundly religious almost in its entirety in spite of divisions into numerous creeds."[20] Another Brazilian observer, Erico Verissimo, who spent two of the war years in the United States, reported that "the American citizen in a certain sense is as religious as the Latin Americans, if not more so."[21] This religiosity of the North Americans, however, was not so apparent to Jorge Fernández, who noted that "their religious spirit does not include either the mystical devotion which inspired medieval man to erect his Gothic cathedrals nor the impassioned zeal which produced the Inquisition and the temples of Spain and Latin America. The Kingdom of the North American is of this earth. He lives here on its soil, in its life currents, in its activity, in the splendor of its richness."[22]

Here was a nation which had been converted by the alarm of war into a prodigy of energy and destructive power. To Latin Americans the quiet, organized rage of this new, hard-hitting industrial colossus was a stirring spectacle of democracy in action. By common consent this people had rushed to arms to defend their nation from attack and with it the entire Western Hemisphere. They were sustaining an unprecedented war effort and were maintaining a high war morale for one purpose—victory over the evil of totalitarianism. Washington Luis later declared that the war effort of that nation was "stupendous and formidable. . . . All, without exception of class or party, of ideas or of sentiments, contributed calmly and with self-abnegation to this effort, which at that time appeared miraculous . . . a united effort of an entire people, with its rulers, which could be possible only with democracy."[23] The degree of social discipline accepted by them was explained by the fundamental consensual relationship between government and people there. A regimentation which if imposed by govern-

19. *O Jornal,* Rio de Janeiro, October 4, 1944.
20. *A Noite,* Rio de Janeiro, September 19, 1947.
21. *O Jornal,* Rio de Janeiro, October 6, 1945.
22. *El Comercio,* Quito, May 6, 1944.
23. Address published in *A Noite,* Rio de Janeiro, September 19, 1947.

ment would have been intolerable—would indeed have smacked of totalitarianism—was freely accepted by the people for the achievement of the greater goal of preserving their way of life, their system of free enterprise, their rights of individual liberty.

* * *

How was it possible, asked *Diario de la Marina* of Havana (April 19, 1942), that a people as intellectual and cultured as that of the United States should display so strong a martial spirit? Answering its own question, that newspaper explained that "culture has decided to use force to punish the brute." The Chilean writer Benjamín Subercaseaux, who visited the United States in early 1943, noted that the habitual self-control of the people of the United States was accentuated by the war. All the little problems resulting from the war were resolved "with calmness and good spirit: no one is agitated, no one gets angry, no one even speaks of the war."[24] These people went about their martial tasks with an attitude of firm and quiet determination. "Since Pearl Harbor," reported Jorge Fernández, "the people have accepted this situation spontaneously and without theatrics, quietly and without passion. They view the war as a problem which has to be solved and solved well, and each one occupies his post and devotes himself to it. There is no warlike demonstrativeness in the worker, the mother, the soldier, or the politician. They go about their business with scientific precision, with cool serenity, with trust and optimism. . . . 'We are not fighters,' the North Americans say, 'but we have to fight the war.' . . . The people have confidence in the conduct of the war. . . . They look forward, in everything, to victory."[25] This earnest and restrained optimism was also noted by the Brazilian writer Erico Verissimo. As he observed the people of the United States, they "did not discuss the war: they worked for the war."[26] They were carrying on "this gigantic enterprise," said the Argentine visitor Nicolás Repetto, "with a firm and serene resolution, without any boasting, and with a full realization of their responsibility and of the magnitude of the struggle."[27]

This almost "sporting attitude" toward the war, said Rómulo Betancourt after his visit to the United States in mid-1945, was "the

24. *Retorno de U.S.A.* (Santiago de Chile, 1943), 244-245.
25. *El Comercio,* Quito, May 5, 1944.
26. *O Jornal,* Rio de Janeiro, October 6, 1945.   27. *Op. cit.,* V.

same spirit of 'what the hell; let's get on with the game,' with which a North American football team takes its opponents' goals during the course of a hard match." He was "struck by the serenity with which a mother speaks of her two sons who were killed on Okinawa, by the comradely gaiety of the trains full of uniformed boys and girls on their way to the Pacific, by the lack of tears in the farewells of women to their men when they leave for the warfronts." Betancourt saw "only one heart-rending scene: that of a girl from Texas, who looked half-Mexican, whom I saw faint one night at the Union Station in Washington when the train carrying her husband off for the Philippines pulled out."[28] Wartime hardships did not appear to grieve the North American. "He knows," commented *El Panamá-América* (May 21, 1945), "that the harvest of those sacrifices will be enjoyed by the men of tomorrow; and he is satisfied. He lacks conceit; it is not any one group of citizens who thinks in this way. It is the millionaire from whom the taxes take up to 90 per cent of his lawful income; it is the man of the liberal professions; it is the manager of a great enterprise; it is the artist and it is the man in the street; it is the workman and it is the housewife; it is the parish priest in his church and it is the professor at the university; it is the farmer and it is the movie house janitor."

This unemotional self-confidence also characterized the armed forces of the United States. As Nicolás Repetto observed the soldiers, sailors, and aviators circulating through the cities of the United States he was not struck "by their martial air, by their parade step, nor by their terrorizing expression. They are excellent boys," he concluded, "citizens of a democratic and free country, separated from home, shop, factory, office, farm, university to defend generously and valiantly a cause which is at the same time theirs and that of all civilized humanity."[29] "The combatant," generalized Jorge Fernández, "enlists in a sporting spirit; he goes to the front without militaristic passion, without hatred, to defend his country on a foreign soil, and there he acts with all his energy."[30] As Enrique Santos of *El Tiempo* traveled to Europe on the troopship "L'Ile de France" he concluded that these soldiers, so heterogeneous in character and in racial origins, were not animated by the heroic spirit, "nor are they much interested in the defense of the four liberties. . . . They were born in a good land where their fathers were able to free themselves from the status of

28. *El País,* Caracas, August 7, 1945.   29. *Op. cit.,* V.
30. *El Comercio,* Quito, May 5, 1944.

serfs which they bore in Europe. It is the land of opportunities, of abundance, of liberty, which many do not understand but which everyone feels; they were told that this nexus of pleasant realities—their people, their homes, their small or their great comforts, their 'way of life'—was threatened by a monster, by an implacable dragon, which must be killed. And simply, without tragic gestures, without black or brown shirts, and without fanaticism, they went to Europe to kill the dragon. . . . They all have no other ambition than to return to their homes, to their town, to their wives, to follow their former mode of living, to work, to be free and happy, to lead a quiet and good life."[31]

The same qualities were observed in United States troops stationed at military, naval, and air bases in Latin America. To the mayor of Recife in Pernambuco, Brazil, the "hundreds of North Americans from high-ranking officers down to plain soldiers and sailors" who thronged his city appeared to be "human, sensitive, and fun-loving spirits who have no hatreds and no prejudices. . . . Their habits, their joy of living, the absence of protocol and studied attitudes, their simplicity of conduct, and their cordial manners give the impression of a young people—especially young in spirit—which is proof that they do not allow themselves to be dominated by human malice in its most ambitious, egoistic, and violent forms."[32] At Natal also, on the northeastern bulge of Brazil, where in 1943 North Americans were "seen by the hundreds day and night in the streets of the city, in the bars and shops, singly or in groups," they were characterized as "expansive, likeable, sincere, consistently good-natured, always well balanced in their demeanor, respectful and orderly."[33] On the other hand North Americans, both troops and civilians, who were stationed in the Latin American countries were sometimes criticized by their hosts for making derogatory comments about them, for maintaining attitudes of aloofness and superiority, for indulging in loose moral practices, and for setting standards of living which the economically poorer Latin Americans could not meet. As the colonies of North Americans in Latin America increased in size during the war these criticisms multiplied.[34]

The military readiness and fighting qualities of the Yankee troops were impressive to Latin Americans. These forces, most of which had

31. *El Tiempo*, Bogotá, July 16, 1945.
32. Antonio Novaes Júnior, in *Folha da Manhã*, Recife, July 1, 1943.
33. *O Globo*, Rio de Janeiro, September 21, 1943. See also article by Agamenon Magalhães in *Folha da Manhã*, Recife, March 15, 1944.
34. Hernane Tavares de Sá, "Camouflage of Harmony," 11-13, 43.

been hastily improvised after the outbreak of war, performed their soldierly duties well. The sudden expansion of the military establishment of the United States into a formidable war machine after Pearl Harbor was an astonishing revelation to Latin Americans. To their surprise, "an army unprepared, reduced, without arms and equipment" was "transformed in a short time—increased fifty to one, with the most efficient arms any army in the world has known, organized to the extreme needs of modern war for use in all regions and climates of the world."[35] The results of this "magnificent military achievement" were daily demonstrated by the valorous action of the North American fighter on each of the far-flung fronts. In his world-wide operations, reported Ramón Manrique of Colombia, "he attacks the Japanese in the Pacific, lands in Africa, places his tanks in Sicily and then on the Italian peninsula, and makes the German retreat to the very cliffs of the Brenner; he improvises a railway in Iran to aid Russia with supplies via the Persian Gulf; he constructs the Burma Road to aid China; he sends foodstuffs and cannons and tanks to Russia, which is being choked in the constricting arms of Germany; . . . his doctors, his scientists, his humane men . . . aid the orphans and those rendered destitute by the war; and later he performs the most fantastic feat seen in centuries: he lands in Normandy and rapidly liberates France."[36] The United States, however, for all its rapid mobilization and fighting activities did not give Latin Americans the impression of militarism. "There is no militarism in the United States," concluded Jorge Fernández, "the civil population is in uniform. That is all."[37] *La Noche* of La Paz (April 6, 1946) even took pains to deny that the North American troops should be called "soldiers." Instead it called them "civil heroes," these "boys from every town and city of the United States in a uniform which distinguished them but did not mechanize them." They were "human beings, . . . civilians who were fulfilling a mission for their country and for democracy."

The general impression made upon Latin Americans by this transformed and travailing nation was one of incomparable greatness. Its energy was boundless, its social restraints admirable, its example exhilerating. To visit the United States, wrote an Argentine physician,

35. Lecture given by Lt. Col. Guillermo López L., Chilean military attaché in the United States from 1940 to 1944, in Santiago, Chile, July, 1944.

36. *Diario de la Costa,* Cartagena, Colombia, March 4, 1945.

37. *El Comercio,* Quito, May 5, 1944. The same idea was expressed by Arturo Aldunate Phillips in *Estados Unidos: Gran Aventura del Hombre* (Santiago, 1943), 337.

Dr. Tiburcio Padilla of Buenos Aires, after a three-month visit, is "the same thing as being born fifty or seventy years later." He was particularly impressed by the efficient organization of the hospitals which he visited and by the cooperative spirit displayed in them between the physicians and their students.[38] "The camaraderie of chiefs and their subordinates, of professors and their students" also was noted by the Uruguayan physician Dr. Baldomir. This, he told an interviewer from *La Mañana* of Montevideo (March 19, 1945), after his return to Uruguay, "is not an ostentatious display of democracy but a prevailing habit." A Brazilian physician, Dr. Alvaro Lopes Cançado, who served for two and a half years in various hospitals in New York City and Chicago, also considered it noteworthy that "the heads of clinics gather their internes together to discuss the facts of the more difficult cases. Everything is done on an equal basis, without regard to degrees or ermine, in the famous Round Table manner."[39]

All these visitors were greatly impressed by the achievements of medical science in the United States. Dr. Baldomir, judging that "in the field of medicine North America leads the world," attributed its pre-eminence to the fact that every new discovery was accepted on its merits and that "liberty, security and quiet" were provided to research workers in the laboratories.[40] Dr. Lopes Cançado considered that in the United States "the great secret in the development of medicine rests in the spirit of collaboration," as shown specifically in the American Medical Association, which not only promotes scientific development but is "above all a force that swings extraordinary weight in the political balance of the country." Another reason seemed to him to be the high requirements, some imposed by the Federal government, for medical practitioners. He was particularly impressed by the attention given to correcting "the deformities of children, brought about by infantile paralysis or other causes," and praised highly the childrens' hospitals maintained by the Shriners where the child undergoing treatment enjoys "surroundings that are gay, a normal life, and every necessary comfort. The patients continue their studies with teachers designated by the school authorities. There are places for sun baths, magnificent parks for children, playgrounds, and even libraries. . . . Whatever they need is supplied. Completely free!" The United States, he summarized, "is attentive to her youth and to her

38. *La Nación,* Buenos Aires, January 20, 1946.
39. Interview in *O Globo,* Rio de Janeiro, July 8, 1944.
40. *La Mañana,* Montevideo, March 19, 1945.

sick."[41] Indeed, the United States seemed to Latin Americans to have made a cult of health. Jorge Fernández pointed out that this cult manifested itself "in milk unimaginably pure and vitaminized, in water without microbes, in selected and nutritious foods, in smooth elevators, in safe and comfortable trains, in hygiene, in social protection." Here was "a civilization which thinks in terms of life, which feels and loves life, and which has surrounded itself with all the pleasures and comforts which it is possible to enjoy. Its great buildings, its marvelous palaces, its trains, highways, the comfort which makes it possible for man to live, all this appears to be basically a song of life, of sacred concern for the body."[42]

It seemed to another observer of this North American people, Oscar Gajardo, executive vice president of the Chilean Corporation for Promotion of Production, that "their democratic, ample, human, comprehensive, optimistic, tolerant life begins with their healthful homes. . . . Their realistic and practical spirit has led them . . . to build houses with two characteristics: first, clean, healthful, and hygienic; and second, at a cost for rent or purchase which puts them within reach of the greatest number. . . . All appearance of superfluous luxury has been eliminated." He noted too that a housing area generally "has attached to it a sector of equal size, or greater, for parks, avenues, or green spaces." Indeed, he spoke of "their fanaticism for the tree." This insistence upon a clean and natural environment, he said, "explains the physical and moral health of that people, their self-assurance in the struggle for life, their faith in work. The child opens his eyes on life in neighborhoods where everything speaks to him of optimism, of certainty for the future, of happiness and human brotherhood." In this circumstance he found also an explanation of the "exceedingly low incidence of delinquency and the honesty which is a distinction of the people of the United States."[43] Latin American visitors were astonished, as was the Argentine Nicolás Repetto, to discover that in the United States shopkeepers would leave their shops at night "without any more protection than a little lock," that "the majority of North American homes had no defenses" such as "iron grillwork, complicated locks, nor high walls," that their owners left their garden furniture outside and their houses open when they were absent.[44]

41. *O Globo,* Rio de Janeiro, July 8, 1944. See also *Gazeta de Notícias,* Rio de Janeiro, July 12, 1944.   42. *El Comercio,* Quito, May 4 and 10, 1944.
43. *El Mercurio,* Santiago, August 23, 1945.   44. *Op. cit.,* IV.

If the people of the United States insisted upon high standards of health and physical comfort for themselves, they were generous in sharing with others the benefits of their enlarged manner of living. Washington Luis was struck by the humanitarian aspect of science, hospitals, schools, and universities in the United States.[45] "Americans . . . are generous and kind," wrote the Mexican diplomatic official Luis Quintanilla in 1943. "They not only have brains; they also have a heart, and a very big one at that. . . . An earthquake in Japan, Mexico, Chile, a flood in China, a famine in Europe, move the citizens of this country to immediate response."[46] *La Prensa* of Lima (July 4, 1945) praised "the role the United States has played in making the world a more healthful place in which to live," particularly through its "splendid work of rehabilitating many of the indigenous peoples of South America." Latin Americans were emotionally moved by instances of the individual philanthropy of North Americans. *El Mercurio* of Antofagasta, Chile (January 10, 1944), editorially commended the United States consul in that city who, hearing about "a poor old woman" of Antofagasta who suffered from a chronic skin disease, ordered medicine for her from the United States "as a personal gesture of 'good neighborliness' " and paid the cost of $81 himself—"a larger amount than the poor woman spent for food in a whole year." The Guatemalan ambassador to the Pan American Union, Rafael Arévalo Martínez, reported in *El Imparcial* of Guatemala City (February 25, 1947) that "in restaurants in Washington and New York" in 1946 he had seen "a boy ask his girl friend not to eat dried plums but to choose fresh ones because the former could be shipped to countries of Europe and Asia which were suffering from hunger" and that he had seen "a mother take a slice of bread from the hands of her son and give him potatoes instead because wheat could be exported. . . . This generous people were taking the bread out of their mouths to give it to the needy beyond the seas. . . . They are truly," he concluded, "a romantic people par excellence, . . . the most public-spirited people in the world." Dr. Juan Boggino, a former rector of the National University of Paraguay, told the Rotary Club of Asunción after a visit to the United States, that these people "do not act in the character of Caliban. . . . If the people of the United States have built the longest bridge, if they have erected the highest building, if they have dug the deepest tunnel . . . this admirable peo-

45. *A Noite,* Rio de Janeiro, September 19, 1947.
46. *A Latin American Speaks* (New York, 1943), 46-47.

ple also have ennobled their gold and their days in many enterprises of an altruistic and brave nature, as when they found and support universities in China, when they restore the cathedrals of France, when they build leper asylums in the Pacific, when they eradicate the yellow fever from Brazil, or when they build roads and hospitals in our own country." As a result of his own observations Dr. Boggino publicly repudiated the Rodó thesis of the United States in which he had been indoctrinated as a youth.[47]

The participation of the United States in World War II was interpreted by many Latin Americans as evidence of the generous spirit of that nation, answering, as *El Popular* of Mexico City (October 7, 1941) expressed it, "humanity's anguished call for help." By this participation the United States, according to *El Tiempo* of Bogotá (July 4, 1945), had effaced erroneous conceptions which had grown up about it in Latin America as lacking "spiritual worth" and as possessing only a "capitalist mentality." These people, said *El Tiempo,* had entered the war not because of any "immediate threat" to the sovereignty of their country but to fight for "the cause of humanity" and to fulfill an obligation "to the world because of their own privileged greatness." In this war, Dr. Boggino told the Asunción Rotary Club, the United States was a "leader of ideals for the redemption of humanity." Through its efforts it was "sustaining a worthy world order and the hope of a better one."[48] Here, then, was a people who had assumed the laudable mission of eliminating injustice from the world. They were "making efforts and sacrifices," it seemed to the mayor of Recife, in Pernambuco, Brazil, "to create a less afflicted, a more just, and a happier world, in which there may be a place for all under the same health-giving and fecund sun of human happiness."[49] To Ramón Manrique they were best personified by Buffalo Bill who carried on an "eternal search for the thieves, scoundrels, and rustlers of the West."[50] This basic Yankee quixotism was a quality that appealed to Latin Americans.

* * *

47. *El País,* Asunción, July 5, 1945.
48. *Ibid.*
49. Antonio Novaes Júnior, in *Folha da Manhã,* Recife, July 1, 1943. For similar sentiments see *Le Soir,* Port-au-Prince, July 4, 1945.
50. *Diario de la Costa,* Cartagena, Colombia, March 4, 1945.

What were the reasons for the greatness of the United States? "I am really amazed by North America," rhapsodized Plinio Brasil Milano, a representative of the Political and Social Organization of Rio Grande do Sul in southern Brazil, after a three-months visit in the United States in 1943. "One cannot imagine, without a prolonged visit, what American greatness actually is."[51] President Medina of Venezuela described the impression of the United States which he received as "immense."[52] It seemed to the Venezuelan poet-politician Dr. Andrés Eloy Blanco to be a country which had "something of everything."[53] A Bolivian engineer, Jorge López Videla, Director of Sewage and Drainage in La Paz, who made a three-months' tour of the United States, pronounced it "the greatest country in the world in every respect." He "saw such great engineering works," he told reporters upon his return to Bolivia, "that we cannot even imagine them here," and attributed this greatness to "the profound religious and moral sense of the people of the United States."[54] The young Brazilian Arnaldo Leão Marques, who spent two years in the United States and published his "Impressions of the United States" in *A Manhã* of Rio de Janeiro (January 28, 1944), considered that "the greatest secret of the rapid progress" of this country, "with its fertile fields, its immense plains, and its many navigable rivers," was its ideal natural suitability "for the establishment of communications systems— railroads, roads, fluvial navigation, etc." He was astonished that he was able to travel from New York to Texas and not "pass through more than two or three tunnels!" The United States could not be interpreted without an understanding of its physical advantages. Its civilization, according to Jorge Fernández, was based upon these advantages and its "prodigious wealth."[55]

In the tradition and practice of freedom in the United States some Latin Americans found the secret of its enterprise and productive genius. The "marvelous ability" of that country "to convert itself from a workshop of peace into a stupendous arsenal of war, from a peaceful and gay people into a war power of the first order . . . was possible," proclaimed one of the largest provincial newspapers of Ar-

51. *O Jornal,* Rio de Janeiro, September 2, 1943.
52. *El Heraldo,* Caracas, February 19, 1944.
53. *El Nacional,* Caracas, January 13, 1944.
54. *El Diario,* La Paz, January 26, 1946. Substantially the same interview was published also in four other La Paz dailies: *Ultima Hora,* January 25, and *La Calle, La Razón,* and *Pregón,* January 26.
55. *El Comercio,* Quito, May 4, 1944.

gentina, "because the democratic system makes liberty the greatest incentive by which man can achieve his highest accomplishments."[56] The course of the United States in the war demonstrated to Roberto García Peña that its "system is efficacious and useful for mobilizing collective effort to accomplish purposes which totalitarianism believed it could accomplish only by violence and by the absolute abolition of individual liberty."[57] The United States was "an exemplary democracy . . . whose principles are not a mere inert juridical formula but a dynamic concept of life."[58]

Individualism was one of the inseparable characteristics of this system. To the Brazilian writer José María Belo "the tradition of the free individual, slightly aloof from the discipline of the state, . . . explains, . . . even today, the power of the spontaneous and secondary form of associations—societies, parties, leagues of all sorts—that frequently break forth into strange collective movements and astound the foreign observer."[59] In that country, generalized Washington Luis, "what counts is individual initiative at the service of daring conceptions and devoted to the task of development by cooperation."[60] According to *Información* of Havana (September 28, 1949), "free enterprise is the queen and mistress of American power and drive." This was manifested particularly in the "very strong commercial imagination" of North Americans, to use a phrase of the Chilean writer Joaquín Edwards Bello. In the United States, he noted, "thousands of inventions are registered annually. On the eve of the boxing match between Carpentier and Dempsey one Yankee had the idea of making thousands of fans, as it was summer time, giving the pictures of the champions and the date. The sale of fans during this match made a fortune for him. . . . A Negro woman invented a hair grease especially for Negro hair. In a short time she was a millionaire. During the war thousands of Yankees had the idea of renting their damp basements, useless until then, for growing mushrooms, which produced millions of dollars."[61]

In this country, then, so "free from what the psychoanalysts call

56. *La Capital,* Rosario, Argentina, May 14, 1945.
57. *El Tiempo,* Bogotá, May 10, 1944.   58. *Ibid.,* July 4, 1945.
59. Lecture sponsored by the Committee on Intellectual Cooperation in the Brazilian Department of Foreign Affairs in September, 1939, translation forwarded to President Roosevelt by José María Belo Filho, September 16, 1939, Department of State Archives.
60. *A Noite,* Rio de Janeiro, September 19, 1947.
61. *La Patria,* Concepción, Chile, March 11, 1946.

inferiority complexes," declared Betancourt, "the 'self-made man,' the man who has gotten ahead by his own efforts, is in evidence everywhere."[62] The strenuous competition among individuals had produced the extraordinary physical and material results apparent everywhere in that country. "In the depths of every North American," observed the Peruvian Luis Alberto Sánchez after his visit to the United States in 1941-1942, "crouches a record-man, or better, a record-maniac. . . . When one arrives in Chicago the letters of many ubiquitous signs strike one's eyes: 'The Stevens Hotel, the biggest in the world'; in San Francisco, 'Oakland Bridge, the longest in the world'; in New York, the Empire State Building, 'the tollest [sic] in the world.' "[63] The "free and easy" manner characteristic of society in the United States as represented in the Hollywood movies was, when rightly interpreted, only somewhat exaggerated evidence of the individual freedom which prevailed there "without the hindrances of old-fashioned ideas." This society was based upon the principle that every individual is responsible for his own conduct, ideas, and attitudes.

But this freedom was counterbalanced by a seemingly spontaneous and voluntary feeling of mutual respect. Tolerance for divergent views, therefore, was a characteristic of the "Yanqui" way of life. "Every idea, every proposal, every attitude," observed Jorge Fernández, is listened to with patience by reason of a kind of " 'collective consent' that every man may do that which will benefit himself."[64] The Brazilian cleric Roberto Saboia de Medeiros, who lived among the people of the United States in 1944, considered it noteworthy that "though they have no one common religion their respect and tolerance of free worship has dominated all their living."[65] "The citizen of the United States," concluded Dr. Baldomir of Uruguay, "is educated in an atmosphere of . . . absolute respect for the rights of others."[66] In "this environment of freedom of discussion," observed the editor of El Tiempo of Bogotá (May 10, 1944), "is the expression of his tolerance, for he freely debates for the purpose of convincing his opponent but without renouncing the idea of being convinced." The people thus educate themselves "in the clubs, in the

62. El País, Caracas, August 5, 1945.
63. Un Sudamericano en Norteamérica: Ellos y Nosotros (Santiago de Chile, 1942), 256.   64. El Comercio, Quito, May 6, 1944.
65. Article datelined São Paulo, distributed by the Brazilian news agency Meridional on October 3, 1944, and published in O Jornal, Rio de Janeiro, October 4, 1944.
66. La Mañana, Montevideo, March 19, 1945.

labor unions, in the press, in books, at simple luncheons with friends; for the North American is essentially an extrovert."

This Colombian editor, Roberto García Peña, was impressed with the role of journalism in forming public opinion in the United States. He considered that journalism in the United States was "more objective than subjective, . . . more a photographic camera of facts than the protagonist of a thesis, . . . for the North American has a permanent hunger for information. Every citizen there buys two or more newspapers, with the result that, as statistics show, more newspapers are purchased daily than the country has inhabitants. . . . The North American people read more than any other people in the world." This avidity for reading was also attested by the fact that "in 1943 they published an average of thirty books daily on all subjects of human learning."[67] The Mexican diplomat Luis Quintanilla noted that "Americans love to read. One finds them reading at home, in restaurants, in streetcars, in busses."[68] But in their reading, noted Nicolás Repetto, they sought primarily "scientific and technical information directly applicable to their professional activity." In that, as in their education generally, they demanded a "certain measurable utility," unlike the Latin Americans who, according to Repetto, "zealously cultivate the purely verbal disciplines, disdaining work with the hands."[69]

This national passion for learning also appeared noteworthy to the distinguished Professor Hernane Tavares de Sá of the University of São Paulo, who lectured in thirty-eight of the states of the United States in the early part of the war. "The American," he wrote in *Jornal do Brasil* of Rio de Janeiro (December 19, 1943), "likes lectures and is ready to attend one on the slightest pretext. . . . The attentive interest and spirit of fair play of the American audience are admirable. One can talk to them with great frankness; they actually take criticism, however harsh, with serenity and good humor; but criticism of the United States must be substantiated." He discovered that audiences wanted, not declamatory speeches so popular in Brazil, but speeches marked by simplicity of expression, even slang, and packed with facts. "The American loves facts, and their crude and bare presentation satisfies him completely. . . . Ideas do not register well, especially if they do not conform to the limited, orderly

67. *El Tiempo*, Bogotá, May 10, 1944.
68. *Op. cit.*, 43.
69. *Op. cit.*, IX.

supply of original thoughts doled out sparingly to the public by the recognized thinkers of the country." Jokes too were needed even in the most serious lectures. In the question period, which Dr. Tavares de Sá considered "perhaps the most typical feature of the lecture system" in the United States, "the participation of the public is active."

Despite all this activity, Jorge Fernández concluded, the United States "has not yet produced its art, its literature, its philosophy. Scarcely has it given form to its architecture. . . . Its thinkers, scholars, and artists were of foreign origin. It has bought everything. . . . From England, France, Germany, Spain, Finland, Sweden, Latin America—men from all these parts of the world give their best thought and produce their art in the United States. They are the teachers of the nation."[70] The same explanation was given by José Vasconcelos, ex-Minister of Public Education of Mexico, to a Mexican audience in 1945. "The United States are a prolongation of European culture in the New World," he declared. "Their religion, their discipline are of European origin, and in the process of being transplanted to this continent those qualities suffered diminution." The United States itself, he said, "has not produced a great philosopher."[71] Another Mexican, Luis Quintanilla, observed that among North Americans there was "a certain fear, . . . a certain shame . . . of being called intellectuals. . . . In contrast, muscular activity is always something to brag about. Football men, basketball men, advertise their status in big letters spread all over their powerful chests."[72] Commenting on this national addiction to sports, Dr. Alvaro Lopes Cançado noted that "the admiration which the American people feel for the champion is something religious."[73]

To Latin American visitors the "democratic museums" in the United States were a constant source of wonderment. Jorge Fernández thought that they included everything that "man has thought, believed, and done throughout all the milleniums of his existence." They were "indescribable in their size, in their riches, in their intelligence. Incessantly, hour after hour hundreds of men and women of every age throng through the museums with the restlessness of students. The technique of Titian is explained in front of an original; Alexander the Great is discussed almost in his home; Greece is given

70. *El Comercio,* Quito, May 6, 1944.
71. *Excelsior,* Mexico City, August 17, 1945.
72. *Op. cit.,* 41.
73. *O Globo,* Rio de Janeiro, July 8, 1944.

many immense rooms where one finds everything from authentic cos-
tume, arms, and sculptures up to reproductions of palaces in minia-
ture." But these museums were not only repositories of the dead past.
In a transportation display in the Museum of Science and Industry
in New York this Ecuadoran visitor saw not only "all the vehicles of
transportation . . . up to the most modern locomotive" but also "the
locomotive of the future, the city of the future, the airplane . . . of
the future." He even noted with interest that visitors could operate
the mechanical exhibits themselves.[74] These museums, "though founded and supported by wealthy people," commented a Brazilian visitor,
Dr. José Antonio do Prado Valladares, director of the Museum of
Bahía, "function and exist for the education of the public. Their
educational activity—guide service, free courses, lectures, temporary
exhibits, loans of material to schools, publications, etc.—is what jus-
tifies their enormous expense to the eyes of the public and their own
boards of trustees. . . . Signs, simple cards, engravings, designs, minia-
tures, pictures, transparencies, projections, loud speakers, and guides,
practically all methods of communications are utilized in an effort to
capture the interest of the average man." But all this educational
effort, he concluded, "does not hinder in any way the true scientific
work" of these institutions.[75]

Equally important with individualism in explaining the achievements of the people of the United States was the cooperation of citizens in society for both material production and social progress. Social
self-discipline was a marked characteristic of almost all citizens. Here
was a people, reported Washington Luis in *A Noite* of Rio de Janeiro
(September 19, 1947), who "collaborate by discussion and by expression of thought efficiently and effectively everywhere in their fundamental law, in the day-by-day laws, in the administrative decrees,
without doctrinaire preoccupations, guided by collective good sense
to a practical solution of their problems, sometimes arduous and delicate, with the objective of worthily establishing the tranquillity, security, and prosperity of all." Dante Costa, writing in *O Jornal* of Rio de
Janeiro (December 19, 1943), succinctly characterized the United
States as "a country of organization and cooperation." The people
whom the Argentine historian Enrique Gandía studied on his visit to
the United States in 1941 observed, as he later wrote, "an admirable
discipline in their daily lives. . . . If the life of that immense country

74. *El Comercio,* Quito, May 6, 1944.
75. *O Jornal,* Rio de Janeiro, October 4, 1944.

did not proceed with the regularity of a clock it would become an inferno."[76]

To some Latin American observers these social disciplines seemed stifling. Jorge Fernández concluded that "the North American is incredibly conscious of his duties and is oppressively disciplined. His field of action is almost cruelly limited to a narrow area, which is all the orbit that he knows, or that he has at his disposal, or that interests him or that he aspires to. It is his place in the shop, his duties in an office or store, services, professorship, route, technical ability. It is specialization to an unprecedented and exaggerated extreme. The complexity and the scope of life in North America, the harshness of work, indeed require this limitation, which, at the price of human personality, is transformed into collective comfort in the life of the country. . . . The North American" therefore had allowed himself to become only "a link in a chain which he accepts without complaints." By reason of this fact and of the "superficiality of his existence" he was unprotestingly badgered by propaganda "on the quality of a food, the advantages of a brand of clothing, spectacles, or any kind of necessity." As "the lowest organism in a human sea, an obscure screw in the phenomenal gears of his economy" and knowing "little of the world outside," he accepts such propaganda as "a kind of guide to knowledge."[77]

All this produced an "exaggerated standardization," according to the young Brazilian Arnaldo Leão Marques. "The average American," whom he found to be "very likeable, friendly, happy, industrious, and honest, . . . dedicates himself zealously to his profession or to his studies, and in his specialty is almost always a supreme authority of the greatest efficiency." The chief fruits of that "efficiency," he felt, which were worthy of admiration and emulation by Latin Americans, were the "numerous achievements in the fields of industrial progress and personal comforts among the masses." But these were accomplished at the expense of " 'charm' and erudition." This efficiency and this organization were harmful to the expression of human personality.[78] The editor of *El Tiempo* of Bogotá (May 10, 1944) also felt that the development of North American life "is producing a phenomenon of dehumanization which can be serious." As

76. *El Gigante del Norte: Una Visión de Estados Unidos* (Buenos Aires, 1942), 78.
77. *El Comercio,* Quito, May 4, 1944.
78. *A Manhã,* Rio de Janeiro, January 28, 1944.

evidence of the uniformity or conformity of North American individuals to type, the Argentine visitor Nicolás Repetto noted the similarities in dress. "In the restaurants and cafeterias," he observed, "all appeared to have the same tastes, to enjoy the same dishes, and to pay the same prices."[79] Other evidence could be found in North American journalism, which, reported a young Guatemalan journalist, Pedro Julio García, who visited the United States under a university training program, showed "a marked tendency toward standardization."[80]

This mode of life made a painful impression upon many Latin Americans. Looked at from their point of view, the people of the United States, observed Benjamín Subercaseaux, "appear to have renounced an immense amount of the pure animal enjoyment which primitive man possessed and which we [Latin Americans] would not renounce for any price. They do not regret this renunciation because they have been born into a society of self-controlled people. But when we go to live in North America," Subercaseaux added, "we feel that life has lost all its attraction and that as each new morning dawns it lacks the hope and stimulus which we need to live out the day. We feel like a Polynesian on whom a missionary has just placed a shirt."[81] To the Latin American, then, life in the United States was an oppressively strait-jacketed mode of living.

The tendency of the North Americans to live by fixed habits, to follow routine procedures even under harrowing and abnormal conditions, was most astonishing to Latin Americans when displayed in politics. Even under the hardships and uncertainties of war, for example, they followed their customary electoral procedures. In the Congressional and state elections of November, 1942, *La Nación* of Buenos Aires (November 5, 1942) was impressed that "the nation conducted itself both during the pre-election campaign and in the election with the normal civic attitude of a democracy which allows no extraneous matter to alter or modify the habitual system which governs its life. . . . The war did not introduce any change in party methods nor abridge the prerogatives of citizens nor diminish the liberties which they enjoy." In this and other wartime elections they displayed a moderation and lack of impulsiveness which seemed noteworthy to

79. *Op. cit.,* II.
80. *Nuestro Diario,* Guatemala City, March 7, 1945.
81. "Así Son Los Norteamericanos," *Continente,* Quito, II, 7 (April 1, 1944), 9-22.

visitors of Latin temperament. The excitement attending the presidential elections of 1944 agitated Erico Verissimo to such an extent that he "became alarmed at the liberty with which the opposition criticized President Roosevelt." But "after the results were announced, nobody discussed the matter any longer. The President, democratically elected, had the support of the whole country, including that of his opponent."[82]

Latin Americans did not fail to notice the stoical and self-sacrificing element in the cooperative effort of North Americans, particularly during the war. At Walter Reed Hospital in Washington, Jorge Fernández, who "was horrified by the spectacle of scores of ex-combatants whose hands had been mutilated," said to a nurse that her work must be horrible. "No," she replied simply, "I like to help the boys learn to manipulate their new hands. That is my contribution."[83] But this rigid sense of social discipline was not regimentation. Latin Americans observed that "outside the shop or the factory the boss and the employee are citizens with equal rights" and that the North American soldier, though "subordinate and proudly respectful toward his superior," nevertheless, "in his free hours, outside the army camp, . . . follows his habits as an American citizen."[84] *La Nación* of Buenos Aires (November 5, 1942) noted that President Roosevelt's call for the election of a Democratic governor in New York State did not result in his election. In the United States, it observed, "the well known 'hint' is not sufficient to swing the elections in favor of one person, nor is the open blessing of even the first magistrate effective in assuring him victory. . . . The people act freely without restraints, without fear." After the election each citizen "returns to his patriotic duties, to unanimous cooperation, and to watching over the common interests of the nation." As evidence of the democracy of the Yankees, José Vasconcelos told a Mexico City audience in August, 1945, that whenever United States troops landed on a Pacific isle they would immediately call the tribe together to elect a chieftain by honest ballot![85]

Had the United States then finally ended the age-old search of mankind for the proper relationship between the individual and society? Luis Alberto Sánchez reached the equivocal conclusion that

82. *O Jornal,* Rio de Janeiro, October 6, 1945.
83. *El Comercio,* Quito, May 5, 1944.
84. Lecture given by Lt. Col. Guillermo López L., *cit. sup.*
85. *Excelsior,* Mexico City, August 17, 1945.

"if anyone in the world has the habit of collective living it is the American citizen; and at the same time if anyone has developed individualism to the utmost it is also he."[86] The Panama *Star and Herald* (May 27, 1945), however, was certain that in the United States the individual was supreme "with the government acting only as a loyal and faithful servant. . . . Under the American way of life, the people, the masses, the majority of an enlightened population that strives to spread enlightenment among all its components are the sovereign over whom stands only God, the Creator." Was it conceivable that such a government could come to dominate the life of its citizens? And yet under President Franklin Roosevelt, it seemed to the Brazilian writer José María Belo, the government, which had formerly been only "a distant shadow" to the individual citizens and had remained so "even when the frontiers were closed and the juridical predominance of the Union was established," was assuming an unprecedented "moral authority."[87] As a result, said José Vasconcelos, "One of the great problems of this people is to decide what is the limit of the liberty of the citizen and at what point the state ought to intervene in the collective life."[88] This seemed to be still unsolved even in the United States.

* * *

Despite evidences of harmony and cooperation, "There are," declared Dante Costa in *O Jornal* of Rio de Janeiro (December 19, 1943), "many imperfections in the United States, fortunately for the North Americans, who therefore have more opportunity for individual and collective improvement." That country, it seemed to *El Liberal Progresista* of Guatemala City (April 17, 1942), fell short of being "a new Utopia, because, as happens in these enormous human communities, misery makes a black and dirty border on the magnificent cloak of riches, and alongside Ford and Rockefeller some millions of unemployed stand idle." President Roosevelt, "having the broad vision of a statesman and a saint," had sought through the New Deal "to remedy in part this social cancer . . . and to give the opportunities of life to the majority of his fellow citizens." But this attempt "to check the monopolies of capitalism" had been interrupted by the involvement of the United States in World War II. The basic problems of poverty

86. *Op. cit.,* 177.
87. Lecture, "The United States and Brazil," September 16, 1939, *cit. sup.*
88. *Excelsior,* Mexico City, August 17, 1945.

and riches, of overwork and unemployment still persisted. *Crisol* of Buenos Aires (December 5, 1941), a tabloid of between 5,000 and 10,000 circulation which was outspokenly critical of the "Yanquis" and which was placed on the Proclaimed List in 1943 as Axis-subsidized, noted that in the United States there were people "who cannot satisfy their hunger and whose houses do not have roofs to keep out the rain," that "92,000 draftees have been rejected for illiteracy," and that "this nation can only be famous for its 'clay eaters,' that is eaters of the soil."

As a "melting pot of races" the United States was especially interesting to Latin Americans. The "North American man," noted Jorge Fernández, "is a combination of many peoples and races who slowly amalgamated themselves." Unassimilated immigrant groups still persisted. "The Polish quarters in Chicago, Harlem, the Latin, Italian, and other quarters in New York are groups where foreign languages are spoken and where their birthplaces, slightly modified, have been transplanted." But out of these various nationalities a new nationality was still being forged. "The country has a personality so powerful that it absorbs the personality and nationality of the immigrant. The rhythm of life and of work in North America imposes its enveloping and overwhelming psychology upon whoever arrives there for a simple visit, even upon one who secludes himself in the 'quarters.' . . . The North American imposes himself inflexibly upon his world and can only see it reflected in that of others." In this way, wrote Fernández, the United States "has absorbed the experiences of all the nationalities of the world and has transformed the condition of all the immigrants, giving a new rhythm to its customs and systems."[89] It had worked "stubbornly," generalized Nicolás Repetto, to form "a strong national sentiment," utilizing for this purpose "the school and the almost mystical cult of the founding fathers."[90]

But of all the "black and dirty" spots on the "magnificent cloak" of the United States, the most puzzling and at the same time the most serious, judged both by the attention which Latin Americans gave to it and by the comments which they made about it, seemed to be the relationship between the white and the colored races. The North American, Manuel Ugarte had noted in 1900, "like the Romans in their palmy days, has as his auxiliaries and servants the subject races,— Indians, Chinese, Africans,—who gather up the crumbs of the feast."

89. *El Comercio,* Quito, May 4 and 6, 1944.
90. *Op. cit.,* VI.

In particular the treatment of the Negro, who was "excluded from the universities, hotels, cafés, theaters, and tramways" and who "only seemed to be in his right place when in the name of lynch law he was dragged through the streets by the crowd," seemed to Ugarte to belie "the sincerity of the principles" of "this equalitarian republic."[91] "Lynch Justice," as *Crítica* of Buenos Aires (June 23 and August 8, 1930) called it, continued to be an object of both derision and apprehension in Latin America.

This situation became a liability to the United States in Latin America after the outbreak of World War II. When the ambassador of the United States to Mexico delivered an address in that country in July, 1939, denouncing the "blinding winds of racial prejudice" which were bringing tragedy to Jews in Germany, *Universal Gráfico* of Mexico City (July 6, 1939) pointed out that "in the United States itself the tradition with respect to the people of color is humiliating. . . . On the day when Mexican children are not discriminated against in the schools of the American region where their fathers work, we shall subscribe with the greatest satisfaction to the emphatic statements against all racial prejudice." Another Mexican newspaper, *El Mexicano* of Ciudad Juárez (April 22 and 29, 1941), explained that in the "southern states of our neighboring country numerous Mexicans and descendants of Mexicans" were denied "various rights in violation of the most elementary human principles," such as "service in barber shops," entrance to "pools and recreation centers," and "admission to restaurants." This practice, it pointed out, was based upon the same "theory of supposed racial superiorities in which totalitarianism pretends to find its right to enslave the world" but was inconsistent "with the new spirit of the Good Neighbor Policy and with the doctrine of continental solidarity."

After the United States went to war some Latin Americans, Mexicans especially, became extraordinarily sensitive to racial discrimination there. José C. Valadés reported in 1942 that while living in California he observed that "some of the most worthy members of the Mexican clergy . . . were not able to officiate at services because the North American Catholic clergy kept them isolated from the faithful and brought them into contempt—all because they were Mexicans."[92] The

91. *The Destiny of a Continent,* 12-16.
92. Article syndicated by ANTA, Mexican news agency, in November, 1942, published in *Hoy,* Mexico City, November 7, 1942, *Acción,* Nogales, Sonora, November 12, 1942, and other Mexican journals.

conservative Roman Catholic *Novedades* of Mexico City (November 28, 1944) alleged that "in Texas . . . in certain Catholic (?) churches 'for whites' baptism is denied to Mexican children." The incident of the "Blue Moon Café" in September, 1943, in which several Texans of Latin American blood, accompanied by the Mexican consul in Houston, were refused service at an eating place in New Gulf, Wharton County, Texas, and were told they would be served in the kitchen, was made the subject of direct protest in an open letter to Governor Coke R. Stevenson of Texas by a labor leader of Ciudad Juárez.[93] An eighteen-year old señorita, Monica Padilla Franco, who belonged to "metropolitan society" in Mexico City, was similarly outraged to discover, after a pleasure trip by air to the United States with her father, that it was necessary "for Mexicans and other 'inferior' races to know what places have been assigned to them by the Yankees so that they may avoid the humiliation of being thrown out into the streets." She told a reporter of *Novedades* (March 27, 1945): "Previously I believed idealistically in democracy; the people in whom I had the most confidence have disillusioned me with their absurd practices." This was the same "prejudice of racial superiority," commented *Novedades* (November 28, 1944), "which is exacting such a high price from the country of Hitler or of Himmler."

In at least partial extenuation, Jorge Fernández pointed out that Latin Americans often assumed an attitude "of miserable humility and humiliation before the richness and power" of the United States. As migrants to that country, he explained, they generally play "an ignoble role. . . . They yield themselves to the low tasks; they are swindlers, gamblers, bohemians of the worst sort, burlesque dancers, and prostitutes." These acts of self-abasement did not appeal to "the North American . . . precisely because he possesses a high concept of human personality."[94] But Latin Americans were more inclined to attribute the racial practices of the North Americans to what *Hoy* of Mexico City (November 11, 1944) called a "most absurd racial concept" held by persons of "a stubborn and truly reactionary spirit." By reason of this concept, it complained, "the situation of Mexicans in Texas," many of whom were "aiding the industry and the general economy of that North American state" in the war, was rendered difficult. According to *Novedades* (September 8, 1944) the lower wage scale of Mexican workers in the United States, as compared

93. *El Continental,* El Paso, Texas, September 24, 1943.
94. *El Comercio,* Quito, May 4 and 6, 1944.

with that of North American workers, was due to the practice of racial discrimination there. In Panama the lower wages and other limitations imposed upon the "silver roll" employees in the Canal Zone were attributed to the same cause.[95]

For all this, which was not only odious to many Latin Americans but also patently inconsistent with the principles professed by the United States, the pattern, in their opinion, was set by the treatment of the Negro. Raymundo Magalhães Júnior, who spent several war years in the United States, reported in *A Noite* of Rio de Janeiro (April 5, 1944) that in the southern states "Negroes do not have the same civic rights as the whites. They suffer restrictions on the right to vote. They cannot buy lands freely, and they have to live in the permanent condition of serfs, tilling the soil and sharing the product of their work with the white parasite, possessor of feudal rights." On the trains he found "cars for the Negroes set apart," and he heard of cases of the "primitive processes" of lynching. Even in the army, he explained, Negro "battalions and regiments lead a life isolated from the white barracks." Rómulo Betancourt wrote in *El País* of Caracas (April 12, 1944) after his visit to the United States that in Miami "Negroes are forbidden to be out in the streets after a fixed hour. . . . After curfew they have to keep to a restricted district, with exact boundaries, a sort of medieval ghetto except that it does not have heavy iron chains separating the racial lepers from the arrogance of the whites." He was particularly shocked to discover that a bus on which he traveled from Washington into Virginia stopped after it had "passed a large bridge across the Potomac . . . so that the passengers could execute a strange regrouping. The colored passengers moved to the rear of the bus" because "police regulations in Virginia prohibited colored persons from sharing public places with members of the privileged white race." The effect upon Betancourt was to produce "a mixture of surprise and anger at the stupidity of it all." Racial segregation was even required at a concert given by the Negro singer Marian Anderson in the gymnasium at the University of Texas, reported a young Guatemalan journalist. But her miraculous singing, he noted, brought the white audience to its feet in fanatical applause while the Negro listeners, forced to sit in the balcony, gloated over the triumph of their race in rapt and solemn silence.[96]

Raymundo Magalhães observed that racial prejudice was a prob-

95. *La Opinión*, Panama, June 13, 1945.
96. Pedro Julio García, *Nuestro Diario*, Guatemala City, April 3, 1945.

lem also in the northern states of the Union. In those states, he pointed out, "certain shipyards and war plants" did "not admit Negro workers in spite of the great scarcity of labor."[97] Another visitor from a country proud of its racial amalgam, the Brazilian Atys Quadros da Silva, who served for two years as an interne at the Ball Memorial Hospital in Muncie, Indiana, noted that the "shameful aspect of racial relations" was not limited to the South. Even in two of the best theaters in Muncie, he declared, "Negroes are not seated. . . . There are primary schools for Negroes and primary schools for whites. They are not mixed." In many other northern states, he reported, racial segregation was practiced in the primary schools. From his survey of racial conditions among the North Americans, he told his fellow Brazilians that "we are at least better civilized than they in many respects."[98] Dr. Tavares de Sá was impressed that during his few hours in Detroit early in the war "all the outstanding citizens" with whom he talked discussed the Negro problem "at length and with much pessimism." Noting that "in certain regions the racial tension is so extreme that it produces an almost tangible conscience about it," he concluded that it constituted "the most acute and difficult of all the domestic problems" still remaining to be solved in the United States.[99]

Altogether the reaction of Latin Americans to this racial tension among North Americans was unfavorable. According to Betancourt, who was to become president of Venezuela after the war, this practice revealed "implications of totalitarian viciousness, of unconscious Nazi tendencies in some of the American people." He explained pointedly that Indo-Hispanic America "is composed in good part of people who have Negroid blood coursing through their veins. . . . The immense majority of the men and women of the mestizo continent, from the Rio Grande to the Straits of Magellan, are proud of their copper, brown, or definitely black skin." In this problem, he concluded, was found a serious deterrent to "a sincere understanding between the two Americas."[100] During the war pro-Axis newspapers, for example *Cabildo* of Buenos Aires, seldom overlooked an opportunity to deride, if not to exaggerate, "the forced political ostracism in which the col-

97. *A Noite*, Rio de Janeiro, April 5, 1944.
98. *O Dia*, Curitiba, reported in Despatch 81, São Paulo, March 15, 1949, Department of State Archives.
99. *Jornal do Brasil*, Rio de Janeiro, December 19, 1943.
100. *El País*, Caracas, August 7, 1945.

ored population is held" in the United States.[101] To those who supported the war effort of the United States the solution of this problem
seemed particularly urgent. "It is," said Quadros da Silva, "a terrible
blot on their civilization, a blot which it is necessary for them to remove as soon as possible."[102]

The agreements under which Mexican laborers were brought into
the United States, negotiated with the Mexican government by the
Farm Security Administration and the War Manpower Commission
in Washington in 1942 and thereafter, provided that there should be
no racial discrimination.[103] Scrupulous efforts were made to enforce
this provision. In the midst of the disturbing instances of racial
antagonism the legislature of Texas passed and Governor Stevenson
promulgated a resolution condemning any discrimination against
members of the Caucasian race, which of course included most Latin
Americans, as violating the Good Neighbor Policy.[104] But the relations
between the United States and its dark-skinned southern neighbors
continued to be troubled by the racial question. In the light of the
idealistic wartime propaganda the usual border incidents which were
provoked by it assumed an unusual importance.

* * *

Did all these traits, customs, manners, and attitudes of the people
of the United States add up to something that was a new and distinctive civilization? Was there such a thing as a Yankee culture? Latin
Americans asked. If so, what might be its significance for the future
of both the Americas?

101. Despatch 7276, Buenos Aires, November 9, 1942, Department of State
Archives.
102. *O Dia, cit. sup.* See also Arturo Aldunate Phillips, *op. cit.,* 79.
103. *Department of State Bulletin,* VII (August 8, 1942), 689-690; VIII
(May 1, 1943), 376-377; and Department of State, *Executive Agreement
Series 278,* "Temporary Migration of Mexican Agricultural Workers: Agree-
ment between the United States of America and Mexico Effected by Exchange
of Notes Signed August 4, 1942"; *Executive Agreement Series 351,* "Temporary
Migration of Mexican Agricultural Workers: Agreement between the United
States of America and Mexico Revising the Agreement of August 4, 1942,
Effected by Exchange of Notes Signed at Mexico City, April 26, 1943"; and
Executive Agreement Series 376, "Recruiting of Mexican Non-Agricultural
Workers: Agreement between the United States of America and Mexico
Effected by Exchange of Notes Signed at Mexico City April 29, 1943, Effec-
tive April 29, 1943."
104. Legislature of Texas, House Concurrent Resolution 105, Regular Ses-
sion, 48th Legislature, 1943, approved May 6, 1943.

Among Americans to the south the notion was widespread that they excelled in culture and things of the spirit whereas the United States was superior only in material accomplishments. To them the mad rush of the New Yorkers, for example, betokened an obsessive preoccupation with physical things. "The people in New York rush along the streets in such haste," reported the Peruvian political leader and journalist Manuel Seoane, after a visit there in 1943, "that many times at first I ran after them, thinking that some exciting event had occurred, which, being a newspaperman, I did not want to miss. After I found out that they were just rushing into some office building, store, or subway station, I relaxed and began to enjoy myself."[105] Their concept of time seemed to allow no place for the contemplative values so highly esteemed by Latin Americans. It seemed to be dictated by their concern with busywork and production—always more and more production, without much thought of its end-use or social utility.

The power of the North Americans, then, seemed to be economic and political, not intellectual or cultural. Their goal was physical comfort, not spiritual well-being. José María Belo told a Brazilian audience in 1939 that the United States was a "business civilization which is alike the glory and the torment of the powerful democracy."[106] This material superiority did not entitle the United States to claim excellence in everything. The bitterly hostile tabloid *Crisol* of Buenos Aires (December 5, 1941) ridiculed the supposition that, because the United States "is . . . the best nourished, the most radio-advertised, the most mechanized nation in the world," it "is therefore the most moral, the most intelligent, the strongest, the most civilized, the happiest in the world." Roberto García Peña of *El Tiempo* of Bogotá (May 10, 1944) alluded to the common belief "in certain intellectual circles of Latin America . . . that the North American is an individual unaccustomed to intellectual discipline, disinterested in matters pertaining to the spirit, enfolded in his pragmatism, without 'wings on his soul,' to use the expression of the French philosopher."

García Peña hastened to repudiate this belief as "ingenuous," "erroneous," "absurd." The North American people, he said, "not only are creating a civilization in terms of progress in science for the service of man but are also at the same time creating a culture." Their art, stimulated by foreign influences, was becoming increasingly

105. "Impressions of a Roving Peruvian," *Tomorrow* (New York), II (March, 1943), 29-30.
106. Lecture, "The United States and Brazil," September 16, 1939, *cit. sup.*

creative, and their advances in science, particularly medical science, seemed to him phenomenal.[107] Erico Verissimo considered it "an error to think that the United States are a people who do not have an art and a literature of real importance."[108] To *Le Soir* of Port-au-Prince (July 4, 1949) "American civilization" appeared to be "a combination of spiritual forces which maintain their strength not-withstanding the materialistic currents which necessarily must flow through a nation of 150,000,000 inhabitants." A Paraguayan musi-cian and author, Señora Haydee de Castaing, writing in *La Unión* of Asunción (March 4, 1949), also argued that the people of the United States had a perfect understanding of the close interdepen-dence of the material and the spiritual. Their "practical monism" had enabled them to achieve a true union of the two and thus to make immense progress not only in the economic and commercial fields but also in the realm of culture, science, and art. They had achieved, said *Correio da Manhã* of Rio de Janeiro (May 11, 1947), "a nice balance between their unequaled idealism and their unequaled zeal for material things." Luis Quintanilla called the notion that "all spiritual culture belongs to Latin America and all material civili-zation to the United States" a "continental prejudice" which had been "more deterimental to mutual understanding in the Americas" than anything else.[109]

The subordination of materialism to idealism in the war effort of the people of the United States tended to demonstrate convincingly to Latin Americans the fallacy of this conventional belief and to dispel Latin American notions about their "decadent democracy" and their "worship of the almighty dollar." As they watched the North Ameri-cans living through those difficult times they acquired a new respect for them, not only because of their material power but also because of their self-denials and their devotion to high moral purpose. But after the war could the United States remain loyal to its innate prin-ciples which had given it moral pre-eminence in the war against the Axis powers or would it again succumb to the forces of materialism? That question remained unanswered.

The characteristic of the United States which perhaps most im-pressed Latin Americans was that it was not a finished civilization. Here was a people, declared an editorial in *El Centroamérica* of San

107. *El Tiempo*, Bogotá, May 10, 1944.
108. *O Jornal*, Rio de Janeiro, October 6, 1945.
109. *Op. cit.*, 43.

Salvador (November 9, 1940), "full of virtues—as are all the peoples of the world—and a people full of possibilities—as is no other people in the world." To José C. Valadés, who was soon to become private secretary to Mexican Foreign Minister Ezequiel Padilla, the North Americans seemed "a people who were working tirelessly, as no other people in the world, to create tradition and culture."[110] Andrés Eloy Blanco also found "among these people an ambition to make the United States a great nation not so much in its military power as in its social and cultural progress."[111] Nicolás Repetto gained the "impression that the North Americans already possess an admirable technical-mechanical culture and that they are gathering together, by patient and well-conceived methods, the requisite elements of a new spiritual culture based on human solidarity and showing a social consciousness."[112] The United States was to Jorge Fernández "still in process of becoming." As it seemed to him, "All the elements of its civilization are fresh, recent, as young as the spirit of its people; its tradition does not go back for centuries, and it has a capacity for ridding itself of the past which enables it to continue in a state of constant renewal."

According to Fernández, "the North American likes tradition precisely because he does not possess it as profoundly as the Spaniard, the Englishman, the Italian." But he "loves the past not as past but only as it serves the future," for "this North American civilization has not yet run its full course." It seemed to him to be dissatisfied with its own achievements. "The North American . . . is always seeking a new formula, a new system of gears (they have already made a square wheel for gears), of pulleys, of resistances, of contacts, of movement in general. . . . He does not really believe in what he has already done but believes only in what he expects to do." These people are constantly "prying into the future." By reason of this "restlessness" their life "is always one step ahead of today." Already, Fernández wrote, this nation "has attained its stage of gigantism, of immensity, and already is raising to the skies its monuments of steel and electricity dedicated to the living, in order to make man live. It is now in the process of surpassing this stage of gigantism, which affords only an infantile pleasure. . . . In material arrangements it

---

110. Article syndicated by Mexican news agency ANTA, in November, 1942, *cit. sup.*
111. *El Nacional*, Caracas, January 30, 1944.
112. *Op. cit.*, IX.

has made everything the greatest, the strongest, and the grandest that the world has ever seen." The United States, he wrote in the spring of 1944, "can now write the second chapter of culture—spiritual refinement," can "finish the two chapters which Egypt and Greece wrote."[113]

World War II, then, was only an unpleasant interruption to this people, a "warlike parenthesis" in their national career, as a Venezuelan visitor characterized it.[114] Their main preoccupation was silently to work for its speedy and victorious termination, and their persistent hope was that this tragedy overseas might not work permanent injury to their nation. The Chilean Oscar Gajardo cited the titles of books which he saw flowing from the printing presses when he visited the United States in mid-1945: "We Are Going to Have a Farm," "We Are Going to Have a Small Mill," "We Are Going to Have a Store," "We Are Going to Have a Dyeshop," and "We Are Going to Organize a Company."[115] The United States had not known the real harassment of war. It had no bombed-out cities. War's devastation had passed it by. It was still a young and buoyant nation which, as Jorge Fernández observed, "knows neither great sorrows nor great tragedies." So complete was the sense of transitoriness of this war experience that, as it seemed to Fernández, "The worker, the employee, the engineer, the producer, the businessman—all of them without exception are thinking of their projects 'after the war.' . . . 'After the war' new buildings will be built, factories will be enlarged, new machines, airplanes, motors will be constructed; they will travel, they will buy and sell, they will live." The North Americans were filled with dreams of "the future which they see coming. . . . They await their opportunity to transform their lives, to better them, to conquer, which, from their point of view means to get more money. They are a people who have learned to hope."[116]

113. *El Comercio,* Quito, May 6, 1944. For similar views see article by Pedro Julio García in *Nuestro Diario,* Guatemala City, March 4, 1945.
114. D. Esteban Chalbaud Cardona, "Viaje al País de la Civilización y de la Justicia," *Revista Militar* (La Paz, Bolivia, September-October, 1945), 776.
115. Address before the Council of the Chilean Corporation for Promotion of Production (Fomento) on August 22, 1945, reported in *El Mercurio,* Santiago, August 23, 1945.
116. *El Comercio,* Quito, May 4, 1944.

Chapter 6

WEAKENING PARTNERSHIP

I have the firmest conviction that the worst evils that can befall the United States will be engendered in Latin America and that without Latin America the United States will not have even the minimum that it needs for its own happiness.
—Daniel Cosío Villegas

*A*T Roosevelt's death the United States, whose armies were sweeping on to victory in the war, was regarded in Latin America as pre-eminently a nation of idealism and altruism. "That people," declared *El Panamá-América* (May 21, 1945), "which was considered without ideals is sacrificing itself for the noblest ideal. . . . The United States represents today the knights of the ideal, the Quixotes of the contemporary era. The Knight of all knights has transferred himself from La Mancha to North America. He has carried his lance and shield; and he has placed them in the service of the ideals of humanity: the service of liberty, of justice and of the dignity of man." To another Panamanian newspaper, *La Estrella de Panamá* (July 4, 1945), it seemed that the recent history of the United States had been so full of examples of altruism as to compensate entirely for any errors it had committed in the past. This country, it pointed out, was even suffering privations for the sole purpose of feeding Hitler's victims.[1] Its attitude, said *El País* of Asunción (October 31, 1945), was one "of pure disinterestedness, at the service of the extension of liberty." To *Jornal do Brasil* of Rio de Janeiro (November 25, 1945) the United States seemed "the champion of the highest ideals and noblest causes."

1. Panama *Star and Herald,* July 18, 1945; and *La Estrella de Panamá,* March 31 and April 1, 1946.

188

As the war drew to a close, there was ample evidence that the stupendous material superiority of the United States would enable it to assume a position of leadership in the postwar world. A Colombian representative to the San Francisco Conference of the United Nations, Dr. Eduardo Zuleta Angel, told a reporter of *El Liberal* of Bogotá (September 5, 1945) that "it is necessary to go back to the era of the greatness of the Roman Empire to find an example of power and of decisive influence in the destinies of the world equal to that presented today by the United States of America." In that country, Jorge Fernández told his fellow Ecuadorans, "the economic power of the nation is felt in the atmosphere, it is seen on the sidewalks of the streets, in the faces of men."[2] The Brazilian visitor Atys Quadros da Silva also observed throughout his stay in the United States that "the Americans consider their nation the most powerful and the most civilized on the earth. No one can escape this omnipresence of greatness."[3]

Latin Americans saw much evidence that the United States would not abuse its power in the postwar era. Its immediate reconversion to peacetime civilian life was convincing proof that it neither nourished ulterior plans of conquest nor expected to be made the object of attack. "As soon as the surrender of Japan was announced by President Truman," reported Dr. Zuleta Angel, "the government began to abolish controls, to liquidate war agencies, to organize civilian production, to stop rationing, to study reduction of taxes, and, in short, to return to normality. . . . When the surrender of Japan was signed on board the 'Missouri,' the United States had already commenced to manufacture automobiles, machinery of all kinds, civilian airplanes, and even nylon hose."[4] Latin Americans deemed it noteworthy that this transition from a state of war to a state of peace was accomplished quickly and without revolutionary dislocations. With the work week now set at "only five days of eight hours per day," reported a correspondent of *El Diario de Hoy* of San Salvador (October 8, 1945), "there is work for everyone, and the United States continues to be an emporium of wealth and a favorable place for the development of all constructive activities."[5] This successful reconversion demonstrated to *Novedades* of Mexico City (November 7, 1945) that "the United

2. *El Comercio,* Quito, May 4, 1944.
3. *O Dia,* Curitiba, reported in Despatch 81, São Paulo, March 15, 1945, Department of State Archives.
4. *El Liberal,* Bogotá, September 5, 1945.
5. Marco Tulio Canjura, writing from San Francisco.

States have achieved the working together of management and labor for the good of their country."

Even more significant in disproving charges of "American imperialism" was the "lightning demobilization" of the armed services, as *A Noite* of Rio de Janeiro (February 6, 1945) called it. That newspaper exclaimed almost incredulously: "The richest country in the world, one of the principal winners of the war, the nation whose interests spread all over the globe—disarmed!" To *La Nación* of San José, Costa Rica (October 25, 1946), this demobilization made clear that "the North American people . . . are essentially peaceful. . . . The American believes that the charms of 'sweet home' are sweeter than the most brilliant cavalry charge. . . . The horse racer in Kentucky, the fruit picker in California, the cotton planter in Georgia, the Mississippi River boatman or the automobile builder in Detroit feel happy in a world of peace and of labor which permits them to live comfortably, to dance nightly if they wish, to engage in sports when they please, to go to church on Sundays, to turn on their radio quietly in the home, to travel at times from coast to coast in their country, to drive their car over the highways, to fish or to hunt, to drink a whisky with a friend, to chat, to go to baseball or the ringside to see world championships, and to vote each four years to elect a President of the United States." These people, it concluded, "are not primarily interested in going out to kill other men or to expose themselves to death."

This peace-loving attitude was particularly noted in the reaction of the United States to its victory in the war. *La Estrella de Panamá* (July 4, 1946) rejoiced that the United States was determined "not to add a single inch of territory to her possessions, nor to establish a 'single sphere of influence,' nor to interfere in the political desires of the freed nations." President Enrique Jiménez of that country told a banquet audience in Colón on July 3, 1946, that "the fact that the United States is not exploiting its victory on the battlefields to oppress other peoples or to gain new territories, but, on the contrary, is granting independence to its richest overseas possession [the Philippines] underlines the sincerity and the loyalty of the American people to the democratic principles of their way of life."[6] *El Tiempo* of Bogotá (July 4, 1945) pointed out as the war ended that the United States had not shown "an exorbitant appetite for conquest" and that its victorious generals had not let "the glory of victory turn their pure demo-

6. *La Estrella de Panamá,* July 4, 1946.

cratic conscience into conceit."[7] Its voluntary withdrawals from its
naval and military bases in Latin America also made a favorable impression. By this action, said *La Opinión* of Valparaíso, Chile (December 28, 1947), "the United States has set a high and edifying
example of respect for the sovereignty of nations."[8] All these evidences of the self-restraint and anti-imperialism of the United States
were heartening to Latin Americans.

From the character of Harry Truman, Roosevelt's successor in the
White House, Latin Americans also took heart. According to *Jornal
do Comércio* of Rio de Janeiro (April 18, 1945) this "simple, unpre-
tentious personality who has just assumed the leadership of his nation
was full of faith in his efforts to respond worthily to the imperative
needs of so heavy and glorious a heritage as the government of Roosevelt." President Truman was characterized in *A Noite* of that
capital (December 18, 1945) by Miss Fernanda Reis, a Portuguese
reporter who had just returned from a visit to the United States, as "a
democrat clear down to the roots of his hair." She added that "as a
politician he impressed me as a profoundly honest man, anxious to
do right." *La Tribuna* of San Salvador (April 20, 1945) was confident that "he will know how to put his brain, his heart, and his
strength to the service of the great cause for which . . . Franklin
Delano Roosevelt gave his life."[9]

Latin Americans were favorably impressed by Truman's first
policy declarations. His statement to Congress on April 16, 1945, that
"the responsibility of the great state is to serve and not to dominate
the peoples of the world" was applauded by *El Universo,* Ecuador's
largest newspaper (April 18, 1945), as agreeing "exactly with the
course which President Roosevelt followed and which was summarized in the word 'cooperation.' " *La Nación* of Santiago, Chile (April
17, 1945), felt that his declarations "are inspired by the very policy of
the great Roosevelt and are the best guaranty that the spirit of the
first fighter for civilization will continue to preside over the destinies

7. See also José Vasconcelos in *Novedades,* Mexico City, June 20, 1946; *La
Esfera,* Caracas, July 4, 1946; and column by "Caliban" (Enrique Santos) in
El Tiempo, Bogotá, October 1, 1947.
8. Editorials of the same tenor were published in *La Patria,* Quito, July
3, 1946; *Diário Trabalhista,* Rio de Janeiro, October 5, 1946; *El Callao,*
Lima, October 29, 1946; and *El Tiempo,* Bogotá, December 27, 1947.
9. See also editorials in *La Hora,* Santiago, April 17, 1945; *El Diario Ilustrado,* Santiago, April 18, 1945; *El Colombiano,* Medellín, Colombia, July 16,
1945; and articles by Mario Valdettaro Nosiglia in *La Crónica,* Lima, June 15,
1945, and J. M. Pérez in *La Esfera,* Caracas, October 3, 1945.

of the world." Truman's statement in his Navy Day address at New York in October, 1945, that his government did not seek "one inch of territory" or any "selfish advantage" was lauded by Latin Americans as evidence that the United States would respect the territorial integrity of their nations. His emphasis upon the service responsibilities of the great powers toward small nations, coupled with his reaffirmation of the Good Neighbor Policy, meant to *El País* of Asunción (October 31, 1945) that "humanity can expect much from this people whose power is unconditionally placed at the service of right."

Moreover, the veneration in which Roosevelt's memory continued to be held in Latin America was an auspicious factor in the postwar relationship between Americans North and South. After his death he was honored throughout Latin America on many anniversaries of his birth and death and on many national holidays. "Promulgator of the Good Neighbor Policy," wrote *La Tribuna* of Asunción (April 12, 1946) on the first anniversary of Roosevelt's death, "he really found the true road to American brotherhood. . . . The Pan-Americanism of Roosevelt is not that of the United States alone but of all the continent; a Pan-Americanism made up of democracy and progressive impulse." Three years later, on another anniversary of his death, *Relator* of Cali, Colombia (April 12, 1949), hailed him as one who, "especially for the New World, was a new discoverer, a new Columbus." Roosevelt, declared *El País* of Montevideo (April 12, 1949) on the same occasion, "created a consciousness of inter-American solidarity and friendship, and the force of that idea will prevail over all contrary maneuvers." In him inter-American fraternity still had a champion.

* * *

The relationship that developed between the United States and most of the Latin American nations after Pearl Harbor, it must be repeated, was quite different from the previous relationship between good neighbors. The natural fruit of the prewar Good Neighbor Policy was hemispheric isolationism. The Roosevelt administration, as long as it pursued that objective, received the virtually unanimous cooperation of the Latin American governments and their peoples. But under the alarms and stresses of World War II the Good Neighbor Policy underwent an almost imperceptible change. When the

United States and its Latin American neighbors, living at peace in their adjoining nations, decided to embark upon a partnership venture in 1940, the feeling gradually developed that the United States should take a position on every problem that arose, that it should support or refrain from supporting new Latin American governments, that it should endorse or refrain from endorsing all courses of action adopted in Latin America, and that it should aid or refrain from aiding the Latin American countries in solving their problems.

As an understandable natural result of the partner relationship created by the war, the nod of the United States came to mean much more than that of any other nation of the hemisphere. So far did this feeling go that the silence of the United States government or its official representatives in the face of actions or developments in Latin America was interpreted as acquiescence in them. By a curious semantics, nonaction was construed to be the same as action. If the ambassador of the United States in Argentina did not speak out against Perón's policies, he was presumed to be identifying himself with them. If the United States ambassador in Nicaragua absented himself from a reception given by the government, it was assumed that a revolution, of which he was cognizant, was being plotted against the government. To apply the term Good Neighbor Policy indiscriminately to the official attitudes of the United States toward Latin America after 1940 is to fail to recognize the subtle alteration that took place in that policy as a result of the felt need for hemispheric solidarity in the face of the Axis menace. The hemispheric unity that was created by the Good Neighbor Policy before the war ceased to exist during the war.

This wartime Good Neighbor Policy, or rather more accurately the Policy of Partnership, depended in part upon the economic power of the United States applied either in the form of aid or in the form of sanctions. When it involved economic aid it was a policy of dollar diplomacy. The difficulties in the way of a complete and effective Pan-Americanism arose, as *El Tiempo* of Bogotá (June 2, 1943) bluntly pointed out, from the basic disparities between "the great democracy of the north and each one of the other American democracies, . . . especially in economic matters." The United States became a generous neighbor, but also an inquisitive neighbor, a demanding neighbor. The favors which it dispensed were, like the apple of Eris, divisive. Paraguay objected that Bolivia was receiving from the United States a threateningly disproportionate amount of

Lend-Lease equipment. Chile protested that for the same reason Peru's military position was being improved over her own. Argentina developed a profound jealousy of Brazil by reason of the latter's military build-up by the United States. Mexico felt that the United States was trying to control its economy on the assumption that the Mexican government lacked the technical capacity and the honesty to allocate fairly the machinery, equipment, replacements, and raw materials sent by the Washington government for the production of strategic materials and the maintenance of the standard of living of the Mexican people.[10]

In this process the essential nonintervention element in the Good Neighbor Policy became weakened. The good neighbor does not pry into his neighbor's affairs nor instruct him as to how he shall behave himself in his own home. To him the principle that "a man's home is his castle" is an essential basis of good neighborliness. But the good partner, particularly if he is the senior partner, must concern himself with these matters. The junior partner's habits and modes of living, his ways of thinking, his character and reputation, the sickness of his children, the leaky roof over his home—all these become objects of understandable and often justifiable concern, which can easily slide into intervention by the senior partner in his affairs. Gift-giving is intolerable except among equals. "The more favors we receive from the Yankees, the less we like them," wrote Enrique Santos in 1945.[11] The distribution of largess by the United States through outright gifts, loans, and guaranteed prices on exportable crops tended to make the Latin Americans feel that Uncle Sam either was a "sucker" or nursed dark ulterior motives toward them. As the Brazilian proverb expresses it: *Esmola demais o santo desconfia* ('The saint distrusts the giving of too much alms in church).

Sometimes, Latin Americans felt, the senior partner acted like a rich uncle distributing his favors in a free, uncalculating, and often inefficient way. He acted as if there was nothing in Latin America that Uncle Sam's money could not buy. The United States was willing to buy from the Latin American peoples and to teach them, but not to learn from them. The sum total of United States policy toward them, it seemed, was that hemispheric security and good neighborliness could be attained if they would only supply the United States with strategic materials at its prices, would grant military bases to the United States, and would accept equipment, supplies, and mili-

10. *Hoy*, Mexico City, September 4, 1943.
11. *El Tiempo*, Bogotá, March 1, 1945.

tary instruction from the United States. On the other hand, when the United States threw its influence against those Latin American nations which were "contrary-minded," as for example Argentina and, for a time, Chile and Bolivia, the Good Neighbor Policy was transformed into a Bad Neighbor Policy. As Sumner Welles later wrote: "The Good Neighbor Policy had undergone a woeful transformation. It had become . . . overbearing. . . . The United States was beginning once more to show signs of an intention to use its overwhelming power to dictate to the people of a sovereign American state what they should and should not do about their internal concerns."[12] In the end it was the preponderating power of the United States, exerted on behalf of a mighty war effort, which caused the disintegration of Roosevelt's Good Neighbor Policy. The mere demonstration of that power was enough to weaken the doctrine of the equality and sovereignty of all the American nations which was the premise and basis of the Good Neighbor Policy. In undertaking to distribute rewards and punishments, the United States ceased to be a good neighbor.

It was perhaps natural that the friendly feelings of Latin Americans for the United States should deteriorate as they ceased to need its assistance against the threat of foreign aggression. Traditionally they had been united to Spain and Portugal by their colonial heritage, to France by strong cultural ties, to Germany by their scientific interests, to England by their commercial and financial relationships, but to the United States only by physical coexistence in a common hemisphere and the corollary need for a common security against threats from outside the hemisphere. Their common racial origins, their history and traditions as Spanish- and Portuguese-speaking peoples, predisposed them toward suspicion of the United States. Although they might consider the people of the United States to be, at least temporarily, "good neighbors," they regarded each other, despite occasional "family rows," as "brothers." The well-understood, if perhaps not always explicitly avowed, condition of their cooperation with the United States during World War II had been that the United States would, through its military action and leadership, safeguard the security of the hemisphere. In retrospect it can be seen that the degree of their cooperation with the United States was determined largely by the seriousness of the Hitler menace to their security. Perhaps indeed, as Professor J. Fred Rippy has somewhat cynically argued, Latin America has never felt the need of intimate relations or a com-

12. *Where Are We Heading?* (New York, 1946), 198-202.

munity of interest with the United States except in times of dire distress, as, for example, during its wars for independence and later in the struggle against Maximilian.[13] During World War II, declared *Marcha* of Montevideo (September 8, 1944), only "the terror of the Nazi danger . . . caused a good part of American opinion to turn its eyes toward the United States." Assis Chateaubriand confirmed this judgment when he wrote in *O Jornal* of Rio de Janeiro on September 3, 1945, "We owe to Hitler and to Japan this new atmosphere of understanding" with the United States. "Paradoxically," wrote Luis Quintanilla in 1943, "it took the armies and blunders of a Hitler to hasten America's discovery of America."[14] This basic condition of inter-American cooperation in the war, therefore, was fulfilled by the successive victories of the Allied armies in Europe and Asia. The unity of allies anxious to win the war to which they were mutually committed began to dissipate as the war was won.

As early as April, 1943, a friendly observer in Brazil noted "a kind of *desconfiança*, of mistrust from our people toward the United States. They are starting to speak in undertones on the 'Yankee danger,' and the 'American imperialism.' "[15] Even from the time of the first announcement of the "Black Lists" by the United States in July, 1941, some Latin Americans had expressed irritation and displeasure over them, objecting particularly to their unilateral character. Some of the hostile comments on the United States had, of course, an Axis origin. The pro-Axis *La Fronda* of Buenos Aires (May 6, 1944), for example, before it was put on the United States Proclaimed List, bitterly charged that the only object of the United States in the war was to find "future markets . . . in order to sell the products of their insatiable industrialists." Even the usually well-disposed *El Tiempo* of Bogotá (June 2, 1943) criticized the wartime Pan-Americanism in general as primarily a unilateral operation of the United States.

As United Nations victories multiplied and the Axis menace correspondingly abated, Latin American criticism of the United States increased. "Anti-U.S. feeling is growing in Brazil," reported Hernane Tavares de Sá in August, 1944, after thoroughly sampling public opinion in his native country.[16] Professor Raúl Cordero Amador told

13. *Latin America in World Politics,* 252.
14. *A Latin American Speaks,* vii.
15. Erico Verissimo, "Cultural and Human Relations between Brazil and the United States of America" [April 19, 1943], files of Coordinator of Inter-American Affairs, The National Archives, 06.1 Brazilian Cultural Agreements.
16. "Camouflage of Harmony," 10.

a group of students from the United States at the National University of Mexico in the summer of 1944 that the United States "should know that it does not have all the sympathy which some of us wish that it had."[17] The Mexican *Hoy* (November 11, 1944), speaking of United States-Mexican relations late in the same year, considered it "clear that certain resentments . . . have not been erased."[18] *Marcha* of Montevideo (September 8, 1944) concluded at the same time that "the United States has not been able to win the confidence of the Latin American countries." It reported that "The policy of good neighborliness is having its troubles and Pan-Americanism, as the northern observers themselves are finding out, has 'cooled off considerably'!" The leftist *La Tribuna* of San Salvador (March 8, 1945) avowed that "our political thought" has taken on "a serious anti-Yankee complex. We have come to hate each and every Yankee citizen."[19] Even the large sums that the United States was pouring into cultural projects were suspected of masking ulterior motives, reported the *New York Times* correspondent in Central America. "The same old criticisms of the United States are rife," he concluded pessimistically.[20]

The slump in Latin America's cordial feelings toward the United States became so marked that it evoked much comment and many reasoned explanations in Latin America. Of these latter perhaps the most cogent was an article by Daniel Cosío Villegas, "Concerning the United States," which was published in *Revista de América* in Bogotá in March, 1945. This distinguished Mexican economist was convinced that friendly hemispheric relations were essential to both the Americas. "Without Latin America," he declared simply, "the United States will not have even the minimum that it needs for its own happiness. As for us, it is hardly necessary to say that relations with the United States are a problem simply of life or death, of being or not being." And yet he reported in this article after a visit through Latin America that in all these countries—"without exception even though in varying degree—there exists today a great animadversion against the United States and a profound distrust of it."

17. *Novedades,* Mexico City, August 13, 1944.
18. See also *Hoy,* August 28, 1943.
19. For additional criticisms of the United States see the statement by Professor Francisco Frola of the National University of Mexico in *El Diario de Hoy,* San Salvador, June 7, 1943; and René Ballivián C., *Hombres de Buena Voluntad* (La Paz, 1945), 105.
20. Milton Bracker in *New York Times,* September 2, 1946.

Could this resurgence of "anti-Yanquismo" be explained, asked Dr. Cosío Villegas, "by the growing power of the United States, which inevitably engenders distrust and rancor in the weak?" A century ago, he noted, "England was as strong as the United States is today, and nevertheless did not arouse this rancor and distrust." Other reasons therefore must be sought to explain why the United States was becoming "detestable in Latin American eyes." One of these was that the United States seemingly "resorts to brute force or proceeds with less skillful methods and that it does not show the fruit of intelligence, of perseverance and of wisdom; it engenders the feeling of power given, but not earned—in short, unmerited." Another obvious cause, he said, was "the lack of international delicacy of the United States and the open errors that it commits in its foreign policy." This cleavage was widened by the conduct of North American travelers in Latin America. "There is nothing in the world so lamentable," generalized Dr. Cosío Villegas, "as a North American who travels, who separates himself from his country, for what counts with him is not the individual but the group." Away from his group he "is the worst enemy of the United States, because all his weaknesses are obvious and offensive." These North American visitors appear "fools and boors, beyond redemption, even those whom we have seen in these last three years, intent on being solicitous and affable with us." In general the North American shows "abysmal ineptitude . . . in matters of propaganda," not because "he is ignorant of it" but because "he has spent all his effort on things and not on persons; while he has succeeded with the publicity that a smoker should walk a mile for a Camel, he has not been able to convince us that he, the North American, is intelligent, human, and capable of understanding, that he is interested in culture, and that he has achievements in this field which would fill any people with pride."

"Hundreds of causes," then, had combined to give Latin Americans a harsh opinion of the United States, to array them against the Yankees. Dr. Cosío Villegas predicted that after the war this dislike would "break loose like an irrepressible wave." It was his opinion that "for years and years" there had "not existed in any of our countries so strong a political force as this animadversion and this distrust." He expected that political leaders would use it to "sweep along not only what in our countries is called 'the masses' but also the entire nation, the rich and the poor, the ignorant and the well-informed alike." It was entirely probable, he concluded prophetically, that as a result "the worst evils that can befall the United States will be engendered in Latin America."[21]

At the same time the Colombian columnist Enrique Santos ("Caliban") declared in his column "Dance of the Hours" in *El Tiempo* of Bogotá (March 1, 1945) that "antipathy toward the United States . . . is growing stronger every day in all the Latin American countries." In order to resist "this senseless movement," as he called it, "to extirpate this evil, which, if unchecked, would bring us the most tragic consequences," he urged that the United States "revise the methods it has employed to promote the Good Neighbor Policy." For all the material benefits of that policy, he declared, "the inhabitants of the countries south of the Rio Grande have only feelings of gratitude toward the United States. In the fight against disease the Rockefeller Mission and the Inter-American Cooperative Health Service have done great work. . . . Money from the 'gringos' has stimulated all our business. . . . All in vain." For "the North Americans," he said, "are the worst propagandists in the world when they try to put themselves across." What was needed then was "an effective *rapprochement* between the north and south, on a basis of perfect clarity and mutual understanding." Such a *rapprochement* could be achieved, he suggested, by more "material help, commercial interchange, industrial development and the cultivation of positive, sincere, and fruitful friendships." But all this would depend upon the postwar policy of the United States. "If we are relegated to the position of colonial countries," he warned, "our industries ruined, our economies mere markets for foreign products, our sovereignty reduced to hopeless mediocrity—then that revulsion, that wave of savage hatred of the United States will explode as an uncontrolled protest." It seemed likely to a prescient writer in the small Panama weekly *Calle 6* (July 20, 1946) that politicians would "take advantage of such a state of affairs to promote a movement of exalted nationalism."

It was obvious then, at least by early 1945, that Latin America's "honeymoon with Yankeedom," as Ramón Manrique called it, was over.[22] Gratitude for the high example and costly sacrifices of the United States in the defense of the Western Hemisphere against totalitarianism in the war would clearly not be enough to sustain Latin America's continued loyalty after the war. Cordiality was being replaced by coolness. Old jealousies, suspicions, and even hatreds were

---

21. *Revista de América*, Bogotá, I (March, 1945), [361]-365.
22. *Diario de la Costa*, Cartagena, Colombia, March 4, 1945.

being revived. Latin Americans detected a deterioration in United States interest in their culture and their ideas. The feeling became prevalent that the United States had taken more from Latin America than it had given in return during the war, that it had taken advantage of Latin America's security dependence upon it to acquire war materials at its own prices, and that as the war ended it was returning to its traditional attitude of neglect, even contempt, toward the Latin American peoples. The changed attitude of the United States was vividly revealed in an impromptu order which an influential senator, who was a member of the United States delegation to the San Francisco Conference of the United Nations, gave to Nelson Rockefeller, Assistant Secretary of State for Latin American Affairs: "Your Goddamned peanut nations aren't voting right. Go line them up."

Latin America's displeasure with the United States was reinforced by the activities of some of the *fomento,* or development, corporations, particularly those in Bolivia, Haiti, and Ecuador, in which the United States either was represented on boards of directors or was otherwise involved. The projects and programs of these corporations in which United States government agencies, including the Rubber Development Corporation, the CIAA, the Commodity Credit Corporation, the Defense Supplies Corporation, the Metals Reserve Corporation, and the Foreign Economic Administration, often had a direct administrative interest were carried forward within another sovereign state and sometimes gave rise to accusations of absentee foreign control. Some of their operations, as was to have been expected, did in fact warp local economies and create wage and employment situations which were disadvantageous to local business.

When the war was over, many of these activities were abruptly terminated. United States purchasers turned once more to producers in the Far East who by reason of their more abundant labor supply and more advanced production methods were able to deliver their products more cheaply than could Latin American producers. In the postwar world Brazilian rubber could not compete with the plantation rubber of the East Indies. Bolivian tin ore is found only in hard rock deposits, requires expensive smelting, and has a lower metal content than the East Indian alluvial tin. Peruvian quinine and Chilean nitrate cost much more than their synthetic equivalents. As a result the imports of the United States from Chile, for example, declined from a peak of $153.6 million in 1944 to only $83.8 million in 1946, and imports from Bolivia from $38.3 million to only $24 million during the same two-year period.[23] As the United States war agencies and businessmen withdrew from Latin America, what did they leave behind? asked a former foreign minister of Bolivia, Gustavo Chacón, in *La Noche* of La Paz (February 26, 1946). "In the rubber regions, empty tin cans, one or more broken-down Frigidaires, rural air strips from which their airplanes took off with their household goods, their office employees, and their blondes. In the tin and wolfram mines, cavities in the ground and cavities among the democratic workers who left their lungs behind in the tunnels in order to save democracy which was under assault in the world!"

In Haiti the failure of the cryptostegia program in late 1943, a program financed by the Rubber Reserve Corporation in the United States, reacted unfavorably not only against all the projects sponsored by the Société Haïtiano-Américaine de Développement Agricole (SHADA) but also against the United States generally. In this program of producing rubber from the cryptostegia shrub 55,000 workers, largely Haitian, were employed over a period of a year on an area of 75,000 acres of land, but only 8,000 pounds of rubber were produced. The general consensus in Haiti was that this program, as well as others which were supervised by SHADA, was detrimental to the labor market, in that Haitian labor was overpaid and accomplished too little work. In 1943 at the peak of its career SHADA was the largest single employer in Haiti, disbursing an annual payroll of $6,248,000—a sum which exceeded the total annual revenues of the Haitian government. The dislocating effect of these United States ventures upon the economy of Haiti can be appreciated when it is realized that in that poor country with annual revenues of less than $6 million and with a total annual average trade of only about $16 million the United States expended during the war a total of more than $20 million. Large quantities of United States dollar bills and coins were shipped into Haiti with disastrously inflationary effects.[24]

These programs, which seemed so necessary to war planners in the United States but which took on an aspect of extravagant wastefulness to Latin Americans, produced a feeling of antipathy to foreign investment and foreign monopolies. Toward the end of the war,

23. Richard F. Behrendt, *Inter-American Economic Relations: Problems and Prospects* (New York, 1948), 37.

24. Marie V. Wood, "Agricultural Development and Rural Life in Haiti, 1934-1950," unpublished doctoral dissertation, The American University, Washington, D. C., chapter VII.

therefore, a serious antiforeign outlook developed with definite indications that government interference and restrictions might inhibit further foreign investment.[25]

Ecuador was often cited as an example of the disadvantageous effects of Latin America's wartime cooperation with the United States. During the war it made bases available to the United States both on its mainland and on the Galápagos Islands, put its armed services under the virtual control of United States missions, and freely contributed its strategic materials—balsa wood, rubber, quinine, and others—to meet the war needs of the United States. The facilities of the single railroad, the only land-transportation link between the port of Guayaquil and the rich interior of the country around Quito, were all but worn out as the heavy trains busily plied to and fro over some of the most mountainous terrain in the Western Hemisphere in their round-the-clock traffic for the united war effort. New towns of Ecuadorans were established near sites of war factories and United States air bases. Old business firms, unable to get their usual foreign merchandise, disappeared, and imported goods ceased to be available in the *almacenes*. Ecuador's entire economy was disrupted by the war, and its accumulated dollar balance, which was considerable, could not be used and became, for all practical purposes, valueless.

By reason of Ecuador's participation in the war effort its exports by March, 1943, were almost 100 per cent greater than its imports by value and approximately 600 per cent greater by volume. Its imports, coming mostly from the United States, had been drastically reduced by war requirements and lack of shipping. The dollar loans received from the United States for road construction, stabilization of currency, rehabilitation of El Oro province, the operation of sanitary projects, dollar expenditures by the United States Rubber Reserve Company and the Ecuadoran Development Corporation, combined with the money brought into the country through the construction of United States military and naval bases and expenditures by the United States armed forces, gave Ecuador an abundance of dollar exchange. As a result inflation became rampant, the price of foodstuffs doubled, and building construction almost entirely stopped because of the shortage of necessary imported construction materials.[26]

When Germany and Japan surrendered to the United Nations

25. *Ibid.*
26. American Consulate General, Guayaquil, Report No. 52, April 13, 1943, Department of State Archives.

the war installations in Ecuador were immediately abandoned by the United States and the populations of the new towns were cast adrift. The shortages of imported goods became more acute than they had been in wartime. Four long years passed before the decrepit Guayaquil-Quito railroad was able to get even one new replacement of rolling stock from the United States. Meanwhile merchandise piled up in its freight yards for months and even years awaiting shipment. And meanwhile resentments also piled up against the United States.

Once again the basic cleavage—historical, cultural, psychological, racial, even economic and political—between Anglo-America and Hispano-Indo-America—this indisputable dichotomy of the Western Hemisphere which had been the starting point for the analyses of Rodó, Ugarte, and all their disciples—began to be stressed, and it appealed to every admirer of the traditions of the Cid, Cervantes, and Camões. The New World was in fact, as Ugarte had written, "cleft in two by origin and speech"—and he might have added "by tradition, attitudes, and political systems."[27] If some of these dissimilarities had been forgotten or submerged in the supposed common danger presented by World War II, they could not be permanently denied. The exceptional cooperation in action between the two Americas in that period had to give way to the more durable "continental dualism," to borrow a phrase of Luis Quintanilla.[28] "The Mexican-Yankee frontier," wrote the distinguished Ecuadoran Dr. Pío Jaramillo Alvarado in *El Comercio* of Quito (March 26, 1944), is a "dividing line between two races and two cultures." In the opinion of the perceptive Jorge Fernández, the psychology of the North American people "differs as profoundly from ours as from the psychology of the European or Asiatic peoples."[29] Roberto García Peña of *El Tiempo* of Bogotá (May 10, 1944) frankly did "not believe that there are similarities of character between Saxon-Americans and Latin Americans. It would be ingenuous to say that they exist and dishonest not to admit that the two cultures, theirs and ours, have different spiritual tendencies." Enrique Santos spoke of the differences between Latins and Anglo-Saxons as "absolute" and cited as an example the enlistment of women in the armed services of the United States, which was profoundly repugnant to Latin Americans.[30]

To many Latin American observers these fundamental differences

27. *The Destiny of a Continent,* 4.   28. *Op. cit.,* 6.
29. *El Comercio,* Quito, May 4, 1944.
30. *El Tiempo,* Bogotá, July 25, 1945.

seemed to be aggravated by each America's ignorance of the other at the end of the war—this despite all the deliberate, painstaking, and costly efforts at understanding which had been made during the war. "A false interpretation of each other creates an abyss between the two parts of the Western Hemisphere," wrote Ramón Manrique in early 1945.[31] North Americans, complained Enrique Santos, belong "to a race which does not understand us. And they are doing nothing to understand us. Have we not been the victims of hundreds of tourists who write all kinds of foolishness and atrocities about us without ever trying to get to the bottom of our souls?"[32] According to Joaquín Edwards Bello, writing in *La Patria* of Concepción, Chile (March 8, 1946), "the North American has traveled through our America either as a tourist or as a merchant, looking either for local color or good business opportunities. He does not know our spiritual struggles and therefore exaggerates or misinterprets our problems." Latin Americans made scathingly derogatory comments on "the North American tourist who tries to understand our customs from 3,000 meters up aboard a Pan-Air plane."[33] Especially loathsome, as it seemed to Rómulo Betancourt, were the "tourist-journalists of United States nationality who deliver authoritative opinions about any of our Latin American countries after having spent a fortnight in them, . . . interviewed only half a dozen of its so-called representative men and sped through half a dozen of its most important cities in a swift automobile."[34] These were the "paratrooper journalists," the "hurry-skurry tourists," as *A Gazeta* of São Paulo (November 24, 1943) called them. From the almost standardized operations of these visitors, warned *El Panamá-América* (January 27, 1947), "there arise many false concepts held concerning Central and South America by the general public of the United States." After such a journalist visits all the capitals of Latin America, it satirically continued, "he returns to New York speaking about the 'Pisco sour' which they make in the Bolívar of Lima, the lobsters they serve at the Carrera in Santiago, the tremendous 'Bifes' of the Alvear-Palace of Buenos Aires, the nights at the Urca and Copacabana in Rio, all of this seasoned up with the 'Planters Punch' of the Queens Hotel of Port-of-Spain." In the articles which he will then prepare for his

31. *Diario de la Costa*, Cartagena, Colombia, March 4, 1945.
32. *El Tiempo*, Bogotá, July 25, 1945.
33. Ramón Manrique, *Diario de la Costa*, Cartagena, Colombia, March 4, 1945.
34. *El País*, Caracas, August 5, 1945.

North American readers he will "recall something he heard in a cabaret in Panama, Buenos Aires, or Havana; and his imagination will do the rest."

From such superficialities, it seemed, came in large measure the misunderstandings in the relations between the people of the United States and their southern neighbors. "They reduce all their knowledge of the twenty republics to one vague and completely false generalization on the basis of picturesqueness, exoticism, sentimentalism for housemaids," complained Professor Hernane Tavares de Sá late in 1943. For them, he added, "Latin America is contained in the two magic words that all Americans know: *fiesta* and *siesta*."[35] They were seldom able to distinguish or identify each one of the Latin American nations.[36] According to a writer in *Diario de Costa Rica* (December 22, 1949), a Costa Rican traveling in the United States would often become involved in the following dialogue:

"Where do you come from?" the North Americans frequently ask when receiving us in a business office.

"From Costa Rica. . . ."

"Oh, Puerto Rico! . . ."

"No; Costa Rica, a Central American country situated between Panama and Nicaragua."

"Oh, South American. . . ."

"And there seems to be no possible means," hopelessly concluded this writer, "by which the majority of North Americans can succeed in locating our little country on the map of America, in spite of the fact that in our country their fellow countrymen have great economic interests and in spite of all the Pan-American preachments. . . . They cannot be good neighbors," he sententiously concluded, "who do not know or only half know each other."

Of the vast South American continent the people of the United States, it seemed to Latin American observers, had only the vaguest notions. The average North American, wrote the Colombian novelist Eduardo Caballero Calderón, "scarcely knows that in Lima there is still the barbarous custom of bullfighting, that there is a great city in Argentina, and that there are tribes of savage Indians in the Amazon jungles. His notion of the continent which stretches south of the Panama Canal has only an economic or rather a digestive basis, since he consumes bananas and coffee from Colombia, coffee and coco-

35. *Jornal do Brasil,* Rio de Janeiro, December 19, 1943.
36. See comment by Jorge Fernández, *El Comercio,* Quito, May 6, 1944.

nuts from Brazil, cocoa from Ecuador, et cetera, never realizing, however, that his automobile also uses South American petroleum and that his wife buys a Panama hat when she goes to the shore for a summer vacation."[37]

For this ignorance Latin Americans were inclined to assign considerable blame to the newspapers and news services of the United States. "For those great newspapers," said García Peña in 1944, "Latin America hardly exists. . . . They say that their readers are not interested in the subject." As a result, he pointed out, "the public is not accustomed to being informed about Latin America."[38] Among North American readers, declared Jorge Fernández in the same year, "Latin American news has no market. . . . Of our affairs they are interested only in sensationalism, revolutions, and crimes or supposed actions of primitive Indians."[39] In their "unrelieved ignorance" of Latin America, complained *El Tiempo* of Bogotá (December 5, 1947), North American newspapers "almost never stress the importance, for example, of a quiet change in government." So serious was this journalistic neglect of Latin America that in December, 1947, the Mexican representative on the Governing Board of the Pan American Union, Luis Quintanilla, spoke out before the board against the "boycott by the American press of everything that refers to the Pan American Union." In this complaint he was supported by the ambassadors of Argentina, Chile, and Venezuela. "We are of less importance to any American newspaperman than is the most mediocre commercial firm in Detroit or Cleveland," lamented Dr. Gonzalo Carnevali, the ambassador of Venezuela.[40] Supporting this criticism *El Liberal* of Bogotá (December 5 1947) declared that even the occasional notices about Latin America printed in newspapers of the United States were "filled with inaccuracies and convenient distortions," and it suggested that perhaps "the real intention of publishers and editors" there was "to poke fun," to present the affairs of Latin Americans "as ridiculous and grotesque." Such an attitude, it concluded, was "inconsistent with a frank, firm, and open policy of good neighborliness, of Pan Americanism, of continental solidarity."

Misinformation and misconceptions of Latin America in the

37. *Suramérica, Tierra del Hombre* (Medellín, Colombia, 1944), 7.
38. *El Tiempo*, Bogotá, May 10, 1944.
39. *El Comercio*, Quito, May 6, 1944.
40. Pan American Union, *Minutes of the Special Meeting of the Governing Board of the Pan American Union Held on December 1, 1947* (Washington, D. C., mimeographed), 16-23.

United States, it was alleged, were not limited to newspapers. Holly-wood films, according to *La Estrella de Panamá* (July 22, 1947), pic-tured Latin America as nothing more than "a motley group of hovels, some palm trees, a maraca orchestra around which dance sweaty people in their shirt sleeves." Radio broadcasts from the United States to Latin America were criticized by *Diario de la Costa* of Car-tagena (October 11, 1945) for "the incomprehension and ignorance which the directors of the radio network have of these countries." Books also, especially textbooks, were written in terms of inadequate information and unwarranted stereotypes about Latin America, as a report of the American Council on Education, published in 1944, re-vealed. That report, which was entitled *Latin America in School and College Teaching Materials* and which disclosed serious defects in those materials, attracted considerable attention in Latin America. Rafael Pérez Lobo, writing in *Información* of Havana (January 16, 1945), endorsed its conclusions, pointing out that when writers in the United States "turn their attention to us they do not gather proof here, nor do they learn from our books, nor are they interested in making even a moderate investigation beyond a little tourist trip." Latin American history or geography "is more or less invented" for their textbooks, and in their bibliographies "is rarely included a work of ours. . . . They study us through their own eyes; and thus the errors keep accumulating with time." All this, he felt, was due not to "malice" but to "that idea of superiority which the North Ameri-cans have with respect to everything Hispanic. They think they know it all; at least they believe that they can learn little from us." Upon this basis no durable relationship of understanding and cooperation could be established between the peoples of the Western Hemisphere.

The United States did not even seem concerned to put its best foot forward in Latin America. Not only the "journalist-tourist" with his "quickie takes" of Latin America but also "the business man of coarse and gross appetites and interests and the usual public official, as incompetent as he is arrogant," to quote Daniel Cosío Villegas, left a trail of disgust wherever they went in Latin America. Their over-presentation of statistics of the physical or material accomplishment of themselves and their nation gave Latin Americans the impression that they were "showing off." The United States seemed unable to impress Latin Americans with its high artistic and intellectual achievements.[41] That country, wrote the Venezuelan critic Mariano

41. *Op. cit.,* [361]-365.

Picón-Salas in *El Nacional* of Mexico City (February 23, 1950), "seriously errs in its international relations when the tradition of Emerson is superseded by that of Vanderbilt and of Morgan, when the old John Rockefeller is made to appear more important than William James." Hollywood films also, to quote García Peña, had undertaken "to give us an absurd idea of the people of the United States." All this mutual ignorance, as he pointed out, "logically engendered distrust."[42]

An element in the widening breach between the two Americas was a kind of moral revulsion in Latin America against the United States as a country of Hollywood morals, free and easy living, commonplace divorce, and irreligion. A leading newspaper of Guatemala complained that United States news services, while neglecting to supply them with the text of Secretary Cordell Hull's speech of April 9, 1944, setting forth the design for a postwar international peace organization, sent them "interminable articles about the foibles of Charlie Chaplin and his harebrained, unconventional ex-wife."[43] Old criticism of Reno, Nevada, as a city "where an industry for the dissolution of the home has been established," still persisted.[44] Adverting to this Reno influence, Enrique Gandía was astonished to note on his visit to the United States in 1941 that "a woman divorced once, twice, or more times is treated no differently than one who lives all her life with the same husband." He concluded that in the United States "the moral concepts of women were totally foreign to Hispano-Americans." But, he added understandingly, if North American women "resort to divorce it is because their anxiety to be loved, to live, and to struggle for illusion, for happiness, is stronger than the religious and social prejudices of the women of other countries."[45]

From the "imperialism of North American immorality" Latin Americans wished to be spared. But the wartime propaganda facilities, the moving pictures, and the opportunities for travel were making the offensive practices of the North Americans all too common in Latin America. Enrique Santos lamented that Latin Americans "are being seduced with this . . . resurrection of paganism . . . which will bring us to the day of divorces and feminists, and WAACs [*sic*] and girls who spend the night away from home, and coeducation,

42. *El Tiempo*, Bogotá, May 10, 1944.
43. *Nuestro Diario*, Guatemala City, April 11, 1944.
44. Nemesio García Naranjo, *La Nación*, Buenos Aires, June 6, 1931.
45. *El Gigante del Norte*, 21, 79-80.

and sexual education, of those who teach girls to protect themselves from the boys and from diseases but who destroy modesty and moral principles." All this, he apprehended, would put an end to the Latin American "way of life." Santos admitted, however, that "there are millions of sanctified homes" in the United States but "with a sanctity different than we conceive it. Neither worse nor better but different."[46]

This difference explained in part the Latin American antipathy to the intensified Protestant missionary activity after the war. In these Roman Catholic countries Protestants are sometimes treated as undesirable intruders. In Colombia between 1948 and 1953, according to the Evangelical Confederation, 57 Protestant churches and chapels were either destroyed or closed as a result of religious persecution.[47] Ramón Manrique, writing in *Diario de la Costa* of Cartagena, Colombia (March 4, 1945), implored the North Americans to "leave us to our religion which we love and understand, and not send us Protestant pastors who come to tell us such nonsense as that Saturday instead of Sunday is the Lord's Day." Competition between Roman Catholic and Protestant forces, then, was and continues to be at the root of much Latin American folk antipathy to the United States.

This antipathy was intensified by the "diplomatic boycott" of Franco Spain by the United States and its successful opposition to the admission of this Catholic Church-supported, but allegedly Fascist, government to the United Nations. After the adoption of an anti-Franco resolution by the General Assembly of the United Nations in December, 1946, six Latin American nations including Argentina, Costa Rica, the Dominican Republic, Ecuador, El Salvador, and Peru refused to recall their ambassadors from Spain, and by 1948 the pro-Franco bloc in the Western Hemisphere included not only those nations but also Honduras and Nicaragua. In the following year further support for Spain was offered by Brazil, Bolivia, Colombia, and several Central American countries. But strenuous opposition to the Franco government was expressed by Mexico, Panama, Guatemala, and Uruguay.[48] As a result partly of the persistent opposition of the Truman administration to the Franco government, it became the target of much criticism from both pro-Franco and anti-Franco

46. *El Tiempo,* Bogotá, July 25, 1945.
47. Ronald Hilton (ed.), *Hispanic American Report,* VI, 8 (September, 1953), 25.
48. *Ibid.,* I, 1 (November, 1948), 2; and II, 2 (January, 1949), [1], 9.

partisans in Latin America, the latter, who were most numerous in Mexico, being especially vociferous and even vituperative.[49]

So strong was the postwar feeling against the United States in 1947 that Enrique Santos felt it necesary to caution in his column in *El Tiempo* (October 1, 1947) that the United States as "the most powerful nation in this hemisphere should not be covered with insults every time a more or less serious incident occurs," because, "whether we like it or not, our individual and national prosperity, our very lives, are tied up with the United States." Several such incidents occurred. Vociferous popular demonstrations against the United States were held in Panama in December, 1947, celebrating the unanimous rejection by Panama's legislative assembly of the defense sites agreement by which the United States sought to secure leases on thirteen Panamanian bases outside the Canal Zone.[50] In March, 1949, phrenetic displays of anti-United States sentiment took place in Havana after three drunken United States sailors, on shore leave from the U.S.S. "Rodman" in that capital, desecrated a statue of José Martí, the apostle of Cuban independence.[51] A similar anti-United States demonstration occurred in the same month in Ciudad Trujillo in the Dominican Republic provoked by the disrespectful conduct of United States sailors on shore leave.[52] Hostile demonstrations, allegedly Communist, were made against both Assistant Secretary of State Edward G. Miller, Jr., and the State Department's policy planning representative, George F. Kennan, on their visit to Brazil in March, 1950. In Mexico strong anti-United States sentiments were systematically propagated by the militantly anti-Communist and pro-Spanish Sinarquista organization, or *Unión Nacional Sinarquista,* which operated after the war as the *Partido de la Fuerza Popular* (Popular Force Party). Charges of "Caliban" and "Colossus of the North" were again leveled against the United States, political leaders sought to make capital from the anti-"Yanqui" feelings, and the belief gained ground that economic misfortunes in Latin America were due to the misplaced assistance rendered to the United States during the war.[53]

* * *

49. *Ibid.,* II, 8 (August, 1949), 8.
50. *Star and Herald,* Panama, December 23 and 24, 1947.
51. *Diario de la Marina,* Havana, March 13, 1949.
52. Hilton, *op. cit.,* II, 4 (April, 1949), 32.
53. Carlos Ibarguren, *De Monroe a la Buena Vecindad: Trayectoria de un Imperialismo* (Buenos Aires, 1946).

The issue that most sharply divided the hemisphere north and south in the immediate postwar period and that contributed most to the growth of anti-Yanquismo in Latin America was the Braden corollary of the Good Neighbor Policy, particularly as it was applied to the colonels' government in Argentina. Implicit in the Atlantic Charter and the Four Freedoms and explicit in much of the wartime propaganda of the United States was abhorrence of dictatorship. In waging the war, the United States daily showed its determination to destroy regimes which it considered to be undemocratic. "The great power of the north," said the Havana newspaper *Alerta* (October 29, 1945), "wants a clear-cut democracy:—nothing in the nature of a single party, or a single capitalist, even though it be the state, nor a single social class. No dictatorship at all. Freedom of speech, of thought, of belief, of action, of initiative" represented its program in international affairs. Thus there developed a widespread belief that the United States, for a variety of reasons including its own security, wanted democratic governments established everywhere. If the people of the United States had this as a global objective they obviously desired that democratic governments should be established and maintained in all the Latin American countries. Did not the logic and momentum of the cause for which they professedly fought in the war require that pressure be applied either to reform or to overthrow governments of a contrary character?

In the beginning the Good Neighbor Policy had not denied that regimes unrepresentative of the majority of the people existed in many Latin American countries. But for the United States the validity of such a regime was determined by its durability. It was presumed to grow out of the aspirations and requirements of its people. If in fact it did not do so, it would be replaced by another regime better suited to their needs. But until and unless it was thus replaced, the United States would deal with it as their government speaking for them. This policy, as Theophilo de Andrade rightly described it in *A Noite* of Rio de Janeiro (November 17, 1945), was the policy "of passive good neighborhood, such as that of codwellers in an apartment building." It was a policy which "recognized the international validity of some Latin American governments which were anything but democratic although in the international field they fulfilled their duties as codwellers and treated the others nicely enough." It repudiated intervention; it was essentially a policy of nonintervention, of anti-imperialism, of "hands-off," of "live and let live."

For this very negative quality, however, that policy was vigorously criticized by self-avowed democratic elements in Latin America and by Don Quixotes who aspired to win glory—and perhaps political power—in another historic Battle of the Windmills. This apparent failure of United States policy to distinguish between dictatorial governments and democratic governments in its relations with the Latin American countries tended to disillusion friends of the United States as to its war aims. In January, 1943, the Costa Rican Dr. Clodomiro Picado criticized Roosevelt's paradoxical policy of combatting "in Europe the supercriminals who have declared war without quarter against liberty, the sciences, and human greatness" while at the same time maintaining "in power the governments of the little tyrants of the Caribbean."[54] Why, asked Dr. Pío Jaramillo Alvarado in an interview published in El Comercio of Quito (March 26, 1944), did the United States, engaged in a struggle to the death against totalitarian dictatorship in Europe and Asia, support Latin American regimes which "follow Fascist constitutional patterns," as for example those in Bolivia, Argentina, and Peru?[55] In the judgment of Dr. Juan José Arévalo, soon to be elected president of Guatemala, Roosevelt, one of "the paladins of democracy," ought to take action against certain nations of Central and South America which though they had joined the United Nations were, by their actions, daily corrupting and destroying democracy.[56]

A strong public opinion developed, therefore, that the Roosevelt administration should repudiate "all forms of dictatorship or regimes of terror in America."[57] The "good neighbor edifice," advised Ultimas Noticias of Mexico City (March 20, 1944), must be reconstructed on a democratic basis to "have its foundation . . . in the people themselves." It must concern itself thereafter with "those unhappy people" who had lived for many years "shackled by the most antidemocratic forms of government." The distinguished Roman Catholic Conservative senator, Eduardo Cruz-Coke of Chile,

54. Diario de Costa Rica, San José, January 5, 1943.
55. For similar comments see the open letter "To the Diplomatic Corps" in Lider, "Organ of the Student Democratic Front," a publication of the University students of San Salvador, September 6, 1944; Professor Raúl Cordero Amador, Novedades, Mexico City, August 13, 1944; Sergio Carbó, Prensa Libre, Havana, December 21, 1945; and El País, Caracas, August 8, 1946.
56. El Libertador, September 9, 1944, reprinted in Juan José Arévalo, Escritos Políticos (Guatemala, 1945), 75-78.
57. J. Gustavo Morales, El Imparcial, Guatemala City, October 6, 1945, Despatch 713, Guatemala City, October 10, 1945.

even went so far as to declare in an address at Princeton University in March, 1945, that "The democracy of the United States will never be safe until all the nations to the southward are also democracies." Respect for the principle of nonintervention must give way to the need of a democratic hemisphere.

Pressure was thus built up for the United States to convert its passive government-to-government relationship into a warm people-to-people relationship, and in October, 1944, the State Department began to espouse the doctrine in Latin America of "a greater affinity and a warmer friendship for those governments which rest upon the periodically and freely expressed consent of the governed."[58] Under the guidance of Ambassador Spruille Braden, later to become Assistant Secretary of State, it adopted a policy of cold-shouldering dictatorial and disreputable regimes in Latin America as enemies to democracy and liberty. Although this corollary of the Good Neighbor Policy was accompanied by frequent and firm reaffirmations of the continuing steadfast adherence of the United States to the principle of nonintervention, it nevertheless signalized that the United States was assuming the responsibility of guiding the destinies of the people of the entire Western Hemisphere. It now recognized, to quote Theophilo de Andrade again, that "passive good neighborhood was a danger to the peace of the hemisphere and of the world and that in place of this policy America should adopt one of active good neighborhood."[59] This seemed to imply that the United States would use at least its moral force to secure more frequent and free elections and better observance of such civil and human rights as freedom of speech and assembly, freedom of the press and religion. It meant that, in the words of *La Prensa Libre* of San José (January 7, 1949), "a regime established against the will of the people will not be able to prosper because it will be put in quarantine of isolation until it has become disinfected." Here, as *Le Nouvelliste* of Port-au-Prince (January 10, 1945) pointed out, was a "new conception," an "enlarged formula of Pan-Americanism," stressing "the opposition of the two terms 'government' and 'peoples.'"

In pursuance of this "enlarged formula" the United States promptly gave its approval to the policy recommendation of the

58. Circular Instructions to United States Embassies in the Other American Republics from Assistant Secretary of State A. A. Berle, November 1, 1944, Department of State Archives.
59. *A Noite*, Rio de Janeiro, November 17, 1945.

Foreign Minister of Uruguay, Dr. Alberto Rodríguez Larreta, in November, 1945, calling for "multilateral collective action" by the American nations to establish "essential rights" in any country "which has been suffering under . . . a harsh regime." This proposal, also enthusiastically endorsed by Costa Rica, Guatemala, Panama, and Venezuela, was hailed by many newspapers in Latin America as marking "the obsolescence of nonintervention"—a principle which was now considered to be "outdated in view of other obligations and of the political and social Pan-American structure."[60] "If intervention is collective," declared Junta President Rómulo Betancourt of Venezuela, "there is no danger whatever in it."[61] Through collective action the American nations could now end tyranny and ensure democratic government throughout the Americas. Restrictions in the general interest must be imposed upon "the archaic concept of absolute sovereignty of states." Besides, this principle of collective action was merely following the principles laid down in the new Charter of the United Nations to maintain peace and security in the modern world.

Nevertheless the Uruguayan proposal did not prosper. Unfavorable in varying degrees were the replies from Cuba, Peru, Argentina, Chile, Brazil, Ecuador, Colombia, Mexico, Haiti, Nicaragua, Paraguay the Dominican Republic, Honduras, and El Salvador. Latin America was not willing to consent to any weakening of the principle of nonintervention. "Intervention, whether collective or unilateral, can only be an attack against the rights of peoples to choose their own government and the regime they desire," declared *Le Soir* of Port-au-Prince (December 5, 1945). To *El Nacional* of Mexico City intervention was still intervention whether "coming from a single state or coming from a large group of states working together, no matter what the motive or the results." That newspaper (December 3, 1945) concluded that "the principle of collective intervention involves serious dangers for the liberty and the sovereignty of the Latin American nations." The Brazilian Foreign Minister, Leão Veloso, in disapproving the Uruguayan doctrine, observed, "We have nothing to do with the internal organization of other countries, so long as the peace and security of the rest are not disturbed." Besides, it was pointed out, the application of the principle of collective action would be to divide the American nations into two groups and thus destroy the unity of the hemisphere. The Uruguayan proposal also aroused fears as to

60. *O Jornal,* Rio de Janeiro, December 3, 1945.
61. *El País,* Caracas, January 30, 1946.

the possibility of new interventions by the United States, which, as the most powerful nation of the hemisphere, would almost certainly be the principal enforcer of collective sanctions.[62] Such fear seemed justified when the United States ambassador to Brazil, Adolf A. Berle, made strictures upon the Vargas regime in a public address in January, 1946. His remarks were widely criticized in Latin America as a manifestation of an interventionist disposition in official circles in the United States.[63] Fear of intervention by the United States was the reason given by the Argentine Foreign Minister, Juan I. Cooke, for Argentina's rejection of the Uruguayan proposal.[64] Even Panama, which accepted the Uruguayan proposal, somewhat apprehensively insisted that collective intervention must not include military action.[65] And furthermore, it was asked in Latin America, how could any sanctions be enforced against the United States if that nation violated human liberties or failed to honor its engagements?

In February, 1946, while the Rodríguez Larreta proposal was still being argued over, the State Department in Washington issued a memorandum on "The Argentine Situation," the notorious Blue Book, charging the Argentine government, which was in effect controlled by Colonel Juan Domingo Perón, with following fascist-totalitarian practices and with aiding the Axis cause. Into the preparation of this 131-page memorandum went considerable fury and prejudice against Colonel Perón and a strong determination on the part of the State Department to defeat him in the campaign which he was then waging for election to the presidency of Argentina. In the election two weeks later Perón won a resounding victory on the slogan "Braden or Perón," receiving 55 per cent of the popular vote.

The tenor of such Latin American opinion as defended this Argentine policy of the United States was that it served a useful purpose to the entire hemisphere by exposing "the danger of Nazification and the predominance of a German-totalitarian ideology" in Argentina and that such an exposure was required under the resolutions of the Inter-American Conference on Problems of War and Peace in which all the American nations except Argentina had participated at Mexico

62. *Star and Herald,* Panama, December 15, 1945.
63. Despatch 27,958, Mexico, January 15, 1946, Department of State Archives.
64. Radio address, November 30, 1945.
65. Minister of Foreign Affairs of Panama, R. J. Alfaro, to the Minister of Foreign Affairs of Uruguay, November 30, 1945, *La Estrella de Panamá,* December 4, 1945.

City in February-March, 1945. By this action, said *El Mundo* of Havana (November 20, 1946), the United States was undertaking to establish "the maximum guaranty of American democracy." Since, it was said, the Good Neighbor Policy from the very beginning had implied that democratic governments should be established in all the Latin American countries, the United States was now finally orienting its policy in that direction. It was laying the basis for true democratic American solidarity. It would no longer act in complicity with tyrants but would instead seek contacts with the people living in the grip of strong-arm governments in order to overthrow them. To *Mediodía* of Guatemala (January 18, 1947) Mr. Braden was "truly a progressive democrat and an authentic spokesman of the Good Neighbor Policy." He was interested in "democratizing the Good Neighbor Policy and in terminating the deception of nonintervention which at bottom encompasses the most degrading forms of intervention known in politics, in social questions and in economic matters." If this meant intervention, it was intervention for a laudable purpose.

But intervention, whether for praiseworthy objectives or not, was odious to many Latin Americans whose recollections of previous foreign interventions still rankled and who remembered as a triumph for their nations the noninterventionist pledges made by all the American governments, including the United States, in the early days of Roosevelt's Good Neighbor Policy. The United States would have done better, wrote Gustavo Chacón in *La Noche* of La Paz (February 26, 1946), referring to the Blue Book, "to *teach the love of democracy* by example and not to make it hated through intervention. By this latter method the North Americans will only succeed in raising up . . . in each one of the twenty Latin American countries . . . a rebellious Sandino with a spirit of exalted nationalism or will bring to triumph in each country a Colonel Perón, who will set in motion elements hostile to democracy and make each country a fortress bristling with hatred against a nation which we all wish to love and to consider as our friend."[66] The judicious *El Tiempo* of Bogotá (January 15, 1946) warned that "the belligerent participation of the United States in the internal policy of these nations is an abominable deed which restores practices that appeared fortunately to have been abolished. . . . The intervention which, under the pretext of safeguarding democracy, is now praised endangers the understanding and friendship which are so propitious for the great undertakings that

66. Italics in original.

America yet has before it in the world."[67] Throughout Latin America wide circulation was given to the views of the former Under Secretary of States, Sumner Welles, criticizing the new policy of the United States as a departure from the nonintervention principle and as violative of the Good Neighbor Policy.[68]

Even less restrained arraignments of this Braden corollary to the Good Neighbor Policy were made in the southern countries of South America. As was to be expected, the pro-Perón press in Argentina denounced it as "an imperialist maneuver of which the only and real objective is to carry the Stars and Stripes to the Straits of Magellan." Because of it *La Epoca* of Buenos Aires (March 17, 1946) characterized "American diplomacy" as "a combination of power politics, indiscretions, and economic scrambles for the riches of its neighbors." To *El Debate* of Montevideo (May 3, 1946), newspaper organ of the Herrerista political faction in Uruguay, the United States, as attested by its policy of intervention in Perón's Argentina, was a "beast . . . still breathing and . . . planning revenge" for Argentina's refusal to follow the will and purposes of the State Department in Washington during the war.

The Communist press throughout Latin America immediately joined in this hue and cry against the new "interventionist policy of Yankee imperialism."[69] The Communist *La Hora* of Buenos Aires (May 31, 1946) alarmingly declared that "It is no longer a question of simple 'dollar diplomacy' nor of the landing of Yankee marines here and there, but of the complete military submission of all Latin states to the orders of the North American army."

Even in the Dominican Republic the unofficial newspaper mouthpiece of the Trujillo government deemed the time opportune to publish a series of articles which recalled the arbitrary and harsh treatment imposed upon the inhabitants of that country by the military intervention of the United States in the 1920's.[70] This new policy of "active good neighborhood," somewhat wryly commented Theophilo de Andrade, "seemed too active" and likely "to degenerate . . . into the Big Stick Policy."[71] Latin American political leaders frankly told United States diplomatic officials in their countries that the United States would have to break away even further from the old policy of the

67. Similar views were expressed by *El Espectador,* Bogotá, January 5, 1946.
68. See, for example, *El Universal,* Mexico, December 13, 1945.
69. *Diario Popular,* Bogotá, January 16, 1946.
70. *La Nación,* Ciudad Trujillo, May 18, 20, 21, 1946.
71. *A Noite,* Rio de Janeiro, November 17, 1945.

Big Stick than it had yet done in order to win the sincere friendship of their nations. The old reactionary spirit, they complained, was still at work seeking to use the power of the United States to dominate the smaller and weaker republics to the south. Unless the United States adopted a policy of greater generosity and respect, they warned, it would receive perfunctory cooperation but not genuine support from them.

The overt abandonment of the Braden corollary, which was implied by Braden's resignation as Assistant Secretary of State in June, 1947, was lauded in Latin America as a return to "the policy of nonintervention," preparing the way for a new "continental solidarity."[72] The United States, pontificated the Brazilian statesman Oswaldo Aranha, "cannot impose its type of American democracy in Latin America."[73] Its new noninterventionist policy was signalized by its immediate withdrawal of troops from the defense sites in Panama after the rejection of its proposed defense sites agreement by the Panamanian national assembly. For this move the United States was commended throughout Latin America, and its action was contrasted with that of the Soviet Union toward its satellite countries. "What a difference there is between the international policies of the democratic nations and the totalitarian states!" exclaimed a former Minister of Foreign Affairs of Chile, Conrado Ríos Gallardo.[74]

At the same time this new phase of United States policy toward Latin America discouraged many of the so-called "liberal" democratic groups as well as the "outs" who had hoped to profit from the application of United States pressure upon existing regimes, and they charged the United States with sacrificing its ideals and principles in favor of a cynical policy of power politics, with being concerned about democracy in Europe but not about democracy in Latin America. "North American diplomacy," bitterly commented *El Diario Latino* of San Salvador (December 30, 1947), "has preferred to support the interests of the unjust ruling groups who, under whatever form, wield power in many Ibero-American states." In doing so, it declared, the United States had "deeply wounded the democratic and liberal sentiment of the peoples on this side of the Bravo [Rio Grande]."[75] After the ousting of legally elected governments in Peru and Venezuela by military

72. *La Razón, El Tiempo,* and *El Liberal,* Bogotá, June 10, 1947.
73. "Bases for Inter-American Peace," *Daily Times Herald,* Dallas, Texas, February 8, 1948, quoted in Smith, *Yankee Diplomacy,* 174.
74. Despatch 17, Santiago, January 8, 1948, Department of State Archives.
75. See also Ricardo Ibarra in *La Tribuna,* Tegucigalpa, August 4, 1948.

juntas in October and November, 1948, the United States issued a general protest against the overturn of popularly elected governments by military force.[76]

Yet the Washington government soon afterward extended recognition not only to these governments but also to other new military governments in Latin America, and this action was severely reprobated by some writers in Latin America. "The democratic countries and the democratic tendencies that exist in all the republics of the continent have . . . been abandoned," wailed *El País* of Montevideo (January 7, 1949). *Acción* (January 24, 1949), the newspaper organ of President Luis Batlle Berres of Uruguay, expressed disappointment that the United States had not returned "to the right path in defense of democracies." By this action, complained *La Nación* of Buenos Aires (June 28, 1949), "the government of the United States appears to be giving indirect encouragement to antidemocratic forces as if other interests carried more weight than the political doctrines the defense of which has given the North American people the moral prestige which they enjoy in the world. . . . This kind of collaboration . . . takes on a symbolic meaning in the eyes of the rest of America and has the effect of spreading a dangerous skepticism respecting the value of the ideas which are invoked to proclaim continental unity."[77] Obviously the United States would be "damned if it did or damned if it did not" support democracy in Latin America.

The real effect, if not the purpose, of the Braden corollary, as exemplified particularly in its application to Argentina, was to oppose the right of national self-determination in Latin America. "The exaggerated nationalisms, now so prevalent everywhere," Assistant Secretary Braden told the National Foreign Trade Convention in New York on November 14, 1945, "must be completely extirpated. . . . To eliminate those nationalisms . . . is our firm purpose."[78] Braden's use of the word "exaggerated" as qualifying nationalisms did not detract from the assumed role of the United States as an opponent of national self-determination in Latin America. As long as it played this role it confronted Latin Americans with the disagreeable dilemma of choosing between continued friendship with the United States, on the one

76. *Department of State Bulletin,* XX (January 2, 1949), 30.
77. Similar views were expressed by *El Liberal,* Bogotá, December 21, 1949.
78. Address by the Honorable Spruille Braden, Assistant Secretary of State, at a Luncheon of the National Foreign Trade Convention, Waldorf Astoria Hotel, New York, N. Y., Wednesday, November 14, 1945, Department of State, *Press Release,* 850, November 14, 1945.

hand, and their own interests as they conceived them, on the other. When Braden criticized Perón, said Carlos Alfonso Vaccaro L. in his column "Comentarios" in *Colón al Día* of Colón, Panama (April 5, 1946), he was "the powerful foreigner who was trying to show the rules to a nation that was attaining its own unity and its own security as a national entity."

* * *

As the vaunted wartime solidarity of the Western Hemisphere thus deteriorated, Latin Americans found additional cause of friction in the race situation in the United States, which, far from showing the improvement that they expected, continued to reveal that country to the dark peoples of Latin America as something less than a model of democracy. Betancourt warned in 1945 that "as long as a contemptuous attitude toward the Negro, reaching even the extremes of rancorous hatred, prevails among a large percentage of the population of the United States, a sincere understanding between the two Americas will be difficult."[79] More important even than old grievances such as "the dismembering of Mexico, the separation of Panama, the occupation of Santo Domingo and Nicaragua" in shaping Latin America's attitude toward the United States, said Cosío Villegas, was the knowledge that "the Mexican is, like the Negro, excluded from public places frequented by the white North Americans."[80] This prejudice of the North American was viewed by Ramón Manrique as "a sediment of loathing for the 'native,' whom he employs as a Negro, mulatto, or Indian."[81] Communists in Latin America gave the same explanation, generalizing that the master classes in the United States considered all darker peoples as inferior.[82] Their newspapers, such as *Hoy* of Havana (May 25, 1947), vigorously condemned "the anti-Negro crime of lynching," as exemplified in a trial at Greenville, South Carolina, in early 1947, calling it a revival of "the barbarous racial practices of the Nazis."

The adverse effect of these practices upon Latin America's atti-

79. *El País,* Caracas, August 7, 1945.   80. *Op. cit.,* [361]-365.
81. *Diario de la Costa,* Cartagena, Colombia, March 4, 1945. See also *Novedades,* Mexico City, March 26, 1945. For critical comments on the election of Herman Talmadge as governor of Georgia on a platform denying Negroes the right to vote see *Correio da Manhã,* Rio de Janeiro, February 1, 1947; and *Panama Tribune,* Panama, February 2, 1947.
82. *Hoy,* Havana, March 14, 1949.

tude toward the United States was clearly pointed up when the Haitian Minister of Agriculture, François Georges, arrived in Biloxi, Mississippi, to attend as an invited guest of honor a meeting of the National Association of Commissioners, Secretaries, and Directors of Agriculture in late 1947. "For reason of color" he was denied a room at the Buena Vista Hotel where he had made a reservation and was assigned instead to an outside cottage where he was told his meals would be served. This affront, as *Le Nouvelliste* of Port-au-Prince (November 17, 1947) called it, to "one of the most distinguished personalities of our Negro community" was denounced by that newspaper as an example of "the stupid color prejudice which is rotting certain southern states of the United States." How was it possible, bitterly asked another newspaper of the Haitian capital, *La Nation* (November 18, 1947), for the people of the United States themselves to "speak of Pan-American solidarity when among themselves they make a fierce discrimination between the peoples of the Americas?" In the light of such incidents, the democratic professions of the United States and its "official declarations of respect for the rights of man" gave out a hollow ring.[83] Brazilian newspapers repeatedly cited their own country as an example to the United States in matters of race tolerance. Upon the basis of the contrast revealed by the race situation the eminent Brazilian sociologist, Gilberto Freyre, generalized: "The Latins have developed the ethnic aspect of democracy more than the political, and the Anglo-Saxons the purely political aspect more than the ethnic."[84]

However vigorously Latin Americans might deplore this race situation in the Democratic southern states of the Union and resist the Braden corollary, they favored the continuance of the Democratic Party in power in the United States, because that party, as *Diario de Costa Rica* (November 7, 1946) expressed it, "recalls to us many fine and noble things: the culture and humanity of two great administrations, that of Wilson and that of Roosevelt, the idea of the League of Nations, the Good Neighbor Policy, the Atlantic Charter, the Act of Chapultepec—all that to which humanity aspires in this tortuous century." The victory of the Republican Party, on the other hand, said *La Razón* of David, Panama (November 6, 1946), would open "poorly healed wounds, which North American imperialism during the eras of Harding and Theodore Roosevelt inflicted on Latin America." *Diário Carioca* of Rio de Janeiro (April 21, 1945) even considered it

83. Felipe San Carlos in *Tribuna*, Buenos Aires, June 23, 1947.
84. *Brazil: An Interpretation* (New York, 1945), 147.

"possible that the Republican Party will launch a large-scale offensive against the Good Neighbor Policy, which constitutes an undeniable triumph of the Democrats." As that party was thought of as pre-eminently the party of the Big Stick and "dollar diplomacy," Latin Americans took a dim view of the future of the Good Neighbor Policy after the Republicans won the Congressional elections in November, 1946.[85] *El Diario Latino* of San Salvador (December 30, 1946) even suggested that Latin America in order to "prepare herself economically and politically for future American Republicanism . . . should notice how the Argentine Republic, whose example will have to be followed by other nations, . . . has managed to pursue a course of genuine freedom in both its internal and external affairs."[86]

So widespread was this apprehension of a watering down of the Good Neighbor Policy by the Republican Congress that Senator Arthur H. Vandenberg was constrained to write a letter to Ambassador Hallett Johnson in Costa Rica reassuring "our Central American and South American friends" that they need not "worry about the continuation of a 'Good Neighbor Policy' under the Republican auspices."[87] Speaking for the new Republican majority in Congress, the Speaker of the House, Joseph Martin, also reassuringly declared that "We should do everything possible to promote and strengthen the good relations with our neighboring republics." Now, optimistically concluded *La Prensa Gráfica* of San Salvador (December 5, 1946), "the Republicans understand that the Good Neighbor Policy has been firmly crystallized in the conscience of all America . . . and we believe that the Republicans, with their efficiency and drive will continue it even further."[88] To do so, under the postwar conditions of discord and resentment, would obviously require mighty efforts at reconciliation and understanding.

The termination of World War II, then, ending the pressing necessity for close cooperation among the wartime allies in the Western Hemisphere, thus brought to the surface again the basic dissimilarities between Anglo-American United States and Hispano-Indo-America which had been temporarily shelved in the interests of hemispheric

85. *Novedades,* Mexico City, November 8, 1946; *El Panamá-América,* November 7, 1946; and *La Mañana,* Montevideo, November 7, 1946.

86. See also *El Diario Latino,* January 2, 1947.

87. Arthur H. Vandenberg to Hallett Johnson, November 16, 1946, and January 9, 1947.

88. See also *El Nacional,* Mexico City, November 11, 1946; *Ultima Hora,* San José, November 14, 1946; and *La Nación,* San José, December 25, 1946, and January 7, 1947.

defense. The wartime cooperation between them, though unprecedented in degree, now appeared to have failed to establish a durable solidarity of the Americas which had been the objective of the prewar Good Neighbor Policy and the wartime Policy of the Good Partner. That objective remained, in the words of Roberto García Peña, "only a pretty myth."[89] This division of the Americas, though not caused by the anti-Perón policy of the United States, was nevertheless hastened by it, for that policy, as Mario Flores, editor of *La Noche* of La Paz, wrote in his newspaper (March 7, 1946), created "what the Nazis failed to create: the atmosphere necessary for the formation of two blocs on the continent." To "this almost violent way chosen by the new Washington officials for their hemisphere policy," *La Razón* of Bogotá (January 15, 1946) attributed "the breakdown of the ideals of spiritual and physical cooperation which America thought it had won a few years ago." Now, predicted the Panama *Star and Herald* (January 17, 1946), "Argentina, whether Nazi-Fascist or democratic, will again resume her leadership in Latin American affairs in proportion to the speed with which fear of the 'Yankee Imperialist' returns. . . . Uncle Sam's stock is on the downgrade in the Americas while that of Argentina is headed for a rising market." To some groups in Latin America such a development opened up a welcome prospect. A proadministration newspaper in Lima, Peru, for example, rejoiced that Argentina would now be able to offer "positive competition to North American penetration, opposing it and liberating us from the exclusive domination which the Great Democracy of the North today exercises."[90]

This postwar rekindling of anti-Yanquismo in Latin America was attributed by some to Soviet influence. "The ghost of Mr. Oumansky," eerily warned Ramón Manrique, "still roams suspiciously through the chancellories of America" and "the Yankee is being craftily betrayed."[91] The Panama *Star and Herald* (September 15, 1947) pointed out that "among the people, the masses, there is always at work a Communist ferment which never lacks supporters from other ideological fields seeking to exploit this condition for their own selfish interest." But this anti-United States attitude seemed to both Enrique

89. *El Tiempo,* Bogotá, May 10, 1944.
90. *Jornada,* Lima, June 7, 1947.
91. *Diario de la Costa,* Cartagena, March 4, 1945. Constantin Oumansky served as Soviet Ambassador in Mexico from 1943 until his death in an airplane accident in January, 1945.

Santos and Cosío Villegas to be merely a "confused, unconscious, and almost intangible force," likely to be channeled and exploited by demagogues whether of the right or the left. It was not the exclusive "political property of the Communists." In like manner, *O Jornal* of Rio de Janeiro (January 27, 1949) explained that the sentiment of Yankeephobia had affected sectors of public opinion which were "the most conservative and most impermeable to any leftist influence." It attracted "all the enemies *à outrance* of the United States," motivated by "old ideological hatreds, old frustrations," and "complexes which now come to the surface."[92]

Others felt that this sentiment was caused by the abandonment of the Good Neighbor Policy and were reluctantly constrained to write *el fin* to that policy. "The Good Neighbor Policy . . . has disappeared as if President Roosevelt had taken it with him to the tomb," lamented Enrique Santos.[93] "With Roosevelt gone," declared *El Panamá-América* (March 4, 1947), "the waters return to their normal course, that course being incomprehension, indifference toward the problems of the hemisphere, and North American preoccupation with their own business enterprises." Some business groups in the United States were believed in Latin America to be dominated by "the imperialistic spirit" and to be "incapable of understanding the value of a 'Good Neighbor' policy." Accordingly, as the forces of "fascism, imperialism, and reaction" regained control in the United States, hemispheric relations deteriorated.[94] A certain Mexican intellectual flippantly denoted the passing of the Good Neighbor Policy with the remark that North Americans and Latin Americans "are truly good neighbors: they, the neighbors and we, the good."[95] "Behind the ponderous United States' façade of wealth and power," exclaimed Carlos Dávila, "there is a perilous hemispheric fragility."[96]

Probably at no time during the decade after 1945 could an avowed pro-United States candidate have won election as president in any Latin American country. The certain way to political oblivion in

92. See also Augusto Frederico Schmidt in *Correio da Manhã,* Rio de Janeiro, January 25, 1949; and speech by Assistant Secretary of State Edward G. Miller, Jr., at Boca Raton, Florida, December 6, 1950, *Department of State Bulletin,* XXIII (December 25, 1950), 1011-1016.

93. *El Tiempo,* Bogotá, January 20, 1948.

94. *La Tribuna,* San Salvador, April 20, 1945; *El Tiempo,* Bogotá, April 14, 1945; and "Rumiñahui" in *El Universo,* Guayaquil, July 4, 1945.

95. *Mañana,* Mexico City, November 3, 1945.

96. *We of the Americas* (Chicago and New York, 1949), 38.

Brazil, wrote Carlos Lacerda, editor of the Liberal Catholic *Tribuna da Imprensa* of Rio de Janeiro (July 6, 1952), is "to defend the thesis of collaboration by Brazil with the United States." The Latin American countries, it seemed likely, could not be depended upon to play the same partnership role with the United States in another war as they, with a few exceptions, played in World War II. Throughout the twenty Latin American nations sentiments favorable to the United States rarely found public expression. The era of good feeling had come to an end. The Western Hemisphere was again polarized as Anglo-America and Latin America drifted apart. The Rio Grande had been allowed once more to become wider than the Atlantic Ocean. The changed attitudes toward the United States in Latin America, so unmistakably widespread and disturbing, could not be attributed solely to the machinations of international Communism. They went far deeper than Communist propaganda. Neither could they be explained simply as defiant gestures of the Latin Americans to disprove allegations that they had allowed themselves to become mere satellites of the United States. Nor could they be dismissed, as was sometimes done, with the cavalier remarks that "Anyway the ruling classes in Latin America are pro-capitalist, and they are the only ones who count" or "The Latin American governments are signing the kind of agreements that we want. Does it matter what their people think?" A much broader approach than was revealed by these remarks would be required to re-establish the harmony of the hemisphere.

Chapter 7

ILLUSION AND DISILLUSION

These [Latin American] countries will receive positive aid in improving their conditions and acquiring a high "standard" which will enable them to produce, consume, and act like any European nation.

—*El Telégrafo*, Guayaquil, Ecuador

*D*URING WORLD WAR II fresh winds had blown through Latin America. There was a quickened consciousness of international prestige, a heady exhilaration of participation in common effort, a new sense of achievement and "belongingness." Latin Americans had been lifted to new levels of hope by President Roosevelt's eloquent speeches on the objectives of the war. They were inspired by his voice of "democratic faith" appealing to the "oppressed of the world" and upholding the very "cause of civilization." The propaganda, leadership, and, more important still, the successful military operations of the United States and its allies had led to a wider acceptance of civil rights and the Four Freedoms, stimulated a desire for increased political democracy, discredited several unrepresentative governments, and resulted in their replacement by new ones more broadly based in the popular will. In some countries the narrow agrarian and commercial classes which traditionally governed were in considerable measure divested of their control. In addition the war had generated powerful mass urges for more abundant living and for the fuller participation of the large "have-not" elements of society in the benefits of the economic system. The competing propagandas of Hitler's nations on the one hand and of the United States and its allies on the other had focused attention upon the physical needs of hungry, underprivileged peoples, perhaps in compensation

226

for the horrors and destruction wrought by the war. This had created a new dynamic of rising expectations.

Hungry, underprivileged peoples are everywhere in Latin America. Culturally some of them are still in the prelithic or pre-Stone Age civilization.[1] In few other areas of the world do so many have so little. In Venezuela the 1941 census revealed that of 406,460 dwellings more than 50 per cent had only earthen floors and straw roofs, more than 73 per cent entirely lacked sanitary facilities, and 63 per cent of the rural dwellings had only one room with an average occupancy of 5.5 persons.[2] In some of the Latin American countries life expectancy at birth is as low as 32 years, and disease and malnutrition seriously impair the efficiency of the great majority of the workers. It has been said that hunger is at the root of most of Latin America's health problems. But even health problems which are not due to food shortages are inadequately handled. In the entire country of Bolivia, the Joint Bolivian-United States Labor Commission reported in 1943, there were only 450 physicians, or one to every 7,682 persons.[3] This ratio was even lower in Haiti which had only one physician to every 11,904 persons. "Millions of inhabitants" of these countries, Dr. Alberto Lleras Camargo, while Secretary General of the Organization of American States, declared, are "without a home or an organized family life, without schools, without land, without even personal belongings."[4] Some of the native Indian peoples in Latin America have never even seen water piped into a house and running out of a spigot. When they see it for the first time they sink to their knees in prayerful awe. The natives of Port-au-Prince, the capital of Haiti, watched with wonderment the new traffic lights installed there in December, 1952.

There are thousands of communities in Latin America which have no machines and no factories, where money, if it circulates at all, circulates only in the smallest denominations, and where the only trade is the trade in merchandise carried on men's backs. Theirs is a "centavo capitalism" truly "out of this world" of the mid-twentieth century. Their horizons and often, too, their interests extend only to the next market town. These people have, to all intents and purposes,

1. Alceu Amoroso Lima, "Men, Ideas, and Institutions," *Atlantic Monthly*, February, 1956, 118.

2. Economic Commission for Latin America, *Economic Survey of Latin America, 1950: Recent Facts and Trends in the Economy of Venezuela*, 40.

3. International Labour Office, *Labour Problems in Bolivia*, 35.

4. "The Bogotá Conference," lecture, the Pan American Union, May 24, 1948, *Bulletin of the Pan American Union*, LXXXII (June, 1948), 308.

never been incorporated in the national economy or given opportunities to enter into the capitalist era of society.

One morning, Federico de Onís has related, he and his wife were walking through the Central Market of Guatemala City on their way to an appointment at the Presidential Palace. "How clean the market was! How colorful the flowers! . . . All the imaginable products of the tropics were piled up in mountains of gay profusion and confusion. . . . In front of a basket of carnations an Indian woman was kneeling with a dignified and graceful air. She was wearing a two-piece dress of colored material, her hair was held back by a thick band, and around her slender neck was a heavy silver necklace which fell to her bosom. Her face was open, frank, sweet; her smile fresh and winsome. . . .

'Madam, Buy my flowers! . . .'
'Thanks, my dear, I cannot carry them with me now.'
'I will give them to you for two cents a dozen. . . . '
'Thanks, my dear, after while. . . . '
'I will give them to you for one cent. . . . '
'Many thanks; I cannot carry them.'
'Then I will make you a present of them! Please come back!'
And with a sweeping gesture and a beautiful smile she placed in the outstretched arms of my wife the twelfth part of her stock in trade. We talked with her. She had left her home at the last blinking of the stars and had traveled three leagues on foot with a basket of carnations on her head from San Juan Sacatepéquez to the capital. And in the basket were twelve dozen carnations, planted by her, cultivated by her, selected by her, and now given away by her! . . . She was happy and sure in what she had done. Would she return to her home with only 22 cents instead of 24? No, it was not a matter of cold calculation, but of an overflowing humanity, . . . of loving, of having, of giving."[5]

In Haiti in 1942 the currency in circulation averaged only $1.20 per person, and the average individual cash income for a considerable part of the population was estimated at less than $4 per year.[6] Throughout Latin America a large majority of the peasant, or *peón*, population live outside the money economy of the nation. Under wartime conditions many of them first began to see, and acquire an appetite for, the advantages of modern living. Yet these new aspirations

5. Raúl Osegueda, *Operación Guatemala* $$ OK $$ (Mexico, 1955), 21-22.
6. Stark, "War Bolsters Haiti's Economy," 4.

could not be gratified, partly because of war shortages but partly because of inadequate purchasing power. It was calculated in 1942 that whereas wage earners in the United States had to spend less than 34 per cent of their income for food, those in Brazil had to spend over 48 per cent, in Mexico over 56 per cent, in Argentina almost 60 per cent, in Colombia almost 64 per cent, and in Chile as much as 80 per cent.[7] Even under wartime conditions of high employment, therefore, these people lived on the margin of subsistence.

In Latin America the emphasis has normally been placed upon the exploitation of natural resources for industrial processing abroad. The region is one of those raw-materials producing areas of the world which, since approximately 1866, has been receiving a diminishing share of the benefits of technical progress.[8] A charting of the terms of trade from 1866 to 1947 shows a steady downward trend indicating a constant deterioration in the profitability of foreign trade for the area. Although these figures fail to make allowance for the enormous decline in transportation costs which has occurred since 1866, Latin Americans have made the most of them. In terms of commodities, a Pan American Union study pointed out in 1950, "Latin America receives today 46% less volume per physical unit of exports than 82 years ago. . . . In order to be able to buy the same volume of imports as 82 years ago, it must export over 80% more than at present." This decline was marked even during World War II. In 1946 the terms of trade for Latin America as a whole were 14 per cent less favorable than they had been in 1937.

The effect of this long-range decline in the purchasing power of Latin America's exports appears even more serious when it is calculated on a per capita basis. In terms of real per capita income from raw-materials exports, the figure for eleven countries of Latin America in 1950 was no higher than it had been during the periods 1901-

7. George Soule, David Efron, and Norman T. Ness, *Latin America in the Future World* (New York, 1945), 13, 343.
8. Department of State, *Data Book, Latin America*, 2 vols. (Washington, 1951), *passim;* and Anibal Pinto Santa Cruz, *Hacia Nuestra Independencia Económica* (Santiago de Chile, 1953), 11. See also H. W. Singer, "Economic Progress in Underdeveloped Countries," *Social Research*, XVI (March, 1949), 2-3; United Nations, Department of Economic Affairs, *Relative Prices of Exports and Imports of Under-Developed Countries* . . . (New York, 1949), 7, 23-24; and Inter-American Conference, Tenth, Caracas, 1954, *Some Problems of Economic Development in Latin America: Report Presented by the Pan American Union for the Information of the Delegates* . . . (Washington, 1953), 3-4.

1905 and 1921-1925. In Argentina it dropped 56 per cent below the figure for the period of maximum value, in Costa Rica 37 per cent, in Brazil 28 per cent, and in Uruguay 15 per cent. Judged in terms of the value of per capita exports, all the Latin American countries except Ecuador and Venezuela were worse off in 1950 than in any previous year. In other words, to the average Juan Pueblo of Latin America the importance of the export trade to his income meant less year by year.[9] Moreover the rates of return to the Latin American countries for their primary products have been marked by extreme instability. A United Nations study of the export markets of a broad group of Latin American primary commodities during the half-century from 1901 to 1950 shows that the year-to-year fluctuation in proceeds from such exports averaged 22.2 per cent. In other words, Latin American exporters in any one year could expect their proceeds for the following year to rise or fall within the enormous range of 22.2 per cent.[10] This meant that the production of even exportable raw materials in Latin America was chronically uncertain and speculative.

Under the stimulus and optimism of World War II the Latin American peoples had become impatient with their traditional status as "hewers of wood and drawers of water." To their backward agricultural and largely raw-materials economies they attributed their economic colonialism which, they felt, had long kept them subservient to the industrial nations of the world, specifically Britain, the United States, and, to a lesser degree, France and Germany. The answer to their plight seemed therefore to lie in the further industrialization of their own countries. They came to regard factories as a necessary step to their "decolonization." They began to look to them as a means of supplying their wants, increasing their national incomes, raising their levels of living, and diversifying and thereby presumably strengthening their economies. With industrialization, declared the Mexican-American Commission for Economic Cooperation in its report in July, 1943, "the industrial worker will be able to buy more of the products of agriculture, the agricultural worker will be able to buy more of the products of industry, and their combined productive and purchasing power will enable Mexico to widen its markets and increase its purchases from other nations. These obvious

9. Inter-American Conference, Tenth, Caracas, 1954, *op. cit.*, 6-10.
10. United Nations, Department of Economic Affairs, *Instability in Export Markets of Under-Developed Countries* (New York, 1952), 42.

economic truths can become actualities more quickly in this hemisphere than in perhaps any other portion of the world."[11]

Latin America's economic development throughout the nineteenth century and down to World War I was limited largely to extractive operations initiated and financed by foreigners. Under the prevailing system of free exchange of goods, capital, and labor, it seemed natural that these countries should specialize in the production of raw materials, should supply them to the industrialized nations of Europe and the United States, and should in turn import from those nations practically all the manufactured goods and even a considerable proportion of the consumer goods that they required. From this cozy arrangement all countries concerned profited. But it was interrupted first by World War I and then by the economic depression after 1929 which cut off the traditional overseas outlets for Latin America's meat, sugar, copper, and other raw materials and deprived Latin Americans of foreign manufactures. They were consequently forced into the development of manufacturing industries of their own.[12]

Machine industry had received its first major stimulus in Latin America in World War I, but at the beginning of World War II, except in a few countries, it was still almost negligible in relation to agriculture. Such as it was, it was largely concentrated in the manufacture of light consumers' goods, specifically textiles, leather goods, building materials, miscellaneous metal products, furniture, paper and paper products, processed foodstuffs and beverages, and pharmaceutical and toilet preparations. Industrial interest and activity continued in the same fields during World War II, but showed a tendency to expand, at least in some of the larger countries, into the development of heavy industry, principally iron and steel.

In this program of industrial expansion, even of expansion into the field of heavy industry, Latin America received encouragement from the United States. The Inter-American Financial and Economic Advisory Committee, which was set up on the initiative of the United States at the Panama Conference of Foreign Ministers in 1939, was authorized to study, among other matters, the possibility of securing closer inter-American financial cooperation between banks and treasuries to promote industrial development and methods of encouraging

11. Printed in *Department of State Bulletin,* IX (July 17, 1943), 46.
12. Richard F. Behrendt, "Economic Nationalism in Latin America," *Inter-Americana, Short Papers I,* The School of Inter-American Affairs, University of New Mexico (Albuquerque, 1941), 2-3.

further industrial production in Latin America. This committee proceeded to create the Inter-American Development Commission to stimulate new productive facilities in the American republics and prepared the framework for an Inter-American Bank which would make possible financial cooperation in long-term developmental projects. The proposal for an Inter-American bank had been endorsed at both the First and Second International Conferences of American States in 1889-1890 and 1900-1902.[13] It had been urged again by the delegations of Peru, Mexico, Uruguay, Chile, Paraguay, and the Dominican Republic at the Seventh International Conference of American States at Montevideo in 1933 and was there unanimously accepted.[14] But the bank had never been set up. Under the stress of war conditions in 1939 the United States threw its influence behind both the Inter-American Development Commission and the Inter-American Bank.[15]

In addition, the Office of the Coordinator of Inter-American Affairs through a series of bilateral agreements provided several Latin American nations with assistance in starting new manufacturing industries to compensate for wartime dislocations. For this latter purpose Latin American governments were encouraged to form local development commissions which would draw up plans for industrial expansion with financial assistance from the Export-Import Bank in the United States, the proposed Inter-American Bank having died aborning. The Chilean Corporación de Fomento de la Producción received the first such loan, amounting to $5 million in 1939. In 1940 the authority of the Export-Import Bank was expanded by law to enable it to make loans "to a political subdivision, agency, or national" of a foreign government for the purpose of assisting "in the development of the resources, the stabilization of the economies, and the orderly marketing of the products of the countries of the Western Hemisphere."[16] Promotion of the development of the Latin American countries thus became an explicit objective of the United States.

---

13. James Brown Scott (ed.), *The International Conferences of American States, 1889-1928* (New York, 1931), 40-65.
14. Carnegie Endowment for International Peace, *The International Conferences of American States: First Supplement, 1933-1940* (Washington, 1940), 66-67; and Felipe Barreda Laos, *¿Hispano América en Guerra?* 21-24.
15. The "Convention for the Establishment of an Inter-American Bank," as drafted by the Inter-American Financial and Economic Advisory Committee, was printed in *Department of State Bulletin,* II (May 12, 1940), 512-522.
16. Export-Import Bank of Washington, *Annual Report for 1942.*

As a result, a considerable increase in industrial activity occurred in many of them. The extractive industries—those concerned principally with getting out minerals and forest products—were stimulated by wartime procurement requirements of the United States. In the field of heavy industry the greatest expansion occurred in Brazil and Mexico where steel mills were constructed with the aid of United States government credits. Brazil's pig iron production more than tripled between 1937 and 1946 to reach 350,000 tons in the latter year. By that year the value of her industrial production exceeded that of her agricultural output.[17] In Mexico the physical volume of industrial production increased by 40 per cent between 1939 and 1946, aided, of course, by the disruption of trade channels with Europe.[18] Plans were made to continue this expansion after the war. A subcommittee of the Mexican-American Commission for Economic Cooperation, which was set up as a result of the meeting between President Roosevelt and President Avila Camacho at Monterrey in April, 1943, reported in June, 1944, that in the few years after the war Mexico would need to spend nearly $383 million on development projects. The committee planned and approved 59 such projects for development in Mexico when machinery and equipment should become available.[19]

Encouragement by the United States government, of both a tangible and an intangible nature, was thus partly responsible for the high level of developmental activity attained in Latin America during the war. But this was not the only cause. The war brought a generally increased demand for most of Latin America's export products. It also caused a shortage of imports at a time when consumer purchasing power, particularly among upper-class urban populations, was unprecedentedly high. It thus stimulated a strong demand among these groups for industrial self-development. The inducements for this development were attractive not only because of rising price levels, both domestic and foreign, but also because of the wartime elimination of foreign competitors. The means for it, they believed, either were at hand or would become available from the increased local investment capital, the access of refugee funds, and, most im-

17. Behrendt, *Inter-American International Relations: Problems and Prospects*, 25-26.
18. Richardson Wood and Virginia Keyser, *United States Business Performance Abroad: The Case Study of Sears, Roebuck de Mexico, S.A.*, National Planning Association (Washington, May, 1953), 9.
19. Coordinator of Inter-American Affairs, *History*, 22-23.

portant of all, continued large loans and direct expenditures by the United States government.

In short, Latin Americans desired suddenly to claim the full benefits of the Industrial Revolution which they felt had previously been denied them and which had been monopolized by the United States and the nations of western Europe. Overlooking the political and human factors in their own domestic situation, which for decades past had largely limited them to extractive production, they now determined to move out of the nineteenth century. These "yesterday countries" of bananas and silver mines were eager to become "tomorrow countries" aspiring to a new life in the modern world. From further development of their natural resources, mainly through industrialization, they optimistically hoped to achieve not only increased productivity, higher levels of living, new sources of revenue for governments, and more diversified forms of national income, but even economic and political stability. All this, they believed, would follow industrialization like a chain reaction. Industrialization was conceived to be not necessarily an end in itself but rather a means of development by which these countries might share in the benefits of modern technical progress. By this means they believed they could raise their living standards to those of western Europe and the United States.

At the close of the war, then, Latin American expectations of the continuance of their wartime industrial activity and prosperity were extravagantly high. These expectations were the product of their reliance upon the wartime commitments made to them, of the aspirations generated in them by wartime propaganda, of the grinding need for assistance which was highlighted by their wartime deprivations, and of a certain amount of wishful thinking. During World War II they had come to consider the United States, personified by President Roosevelt, as the guardian of their interests, the resolver of their problems, the unselfish champion of their welfare, the generous neighbor, the answerer of prayers, the magnanimous knight-errant. After the war those nations, with the possible exception of Argentina, expected to move along the path of the future hand in hand with the United States.[20] They had received preferential treatment from the United States during the war, and they hoped that that nation would continue its purchases of strategic materials at guaranteed prices into the postwar period, would provide a continuing market for some of their basic raw products, specifically metals, rubber, cinchona, and

20. Guillermo Martínez Marquez in *El País,* Havana, October 20, 1945.

nitrates, would send them consumer goods to meet pent-up civilian needs, would furnish materials to complete half-finished construction projects, and in general would give them such financial and technical assistance as would enable them to raise their low levels of living and would elevate them into the ranks of the more advanced nations of the world. From their viewpoint the main problems of inter-American relations after the war were social and economic, and they expected the United States with its Policy of the Good Partner, which had achieved a strikingly successful political *rapprochement* among the nations of the Western Hemisphere, to satisfy their requirements in these other clamorous areas of action.

So roseate were Latin America's expectations that *El Telégrafo* of Guayaquil (December 7, 1944) predicted that "the whole continent is definitely on the road toward the attainment of higher goals which will make it the center of a new Humanity. . . . These countries," it said, "will receive positive aid in improving their conditions and acquiring a high 'standard' which will enable them to produce, consume, and act like any European nation." To this end Latin American writers, economists, industrialists, and politicians expected, in the words of Jorge Martí, writing in *El Mundo* of Havana (May 19, 1946), a "bold program" of economic development aided by foreign capital, immigration of foreign agriculturists, technicians, and industrial workers, and industrialization on a continent-wide basis, for which a "continental bank" should be established, underwritten by both Latin America and the United States. "Thus," as Martí optimistically forecast, "Europe would contribute the human material; the United States of America part of the capital and the means of transportation as well as its counsel and experience in industrial and financial techniques; and Latin America the geographic area with a society anxious for progress and democracy." This seemed to him to be "a feasible Utopia."

All this represented a goal of stupendous proportions, the realization of which was deemed to necessitate large dollar credits from the United States. Assistance seemed to be required if the Latin American countries were to lift themselves out of the vicious circle formed by a low standard of living, lack of skills, low output, small savings accumulations, and inadequate capital equipment, all of which in turn produced a low standard of living. Midway through the war the Foreign Minister of Mexico, Ezequiel Padilla, had urged that the United States "employ its vast wealth to make available enormous credits to finance a program to fight all the forces that undermine the health and strength of the nations of America."[21] After the war Latin Americans expected the United States to show, as *Información* of Havana (November 7, 1947) explained, the "spirit of sacrifice, of effort or help in defense of the material interests of our countries." They even bluntly suggested that it had put itself under obligations to do so by reason of the partner relationship which it had encouraged during the war. This was illustrated by Brazil's request for aid from the United States in the same year. The Brazilian Minister of Finance, Pedro Luis Corrêa e Castro, stressed that Brazil had "contributed valuably to a common victory in the last war . . . without receiving material compensation of any sort," that in the event of a third world war Brazil could not "in its present circumstances lend valuable assistance to the United States," and that therefore it deserved to receive loans for its "financial recuperation" and "future economic development" in the total amount of $1,800 million! "Lend me your hand," he enjoined, citing a popular Brazilian proverb, "if you do not wish to carry me on your back."[22]

There is no doubt, then, that Latin Americans expected that the wartime momentum of inter-American cooperation would continue into the postwar period. They wanted a good neighbor who, in the words of *La Prensa Libre* of San José, Costa Rica (January 7, 1949), "understands our anxieties and tries to alleviate them, who knows our errors and prudently corrects them, who shelters our very fears and making them his own comes to our side, who assists in our poverty with a gesture of aid honorable to both sides; we want a neighbor who is a loyal friend, disposed to assist on a mutual basis in the heavy load of the destiny of the continent." For them the Good Neighbor Policy of the United States had been transmuted into the simple principle, "Thou shalt love thy neighbor as thyself." They expected that the Americas would become a hemisphere of brothers, an *hermandad* of participants in mutually helpful, joint efforts at reconstruction and development, in which the United States as the wealthiest member would be largely responsible for their future well-being and progress.

These dreams were shattered. As World War II neared its end, the interest which the United States had shown since 1930 in Pan-American regionalism, almost to the exclusion of interest in other

21. *Free Men of America*, 100.
22. *Correio de Manhã*, Rio de Janeiro, June 8, 1949.

areas of the world, diminished and was replaced by a new zeal for world-wide organization. The Western Hemisphere system had to yield priority to the international security system which Roosevelt and Hull worked out with Churchill and Stalin and which was established at San Francisco in June, 1945. At the same time the preferential treatment which the Latin American countries had enjoyed under the Western Hemisphere system of economic cooperation during the war was threatened by the postwar insistence of the United States upon world-wide trade expansion through removal of all obstacles to the free international exchange of goods. As the United States swung over to a position in favor of a unified world economy, it seemed to render impossible the continued "togetherness" of the American nations. The deterioration of relations between the United States and Latin America after 1944 was due in large part to the preoccupation of the United States with world-wide organization. As the United States strenuously campaigned against regional blocs in any part of the world, it could not consistently show favoritism for its own Pan-American bloc.

By the end of the war the Latin American countries had accumulated gold and foreign exchange holdings amounting to almost $4.4 billion, an unprecedentedly large foreign exchange reserve built up primarily by reason of the favorable balance-of-payments position of those countries in relation to the United States as well as other areas of the world during the war when demand for their raw-materials exports was high and the availability of imports low.[23] The end of the war, therefore, left them with a large reservoir of unexpended credits and an even larger urge to spend them. But postwar prices of many of the commodities which Latin Americans wanted to import from the United States rose sharply as the Truman administration removed domestic price ceilings. At the same time the value of the dollar declined. Studies made by the International Monetary Fund and the United Nations show that Peru, for example, had to pay more than twice as much per unit for durable consumer goods, including radios, housewares, and motor cars, in 1946 as in 1938. With a given quantity of its prewar exports it could buy after the war only 61 per cent as much imported textile manufactures and 63 per cent as much imported food as before the war. Similarly Brazil could buy only 81 per cent as much textiles and 78 per cent as much food, Mex-

23. Department of Commerce, International Economics Division, *International Transactions of the United States during the War, 1940-45*, 134.

ico only 87 per cent as much textiles and 71 per cent as much food, and Chile only 58 per cent as much textiles and 46 per cent as much food.[24] As under these conditions the Latin Americans sought to relieve their wartime commodity shortages and to satisfy their pent-up consumer demands, they incurred during the first three postwar years debits of $2.7 billion, the financing of which largely depleted their dollar reserves. As their accumulated savings thus disappeared in the postwar inflation, they were quick to blame the United States. As the official *Democracia* of Buenos Aires acridly explained in an editorial published six years after the war, "In 1945, when the war ended, the United States owed Argentina a large sum representing supplies which had not been paid for. These credits were blocked at the end of the war. In other words the debtor refused to pay, did not include any interest, and meanwhile manipulated prices in such a way that half of this blocked Argentine credit evaporated. As a result of this maneuver this country was swindled out of an immense sum."[25]

Since the procurement and developmental operations of the United States in Latin America during the war period had been carried on in pursuance of government-to-government agreements—a method which was followed in order to ensure both an orderly expansion of production and a stabilization of prices—Latin Americans became accustomed to look to the United States government for aid and guidance in such operations and to expect large assistance from it after the war. American public capital was being used to provide purchasing power to Europe. But Latin Americans were profoundly disappointed that the government aid from the United States to their area was so small a trickle in comparison with the broad stream of that aid to other parts of the world. The new United States government capital made available to them in 1945 was only approximately equivalent to their own repayments of outstanding obligations to the United States.[26] The $110 million of grants and credits which they received from the United States in 1946 declined to $99 million in 1947 and only $68 million in 1948. Early in the year 1948 an offer of large assistance to at least one Latin American country, Mexico,

24. International Monetary Fund, *Terms of Trade in Latin American Countries* (Washington, 1949); and United Nations, Department of Economic Affairs, *Relative Prices,* 15, 63-65.

25. Editorial "Así Paga el Diablo" by "Descartes" in *Democracia,* Buenos Aires, October 11, 1951.

26. Department of Commerce, International Economics Division, *International Transactions,* 143.

was made by the Assistant Secretary of the Treasury in Washington, Harry Dexter White. He proposed to the Director General of the Bank of Mexico, Carlos Novoa, that the United States assist his country in the amount of about $2.5 billion, $1 billion of which would be a stabilization commitment that would probably not have to be used. The rest would be made available over a period of approximately ten years and would be arranged on terms similar to the terms granted to the British in their $3.25 billion loan of 1946.[27] But this generous proposal did not prosper. From July, 1945, to July, 1950, Latin Americans saw the government in Washington pour into foreign countries the fabulous total of more than $28 billion, of which it channeled only $514 million, or 1.8 per cent, to them. To Latin Americans there appeared to be, as Argentina's Perón said, a Dollar Curtain as well as an Iron Curtain.[28]

It seemed to Latin Americans that while the United States was distributing its wealth with amiable prodigality to nations outside the American hemisphere it was making only a "poor mouth" to them. In its relations with them, they complained, the United States was acting in the spirit of the cynical folk maxim *Yo no olvido las deudas, pero no las pago* (I do not forget debts; I just do not pay them). The United States, protested *Le Nouvelliste* of Port-au-Prince (April 16, 1946), was being generous to Germany, which had caused incalculable destruction during the war, but was doing nothing for Haiti, which had met all her responsibilities to help the United States by granting the use of her air bases, her territory, and her strategic commodities for the defeat of Hitler's Germany. "Those who ask and do not give," pointedly warned *Noticias Gráficas* of Buenos Aires (February 23, 1951), "are in danger of seeing their good neighbors turn their backs when they are summoned in the name of a fraternity which is only preached but not practiced." According to *El Crisol* of Havana (December 11, 1947), "in many of our countries there are more hunger, more epidemics, more want than in the European countries devastated by the war." The real enemies of Latin America, it insisted, were hunger, sickness, ignorance, and misery. Should not the United States, in its own interest, if not in the interest of the

27. "Suggestions for a Program of Close Economic Co-Operation between Mexico and the United States," January 12, 1948, Harry Dexter White Papers, Princeton University, Item 28.

28. Address to the First World Congress of College Youth, Buenos Aires, April 30, 1952.

Latin American countries, asked *La Estrella de Panamá* (September 3, 1949), show toward them some of the concern which had prompted it to help the European nations to reorganize their productive machinery, to restore their economies, to relieve unemployment and poverty, and thus "to thwart the sinister plans of the Soviet"?

To Latin American eyes it seemed that their area of the world was being stingily "measured and weighed" by the United States, as *El País* of Montevideo (May 16, 1952) concluded, "like a strategic commodity needed for a possible conflict." A grim story, attributed to Dr. Oswaldo Aranha, a former foreign minister of Brazil, was told in some of these countries to highlight one of the difficulties in the way of securing loans from the United States. According to the story, when a representative of Monaco asked President Truman for a loan for his country, he was asked if there were any Communists in Monaco. When he replied that there were none, he was told that a loan could not be given. The Monaco representative then went to France to borrow a few Communists but was informed, "We cannot lend our Communists because then the United States will make no loans to us."[29] For Monaco in this story each Latin American could substitute the name of his own country. But anti-Communist governments in Latin America were disappointed that they received so little aid from the United States in their resistance to Communist doctrine and activity.[30]

As the United States reoriented its world policy after the war, Latin Americans felt that their wishes and interests were not taken into consideration. Evidences of their disappointment were abundant. "The relations of Pan-Americanism to the new world conceptions" of the United States should be defined, urged *Correio da Manhã* of Rio de Janeiro (April 24, 1947), "before the great Republic of the North buries itself to its ears in new world commitments and duties at the same time that its oldest and most proven allies of the Hemisphere go neglected." But this was not done, and the Good Neighbor Policy was allowed to become, as Angel Guerra, a columnist of *El Liberal* of Bogotá (January 17, 1948), called it, only a "Good Spectator Policy." As the United States was now largely preoccupied with its formidable postwar problems outside the Western Hemisphere, Latin Americans were relegated to the periphery of its interest and their expectation of enlarging tomorrows evaporated. "The

29. *El Tiempo,* Bogotá, January 15, 1948.
30. *El Diario Ilustrado,* Santiago, April 4, 1947.

tasks of the United States in other parts of the world," declared *El Liberal* (April 15, 1946), "are delaying the development of the American Good Neighbor Policy and postponing the date of arrival for us of the message of the better world that was promised."[31] By January, 1948, Dr. Eduardo Zuleta Angel, who soon afterward became the foreign minister of Colombia, reported that he found in the United States a "total indifference toward Latin America." Latin Americans, he said, "are becoming a kind of poor relative, troublesome, tiresome and unnecessary."[32] They had begun to feel abandoned, useful in times of international emergency but fit only to be discarded after the return of peace. "In the North American republic," said the outstanding Brazilian newspaper *Correio de Manhã* (March 27, 1947), they had been *"à la mode* only during the war," the period of "close collaboration" had passed, and they were regarded now only vaguely as friends, useful in giving occasional help. For the past four years, asserted that influential newspaper (May 10, 1949), the United States had shown no special interest in Brazil, had furnished it with no sufficient economic assistance, and had denied its markets to Brazil's primary products.

During the war the United States in many public statements created expectations among the Latin American peoples that it could not possibly fulfill in the postwar period. Its wartime propaganda promises came back only as a hollow echo to plague it when the war ended. The United States thus created its own psychological problem—a problem of the first magnitude—in Latin America. As it assumed responsibility for the welfare and prosperity of the entire non-Soviet world, it began to cut the Latin Americans down to size in relation to other peoples, and by its world-wide commitments complicated its own problems of postwar readjustment in inter-American relations.

When two South American presidents-elect, Dr. Mariano Ospina Pérez of Colombia and Tomás Berreta of Uruguay, visited the United States in 1947 their visits were scarcely even noticed in the United States press—even in the New York press. Latin Americans were repeatedly—and sometimes bluntly—told by officials of the United States that they were less important in the postwar world than the people of other areas, particularly Europe and the Far East. Since Latin America had not, like Europe, suffered the direct ravages of

31. See also Luis Rivas in *El Liberal,* Bogotá, December 5, 1947.
32. *El Tiempo,* Bogotá, January 15, 1948.

World War II nor, like Asia, emerged from the war as a power vacuum, it seemed to become a "forgotten land" in the matter of economic aid. Indeed Latin Americans thought they saw evidence that they were not being treated even as well as some of the African peoples.[33] The close, mutually beneficial relationship which most of them had established and maintained with their powerful northern partner during the war was replaced by dashed hopes, sore resentments, and disheartened cynicism about the motives and aims of the United States. They even complained that the United States as the industrial nation of the world par excellence was only interested in keeping them undeveloped so that they might continue as purchasers of its manufactured products.[34] Its European Recovery Program, which was deliberately intended to restore Europe to its prewar position in world trade, would have the effect of reducing them again to a virtual colonial status, ignoring the considerable changes brought about by wartime industrialization and reorientation of their trade.[35]

* * *

Government loans are more attractive to Latin American countries than private loans because they draw a lower interest and therefore make a smaller drain on their foreign exchange holdings. They may also be susceptible to interest readjustments whereas private loans usually carry fixed interest rates. But Latin Americans were repeatedly told after the war that the United States favored the use of private rather than public capital in the development of their countries. The long-term economic development which they needed, Secretary of State Marshall told the Inter-American Conference for the Maintenance of Continental Peace and Security at Quitandinha, Brazil, in September, 1947, required "a type of collaboration in which a much greater role falls to private citizens and groups than is the case in a program designed to aid European countries to recover from the destruction of war."[36]

33. Augusto Frederico Schmidt in *Correio da Manhã*, Rio de Janeiro, May 13, 1949; *Diário Carioca*, Rio de Janeiro, May 15, 1949; and Carlos Dávila, *We of the Americas*, 53-62.
34. *Nuestro Diario*, Guatemala, August 31, 1949; and *El Universal*, Caracas, December 29, 1950.
35. Speech by João Carlos Muniz of Brazil, Sixth Session of United Nations Economic and Social Council, Official Record, 146th Mtg., 18 February 1948, 196.
36. *Department of State Bulletin*, XVII (September 14, 1947), 500.

The main objective of the United States in its Latin American policy after the end of World War II, as it seemed to Latin Americans, was the promotion of private capital investment. During the 1930's United States direct investments in Latin America had declined in value from the depression level of $3.52 billion in 1929 to only $2.77 billion at the beginning of World War II, or by about 21 per cent.[37] After the United States became involved in the war, efforts were made to open up new opportunities for private investment in Latin America. Under the Western Hemisphere Trade Corporations clause, which was added to the Internal Revenue Code in 1942, United States companies which received substantially all their gross income from sources within the Western Hemisphere outside the United States were given total exemption from excess profits taxes and partial exemption from corporate income taxes by a rate pegged at 14 percentage points below the regular corporate rate.

But the incentives provided by the Western Hemisphere Trade Corporations legislation appeared to be insufficient, judged by their results. Private loans to Latin American governments through bond flotations in the United States continued to be unpopular largely because of the unsatisfactory experience of United States investors with the servicing of Latin American bonds during the period 1929-1940. As a result no Latin American government bonds were floated in the United States, though Latin American governments were enabled to satisfy some of their capital needs after the war by loans from the International Bank for Reconstruction and Development. United States investors were loath to go into the region. They regarded investment there as subject to high and unpredictable risks, including currency depreciation, exchange controls, the possibility of nationalization, restrictive labor legislation, and unfamiliar property laws, all of which were deemed to create an unfavorable climate for private investment. Besides, United States investors found that after the war they could employ their funds to better advantage in profitable local undertakings. The opportunities for utilizing capital in the United States were so attractive that in general the volume of private long-term foreign investment in the postwar period was small in relation to the volume of private domestic investment. As a result the net new private United States capital which went into Latin America

37. Department of Commerce, *American Direct Investments in Foreign Countries, 1936* (Washington, 1938), 11; and *American Direct Investments in Foreign Countries, 1940* (Washington, 1942), 5, 8.

in the first three postwar years amounted to only $975 million and thus fell far short of meeting both the requirements and the expectations of Latin America. By 1948 the total private United States investment in that area amounted to $3.68 billion, a figure which was only slightly higher than the total for 1929.[38] At the same time British investments in Latin America, which had reached almost 1.13 billion pounds sterling before the war, were being substantially liquidated, declining by more than a third between 1945 and 1951.[39]

The Truman administration, inspired particularly by Secretary of Commerce Averell Harriman, began forthwith to push with increased aggressiveness a program to foster private United States capital investment in Latin America. This program included the negotiation of bilateral agreements of friendship, commerce, and navigation, which sought to reduce the risks of private capital investment abroad by assuring through treaty arrangements that such investment would receive nondiscriminatory and equitable treatment. They also sought to ensure that in general the treatment of such investment would be no less favorable than that accorded to nationals of the foreign country and to nationals of a third country. Moreover, these agreements provided for prompt, adequate, and effective compensation in the event of the expropriation of an investor's property, for conversion of such compensation into the investor's currency on a basis that would protect his interest, and for the withdrawal of earnings and reasonable amounts of the principal of the investment. The purpose was to establish new legal bases for United States private investment and business operations abroad. But none of these treaties was immediately ratified and put into force.

At the Ninth International Conference of American States at Bogotá in 1948 the United States sought to secure the cooperation of all the American nations in a collective effort toward the same end. The so-called Economic Agreement of Bogotá, drawn up there, was written largely in accordance with Harriman's suggestions to conform to the requirements of United States capital, but it was signed by several of the Latin American delegations only with reservations to the articles dealing with private investments and was subsequently ratified by only three governments—Costa Rica, Panama, and Hon-

38. Department of Commerce, *The Balance of International Payments of the United States, 1946-1948* (Washington, 1950), 94.

39. Pan American Union, *Foreign Investments in Latin America: Measures for Their Expansion* (Washington, 1954), 2-3.

duras, the last with a reservation. Latin Americans generally complained that it did not sufficiently recognize the principle that foreign capital must be subject to the national laws and national courts.

As another means of stimulating private capital investment in Latin America the United States sought to eliminate double taxation —that is, taxation of the earnings of capital both in the United States and in the Latin American country where the earnings originate. Soon after the end of the war it showed an interest in developing a cooperative program which would avoid this duplication of taxation or double collection of taxes on the same earnings. United States officials exchanged views and held conferences with representatives of Colombia, Venezuela, Mexico, Brazil, Paraguay, and other Latin American countries in an attempt to discover whether a sufficient similarity of tax systems existed to warrant the conclusion of bilateral agreements. But whereas federal tax law in the United States taxes the income of United States citizens and corporations whether it is earned in the United States or in a foreign country, most of the Latin American governments insist that earnings shall be taxed according to their source. They contend that the privilege of prior taxation should be acknowledged to reside with the government of the capital-importing country, since it is the locus of the earnings. The United States, making an effort to mitigate the effects of double taxation without surrendering to this source principle, offered to credit United States investors with the amount of taxes paid to a Latin American government. But despite protracted negotiations no agreements for avoidance of double taxation could be reached. The Economic Agreement of Bogotá contained a recommendation that the American governments should "seek to conclude as soon as possible agreements to prevent double taxation" (Article 27), but this recommendation suffered the fate of the agreement as a whole.

A still different method of encouraging private capital investment in Latin America was proposed by the Truman administration in 1949 as a part of the Technical Assistance, or Point Four, program. By this method the President proposed to stimulate United States private capital to go into overseas investment fields by providing governmental guaranties against the hazards of foreign investment.[40] The method was already being tried under the Economic Cooperation Act of 1948 for those countries—none of them Latin American—which were participating in the Economic Recovery Pro-

40. President Truman's Message to Congress, June 24, 1949.

gram. In late 1949 specific legislation was introduced into Congress providing guaranties to new capital against the "risks peculiar to foreign investment." These were intended to make the United States responsible for, first, investment losses arising from inability to transfer investment yields or to make capital withdrawals, and, second, capital losses resulting from expropriation without "prompt, adequate, and effective compensation."[41] But this proposal was not acceptable to Congress. It seemed likely to impose upon the United States government the disagreeable alternative of either itself paying for the obligations for which it had assumed responsibility or contriving some means of forcibly collecting them from foreign governments.

Moreover this proposal did not gain the support of private investors in the United States. "Governmental guarantees [sic] by this country," declared the National Planning Association, "are not nearly as effective in safeguarding such investments as the enlightened attitudes of the U.S. businessmen who manage the investments."[42] All the major business organizations publicly declared their objections to the Truman administration's new plan. They felt that the responsibility for removing obstacles to private investment rested solely upon those Latin American and other countries which desired outside capital and that if those countries did not choose to create and maintain a favorable climate for private foreign investment they must suffer the consequences. Governmental efforts could not induce private capital to flow into other countries, even the most friendly. Only the nation desiring the capital could attract it there. Private investors agreed, further, that this guaranty proposal, as well as any other measures taken by the United States to increase the investment of its nationals abroad, would serve only to weaken the incentive of capital-importing countries to take the steps required to attract foreign private capital. Besides, private investors generally eschewed governmental directives and preferred to operate outside officially privileged channels.

Nevertheless, toward the end of 1952, officials of the Truman administration began to advocate a virtually all-out effort to force United States private capital into foreign areas. They proposed that all the agencies of the government which were concerned with promoting private investment abroad "should launch a program of total

41. Department of State, *Point Four: Cooperative Program for Aid in the Development of Economically Underdeveloped Areas* (Washington, 1950), 73-75.
42. Wood and Keyser, *op. cit.*, x.

diplomacy directed towards improving the climate for foreign investment in friendly, foreign countries" and forestalling "discriminatory
or other actions by foreign governments adversely affecting the interests of American investors." Negotiations for bilateral investment
treaties would be pushed, though none of them had yet aroused any
enthusiasm in Latin America. "Industry advisors" would be assigned
immediately to key diplomatic missions in order to push private investment abroad. The Export-Import Bank would "aggressively
extend its activities" by entering into partnership with a selected few
United States corporations and supplying them with capital on easy
terms to enable them to extend their operations in foreign countries.
"A government investment guaranty system" would be established
providing "all risk coverage," including protection against losses resulting from "international or civil war," and tax inducements similar
to those granted in the Western Hemisphere Trade Corporations Act
would "be offered to individual and institutional purchasers of foreign
securities." The government, it was urged, "should assist in every
way possible the efforts of individual private investors to obtain concessions from foreign countries." Emphasis was to be placed upon
the stimulation of the flow of private capital into "the industrialized
countries of Europe and Japan in order to enable them to send venture capital in turn to the underdeveloped areas of Asia, Africa and
Latin America." This comprehensive program for governmental
stimulation of private investment was conceived to be the only satisfactory method of assisting "friendly foreign countries to achieve balanced economic development."[43]

The effectiveness of governmental effort in this direction, it was
argued, was demonstrated by the fact that of the total new United
States private investment that flowed into Latin America in the postwar years, almost 30 per cent represented investment by United States
petroleum interests, which received the active support of the United
States government for reasons of policy in their attempts to secure
and consolidate concessions abroad.[44] But perhaps an even more
important reason than active governmental support for this outflow
of petroleum investment was the high rate of return on such investment in Latin America, which rose from 20.4 per cent in 1945 to 28.4

43. August Maffry, "Program for Increasing Private Investment in Foreign
Countries: Report Prepared for Technical Cooperation Administration, Department of State, Department of Commerce, Mutual Security Agency, December
18, 1952," mimeographed.

44. Department of Commerce, *The Balance of International Payments*, 139.

per cent in 1948 and which represented the highest rate of return for any major category of investment.[45]

From the Latin American viewpoint the investment guaranty program was particularly objectionable because it made all claims arising out of such guaranteed investment immediately the subject of diplomatic negotiations between the governments concerned, thus removing them from the jurisdiction of local courts and derogating from the sovereign right of a government to exercise supervision over the activities of foreign private capital within its national boundaries. This feature, giving all governmentally guaranteed private investment a semiofficial status, raised the specter of a new dollar diplomacy. For this and other reasons Latin Americans showed little or no interest in it, and only one country—Haiti—concluded an investment guaranty agreement with the United States permitting the program to be put into effect.[46] The postwar emphasis of the United States upon private investment was often interpreted in Latin America as an attempt by the United States to push the very types of economic enterprise which had long been made the object of political attack by the economic nationalists and the social revolutionaries, who rose to the ascendancy in many countries of Latin America after the war. Moreover, as it was often coupled with the creation of a hemisphere defense framework for the United States, it aroused deep-rooted suspicions in Latin America that the United States was here employing an economic weapon which would reduce their sovereign countries to satellites in preparation for a new world war.

The Truman administration's hope of putting the United States government squarely and officially behind United States capital exporters was, therefore, not realized. But an alternative plan for a government-backed international financial consortium to stimulate and direct private capital investment into underdeveloped areas, including Latin America, was put forward in March, 1951. This proposed International Finance Corporation, to be organized as an affiliate of the International Bank for Reconstruction and Development, would finance private developmental projects through equity investments or loans without government guaranties in underdeveloped countries which were members of the International Bank and which subscribed to the capital of the corporation. The corporation would supply potential private investors with information about such

45. *Ibid.*, 94.
46. *Department of State Bulletin*, XXVIII (May 11, 1953), 682.

projects, would assist financially in launching them, would provide an informed and continuing supervision over them through an international directorate representing all the member governments, and might, by reason of its international character and prestige, afford cooperating private investors some measure of protection against the possibility of discriminatory treatment. This plan was endorsed by spokesmen for all twenty of the Latin American nations, but it was not put into operation during the Truman administration.[47]

Meanwhile, certain United States companies discovered that they could operate profitably in these countries if they took pains not to give the Latin Americans opportunities to equate their operations with "capitalistic exploitation." If they abstained from interference in local politics, accepted conditions as they found them, or when dissatisfied with such conditions sought to improve them through cooperative efforts with local governments and local associates, they could gain and retain the confidence of Latin Americans. If their main purpose appeared to be to contribute to the economic and social development of the host country and to identify themselves with the welfare of that country, they would not run serious risk of expropriation and generally need not fear that even their remittances of reasonable profits to stockholders in the United States would be inhibited by the local government. The policy of one such company, for example, operating in Cuba, Mexico, Brazil, and Venezuela, is to make itself more and more a part of the economy of the country in which it operates; to buy the largest possible amount of merchandise items there, even setting up local manufacturers in business wherever possible; to reinvest 100 per cent of the profits in the country; to use native employees to the fullest extent possible; and to emphasize profit-sharing and in-service promotions as means of giving these employees a sense of identification with company interests. Its purpose, says a company official, is to make the company "a window through which Latin America can view the system of the United States."[48]

47. International Development Advisory Board, *Partners in Progress* (Washington, March 1951), 84-85; International Bank for Reconstruction and Development, *Report on the Proposal for an International Finance Corporation* (April, 1952); *Report on the Status of the Proposal for an International Finance Corporation* (May, 1953); *A Second Report on the Status of the Proposal for an International Finance Corporation* (June, 1954); Foreign Operations Administration, Office of Research, Statistics and Reports, *Report on the Economic Situation in Latin America, Prepared for the International Development Advisory Board* (Washington, 1954), 201-202.

48. Wood and Keyser, *op. cit., passim.*

Another such company is the Venezuelan Basic Economy Corporation created in 1947 and capitalized at $4 million. Largely financed by the International Basic Economy Corporation, a Rockefeller enterprise, it seeks to assist in reducing the cost of food to consumers in Venezuela by inproving its productivity and distribution. One-half of the common stock in the corporation was opened up for purchase by the Venezuelan Development Corporation, a branch of the Venezuelan government, which by 1949 had actually taken preferred stock in its two main subsidiaries, Productora Agropecuaria and Pesquerías Caribe. It was intended that when a subsidiary company should begin to show a profit, its common stock would be offered for sale on the Venezuelan market and that by 1957 the corporation would offer stock control to Venezuelan buyers.[49]

The system of a mixed company, composed of both private United States capital and local Latin American capital, has therefore been experimented with since the war. It has the large advantage that a Latin American government is not likely to expropriate a company in which its own citizens are heavily interested. Even the problem of exchange convertibility for profits ceases to be serious when local Latin American capital is permitted to participate on equitable terms with United States capital in mixed-company undertakings and when profits are plowed back into the country through reinvestment or profit-sharing arrangements with local employees. Reinvestment of the earnings of a United States company in the foreign country in which it operates is encouraged by United States tax laws which permit the company to defer the payment of income taxes on the earnings of a foreign subsidiary until the company distributes its dividends.[50] One of the recommendations of President Truman's International Development Advisory Board, submitted on June 5, 1952, was that "foreign capital should be encouraged to invest in the underdeveloped countries in partnership with local capital and in a spirit of cooperation rather than of exploitation. . . . Foreign capital in these countries should be creative as well as profitable; contributing to economic growth and better lives for the people of the country, recognizing their national pride and national interests. It should make friends, not lose them."[51]

49. John Chamberlain, "The Good Partner," *Barron's,* January 31, 1955; and "Development Ideas That Pay," *Business Week,* September 10, 1955.
50. United Nations, Economic and Social Council, *Taxation in Capital-Exporting and Capital-Importing Countries.*
51. *Guidelines for Point 4: Recommendations of the International Development Advisory Board* (Washington, June 5, 1952), 3.

United States private capital, it was felt, taking its technology with it, could make a fundamental contribution to Latin American economic development. To the extent that foreign capital in the past, it should be noted, had failed to relieve Latin American countries of dependence upon foreign exchange, it had encouraged nationalist restrictions upon foreign capital generally.[52]

Latin Americans asserted that private capital which entered Latin America on this basis after the war would be generally accepted. "We are truly interested," declared *El Panamá-América* (April 6, 1945), "in the North American or the European who comes to these Spanish-speaking countries in order to collaborate with us in promoting the general welfare." President Alemán informed President Truman on the latter's visit to Mexico City in 1947 that "your capital, respecting our laws, will find in our country a welcome which will be in proportion to the spirit with which it is inspired, within the limits of a collaboration that stands above all egoism and all attempt at hegemony." The Mexican government assured the United States in October, 1952, that the climate in that country was completely favorable to foreign investments which were willing to submit to Mexican law and the jurisdiction of Mexican courts. The Finance Minister of Brazil, Oswaldo Aranha, declared, in his first public statement after his appointment in mid-June, 1953, that he was not opposed to foreign capital in Brazil as long as it did not hold a privileged status. In general the Latin American countries were willing to assist in the investment of private capital provided it came not as *émigré* capital but as resident capital. While not denying due guaranties to foreign investment they were determined to protect their people from the foreign intervention in their affairs and the foreign monopolistic control of natural resources which had often been the bane of Latin America in the past. If foreign investment helped to promote their national development, to raise living standards, and to diversify their economies, if it contributed to the progress and benefit of the country without unduly disturbing native cultures, patterns of living, and political processes, and if it operated under the nation's own invest-

52. Both the National Planning Association and the Latin American Investment Council have described the attractive opportunities awaiting United States business enterprise in Latin America and have suggested many excellent practical ways in which it may profitably operate there. Wood and Keyser, *op. cit.;* and Thomas A. Gaines, *Profits with Progress: Latin America's Bright Investment Future,* Latin American Investment Council (Stamford, Connecticut, 1954).

ment laws and not under foreign laws, it was welcomed. If it did not do these things, it might be dealt with as the hostage of a hostile foreign nation set down in their midst. It remained subject to the prior and inalienable right of a Latin American country and people to exploit their own national resources without interference and dictation from outside.

This reservation was made explicit in a Bolivian-Uruguayan proposal which was passed in a session of the Second Committee of the General Assembly of the United Nations in December, 1952, with the almost unanimous support of the Latin American delegations. In that resolution the right of nationalization was sustained by twelve Latin American states over the objection of the United States. Even a subsequent amendment by the United States to eliminate from nationalization proceedings "action contrary to the applicable principles of international law and practice, and to the provisions of international agreements" was rejected by the Latin American delegations, not a single one of whom supported the United States in the final vote.[53] Their strong feelings of nationalism thus prevailed even over their need for foreign capital.

By the end of 1952, private United States investments in Latin America amounted to almost $5.8 billion, comprising over 38 per cent of the total investment of citizens of the United States in foreign countries. Of this total the largest amounts were invested in Venezuela ($1.2 billion), Brazil ($1 billion), Cuba ($0.7 billion), and Chile ($0.6 billion), and the new postwar capital had flowed principally into those countries.[54] By this means the United States was, in effect, making not only its dollars but also its inventions, its manufactures, its gadgets, its technical skills, and perhaps indeed its whole way of life available to Latin America. As a result new sources of wealth were opened up in Latin America and the sum total of goods and services there was enlarged. The tools, skills, goods, craftsmen, and teachers supplied by such capital had accelerated the rate of material

53. United Nations, General Assembly, Seventh Session, 1952-1953, *Official Records, Annexes, Agenda,* Item 25, 7-8; and General Assembly, Seventh Session,1952-1953, Second Committee, *Official Records,* 271-283. The vote as given in this official record appears to be inaccurate, as Nicaragua, which was chosen by lot to vote first, is not recorded as voting either in favor or against or as abstaining.

54. Department of Commerce, *Foreign Commerce Weekly* (January 25, 1954), 11; and United Nations, Department of Economic and Social Affairs, *Foreign Capital in Latin America* (New York, 1955), 12.

progress in all these countries, providing new incentives to progress and eliminating much of the otherwise inevitable and costly process of trial and error in achieving it.

But the rate of increase of United States private investment in Latin America was slower than it had been in the 1920's. The outflow of direct investment capital from the United States to all foreign areas after the war was, in general, disappointing to them as well as to the Truman administration. Of the less than $750 million of new United States private direct investment in all such areas during the period 1948-1953 less than 30 per cent went to Latin America.[55] During the four-year period starting in 1950 the net new dollars flowing to Latin America from the United States averaged only $15 million a year.[56] Besides, as was perfectly natural, this capital tended to go into already established and proved industrial lines, such as the extractive industries and the export of foodstuffs, and not into production to satisfy local needs nor into new industries such as the manufacture of newsprint. During the years 1946-1949, for example, over 72 per cent of all the new investment capital that went from the United States into Latin America was invested in the petroleum industry of Venezuela.[57] In addition, much of the apparent increase in United States investment in Latin America after 1948 resulted from back earnings; a census of United States foreign investments taken in 1950 showed that about 30 per cent of all United States assets in Latin America represented reinvestment of profits. Indeed, United States private investment in agriculture, manufacturing, and commerce in Latin America had suffered severe cutbacks.[58] Nor, for obvious reasons, had new private investment been attracted to basic projects in the fields of education, health, road construction, irrigation, and reclamation, which were considered by Latin Americans to be socially essential. Nor had it gone into the more backward countries such as Ecuador, Haiti, and Paraguay, which desperately needed economic development. Private capital is not venturesome, and

55. Raymond F. Mikesell, *Foreign Investments in Latin America* (Washington, 1955), 49.
56. International Development Advisory Board, *An Economic Program for the Americas* (Washington, September, 1954), 12.
57. United Nations, Department of Economic Affairs, *A Study of Trade between Latin America and Europe* (Geneva, January, 1953), 8.
58. Samuel Pizer and Frederick Cutter, "Growth in Private Foreign Investments," Department of Commerce, *Survey of Current Business* (January, 1954), 5-9.

neither the method nor the area of its operation was large enough to satisfy Latin America. Moreover, United States private capital still operated in Latin America largely as foreign capital, allowing only a minimum of participation by local investors. The participation by foreign investors in United States direct-investment operations in Latin America was shown by the census of 1950 to amount to only 10 per cent as contrasted with a world average of about 22 per cent.[59]

* * *

"We need, ask for, and hate foreign capital at the same time," generalized Augusto Frederico Schmidt in *Correio de Manhã* (January 25, 1949). Schmidt, a wealthy Brazilian newspaper columnist, reflected the views of Brazil's prosperous and powerful industrial class. "Yankee foreign business," he concluded, has a colonizing effect, which, though usually unintentional, is "profoundly contradictory to the idealism and generosity of that great country." "Dollar imperialism" was considered one of the more subtle forms of intervention. A writer in *El País* of Caracas (June 14, 1946) spoke of the nascent imperialism of the United States "swaddled in candy wrappers." The aim of the United States as interpreted in that same year by *La Hora* (October 24, 1946), a newspaper representing the rightist wing of the administration party in Chile, was to "control world markets" in "the interests of capitalists and bankers." To Latin American intellectuals of Marxist-Leninist convictions the United States, of course, was "fatally imperialistic" because, as the director of the Mexican *Cuadernos Americanos,* Jesús Silva Herzog, explained, it was a nation which because of its capital accumulations is bound to export its capital to "nations in a backward stage of development and there invest it in businesses that produce high profits. . . . Excess capital spills out and overflows both neighboring and distant lands in the same way that water when it bursts its bounds . . . inundates the countryside both near and far. This is economic imperialism which inevitably becomes political imperialism."[60]

Latin Americans hold a deeply ingrained conviction that they have suffered painfully and are still suffering painfully at the hands of foreign private capital.[61] Their attitude is, in part, a long-standing

59. United Nations, Economic Commission for Latin America, *Economic Survey of Latin America, 1953,* 41.
60. *El Tiempo,* Bogotá, February 15, 1948.
61. See, for example, editorial in *La Tribuna,* San Salvador, March 9, 1945.

reaction against the alleged usurious activities of business firms identified with foreign nations, particularly the United States, and operated for what has seemed to be the primary benefit of absentee owners. They know that for more than a century foreigners have taken the lead in the development and industrialization of their countries. They have had unpleasant experiences with foreign business interests which acted as if the moral law does not run south of the Rio Grande. They know that United States businessmen not infrequently have gone into Latin American countries under long-term concessions with the deliberate intention of recovering their initial investment within a year or two. As one of these businessmen, who served as ambassador under the Truman administration, has said, they do not fear expropriation of their investment after two years because by that time they will have completely recovered their original investment and meanwhile will have taken, in addition, a considerable profit out of the Latin American country in which they have been operating. This practice naturally does not create a desire for foreign capital.

The rates of return on investment in Latin America have, in fact, been high. According to Department of Commerce statistics, United States investors received in 1948 an average return of 17.4 per cent on their direct investments in Latin America, after deducting foreign taxes. By 1948 their average rate of earnings on such investments had increased to 21 per cent and remained substantially the same, 20.5 per cent in 1951, the last year for which statistics are available. Surpassing these averages, investors in the petroleum industry received average earnings of 31.1 per cent during the years 1948-1951.[62] President Vargas declared in his final testament to the Brazilian people that when he returned to power in 1950 "profits of foreign enterprises reached 500 per cent yearly."[63] Furthermore, some of these enterprises have sometimes failed to allow the degree of local participation and consultation which was expected of them. That the Latin American resentment of this practice had some basis in fact was shown by a United States Treasury Department census of United States-owned assets in foreign countries in 1943 which showed that the participation of foreign nationals in United States-controlled enterprises oper-

62. Department of Commerce, *The Balance of International Payments,* 94; United Nations, Statistical Office, *National Income and its Distribution in Under-Developed* Countries (New York, 1951), 11; and United Nations, Department of Economic and Social Affairs, *Foreign Capital in Latin America,* 13.

63. Vargas' farewell letter, published in Rio de Janeiro, August 25, 1954, *New York Times,* August 26, 1954.

ating in their countries was less in the case of Latin America than of any other geographical area of the world except India. Nationals of the Latin American countries, said the Treasury, "did not participate to any significant extent in the ownership of the American-controlled enterprises located therein."[64] Moreover, some United States and other foreign companies long operated in Latin America under contracts which exempted them from the payment of taxes without their consent and which entitled them to enjoy a virtually sovereign status in relation to the government of the country in which they carried on their business.

In many Latin American countries, therefore, the burden of proof is still on foreign companies to show that they are truly interested in the improvement of the country in which they operate. "We do not look with favor," commented *El Panamá-América* (April 6, 1945), "upon those who come to our cities, to our countries, in order to organize a fabulous business and then to depart quietly and enjoy their gains in their own countries. Our eyes have been opened in this part of the continent. . . . The days have passed when a businessman can live in New York or Chicago or in San Francisco and draw thousands of dollars from his business in these countries." The editor-in-chief of *O Jornal* of Rio de Janeiro (January 27, 1949) referred circumspectly but critically to "some of the gross errors of perspective committed by representatives of American commercial interests among us." The lingering resentment among Latin Americans at such past errors can hardly be overstated. They are quick to place the blame upon these business entities around which, by the very nature of their situation, their most immediate contacts with North Americans have developed. Latin Americans feel that the exploitation of the national resources by foreign companies not only is not increasing the national income but is diverting part of their national wealth into foreign hands. Under that system the profits are transmitted to the countries of capital origin, part of the income of the foreigners employed by that capital goes abroad, and the machinery and equipment used come from abroad.

In Latin America as a whole the inflow of foreign capital has seldom exceeded the transfer of profits and interest outside the area. In other words, more capital has been removed from Latin America in the form of profits than has been brought to it. After the war,

64. Treasury Department, *Census of American-Owned Assets in Foreign Countries* (Washington, 1947), 31.

therefore, Latin Americans often expressed disillusionment as to both the ability and the willingness of foreign capital, governmental and private, to meet their importunate requirements for economic development. Between 1946 and 1952 the new foreign capital investment in Latin America as a whole, amounting to $2,090 million, was more than offset by the remittances of profits and interest to investors outside the area, amounting to $5,830 million. This disparity between the inflow of foreign capital on the one hand and remittances abroad on the other was thus in the ratio of almost one to three. In 1951 the transfer of profits and interest on foreign investment accounted for 70 per cent of Latin America's dollar deficit.[65] It continued through 1955 to be far in excess of the inflow of new private capital, amounting in that year to approximately $750 million.[66] This situation furnishes an opportunity for local political leaders to drain off the resentment of the working classes at low wages and low levels of living in campaigns against foreign ownership and foreign exploitation.

For all these reasons the attempt by the United States to promote private investment aroused widespread criticism in Latin America. The conservative *Diario Nicaragüense* of Granada, Nicaragua (April 7, 1948) called it "The New Filibusterism." Acording to Samuel Wainer, editor of *O Jornal* of Rio de Janeiro (January 27, 1949), it gave to inter-American relations "a character strictly and plainly commercial, eliminating from them all their powerful and fertile human content." If the United States persistently pursued a mercenary policy toward Latin America and reduced "everything to accounting and to the current price of the dollar in international exchange," *Novedades* of Mexico City (September 8, 1944) warned, they must understand "that they cannot depend on anything more than a transitory, formal friendship." At the height of the movement to write official guaranties of private capital investment into the Point Four program, Julio E. Huertematte of Panama, chairman of the Inter-American Economic and Social Council, voiced "suspicions that the prime intention of the investors is undue exploitation rather than participation . . . in a manner reciprocally beneficial to all the parties concerned."[67] The insistence of the United States upon forcing private capital upon

65. United Nations, Economic Commission for Latin America, *Economic Survey of Latin America, 1951-52*, 9, 55.
66. United Nations, Economic Commission for Latin America, *Economic Survey of Latin America, 1955*, 28.
67. Address at the First Plenary Session of the Special Meeting of the Inter-American Economic and Social Council, Washington, March 20, 1950.

Latin Americans aroused their apprehensions that the United States intended to buy up all they had, and impelled them to take counter-measures. However advantageous and even necessary this capital might be, Latin Americans still regarded the policy under which it was being furnished as falling short of the promise of the policies of the Good Neighbor and the Good Partner. Those policies seemed to have dwindled into an effort by the United States to send the capital of its citizens into their area. Viewed in its best light, this new policy could be considered as only a diluted Good Neighbor or Good Partner policy; viewed in its worst light, it took on the aspect of a new dollar diplomacy.

The direct investment which has predominated over portfolio investment in government bonds since the war implies entrepreneurial control by the investor.[68] Latin Americans, resentful of their traditional colonialism, of the absentee ownership of their resources, and of their often minor role in the exploitation of their own national patrimonies, therefore insisted that foreign entrepreneurs should not be permitted to drain off the riches of their countries but rather must be subjected to local controls. To this end they maintained and even extended their old barriers against foreign private capital as a necessary precaution, as they said, to avoid "economic slavery."

These barriers took various forms, including restrictions upon the ownership of property by aliens, the employment of aliens in foreign companies operating within their territories, and the exchange convertibility of profits from foreign investment. Some governments required at least 50 per cent participation of local capital in new industries seeking franchises to operate in their countries, their purpose being not only to force idle local capital into productive operations but to keep dividends within the country. Legislation was also enacted compelling foreign insurance companies doing business in certain countries to make increased investment of their assets in those countries. Venezuela increased its "take" to 50 per cent of the net profits of the foreign oil companies operating in that country.[69] The Chilean government moved to collect about 65 per cent of the profits of its foreign-owned copper-mining companies. After the war Mexico began

68. United Nations, Economic and Social Council, *Economic Development of Under-Developed Countries: Methods of Financing Economic Development of Under-Developed Countries. Survey of Policies Affecting Private Foreign Investment* (8 March 1950).

69. United Nations, Department of Economic and Social Affairs, *Foreign Capital in Latin America*, 18.

a stringent enforcement of its regulations against the admission of aliens to assume positions of responsibility with foreign firms. Guatemala required by law that any enterprise which operates or is established in that country may not have more than 10 per cent of foreign workers and must pay 85 per cent of its total wages to Guatemalan workers. Similarly a Salvadoran law, passed in July, 1949, stipulated that not less than 90 per cent of the employees of all foreign firms operating in the country must be native Salvadorans and that they must receive at least 85 per cent of the payroll.[70] By 1955 all but four of the twenty Latin American governments had similar legislation, the minimum percentage of foreign personnel permitted ranging from 50 per cent in Cuba to only 10 per cent in several other countries, including Mexico, and only 5 per cent in Haiti.[71] Many of the Latin American countries also put forward again the so-called Calvo doctrine requiring foreign enterprises to consider themselves subject only to the laws of the country in which they operate, their purpose being to assert and maintain control over the operations of such enterprises in order to safeguard their economies against what they regard as exploitation and to fulfill their own developmental programs.[72] But they were unable to secure the recognition of this doctrine by the United States in the Economic Agreement signed at Bogotá in 1948.

At the same time these restrictions both heightened and were heightened by the trend toward national protection or economic nationalism, which has been a notable phenomenon in postwar Latin America. Against it the United States set its face, favoring instead "practical and effective cooperative measures to reduce barriers of all kinds to the flow of international trade" and "elimination of economic nationalism in all its forms," as stated in the draft proposal for an Economic Charter of the Americas which Assistant Secretary of State William L. Clayton presented at the Inter-American Conference on Problems of War and Peace at Mexico City in early 1945. But this draft had to be toned down at the insistence of the Latin Americans. To them the Clayton Plan, as it was called, seemed in-

70. Ronald Hilton (ed.), *Hispanic World Report*, II, 8 (August, 1949), 12.
71. United Nations, Department of Economic and Social Affairs, *Foreign Capital in Latin America*, 20-21, 103.
72. The laws, regulations, and policies of the Latin American governments affecting private foreign investment are summarized in United Nations, Economic and Social Council, *Economic Development of Under-Developed Countries*, 72-92. See also United Nations, Department of Economic and Social Affairs, *Foreign Capital in Latin America*, 97, 114-115.

tended to thwart their national development, to discourage industrialization of their countries, and to blight their aspirations for balanced economic development to benefit the foreign trade interests of the United States. It was, declared the First National Congress for the Transformation of Industry (Primer Congreso Nacional de la Industria de Transformación) at Mexico in April, 1947, "nothing but a plan for world dominion and for the abolition of competition and freedom, in which the United States plays the role of a metropolitan country and other states the role of satellite countries."[73]

After the war Latin American governments undertook to give preferences to local industries in various ways. Several of them, including Mexico and Argentina, provided by law that at least 50 per cent of the screen time of all theaters must be devoted to the showing of national, that is, locally made, moving-picture films. An Argentine government decree in January, 1950, required that all music played on any program must be at least 50 per cent Argentine in origin.[74] The Chilean government reserved to itself all production and refining of its petroleum resources, letting foreign companies handle only some of the distribution. Brazil, after a vigorous campaign centering around the slogan "The petroleum is ours," passed the so-called "Petrobras Bill" in 1953 which created a government corporation (Petroleo Brasileiro S.A.) to handle all phases of oil exploration, development, and processing and excluded all foreign participation from any of these operations.[75] In addition, the desire of the Latin American countries to continue their development programs impelled some of them to look askance upon their trade agreements with the United States, negotiated under the Roosevelt-Hull reciprocal trade-agreements program. Considering these agreements restrictive of their commercial action, several governments denounced them or called for their renegotiation.[76] They also required importers to match their imports with purchases of equivalent or at least specified amounts of domestic goods. Some imposed new tariff and quota restrictions upon foreign goods

73. "Primer Congreso Nacional de la Industria de Transformación," *Revista de Economía*, Mexico, X (May 31, 1947), 58.

74. Ronald Hilton (ed.), *Hispanic American Report*, III, 2 (February, 1950), 28.

75. United Nations, Department of Economic and Social Affairs, *Foreign Capital in Latin America*, 19, 57.

76. For example, the United States-Costa Rican trade agreement of 1936 was terminated for this reason at Costa Rica's request in April, 1951. Ronald Hilton (ed.), *Hispanic American Report*, IV, 5 (May, 1951), 14.

and sought to encourage infant industries by adopting protective measures for products which were formerly of only secondary importance,
treating them now as new and important elements in their economies.
They made a shift away from tariffs for revenue primarily to tariffs
for protection of native industry in compliance with the new emphasis
upon economic nationalism. They realized that they could not expand
the industrial element in their economies without the aid of tariffs
which would protect new industries during their infancy. The already
industrialized countries—England, the United States, Germany, Japan
—had so great an advantage in the production of industrial commodities that these nonindustrialized countries felt that they could not
build up competing industries without traiff protection or subsidy.

In an effort to conserve dollar and other foreign exchange and at
the same time to lessen their vulnerability to foreign price fluctuations
the Latin American countries stiffened their controls over imports and
foreign exchange at the very time when the United States was relaxing
its controls. By the end of 1948 thirteen of the Latin American nations
had instituted some form of import restrictions or exchange controls
other than tariff regulations. These varied from the relatively few
import restrictions established by Mexico to the virtually complete
control over imports and foreign exchange established by Brazil and
Argentina.[77] When the price of tin declined in April, 1950, Bolivia's
President Mamerto Urriolagoitia ordered a reduction in the expenditure of dollar exchange and implored his people to accept an austerity
program and to refrain from succumbing to Communist and other
subversive propaganda.[78] Remittance of profits from Argentina to
United States investors was frozen in 1948. Later Brazil limited to
8 per cent of original capital investments the profits that might be sent
out of that country to foreign investors.[79] Nicaragua prohibited transfer abroad of more than 10 per cent annually of the foreign capital
invested there.[80] By such means the Latin American nations were able
finally to achieve balance of payments surpluses. But in doing so they
drastically reduced the supply of goods available for domestic consumption, increased inflationary pressures, and created an unfavorable
climate for foreign investment.

77. Department of Commerce, *The Balance of International Payments,* 34.
78. Message to the people of Bolivia by President Urriolagoitia, *La Razón,*
La Paz, April 9, 1950.
79. United Nations, Department of Economic and Social Affairs, *Foreign
Capital in Latin America,* 23, 58.
80. *Ibid.,* 123.

In the matter of exchange controls Latin Americans contend that any country dependent upon only one export or a few exports for its dollar exchange may be obliged, when the world price of these commodities declines, to lay restrictions upon the remittances of exchange abroad in order to prevent depletion of its exchange reserves, to sustain its economy, and perhaps to prevent social catastrophe. Most of the Latin American countries have depended on only one or a few products for the bulk of their exports. For example, 92 per cent of Venezuela's exports in 1938 consisted of petroleum and 87 per cent of El Salvador's exports consisted of coffee.[81] In nine of the twenty Latin American nations the leading export accounted for more than 50 per cent of the total, and in seven other Latin American nations the two leading exports together accounted for more than 50 per cent of their total exports.[82]

The same situation continued after the war. During the fiscal year 1948-1949, 73 per cent of the value of Haiti's exports came from coffee and sisal only. A slight decline in the world market for these crops would inevitably plunge Haiti into economic misery. Some 70 per cent of Bolivia's foreign trade receipts and 40 per cent of its governmental revenues come from tin. These are needed largely to provide imports of foodstuffs, for less than 1 per cent of the agricultural area of the country is cultivated. This considerable dependence of the entire Bolivian economy upon tin has lent support to the contention of the *MNR* (*Movimiento Nacional Revolucionario*) in that country that the mines should be considered as public works and nationalized. Similarly sensitive to foreign market situations are several other Latin American governments, specifically those of Cuba, Venezuela, Brazil, El Salvador, Colombia, and Chile. Cuba's principal export, sugar, accounts for almost 80 per cent of its foreign exchange; Venezuela depends upon petroleum, which since the war represents 98 per cent by value of all its exports; Brazil's coffee represents between 68 and 74 per cent of its exports; El Salvador and Colombia depend upon coffee to supply 90 and 84 per cent respectively of their foreign exchange; and Chile depends upon copper,

81. United Nations, Department of Economic Affairs, *Relative Prices,* 34-35.
82. Department of Commerce, International Economics Division, *International Transactions,* 132. Slightly different figures are given in International Development Advisory Board, *An Economic Program for the Americas* (Washington, September, 1954), 7.

which provides 65 per cent of the total value of its exports, as almost its sole source of dollars.[83]

For this reason the opportunities available to Latin Americans to carry out their developmental programs through manipulation and control of their own exports are strictly limited. This has been particularly true of those countries which are members of the dollar bloc. This bloc includes fourteen countries of Latin America—all except Argentina, Brazil, Chile, Paraguay, Peru, and Uruguay. In other words the United States dollar area extends southward below the equator. Membership in the dollar bloc regulates the convertibility of the exchange which the member nations derive from foreign trade. Latin American nations, whether members of the dollar bloc or not, are dependent upon world prices on all except a few commodities in which they enjoy a monopoly position. The postwar rise in the price of coffee—one of the exports on which Latin America has such a monopoly, at least in relation to the United States—has tended to compensate several of these countries for their loss of exchange and their general susceptibility to foreign market pressures in other export lines. The hope of creating the same situation with reference to another monopoly export—bananas—may have been one of the motives behind the policy of the Arbenz government of Guatemala in its dealings with the United Fruit Company. But the possibilities for the Latin American countries of establishing bases for a new reciprocity in their relations with foreign countries in this way are soon exhausted. The most feasible alternative method seems to be industrialization.

The postwar emphasis upon development and protection in Latin America seemed to point toward national and regional self-sufficiency as a probable goal. Latin Americans felt that as long as they continued dependent or, at least, mainly dependent upon foreign demand for their commodities and foreign sources of supply for their manufactures, their economies would remain precarious and the success of their programs for economic security and social welfare would be jeopardized. Their economies would be adversely and perhaps even tragically affected by slight restrictions of trade by a foreign country, by the reduction of production costs or opening up of new sources

83. United Nations, Economic Commission for Latin America, *United States Capacity to Absorb Latin American Products* (Mexico City, May 28, 1951), 26; and *Recent Developments and Trends in the Economy of El Salvador* (New York, 20 April 1951), 16. Slightly different figures are given in International Development Advisory Board, *An Economic Program for the Americas*, 7.

of production in another part of the world, or by the replacement of their products by synthetic substitutes. They were aware that the United States, for example, by merely threatening not to buy coffee or not to sell flour or machinery can effectively influence the domestic policy of several of their governments. Cuban Senator José Manuel Casanova complained in 1948 that whereas the United States had called upon Cuba to supply 65 per cent of its sugar needs during the war, it was purchasing only 28 per cent of its postwar sugar in Cuba.[84] Cuba's resentment against this sort of pressure, which was applied, as Cuba believed, by the United States in Section 202E of the Sugar Act of 1947, inspired the successful drive of the Cuban ambassador in Washington, Dr. Guillermo Belt, to include in the Economic Agreement of Bogotá an article prohibiting the use of "coercive measures of an economic and political character in order to force the sovereign will of another State and to obtain from the latter advantages of any nature."[85] A decline of one cent in the price of coffee in the United States costs Brazil $15 million and Colombia $7 million. The dependence of Latin Americans upon foreign nations is emphasized anew whenever a foreign monoply purchaser terminates his purchase contracts with them. When the Wrigley Company, for example, which has been the only buyer of Guatemalan chicle, announced in August, 1952, that it would not contract for the purchase of the 1952-1953 harvest, the Guatemalan government was obliged to go to the aid of the local chicle industry in order to prevent distress among the chicle harvesters.

In an effort to soften the impact of such shocks for Argentina, Perón issued a "Declaration of Economic Independence" on July 9, 1947, and followed it up with action in the economic field. He had earlier announced, in a message to the Argentine Congress on June 26, 1946, that his purpose was "the Argentinization of our economy." For reasons almost purely political and certainly not economic, he used his foreign currency balances to purchase the British- and French-owned railroads which had long operated in his country. Similarly the Brazilian government used blocked sterling balances in 1946-1949

84. Ronald Hilton (ed.), *Hispanic World Report*, II, 2 (January, 1949), 29.

85. Inter-American Conference, Ninth, Bogotá, 1948, "Proposal Relating to the Project of Basic Agreement of Inter-American Economic Cooperation Submitted by the Delegation of Cuba" (CB-22-E/SG-4) ; "Discurso del Doctor Guillermo Belt, Presidente de la Delegación de Cuba a la Novena Conferencia Internacional Americana," April 8, 1948; and *Final Act*.

to take over the British-owned São Paulo Railway Company and other British companies. In Cuba the government of President Carlos Prío Socarrás expropriated and nationalized the transportation system of Havana, Autobuses Modernos, S.A., owned by private United States interests, and between 1939 and 1949 the proportion of sugar produced by Cuban nationals increased from 22 per cent to 45 per cent of the total Cuban sugar production.[86] Several governments gave preferences to national shipping lines and created state-trading corporations and state-planning agencies as new instruments for freeing themselves from foreign control. Carlos Ibáñez, in his successful campaign for the presidency of Chile early in 1952, warned foreigners not to forget that "Chile is neither a warehouse nor a colony."[87] The program of the Arévalo-Arbenz government in Guatemala called for the "liberation" of that country also from foreign economic domination.[88]

These programs aiming at national economic self-sufficiency and diversification had the effect of increasing the amounts of foreign capital reinvested in Latin America. As the transfer of such capital abroad was inhibited both by nationalist restrictions and by exchange difficulties, it was perforce retained in increasing amounts in the Latin American countries in which it was invested. For the period 1946-1951 reinvested earnings of United States capital provided 38 per cent of the total increase in United States private investments in Latin America, and for the year 1951 such earnings provided 55 per cent of the total. In the latter year reinvested earnings accounted for the entire net capital increase in Venezuela.[89]

But in general these nationalist programs met with only limited success in enabling the Latin American countries to diversify and strengthen their economies. Unprocessed agricultural and mineral exports continued to represent the great bulk of Latin America's total exports. In the case of Mexico, for example, one of the most highly industrialized of the Latin American countries, raw materials still accounted for 70 per cent of the country's total volume of exports in 1952. As President Alemán pointed out on September 3, 1952, in his address opening the seventh annual meeting of the International Monetary Fund and the International Bank for Reconstruction and

86. United Nations, Economic Commission for Latin America, *Economic Survey of Latin America, 1955*, 172.   87. Address of February 7, 1952.
88. See address by President Juan José Arévalo, March 15, 1951, in his *Escritos Políticos y Discursos* (Havana, 1953), 493-507, especially 497.
89. United Nations, Economic Commission for Latin America, *Economic Survey of Latin America, 1951-52*, 1-57.

Development, the Latin Americans were still very much under the influence of factors beyond their control—principally the activity of highly industrialized nations.[90]

The people in every country of Latin America are far more dependent upon exports than are the people of the United States. They stress that their high export coefficient which is due to their concentration upon a few commodities has worked to their disadvantage for

PER CENT OF EXPORTS TO GROSS NATIONAL PRODUCT FOR THE LATIN AMERICAN COUNTRIES AND THE UNITED STATES

	1953	1954	1955	1956
Argentina	14.9	13.3	11.4	10.0
Bolivia	n.a.	n.a.	44.1	47.5
Brazil	9.3	8.7	7.7	8.0
Chile	17.5	16.7	18.8	20.5
Colombia	16.0	16.3	13.7	14.0
Costa Rica	29.0	29.8	26.5	22.8
Cuba	32.3	25.7	26.1	26.6
Dominican Republic	24.4	25.5	22.3	23.7
Ecuador	15.2	18.4	17.0	17.1
El Salvador	21.1	23.8	22.7	22.6
Guatemala	18.5	20.0	18.6	19.5
Haiti	n.a.	17.1	13.8	15.3
Honduras	22.6	18.4	16.8	20.7
Mexico	9.3	9.1	9.9	9.5
Nicaragua	16.4	18.6	23.2	19.6
Panama	16.6	23.8	25.2	24.7
Paraguay	n.a.	17.4	17.5	18.0
Peru	16.5	17.7	17.8	19.8
United States	4.3	n.a.	3.9	n.a.
Uruguay	17.4	15.5	11.6	11.6
Venezuela	39.0	41.2	42.4	42.3

Source: Data supplied by the International Cooperation Administration, June, 1957.

n.a.—not available.

decades. In 1947 Argentina, for example, exported 21 per cent of its gross national production. The ratio of its exports to its total production declined thereafter, but in 1953 it still stood at almost 15 per cent, a figure which is almost five times as high as the corresponding figure for the national production of the United States. Guatemala is more typical of the general dependence of the Latin American countries upon exports. The ratio of its exports to its entire national production, which averaged around 14-16 per cent during the prewar

90. International Bank for Reconstruction and Development, *Seventh Annual Meeting of the Board of Governors, Mexico City, D.F., September 3-12, 1952, Summary Proceedings* (Washington, December 15, 1952), 1-2.

years 1937-1939, reached a high of 18.1 per cent in 1945. It stood at 17.4 per cent in 1947, 15.7 per cent in 1952, 18.5 per cent in 1953, and rose to 19.5 per cent in 1956. In other words, Guatemala in 1956 was dependent upon foreign markets as an outlet for almost one-fifth of its entire production. The ratio of exports to gross national product is still greater in the case of certain other countries of Latin America. In nine of them, namely, Bolivia, Chile, Costa Rica, Cuba, the Dominican Republic, El Salvador, Honduras, Panama, and Venezuela, it exceeded 20 per cent in 1956, and actually reached 42.3 per cent for Venezuela and 47.5 per cent for Bolivia. The ratios for these and all the other countries of Latin America as well as for the United States for the years 1953, 1954, 1955, and 1956 are shown in the accompanying table.

In general, the dependence of the Latin American peoples as a whole upon foreign outlets for their exports has been increasing since the end of World War II. Moreover, although Latin America's exports have shown a slight increase in terms of value since the war, they leveled off in 1948 in terms of physical volume and showed almost no increase thereafter.[91] These facts strengthen the claim of the Latin American countries that their economies are largely dependent upon foreign markets and foreign prices and that they must develop their resources for their own needs in order to achieve increased self-sufficiency, to gain their economic independence, and to raise their levels of living.[92]

* * *

In the Latin American area since the war the most rapid industrial progress has been made in Brazil, Chile, Colombia, Mexico, and Venezuela. The rate of industrial growth in other countries, in particular Ecuador, Peru, and Uruguay, has lagged behind. In the remaining twelve Latin American countries manufacturing has not developed to any significant extent. For the Latin American area as a whole the industrial peak was reached in 1945-1947 and declined in 1948-1951 generally, except in Chile and Mexico. This decline re-

91. United Nations, Statistical Office, International Monetary Fund, and International Bank for Reconstruction and Development, joint publishers, *Direction of International Trade* (Statistical Papers, Series T), IV, 2 (no place or date of publication), 430.

92. International Monetary Fund, *International Financial Statistics*, VII (October, 1954). See also Pinto Santa Cruz, *op. cit.*, 113-124.

sulted in part from increased competition from imports, from inflationary developments which reduced consumer buying power, and
from the prevailing patterns of wealth and income distribution which
limit the consumption possibilities of the majority of the population.[93]

Latin Americans therefore relapsed once more into their historic
role of supplying foodstuffs and raw materials to foreign industrial
nations. The arguments of those who believed in agrarian and mining wealth rather than industrial manufactures as a source of economic well-being once again prevailed. As a result Latin Americans
were obliged to adjust their economies, which had been largely geared
to the needs of the United States during the war, once more to Europe's requirements. Though they were not averse to reopening their
European trade channels, they deplored the consequent jettisoning of
their plans for industrialization and for the diversification of their
economies. They found themselves forced back again into the triangular trade pattern, exporting raw materials to Europe and importing, in exchange, manufactured goods from Europe and the United
States. It became evident that under these conditions the execution
of their developmental programs would be slow and only incidental
to their traditional trading operations.

Their indecisive and subservient role in those operations was emphasized anew in 1949 by the adverse effect of the decline in foreign
purchases upon their export trade which, as a result, dropped to only
$5,570 million, or by more than $900 million in comparison with
1948. As the foreign demand for Argentina's cereal products and for
the mineral products—lead, copper, and tin—of Chile and Bolivia
sharply dropped, the economy of these countries and of others in
Latin America worsened, and they became apprehensive as to the
future dependability of their foreign markets. It was made painfully
obvious to them that their economic situation would depend upon
the level of prosperity in the United States, the continuance of its
purchases of strategic materials, and the maintenance of its support
of the economy of western Europe through Marshall Plan and other
aid. One of the purposes of the currency devaluations carried through
by many of the Latin American countries in September, 1949, was
to improve their position in foreign trade and to free themselves from
too much dependence upon manipulated dollar and sterling curren-
cies.[94] Nevertheless by mid-1950 they were accumulating surpluses

93. United Nations, Economic Commission for Latin America, *Economic
Survey of Latin America, 1951-52*, 298-341.   94. *Ibid., 1949*, 508-525.

of many of their staple products, particularly sugar, petroleum, tin, and copper, and were suffering from consequent declines in world prices and inevitable further shrinkages in domestic levels of living.

For all these reasons industrial development was allowed to taper off in Latin America or rather was forced to yield priority to agricultural development. This de-emphasis of industrialization became apparent in 1949. It was shown by Argentina's new policy, adopted early in 1950, of paying premium prices for increased agricultural production and of allowing enlarged imports of agricultural machinery, by various measures of the Mexican government to encourage agriculture at the expense of industry, by the Chilean government's price-support program for certain agricultural crops, and by the emphasis placed upon agriculture in Brazil's *SALTE* Plan *(Saude, Alimentação, Transporte, e Electrica)*. So long as any Latin American country remained a deficit area in the matter of food production for the consumption of its own population and was obliged to import any of its food supplies, it suffered a drain on its foreign exchange. Many of the Latin American countries continued to be thus dependent upon foreign sources of foodstuffs after the war.[95] Their new emphasis upon agricultural production after 1949 therefore served both to promote their economic self-sufficiency and to conserve their foreign exchange. But Latin Americans retained an abiding, almost passionate zeal for industrialization as a means of diversifying their economies and of rendering them less vulnerable to shocks from abroad. Heavy industry, such as a steel mill, has become for them a symbol of national pride and sovereignty. There is scarcely a country that does not want its own Volta Redonda. Dr. Milton S. Eisenhower and his party, who traveled through South America in mid-1953, "encountered everywhere a widespread desire for steel mills, metal fabricating plants, food processing plants, textile industries and a wide variety of consumer-goods fabricating facilities."[96] To the "have-not" peoples of Latin America industrial undertakings appear as alluring and dramatic forms of development.

These dreams were spun out of the substantial wartime coopera-

95. For data on the dependence of selected Latin American countries upon imported food supplies see Moisés Poblete Troncoso, *La Economía Agraria de América Latina y el Trabajador Campesino* (Santiago de Chile, 1953), 22-23. See also Philip C. Newman, John E. Ellman, and Robert S. Aries, *Technical Cooperation with Underdeveloped Countries* (New York, 1952), 33.

96. Milton S. Eisenhower, "United States—Latin American Relations," 707.

tion between the United States and Latin America. "During the war," wrote Augusto Frederico Schmidt in *Correio da Manhã* (January 25, 1949), "we obtained . . . some facilities from the North Americans and these facilities supported our fantasy. And we dreamed more. We imagined on the part of our allies a total solidarity, a desire to do everything for us, a watchful attention for the South American brother who was irresolute and unsure of the method of solving his great difficulties and crucial problems. We began to live chimeras by hopes and dreams." When these dreams were shattered, Latin Americans not only blamed the United States for having permitted the dreams to be dreamed at all but also tended to blame it for all their economic and social ills. They were disappointed, even antagonized by the frequent and painstaking reaffirmations of the Good Neighbor Policy after the war which stressed its original noninterventionist element. *Información* of Havana (November 7, 1947) was shocked by the suggestion that good neighborliness might consist merely of respect for the sovereignties of the Latin American states, of noninterference in their affairs, of according equal treatment to them, and of other "principles of a juridical nature."[97] They expected more than mere promises of nonintervention which had seemed desirable in the 1930's. They hoped to be enabled to expand their exports to the United States through the cooperative assistance of that country in reducing or eliminating its tariff and other barriers to their trade, especially with respect to their manufactures and semi-manufactures. They wanted to receive higher prices for their exports than they had been receiving because, as they said, the terms of trade had become increasingly disadvantageous to them and to other raw-materials producers through the years. They also wanted increased financial assistance from the Export-Import Bank and the International Bank for Reconstruction and Development to finance their programs of economic development. In all this Latin America's attitudes were often inconsistent, probably because they were rooted more in emotion than in reason. But these emotional reactions, which are deep, are themselves a factor of the highest importance in inter-American relations. They are symptomatic of the growing pains which Latin America is experiencing as it attempts to "keep up with the Joneses" in this modern industrial world.

In today's world the nations which can most successfully fulfill

97. Similar views were expressed by *El Panamá-América,* Panama, February 23, 1947.

the expectations of their citizens are those which are best able to solve their foreign exchange problems and to maintain their balance of payments position. This they can do in two ways: either by maintaining a position of monopoly or virtual monopoly in respect to one or a few exports or by creating and maintaining an economy so delicately balanced between agriculture and industry as to render foreign exchange problems of little effect. The former can be characterized as a kind of neomercantilism, the latter as autarchy or national self-sufficiency. By both these methods the requirements of their citizens can be met. The Latin Americans have been unable, however, to pursue a policy of neomercantilism because they do not normally possess a monopoly source of any commodities except perhaps coffee, cocoa, bananas, and cinchona. Their monopoly with respect to a host of other products during the war, including manganese, petroleum, copper, tin, and even sugar, catapulted them into an artificial position and gave them illusions of the possibility of pursuing a postwar mercantilist policy. To the extent, however, that their monopoly was lost after the war and they relapsed into the normal system of competition, they felt that their freedom was impaired and that they were being forced again into a position of subservience where the prices of their exports were fixed abroad to their disadvantage. The natural reaction to this disillusionment was a new effort to create self-sufficient national economies which would be better able to withstand foreign pressures. But this necessitated diversification of their economic systems, which in turn would be possible only through imports of technical processes and machinery from more advanced industrial countries. This in turn called for capital imports which their own desires for national self-sufficiency and independence resisted. As a result many an "Operation Bootstrap" was undertaken without the bootstrap which, as it happened, could only be imported from abroad.

Latin Americans thus learned the hard truth that there is no such thing as love between nations. They were disposed to conclude that to the United States the Latin American situation appeared to be not, as they themselves supposed, primarily a social and economic situation, but a political problem of how to secure their support in the cold war against the Soviet Union. They had looked forward to the adoption of a guaranty after the war that if any American nation had a serious economic problem, all the other American nations would help in its solution. This idea, engendered by their wartime experience, of Americans helping Americans depended upon the support of the United States, which, however, seemed more concerned with a military than an economic collective security pact for the hemisphere. Even the promised economic conference at which they hoped to discuss this plan as well as the general economic situation of their countries was repeatedly postponed at the suggestion of the United States and was not finally held until 1957. Moreover, at the Ninth International Conference of American States at Bogotá in 1948 the project of an inter-American bank which they had hopefully revived as a means of cooperatively financing their developmental programs was shelved by the United States. By 1950 both their postwar economic growth and their dreams of unlimited future development were fading away.

Latin Americans felt that they had been neglected by the United States. After an elaborate and fair investigation a sober Brazilian journalist, Samuel Wainer, concluded in his *O Jornal* of Rio de Janeiro (January 27, 1949) that, whereas "the anti-American wave" which had been spreading over Latin America constituted "still a superficial phenomenon" in Brazil, "in the majority of the American countries of Spanish tongue . . . that wave has already become a permanent dividing factor." His reservation as to Brazil was denied by Brazilian journalist Carlos Lacerda, who concluded in his *Tribuna da Imprensa* (July 6, 1952) that "today in Brazil the public man who wants to be unpopular has one easy resource: to defend the thesis of collaboration by Brazil with the United States." At almost no time in the decade after World War II, either in Brazil or in any of the Spanish American countries, could this wave have been characterized accurately as only "a superficial phenomenon."

It was more than that. Anti-United States sentiment was particularly strong among articulate laboring groups in Latin America. Organized labor there, which developed precociously after World War II, was predominantly antagonistic to the United States. Of the three regional labor federations in the Western Hemisphere both the Argentine-sponsored ATLAS (Agrupación de Trabajadores Latino Americanos Sindicalistas) and the Communist-line CTAL (Confederación de Trabajadores de América Latina) displayed a strong anti-United States character; the third, the ORIT (Organización Regional Interamericana de Trabajadores), composed of representatives of all the leading non-Communist and non-Peronista labor federations in the American nations, divided into sharply drawn pro-United States and anti-United States blocs at its meeting in Rio de Janeiro in December, 1952. In these circumstances, declared *La Prensa* of Lima (June 16, 1952), "it is gross fraud to talk about Pan-Americanism."[98] Lacking the means to produce the manufactured commodities and even some of the foodstuffs which they required, denied the dollar exchange which would enable them to acquire those commodities from the United States, and unable to satisfy their commodity needs in Europe, Latin Americans saw their golden wartime hopes of expanded economies yield to the cold postwar realities of business depression, unemployment, desperate want, and acute political and social maladjustments.

98. For a report on this growing Latin American sentiment against the United States see Sam Pope Brewer in *New York Times,* April 27, 1953. See also statement of Ezequiel Padilla in *New York Times,* May 20, 1953.

Chapter 8

NEW DIRECTIONS IN LATIN AMERICA

*The ideals of Peronista Justicialism . . . proclaim that mankind
is to consist of only one class of men—those who work; that all
shall be for one, and one for all; that there is to be no one with
special privileges except the children; that the governments of
nations are to do what the people want done; that each day all
men are to be a little less poor.*

—EVITA PERÓN

*I*F LATIN AMERICANS could not realize their hope of
being able "to produce, consume, and act like any
European nation" by means of large outside assistance their only alternative was to develop their tremendous resources by the mobilization
of their own local assets, both material and human, to the fullest possible extent. They were forced to conclude that they could not escape
from their colonial economy or relieve themselves of dependence upon
foreign investment until they themselves developed the beginnings of
a healthy economic system for their countries. They decided, therefore, as Ramón Manrique expressed it in 1945, to "dispense with the
policy of kneeling, of absolute submission, because . . . no one, much
less the Yankee, likes the Brotherhood of the Humble."[1] Augusto
Frederico Schmidt, writing in *Correio da Manhã* (January 27, 1949)
severely scored the "stupid mania" of his countrymen "of waiting for
our protectors, our saviours, our friends and neighbors to come to our
salvation." Like the "Little Red Hen" in the children's story they
would do it themselves. They quite naturally concluded that if they
were weak and their claims were being ignored, their only course was
to become strong.

1. *Diario de la Costa,* Cartagena, March 4, 1945.

274

During the decade after the war Latin Americans were strongly encouraged to follow precisely this course. The responsibility for solving their social and economic problems and meeting their developmental requirements largely devolved upon themselves. The Economic Agreement signed at the Ninth International Conference at Bogotá in 1948 stressed "the obligation of each country to take the domestic measures within its power for such development," and this obligation was repeatedly reaffirmed by the International Bank for Reconstruction and Development. "Certainly no amount of external aid, technical or financial," declared the bank in its Fourth Annual Report, dated September, 1949, "can replace the essential will and determination on the part of the government of the country concerned to adopt the often difficult and politically unpopular economic and financial measures necessary to create a favorable environment for development."[2]

Since World War II, Latin Americans have been obsessed as never before with the desire for material progress and improved living conditions. In their rampant postwar aspirations for more abundant living, industrialization, and economic development they have been faced, as they have been faced for over a century in varying degrees from country to country, by the dilemma: should they achieve their aspirations by private or by governmental action? The decision in the past had often been made in favor of the latter.

Both the native Indian regimes in New Spain and Peru and the Hispanic imperial regime which succeeded them were totalitarian and monolithic with respect to private enterprise and activity. The Spanish government was inflexible, authoritarian, and highly centralized. It was operated by an army of bureaucrats which included not only soldiers, but also clergy, tax collectors, royal inspectors, inspectors of inspectors, and a host of other officials. Under the old Spanish monarchy the crown exercised juridical sovereignty over private wealth and regulated the life of his subjects under an elaborate set of protective doctrines. The conquistadores who carved out new empires for Spain and Portugal in the Western Hemisphere looked to the crown for authority and support for their explorations and colonizations. The new lands were claimed as the private estate of the sovereign, and their resources were considerd to be subject to distribution and use only by the ruler. Business operations were carried on

2. International Bank for Reconstruction and Development, *Fourth Annual Report, 1948-1949* (Washington, 1949), 8.

under the grant of privileges or concessions (*fueros*) by the government, and in general they were handled as exclusive monopolies abhorring the idea of individual enterprise and free competition. The authority of the state, closely allied as it was with that of the church, was the greatest single factor in the life of the Spanish and Portuguese colonists in America. The continuance down to our own day of the old Spanish theory that title to all subsoil resources is vested in the national government, which was used to justify the expropriation of foreign oil companies by the Mexican government in the late 1930's, is only one example of the superior claims of government in Latin America over private wealth.

Acceptance of the supreme and overriding power of the state, then, is the inheritance of Latin America. The Roman law and its derivative, the Napoleonic Code, which form the basis for the legal system of Latin America, exalt the authority of the state. Despite the successful resistance of the Latin Americans to Spain, Portgual, and France in their wars of independence, the tradition of governmental absolutism and centralized authority of the state as the decisive factor in human life, which Philip II, Pombal, and Napoleon exemplified, casts its long shadows over modern Latin America—not only as an idea but also as a basis for action. After independence the national governments, quite understandably, continued to claim the prerogatives and act in the tradition of their Hispanic mother countries. "Washington and his contemporaries," the Argentine publicist Juan Bautista Alberdi once acutely wrote, "struggled more for individual rights and liberties than for the simple independence of the country. But in winning the former they gained the latter. On the other hand the countries of South America won political independence but not individual liberty." As a result Latin Americans are disposed to expect government to do many things which their Anglo-American neighbors to the north customarily leave to private initiative. In particular the normal tendency of the Latin Americans is to expect their governments to take the lead in developing new economic enterprises.

Since the end of World War II the main problem and preoccupation of Latin American governments has been to expand national production in such a way as to increase the real per capita income and to see that it is so distributed as to raise the general standard of living. The most pressing political force in Latin America has been a social and economic force, namely, the demand of the peoples for satisfaction of their basic human needs. The main causes of Latin American unrest in recent years are the ancient ones of pressure of population on the food supply and the manipulation of the physical resources by uncontrolled capital, largely foreign. Bread and land! this has been the proverbial cry of the restless in Latin America. Among them, as indeed among many other peoples throughout the world, the sum total of human suffering and want was enormously increased during the past generation by two world wars and a severe world-wide economic crisis. Although the wars did not bring devastation to Latin America they, along with the depression, retarded the progress of these peoples toward higher levels of living while at the same time broadening their horizons and stimulating their desires. As a result a level of living which was considered tolerable before the war became quite unacceptable after the war.

The living conditions of the peoples of Latin America did not show the improvement that was expected in the postwar period. Making no allowance for fringe benefits, which are a considerable factor in feudal-type sectors of the Latin American economy, in 1946 the average hourly wage for industrial workers in Ecuador, El Salvador, and Haiti was only five cents and in Bolivia only six cents, and it ranged from only fourteen to twenty cents in Chile, Colombia, Costa Rica, the Dominican Republic, Guatemala, Nicaragua, Paraguay, and Peru. To earn sufficient wages to buy a one-pound loaf of bread an industrial worker in Brazil had to work 52 minutes, in Guatemala 69 minutes, and in Colombia 80 minutes, as compared with only 4.4 minutes in the United States. To earn a pound of rice he had to work 77 minutes in Colombia and 96 minutes in Bolivia, as compared with less than 6 minutes in the United States. To earn a pound of sugar he required 81 minutes in Ecuador, 96 minutes in Bolivia, and 121 minutes in Peru, but only 3 minutes in the United States. Although the wages of Latin American workers increased from the middle of the war on and showed considerable improvement in certain sectors, inflation since the war has reduced many of their economic gains. By June, 1948, living costs in thirteen of the Latin American countries ranged upward from almost two, to almost four and one-half times the prewar level.[3] Every one of the fifteen Latin American countries for which cost-of-living statistics are available showed increases in retail prices for 1947 and 1948, some annual

3. Donald M. Dozer, "Roots of Revolution in Latin America," *Foreign Affairs*, XXVII (January, 1949), 275.

increases going as high as 33 per cent.[4] In 1950 the cost-of-living index calculated upon the base of 1937 as equivalent to 100, stood at 322 for Argentina, 366 for Colombia, 402 for Brazil, 434 for Peru, 619 for Chile, 776 for Bolivia, and 1,176 for Paraguay.[5] In particular, increases in the prices of basic foodstuffs made it difficult and often impossible for workers to buy more than food, and sometimes they could afford only inadequate amounts or improper kinds.

The decline in real levels of living, resulting from war shortages and postwar inflation, was aggravated by the perennially depressed social conditions. Of the total population of Latin America it is reliably estimated that approximately one-half above the age of fourteen are illiterate. Among the rural population in several countries this proportion exceeds 70 per cent; and in Haiti it reaches 89.48 per cent of the total population fifteen years of age and over.[6] According to studies made by the Inter-American Institute of Statistics, more than 19 million children of school age lack schools and the average length of schooling for those who attend school throughout Latin America is only two years. The 1950 national census of Mexico, one of the most highly developed of the Latin American countries, showed that 50 per cent of the population of that country over six years of age could not read and write, that almost 20 per cent owned no shoes and always went barefoot, and that over 8 per cent of Mexican dwellings had no regular water supply.[7] In Latin America as a whole the average per capita consumption of footwear is less than one pair of shoes or boots a year, and this holds for all countries except four— Argentina, Chile, Cuba, and Uruguay—as compared with 3.2 pairs in the United States.[8]

These illiterate, ill-housed, barefoot people suffer also from lack of adequate and proper food. According to Dr. Federico Gómez of the World Health Organization,[9] 70 per cent of the people of Latin

4. United Nations, Economic Commission for Latin America, *Economic Survey of Latin America, 1949*, 492.

5. Department of State, *Data Book, Latin America*, 2 vols. (Washington, 1951), *passim.*

6. Pan-American Union, *La Educación Fundamental del Adulto Americano,* Seminario Interamericano de Educación, No. 7, Rio de Janeiro, 1949, Washington, 1951; and *New York Times,* August 2, 1953.

7. *New York Times,* August 2, 1953.

8. United Nations, Economic Commission for Latin America, *Economic Survey of Latin America, 1955,* 62.

9. Address before American Conference on Nutrition, *New York Times,* June 14, 1950.

America suffer from chronic hunger. Indeed they can hardly keep body and soul together. They want food, better health, and greater material comfort. The average per capita income in Latin America in 1950, according to studies made by the Economic Commission for Latin America, was only $244. Even in Argentina, one of the most prosperous and highly industrialized of all the Latin American countries, the average per capita income in that year was only $496. In Paraguay it was only $95.[10] Moreover the rate of increase of real per capita income is so small that at this rate Latin Americans will require almost two and a half centuries to reach one-third of the per capita income in the United States.[11] As in many other parts of the world, millions of people in Latin America are inexorably attempting to work out for themselves the solutions to the problems created by their own needs and desires. They demand that governments respond to their pressures. From the depths of their misery they look upward to a leader, even a messiah, who will lead them forward to better days. They will not be satisfied with promises nor will they be limited by traditional procedures. For to them the established system by whatever name it is called has not produced economic welfare and social justice.

The postwar social ferment among the Latin American peoples has been a tangled nexus of both their wartime aspirations and the perhaps inevitable resulting frustrations. It was caused in part by their resentment against special privilege, their long-sustained lack of modern physical comforts, their antagonism to foreign private capital and foreign control, and their sensitivity to the habitually weak national status of their governments. In part also it has been due to their hunger for land and other property, their longing for more adequate self-expression, and their desire to participate more actively in national and world life. Some or all of these factors of unrest are constantly present in all the Latin American countries. They cannot be said to have any special area of geographical concentration. They vary in intensity from place to place. Not all of them occur in conjunction in any one country. In the aggregate they

10. United Nations, Statistical Office, *National Income,* 3; Department of State, *Data Book, Latin America,* Vol. I, *South America,* 3, 22; and United Nations, Economic Commission for Latin America, *A Study of Inter-Latin American Trade,* Sixth Session, 29 August 1955, Bogotá, Colombia, 19.

11. United Nations, Department of Public Information, *The Economic Growth of Twenty Republics: The Work of the Economic Commission for Latin America,* Third Revised Edition (New York, 1956), 28.

may actually have tended to become weaker or at least less apparent than they were during World War II or in the early postwar period. But they must be reckoned with by all local political leaders and by all foreign governments that wish to deal successfully with the international problems of Latin America.

All these popular pressures upon government have been aggravated by the notorious predilection of the Latin Americans for direct action as a means of solving their problems. In parts of Latin America the standard method not only of overturning governments but also of effecting social and economic change is the method of violence. Changes are sometimes sudden and severe. Yesterday's exile may be tomorrow's president. Blood may flow in the streets. Revolution with a capital R—*Revolución* as distinguished from a mere *cuartelazo* or barracks revolt—has been talked about for decades by the "eternal café revolutionaries" in these countries as a means of purging the body politic of poisons; it sometimes obtrudes as a grim reality, as in the Bogotá riots in April, 1948. The inequitable distribution of the national wealth has created conditions of political unrest and instability which stimulate community impulses of a leveling nature. In Panama, for instance, the average annual cash income for a rural lower-class family in 1950 was only $14, as contrasted with a minimum of $5,000 per person for members of the upper class.[12] Friction between the hut dweller and the neighboring *estanciero* is chronic. The *rotos* and the *inquilinos* have traditionally resented the *ricos;* the *comunes,* or the communal agricultural villages that have collective ownership in land, as in Guatemala, Mexico, Peru, and a few other countries, have often made war upon the *latifundistas.* In general the disposition to stay within legal bounds is weaker among the peoples of Latin America than among those of the Anglo-American world, as evidenced, for example, in such a seemingly trivial matter as their almost habitual disregard of traffic lights. The law is seldom allowed to stand in the way of the consummation of social, economic, or political change.

Prior to World War II few Latin American governments had any experience in national planning in solving their problems. Uruguay was almost unique with its quasi-Socialistic constitution of 1917. The

12. Carolyn Campbell and Ofelia Hooper, "The Middle Class of Panama" in *Materiales para el estudio de la clase media en la América Latina,* Publicaciones de la Oficina de Ciencias Sociales, Unión Panamericana, IV (Washington, 1950), 38-75.

Mexican revolutionary government also did something along this line with its agricultural credit banks and its national programs of irrigation and reclamation. In Argentina, Alejandro Bunge and his disciples engaged in some national planning through the *Revista de Economía Argentina* and other publications after 1920. World War II, however, generated a lively brood of developmental agencies in Latin America. Government initiative and government investment came to be considered essential to the development of important segments of the economies of the Latin American nations. The earliest of the agencies for these purposes was the Chilean Corporación de Fomento de la Producción, created in 1939. In 1942 Bolivia established a similar development corporation as a result of the recommendations of the United States Economic Mission, headed by Merwin Bohan. By 1949 Mexico also had its Nacional Financiera, Argentina its Five-Year Plan with all its subordinate administrative agencies, Brazil its SALTE Plan, Venezuela its Corporación Venezolano de Fomento, Guatemala its Instituto de Fomento de la Producción, Ecuador its Corporación Ecuatoriana de Fomento and its Banco Nacional de Fomento, and Honduras its Banco Nacional de Fomento. In Panama the Remón administration began in January, 1953, to plan for the establishment of an institute of economic development to serve as an instrument through which the national government could plan, diversify, and ration production. In general national governments have assumed an active role in promotion of economic development. This trend has been encouraged by the wartime and postwar insistence of the United States that Latin American governments present broad blueprints of national development as a condition of receiving loans from this government. It has been encouraged also by the failure of private capital to undertake such massive social projects as the construction of railroads, highways, ports, and irrigation works, private housing, and school facilities, thus devolving the responsibility for the financing of such projects upon government.

Attempts have been made by these national planning agencies to utilize voluntary capital to finance developmental projects deemed nationally desirable. For example, Nacional Financiera, the official industrial development organization of Mexico, collected 150 million pesos from the public in 1949 by sale of bonds and shares in an effort to expand its developmental operations through voluntary savings. But in Latin America facilities such as stock exchanges and banks of deposit for the mobilization of local capital are either lacking or inadequate.

In general, capital and capitalists are not provided with the buying, selling, and pooling facilities which have long been available to agriculturists. Almost every Latin American town possesses a central food market, but the Latin American cities that have capital markets can be counted on the fingers of one hand. Dr. Milton S. Eisenhower and his party "found no well established capital markets in South America in the sense we know them in this country." They reported that "constructive efforts are being made in Brazil, Colombia, and Venezuela; Argentina, Uruguay, and Chile have markets for bonds and stocks. But much remains to be done."[13] To imagine the degree of chaos that would result from the sudden blotting out of food markets suggests the chronic starvation of capital-consuming projects which results from the lack of capital markets.

Besides, many of the Latin American countries are unable to increase local capital formation with their own resources. The local capital available for investment does not normally exceed 15 per cent of the national income in any Latin American country; and the rate of accumulation of such local capital is no greater than the rate of population increase for Latin America as a whole, namely about $2\frac{1}{2}$ per cent, thus providing almost no margin for new development. Although the rate of investment is not excessively low in relation to that of other countries, its flow has been discontinuous and its quality poor. Local capital is seldom invested in local projects because of political hazards and the greater attractiveness of more highly developed foreign areas as investment outlets. More than $270 million of Latin American assets were deposited in the United States in 1952.[14] Considerable Cuban capital, for example, was transferred during and after World War II to beach property in Miami, Florida. At the end of 1953 deposits in the United States by Cuban firms and individuals were estimated at $69 million.[15] At the same time a credible estimate was made that $50 million of Colombian capital was then on deposit in New York banks.[16] By 1954 Guatemalan citizens were reliably reported to have sent the same amount to New York for investment. In the same year Mexican private capital in the United States reached $140 million. Indeed, during the postwar years the transfer of private

13. *Op cit.,* 711.   14. Newman, Ellman, and Aries, *op. cit.,* 58.
15. United Nations, Department of Economic and Social Affairs, *Foreign Capital in Latin America,* 81.
16. Senate Committee on Banking and Currency, Interim Report, 83d Congress, 2d Session, Senate Report No. 1082, *Study of Latin American Countries* (Capehart Report) (Washington, 1954), 267.

Latin American assets to the United States has exceeded the rate of private United States investment in Latin America.[17] By 1954 Latin American investment in the United States had reached a total of $1,747 billion.[18] Because of this flight of local capital these underdeveloped countries appear, paradoxically, as exporters of capital.

When Latin American capital is reinvested locally it traditionally goes into real estate—largely urban—for reasons of security and prestige. It is also often inhibited from investment in industry and trade by a "high-unit-profits" mentality. These archaic and essentially unpatriotic investment habits have tended to perpetuate stagnant economies. They constitute a serious obstacle to planned national development through voluntary participation of investors. Governments which have wished to promote such development have had to try to overcome these seemingly perverse investment habits. As a result few of them have been able to make even a start toward channeling the capital assets of local entrepreneurs into socially productive developmental enterprises by this method.

The alternative is government financing to promote national development and to increase productivity. This requires enlarged budgets and the discovery of new sources of revenue. The search for such new sources was necessitated by the wartime decline in revenue that governments were able to derive from imports and exports. By 1948 a few Latin American governments in their need for increased revenues had experimented with an increased income tax. In Chile, for example, this tax supplied more than one-third of the ordinary government revenues, and in Argentina, Brazil, Mexico, Peru, and Venezuela it supplied from one-fifth to one-fourth, but in most of the other Latin American countries it contributed only negligible amounts. In Guatemala the Arbenz government inaugurated a moderate, graduated income tax, which went into effect on July 1, 1954, but which was soon afterward abolished by the new Castillo Armas administration. The recommendation by the Lauchlin Currie mission to Colombia of the imposition of a progressively higher tax penalty on underutilized land suggests another approach to the problem of securing additional revenue not only in Colombia but also in the other Latin American coun-

17. United Nations, Economic Commission for Latin America, *Economic Survey of Latin America, 1954*, 48.
18. Clement G. Motten, "The Historical Background," in [Northeastern Council for Latin American and Inter-American Studies] *Latin America: Development Programming and United States Investments* (Philadelphia, [1956]), 13.

284 ARE WE GOOD NEIGHBORS?

tries which suffer from land monopoly.[19] This principle was followed
in the income-tax law that Nicaragua put into effect in January, 1953,
to finance its long-range development program when provision was
made for exemption of expenses incurred in clearing, terracing, and
irrigating land, improving farms and cattle ranches, and establishing,
enlarging, or improving industrial plants.[20] Panama under the Remón
administration in early 1953 likewise sought additional revenue by
imposing increased taxes on uncultivated land.

Some Latin American governments resorted to more drastic programs of forced lending, including assessments upon pension funds,
institutes, insurance firms, and credit establishments in order to
finance their postwar developmental projects. But the essential thing,
it was realized, was to increase the per capita rate of productivity. This
could not be accomplished unless the manual workers were given reasonable assurances that the returns from their productive efforts would
be equitably distributed. To expand production and at the same time
to assure the fair distribution of the fruits of productive effort would
require dynamic, inspiriting, courageous political leadership.

* * *

Latin American governments have responded to the postwar
social and economic imperatives confronting them in three general
ways. First, some of them sought to redress social and economic
inequities, to create more homogeneous national societies, and to promote maximum individual development by orderly evolutionary methods within the framework of the existing constitutional system with its
legislative, executive, and judicial branches and its mechanism of
checks and balances.[21] As these constitutional methods proved slow
and ineffective, these governments sometimes offered belt-tightening
programs. Dr. Oswaldo Aranha, for example, who assumed the position of finance minister of Brazil in mid-1953, immediately announced a policy of "making the family live within its income."

19. International Bank for Reconstruction and Development, *The Basis of a
Development Program for Colombia, Report of a Mission Headed by Lauchlin
Currie and Sponsored by the International Bank for Reconstruction and Development in Collaboration with the Government of Colombia* (Washington,
1950), 10-12.
20. United Nations, Department of Economic and Social Affairs, *Foreign
Capital in Latin America*, 122.
21. Galo Plaza, *Problems of Democracy in Latin America* (Chapel Hill,
1955), [20]-42.

But austerity programs make no appeal to populations that live habitually on the margin of subsistence. Governments in Latin America cannot govern on the assumption that their people are living beyond their means and must therefore eat less. To do so is to invite either national suicide or, more probably, their own overthrow. All but two or three of these governments eventually found themselves caught in the toils of existing social and economic rigidities, fixed largely for the benefit of traditional ruling groups. They either antagonized such groups or unleashed new forces which they could not control. Thus confronted with literally insuperable obstacles they were overthrown, usually by palace coups, and replaced by new governments more obsequious to vested interests than they were willing to be. Since World War II, and particularly since 1948, several of these popular, constitutionally elected administrations have been toppled by military regimes largely representing these interests. As examples may be cited the overturn of President José Luis Bustamante in Peru by a military junta in October, 1948, the ouster of the popularly elected Rómulo Gallegos regime in Venezuela by a military group in November, 1948, the subversion of the constitutional government of Panama by the police in December, 1949, which brought Arnulfo Arias back into the presidency, and the overthrow of the Cuban regime of Carlos Prío Socarrás by General Fulgencio Batista in March, 1952.

As a result, in many countries oligarchic groups whose standing was weakened during the war have been able to regain their dominant positions in government and society. Their methods are quite different from those of the doctrinaire-liberals whom they have supplanted. Their objectives are order, peace, and a minimum of social change; they seek to achieve greater production without altering traditional patterns of property and power. Governments operating in their interests, regardless of the methods of their accession to office, have usually found it politically expedient at least to go through the motions of trying to satisfy the basic demands of the "have-not" masses of their populations. As social turbulence has nevertheless increased they have taken refuge in either obscurantism or persecution of political troublemakers or both. If vague, flamboyant, and bellicose talk has not abated social pressures, they have resorted to restriction and repression of dissident groups as being subversive to groups in power, as indeed they often are.

Some of these governments have found it necessary to trump up "plots" of various sorts to justify the imposition of censorship, the further strengthening of the military, and the suppression of political opposition. They have taken advantage of the postwar conflict of ideologies to demonstrate their anti-Communist orientation and their identification with the "free world." To all the elite classes in Latin America, communism as an ideology is repugnant, and they are willing to sign all kinds of international agreements to that effect. Under the guise of fighting communism they are able to tighten their restrictions upon all who threaten their control, sometimes ascribing the Communist label to groups who have genuine economic grievances or who may be trying only to raise the living standard of their people. Some of these governments may even welcome opportunities to thrust their people into foreign military ventures in order to direct attention away from unsolved domestic problems. As their local situation deteriorates they may blame their difficulties on outside market forces, lack of foreign assistance, or, conversely, the intervention of foreign nations. Saber-rattling and foreign wars are traditional diversionary tactics against revolution. Governments which have a primarily conserving or constricting outlook will gladly support foreign ventures in exchange for material assistance which will enable them to pursue a "bread and circuses" policy toward their people and build up military forces to suppress domestic subversive groups.

Still a third method of dealing with postwar political realities in Latin America is being tried. Similar in some superficial respects to the method just described, it nevertheless has its own distinctive basic quality. Its method is community action on a national scale of, by, and for the majority of the population. In this sense it seeks the objective of the nineteenth-century utilitarians—"the greatest happiness of the greatest number." But the character of the "greatest number" in many Latin American countries is different from what we seem or want to think it is. In most of them it consists of a horde of uneducated "have-nots," a melancholy sea of misery. Countering them are only a small but powerful elite class and a middle class which is almost everywhere both numerically and politically insignificant. In almost no Latin American country is there a possibility of a middle-class majority government such as exists in the United States. In this fact lies the disturbing element in this new political development. Moreover, the postwar inflation further weakened both the elite and the middle classes in Latin America, as elsewhere, while often strengthening the economic and political position of the working class, both urban and rural.

Latin America has been profoundly influenced by the trend so apparent in the second quarter of the twentieth century toward government intervention in the life of individuals and the use of fiscal policy for the reconstruction of the social and economic life of a nation. Government has assumed an ever-increasing responsibility for the maintenance of a healthy national economy, for correcting maladjustments in individual income, and for using the national income in such ways as to promote social harmony and happiness. The compelling ideal of many political groups in the region is the achievement of a broader community and national life, collectivist in nature and aiming at a social security largely conceived in materialistic terms. They know that as long as Poverty and Hunger stalk through Latin America a potentially revolutionary situation exists, quite apart from Soviet motivation and direction, and that it is these which basically threaten the stability of governments and society. They are aware that pent-up social pressures, like underground volcanism, may some day erupt. They have therefore sought to make the state an instrument of social reform and economic change and are modifying the theory and institution of private property in favor of state regulation and control.

This movement was led in Argentina by President Juan Domingo Perón until his fall from power in September, 1955, in Chile by President Carlos Ibáñez, in Venezuela by Rómulo Betancourt and his *Acción Democrática,* in Guatemala by ex-Presidents Juan José Arévalo and Jacobo Arbenz Guzmán, and in Bolivia by Víctor Paz Estenssoro of the *Movimiento Nacional Revolucionario (MNR).* In the latter country the small Marxist *Partido de la Izquierda Revolucionaria (PIR)* also has had much in common with it. It includes also the former followers of Jorge Eliecer Gaitán of Colombia, who have lacked leadership since his assassination in April, 1948, the members of Víctor Raúl Haya de la Torre's *Alianza Popular Revolucionaria Americana (APRA)* or People's Party of Peru, the followers of José Figueres in Costa Rica, and the supporters of President José María Velasco Ibarra in Ecuador. In Brazil it was led for a time by President Getúlio Vargas, who was still seeking to control it when he committed suicide in mid-1954. His successor is Juscelino Kubitschek, who was elected president of Brazil in October, 1955. Similar also is the Popular Party of Luis Muñoz-Marín in Puerto Rico with its "Operation Bootstrap."

The kinds of drastic expedients which the United States found it necessary to adopt during the crisis of 1933-1935 may be frequently resorted to in these Latin American countries where crisis is chronic. While these new movements profess to preserve many of the liberal and democratic forms of the nineteenth century, they seek to swing them in the direction of social justice and national security. Their avowed objectives are to establish governments which will better respond to popular aspirations and provide fuller opportunities for individual self-fulfillment and community action than previous governments have been able to do. They seek to destroy the feudal structure in agriculture, to incorporate the Indian into the economic, social, and political life of the country, to break the political power of the traditional oligarchy, replacing it with a mass-supported government, and to diversify the economy of the country and thus eliminate its dependence upon a single or a two-fold productive enterprise. Its social program has been strongly influenced by the encyclicals *Rerum novarum* of Pope Leo XIII in 1891 and *Quadragesimo anno* of Pius XI in 1931. Its general aims coincide with those of the prevailing Roman Catholicism of Latin America. There is in all this, from the ideological or philosophical standpoint, a strong element of Christian Socialism, not unlike that of the Christian Democratic parties of central and southern Europe.[22] Or to suggest a Latin American analogue, it represents a neopositivism which has a deep overlay of humanitarianism and is therefore "liberal" in the traditional Latin American sense.

Though communism, particularly of the U.S.S.R. variety, is an ideology alien to Latin America, the same cannot be said of socialism. Upon a Latin America traditionally committed to state intervention and control, European Socialistic thought made a deep impression, particularly after 1885. Ex-President Carlos Dávila of Chile has pointed out that Latin American economies have traditionally been managed economies but that they have been managed from abroad.[23] Some of the Latin American countries, notably Uruguay, Mexico, Guatemala, and Argentina, have already gone much further or are moving much faster along the road to socialism than the United States. Socialist innovations began in Uruguay nearly a half century ago under President José Batlle y Ordóñez.[24] The *APRA*

22. Carlos Moyano Llerena, *et al., Argentina, Social y Económica* (Buenos Aires, 1950), 294.   23. *We of the Americas,* 225.
24. George Pendle, *Uruguay, South America's First Welfare State* (London and New York, 1952), 15-34; and Simon Hanson, *Utopia in Uruguay: Chapters in the Economic History of Uruguay* (New York, 1938).

movement of Haya de la Torre has been crusading for agrarian socialism since the mid-1920's. In Mexico socialist indoctrination has been
perhaps the principal objective of the national educational system
since 1917. "The education imparted by the State," declared the
Mexican constitution of 1917, "shall be a socialistic one."[25] In many
parts of Latin America the capitalist system has already been considerably modified by substantial social welfare concepts carried out
through state controls and state interventions. The principle underlying this new national socialism in Latin America was well expressed
by President Higinio Morinigo of Paraguay as early as 1941 when
he declared that "the inertia of the liberal State must yield to the
dynamism of the protecting and directing state."[26]

The people of many parts of Latin America still live in a pre-
capitalist economy. Since they either have never had an opportunity
to make free-enterprise capitalism work for themselves or have come
in contact with it only as operated by foreign business concerns, they
can readily make the transition to state capitalism or state socialism.
As the international system of the World War II period disintegrated
into its prewar component national parts it left a thicker residue of
faith among Latin Americans in programs of socialistic action for
national ends than existed before the war. In Guatemala the *Partido
Acción Revolucionaria,* which controlled the country until its ouster
in 1954, favored national ownership of natural resources. This "spiritual socialism," as former President Arévalo called it, sought to
assure the workers of Guatemala, predominantly Indian, that the
wealth of the country would be controlled by the state for their benefit.[27] To this end the Arbenz government, which succeeded the
Arévalo government in March, 1951, submitted to the Guatemalan
Congress for its approval in early November, 1952, a new five-year
public works program to cost $20 million.[28] In Brazil the program
of President Vargas' Brazilian Workers Party *(Partido Trabalhista
Brasileiro)* gave a large role to the national government as the plan-
ner, organizer, and in some cases the operator of Brazil's economy.
Vargas defined its orientation as "anti-capitalistic and socialistic"
and called for the socialization of "waterpower resources, mineral

25. George I. Sánchez, *Mexico: A Revolution by Education* (New York
1936), particularly Chapter VI, "The Socialistic School."
26. *La Prensa,* New York, October 25, 1941.
27. Juan José Arévalo, leaflet dated October 31, 1944, reprinted in his
Escritos Políticos (Guatemala, 1945), 143-149.
28. *El Imparcial,* Guatemala, November 4, 1952.

deposits, electrical supply facilities, means of transport—in short, the program" of "the British Labor party."[29] The Brazilian *SALTE* is an example of state planning to this end. Latin Americans do not have to look to Krushchev's Russia or to Nasser's Egypt for lessons in nationalization. The railroads of Colombia have been nationalized for many years. Since 1917 the Mexican government, under its revolutionary constitution of that year, has assumed the management of the greater part of the economy of the nation. It has nationalized the transportation, petroleum, and many other industries and has largely broken up the feudal *hacienda* system through distribution of lands to the *peones*. In the depression years after 1929 nationalization of industry and natural resources became an objective of many reform parties in Latin America, as for example, the *Auténtico* Party of Cuba. As a result of a long campaign carried on by the *Partido de la Izquierda Revolucionaria (PIR)* and the *Movimiento Nacional Revolucionario (MNR)* the Bolivian government of President Víctor Paz Estenssoro nationalized the mining properties of Patiño, Hochschild, and Aramayo by decree on October 31, 1952.[30] In Colombia the government of President Gustavo Rojas Pinilla was reported in 1954 to be planning a large-scale nationalization program in order to achieve the objectives of "social justice" proclaimed by the president.[31] In the Dominican Republic, also, the government of President Rafael Leonidas Trujillo has talked about nationalizing the sugar industry, which is largely controlled by United States capital.[32]

Argentina has been particularly conspicuous for its nationalizing activities since the end of World War II. The traditional advocate of this program for Argentina has been the Radical Party *(Unión Cívica Radical)*, which from the beginning of its party organization in the 1890's emphasized economic nationalism in foreign relations and governmental intervention in the domestic economy. As the modern heir of this program the Perón government followed an un-

29. Newspaper interview with Vargas in *Correio da Manhã*, March 9, 1949.
30. See Ricardo Anaya, *Nacionalización de las Minas de Bolivia* (Cochabamba, 1952); Harold Osborne, *Bolivia, A Land Divided* (London, 1955), 107; Economic Commission for Latin America, *Economic Bulletin for Latin America*, II, 2 (October, 1957), 19-72; Alberto Ostría Gutiérrez, *The Tragedy of Bolivia: A People Crucified* (New York, [1958]), 145-148; and Robert J. Alexander, *The Bolivian National Revolution* (New Brunswick, New Jersey, 1959), [94]-103.
31. Speech by President Gustavo Rojas Pinilla at San Gil, Colombia, December 12, 1954.
32. Press statements by President Trujillo, January, 1954.

precedentedly ambitious policy of nationalization after 1946. In that year the Central Bank was nationalized and was given control over the entire banking system of the country. Nationalized industries include the railways, merchant marine, aviation lines, telephones, port facilities, grain elevators, and many others. In addition a government agency, the YPF (Yacimientos Petrolíferos Fiscales), dominates both the production and the marketing of petroleum, and the government has moved into the meat-packing business. Through another government agency it administers a large group of expropriated German companies including metallurgical plants, chemicals and pharmaceuticals, construction firms, and others, and through its Fábricas Militares (Military Factories) it controls many other manufacturing activities. The operations of the state trading corporation, the Instituto Argentina de Promoción de Intercambio (IAPI), also established by Perón, limit the internal free competitive market. Perón's two successive Five-Year Plans were intended to marshal and develop the maximum resources of the country under government auspices.[33]

This type of mass movement, as already suggested, has deep roots in the Latin American past. The new directions in postwar Latin America are really old directions. But they were stimulated by the war with its idealism, its Atlantic Charter, and its mass evangelism, on the one hand, and its materialism, its power politics, and its rough treatment of minorities, on the other. The process of socialization or nationalization was encouraged, it should be noted, in many Latin American countries, particularly Argentina and Guatemala, by their compliance with wartime inter-American commitments to expropriate Axis-owned or Axis-operated businesses and to impose controls of various sorts over the strategic and critical raw materials produced in their countries. The oligarchy of the very rich who had always managed to impress its wishes upon the political leaders of those countries in the past was demoralized by the war. Under wartime conditions it followed the primary object of selfishly looking out for its own interests and pleasures, leaving the newly awakened democratic forces leaderless and disunited. The latter had never had the upper hand in running the country, lacked the organization necessary for sustained political effort, and were susceptible to demagogic blandishments.

33. Edward J. Chambers, "Some Factors in the Deterioration of Argentina's External Position, 1946-1951," *Inter-American Economic Affairs,* VIII (Winter, 1954), 27-62; and United Nations, Department of Economic and Social Affairs, *Foreign Capital in Latin America,* 39-41.

In a broad sense the mass movements which have occurred in Latin America since World War II are a part of the surge toward collectivism which has been growing since the Industrial Revolution and which seems to accompany that Revolution as it advances in country after country. It represents a continuation, in accelerated and intensified form, of the world-wide movement of the 1930's, exemplified by the New Deal in the United States, toward collective action by the people in the hope of obtaining security for themselves and an improvement in their living conditions. It is a part of the world-wide surge of revolt among underprivileged peoples against feudalism, colonialism, imperialism, and capitalism, all of which are associated with traditional local elites, with the United States, and to a certain extent also with other nations of the North Atlantic community. It emphasizes numbers or quantity and requires that the majority element in a society should, in its own interest, assume control. In thus serving its own interest the majority presumably also serves the interest of society as a whole.

The accession of the underling class to power in Latin America represents, from the point of view of that class, progress toward democracy because it enables a larger number of people than ever before to govern. The emphasis of this new self-conscious class is upon the economic rights of man including the right to work, the right to a living wage, the right to adequate housing—all of these for the purpose of achieving freedom from want, freedom from fear, and freedom from exploitation. These rights seem much more important that the civil liberties of ninteenth-century libertarian democracy, such as habeas corpus, freedom of speech, freedom of press and religion, and freedom of assembly, which usually in the Latin American past have been honored only with lip service or, when actually permitted, have seemed only to mean freedom to go hungry.

As comparable movements in the United States have been associated with a magnetic popular hero such as Woodrow Wilson or Franklin Roosevelt, so in Latin America the modern movement is spearheaded by *caudillos* of the people. In the course of the development of the Latin American nations the power of the state has often been embodied in a single national leader. The history of both Spaniards and Indians is replete with examples of the exaltation of the *caudillo*. Strong government by a *cacique* or a *caudillo* has been the rule in Latin America, regardless of constitutional forms.[34] The spec-

34. García Calderón, *op. cit.*, 365-366.

tacle of a modern president of Mexico, for example, regularly traveling about the country to listen to complaints by humble *peones* and
to redress wrongs emphasizes the continuing role of the state as the
source of all authority and the dispenser of all justice in Latin America. Historically the Latin American *caudillo* has usually been the
official representative of the oligarchic clique in power, and has been
able to remain in office as long as he satisfied it and could resist overthrow by an opposition clique. But the prevailing social and economic conditions require a Latin American president, even in those
countries which give only lip service to the popular will, at least to
pose as a "little father of the poor." The modern *caudillo* of the welfare state, therefore, is likely to consider himself the first servant of
the underprivileged masses of the people. He organizes and makes
himself the leader of the increasingly articulate and powerful class of
urban and rural workers and usually concerns himself with their
needs. His leadership is intensely personal, and his followers succumb
almost ecstatically to a new cult of personality which is built around
him.

Throughout Latin America far-reaching adjustments between
classes are taking place. The political idea of government by the
majority is being used to promote the economic well-being of the
working classes through national planning of production and a calculated redistribution of wealth. If through the efforts of such a government the majority of citizens become well fed, well clothed, and
well housed—or even better fed, better clothed, and better housed
than before—the government may continue to win elections and to
exercise power. In the Argentine elections in November, 1951, Perón
was re-elected by more than 66 per cent of the popular vote. The
problem of gaining and keeping political power in Latin America
cannot be dissociated from the problem of social justice.

Such a regime, from the standpoint of its followers and its bene-
ficiaries, seems to be motivated by the highest possible principle,
namely, advancement of the welfare of the underprivileged majority
and so the interests of the nation. To the *descamisados*—the shirtless,
the underprivileged, the underdogs—it is a "do good" regime, is more
responsive to the majority will than previous oligarchic governments
have been, and is capable of acting more efficiently in the interest
of that majority. In Argentina the lower classes have been made
more aware of their worth and power than ever before in history.
Their leader, Perón, has been called not so much "a soldier or an

individual" as "a mental state of the proletariat."[35] To them the old governments represented only "a false and empty democracy," to use a phrase of Carlos Ibáñez of Chile. With power in their hands now, they are bent upon establishing a new "authoritarian democracy," as it has been called, or, perhaps better still, a "majoritarian" government, for it is government of, by, and for the majority of the people. For them the breakdown of the patriarchal tradition represents progress toward democracy. Their ideal society is a democratic collectivism.

The apparent objective, or at least the logical end result of such a system is a workers', or at least, a producers' commonwealth. It has seemed to require the integration of organized labor into the mechanism of the state. In the past the human resources of many of these countries have been carelessly used. Their new governments profess to want to increase the human potential by placing enlarged opportunities for self-improvement in the hands of the workers, workers who from centuries of experience have become accustomed to the paternalism of the *hacendado* or the *patrón* and find it easy to accept the paternalism of the welfare state. Under Vargas in Brazil the labor "syndicates," as they are called, were brought under the complete supervision of the Ministry of Labor. The same identification of the government with the producing masses was attempted in Guatemala under the Arbenz government. In Venezuela the government of President Marcos Pérez Jiménez also sought to unify organized labor under the control of the government-sponsored labor federation MOSIT (Movimiento Sindical Independiente de Trabajadores), which serves as the only effective representative of Venezuelan labor.

In the postwar movement in Latin America toward national integration industrialists, nationalists, and labor organizations find a common meeting ground. Nationally minded governments have won the support of both industrial groups and labor unions for their nationalistic programs directed against the alleged attempts of the industrialized countries, particularly the United States, to block their achievement of economic independence. In postwar Argentina such a program was given a humanitarian character under the name of *Justicialismo* (Justicialism). Perón's labor program, as announced in his speech of May 1, 1944, while he was still head of the National Secretariat of Labor and Social Planning, was to bring all industry and all labor into a single syndicate in order "to suppress the class

35. Joaquín Edwards Bello, *La Patria*, Concepción, Chile, March 8, 1946.

struggle, supplanting it by a just agreement between workers and employers in the shelter of the justice emanating from the state." As a result, the attempt was made in Argentina to substitute the force of organized labor for that of the former landed oligarchy. By late 1946 all wage rates and hours had been brought under exclusive jurisdiction of the national government and labor unions were deprived of their rights of free bargaining and contracting. Labor was thereby not only encouraged but virtually forced to look to the government for benefits in wages, hours, and working conditions. No independent labor movement existed after the port and meat workers unions came into the government-directed Confederación General de Trabajadores in the autumn of 1950. "Workers constitute the great social force of the new Argentina," Perón told an Argentine audience in 1951.[36]

The Perón government's labor policy produced a considerable class shift in income distribution in Argentina. Between 1946 and 1950 workers and small businessmen increased their share of the national income from 58.3 per cent to 77.2 per cent and the real income per worker rose by almost a third.[37] The position of Argentine workers was also strengthened by the government's encouragement of cooperatives in both industry and agriculture. In February, 1955, for example, Perón announced the expropriation of the gigantic Bemberg brewing monopoly and its conversion under government auspices into a cooperative corporation owned by the brewery workers.[38] In addition Argentina's second Five-Year Plan, covering the years 1953 through 1957, provided for a national system of cooperatives to assist the government in all phases of agricultural policy and administration. By these means the government may strengthen its position, using organized labor to offset the pretensions of foreign capital as well as the vested strengths of local magnates. The late Señora Evita Perón declared in her last Christmas broadcast on December 25, 1951, that the ideals of Perón's government "proclaim that mankind is to consist of only one class of men—those who work; that all shall be for one, and one for all; that there is to be no one with special privileges except the children; that the governments of nations are to do what the people want done; that each day all men are to be a little less poor."

36. Speech to Argentine farmers, Buenos Aires, June 5, 1951.
37. United Nations, Economic Commission for Latin America, *Economic Survey of Latin America, 1953,* 13-14.
38. Speech at the Quilmes Brewery, February 5, 1955.

This system has also seemed to require modification of the institution of private property. *Peronismo* has been defined by the Chilean writer Joaquín Edwards Bello as "the reform of the life of the laboring class in its relation to capital."[39] The Argentine constitution of 1949, which embodied the political philosophy of the Peronistas, declared that "private property has a social function" and that "capital shall be in the service of the national economy and shall have social welfare as its principal object." Perón boasted in a speech on December 20, 1950, "We have transformed the economic order and established economic socialism, that is, whereas capitalism put the national economy at its service, we now put capital at the service of the national economy." He later declared that "the basic tenet of our doctrine is to give to the people access to property and riches. Everything in our country belongs to the people." His speeches and actions were obviously predicated upon the conviction that capitalism as a form of social organization is not sufficiently flexible to adjust itself to the requirements of the modern world and will not long survive. He appealed to his *descamisados* to replace it with *Justicialismo*, which ostensibly aims at social justice and welfare through state action. "Justicialism," Perón is reported to have declared in the speech cited above, "will not be able to destroy capitalism all at once. It will be necessary to dismantle the entire capitalist system and build up a new one, unless we are willing to see the misery of the masses increase." He depicted the enemy of his movement as "international capitalism."[40]

39. *La Patria,* Concepción, Chile, March 8, 1946.
40. The best expositions of Perón's program and philosophy of government are found in his speeches published officially at various times by the Argentine Subsecretaría de Informaciones, Dirección General de la Prensa, and in other collections as for example, Juan Perón, *El Pueblo Quiere Saber de qué se Trata* (Buenos Aires, 1944); *Doctrina Peronista: Filosófica, Política, Social* (Buenos Aires, 1947); and *Doctrina Peronista: Perón Expone su Doctrina* [Buenos Aires], 1951. Journalistic expositions of Peronismo are given in Descartes [pseudonym], *Artículos de Descartes: Política y Estrategia* (Buenos Aires, 1951). The Peronista movement has inspired many eulogistic books in Latin America including the following: P. Nuñez Arca, *Perón, Man of America* (Buenos Aires, 1950); Pedro González-Blanco, *Un Gobierno Popular sin Demogogia (la Argentina del General Perón)* (Mexico, 1951); and Benjamín A. M. Bambill, *Hacia la Realización de una Democracia Responsable . . .* (Buenos Aires, 1953). See also Lucien Duquenne and Pierre Biondini, *L'Argentine de Perón* (Bordeaux, 1954). The following studies in English may also be mentioned: Robert J. Alexander, *The Perón Era* (New York, 1951); George I. Blanksten, *Perón's Argentina* (Chicago, 1953); Arthur P. Whitaker, *The United States and Argentina* (Cambridge, 1954), and *Argentine Upheaval*

In several Latin American countries this movement has also emphasized the division, or *parcelación* of large landed properties among the landless, following the pattern set by Mexican governments since 1915.[41] The basic problem is to support ever-increasing populations on shrinking land resources. In general the trend is away from a semifeudal regime of monoculture and *latifundio* toward economically and socially democratic regimes marked by diversification of crops and fragmentation of large estates. The renewed postwar emphasis upon agriculture has run into difficulties of both an agronomic and an institutional nature, namely, sterile soils depleted by centuries of careless agriculture and unchecked erosion, and uneconomic conditions of land tenure. These new-type governments feel that their predecessors have been too tolerant of land monopoly and have not had a proper appreciation of the social function of land. In societies in which political power proceeds from landownership, a diffusion of landownership may be expected to produce a diffusion of power. If everyone owns real property then everyone may rule. A nation of landowners, moreover, is a nation of conservatives. They oppose revolutionary action against the *status quo* because they derive advantage from stability.

The concentration of landed wealth in the hands of a few individuals or families resulting in an uneconomic utilization of the land and the creation of a numerous class of disinherited citizens has been a major problem in most of the Latin American countries since colonial days. According to a report made by the Director-General of the International Labour Organization to the Fifth Conference of American States Members of that organization at Rio de Janeiro in April, 1952, in Argentina 85 per cent of the privately owned agricultural land is in estates of more than 1,200 acres; in Brazil almost half the land is held in estates of more than 2,400 acres; in Chile 64 per cent of the privately owned land belongs to 750 owners; and in Uruguay 16 owners control almost half the cultivated land area of the country.[42]

(New York, 1956). For an analytical exposition of the attitude of the Perón government on private property see Carlos Moyana Llerena, *op. cit.*, [289]-375.

41. The best studies of the Mexican program of land distribution are Eyler N. Simpson, *The Ejido, Mexico's Way Out* (Chapel Hill, 1937); Frank Tannenbaum, *Mexico: The Struggle for Peace and Bread* (New York, 1950); and Nathan L. Whetten, *Rural Mexico* (Chicago, 1948).

42. International Labour Office, *Report of the Director-General to the Fifth Conference of American States Members of the International Labour Or-*

In an attempt to cope with this problem Mexican governments between 1916 and 1945 expropriated and made available to agricultural workers 15.5 per cent of the total area of the country, or an area almost as large as all of New England and New York.[43] This redistribution of land under government auspices appears to have been one of the essential preconditions of Mexico's phenomenal economic development in the second quarter of the century. In Chile legislative moves to expropriate the *latifundios* and to distribute these lands among agricultural workers began in 1928.[44] In Colombia land distribution was carried through on paper in 1936 as one of the reforms of the Alfonso López administration. Venezuela, after making several attempts to deal with the problem of inequitable land tenure after 1936, finally adopted an agrarian statute in June, 1949, the purpose of which was to channel state policy "toward a gradual improvement of rural living conditions through an equitable distribution of land." The statute set up a National Agrarian Institute (Instituto Agrario Nacional) endowed with authority to break up estates, to form agricultural units or colonies, to extend agricultural credit, to undertake the technical training of agricultural workers, to promote cooperatives, and to facilitate the more efficient utilization of land. Operating with a capital of 100 million bolivares contributed by the national government, it was authorized to acquire lands either by direct purchase or by expropriation, and to expropriate lands which are not being efficiently utilized.[45]

This method of land control was given impetus by the recommendations favoring the division of agricultural lands adopted by the Fourth Inter-American Conference on Agriculture meeting in Montevideo in December, 1950, in joint session with the Second Latin American Conference on Food and Agricultural Programs and Outlook.[46] In the following year the United Nations Economic and Social Council adopted a resolution which recognized that land reform designed to improve the conditions of agricultural populations and to

ganization, Rio de Janeiro, April, 1952 (Geneva, 1952), 81. For Chile see Pinto Santa Cruz, *op. cit.,* 134-136.

43. Whetten, *op. cit.,* 124; Tannenbaum, *op. cit.,* 136-153; and Simpson, *op. cit.,* 192-210.   44. Poblete Troncoso, *op. cit.,* 56, 97-99.

45. United Nations, Economic Commission for Latin America, *Economic Survey of Latin America, 1950,* 50-51.

46. Fourth Inter-American Conference on Agriculture, Montevideo, December 1-12, 1950, *Final Act,* Conferences and Organizations Series, No. 9 (Washington, 1951).

increase agricultural production must, in many countries, be regarded as a necessary part of any effective implementation of comprehensive programs for economic development. It accordingly recommended that governments should institute land reforms in the interest of landless, small, and medium farmers.[47]

Several Latin American governments thereafter initiated such programs. In Guatemala the distribution of lands was begun in mid-1952 by the legislature after President Arbenz had pointed out to Congress that 22 families owned about 1,250,000 acres of land in Guatemala, whereas some 300,000 other families owned only about the same amount. This land reform was necessary, said President Arbenz in his annual message to Congress in March, 1953, as a beginning of the economic transformation of Guatemala into "a modern capitalist economy."[48] In Argentina, which is not so well suited to small-scale agricultural operations as certain other Latin American countries, the Perón government nevertheless showed an awareness of the problem of land monopoly.[49] Between 1946 and 1950 it expropriated *latifundios* comprising almost 1,125,000 acres, and in the year 1947 alone it established about 34,000 persons on the land.[50] In Brazil, President Vargas announced in April, 1952, the inauguration of "a peaceful revolution of the utmost importance . . . an agrarian reform which finally will liberate the rural workers from their ageless servitude and will transform the farm workers into farm owners through the division of public lands and the gradual elimination of the backward and harmful feudalistic landholdings which control large areas of rich, virgin lands now kept deserted and unproductive."[51] In Bolivia, President Paz Estenssoro issued a land reform decree on August 2, 1953, which provided for the expropriation of *latifundios* and their distribution to the peasants living on them, estimated to number about 2,500,000 people, mostly Indians, out of a

47. United Nations, Economic and Social Council, 6th Year, 13th Session, Geneva, 30 July-21 September, 1951, Official Records, Supplement No. 1: *Resolutions*, 10-14.

48. *Informe del Ciudadano Presidente de la República, Coronel Jacobo Arbenz Guzmán al Congreso Nacional en su primer período de sesiones ordinarias del año de 1953 . . . 1° de marzo, 1953* (Guatemala).

49. See Perón's speech to the Argentine Congress on October 28, 1946, presenting his first Five Year Plan; and Poblete Troncoso, *op. cit.*, 94-96.

50. International Labour Office, *Report of the Director-General*, 99. See also Duquenne and Biondini, *op. cit.*, 173-174.

51. Address to Fifth Inter-American Regional Conference of the International Labour Organization, Rio de Janeiro, April 17, 1952.

total population of about 3,500,000.[52] In Chile, also, the Ibáñez government has planned an agrarian reform program under which large, uncultivated landholdings will be divided into small plots of land for development by agricultural cooperative societies. And in Cuba the revolutionary government of Fidel Castro unveiled a plan for breaking up large estates in May, 1959.

A majority government in Latin America, run by a *caudillo* in the interests of the majority, will make little provision for either an elite or a middle class. The proletariat, both urban and rural, which comprises this majority is often actuated by deep-seated prejudices against both of these classes and against the "democratic forms" to which they have traditionally adhered. But in their attitude toward minority rights and civil liberties these new movements, as they have come to power, have followed the usual Latin American practices. If the source of power and the objectives of the new *caudillo* are new, the methods by which he remains in power are those of the old-type *caudillo*. A political victory by the traditional parties or elites has customarily been followed by a proscription, more or less thorough-going, of political opponents and a denial of civil liberties. The rights of minorities are preserved mainly by permitting dissidents to seek asylum in foreign embassies or freedom in foreign countries. A new working-class majority which attains power can be expected to follow the pattern of intolerant government already set by previous administrations. Such a majority, if it has been long suppressed by either constitutional or unconstitutional means, is likely to be extremist when it finally comes to power. If it shows a too tender regard for the rights of minorities, it invites its own destruction, for in some of the Latin American countries the older oligarchies have been long and strongly entrenched in power, and when they are thrown into the opposition they become recklessly belligerent. To them the new regime is truly revolutionary. It not only threatens their traditional power and property, but it denies to them the means of regaining popular favor.

For these reasons the fierce determination of the new regime to live is not tempered by a willingness to let live. It is rough and ready, impatient, experimentally minded, and lacking in appreciation of the social value of disagreeing viewpoints. In its bureaucracy it feels need only of lawyers and apologists—not thinkers, philosophers, scholars,

52. Ronald Hilton (ed.), *Hispanic American Report*, VI, 8 (September, 1953), 31; and Ostria Gutiérrez, *op. cit.*, 158-170.

or even impartial journalists. "As for liberty," declared Perón in an address in August, 1951, "we already offer the greatest amount of personal liberty which can be offered while still guaranteeing liberty for all. No one can enjoy liberty to the extent that all others are enslaved. . . . While there is no freedom extended for disrupting public order, there is ample freedom for living decently and doing things right."[53] A political doctrine such as this requires an intensification of social curbs and the imposition of an overwhelming society upon the individual in the interest of the majority and, as its proponents believe, also in the interest of all. By such means the regime aggrandizes itself, seeks to become self-perpetuating, and in its search for increasingly wider support builds a state which tends to become unipartite or monolithic. Its leaders do not even repudiate the label of authoritarian so long as they themselves are convinced that they are giving men more power, more mastery, more vigor, and more opportunities. The aim of their government is not liberty; it is rather the satisfaction of basic social needs as they conceive them in order to achieve an integrated society.

* * *

Nationalism and statism are the outstanding phenomena in modern Latin America. Postwar nationalism is different from the traditional nationalism of thirty, forty, fifty years ago when the ruling "haves," the elites, thought of it primarily as a means of stimulating national consciousness for their own property ends or of diverting attention from their own misdeeds and extortions. The new nationalist movements seek national integration, that is, the national unification of their peoples around certain social, cultural, economic, political, and psychological ideals, the revivification of the national will and spirit, and the recuperation of the national patrimony which they feel has been dissipated by internal disruptive forces or alienated by previous disloyal leaders to foreign interests. "Some oil fields of Venezuela, some copper mines of Chile, some zinc or lead mines of Mexico, some banana plantations in any Central-American country, although lying inside the economies of these nations, are splinters or 'exclaves' of the foreign economy," points out Alfonso Cortina.[54] To

53. Address at a meeting of producers, Buenos Aires, August 16, 1951.
54. "Latin America and the United States Materials Policy," *Social Science,* XXVIII, Autumn Issue (October, 1955), 233.

change this situation leaders of the new nationalism in Latin America are seeking to consolidate their national economies and to do so by means of a mass upsurge, vertical rather than horizontal, embracing all classes in a nation. Even when they use it for demagogic and self-seeking ends they are acknowledging the force of the popular pressures for national self-expression and integration. The shibboleths which politicians find it convenient to use are indicative of popular aspirations.

Postwar nationalism in Latin America has manifested itself in various forms. In Brazil nationalists prevailed upon the government of President Kubitschek in 1956 to refuse to give the United States permission to prospect for uranium within the country and to transport nuclear materials out of Brazil to the United States. In black Haiti the postwar nationalism emphasizes the necessity for peoples of color to "free themselves from the colonial yoke of the white nations," as the Haitian delegate to the United Nations, Pierre Hudicourt, expressed it in a speech before the United Nations in December, 1953.[55]

These movements present many resemblances to the Mexican revolutionary movement of the 1910's and 1920's. They have been presaged by the regimes of many earlier *caudillos,* including Hipólito Yrigoyen in Argentina (1916-1922, 1928-1930) and Arturo Alessandri in Chile (1920-1925, 1932-1938). But they are now taking place under the changed conditions of the 1950's. Many of the ingredients are the same—social restlessness, economic dissatisfaction, opposition to foreign capitalism—but some new ingredients have been added and the potency of the mixture has been intensified by the economic forces, the social changes, even the democratic expectations generated in World War II. These new movements have come to embody the postwar aspirations of the Latin American peoples for increased national strength, independence, and dignity. Their aims are to stimulate and encourage pride of nation and race, to integrate and make the nation more homogeneous than ever before, to increase the sense of national responsibility, to develop the national resources, and to organize the national life in such ways as to benefit all or a majority of the people of the nation. Their objective is the harmonious *convivencia* of their people in a well-integrated society. They resent dictation and imposition, they spurn foreign models of beauty and artistic expression, they view the local scene with new eyes, and they

55. *Le Nouvelliste,* Port-au-Prince, December 18, 1953.

seek to use native modes of expression, native subjects, and native materials. They look to their own earth for their inspiration.

All of this has come about by a peaceful change in the outlook of Latin Americans, as a reaction against their continuing colonial-like servitude, as a protest against their heritage from a feudal social and economic system. Their effective dynamics are provided by the rising groups of industrialists who wish to break their country's position of economic inferiority and to develop a largely independent national economic life. In the words of José R. Colín, one of Mexico's industrialists who is working for the development of Mexico along these lines, this movement in Mexico calls for a new "national ethos" requiring "discipline, determination to reach an objective, a spirit of sacrifice, a clear idea of fulfilling a duty, and a feeling of national enthusiasm in working for the interests of the country."[56] As Colín has pointed out in *Excelsior* of Mexico City, the appeal of these new nationalist movements springs from the fact that they are frankly revolutionary and anti-imperialistic.[57] In short, this new *nacionalismo integrado* emphasizes national and racial unities and seeks to harmonize dissimilarities in the interest of the nation if not indeed of all the Hispanic-American peoples. As a social movement its objective is national homogeneity and unity to be achieved through state action.

This is a new force in several Latin American countries where nationality has been heretofore a virtually unknown quality. Some of the so-called national entities that are marked off with their own geographical boundaries on maps of Latin America are not and never have been nations in the modern meaning of the term. They have lacked "the community of interest and homogeneity of purpose associated with the concept of nationhood."[58] Millions of their residents have remained outside the effective economy and political life of the nation under whose nominal jurisdiction they live. Especially in the predominantly Indian countries of Latin America the Indian peoples are *in* but not *of* the nation. But the modern nationalist movements are exerting themselves to bring these people into the national life and to raise the living levels of all. They have been born, as Robin A. Humphreys has pointed out, "not of the assurance of national unity but of the absence of assurance."[59] They are searching for a nation.

56. *Requisitos Fundamentales para la Industrialización de México* (Mexico, 1945), 12.   57. Reported in radio broadcast on June 4, 1953.
58. Bernard Mishkin, " 'Good Neighbors'—Fact and Fancy," *The Nation,* CLXIX (November 26, 1949), 511.
59. *The Evolution of Modern Latin America* (Oxford, 1946), 88.

To the landless *peón* living in almost feudal servitude the national government may be only a dim, scarcely existent reality. The land which the *peón* tills is his only fatherland, and only when the national government bestirs itself to make the land available to him does it begin, for the first time perhaps, to enter into his consciousness. With such an act the *peón* may emerge with increased dignity as a citizen in a more broadly based and more closely integrated nation.

Through their new nationalism the Latin Americans hope not only to be able to retain but also to dignify the authentic, distinctive qualities of their nationality and race. "The natural peculiarities of any region give rise to customs and practices of a corresponding peculiarity," wrote Domingo Faustino Sarmiento in his famous *Facundo* over a century ago.[60] Pride in these "customs and practices" is of the essence of modern *Argentinidad, Peruanidad, Mejicanidad, Cubanidad, Brasilidade, Hispanidad, Latinidad,* and other such movements. Following in the tradition of a long line of Latin American patriot-nationalists since Simón Bolívar, José Enrique Rodó, writing in his *Ariel* in 1900, strongly repudiated attempts to "denaturalize the character" of the Latin American peoples. "Concern for one's own independence, personality, judgment," he wrote, "is the highest form of self-respect."[61]

Appeals for national self-respect, sometimes taking the form of lyrical panegyrics to patriotism, have been made by a long line of Latin American publicists. The imperialism of European cultures superimposed upon Latin America was criticized by the Argentine intellectual Ricardo Rojas in 1924. "We need," he wrote, a culture "growing out of the experience of our own history, produced here, for us and for America, as a declaration that Argentine nationality has reached maturity." This broad feeling of *Argentinidad,* he continued, must be based on "the emotion of the native landscape, the psychological vigor of the race, the original themes of its tradition, the new ideals of our culture."[62] Similarly, Manuel Ugarte in 1923 stressed the importance to Latin America of "her own peculiar possibilities of development, her own clearly defined personality, her ineradicable traditions, her faculty of self-determination."[63] The modern neo-nationalists in Latin America do not propose to renounce these things

60. *Facundo,* 2d ed. (Buenos Aires, 1940), 31.
61. *Ariel,* 4th ed. (Barcelona, 1930), 73-74.
62. *Eurindia* (Buenos Aires, 1924), 42.
63. *The Destiny of a Continent,* 15.

in favor of any foreign importations which will injure or detract from their own national and racial character. They are rediscovering these national and racial values and are not only developing philosophical justifications for asserting them, but also giving them a new positive character, as in the writings of Enrique V. Corominas of Argentina, Leopoldo Zea of Mexico, and Eduardo Caballero Calderón of Colombia.[64]

"Although we Latin Americans," Mariano Picón-Salas has commented, "are requiring a technology as effective as that of the North American for the improvement of our material conditions, at the same time we wish to preserve our conception of life and culture which, from many points of view, is opposed to that of the United States. The worst thing that could happen to us would be to transform ourselves into second-class Yankees or to have their culture imposed upon us or to suffer an adulteration of native spiritual values, like that which a badly organized North American education has produced in Puerto Rico."[65] Such reasoning explains in part why the Colombian ambassador in Mexico suggested a common "Iberian-American" citizenship in January, 1948, and why the Mexican government has objected to the free exodus of Mexican *braceros,* or manual workers, to the United States to help with harvesting operations. The *braceros,* it feels, ought to remain in their own country where they can contribute to the progress of Mexico's own agricultural and industrial program. This same reasoning also explains the attempt by the governor of Mexico's Federal District in 1953 to ban the use of such bastard Spanish words as *lonchería* (lunch room), *nocout* (knockout), and *pay de manzana* (apple pie) in signs and public buildings.[66]

These Latin Americans, then, are working for vigorous, self-initiated action by their own peoples to produce a strong Latin America possessing its own distinctive Hispanic culture and playing a more worthy and dignified part in the world balance of power than it has

64. Enrique V. Corominas, *La Práctica del Hispanoamericanismo* (Madrid, 1952); Leopoldo Zea, *América como Consciencia* (Mexico, 1953); and Caballero Calderón, *Suramérica, Tierra del Hombre,* 229-235, 239-256. See also Lewis Hanke, "The Americanization of America," in *Latin American Viewpoints, L. S. Rowe Lectures on Latin America delivered at the Wharton School, University of Pennsylvania, in the fall of 1941,* The American Academy of Political and Social Science (Philadelphia, 1942), 24-36.

65. *El Tiempo,* Bogotá, February 15, 1948.

66. *New York Times,* April 21, 1953.

customarily played. They are finding their inspiration in their own reality and tradition. Their strength is proportionate to their union with their own earth.[67] Their *pronunciamientos* and programs have the ring of the old *gritos* of independence. They will accept the mechanical contributions of modern Anglo-American civilization, but without abandoning their own ways of living and systems of thought. As they diversify their production and enlarge their facilities for industrialization, their economies, they hope, will cease to be passive or semicolonial. Their new nationalism, it must be remembered, is a natural reaction from a wartime internationalism that ceased to have effectiveness and beneficence for them.

The changes which they are introducing point toward a further shrinkage of the area in which *laissez-faire* capitalism may operate. In Argentina even the principal opposition party, the *Unión Cívica Radical*, would outdo Perón in its defense of the economic sovereignty of the nation in opposition to foreign concessions.[68] That party's leading exponent of this policy, Arturo Frondizi, was chosen president of Argentina in national elections in early 1958 with the support of the Peronistas. Soon after his election Frondizi let it be known that his government would re-establish the Peronista system of virtual state monopoly over the export-import business of the nation which had been abandoned after Perón's downfall. This policy runs counter to the free trade policies strongly advocated by the United States since World War II.[69]

The economic development of modern Latin America is not being left exclusively to the free interplay of economic forces as was the case, for example, in the United States and other great industrial powers. It is true that (1) the United States developed its resources by turning its capitalists loose and also by holding the door open for British and European capitalists to invest their money in railways, mines, and steel plants in the United States, and that (2) this *laissez-faire* policy of free enterprise plus foreign capital produced the fabulous industrial expansion of the United States between the Civil War and World War I. But in Latin America industrialization is being attempted under different conditions. No wide-open investment field

67. See, for example, Eduardo Caballero Calderón, "El Hombre y el Paisaje en América," *Continente*, Quito, II, 7 (April 1, 1944), 12-17.
68. Speech of Arturo Frondizi, President of the National Committee of the *Unión Cívica Radical*, July 28, 1955.
69. *Washington Post*, March 23, 1958.

is available there for either native or foreign capitalists. The Fomento Corporation in Chile, for example, when organized in 1939, was to confine its credit operations to industrial enterprises, but it later not only extended its credit operations into the fields of agriculture, power, petroleum, and other areas of economic activity but also required that no new business enterprises should be undertaken nor established plants expanded without its approval. In these circumstances capitalism cannot be expected to develop in Latin America as it has historically developed in the United States. Governments have long been accustomed to supplying the services which private capital was either unable or unwilling to furnish.[70] Capitalists in Latin America, therefore, now find themselves confronted with the tradition of government intervention in business and with the widespread popular demand for an expanding service or welfare state. Governments, it is reliably estimated, now account for more than one-quarter of all the economic activity carried on in Latin America. And yet they have in fact allowed large segments of economic life to remain under private enterprise.

In these postwar developments there is the possibility of a radical change in the political pattern of the American hemisphere. The growing rural and industrial working classes are developing a politics responding to their class interests. The Peronista revolution in Argentina, for example, may be appropriately compared in significance and effect with the Mexican Revolution after 1911. The disappearance of any single leader is relatively inconsequential since the underlying economic, political, and social phenomena will remain to engage the efforts of his successors. Shrewd politicians in those countries which accept the principle of majority government and follow electoral procedures must court the electorate; that is, they must try to gain and retain the support of the masses of the people, of the often forgotten majorities. In Argentina the *Unión Cívica Radical* began a year before the overthrow of Perón to woo back organized labor, realizing that they had lost this important segment of Argentine public opinion which had once been a source of strength to them. Popular leaders, whether put in office by election or by *golpes de estado,* are obliged to present themselves as men of the people and guardians of their interests. In those countries in which government has been traditionally monopolized by minorities the intensity of the struggle necessary

70. Alberto Lleras Camargo, "The Government's Role in Latin American Business," *Mexican American Review,* XVI (October, 1948), 16-18.

to establish or re-establish majority rule may be proportional to the degree of its previous denial. The methods which must be resorted to in this process do not look pretty to those who have benefited from the traditional system. But if to the traditional oligarchies this process appears as an abhorrent, leveling movement, to the *peones* and urban workers it holds out alluring promises of more bountiful lives. The new features of these movements are the character of the majorities and their abounding vigor. The broadening of the political base may well be the most significant contribution which they are making and have made to the Latin American way of life. They represent a democracy *sui generis*, responding to the importunate needs of the present and possessing its own internal dynamism. It is frighteningly quantitative and is governed by President Numbers. But to recognize that government should be of the majority, by the majority, and for the majority of the people is a long step forward.

Perhaps the genuine long-term interests of the Latin American peoples will not be served by these new forces which either direct or aspire to direct their destinies. Many a Latin American leader confuses democracy with the techniques of totalitarianism and thus slides into dictatorship. For him the ends—social and economic justice and the continuation of his own regime in power—may justify the use of dictatorial means. His followers, resentful of long-continued injustice, espouse the new collectivism which promises justice without comprehending its tyrannical implications. But results may fall short of intention, as indeed results generally do, objectives may become distorted, and methods may prove faulty. From the Anglo-American viewpoint the desirable thing undoubtedly would be majority government held in restraint by constitutional checks and limitations, but Latin America has not achieved the balance between political stability and social liberalism which exists in the United States. Constitutional prescriptions and proscriptions and traditions of civil liberty do not have the same force there as here. Though these controlling majorities in Latin America do not have the same conception of the responsibilities, procedures, and limitations of government as do the people of the United States, perhaps eventually even they will come to appreciate that their own interests will be best served by a recognition of the civil liberties embodied in the constitutional system of the United States and dear to nineteenth-century libertarians.

It must be remembered that ideals of personal liberty and individualism have run side by side with the practice of authoritarianism and governmental centralization in the Latin American tradition since colonial times. The institutional machinery for maintaining individual liberties has not always been firmly established or, when established, has not always been scrupulously used, but the concept of personal liberty, even when it lacked the safeguards considered essential under the Anglo-Saxon tradition, has been cherished in Latin America. It is omnipresent as a latent force which is sometimes asserted to achieve revolutionary results. Assuredly the merit of any system of social and political organization will ultimately be measured in terms of its effect upon individual worth and virtue. But the absence of the Anglo-Saxon liberties in Latin America must not be allowed to derogate from a proper estimate of the significance for democracy of the changes in outlook and ideology which are occurring there.

Chapter 9

REACTION TO THE COLD WAR

One cannot expect an effective and positive attitude of defense against totalitarian aggression from those who have not yet learned the exact significance of the benefits of liberty and democracy which involve their very existence.
—*La Estrella de Panamá*, Panama

7HE RAMPANT NATIONALISM and the concomitant antiforeignism prevalent in postwar Latin America have offered fertile soil for foreign groups antagonistic to the United States. During World War II the enforced cutback in the activities of France, Great Britain, Italy, Germany, and Japan provided the United States with unexampled opportunities to consolidate its position in Latin America and gave it the opportunity to assume, as it were, the role almost of a residuary legatee of those nations—a role which after 1944 the United States seemed unable or unwilling to play. It failed to take advantage of the tremendous postwar dynamic of rising expectations in Latin America. Its failure to do so has tended to make it the scapegoat for Latin America's ills. The remoteness of the Soviet Union and the paucity of Latin America's contacts with it made the Soviets appear almost beneficent in comparison. Since the end of World War II the attitude of the Latin American peoples toward the United States has been profoundly influenced by the conflict between it and the Soviet Union. That conflict has seemed not only to divert the attention of the United States away from them and their problems to their apparent disadvantage but has also tended to sharpen up class attitudes toward

310

the United States. On the other hand, it has necessitated modifications in the inter-American system which would ensure the collective security of all the American nations against attack by any non-American nation or coalition.

The prevailing Roman Catholicism of Latin Americans predisposes them to an anti-Communist position. The wartime collaboration of the anti-Axis nations with the Soviet Union was a persistent source of complaint by conservative groups who refused to see any possibility of good in it and gave only grudging praise to the Soviet armies for their victories over the Germans.[1] In many parts of Latin America, however, these Soviet victories gradually broke down resistance and transformed criticism of the Soviet Union into admiration. Late in 1944 the government-owned *A Manhã* of Rio de Janeiro (November 19, 1944) was praising Stalin's "policy of fraternization with the peoples of the west." The Soviet government, it observed, by extinguishing the Komintern, had demonstrated its lack of intention to intervene in the domestic affairs of other states. Newspapers which had mass appeal or which represented the views of laboring classes tended to develop enthusiasm for the Soviet Union and its policies.

This enthusiasm was stimulated by the shrewd Constantin Oumansky, one of Russia's outstanding diplomats, who became Soviet ambassador to Mexico in 1943. As was to be expected, Communist newspapers, such as *Hoy* of Havana and *Siglo* of Santiago, Chile, lauded the Soviet military achievements and the Soviet system as advancing the interests of workers throughout the world. A poll taken in São Paulo, Brazil, in November, 1943, revealed that the nation which was considered by those interviewed to have done the most toward winning the war was Russia (37.7 per cent), the second being the United States (35.9 per cent). As the Soviet Union thus rose in the estimation of the Latin American peoples it was given official recognition by Cuba and Mexico in 1942, by Uruguay in 1943, by Costa Rica, Chile, and Nicaragua in 1944, by the Dominican Republic, Venezuela, Brazil, Bolivia, and Guatemala in 1945, and by Argentina in 1946—by twelve Latin American governments in all between 1942 and 1946.

As the Soviet Union and its western allies drifted apart after the war, conservative opinion in Latin America praised the Truman policy of resisting Soviet pretensions and aggressions. Propertied groups,

1. See, for example, *Novedades*, Mexico City, December 7, 1943, and *Excelsior*, Mexico City, December 8, 1943.

who regarded communism with abhorrence as a leveling doctrine hostile to monopoly and private property, supported this "Stop Russia" policy. *Excelsior* of Mexico City (March 2, 1946) pronounced "Russian imperialism, direct or indirect, a dark threat to the peace of the world." The United States seemed to have "the historic destiny," declared *Ultimas Noticias* of the same capital (September 10, 1946), of serving "as a barrier against barbarians wherever they cross the frontiers of our western world." The weekly magazine *Mañana*, also of Mexico City (September 14, 1946), rejoiced that the United States "is ready to defend, together with democratic ideals, the treasures of western culture." In Rio de Janeiro the newspapers *A Noite, Folha Carioca, Vanguarda,* and *Brasil-Portugal* (February 22, 1947) lauded the efforts of the United States to check Communist infiltration. In adopting this course, said *A Manhã* of Rio de Janeiro (September 23, 1946), "the United States is finally on the road to a real foreign policy." As "between Communist Russia and the North American people, who represent true democracy, the choice of the continent," said *La Esfera* of Caracas (September 21, 1946), "must, for reasons of loyalty, solidarity and its own defense, be with the United States."

But a considerable portion of Latin American opinion was slow to accept this reorientation of foreign policy. Both *Le Nouvelliste* (November 12, 1945) and *Le Soir* (November 13, 1945) of Port-au-Prince deplored the alienation of Russia, "whose cooperation with the United States and Great Britain," said *Le Soir,* "is the *sine qua non* for enduring peace." President Truman's commitment in March, 1947, to aid Greece and Turkey in order to prevent their subversion by Communists sharply pointed up to Latin America the implications of this anti-Soviet policy. His action was acclaimed by many Latin American journals.[2] But Latin Americans also, especially after sober second thought, expressed misgivings about this policy declaration as a possible step toward a third world war. *La Razón* of La Paz (March 29, 1947) said that it meant "danger, particularly if this action should be considered as a precedent for further imitations." *Correio da Manhã* of Rio de Janeiro (March 14, 1947) reached "the inevitable conclusion that the United States are preparing for the

2. Especially *El Diario Latino,* San Salvador, March 18, 1947; *La Razón,* Asunción, April 16, 1947; *La Mañana,* Montevideo, March 15, 1947; *El Plata,* Montevideo, March 19, 1947; *Jornal do Brasil,* Rio de Janeiro, April 13, 1947; *Correio da Manhã,* Rio de Janeiro, May 11, 1947; *La Esfera,* Caracas, March 21, 1947; and *Diario de la Marina,* Havana, March 14, 1947.

third world war and are not concerned to hide this fact." *El Tiempo* of Bogotá (March 28, 1947) saw in this policy "the evident peril of a great conflict." Another newspaper of the Liberal Party of Colombia, *El Liberal* (April 13, 1947), wondered "if the United States can really go to the defense of democracy wherever it may be threatened." Furthermore, it asked, "What form of democracy does the United States intend to defend against Communism? That of Italy or that of Spain? Or all, indiscriminately, with the simple aim of containing bolshevik imperialism?"

Stronger criticism of the new "Truman Doctrine" came from Communist and Socialist groups. Communist organs such as *La Hora* of Buenos Aires, *El Diario Popular* of Montevideo, *Tribuna Popular* of Rio de Janeiro, *Hoy* of Havana, and *Labor* of Lima condemned it vociferously as only serving the interests of "Yankee imperialism" and aiming at "vassalage and oppression" of weak nations. The Marxist *Partido de la Izquierda Revolucionaria (PIR)* of Bolivia denounced it as preparing the way for a third war which would "cover the world anew with blood" and would further deprive the Bolivian people of "good food and conditions for a better life."[3] Both the Communist *Vanguardia* of Lima (March 18, 1947) and *El Trabajo,* newspaper organ of the *Vanguardia Popular* of Costa Rica (March 15 and August 21, 1947), predicted that the results for Latin America would in the long run be the same as for Greece and Turkey, namely subjugation to the United States.

Imperialism, whether from Russia or the United States, Latin Americans insisted, could only be resisted by the example of "authentic democracy," which in turn could come only from increased attention to the physical necessities of food, clothing, and shelter. For this reason, they enthusiastically hailed the proposals for improvement of the social and economic conditions of the underprivileged which President Truman advanced in his campaign for the presidency in 1948. By this program, said *Correio da Manhã* of Rio de Janeiro (January 7 and 9, 1949), Truman had placed himself "at the head of what we might perhaps call North American Socialism." His election showed that the American people were "willing to abandon a good part of their old principles of individualism in favor of stability and tranquillity." The Americans, like the British, commented the conservative *Jornal do Brasil* of the same capital (January 7, 1949),

3. *La Noche,* La Paz, September 2, 1947, reporting a speech in the Bolivian Senate by Gustavo Henrich, Minister of Public Works.

were turning socialist, following "the road of evolution, in the direction of a democracy of justice in the distribution of the wealth produced by all. . . . It will not be difficult," it significantly added, "for Pan-Americanism to accept the socialism of the North American government." The Argentine ambassador to the United States, Dr. Oscar Ivanissevich, reported to newspapers in his country that there was a strong trend of opinion in the United States away from "the old selfish, monopolistic economy and toward a social economy . . . a regimen of social planning analogous to what we [in Argentina] already have." Truman's election was therefore interpreted in the Argentine press as a victory for the Yankee *descamisados*. It meant a "resurrection of the New Deal," which, by emphasizing the welfare of the working classes, would cut the ground out from under communism.[4]

The intensification of Truman's anti-Soviet policy after his re-election was lauded by many newspapers.[5] As the United States assumed leadership of the developing anti-Soviet bloc of nations Latin Americans of conservative views increasingly emphasized their identity of heritage and interest with the European community of nations. "We belong to an orbit of juridical conceptions whose like is found in France, Italy, Canada, the United States and England," wrote Assis Chateaubriand, owner of the *Diários Asociados* chain of Brazilian newspapers, in *O Jornal* of Rio de Janeiro (March 26, 1949). Once again, as in 1939-1945, Latin America's security seemed to be closely linked to that of the United States and western Europe. For the defense of the American-West European system of life these Latin Americans felt a common responsibility. When the United States moved aggressively to unite these nations in the Atlantic Pact, they acclaimed it as effecting "the consolidation of the West."[6] Its anti-Soviet attitude, said *Jornal do Comércio* of Rio de Janeiro (December 17, 1948), "constitutes one of the fundamental elements in the security of the world. . . . Between the White House and the Kremlin there can be no third position."

But a "third position" for Latin America had already been fore-

4. *Correio da Manhã*, Rio de Janeiro, November 6, 1948. For additional comment see *El Diario Ilustrado* and *La Hora*, Santiago, November 5, 1948.

5. See among many others: *La Esfera*, Caracas, November 4, 1948; *La Razón*, Asunción, November 5, 1948; *Diário Carioca*, Rio de Janeiro, November 8, 1948; *Diario de la Marina*, Havana, January 22, 1949; *La Mañana*, Montevideo, March 19, 1948; and *El Diario Ilustrado*, Santiago, May 9 and 10, 1949.   6. *El Mercurio*, Santiago, April 2, 1949.

shadowed. The disillusionment with war in general and with World War II in particular, together with the optimistic hopes for world peace which were engendered by the United Nations, indicated that Latin Americans should make their peace with all the nations of the world. As early as September, 1946, *El País* of Caracas (September 19 and 21, 1946), the newspaper organ of the anti-Communist *Acción Democrática* government in Venezuela, was insisting that the policy of the United States was essentially the same as that of Russia, namely, the maintenance of its rights and consolidation of its power within its own sphere of influence while insisting upon territorial gains for strategic purposes. This interpretation of the United States-U.S.S.R. conflict was also set forth by the newspaper organ of the minority Herrerista political party in Uruguay, the anti-Communist *El Debate* (March 16, 1947). "What Russia and the United States dispute," it said, "are 'zones of influence,' the moral or material gathering-in of the territory of others, from Asia and Oceania to Persia and the Dardanelles." Latin Americans, it added, would "have nothing to do with the gigantic collision of the greatest militarisms that the universe has ever known or suffered." They "do not desire," declared the Venezuelan Mariano Picón-Salas, "to be thrown docilely into the flames of a future conflagration. We demand our right to peace in order to prosper and grow."[7] This same plaint was expressed by a leader of the non-Communist *Alianza Popular Revolucionaria Americana (APRA)* or People's Party of Peru, Dr. Luis Alberto Sánchez, on May 12, 1950, when he told the non-Communist Inter-American Democratic Congress, meeting in Havana, that two implacable imperialisms confront Latin America—Wall Street and Moscow.[8] The essence of this neutralist attitude was summarized by Alberto Ostría Gutiérrez, Bolivian ambassador to Chile and representative to the United Nations, in late 1949 when he hoped that communism might gravitate "toward liberty and capitalism toward social justice."[9]

The movement to place Latin America in this third bloc was stimulated by the growth of the "third national force" in France after the war. In Latin America it was spearheaded by Argentina. For that country the postwar dislocation was particularly acute because the war appeared to mark the end of the British era, which

7. *El Tiempo,* Bogotá, February 15, 1948.
8. Telegram 228, Havana, May 13, 1950, Department of State Archives.
9. Despatch 784, Santiago, Chile, December 21, 1949, Department of State Archives.

had been gradually terminating since about 1930. Argentina was faced with the necessity of making new and uncertain adjustments. Could it and other Latin American countries which had traditionally been culturally and economically dependent upon western Europe be certain that they were entering the era of the United States? They appeared to move into a twilight zone, with western Europe receding into the mists and with the United States and the Soviet Union looming up as the new world powers. Those Latin American nations which had traditionally swung in the orbit of the United States of course continued to do so, but others were uncertain which way to turn. Their tendency toward neutralism, toward an attitude of contrary-mindedness in relation to the United States, was undoubtedly accentuated by their conception of the postwar attitude of the United States toward their economic problems, which they considered to be one of indifference if not outright callousness. "These great statesmen of the United States," protested *Tribuna* of La Paz (March 2, 1950), "have the brutality of the man who enjoys abundance when he has to assist a poor man." Therefore, it concluded, "we have to think, first, about defending ourselves and afterwards we will think about defending the interests of the United States."

In mid-1947 Perón made a bid for leadership in a "Third Position" bloc of nations which would presumably include several or all of the Latin American nations, Spain, and possibly other Roman Catholic countries and which would seek to find a middle course between capitalism and communism. He made this program the keystone of his foreign and domestic policy, and his followers incorporated it as a fundamental tenet in Argentina's new constitution, which was approved by the National Constituent Convention in March, 1949. *La Tribuna,* a government newspaper of Buenos Aires (March 15, 1947), advised that Argentina should not take part in a contest between "plutocratic-democratic imperialism" and "Soviet-totalitarian imperialism." In accordance with this neutralist policy the Argentine delegation to the United Nations, headed by Argentine Foreign Minister Juan Atilio Bramuglia, at the United Nations meeting in Paris in October, 1948, took the lead in an unsuccessful attempt to mediate the question of the Berlin airlift.[10] After the outbreak of the Korean War Argentines argued that from a position of neutralism

10. United Nations, Security Council, Official Records, Third Year, 370th Meeting, 22 October, 1948, No. 119, 5-16; and 372d Meeting, 25 October, 1948, No. 120, [1]-14. See also Houston, *op. cit.,* 115-117.

in the Soviet-United States quarrel, Argentina and Latin America
as a whole could draw advantages for themselves. This crisis of western civilization, far from being a problem to them, appeared rather
to be a solution encouraging their hopes of greater liberty. If it were
not for the Soviet threat, declared *El Lider* of Buenos Aires (August
12, 1950), all countries west of the Iron Curtain including those in
Latin America would fall directly under the control of the United
States. "This alone," it said, "keeps the United States in check, limiting the exercise of its hegemony and increasing the value to it of
the friendship of lesser countries, since if Washington were the master of the world the friendship of these countries would be of no importance whatsoever to the powerful neighbor of the north." Perón
now deemed the time opportune to call for the establishment of a
union, or *entente,* of the ABC nations—Argentina, Brazil, and Chile
—which "will provide them with a better defense against Yankee
imperialism" and will enable them to present "a solid front in the
coming struggles, which will be terrible."

* * *

This idea of a union of some or all of the Hispanic-American
nations banded together for their own defense has a long history
going back to the wars of independence.[11] Simón Bolívar, the Liber-
ator, advocated a Hispanic-American league of states for defense on
several occasions after 1815. This proposal was subsequently discussed and embodied in treaties and protocols at conferences of
Spanish-American nations during the nineteenth century.[12] The pos-

11. Juan Egaña suggested such a union in his *Proyecto de una reunión
general* in 1811. Juan Egaña, *Escritos Inéditos y Dispersos,* ed. Raúl Silva
Castro (Santiago de Chile, 1949), [43]-52.
12. See Colombia's treaties with Chile and Peru in 1822, with the United
Provinces of the Río de la Plata and Mexico in 1823, and with Central America
in 1824 in *American State Papers, Foreign Relations,* V, 843; the "Treaty of
Perpetual Union, League, and Confederation," signed at the conclusion of the
Congress of Panama on July 15, 1826; the treaty of confederation signed at the
Conference at Lima in 1847 in República del Perú, Ministerio de Relaciones
Exteriores, *Congresos y Conferencias Internacionales en que ha tomado parte
el Perú,* ed. Ricardo Aranda, 4 vols. (Lima, 1909-1913), I, 172-174; the Continental Treaty of 1856 in *ibid.,* 233-234; Gustave A. Nuermberger, "The
Continental Treaties of 1856: An American Union 'Exclusive of the United
States,' " *The Hispanic American Historical Review,* XX (February, 1940),
[32]-55; the Treaty of Union and Defensive Alliance, signed at Lima in 1865
in Aranda (ed.), *op. cit.,* I, 421-422; and the protocol formulated at Caracas
in 1883 in *ibid.,* I, 920-921.

sibility of the mediating role of such a Latin American league in embroilments in which the United States was involved was opened up by President Woodrow Wilson's acceptance of the mediation of the ABC nations in his difficulties with Mexico. It was implicit also in José Vasconcelos' concept of Latin Americans as a "cosmic race." Later, in the same vein, as the conflict between the Axis and the anti-Axis nations developed during the 1930's, the Mexican scholar and humanist Alfonso Reyes urged that Latin America was peculiarly fitted by its "Latinism," combining action with moral and esthetic wisdom, to assume an integrating role and to restore harmony to a strife-torn world.[13]

During World War II the idea of a *groupement* of some or all of the Latin American peoples was again put forward as an attempt to strengthen their sense of independence and solidarity, to weaken their subordination to "foreign" nations, and to improve their international bargaining power. "Today we are Mexico, Venezuela, Chile, the Aztecan Spaniard, the Quechuan Spaniard, the Araucanian Spaniard, but tomorrow our common suffering will melt us into one," exclaimed the mystic Chilean poetess Gabriela Mistral. "Let us direct all our activity like an arrow toward that inevitable future: one only Spanish-America united by two stupendous factors—the language which God gave us and the misery which the United States gives us."[14] In a more practical vein *El Tiempo* of Bogotá (June 2, 1943) proposed the formation of "a solid and permanent economic, spiritual and international relationship between the non-Saxon countries of the Western Hemisphere" in order to strengthen their position in relation to the United States. The same objective appeared to motivate the abortive efforts of the Colombian president, Alfonso López, at the same time to organize a South American bloc of belligerents.

The movement for the formation of such a bloc was encouraged by the expansion of trade among the Latin American nations which occurred during World War II and which proceeded apace after 1945. Their traditional outlook had been toward the outside world. Brazil and Colombia customarily found the principal markets for their coffee in the United States, Bolivia for its tin, Cuba for its sugar, Venezuela for its petroleum, Uruguay for its wool, Chile for its copper and nitrates. Argentina looked to England for outlets for its meat and grain. But intra-Latin American trade, which was almost non-existent before World War II, was accelerated during the war.

13. *Ultima Tule*, 139-141.   14. "El Grito," *cit. sup.*

At a conference held in Montevideo in 1941, which was the first regional trade meeting of its kind in Latin America and which significantly pointed the way toward future developments, Brazil and Argentina agreed on the broad idea of a customs union and reduction of trade barriers.[15] As the trade of the Latin Americans with the outside world was reduced by the war, their trade among themselves increased. By 1944 imports of the Latin American countries from one another accounted for about one-fourth of their total imports.[16] As a market for Chilean goods, Argentina, for example, rose from ninth place in 1938 to second place in 1944.[17] By 1951 the exports of Latin American countries to other Latin American countries were twice as large as before the war, constituting 8 per cent of the total export trade of Latin America. In that same year intra-Latin American trade also accounted for 8 per cent of the total imports of Latin America.[18] Between 1938 and 1951 the value of Latin America's trade with itself increased almost sevenfold, rising from $102 million in the former year to $708.5 million in the latter.[19] The principal commodities involved in this trade were wheat, wheat-flour, fats and oils, cattle products, sugar, fruits, coffee, maté, petroleum, malted barley, lumber, cotton, copper, sulfur, and wool. This substantial expansion of intra-Latin American trade by a process of "mutual discovery" not only reduced the dependence of the Latin American countries upon earnings from trade outside the area but also simplified their problems of convertibility of foreign exchange. It appeared to be capable of transforming not only the economic relations of the Latin American nations among themselves but also their political relations with the outside world, particularly the United States.

15. Harry Bernstein, "Power Politics on the Río de la Plata," *The Inter-American,* II (September, 1943), [11]. For the wartime interest in regionalism in Latin America see Arthur P. Whitaker (ed.), *Inter-American Affairs, 1943* (New York, 1944), 34-36.

16. Department of Commerce, International Economics Division, *International Transactions,* 137.

17. William L. Schurz, "The Southern Republics of South America: A Regional Economy," Latin American Studies VI, University of Texas (Austin, 1949), 63.

18. International Monetary Fund, *International Financial Statistics,* VII (October, 1954), 32; and Pan American Union, *Selected Economic Data on the Latin American Republics* (Washington, 1954), 5-6.

19. United Nations, Statistical Office, International Monetary Fund, and International Bank for Reconstruction and Development, joint publishers, *Direction of International Trade: Annual Issue,* IV, No. 2, 430-431. See also United Nations, Economic Commission for Latin America, *A Study of Inter-Latin American Trade, passim,* but particularly chapter II.

The aspiration for closer economic relations among the Latin American states was a strong factor in the early postwar policy not only of Argentina but of several other countries. Chile's foreign policy, for example, was set forth by the Foreign Minister of the Ibáñez government in his statement to the Chilean Senate on December 23, 1952, as aiming to promote the economic unity of the Latin American countries for the purpose of securing higher prices for their raw-materials exports and of maintaining their sovereignty and independence. This was deemed to call for elimination of Chile's economic frontiers with Argentina and closer cooperation with Bolivia and Peru, and eventually with Brazil, Colombia, and Ecuador. In a later speech, the Chilean Foreign Minister proclaimed that Chile, in cooperation with all these countries, was on the road toward the creation of a Latin American confederation.[20] "The Latin American nations need greater economic interrelations," declared President Ibáñez of Chile in early July, 1953, "if they are successfully to supply the needs of their peoples, raise their standards of living, and bring their social progress up to the level of present-day civilization and culture."[21] These were some of the objectives sought in the Chilean-Argentine trade pact which was signed in Buenos Aires in the same month, an agreement to which Ecuador also subscribed six months later.[22]

Closer Latin American economic integration—either on a continental or a regional basis—has been the objective of the general postwar movement toward the negotiation of what *El Comercio* of Lima (January 30, 1955) has called "economic-complementation-type agreements among the American nations."[23] The purpose of these agreements is to encourage the development of their respective national economies through the expansion of trade both in traditional products and in new industrial products, to promote the diversification of their economies, and to increase their national incomes. Examples that may be cited are the trade negotiations between Argentina and Bolivia in December, 1951, and between Argentina and Brazil in July, 1953, the organization of the *Flota Mercante Grancolombiana*, or

---

20. Speeches by Foreign Minister Olavarría before the Chilean Senate on December 23, 1952, and at Coquimbo on January 31, 1953.

21. *El Mercurio,* Santiago, July 5, 1953.

22. Hilton (ed.), *Hispanic American Report,* VI, 12 (January, 1954), 26.

23. See also *Acción,* Montevideo, February 10, 1955; and United Nations, Department of Economic Affairs, *Study of Inter-Latin American Trade* (New York, 1957), 68-70, 94, and 101.

Great Colombian Merchant Fleet, in 1947, sponsored by Colombia, Venezuela, and Ecuador[24] and the movement for reduction of commercial barriers among the Central American nations. An important step in this latter movement occurred with the setting up of the Organization of Central American States in 1951. Under the leadership of the United Nations Economic Commission for Latin America, the Central American countries have embarked upon a far-reaching program of economic integration which has resulted in the ratification of reciprocal trade agreements by several of the governments. As a result of the efforts of these governments to achieve the integration of their region the value of inter-Central American trade has increased from a mere $900,000 before World War II to $10,800,000 in 1952. At the meeting of the Central American Economic Cooperation Committee in San Salvador in May, 1955, plans were made for drawing up a multilateral Central American free-trade treaty.[25] The basis for such a treaty had already been laid in the bilateral free-trade treaties concluded by Nicaragua and El Salvador in 1951, El Salvador and Guatemala in the same year, El Salvador and Costa Rica in 1953, and El Salvador and Honduras in 1954.[26]

This movement for closer Latin American cooperation was inspired, in part, by the desire of some Latin Americans to free themselves from "domination" by the United States. The point was sometimes significantly made as, for example, in *El Espectador* of Bogotá (January 16, 1948), that Latin American votes in the United Nations, amounting to approximately one-third of the total, "if adequately utilized, could improve the condition of inferiority in which we find ourselves." In April, 1948, the Argentine press triumphantly reported that the United States had been "reduced to a defensive position against a solid bloc of Latin American nations on both the political and economic fronts," and this assertion was enthusiastically echoed in the conservative *La Prensa* of Managua, Nicaragua (April 11, 1948).[27]

24. Robert S. Willis and Clifton R. Wharton, Jr., "Flota Mercante Grancolombiana," *Inter-American Economic Affairs*, II (Summer, 1948), 25-40.

25. United Nations, Economic Commission for Latin America, *Progress Report on the Central American Economic Integration Programme* (17 October 1953-9 May 1955), Sixth Session, Bogotá (29 August 1955); and *Analysis and Prospects of Inter-Central-American Trade*, Sixth Session, Bogotá, 17.

26. United Nations, Economic Commission for Latin America, *A Study of Inter-Latin American Trade*, 120.

27. See also editorials by Geraldo Roche in *O Mundo*, Rio de Janeiro, July 10, 1948.

But many advocates of Latin American unification have taken pains to point out that it is not necessarily hostile to any outside nation. It represents, according to *Excelsior* of Mexico City (April 28, 1953), an effort by Latin America to "coordinate the defense of its interests abroad." It is therefore not so much "against" the United States as "for" the progress of the peoples of Latin America as a whole, recognizing that this progress requires the help of the United States. "The time has come," it concluded, "for our America to cease being a disorganized group of countries and to become a real family with a full awareness of their common destiny."[28] Such a family, which was envisaged as a Latin American League by the head of the *Partido de la Izquierda Revolucionaria* of Bolivia, José Antonio Arze, would be, in his words, "independent and not subordinate to the United States, nor to Spain, nor to any other foreign power."[29] The potentialities and advantages for Latin Americans of the role of developers of a new world culture, uninhibited by the weight of tradition, have also been glowingly presented by the Colombian publicist Eduardo Caballero Calderón.[30]

Latin Americans have been encouraged in this "Third Position" by widely accepted views as to the probable strategy of World War III. If the war is fought over the North Pole only Canada, the United States, and possibly Mexico and the Caribbean countries will be the first line of defense. Even the Panama Canal will have minimal strategic value, and all the South American continent will be only a second line of defense lying outside the battle zones and useful principally as sources of raw materials. Relying upon their neutral location the people and governments of this area seek to maintain good relations with both the United States and the Soviet Union. In this they feel an affinity and the need for common action with India and the countries of the Middle East.[31] They can therefore regard the cold war as only a political struggle between the United States and the Soviet Union; they must look out for their own welfare first and

28. For similar views see the speech by Senator Dardo Regules of the Catholic Party of Uruguay at a luncheon of the American Association of Montevideo on September 30, 1949.

29. Speech in the Municipal Theater, La Paz, October 18, 1949, reported in *La Razón*, La Paz, October 19, 1949.

30. *Suramérica, Tierra del Hombre,* and "Lo Que Hispanoamérica Representa en el Mundo Contemporáneo," *Cuadernos Americanos* (Madrid), III, 381-406.

31. Ricardo de Labougle, *Dos Mundos Frente a Frente* (Buenos Aires, 1953), 326-333.

cultivate both friendly political relations and advantageous commercial relations with the Soviet bloc.

In the postwar efforts to form a Latin American bloc Brazilian army leaders showed some interest, but Brazilian public opinion remained generally indifferent, partly because the Brazilian people were impressed by the results achieved by their cooperation with the United States in World War II and partly because such a bloc would presumably be dominated, at least numerically, by the Spanish-speaking nations, which are traditional rivals to Brazil for influence in South America.[32] Nevertheless *O Mundo* of Rio de Janeiro published editorials by Geraldo Rocha in July, 1948, advocating an *entente* with Argentina to strengthen Brazil "in defense of continental interests vis-à-vis the United States."[33]

Latin Americans who accept this Third Position have sought to play upon the chords of international hostility to improve the position of their own countries and their own region. Some of them even venture to hope that their countries will assume a mediating role in the United States-Soviet conflict. "We know that war is coming," declared Federico More, editor of the progovernment newspaper *Nuevo Tiempo* of Lima (January 3, 1949), "but let us do as much as possible to postpone it." They have found, however, that, as they deliver themselves over to the complicated game of balance of power in their international relations, they are not able, as Mexico, for example, was in the nineteenth century, to balance European influence and capital against those of the United States, because wherever they now turn in Europe they find ineluctably facing them the "country of the dollar."

To the advocates of a "Third Position" for Latin America the basic struggle in the postwar world has appeared to be a struggle not so much between communism and capitalism or between the Soviet Union and the United States as between those who desire and those who do not desire to advance their social and economic welfare. The inexorable drive for social justice in Latin America since World War II forced governments into an intense preoccupation with the social and economic needs of their own people and the elevation of their

32. *O Jornal,* Rio de Janeiro, October 5 and November 5, 1946; and Austregesilo de Athayde in *Diário da Noite,* Rio de Janeiro, October 12 and November 4, 1946.

33. Report 850, Rio de Janeiro, July 27, 1948, Department of State Archives.

levels of living. The social and economic development of Latin America has therefore been represented as an essential part of any defense program for the hemisphere and as more important than a mere standardization of arms and tactics or even signed agreements for collective military action. "It is necessary," declared Acting Foreign Minister of Mexico Manuel Tello in a public statement in February, 1951, "to recognize that the threats to peace not only come from external sources but that they are latent in the ignorance, sickness, and misery . . . which in greater or lesser degree exist in America and which by creating discontent are a favorable soil for ideologies contrary to the democratic-republican traditions which are our precious heritage."[34]

The urgency and priority of Latin America's social and economic needs were strongly emphasized by the Latin American delegations to the Inter-American Conference for the Maintenance of Continental Peace and Security at Quitandinha, Brazil, in August-September, 1947, the Ninth International Conference of American States at Bogotá in March-May, 1948, and the Fourth Meeting of Consultation of Ministers of Foreign Affairs of American States at Washington in March-April, 1951. The importance of satisfying them was recognized in resolutions adopted at all these meetings. Summarizing the results of the last-named meeting, President Vargas of Brazil told workers attending a sports festival on May 1, 1951, that the Latin American delegates to the meeting had agreed that the principal cause of political crisis in the American continent was social unrest produced by low standards of living and economic insecurity. Speaking with reference to the results of the same meeting later in that month Mexico's Minister of National Economy, Antonio Martínez Báez, declared that "the continued development of our economies will constitute our best safeguard by raising the people's living standards and reinforcing their confidence in democratic institutions." He expressed his "apprehension lest the defense program may impede the importing of equipment and other essential articles while involving expenditures on goods that will not contribute directly to our economic development."[35] The general feeling among Latin Americans was that, in the words of *La Estrella de Panamá* (February 21, 1950), "one cannot expect an effective and positive attitude of defense against totalitarian aggres-

34. *Novedades,* Mexico City, February 22, 1951.
35. Address opening the meeting of the United Nations Economic Commission for Latin America, *New York Times,* May 29, 1951.

sion from those who have not yet learned the exact significance of the benefits of liberty and democracy which involve their very existence. . . . When our countries have a stable economy, when illiteracy has been reduced, when there are schools, roads and hospitals for all, and when democracy has become a reality for the entire continent, a firmer and more effective base will be given to continental solidarity, or to say the same thing, to the defense of the standards and principles which totalitarian imperialism is endeavoring to destroy."

When President Truman set forth in his inaugural address in January, 1949, his so-called Point Four proposal of technical assistance to underdeveloped countries in order to combat those "ancient enemies—hunger, misery, and despair" Latin Americans were encouraged to expect large assistance in meeting their urgent social and economic needs. "Well could this speech have begun with the sacramental words *Urbi et orbi*," chanted *Flecha* of Managua (January 22, 1949). Colombia's Foreign Minister, Dr. Eduardo Zuleta Angel, hailed it as "the most important and transcendental" development for Latin America since President Roosevelt's announcement of his Good Neighbor Policy.[36] According to *La Nación* of Ciudad Trujillo (January 24, 1949), it was a noble admission that the conscience of the North American nation "cannot be clear if there is abundance in the midst of scarcity, wealth in the midst of misery." The laudable aim of the United States, according to Gustavo Wills Recaurte, a columnist in *El Espectador* of Bogotá (January 31, 1949), was now to create "a strong American continent, uniform in its standards of living and homogeneous in its aspirations." A former Brazilian Minister of Labor[37] was quoted in *Correio da Manhã* of Rio de Janeiro (January 22, 1949) as saying that President Truman's proposal "constituted the greatest hope against Communist actions." But the delay in enacting the Point Four proposal into law and the relatively modest scope of the program as finally enacted in June, 1950, produced disillusionment in Latin America.[38]

Some of the Latin American countries had experienced a recession from the high levels of trade that they had enjoyed during the war and in the early postwar period. This recession emphasized the precarious nature of their economic situation, dependent as it was upon foreign demand for a few of their staple commodities. The outbreak

36. *El Espectador,* Bogotá, April 25, 1949.
37. Morvan Dias de Figueiredo.
38. *La Prensa Libre,* San José, Costa Rica, June 8, 1949.

of the Korean War in June, 1950, came as an act of salvation. As a result of the war and the accompanying mobilization in the United States these governments were able to improve seriously deteriorating economic conditions in their countries and to strengthen their own political positions. The imports of the United States from Latin America increased by more than one-fourth in 1950 over both 1948 and 1949 and increased 15 per cent further in 1951. The new war demands, for example, bailed Cuba out of a desperate sugar glut, averted a threatened cutback in petroleum output in Venezuela, revived the languishing tin industry of Bolivia by spiraling the price of tin to a new high level, and created large new demands for Chilean copper. For the first time since World War II Latin America enjoyed the commercial advantages of preferential treatment from the United States.

The increase in the prices of raw materials which the United States bought during the Korean War enabled Latin American governments to acquire surpluses of dollar exchange for the first time in four years. According to joint studies made by several United Nations agencies including the Economic Commission for Europe, the Economic Commission for Latin America, and the Food and Agriculture Organization, the export earnings of Bolivia, for example, increased by from 80 to 100 per cent. For the same reason, according to other studies, Brazil's annual dollar income from exports to the United States increased from $551 million to $715 million, and Mexico's from $435 million to $517 million. Even Argentina's trade with the United States showed a favorable balance as compared with a previously unfavorable one. But these gains were unevenly distributed among the Latin American countries, being highest for the metals-producing countries and lowest for the banana-producing countries, in none of which the increases amounted to more than 10 per cent. They were also more impressive in monetary than in real terms because of the unavailability of Latin America's import requirements during the western rearmament drive.[39] Moreover these gains represented only a war-induced prosperity due to increased stock-piling demand, to artificial shortages caused by speculation, and to forward-purchases. They did not prove durable, for by the middle of 1951 the world prices of tin, coffee, wool, cotton, cocoa, and sugar, which had accounted for approximately 60 per cent of Latin America's exports to the United States in the previous year, had begun to decline while

39. *New York Times,* June 4, 1951.

the prices of the manufactured goods which they obtained from the United States had increased by 16 per cent over those of 1950. By the end of the first year of the Korean War living costs had risen in every one of the Latin American countries, in some by as much as 25 per cent.[40] By 1953, when the Korean War ended, nothing remained of the high prices which had benefited Latin America during the peak period 1950-1951.[41]

* * *

All this helps to explain the Latin American reaction to the Korean problem. The consensus was that "Muscovite Imperialism," like every imperialism, is hateful and must be opposed. In action in the United Nations on resolutions bearing on the Korean War the Latin American delegations supported the position of the United States with a fair degree of consistency, although on some crucial questions a few delegations, including those of Argentina, Chile, Cuba, Ecuador, El Salvador, Guatemala, and Uruguay, significantly abstained from voting.[42] Toward the end of 1950 the United States, in order to secure a coordinated inter-American effort against "the aggressive policy of international Communism, carried out through its satellites" and producing a situation "in which the entire free world is threatened," requested a meeting of Ministers of Foreign Affairs of the American States. In this meeting, which met in Washington in April, 1951, a recommendation was adopted that each of the American governments should "determine what steps it can take to contribute to the defense of the Continent and to United Nations collective security efforts."[43] In terms of tangible assistance, however, Latin America's contribution was slight. Costa Rica offered the use of its territory for sea and air bases, and Panama the use of its merchant marine and highways. Cuba furnished 2,000 tons of sugar and 10,000 gallons of alcohol, Ecuador 500 tons of rice, Mexico chick peas and miscellaneous food and medical supplies, Peru clothing and cloth,

40. Richard P. Stebbins, The Council on Foreign Relations, *The United States in World Affairs, 1951* (New York, 1952), 316-317.
41. United Nations, Economic Commission for Latin America, *Economic Survey of Latin America, 1953*, 46.
42. Houston, *op. cit.*, 118-132.
43. Department of State, *Fourth Meeting of Consultation of Ministers of Foreign Affairs of American States, Washington, D. C., March 26-April 7, 1951, Report of the Secretary of State*, Department of State Publication 4928 (Washington, May, 1953), Resolution II.

Uruguay 70,000 blankets, and Venezuela medical supplies, blankets, soap, and food. That was all. Only Colombia sent troops to Korea, consisting of a battalion of 1,080 ground forces, and furnished a frigate. A few other governments offered troops but only on condition that the United States undertake to train, equip, and transport them.[44]

More typical were the replies to Secretary General Trygve Lie's appeal for additional ground troops. Venezuela, replying in July, 1951, refused to divert its forces outside its own territory because it considered that it could best collaborate in the collective action of the United Nations by guaranteeing the security of its own territory and the continued production of its strategic materials.[45] Guatemala informed the Secretary General of the United Nations that its economic condition would not permit it to make any of its armed forces available for service with the United Nations.[46] The Chilean Foreign Minister announced that in no circumstances would Chile send troops outside its borders.[47] Perón repeatedly assured his people that not one Argentine soldier would be sent out of the country and that his government neither had made nor would make any pacts requiring such use of Argentine troops.[48] President Miguel Alemán of Mexico was quoted as saying that Mexico would fight only if the American continents should be attacked. In his sixth and last annual message to Congress on September 1, 1952, he disclosed an attitude of detachment toward the efforts of the North Atlantic Pact nations to

44. Following mimeographed publications of the Department of State: "Summary of Offers of Assistance for Korea, 2 January 1951"; "Korean Non-Military Assistance Program—Status of Offer as of January 2, 1951 (excluding personnel)"; "Status of Offers of Military Assistance to the UN for Korea," January 8 and March 7, 1951; "Status of Offers to Unified Command for Korean Civilian Relief Program," March 22, 1951; and United States Mission to the United Nations, "Status of Offers to Unified Command for Korean Civilian Relief Program," March 13, 1951. See also United Nations, *Report of the Agent General of the United Nations Korean Reconstruction Agency: Organization and work of the Agency from its activation in February 1951 to 15 September 1952*, General Assembly, Official Records: Seventh Session, Supplement No. 19 (New York, 1952), 40-41.
45. United Nations General Assembly, Official Records, 6th Session, Supplement 13, 37-43.
46. Address of President Jacobo Arbenz, March 1, 1952.
47. Statement, September 13, 1951.
48. For example, in his speech to the national convention of the General Confederation of Commercial Employees on December 20, 1950, and in his speech to the magistrates attending the First National Congress of Justice on January 31, 1952.

contain Soviet aggression and of avoidance of international military commitments.[49]

The Latin American nations in general were still preoccupied with the dislocations that had overtaken their economies as a consequence of their cooperation with the United States in World War II. While professing agreement with the course which the Truman administration adopted toward North Korea they nevertheless tried to ensure that their economies would not again be seriously disrupted. The Cuban ambassador to the United States, for example, after reminding Assistant Secretary of State Edward G. Miller, Jr., that his country was providing essential war minerals, asked for guaranties that the United States would not reduce its shipments of essential goods to Cuba, particularly paper, fertilizer, cotton, and sulfur.[50] Similarly the Brazilian Foreign Minister, João Neves da Fontoura, made plain that his government did not intend to repeat the mistakes which it had made in swinging into the war orbit of the United States in late 1941. Brazil would cooperate with the United States in the Korean crisis but only on a fully reciprocal basis. The nation's needs, he announced, must be "heeded, understood, and met by our powerful ally, the United States."[51] President Vargas received a visit in 1952 from Secretary of State Acheson, who made a special trip to Rio de Janeiro to request Brazilian troops for action in Korea, but Vargas responded only with icy silence.

Latin Americans did not accept the relevancy of the military operations in Korea to the defense of the Western Hemisphere. The war did not become their war; it did not concern them. They were not convinced by anything the United States said or did that that war was a defense of western civilization. They did not consider that "international Communism" had yet become a menace to their security nor did they see the necessity of resisting it by armed action outside their own borders or at least outside the territorial limits of the Western Hemisphere. Moreover, the emphasis which the Communist program placed upon social justice, as the Liberal-Catholic Carlos Lacerda pointed out in *Tribuna da Imprensa* of Rio de Janeiro (August 15, 1950), caused many Latin Americans to identify commu-

49. Mexico, Secretaría de Gobernación, *Informe que Rinde al H. Congreso de la Unión el C. Presidente de la República, Lic. Miguel Alemán, Correspondiente a su Gestión del 1° de Septiembre de 1951 al 31 de Agosto de 1952* (Mexico, 1952).
50. Hilton (ed.), *Hispanic American Report*, IV, 2 (February, 1951), 18.
51. *Ibid.*, IV, 3 (March, 1951), 34-35.

nism with the cause of the liberation of man and was responsible for a certain "neutralization of consciences" toward the Korean War.[52]

This attitude of course did not deny Latin America's zeal for the defense of the hemisphere. When the Mexico City Inter-American Conference on Problems of War and Peace recommended in 1945 that the American governments adopt "measures for a closer military collaboration . . . and for the defense of the Western Hemisphere" (Resolution IV), the United States, as the military leader of the hemisphere and the only considerable producer of military equipment among the American nations, immediately undertook to persuade the Latin American governments to adopt its military methods and its standards of military equipment, to utilize the services of its military missions for training purposes, to cooperate with it in making joint plans for the defense of the hemisphere, and to procure from it their necessary supplies of arms, ammunition, and implements of war conforming to the types used by the armed forces of the United States. This interim arms program, as it was called, was hedged about by the caveats that it should not impose hardships upon the economies of any of the Latin American countries, that neither training nor arms should be furnished to any country bent upon aggression against one of its American neighbors, and that the training and arms should not be used to deprive any people of their democratic rights and liberties.

But the interim program when it was submitted to the United States Congress in early 1946 was criticized for violating these very conditions, and it was not brought to a vote in that Congress. In 1951, however, after the outbreak of the Korean War, a later Congress voted $38,150,000 for direct military assistance to Latin America and in the following year added $51,685,750 to that sum. This money was to be expended after the negotiation of bilateral military assistance agreements with those Latin American nations which were deemed important to the defense of the Western Hemisphere. By October, 1954, such agreements had been concluded and were in force with ten governments—Brazil, Chile, Colombia, Cuba, the Dominican Republic, Ecuador, Honduras, Nicaragua, Peru, and Uruguay. Military assistance was accordingly furnished to those governments in the form of direct grants of equipment, opportunities

52. See also *Noticias Gráficas,* Buenos Aires, February 15, 1951; N. Viera Altamirano, Director of *El Diario de Hoy,* San Salvador, in *La Prensa,* New York, June 12, 1958; and Jorge Castañeda, *Mexico and the United Nations* (New York, 1958), 140.

for the purchase of equipment in the United States, and the establishment of United States army, navy, and air force missions to help train their armed forces. By the end of June, 1955, additional bilateral military assistance agreements had been signed with Haiti and Guatemala.[53]

The outbreak of the Korean War further caused an increase in the official aid program of the United States in Latin America. Loan authorizations to Latin America by the Export-Import Bank expanded from approximately $43 million, or 25 per cent of its total loans for all areas in 1949, to almost $200 million, or more than 53 per cent of its total for all areas in 1950.[54] In the two and a half years after the beginning of the Korean War, from June 25, 1950, through December 31, 1952, the United States extended aid of $427 million to the Latin American governments. In other words, over 45 per cent of the total postwar aid of the United States to Latin America was given in the period of two and a half years after mid-1950.[55] The United States even made a loan of $125 million to Argentina— to the discomfiture of Brazil. At the close of the Truman administration, as Assistant Secretary of State Edward G. Miller, Jr., pointed out, the United States government was officially helping to modernize the entire Mexican railway system, to increase Mexico's electric power by a projected total of about one million kilowatt hours, to expand Mexico's steel capacity, and to develop its sulfur deposits, coal mines, sugar mills, and slaughterhouses; it was helping Chile to construct six major hydroelectric plants, to develop industries for the fabrication of copper and the production of cement, cellulose, pulp and paper, and rayon, to expand a ferro-manganese plant, and to carry out irrigation and land clearance programs; and it was extending similar assistance to many other Latin American countries.[56]

53. Department of State, Office of Public Affairs, *Military Assistance to Latin America*, Department of State Publication 4917, Inter-American Series 44 (Washington, March, 1953); Department of State, *Press Release* No. 367, June 20, 1955; *Department of State Bulletin*, XXXII (February 7, 1955), 244; (June 20, 1955), 1019; and XXXIII (July 11, 1955), 85.

54. House of Representatives, 81st Congress, 2d Session, House Document No. 548, *Report on Audit of Export-Import Bank of Washington, 1949*, 4; and House Document No. 725, *Report on Audit of Export-Import Bank of Washington, 1950*, 5.

55. Department of Commerce, Office of Business Economics, *Foreign Aid by the United States Government: Basic Data through December 31, 1952*, A-12.

56. Address at the Third Kentucky World Trade Conference, Louisville, Kentucky, October 14, 1952.

The United States now realized, commented Carlos Lacerda in *Tribuna da Imprensa* of Rio de Janeiro (August 15, 1950), that the economic recuperation of peoples and democratic reforms "are the only means of conquering communism." It took the Soviet menace, concluded *Ultima Hora* of La Paz (January 10, 1951), to awaken the United States and make it see the light.

The Mexico City conference of March, 1945, had also traced out the main features of a postwar regional security system for the American hemisphere in the Act of Chapultepec. In this act all the American nations, after reaffirming the principle that every attack upon the integrity, the inviolability, the sovereignty, or the political independence of an American state would be considered as an act of aggression against all the other American states, recommended the conclusion of an inter-American treaty which would establish procedures for meeting such acts of aggression. After the emergence of the Soviet threat and the development of the United Nations system of international security the American security system contemplated by the Act of Chapultepec was created by the Inter-American Treaty of Reciprocal Assistance, negotiated at Rio de Janeiro in 1947. That treaty, which has since been ratified by all twenty-one of the American governments, declares that "an armed attack by any State against an American State shall be considered as an attack against all the American States" and pledges each one of them "to assist in meeting the attack in the exercise of the inherent right of individual or collective self-defense recognized by Article 51 of the Charter of the United Nations." In the event of any other threat that "might endanger the peace of America, the Organ of Consultation shall meet immediately in order to agree on the measures which must be taken." The sanctions which may be imposed by the Organ of Consultation range in order of severity from "recall of chiefs of diplomatic missions" to "use of armed force," but "no State shall be required to use armed force without its consent." For purposes of this treaty the Organ of Consultation is the Meeting of Ministers of Foreign Affairs of the American Republics, but until or unless it convenes the Council of the Organization of American States may act provisionally in its place. Decisions are made by a vote of two-thirds of the members, without the participation, however, of the parties to the dispute. The obligations for the security of the hemisphere which President Monroe assumed for the United States in 1823 were thus accepted as a common obligation of all the American nations. But up to mid-

1958 Argentina, despite its ratification of the Inter-American Treaty of 1947, had made no arrangements to cooperate in continental defense. It had not agreed with the United States to any exchanges of personnel or information, and the new Argentine vice-president inaugurated in early 1958, Alejandro Gómez, was demanding that Argentina withdraw from its existing defense obligations.[57]

After the United States took the initiative in promoting inter-American organization in 1889, emphasis was placed upon the promotion of trade, the development of machinery for the preservation of peace in the hemisphere, and the encouragement of cultural interchange. From its inception the modern inter-American system did not assume political responsibilities. The Third Inter-American Conference, which met in 1906, specifically denied "political functions" to the organization. The Sixth Conference in 1928 also declared that the Pan American Union "shall not exercise functions of a political character." Purely political questions as a class were consistently avoided until after World War I when the Latin American nations, disturbed by the course and results of intervention by the United States in their internal affairs, began to agitate such problems as the equality, the rights, and the duties of states, particularly at the inter-American conferences in 1923, 1928, and 1933. Meanwhile the political cooperation of pairs or larger groups of the American states in acts carried on outside the machinery of the Pan-American organization, such as the settlement of boundary and claims disputes and other threats to peace, prepared the way for the assumption of an obligation of political cooperation on a broad inter-American scale. In the inter-American conferences of the 1930's, as the Axis threat became increasingly menacing, the inter-American system was largely converted into an outright system of political cooperation. The procedure of consultation of foreign ministers of the American nations which was developed in the conferences at Buenos Aires in 1936 and Lima in 1938 opened up a new area of action by the inter-American organization. At the Meeting of Foreign Ministers held in 1939, when this new procedure of consultation was first tested, Pan-Americanism first began to operate along political lines. The beginning of World War II, then, was the occasion for a new departure of Pan-Americanism into the area of political action.[58] After World War II as the

57. *Christian Science Monitor*, June 7, 1958.
58. J. M. Yepes, *Philosophie du Panaméricanisme et Organisation de la Paix* (Neuchatel, 1945), 122-123.

collective security system of the hemisphere was interlocked with the established organs of the inter-American system political questions assumed primary importance.

From 1889 to 1948 the inter-American organization functioned with no other charter than the occasional resolutions of inter-American conferences. Neither the traditional respect of the people of the United States for constitutional arrangements nor the Latin American penchant for devising new ones had been utilized to give a constitutional basis to the inter-American organization. To suggest the absence of a constitution to the long-time Director General of the Pan American Union, Dr. Leo S. Rowe, was sufficient to invite a lecture on its superfluousness. As early as the Fourth Inter-American Conference, which met in Mexico City in 1910, consideration was given to the need for a convention which would serve the Pan American Union as a constitutional foundation, but the Project of a Convention which was drawn up at that conference was never ratified. A new but similar convention prepared by the Sixth Inter-American Conference in 1928 also failed of ratification.

During World War II the inter-American organization acquired new importance as it helped to mobilize the hemisphere for war. It was required to assume many emergency duties without being given opportunity to make commensurate organizational adjustments. Of these duties may be mentioned particularly those assigned to the Inter-American Financial and Economic Advisory Committee, the Inter-American Defense Board, the Inter-American Coffee Board, the Emergency Advisory Committee for Political Defense, and the Inter-American Juridical Committee, all of which operated under the broad purview of the Pan American Union. The performance of these responsibilities stretched the Union's capabilities to unprecedented limits and emphasized its need for a clear and broadly defined constitutional authority. Not intended to serve as an instrument of inter-American collective security, it nevertheless became one. Specifically denied the power to perform political functions, it performed them. Lacking a constitutional basis, it acted as if its new *ad hoc* mandates were equivalent to one.

After the war, therefore, a charter was deemed necessary for the inter-American organization in order to regularize and give continuing sanction to the enlarged powers which it had exercised during the war. Moreover, the preparations for the launching of the new international organization of the United Nations, which was expected to affect both the structure and the operations of regional organizations, seemed to make imperative the strengthening of the inter-American system as a means of maintaining regional peace and security within the larger world system. The exclusion of the Latin American nations from the Dumbarton Oaks meetings in Washington in late 1944, at which the plans for the United Nations organization were drawn, aroused their suspicions that the inter-American regional system might not fare well in the postwar world.[59] The Dumbarton Oaks proposals when finally made known to the Latin Americans seemed to give too much power to the Soviet Union and to show the need for a better unified inter-American organization able to cast twenty-one votes in the United Nations.

If the Dumbarton Oaks draft of the Charter of the United Nations had not existed, Dr. Alberto Lleras Camargo, Secretary General of the Organization of American States, has written, "it is possible that the Inter-American system would have been permitted to continue its gradual evolution and its biological growth, determined solely by circumstances, experience, and necessity." But that draft appeared to impose an impossible barrier to the development of the inter-American system and to necessitate, as a consequence, that a written charter or constitution be adopted which would guarantee its survival. Otherwise "it would be able to develop only within the limits traced out for it by the United Nations," in which the Soviet government exercised a veto power.[60]

Accordingly the Mexico City conference of March, 1945, directed the Governing Board of the Pan American Union to draw up "a draft charter for the improvement and strengthening of the Pan-American system."[61] Nevertheless at the conference for the organization of the United Nations held at San Francisco three months later the inter-American system was almost scrapped. Certain members of the United States delegation were unwilling that it, along with other regional systems, should detract from the authority of the new international organization. They argued that regional agreements in general were incompatible with the new world organization then

59. Houston, *op. cit.*, 13-14.
60. Inter-American Conference, Ninth, Bogotá, 1948, *Informe sobre los Resultados de la Conferencia* (Washington, 1948), 12.
61. Organization of American States, *Annual Report of the Secretary General for the Fiscal Year July 1, 1951-June 30, 1952* (Washington, 1952), 26; and Inter-American Conference, Tenth, Caracas, 1954, *Final Act* (Washington, 1954), Resolution LXXXIX.

being formed and that in particular the United States must abandon its preoccupation with its neighbors in the Western Hemisphere in order to be able more freely to discharge its new world-wide responsibilities. Against this plan the Latin Americans squarely set their faces. They were supported by Senator Arthur H. Vandenberg, Nelson A. Rockefeller, and a few other members of the United States delegation, as well as by President Truman, who let the United States delegation know by telephone that he proposed to carry out the recommendation of the Act of Chapultepec. Accordingly a new formula was worked out to protect regional security arrangements, and it was written into the United Nations charter as Article 51.[62]

It became possible, therefore, to proceed with the Chapultepec plan. The resulting project for an Organic Pact of the Inter-American System, which was submitted by the Governing Board of the Pan American Union and published in 1946, served as the basis for the Charter of the Organization of American States which was signed at the Ninth International Conference of American States at Bogotá in April, 1948. A resolution of that conference made the charter legally operative at once without receiving the ratification of two-thirds of the member states, which, however, was supplied on December 13, 1951, when Colombia became the fourteenth member to deposit its ratification. From the postwar Soviet pretensions, therefore, particularly as they were manifested in the United Nations, emerged a stronger, constitutionally based inter-American regional system.

* * *

The defense of the American hemisphere has also been deemed to require both national and inter-American action against local Communist parties operating at the behest and in the interest of the Soviet Union. This has been a matter of particular concern to the United States which under the Monroe Doctrine has long considered any attempt by European nations to extend their system to any

---

62. George A. Finch, "The Inter-American Defense Treaty," *American Journal of International Law*, XLI (October, 1947), 863; Galo Plaza, "Latin America's Contribution to the United Nations Organization," *The Americas and World Order*, International Conciliation Pamphlet No. 419, March, 1946, Carnegie Endowment for International Peace (New York, 1946), 150-157; Arthur H. Vandenberg, Jr., *The Private Papers of Senator Vandenberg* (Boston, 1952), 186-193; and Houston, *op. cit.*, 46-50.

portion of this hemisphere as dangerous to its peace and safety. During World War II many Communist parties in Latin America developed considerable strength, profiting from the widespread popular sympathy with the heroic defense of Stalingrad. While making no secret of their loyalty to the Soviet Union they ardently supported the United States and the United Nations and represented their aims to be identical with the objectives of political democracy and the Four Freedoms which Roosevelt was seeking. They were therefore accorded more freedom of action in many Latin American countries than they had ever enjoyed before, and they in turn collaborated with existing pro-United Nations governments so far as to participate in Popular Front governments dedicated to the allied cause. They abandoned all criticism of the "imperialism" of the United States in their crusade to crush the enemies of Soviet Russia.

When the war ended, Communist parties occupied a strong position throughout Latin America. In the difficult postwar years of frustrations and readjustment Communist propaganda addressed to the underprivileged masses was especially appealing. Communist parties showed their greatest voting strength in Brazil, Chile, and Cuba. They reached their peak in the first-named country in the national elections of 1945 in which their candidate polled 569,-000 votes, or 9.7 per cent of the total popular vote for president. In the Brazilian Congressional elections in 1947 Communist voting strength declined to 450,000, or 8.5 per cent of the total for all parties, but the party nevertheless elected one senator, fourteen deputies, forty-six members of state legislatures, and the largest single-party bloc of members, eighteen, in the city council of Rio de Janeiro. As a result of the elections in Chile in 1946 Communists took over three seats in the cabinet of President Gabriel González Videla. In that year Communist Party registration in Cuba mounted to 150,000. In the elections in Uruguay the Communists for the first time won a Senate seat and they enlarged their delegation in the Chamber of Deputies from three to five. The Communists in Argentina also, though they were losing out to Perón in the contest for the support of labor, made a better showing than ever before. Immediately following the war Communists were represented in the national legislative bodies of Brazil, Bolivia, Chile, Colombia, Costa Rica, Cuba, Ecuador, Peru, and Uruguay.[63]

63. Robert J. Alexander, *Communism in Latin America* (New Brunswick, New Jersey), *passim.*

But as public opinion turned against Soviet Russia the Communist parties in Latin America went into eclipse. As they sought to capitalize upon the postwar ferment in Latin America they accomplished surprisingly little, partly because they were checkmated by more popular social and political movements of native origin, as, for example, *Acción Democrática* in Venezuela, *APRA* in Peru, the *Auténtico* movement in Cuba, the National Liberation movement in Costa Rica, and *Peronismo* in Argentina. In Brazil Communist voting strength decreased to only 20,000 in 1950. In the presidential election in 1952 in Chile the Communist vote was negligible. In the 1951 registration in Cuba the Communist *Partido Socialista Popular (PSP)* barely reached the 2 per cent figure required to survive as a national party. In Argentina the Communist vote dwindled from a high count of 116,000 in 1946 to 80,000 in 1948. In Uruguay it was reduced from 32,000 in 1946 to 15,500 in the election of November, 1950. In Guatemala, however, Communists gained 4 of the 56 seats in Congress in the elections of 1950 and not only were able to maintain the same Congressional strength in the elections of 1953, but were given high nonelective positions in the Arbenz government.

In general, postwar organized Communist forces were very small in Latin America as compared with those in Europe. They were unofficially estimated to number only 350,000 for all of Latin America in 1954. The Communists themselves claimed only some 400,000 members, a figure which represented one Communist to about every 400 persons in the total population of Latin America. But no more in Latin America than in other parts of the world do true Soviet Communists stake their success upon large numbers of overt followers. Adopting the precepts of Marx they disdain the *Lumpenproletariat*—the half-men who lack the power of independent thinking—and try rather to develop a nucleus of leaders, who will know how to encourage discontents and thus to put themselves in a position to furnish leadership to the mass of helpless workers when they judge the time to be opportune for their cause. "Whatever may be said to the contrary," reported the conservative *Universal* of Mexico City (July 7, 1950), "the actual influence of the Communists of the Ibero-American countries is very slight. The things that make them dangerous are the deplorable social, political, and economic conditions suffered by the people among whom they operate and whose discomfort they exploit." President Vargas of Brazil made the same generalization specifically for his own country early in 1951 when he told a

United States journalist that "what appears to some as Communist tendencies in Brazil is simply a reaction and a protest against the poor living conditions to which so many of our people are subjected and which Communist propagandists are exploiting."[64] In such circumstances, however, the activities of even a few Soviet-directed Communists may produce seriously disruptive effects. It is scarcely surprising that their promises of higher levels of living and fuller community action than seem possible under existing conditions should appeal to Latin Americans who are restive and even desperate under the traditional feudal or oligarchic pattern of control. These promises and attitudes are not peculiar to Communists, but often parallel those of non-Communists and anti-Communists.

In the early postwar years Communist leaders in Latin America overplayed their hand. After cooperating with several successful "liberal" presidential candidates, as, for example, José María Velasco Ibarra in Ecuador and González Videla in Chile, and receiving in return cabinet positions in the new governments, they sought to impose exorbitant demands which alienated these same "liberal" administrations. The diminution of overt Communist strength was attributable also in part to the struggles for power and ideological disagreements within the local Communist parties. Moreover, their cause was weakened by the intensified social action of some of the Latin American governments. President Galo Plaza of Ecuador, for example, took the position that the Communist Party should be permitted to operate in his country because he did "not believe in the persecution of ideas by police methods" and because his government was demonstrating to the people that it could satisfy their necessities and hopes by orderly constitutional processes. Similarly, the policy of the Arévalo government in Guatemala toward the Communists was, in Arévalo's words, "neither to persecute them nor to encourage them." But almost all the Latin American governments have taken measures to control these parties. Between 1945 and 1955 sixteen Latin American governments, namely, Bolivia, Brazil, Chile, Colombia, Costa Rica, Cuba, the Dominican Republic, El Salvador, Guatemala, Haiti, Honduras, Nicaragua, Panama, Paraguay, Peru, and Venezuela, outlawed the local parties at various times and with varying degrees of effectiveness. In Brazil, for example, President Eurico Gaspar Dutra's government ruled that the Communist Party was illegal in May, 1947, and closed its offices. Attempts were made, also

64. Edward Tomlinson in Washington *Sunday Star,* March 4, 1951.

with varying degrees of effectiveness, to control other Communist activities in consonance with inter-American agreements adopted at the Ninth International Conference of American States at Bogotá in 1948 (Resolution XXXII), the Fourth Meeting of Consultation of Ministers of Foreign Affairs in 1951 (Resolution VIII), and the Tenth Inter-American Conference in 1954 (Resolution XCIII).

The conference of 1948 condemned "the political activity of international communism" as a system "tending to suppress political and civil rights and liberties." Three years later the foreign ministers of the American governments, called into their Fourth Meeting of Consultation because of the need "for common defense against the aggressive activities of international communism," charged the Inter-American Defense Board "with preparing, as vigorously as possible, . . . the military planning of the common defense." The Tenth Inter-American Conference went still further in March, 1954, in declaring that "the domination or control of the political institutions of any American State by the international communist movement, extending to this Hemisphere the political system of an extracontinental power, would constitute a threat to the sovereignty and political independence of the American States." So, in phrases reminiscent of the Monroe Doctrine, the bases were laid for united Pan-American action against the international Communist movement as a non-American political and conspiratorial system.

The threat which inspired this resolution at Caracas was the Arbenz government of Guatemala. That government was ringingly defended by its Foreign Minister, Guillermo Toriello, in an address at the Caracas conference. The policies of his government, he asserted, conformed "to the economic resolutions adopted by the United Nations and its specialized agencies, by the International Labour Organization, and by the Organization of American States with regard to economic development, agrarian reform, capital investment, social policy, and the exploitation of natural wealth and resources in behalf of the people." But these non-Communist efforts of his government to modernize Guatemala's semi-feudal economy, Toriello charged, had been twisted into a "Communist threat against the Americas" because they trenched upon the privileges of certain United States business concerns operating in Guatemala "which were holding back progress and the economic development of the country." The operations of these concerns, he said, were inimical to the interest of the countries in which they operated because they were not paying equitable taxes, and the pressures applied by the United States on their behalf violated the principle of nonintervention. They represented a return to the policies of the " 'big stick' and the lamentable 'dollar diplomacy.' " Guatemala, he said amidst the enthusiastic acclaim of the other Latin American delegations, could not accept the view that any government in Latin America which touches the interests of foreign companies that control basic resources in Latin America will be called Communist, will be accused of jeopardizing continental security, and thus will be threatened with foreign intervention.[65]

In all its postwar efforts at concerted Pan-American action, the Latin Americans have shown a vigorous insistence upon the maintenance of the principle of nonintervention. As the American nations have united in collective defense measures against the interventionist activities of international communism, they have repeatedly insisted upon this principle in their relations one with another. The Charter of the Organization of American States defined the principle very broadly as follows: "No State or group of States has the right to intervene directly or indirectly, for any reason whatever, in the internal or external affairs of any other State. The foregoing principle prohibits not only the armed force but also any other form of interference or attempted threat against the personality of the State or against its political, economic and cultural elements" (Article 15).

In specific connection with proposed measures of inter-American action to deal with the threat of international communism the Guatemalan government took the lead in pointing to the possibility that such measures might lead to violations of the principle of nonintervention. For this reason Guatemala voted against the anti-Communist resolution at the Tenth Inter-American Conference at Caracas in March, 1954, and both Mexico and Argentina abstained from voting. At the same time the American governments coupled with it a reaffirmation of "the inalienable right of each American State freely to choose its own form of government and economic system and to live its own social and cultural life" (Resolution XCIII). Even measures of collective defense, therefore, must be taken without prejudice to the sacrosanct American concept of the juridical

65. Guillermo Toriello Garrido, Address in the Third Plenary Session, Tenth Inter-American Conference, Caracas, Venezuela, March 5, 1954, Doc. 95, English; and Guatemala, Government Information Bureau, No. 17, March 15, 1954.

342 ARE WE GOOD NEIGHBORS?

equality and sovereignty of all the American states. This concept requires that there must be no interference with the natural economic and social evolution of the Latin American peoples. Such evolution even when it takes revolutionary forms must not be assumed prima facie to be a manifestation of international communism.

As the antagonism of the United States to the Arbenz government, which had been made manifest at Caracas, became more intense in the ensuing weeks, even strongly anti-Communist newspapers in Latin America condemned the United States for supplying arms to Guatemala's neighbors, Honduras and Nicaragua. Within a month after Guatemala received an arms shipment purchased from Sweden, the United States forwarded to Honduras and Nicaragua enough arms and other military equipment to fit out an infantry battalion in each country. "The North American government," sharply declared the generally pro-United States *El País* of Montevideo (May 29, 1954), "in pressuring the government of Guatemala to accept the conditions demanded by the United Fruit Company . . . under a leprous contract concluded the 30 of April 1923 under the dictatorship of General Lázaro Chacón . . . is returning to a policy which will alienate the sympathy of the continent and rouse a clamor of disapproval." At that time the Arbenz government under its land reform program had expropriated 233,973 acres of United Fruit Company land and was planning expropriation of an additional 174,000 acres.[66] As the United States undertook to line up other anti-Communist nations to embargo arms shipments to Guatemala and imposed an economic squeeze on that government by withdrawing its already limited technical assistance, it roused further protests. To these protests the State Department replied, first, that it was no more concerned with the United Fruit Company than with any other United States interest in a foreign country and, second, that it was not intervening in the internal affairs of Guatemala but was merely trying to check the aims of the Soviet Union in this hemisphere.[67] But only nine Latin American governments joined the United States in calling for a fifth meeting of ministers of foreign affairs to deal with the "intervention of the international Communist movement in the republic of Guatemala and the danger which this involves for the peace and security of the continent."[68] Absent from this list were the leading nations: Argentina, Mexico, Chile, Colombia, and Vene-

66. *New York Times,* June 19, 1954.
67. *Ibid.,* June 24, 1954.   68. *Ibid.,* June 27, 1954.

zuela. The meeting thus called was rendered unnecessary by the overthrow of Arbenz and was indefinitely postponed on July 2, 1954.[69]

For the overthrow of the Arbenz government by invading forces from Honduras under Colonel Castillo Armas, assisted mysteriously by three F47 airplanes built in the United States, the United States was held responsible in Latin America. Toriello's charge in his complaint to the Security Council of the United Nations that the invasion had been incited by "certain foreign monopolies whose interests have been affected by the progressive policy" of the Guatemalan government was echoed in the Latin American press. Demonstrations against the United States, some of them allegedly Communist-inspired, were held in Chile, Argentina, Uruguay, Bolivia, Cuba, Panama, Puerto Rico, and Honduras.[70] Even in countries where the strong stand of the United States against the Communist-infiltrated Arbenz government had been applauded, questions about United States intervention were raised. *El Tiempo* of Bogotá (June 26, 1954) proclaimed "its devotion to the cause of Guatemala," because it believed in the principle of "nonintervention and in the peaceful solution of the problems of the hemisphere."[71] The so-called "liberal" press, preoccupied with the problem of low living standards and with the attempt of the Arbenz government to raise them by national action, condemned the intervention which overthrew that government. Even conservative papers did not blame the Arbenz government for seeking to secure better treatment at the hands of North American capital. But, said *El Comercio* of Lima (June 29, 1954), Latin America should not allow the exploitations of North American capital, supported by the government in Washington, to "serve as a pretext for the introduction of Soviet imperialism into the Western Hemisphere."[72] The revolutionary overthrow of the Arbenz government

69. Department of State, *Penetration of the Political Institutions of Guatemala by the International Communist Movement: Threat to the Peace and Security of America and to the Sovereignty and Political Independence of Guatemala* (Washington, June, 1954). For a reply by the former secretary to President Arbenz of Guatemala, see Raúl Osegueda, *op. cit.* Certain aspects of this Guatemalan case are penetratingly reviewed by Arthur P. Whitaker in "Guatemala, OAS and U.S.," *Foreign Policy Bulletin*, XXXIII (September 1, 1954), 4-7. See also Robert J. Alexander, *Communism in Latin America*, 357-364; and Ronald M. Schneider, *Communism in Guatemala, 1944-1954* (New York, 1958).

70. *New York Times*, June 21, 22, 23, 24, 1954. See also Ezequiel Ramírez Novoa, *La Farsa del Panamericanismo y la Unidad Indoamericana* (Buenos Aires, 1955), [23].   71. See also *El Tiempo*, June 19 and 29, 1954.

72. See also *El País*, Montevideo, June 29, 1954.

344 ARE WE GOOD NEIGHBORS?

was due, concluded *El Mercurio* of Santiago (June 30, 1954), not to Washington but to "Soviet penetration in Guatemala."

The attitude of Latin American Communists toward the United States has been to criticize and oppose it on almost every issue. They have pictured it as a country ridden by "trusts and cartels."[73] Its postwar prosperity and prestige, they allege, has been due to its exploitation of millions of workers throughout the world, particularly in Latin America. Its ultimate purpose is to compel "all peoples and all races to bow the knee before the Moloch of Wall Street."[74] Monopoly capital, they say, has been determining its domestic and foreign policy, and has made it "the principal bulwark of the reactionary forces of the entire world, replacing the Fascists of Germany, Italy, and Japan."[75] The United States is a "warmonger," they assert, preparing conditions for "a new world hecatomb,"[76] and they declare that they will refuse to "allow themselves to be used as cannon fodder of the imperialist armies in a World War III. . . . They will not fight under the North American flag crushed by the bankers and Wall Street."[77] According to the Central Committee of the Communist Party of Ecuador, Communists will try to transform such a war "into a war of national liberation from imperialist oppression" in order "to liquidate the feudal system and to erect a true democracy."[78] Their expectation is that existing elite or master classes would not be able to survive such a war.

In preparing for this war, the United States, according to the Communist "line," regards the entire Western Hemisphere as its own "sphere of influence for Yankee imperialism."[79] All that it offers to Latin America, declared the Communist *Diario Popular* of Montevideo in July, 1946, is "the possibility of living—economically, militarily, and politically—subordinated to the generous Yankee imperialism."[80] The relationship between the United States and Latin

73. *Diario Popular,* Montevideo, October 23 and 24, 1946.
74. *Hoy,* Havana, March 13, 1949; and Eugenio Gómez, *Europa, Nuevo Mundo* (Montevideo [1948]), [13]-24, [245]-256.
75. Francisco P. Vázquez in *Hoy,* Havana, March 7, 1947; and *Tribuna Popular,* Rio de Janeiro, March 17, 1947.
76. *Tribuna Popular,* Rio de Janeiro, March 4, 1947; and *Folha do Povo,* Rio de Janeiro, March 17, 1949.
77. Fernando Siñani in *El Pueblo,* La Paz, March 26, 1949.
78. Resolution of April 5, 1949.
79. Juan Antonio Corretjer in *Hoy,* Havana, March 29, 1946; and Sergio Aguirre in *Hoy,* March 14, 1947.
80. Quoted in Despatch 7460, Montevideo, July 10, 1946, State Department Archives.

America, they say, is that of the rider and the horse.[81] The United States is thwarting the legitimate desires of the Latin American nations for industrialization. It is interested in them only to the extent necessary to bring them into its power bloc in the cold war against the Soviet Union. At the same time it is contemptuous of their sovereignty and its ultimate aim is to subjugate them.[82] In particular, Communists accused President Truman of abandoning Roosevelt's Good Neighbor Policy toward Latin America in order to follow a policy of intervention and imperialism.[83] They even allege that the United States is preparing to launch military expeditions against the Latin American countries to protect its business corporations there from "communism."

Despite all this criticism Jorge Castellanos was able to write in the Communist *Hoy* of Havana (March 5, 1947) that the Communists are not anti-United States but are simply "anti-imperialists," and to avow: "We love the country of the Good Neighbor just as much as we fear and hate the country of the Big Stick." According to *Hoy* (February 23, 1947), this policy of the Big Stick was being "advocated by high financial and industrial circles in the United States." But the Communist *Diario Popular* of Bogotá (July 4, 1945) explained that "the North Americans do not sympathize with the imperialist agents of their country." In this way the Communists have sought to draw a distinction between the masses of the people of the United States, who are well disposed toward Latin America, and their imperialistic masters who are seeking world hegemony at the risk of a third world war.[84]

The attraction that communism makes to societies that are feudally organized and have rigid class stratifications must not be underestimated. But its appeal is less ideological than material, for it has a demonstrated capacity to achieve desirable material results and to achieve them in a hurry. Communist and other extremist movements in Latin America gain advantage from the failures of existing governments and ruling groups to solve the problems, first, of mere existence

81. Francisco P. Vázquez in *Hoy*, Havana, March 7, 1947.
82. *Tribuna Popular*, Rio de Janeiro, September 19, 1946; Francisco P. Vázquez in *Hoy*, Havana, March 7 and December 11, 1947; and Sergio Aguirre in *Hoy*, March 14, 1947.
83. *Diario Popular*, Bogotá, July 4, 1945; *La Voz de México*, Mexico City, May 5, 1946; Hernán Laborde in *Todo*, Mexico City, August 29, 1946; and José Mancisidor in *Hoy*, Mexico City, August 31, 1946.
84. *Diario Popular*, Bogotá, January 20 and November 14, 1946.

in some countries and, second, of a comfortable existence in all countries. The annual per capita income in eleven Latin American
countries in 1955 was below $200, it ranged from $200 to $450 in
seven others, and in two only did it exceed $450.[85] The political insta-
bility which is so marked a characteristic of many of these countries
is a reflection of a deep-seated economic and social malaise. Since
the war Bolivia, for example, has had as many as eighteen ministers
of labor in four years and eight ministers of finance in eighteen
months.[86] The frequent changes of presidents, finance ministers, and
ministers of labor generally represent desperate expedients by the ruling
groups to find solutions to hitherto insoluble problems or to give the
appearance of change while actually suppressing it. As long as these
problems remain unsolved the position of existing non-Communist
governments continues to be precarious. Nor can Communist con-
spiracies in Latin America be thwarted by denying or ignoring the
existence of the discontents which produce them. What is required
is an intelligent appraisal of them and remedial action which will
remove the basic and chronic factors of instability. This is being
done in many parts of Latin America by native leaders who have
won the confidence of the people. The announced policy of Brazil's
President João Café Filho toward communism in early 1955, for
example, was "to suppress Communist subversive activities by utilizing
all legitimate means, including, particularly, promoting the establishment of social conditions that will make it difficult for antidemocratic
ideas to thrive."[87] In the opinion of such leaders and their followers,
who constitute the great mass of the people in Latin America, the
cold war is not their war. The war that they must wage is a war
against hunger, poverty, and disease, against illiteracy and superstition,
against entrenched privilege, against ossified institutions, against the
inheritances of colonial rule, against a long accepted position and
habit of inferiority which has resulted in oversensitivity and over-
compensation, in short, against national weakness and the forces of
national disintegration. They feel that they can best repel communism with prosperity, not with bullets.

* * *

85. United Nations, Economic Commission for Latin America, *Economic Survey of Latin America, 1955,* 8.
86. Albert Lepawsky, *The Bolivian Operation: New Trends in Technical Assistance,* International Conciliation Pamphlet No. 479, March, 1952, Carnegie Endowment for International Peace (New York, 1952), 106.
87. *El Mercurio,* Santiago, Chile, January 11, 1955.

Though Latin America belongs both culturally and geographically to the western world, its support of the ideas and strategy of the West in the postwar East-West conflict cannot be taken for granted. Unlike the Anglo-Americans, the Latin Americans are not the heirs of a primarily capitalist tradition. Long schooled in the doctrine that certain economic activities must be carried out and controlled by the central government, they find it difficult to accept the preachments of Washington that capitalism is the only means by which they can improve their living conditions and enter more actively into the life of the modern world. They are convinced that it is not the only technique that can be used to conduct business under freedom or to eliminate poverty from their countries. In a broad sense the issue for Latin America is indeed capitalism versus communism. But the burden of proof is on those who believe that capitalism can provide the Latin Americans with all the satisfactions and all the "goods" that they desire. The free enterprise system and the United States as the exponent of that system must meet their requirements for industrial development, for agricultural progress, for higher levels of living, and, particularly, for a lift in spirit and morale. It must stand up and deliver. If it does not do so the Latin Americans are prepared to turn from it to something else. They will take help wherever they can get it. The satisfaction of their basic requirements and demands may override their ideological predilections for the free enterprise system which, as has been shown, has been seriously weakened anyway in the last quarter of a century when it has been increasingly challenged in many parts of Latin America. The counterappeal of a state-directed and state-integrated economy to Latin Americans must not be underestimated, and it will surely become stronger if their wants are increasingly satisfied by it.[88] To people who have never enjoyed the full experience of freedom, communism appears attractive. If adequate private capital and technology are not made available from outside Latin America, governments, even in those countries where in the past private efforts have played a major role, may find it necessary to establish and operate productive enterprises themselves. The result may not, almost certainly will not, be the adoption of Soviet Communism, but it may well take the form of intensified social action along nationalist lines.

For the satisfaction of their basic requirements Latin Americans have been turning increasingly to other areas of the world than the

88. On this general subject see Pinto Santa Cruz, *op. cit.*, 97-112.

United States since the end of the war. Both their postwar economic needs and their changed political orientation have inspired them to reconsider their relations with Spain in particular. The overthrow of the *Acción Democrática* government of Venezuela gave the military junta which succeeded it an opportunity to recognize the Franco government in March, 1949. Two months later a resolution opening the way for diplomatic recognition of Spain was pushed through the Political Committee of the United Nations by Brazil, Bolivia, Colombia, and Peru over the opposition of Costa Rica, Guatemala, and Uruguay. Despite the subsequent defeat of the resolution in the General Assembly of the United Nations, several American nations, not including the United States, either re-established or continued to maintain diplomatic relations with Spain. When the United States finally abandoned its opposition to Franco after the outbreak of the Korean War in early 1950 it became possible for a bloc of Latin American nations including Bolivia, Costa Rica, the Dominican Republic, El Salvador, Honduras, Nicaragua, and Peru to spearhead a final successful drive in the United Nations to rescind the anti-Spanish resolution in November, 1950[89] In the voting an anti-Franco position was maintained to the end by Mexico, the Arévalo government of Guatemala, and Uruguay, while Cuba and the United States abstained from voting.[90] This action of the United Nations prepared the way for a *rapprochement* between Spain and most of the nations of the American hemisphere and for General Franco's acceptance of a defense-aid pact with the United States in September, 1953, in which he promised to aid the United States in resisting Soviet aggression. It has also been followed by an increase in Latin America's trade with Spain.

It will be recalled that World War II cut across established trade patterns in the Western Hemisphere and brought new alignments. It temporarily suspended Latin America's commercial dependence upon Europe and moved the United States into first place as both the supplier and the customer of all the countries of Latin America. But after World War II the United States lost its special commercial position in Latin America, and the Latin American countries, unable to meet their commodity and dollar needs in the United States, once

89. Houston, *op. cit.*, 88-97.
90. Hilton (ed.), *Hispanic World Report*, II, 6 (June, 1949), [1]-3; *Hispanic American Report*, III, 2 (February, 1950), 5-6; and 11 (November, 1950), 6.

again began to depend upon supplies and even dollars received from European countries. "Foreign competition with the United States for the Latin American market is growing," concluded the Senate Banking and Currency Committee, chairmaned by Senator Homer Capehart, after a thorough study of Latin American conditions and a journey through that area in the fall of 1953.[91] Brazil's imports from the United States, for example, amounting to only $71,342,000 in 1938, reached $746,273,000 by 1947, or more than ten times the prewar figure, but declined to $474,000,000 in 1949 and to only $295,-000,000 in 1953. Brazil's imports from the United Kingdom and Europe, meanwhile, rose from $265,929,000 in 1947 to $363,700,000 in 1949.[92] Similarly Argentina's imports from the United States, which amounted to only $74,648,000 in 1938, reached $594,400,000 in 1947 but fell back to $129,100,000 in 1949 while its imports from the United Kingdom and Europe were increasing from $398,100,000 to $584,-900,000.[93] By 1953 Argentina's imports from the United States had declined to only $104,200,000. The same pattern of three- to tenfold increases in trade with the United States during the war period until 1947 or 1948 and then sharp declines by 1949 or 1950 with corresponding increases in trade with Europe was traced by many other Latin American countries. Imports of goods from the United States into Latin America, which stood at 69.4 per cent of all Latin America's imports in 1947, sank to only 52.3 per cent in 1952, and in the case of some commodities United States producers have been almost entirely eliminated from the Latin American market by European competition.[94] As a result those countries were able to say to the United States, using words addressed to Senator Capehart's committee by the Federação do Comércio do Estado de São Paulo in November, 1953, "It was only in consequence of the world wars that our market was conquered by your industries and your products. To keep it as you have had it until now, you must offer us more, not less, than the European countries."[95]

After the war, therefore, Europe moved back to resume its prewar

91. *Congressional Record,* Vol. 100 (March 16, 1954), 3105.
92. Department of State, *Data Book, Latin America,* I, *South America,* 44.
93. *Ibid.,* 11.
94. United Nations, Economic Commission for Latin America, *Economic Survey of Latin America, 1953,* 31-32, and *1954,* 63.
95. Senate Committee on Banking and Currency, Interim Report, 83d Congress, 2d Session, Senate Report No. 1082, *Study of Latin American Countries,* March 16, 1954, 145.

trade position in Latin America, and the prewar international competition for the products and markets of Latin America was reopened.
The governments, capital markets, and industrialists of Europe, sustained and revitalized by the generosity of the United States, began
to compete again with the United States in that area, adopting as techniques for trade expansion their successful prewar methods of bilateral
trade agreements and liberal credit terms. The countries of western
Europe, as well as those of eastern Europe and Japan, have used these
methods to increase their exports and to open up new markets in the
nonconvertible currency areas of Latin America. As a result, in 1951
Europe increased its sales to Latin America 62 per cent over 1950.

One of the most striking examples of the revival of international
rivalry in Latin America is the reappearance of western Germany as
a relatively large trader and investor there, just as in the period between World Wars I and II. West Germany's export trade to Latin
America increased by 43 per cent in 1951 over that of 1950 and made
further spectacular rises in 1952 and 1954.[96] By 1954 West Germany
was Argentina's third most important customer, ranking respectively
after Britain and the United States, but as a supplier of Argentina's
imports it had edged out both Britain and the United States to head
the list. West Germany's investment in Brazil alone in 1956 and 1957
reached approximately $50 million and was concentrated notably in
the automobile industry. Between 1952 and 1957 about 30 per cent of
West Germany's total foreign investment of $120 million went into
Latin America.

Europe has largely recovered its prewar position in Latin America.
By 1951 the United Kingdom and Europe were absorbing 30 per cent
of Latin America's exports, as compared with 39 per cent in 1937;
in the same year 1951 they were responsible for 25 per cent of Latin
America's imports.[97] French and Italian manufacturers of automobiles
and agricultural machinery have set up factories in Brazil. The
government, banks, and industry of France supplied the loans and
materials that made possible the new steel mill that was inaugurated
at Paz del Río in Colombia on October 14, 1954, by President Gustavo
Rojas Pinilla. During 1953-1954 three large French, West German,

96. *United Nations Bulletin,* "Need for More Trade between Latin America and Europe," XIV (February 15, 1953), 147; and United Nations, Economic Commission for Latin America, *Economic Survey of Latin America,
1954,* 46.
97. International Monetary Fund, *International Financial Statistics,* V
(October, 1952), 32.

and Italian manufacturers concluded agreements with the Argentine government to establish tractor factories there with a total investment of more than 1,000 million pesos, and by February, 1955, a French consortium was completing new steel plants at Chimbote in Peru and in Minas Gerais, Brazil.[98] England's commercial position in Argentina was enhanced by the overthrow of the Perón government there in September, 1955. These are only a few instances among many of the ways in which non-American trade rivals of the United States are moving into Latin America.[99]

The Soviet Union and its satellites in eastern Europe are increasingly entering the markets of Latin America as both buyers and suppliers, thus introducing a new factor, virtually nonexistent before World War II, into the international competition for the trade of that area. In 1951 the countries of eastern Europe exported to Latin America some 20 per cent more than during 1950, including, especially, electric motors and machinery, machine tools, textile machinery, tractors, and rolling stock. Taking advantage of Latin America's postwar dollar difficulties and shortages of needed goods from the United States, they have concluded several bilateral trading agreements with Latin American countries, thus setting up nondollar trade blocs. Czechoslovakia, Hungary, and Poland concluded trade agreements with several Latin American countries prior to 1952, but in that year they and other eastern European countries, including the Soviet Union itself, began to establish a network of such agreements with Latin American countries, starting with an agreement between Czechoslovakia and Brazil in July, 1952. By early 1955 fourteen trade pacts of this sort had been concluded between the countries of eastern Europe and Argentina, Brazil, Paraguay, and Uruguay alone, excluding some barter agreements with Chile and Colombia. As a result the trade

98. Illustrated brochures entitled *Paz del Río,* no author but published by Antares, Bogotá, 1954, 10; and *Paz del Río, Una Grande Realización Francesa en Colombia: Estudio presentado ante el Instituto de Estudios Americanos del Comité Francia-América, el 11 de junio de 1954, por Jacques Wetzel, Director General de los Establecimientos Delattre & Frouard Réunis* (Bogotá, [1954]). This Paz del Río project was earlier turned down by United States investors after, as it is alleged, an unfavorable report on it was presented by Lauchlin Currie.

99. United Nations, Economic Commission for Latin America, *Economic Survey of Latin America, 1954,* 63-69. The postwar relations of the Caribbean nations with countries outside the Western Hemisphere are described in Donald M. Dozer, "Caribbean Relations with Non-American Countries," *The Caribbean: Contemporary International Relations* (Gainesville, Florida, 1957), 20-38.

developed by those countries with Latin America reached $300 million in value during 1954 and surpassed $500 million in value during 1955.[100]

The commodities exchanged in this new East-West trade are predominantly coffee, rye, wheat, meat, hides, wool, and sugar from Latin America and machinery, fuel, steel products, and cement from eastern Europe. Under the terms of a Soviet-Argentine commercial agreement, for example, concluded in August, 1953, the Soviet Union has exported to Argentina coal, aviation gasoline, tires, crude oil, and many iron and steel manufactures including pipe line, steel rails, boiler plate, and sheet steel in exchange largely for Argentine meat and other animal products. By 1954 the Soviet Union ranked fourth among Argentina's foreign markets and was acounting for between 5 and 8 per cent of Argentina's total foreign trade. In May, 1955, the two governments extended their trade agreement in a protocol which provided for an exchange of products valued at $100 million. Early in 1958 they signed another trade agreement providing for the shipment to Argentina of Soviet oil-drilling and other equipment.

With Colombia, or rather with the semi-official Federación Colombiana de Productores de Café, trade representatives of the East German government concluded an agreement in early 1955 providing for the transfer of Colombian coffee valued at $7 million in exchange for East German industrial equipment, agricultural machinery, and fertilizers.[101] With Cuba, agents of the Soviet Union concluded a purchase contract in early 1955 for the delivery of 350 thousand tons of sugar and actually purchased 568 thousand tons.[102] With several other Latin American countries, both the Soviet Union and Hungary made agreements in 1953 and 1954 covering the barter of electrical machinery for raw materials.[103] The Soviet Union has also procured 20,000 tons of copper wire from Chile, quantities of sugar from Cuba, and wool from Uruguay. Black market operations with the Soviet Union are extensive.

Since World War II the Soviet Union has participated in all the trade expositions held in Latin America. The propaganda efforts which it and its eastern European satellites are making for expanded trade with Latin America were particularly noted at the Sixth Session of the United Nations Economic Commission for Latin America in

100. United Nations, Economic Commission for Latin America, *Economic Survey of Latin America, 1954,* 71.   101. *Ibid.,* 61.
102. *Ibid.,* 62; and *1955,* 49.   103. *Ibid., 1954,* 65.

Bogotá in September, 1955, where it was pointed out, for example, that Poland's trade with Argentina had increased from $13 million in 1953 to more than $28 million in 1954 and that Poland's trade with Brazil was growing at an even greater rate. In the following year Soviet wheat was even shipped to Brazil.[104] But these closer commercial relations, which are interpreted by some observers as presaging closer political relations, appear to have only limited possibilities for development because of the substantial lack of complementarity in the Soviet and the Latin American economies. They have also been attributed to the genuine need of the Soviet Union for South America's exports to meet its own agricultural deficiencies rather than to ulterior political motives. Thus far in the postwar period the Soviet Union has been important only as an importer of a few Latin American commodities which she cannot procure in eastern Europe and her commerce with Latin America has been limited to what is necessary to supplement her own economy.

Latin American attitudes toward the Soviet Union are as various as their attitudes toward the United States after 1930 and their attitudes toward the Nazi and Fascist nations between 1933 and 1940. Not only do they vary from country to country, but throughout Latin America they are strongly influenced by social and economic factors. The attitudes, for example, of the owner of a Central American coffee *finca* and the president of a Caribbean republic may differ considerably from those of a coffee worker and a labor organizer. But Latin Americans can be depended upon to adopt a solidary opposition to Soviet and every other imperialism, whether military or economic or ideological, in defense of their independence and their institutions. In this direction they are impelled by their strong nationalist convictions. So strong are those convictions that Latin America, like Spain in its resistance to the French invasion in 1808, might refuse in a showdown to join a foreign nation which like the France of Napoleon I claimed to be the leader of the free world, if it felt that its own nationality was threatened. In such a situation Latin Americans would give priority to the protection of their own nationalism. "We are small nations," they argue, "and suspicion must be our defense." As their delegates to the Tenth Inter-American Conference at Caracas in 1954 made plain, their opposition to communism is derived from their determination to prevent all foreign elements directed from abroad from undermining their economy and subverting their political institutions.

104. *Ibid.,* 61.

354 ARE WE GOOD NEIGHBORS?

In the cold war considerable numbers of Latin Americans will be more strongly influenced by trends in western Europe than by the policies of the United States. They appreciate that for several centuries the fate of the Indo-Iberic peoples of the Western Hemisphere, like that of the Anglo-American peoples, has been inextricably and mystically bound to that of western European culture. To Latin Americans no bond is more fundamental than this cultural bond which is based upon a few essential principles and common institutions and which is all the more powerful because it is spiritual and not mechanistic. Nevertheless, they have profoundly hoped that peace can be maintained between the east and west. For this reason they have generally hailed with gratification the waning of the cold war after the "summit meeting" at Geneva in July, 1955. Their feelings of relief and hope for a continuance of world peace were expressed by the delegations of several of these nations at the opening session of the United Nations General Assembly in September, 1955.[105] Their hopes for the economic development and improvement in living standards which will give them new standing in the modern world depend upon a long period of peace.

105. See, for example, speeches by Messrs. Cyro de Freitas-Valle of Brazil, the Reverend Benjamín Nuñez of Costa Rica, José Vicente Trujillo of Ecuador, Víctor A. Belaunde of Peru, Rudecindo Ortega of Chile, Alberto A. Boyd of Panama, Hernán Siles Zuazo of Bolivia, Guillermo Enciso Velloso of Paraguay, Jean Price-Mars of Haiti, Vicente Basagoiti of Uruguay, and Santiago Pérez-Pérez of Venezuela, United Nations, General Assembly, *Tenth Session, Official Records, Plenary Meetings,* Nos. 516-528, September 20-30, 1955 (New York, 1955).

Chapter 10

CHARTING THE FUTURE

I earnestly hope that the meeting as a whole may join with the Delegation of the United States in common dedication to the Policy of the Good Partner.
—PRESIDENT DWIGHT D. EISENHOWER

THE POSTWAR DISILLUSIONMENT with the United States in the countries to the South continues and has left its heritage of illwill. Latin Americans still charge that the prices of their raw materials during World War II were fixed unilaterally by the United States. More than nine years after the end of World War II *La Nación* of Santiago, Chile, complained that if during the war the United States had bought Chilean copper at world market prices, which went up as high as 40 and even 50 cents a pound, and not at the frozen rate of 10.9 cents a pound, a price, said *La Nación* (October 27, 1954), "which was imposed upon our country as its war contribution, then there would have been no need for us to have recourse to any foreign loan." Furthermore, Latin Americans recall with bitterness that the dollar exchange that they acquired during the war could not be utilized until its purchasing power had seriously deteriorated and was no longer able to purchase the machinery, equipment, and other goods required after the war for rehabilitation and modernization of their economies. This reduction in the purchasing power of their dollar holdings amounted in effect, they say, to a retroactive decrease in the prices of their raw materials. After the war the United States concentrated its attention upon Europe at the expense of its allies in the Western Hemisphere. In the Marshall Plan it lavished billions of dollars upon Europe, thus creating competition

355

356 ARE WE GOOD NEIGHBORS?

for the war-born industries of Latin Americans and inflating the prices of things they had to buy. At the same time the United States repeatedly postponed the promised inter-American economic conference and then sabotaged their legitimate economic aspirations by insisting upon provisions in the Economic Agreement of Bogotá which they could not accept. From the viewpoint of Latin Americans all the economic conferences held since have been largely failures.[1]

All these grievances, whether they can be factually substantiated or not, have been repeatedly voiced by Latin Americans in newspapers, speeches, radio broadcasts, and international conferences since the end of World War II. Latin America is convinced that it remains, to use the word of *Correio da Manhã* of Rio de Janeiro (January 9, 1954), only a "postscript" to the United States. At the Tenth Inter-American Conference held at Caracas in March, 1954, for example, Latin American delegates complained that in both World War II and the Korean War the prices of Latin America's primary products were, in effect, frozen. The price of coffee increased by only 12 per cent during the Korean War, explained Salvadoran Foreign Minister Roberto Canessa, while the price of steel increased by 27 per cent. Since the United States failed to equalize the prices paid for Latin America's raw materials with the prices charged for its manufactured products, Latin Americans were caught in a "price scissors." Unless they could receive aid in the form of "parity prices" for their raw materials, an increased flow of capital at low interest rates or in the form of grants which would enable them to meet developing competition from Africa and Asia, and freer access to United States markets, their political stability and their standards of living, they declared, would then become more susceptible to communism. "If we fail to raise the standard of living of our population to a level compatible with human dignity," Brazilian Foreign Minister Vicente Rão told the Tenth Inter-American Conference, "we shall be weak nations, and weak nations constitute the most favorable environment for proliferation of the infectious germs of subversive ideologies." This dire fate could be prevented only by a common inter-American effort to raise the standard of living of the Latin American peoples. Such an effort should receive the support of the United States as a means, as Peru's

1. "Palabras pronunciadas por el Sr. Washington P. Bermudez el 18 de noviembre de 1957, al concluir su mandato como presidente del Consejo Interamericano Económico y Social," Pan American Union, ES-RAE-Doc. 10/57, mimeographed, 4.

Minister of Foreign Relations Ricardo Rivera Schreiber declared, of quarantining itself "against disrupting reverses, while contributing to the development and more equitable distribution of wealth throughout the hemisphere." This Latin American conception of what a good neighbor and a good partner ought to be was embodied in resolutions sponsored by the Latin American delegations both at the Tenth Inter-American Conference at Caracas, and at the Meeting of Ministers of Finance or Economy at Quitandinha, Brazil, in 1954.[2]

Again, at the meeting of presidents of the American nations at Panama in mid-1956 and at the continuation meeting of the representatives of the presidents in Washington in September, 1956, the stress was placed by the Latin Americans upon the need for raising the living levels of their peoples through a joint inter-American effort in which the United States would play a large role.[3] The cooperation of the United States with the Latin American nations in raising living standards, maintaining the peace of the hemisphere, and guaranteeing hemispheric security—all obligations which it assumed during World War II—must be given in accordance with the principle of nonintervention, respecting the individuality and sovereignty of every other nation of the hemisphere. Aid from the good partner to the north would be welcomed in the form of private capital, but such capital must not seek to monopolize the resources of the Latin American peoples or claim a privileged status above the national laws. But much of the United States insistence upon private entrepreneurial action is galling to the Latin Americans. They consider it inadequate to meet their programs of economic diversification. Moreover, the type of investment that Latin America needs, Bolivian Foreign Minister Walter Guevara Arze told the delegates to the Caracas meeting, "is exactly the kind that yields a low return, that is, highway construction, hydroelectric works, and agricultural development." Many economic activities, particularly in countries which are still

2. Inter-American Conference, Tenth, Caracas, 1954, *Final Act;* and Organization of American States [Inter-American Economic and Social Council], *Resoluciones Aprobadas en la Reunión de Ministros de Hacienda o de Economía en IV Sessión Extraordinaria del Consejo Interamericano Económico y Social, 22 de noviembre-2 de diciembre de 1954* (Quitandinha, Petropolis, Brasil, 1954).

3. Organization of American States, *Acta de la Sesión Conmemorativa del Congreso de Panamá de 1826, 18-22 de Julio de 1956* (Washington, 1956); and Inter-American Committee of Presidential Representatives, *Summary of Proposals Made by Representatives at the First Meeting of the Committee,* Doc. 5 (Rev. 2), September 19, 1956 (Washington, 1956).

underdeveloped, must therefore be carried on by government action and under government control. Only in this way, Latin Americans insist, can they successfully meet the challenges of communism.

Latin America has a higher rate of population growth than any other major area of the world, averaging 2.5 per cent per year and reaching 3.1 per cent in some countries, as compared with 1.7 per cent for the United States and only 1.0 per cent for the world as a whole. This rate of increase, which is two and a half times the world average, is preponderantly the result of excess of births over deaths in these predominantly Roman Catholic countries and has been rising at a progressively faster rate for many years. Every country in Latin America has a higher birth rate than the United States. In 1950 the population of Latin America as a whole was four-fifths greater than it had been in 1920 whereas the total population of the world had increased by only an estimated one-third during the same period. A projection of present trends indicates that the population of Latin America may increase at an even more rapid rate in the future. By 1980 it is expected at least to double and in some areas even to attain two and a half times its present numbers. Mexico's population will equal that of Germany, and Brazil will become a "veritable giant" with a population approaching 100 million inhabitants—a figure exceeded at present by only four nations—China, India, the Soviet Union, and the United States. By the year 2000 Latin America's population is expected to reach 500 million, outnumbering the combined populations of the United States and Canada by as much as two to one. Barring unpredictable cataclysmic developments, the present population balance between Latin America and Anglo-America, therefore, will be radically altered within the next half-century to the great advantage of the former. If to populate is to govern, as it must be as long as the principle of majority rule is followed, Latin America can be expected to assume a more commanding role in world affairs than ever before.[4]

This explosive population trend highlights both the problem and the promise of Latin America. As population increases, both the problem and the promise will increase. The problem presented by an overflowing Latin American population may become insuperable

4. Department of State, Office of Intelligence Research, "Population Growth and Economic Development in Latin America," Intelligence Estimate Number 56, July 13, 1953; United Nations, Bureau of Social Affairs, *The Population of Central America (Including Mexico), 1950-1980* (New York, 1954), 11-14; and *The Population of South America, 1950-1980* (New York, 1955), 12-17.

unless the promise held out by that population is constantly kept in mind. It must be viewed against the social forces that have appeared in Latin America during and since World War II. The Latin America of the 1950's cannot be pushed around as was the Latin America of the 1910's and 1920's. Self-consciousness and assertiveness are the hallmarks of modern Latin America. The newly forming and increasingly articulate middle classes and the new, vigorously class-conscious, well-organized working classes will not easily yield to the kind of pressures that have been applied in the past. These are inextricably allied, moreover, with the intensified nationalist forces, which are determined to generate a new self-esteem in the Latin American peoples and to give them an enlarged role in the future world commensurate with their growing numbers.

Latin American aspirations for national and regional self-aggrandizement are being assisted by the general increase in production of material goods in this area. Since the end of World War II the annual increase in total production in Latin America has averaged nearly 5 per cent. When set over against the 2.5 per cent annual rate of population increase, this means a net gain of approximately 2.5 per cent in per capita output, which is larger than the net gain of only 2.1 per cent registered by the United States during the entire period 1869-1952.[5]

But although this increase in gross output gives Latin Americans a temporary advantage in their terms of trade with the more highly industrialized areas of the world it remains to be seen whether they truly are acquiring a spirit of business enterprise, whether they can maintain their present level of economic development, and whether they can make it self-generating and self-perpetuating. When reckoned in terms of trade, their economic growth has been significant only in those relatively few countries that have benefited from the high prices of coffee and cocoa. For Latin America as a whole a downward economic trend began in late 1956, and since that year the prices of all Latin America's raw materials, except cocoa, have declined. The trade relations of most of the Latin American nations with the foreign world continue to be unsatisfactory to them and are marked by violent seasonal oscillations. Since 1953, the date of the termination of the Korean War and the consequent reduction of stockpiling operations in the United States, both actual production and net capital investment in Latin America have declined. Governmental investment in that area

5. Milton S. Eisenhower, *op. cit.*, 706-707.

tapered off after 1950, and private investment began its downward trend in 1953. Latin America's level of economic growth therefore passed its postwar peak in the early 1950's.[6] By 1954 the gross rate of investment there had declined from an earlier 17 per cent to only 14.9 per cent, which meant a net rate of less than 9 per cent a year.[7] During 1956 Latin America's rate of economic development slowed down to the point where it was barely keeping pace with the rate of population increase.[8]

The basic wants of Latin Americans are still unsatisfied. Some of them have been aggravated by the postwar increases in population. The total food production of Latin America has shown a considerable increase in every year except one since the end of World War II, reaching a volume in 1954-1955 which was almost two-fifths greater than in the prewar period, and in addition the volume of food exports from Latin America has declined since the war by about 10 per cent below the prewar level. But Latin Americans remain underfed. Populations have grown so fast that per capita food production and food consumption are below prewar levels, whereas both per capita food production and food consumption considerably exceed prewar averages in other major areas of the world. Calculated on the basis of 100 as the prewar average, per capita food production reached an index number of 106 in 1954-1955 in the Near East, 109 in both western Europe and Africa, 113 in the United States, but only 94 in Latin America. In the matter of food consumption the same relative situation exists in several countries of Latin America where food consumption remains below the very inadequate prewar figures, despite the considerable rise in food consumption since the war in most other areas of the world. In Latin America the problem of enabling people to obtain the food which they need for healthy and productive living has not yet been solved.[9] This problem is aggravated by the continuing, almost astronomical increases in the cost of living. In the year between December, 1955, and December, 1956,

6. United Nations, Economic Commission for Latin America, *Economic Survey of Latin America, 1953,* 3-9.
7. Dr. Raúl Prebisch, Address at the Twentieth Session of the United Nations Economic and Social Council, July 14, 1955, *Official Records,* 875th meeting, 73.
8. United Nations, Economic Commission for Latin America, *Economic Survey of Latin America, 1956* (New York, 1957), 3.
9. United Nations, Food and Agriculture Organization, *The State of Food and Agriculture, 1955: Review of a Decade and Outlook* (Rome, Italy, September, 1955), 7-8, 95-97, 223.

the cost of living in Argentina, for example, rose by almost 17 per cent, in Brazil by 20-22 per cent, in Chile by 56 per cent, and in Bolivia by more than 169 per cent![10]

Visitors to Latin America are often shocked at the monotonous dietary regimen of the *peones*—beans, *tortillas, tortillas* and beans. They complain of the lack of meat, eggs, fish, milk, fruits, and sweets. In some of the cattle-raising countries they disapprove of the excessive consumption of meat. But many of these native diets are healthful diets, proved so by centuries of experience. The lack of milk and white potatoes does not necessarily make them deficient in body-building and energy-producing elements. We are unrealistic and lacking in comprehension if we conclude that Latin Americans are not healthy unless they eat our foods.[11] Besides, attempts to change the dietary habits of a people are often fiercely resented and can become a fertile source of international discord. Only educational effort and suggestion gradually and persuasively applied will effect any constructive or durable change in their dietary regimen. That deficiencies exist in the diets of large populations in Latin America is undeniable, but the means for remedying them are usually found near at hand, requiring only education and a little knowledgeable industry to make them available. Unintelligent or hasty attempts to remedy them may throw the reasonably satisfactory customary diets out of balance and produce more serious deficiencies than now exist.

In Latin America agricultural techniques, health and sanitation practices, and educational activities are generally less advanced than in the United States. The forms that technical assistance may take include the preparation of studies and surveys of economic problems, needs, and potential lines of development; the furnishing of expert advisers on administrative problems and development projects; the establishment and operation of research and experimental centers; the furnishing of instruction in the use of materials and equipment; the translation of textbooks and reports; the exchanging of students and teachers; and the operating of technical libraries and film services. Among the serious problems in agriculture which need to be

10. United Nations, Economic Commission for Latin America, *Economic Survey of Latin America, 1956,* 10, 12, 15.
11. René Cravioto B., *et al.,* "Composition of Typical Mexican Foods," *Journal of Nutrition,* XXIX (May, 1945), 327-328; and R. K. Anderson, *et al.,* "A Study of the Nutritional Status and Food Habits of Otomi Indians in the Mezquital Valley of Mexico," *American Journal of Public Health and the Nation's Health,* XXXVI (1946), 902.

dealt with by means of both local programs of self-help and technical assistance from abroad may be mentioned those involving land tenure, credit facilities, transportation services between centers of production and centers of consumption, fertilizers, irrigation, soil surveys, market reporting, storage facilities, grading operations for agricultural produce, agricultural extension services, and mechanization of agricultural processes. Development along these lines is required in the interest of a fair balance between these primary activities and industrial expansion. An increase in agricultural productivity, which will result from the solution of these problems, will be urgently called for as populations increase. It is also a necessary prerequisite to industrial development, for industry depends upon crop production and livestock for many of its basic supplies of raw materials as well as for the feeding of newly recruited industrial workers. Such forms of technical assistance offer the possibility of reaching the vast majority of Latin Americans who cannot be reached by costly spending programs. These are the underprivileged *peones* to whom the promises of Communist and other leveling movements hold out constant allurements.

But all such assistance should be offered only when the social environment in a Latin American country is ready to receive it, and it should be provided with the utmost diplomacy by officials who like and understand Latin Americans.[12] In Mexico, Guatemala, and many other Latin American countries instruction in needlework, for example, is a work of supererogation. Technical assistance in that field, where the women of Latin America have skilled themselves for centuries in superlatively beautiful needle handicraft, might well be the other way around—from them to the women of the United States. In weaving, leather craft, and ceramics Latin Americans also excel.

A successful early experiment in inter-American technical assistance was carried through by President Domingo Faustino Sarmiento of Argentina in the 1870's, when he employed school teachers from

12. National Planning Association, *Technical Cooperation in Latin America: Recommendations for the Future by the NPA Special Policy Committee on Technical Cooperation* (Washington, 1956), 24. For other studies of the problems and achievements of technical assistance in Latin America see in the same series by the National Planning Association, *Technical Cooperation—Sowing the Seeds of Progress* (Washington, 1955), *The Role of Universities in Technical Cooperation* (Washington, 1955), *Case Study of the Agricultural Program of ACAR in Brazil* by Arthur T. Mosher (Washington, 1955), and *Administration of Bilateral Technical Cooperation* (Washington, 1956). See also Philip M. Glick, *The Administration of Technical Assistance: Growth in the Americas,* Chicago, 1957.

the United States to serve as teachers in Argentina's new normal schools. It was arranged at Argentina's request and was assisted by educational authorities in the United States, including Sarmiento's friend Horace Mann.[13] Projects of technical assistance to Latin America can be successfully carried out only in full cooperation with the host country; they should be undertaken only in response to expressed needs. Moreover, they must be susceptible of being readily adapted and retained by the recipient country. An example of the wrong kind of project was the "latrine project" in World War II. Certain sanitary engineers from the United States, convinced that latrines were indispensable, finally observed that in certain areas of tropical Latin America latrines, instead of lessening the incidence of enteric diseases, actually increased it. The underground latrines which they were so assiduously constructing hampered the germicidal effect of the sun's rays. The latrine regimen was found not to be desirable.

Progress in agriculture and manufacturing industry are closely linked. Underdeveloped countries believe they remain poor because they have few factories. They see that industrial undertakings and the technical progress achieved by the Anglo-American peoples enable men to gain control over their environment, to reach new levels of productive efficiency, and to rise above a mere vegetable existence. Industrialization is considered to be synonymous with civilization. It is expected to provide the means of raising levels of living, of incorporating the Indian in the national society, of promoting labor specialization, of creating modern forms of wealth, and of converting time into a significant factor in living. It will diversify the economy of a country and reduce its vulnerability to shocks from abroad.

Latin America is today at about the stage of industrialization reached by the United States in the 1870's.[14] It has passed the first stage of industrialization, which is the manufacture of simple consumer goods, and some of the countries are advancing to the next stage, which is the manufacture of intermediate products and capital goods.[15] Seven countries of Latin America were reported in 1956 as either already having an iron and steel industry or being in a position to establish one: Argentina, Brazil, Chile, Colombia, Mexico, Peru,

13. Tristán Enrique Guevara, *Las Maestras Norteamericanas que Trajo Sarmiento* [Buenos Aires? 1954], *passim*.
14. George Wythe, *Industry in Latin America*, 2d ed. (New York, 1949), [12].
15. Dr. Raúl Prebisch, address at the Twentieth Session of the United Nations Economic and Social Council, July 14, 1955, *cit. sup.*, 73.

and Venezuela.[16] Like the United States in the 1870's, Latin America still has vast natural resources to be exploited. Besides, it has an enormous actual and potential demand for manufactured products in the widespread lack of the basic goods of life. The previous unawareness and wantlessness of the people in relation to these goods largely disappeared during World War II, and now their demands are insatiable. Their increased earnings during both the war and postwar periods led to the development of higher living requirements than ever before and the creation of new needs.

* * *

Latin Americans have no more urgent concern than the hastening of their material progress. In many towns of considerable size and even in some cities electrical power is not provided to dwellings from noon until dark because the electricity-producing facilities are inadequate. When the lights come on in the gathering darkness of evening, the residents hail it with cheers. Latin America needs more electrification, improved facilities for transportation and communication, works of irrigation, better housing, and mechanization of agriculture.[17] This type of development is a fundamental prerequisite to any increase in the gross product of Latin America, to a diversification of domestic production, and to reduction of dependence on foreign trade. In certain countries the pressure of population and urban congestion compel the conclusion that expanded public health and sanitation campaigns, which will lower the rate of infant mortality, increase adult resistance to disease, and lengthen the life span, will be ineffective in solving basic social and economic problems unless they are accompanied by at least modest programs of industrialization which will provide an adequate livelihood for urban workers on a cash-wage basis. By 1975 Latin America's economically active population, it is estimated, will have increased by approximately 38 million, of whom some 33 million will have to seek productive occupations outside agriculture, that is to say, in industry.[18] Full employment,

16. United Nations, Department of Public Information, *The Economic Growth of Twenty Republics*, 13.
17. Needed areas of investment and specific investment proposals in Latin America were discussed at the Inter-American Investment Conference which met at New Orleans in February-March, 1955.
18. Economic Commission for Latin America, Press Section, "Conclusion of the First Meeting of the Group of Latin American Experts on the Regional Market," Santiago, Chile, February 11, 1958, typewritten, 2-3.

then, will require increased industrial activity, but such activity will not be incompatible with the maintenance and even the expansion of traditional agricultural activity.[19]

As mentioned earlier, the pace of Latin America's industrial development, at least temporarily, slackened after 1950. The rate of increase in its industrial output fell from an average of 7.7 per cent for the period 1945-1950 to 4.1 per cent in 1952 and only 1.3 per cent in 1953. Both capital investment in industry and the proportion of Latin America's total labor force employed in industry correspondingly declined.[20] But industrialization need not always be thought of exclusively in terms of steel plants. It should be adapted rather to special conditions in each country and should serve not as an end in itself but as a means to the balanced development of the country, supplementing the necessary agricultural and other extractive occupations.[21] It may mean, and perhaps in most of the Latin American areas where agricultural activities predominate ought to mean, the development of rural industries which will use locally available raw materials, will meet the need of farmers for industrial products, and will at the same time provide work for farmers who may be expected to leave the farms as agriculture becomes modernized and mechanized. Such a rural industry already exists in the sugar *centrales* of Cuba which provide seasonal occupation for farm labor. Agricultural processing industries offer some of the most promising forms of industrial development in Latin America. Other industries that are susceptible of this same decentralized development include the manufacture of small tools, glass, textiles, and cement. The manufacture for export of instant coffee from Latin America's own washed coffee beans offers large possibilities. But unless such industries, even if they are only small enterprises, are developed as part of a general rehabilitation of the nation's economy, they may actually depress the economy of adjoining areas.

In estimating the future capabilities of the Latin Americans for industrial development it must be remembered that, as a committee

19. United Nations, Department of Economic and Social Affairs, *Inter Latin American Trade: Current Problems* (New York, January, 1957), 8.
20. United Nations, Economic Commission for Latin America, *Economic Survey of Latin America, 1953*, 10-11, 205.
21. Alberto Lleras Camargo, "The Two Americas," *The Lamp* (Standard Oil Company of New Jersey), XXXVI, 3 (September, 1954), 4. See also United Nations, Department of Economic Affairs, *A Study of Trade between Latin America and Europe* (Geneva, January, 1953), 27.

of the National Research Council pointed out in 1941, "the entire culture of the people is one of art rather than of science."[22] Their educational systems have stressed the so-called cultural and legalistic studies. Latin Americans have not set a premium on entrepreneurial enterprise nor cultivated a standard of values which made physical welfare or business success a primary objective. Their ruling classes have not done what they should have done to bring their countries into step with the modern world. They have not created the right conditions for economic development but have allowed foreigners to take the initiative. And yet Latin Americans are proving as expert at technical operations as their Anglo-American contemporaries. They have at their disposal the enormous wealth of modern techniques which have been developed in the pioneering industrial nations. But they cannot take advantage of them except through the interest and technical knowledge of outsiders. In the fields in which Latin Americans are not proficient they need technological assistance from the technologically advanced nations unless they are to be obliged to recapitulate for themselves the inventive experience of those nations. But up-to-date technology is private property and can be had only at a price. Operation Bootstrap is difficult when even the bootstraps have to be imported. As a method by which the Latin American nations may obtain the necessary means of progress the United Nations Economic Commission for Latin America has emphasized the need for national programming of economic development. Each Latin American government should, under the recommendation of the commission, devise "a well-conceived programme based on careful projections of future demand for consumer and capital goods and of the capacity to import" and should then "take advantage of periods of foreign exchange ease to restrict non-essential imports and to purchase the capital goods required."[23]

For the further development of Latin America along these lines the capital and other resources of the United States are indispensable.[24] After 1939 the United States government assumed large responsibilities toward Latin America. As it took the lead in both

22. Quoted in J. Fred Rippy, *Latin America and the Industrial Age,* 2d ed. (New York, 1947), 7.
23. United Nations, Economic Commission for Latin America, *Economic Survey of Latin America, 1954,* 21.
24. See address by President Juscelino Kubitschek before the Commercial Association of Santos, São Paulo, Brazil, January 29, 1957, *Diário Oficial,* Rio de Janeiro, January 20, 1957, 2189-2190.

broadening and fulfilling the political guaranties of the Monroe Doctrine, it also established, in effect, an economic Monroe Doctrine for the American hemisphere, in response to both its own and Latin America's requirements.[25] During World War II the United States furnished economic assistance to Latin America by constructing highways, by extending official credits to needy governments, by financing developmental projects, by shipping medical supplies and foodstuffs for emergency relief, by subsidizing experimentation on new crops, by supporting health and sanitation projects, and in many other ways. During the period of World War II, as noted above, the dollar aid furnished to Latin America in the form of grants and credits by the United States government totaled $742 million. In the postwar period from July 1, 1945, through December 31, 1952, this government's assistance to Latin America reached $941 million. During the twelve-year period 1940-1952 the United States therefore gave dollar aid to Latin America in the total amount of $1,683 million.[26] This total does not include indirect aid given by the United States in the form of contributions to the United Nations, the Organization of American States and its specialized organizations, the International Children's Fund, the International Bank, the International Monetary Fund, and several other organizations. In the postwar period the major recipients of United States government aid to Latin America were Argentina, Brazil, Chile, and Mexico; but every Latin American country received some grants, loans, and other credits during that period.[27]

The Latin American countries need the participation of the United States in their economic development. During the nineteenth century foreign capital invested in Latin America was directed mainly toward the expansion of exports and corollary transportation activities. It was not much concerned with the domestic consumption requirements of the Latin American countries. The cooperation of United States private capital with local Latin American interests,

25. Carlos Saavedra Lamas, "Monroismo Económico," *Desfile* (weekly newsmagazine), Buenos Aires, September 12, 1941.
26. Department of Commerce, Office of Business Economics, *Foreign Aid by the United States Government.* See also Library of Congress, Legislative Reference Service, *Total Economic and Military Aid Extended by the United States Government to All Foreign Countries, July 1, 1940-December 31, 1951* (Washington, May 27, 1952).
27. J. Fred Rippy, "U.S. Government Assistance to the Underdeveloped Countries, 1945-1953," *Inter-American Economic Affairs,* VIII (Spring, 1955), 45.

both private and governmental, for the satisfaction of these pressing consumption requirements, representing a relatively new area of foreign capital interest, offers great possibilities for mutually helpful activity.[28] Industries primarily designed to serve Latin America's needs, and combining the resources, equipment, capital, and technical skills of the Latin American nations with those of the United States, furnish a fruitful field for the best type of economic cooperation.

Such cooperation can offer large benefits to the United States. Well-developed, industrialized countries in Latin America will supply not only the raw-materials imports which the United States requires but also enlarged markets for its exports. The rational development of industry tends to expand international trade. It is useful to note that the 15 million people of Canada, a well-developed and industrialized country, bought almost as much from the United States in 1952 as the 162 million people of Latin America.[29] The lack of coal, which has been considered a deterrent to Latin American industrialization in the past, ceases to be important as Latin America's enormous petroleum resources are further developed. Its hydroelectric energy has scarcely been tapped. Five Latin American countries—Brazil, Peru, Venezuela, Colombia, and Argentina—have appreciable hydroelectric potential, but only Brazil has yet developed any significant amount of its hydroelectric energy.[30]

Rapid industrialization offers the only means by which these countries can hope to escape the pressure of their exploding populations against their limited agricultural resources. But the industrialization which is required cannot be brought about because of the scarcity of capital. For this reason some of them have already begun to look to atomic power as a means of reducing the foreign capital required for their industrialization.[31] Intensive prospecting for radioactive

28. See Dr. Raúl Prebisch, Address at the Informal Discussion on Economic Development During the Seventh Annual Meeting of Governors of the International Bank for Reconstruction and Development, September 10, 1952, International Bank for Reconstruction and Development, Seventh Annual Meeting, Board of Governors, Mexico, D.F., Document No. 19.

29. United Nations, Statistical Office, International Monetary Fund, and International Bank for Reconstruction and Development, *Direction of International Trade: Annual Data for the Years 1937, 1938, and 1948-1952*, 10, 394.

30. President's Materials Policy Commission, William S. Paley, Chairman, Report to the President, *Resources for Freedom*, III, *The Outlook for Energy Sources* (Washington, June, 1952), 40.

31. Sam H. Schurr and Jacob Marshak, *Economic Aspects of Atomic Power* (Princeton, 1950), 270-273; and United Nations, Department of Economic and Social Affairs, *Energy in Latin America* (Geneva, 1957), 70-71.

minerals is being carried on in several Latin American countries with gratifying results. Brazil has been discovered to be one of the countries of the world most richly endowed with this resource and is working its monazite deposits. Argentina has developed facilities for producing metallic uranium. Uranium, plutonium, and other fissionable elements are usually found wherever the heavy metals are found. These latter were deposited in Latin America more abundantly perhaps than in any other major area of the world. The mines of Guanajuato and of Potosí may again become as profitable in our atomic century by reason of their deposits of fissionable elements as they were in the sixteenth and seventeenth centuries as sources of silver and gold.

To stimulate industrial and other types of economic undertakings which will move Latin America forward into the modern age, the Eisenhower administration has increased the lending authority of the Export-Import Bank operating in the field of public loans. Secretary of State Dulles informed the Tenth International Conference of American States, meeting in Caracas in March, 1954, that the bank would give increased consideration to loans for developmental purposes.[32] The Eisenhower administration has also given the bank a new authority to underwrite exports which are privately financed. Accordingly the total of loans to Latin America authorized by the Export-Import Bank increased considerably, reaching $420 million in 1956.

In a message to the Meeting of American Ministers of Finance or Economy, held at Quitandinha, Brazil, in November-December, 1954, President Eisenhower revived President Roosevelt's phrase of 1942 by calling upon all the Latin American nations to "join with the Delegation of the United States in common dedication to the Policy of the Good Partner." But at that conference the United States was confronted with a strong Latin American demand, led by the Chilean delegation, for the establishment of an Inter-American Bank which would finance economic development in Latin America with Latin America's own resources. According to figures supplied by the International Monetary Fund, asserted the principal Chilean delegate, Arturo Maschke, president of the Central Bank of Chile, the twenty Latin American countries possessed, as of March 31, 1954, some $3,475 million in gold and securities which could be used as capital for the bank. When the Latin American nations unanimously voted to draft plans for such a regional banking institution, the

32. *Department of State Bulletin,* XXX (March 15, 1954), 379-383.

United States alone abstained. Countering the Latin American decision, the United States delegation then offered to furnish technical aid which would assist Latin America in creating their institution and finally agreed to the setting up of an International Finance Corporation, which had been discussed since 1951, to encourage and invest in private business undertakings in the Latin American countries.[33] Of the total of $100 million capital of this new corporation the United States offered to furnish $35,168,000, or more than one-third.

These actions were supplemented by increased financial assistance by the United States government. During the first year of the Eisenhower administration the dollar aid which the United States made available to Latin America reached $400 million, or 6.2 per cent of the total United States aid to all countries of the world. This was more than a twofold increase over the dollar aid furnished to Latin America during the last year of the Truman administration. But this amount was cut back to $124 million in 1954 and $102 million in 1955. In the latter year United States deliveries of military supplies and equipment to Latin America reached the lowest point in any year since the inauguration of the Mutual Defense Assistance program. At the same time the Technical Assistance program was considerably increased in Guatemala because of the accession of the Castillo-Armas government to power.[34]

Looking broadly at the technical assistance program of the United States in Latin America since the end of World War II, the accompanying table shows the total direct aid furnished to Latin America by the United States government from July 1, 1945, through December 31, 1955. The largest grants have gone respectively to Mexico, Bolivia, and Brazil, with substantial amounts also to Peru, Chile, Haiti, and Guatemala. Of these amounts large sums were spent in Mexico in efforts to eradicate the hoof-and-mouth disease which was threatening to spread to herds in the United States; considerable financial assistance was given to relieve starvation in Bolivia; and Technical Assistance projects were generously financed in these and

33. Address of Secretary of the Treasury, George M. Humphrey, at the Meeting of Ministers of Finance or Economy at Quitandinha, November 23, 1954, *Department of State Bulletin*, XXXI (December 6, 1954), 868; and Organization of American States [Inter-American Economic and Social Council], *op. cit.*

34. Department of Commerce, Office of Business Economics, *Foreign Grants and Credits by the United States Government*, December, 1955, Quarter, 6, and March, 1956, Quarter, S-6.

several other countries, particularly Brazil, Guatemala, Haiti, Costa Rica, and Panama. Nevertheless all the economic aid furnished by the United States from public funds ($625 million) to all the Latin American countries, with their 175 million people, from the end of World War II to the end of the calendar year 1958 was less than that furnished to Yugoslavia with only 20 million people ($795 mil-

DIRECT AID TO LATIN AMERICA
BY THE UNITED STATES GOVERNMENT
July 1, 1945-December 31, 1955
(thousands of dollars)

Country	Grants	Credits Utilized	Total
Argentina	$ 198	$ 101,675	$ 101,873
Bolivia	42,554	39,912	82,466
Brazil	23,707	599,692	623,399
Chile	10,504	121,746	132,250
Colombia	7,166	61,045	68,211
Costa Rica	13,899	3,857	17,756
Cuba	1,437	26,490	27,927
Dominican Republic	2,005	——	2,005
Ecuador	8,514	26,500	35,014
El Salvador	5,026	576	5,602
Guatemala	22,311	494	22,805
Haiti	11,719	20,408	32,127
Honduras	6,005	223	6,228
Mexico	105,311	229,144	334,455
Nicaragua	10,530	600	11,130
Panama	9,113	4,000	13,113
Paraguay	8,273	825	9,098
Peru	14,940	27,621	42,561
Uruguay	1,994	11,554	13,548
Venezuela	2,152	13,301	15,453
Unspecified	300,109	6,069	306,178
Totals (rounded)	$607,469	$1,295,733	$1,903,200

Source: Adapted from Department of Commerce, Office of Business Economics, *Foreign Grants and Credits by the United States Government,* December, 1955, Quarter and March, 1956, Quarter, tables 3 and 6.

lion). Besides, the United States was discriminating among the Latin American countries. It was distributing its largess unequally, giving candy to one child and not to another.

Direct aid in the form of dollar grants and credits supplied by the United States to Latin America in the postwar period totaled $1,295 million at the end of 1955. This represented 2.4 per cent of the total direct aid furnished by the United States to all foreign countries during that period as compared with an allocation of

8.7 per cent to the Near East and Africa during the same period and more than 20 per cent to non-Communist Asia and the Pacific area. The share allocated to Latin America was the smallest furnished to any major area of the world except eastern Europe. This proportion was altered somewhat in favor of Latin America when the Eisenhower administration recommended increased direct aid to that area in both fiscal years 1956 and 1957, and in both years Congress voted larger appropriations for the Latin American countries than the administration requested.[35] But all this left Latin America still a long way from the position of strength in our "Western Hemisphere Gibraltar of Western Civilization" which was envisaged for it by former President Herbert Hoover.[36]

Figures on direct aid do not tell the whole story. Indirect aid must also be taken into consideration in the computation of the total aid furnished by the United States to Latin America as well as other areas of the world since World War II. In the case of Latin America the totals given in the table would have to be supplemented by approximately $25 million contributed by the United States toward the construction of the Inter-American and related highways, the largest amounts having gone respectively to Costa Rica, Guatemala, Nicaragua, and Panama. In addition more than $4.5 million has been furnished as the share of the United States in the technical aid projects of the Organization of American States in Latin America, financing the work of such agencies as the Pan American Union, the Pan American Sanitary Bureau, the Inter-American Institute of Agricultural Sciences, the Pan American Institute of Geography and History, the American International Institute for the Protection of Childhood, the Pan American Railway Congress Association, the Inter-American Indian Institute, and the Inter-American Radio Office. These totals should also be supplemented by the substantial aid furnished by the United States to Latin America through the United Nations and its various agencies. The United States has supplied a major part of the capital for World Bank loans to many Latin American countries, which totaled $579.2 million during the fiscal years 1948-1955; it contributed more than 51 per cent of the grants allocated by the United Nations Technical Assistance Board

35. J. Fred Rippy, "Contributions of the U.S. Government to Latin America, Fiscal Year 1956," *Inter-American Economic Affairs*, IX (Autumn, 1955), 87-96.
36. Speech of December 20, 1950, *New York Times*, December 21, 1950.

to Latin America, which totaled almost $20 million during 1950-1955; and it supplied over 67 per cent of the grants made by the United Nations Children's Fund to Latin America, which have amounted to almost $16 million. The United States also contributes a large part of the maintenance cost of other world organizations in which the Latin American countries are represented and from which they derive benefits. In addition, United States government funds support educational exchange programs and several educational institutions— elementary and secondary—in Latin America. But this indirect aid which is made available to Latin America in the name of the disbursing organizations is not widely recognized as coming from the United States.[37]

As new foreign investment in Latin America has tapered off, several Latin American governments have relaxed their restrictions against it. An Argentine law of August, 1953, accorded to certain kinds of foreign private capital, if duly approved by the government, the same treatment as domestic capital. Profits up to 8 per cent may be transferred to the home country after two years, and from 10 to 20 per cent of the original capital may be repatriated after ten years. Foreign investments which are declared to be "of national interest" may even be given tariff protection, import quotas, and export subsidies.[38] In early 1955, after the downfall of the Perón government, Argentina authorized the large-scale participation of foreign oil companies in developing the petroleum resources of that country. By the end of 1956 Argentina had abolished all restrictions on remittances of profits on new capital invested in that country.[39] Chile, Bolivia, and Paraguay have also offered special inducements to foreign private capital, and in 1954 Costa Rica and Peru joined Haiti in concluding investment insurance agreements with the United States, which had been provided for in the Mutual Security Act of 1954.[40] But a different course was followed by Brazil. When Dr. Oswaldo

37. Credit is due to Professor J. Fred Rippy of the University of Chicago for useful leads to some of this statistical information, particularly for information contained in his manuscript article "A Decade of Assistance to Latin America by the Government of the United States," which was subsequently incorporated as Chapter 5 in his *Globe and Hemisphere*, Chicago, 1958.
38. United Nations, Department of Economic and Social Affairs, *Foreign Capital in Latin America*, 41-42.
39. United Nations, Economic Commission for Latin America, *Economic Survey of Latin America, 1956*, 38.
40. International Development Advisory Board, *An Economic Program for the Americas*, 27-30.

Aranha became Finance Minister of Brazil in late 1953 he announced that foreign capital was not necessary to his country and that if foreign companies objected to proposed new taxes "they can leave; it makes no difference." Brazil, he declared, had "depended too much on outside aid . . . we must learn to stand on our own feet."[41]

An upswing in private foreign investment in Latin America began to appear in 1955. The total net inflow of capital into the area in that year reached $250 million and in 1956 rose to $600 million. By the latter year this investment was large enough to replace 60 per cent of the capital outflow of profits and interest from Latin America. But much of this new investment, as formerly, was channeled into production for export and did not meet the domestic consumer needs of the recipient countries. It has been directed principally into metallurgical, mechanical, and chemical industries in Brazil, copper in Chile, petroleum in Venezuela, and the same categories of industries in Peru and Mexico.[42]

Foreign assistance in national development cannot take the place of the will and determination of the recipient nation itself. All the people of a country must be made to feel that they have a stake in economic progress and will benefit from it. "National development must be based primarily on national resources and must come largely from the people concerned. . . . It is closely related to their habits and attitudes of work, saving, venturesomeness, and adaptability"[43] For example, the habit of privately endowed philanthropy and organized social service, which has provided the accumulated capital for many technical advances in health and education in the Anglo-American world, has not become prevalent among Latin Americans. The wealthy have an inordinate propensity for high living and for flaunting their riches in socially unproductive and almost defiantly provocative ways. The moral climate does not set a high premium on thrift and industry. Nor is it realized that the social value of money which is spent on luxuries and riotous living is negligible or perhaps even negative. Latin Americans need to learn, for example, that municipal pure-water systems will give greater benefits to their economies than many hundreds of high-powered motor cars.

41. *New York Times*, November 14, 1953.
42. United Nations, Economic Commission for Latin America, *Economic Survey of Latin America, 1956*, 38-40.
43. Department of State, *Point Four: Cooperative Program for Aid in the Development of Economically Underdeveloped Areas*, 3.

In many of these respects the United States, with the multifarious products of its industry and its inventive genius, is working a silent, and perhaps unintended revolution. Its gospel of progress is making its conquests. Its formulas and processes of economic efficiency are becoming partially acclimated in some Latin American countries. The shiploads and trainloads of refrigerators, deep-freeze units, late-model automobiles, television sets, and all the other manufactures of its industrial civilization are altering the character of Latin American life, serving as impressive examples not only of Anglo-American wizardry but also of Anglo-American habits of industry and team-work. They are jolting the extreme traditionalism of many of these countries, based upon distinctions of race, sex, class, and inherited economic status. They are resulting in what has been called the "Cocacolazation" of Latin America. The impact already made upon certain Latin American countries by Yankee materialism is shown not only by their tremendous material development since World War II but also by their imitation of Yankee business ingenuity.

But, it must be understood, the very material wealth and power of the United States, symbolized by the outpourings of its money and its manufactured products, make a closer *acercamiento* between it and the Latin American countries difficult. Those countries feel a natural apprehensiveness in cultivating closer relations with a neighboring colossus, for by doing so they run the risk either of succumbing too completely to its influence or, as dependents weak in bargaining power, of being repulsed by it. They feel that they excel in human and spiritual qualities while in contrast the United States, though possessing an admittedly distinctive and profound culture, nevertheless is mainly dedicated to pragmatic and material values. They fear that they cannot cultivate their own values and perfect their own nationality and culture in too close alliance with the United States. "We are two complementary civilizations," declares the distinguished Brazilian exponent of closer inter-American relations, Dr. Alceu Amoroso Lima, "that are tied together in a natural alliance which we ought to cultivate and develop. Let us not imitate the United States," Dr. Lima enjoins his fellow Latin Americans, "if we wish, as we should, to live intimately allied with it. It is not through our similarities but rather through our diversities that we ought to come together."[44]

Latin Americans, in following the cultural, technological, and in-

44. *A Realidade Americana* (Rio de Janeiro, 1954), 245.

dustrial progress of the United States, will, it is hoped, avoid imitating it too closely and will never sacrifice their own national identity —whether intellectual, spiritual, or even political—in order to adopt wholesale its institutions and ways of living. There is much in the United States that may be wholly unsuitable for transplantation into Latin America and much in Latin America that may be wholly unsuitable for transplantation into the United States. Plagiarism between them is to be deplored. "In order to achieve closer relations," wrote Roberto García Peña of Colombia in 1944, "it is not necessary to assimilate one another; and perhaps it would be more beneficial for the future of our relations to accentuate our respective natures."[45] *La Mañana* of Montevideo (November 15, 1945) observed, "The people of the United States have created their own national character—peculiar to themselves and vigorous; we Latin Americans have ours." The two can be accommodated without assimilation and without "the necessity of hybrid imitations." Elephant's ears would have looked grotesque indeed on Don Quixote's mule.

Advances in industrialization are expected, however, to bring to Latin America not only a new emphasis upon the spirit of business enterprise, new attention to technical training and qualities of inventiveness, and the multiplication of means for the production and accumulation of wealth but also changes in social structure and points of view. The development of industry cannot be separated from a process of radical social and economic change for most of Latin America. It can be expected to strengthen national feeling and to intensify the demand for economic and political freedom. Since its benefits cannot be maximized as long as large numbers of the population remain at a low economic level and are unable to buy the products of the new industries, it will undoubtedly lead to change in the values of human labor and will thus serve as a means toward the creation of middle-class societies, as it has done in countries already industrialized. If the experience of these countries can be used as a guide, industrialization will have a homogenizing effect upon the existing social system tending to reduce the level and numbers of the upper class and to raise the level and numbers of the lower class. It may be the means of effecting the bourgeois revolution in Latin America and of creating a middle-class society with all that such a society connotes for political stability and economic progress. It may

45. *El Tiempo*, Bogotá, May 10, 1944.

also tend to reduce the power of the traditional landholding elites and to transfer it to the rising industrial, labor, and commercial interests, with resulting changes in cultural values and economic relationships. These new interests will demand entry into the seats of power and into the upper social strata.[46]

* * *

The remodeled inter-American system holds great potentialities for future cooperative action among the nations of the Western Hemisphere. The objectives of the Organization of American States, as stated in Article 4 of its charter, are

(a) To strengthen the peace and security of the continent;
(b) To prevent possible causes of difficulties and to ensure the pacific settlement of disputes that may arise among the Member States;
(c) To provide for common action on the part of those States in the event of aggression;
(d) To seek the solution of political, juridical and economic problems that may arise among them; and
(e) To promote, by cooperative action, their economic, social and cultural development.

All the American nations are entitled as of right to membership in the new Organization of American States and may be represented at the Inter-American Conference, which under the charter is the supreme body of the inter-American system and which decides general questions of action and policy relating to the functioning of the organization. This conference is expected to meet every five years but may be convoked in extraordinary session at any time by two-thirds of the members.

The second ranking body of the Organization of American States is the Meeting of Consultation of Ministers of Foreign Affairs, which was originally provided for in the Inter-American Conferences at Buenos Aires in 1936 and Lima in 1938. Three such meetings were held during World War II—at Panama in 1939, Havana in 1940, and Rio de Janeiro in 1942. A fourth, convened for the purpose of strengthening the Americas against the "aggressive policy of international communism," met at Washington in March-April, 1951;

46. Ralph L. Beals, "Social Stratification in Latin America," *American Journal of Sociology*, LVIII (January, 1953), 336.

and a fifth met in Santiago, Chile, in August, 1959, to consider the problem of maintaining peace in the Caribbean area. This body meets not at regular or stated times but only in emergencies when time does not permit the slower processes of the Inter-American Conference to operate. Meetings of Consultation are to be held under the charter when requested by a member state and summoned by a majority of the members of the Organization of American States. Or in cases of aggression against an American state a Meeting of Consultation may be called immediately by the chairman of the Council of the Organization to agree upon measures which must be taken to assist the victim of the aggression and to protect the security of the hemisphere. In this latter case the foreign ministers are assisted by the Advisory Defense Committee, which is concerned with problems of military cooperation under existing treaties on collective security.

The permanent or continuing bodies of the Organization of American States are the Council of the Organization and the Pan American Union. The former, which takes the place of the old Governing Board, sits continuously in Washington and includes a representative of each of the twenty-one member nations especially designated as its representative with the rank of ambassador. The council is charged with carrying out specific assignments of the Inter-American Conference and the Meeting of Consultation and with serving provisionally as the Organ of Consultation under the above-mentioned Inter-American Treaty of Reciprocal Assistance. The council is also responsible in a general way for the operation of both the Pan American Union, which serves under the charter as the permanent central secretariat of the Organization of American States in Washington, and its three subsidiary organs, the Inter-American Economic and Social Council, the Inter-American Council of Jurists, and the Inter-American Cultural Council; and it coordinates the relations of the Organization of American States with the specialized agencies.

In the Charter of Bogotá these specialized agencies are defined as those which are intergovernmental, which are established by multilateral agreements, and which perform specific functions in the inter-American system. Totaling some thirty in number in the early 1950's they had grown up over the years to carry out technical programs in such fields as public health, agriculture, child welfare, cartography, geography, and history. By 1959 their number had been reduced to six. Though they enjoy "technical autonomy" they submit periodic reports to the council and enter into agreements with it determining their relationship to the organization. Since the specialized agencies have been criticized as having a tendency to convoke too many technical conferences, the charter stipulates that specialized conferences shall be convened to "deal with special technical matters or to develop specific aspects of inter-American cooperation" only when an Inter-American Conference or a Meeting of Consultation of Foreign Ministers approves, when inter-American agreements call for them, or when the Council of the Organization authorizes them.

Just as the Organization of American States negotiates agreements with the specialized agencies already operating in the Western Hemisphere, so it negotiates agreements with the specialized agencies of the United Nations. As its first formal arrangement with a world body it approved in May, 1950, an agreement with the International Labour Organization (ILO) defining the relationship that should exist between them. It concluded similar agreements with the United Nations Educational, Scientific, and Cultural Organization (UNESCO) in December, 1950, and with the Food and Agriculture Organization of the United Nations in May, 1952. Jurisdictional problems raised by the work of the long-established Pan American Sanitary Bureau have been solved by an arrangement under which the Bureau serves both as a specialized agency of the Organization of American States and as a regional branch of the World Health Organization (WHO) of the United Nations. The most controversial relationship to be worked out was that between the Economic Commission for Latin America (ECLA) of the United Nations and the Inter-American Economic and Social Council (IA-ECOSOC) of the Organization of American States, which, according to a declaration of the Tenth Inter-American Conference in March, 1954, will continue to function as separate entities.[47]

In its larger relationship with the United Nations, the Organization of American States not only cooperates with it in these and other fields of international action but also serves as a regional agency for security purposes. The problem of collective security or mutual defense of the nations of the American hemisphere was not included

47. Organization of American States, *Annual Report of the Secretary General for the Fiscal Year July 1, 1951-June 30, 1952,* 26; and Resolution LXXXIX, Final Act of the Tenth Inter-American Conference, Caracas, Venezuela, March 1-28, 1954.

on agendas or discussed at inter-American conferences from 1889 until the 1930's. A proposal which was made by President Baltasar Brum of Uruguay in 1920 that an "American League" be formed to defend each of its members against aggression from Europe or from another American nation did not prove acceptable. Even the conferences at Buenos Aires in 1936 and Lima in 1938 cannot be said to have established a security system for the hemisphere, although they recognized the collective concern of all its governments in case of war or threat of war. As long as the United States remained un-involved in World War II, the consultative meetings of foreign min-isters premised the security of the hemisphere upon the maintenance of neutrality. But after Pearl Harbor collective security was deemed to require that the Latin American nations break relations with the nations which were at war with the United States and that they take strong action against subversive activity. The Third Meeting of Foreign Ministers, which convened in January, 1942, prepared the way for the establishment of an Emergency Advisory Committee for Political Defense, and charged it with the duty of recommending to the governments of the American states measures dealing with such matters of political defense as the control of dangerous aliens, the prevention of abuse of citizenship, clandestine crossing of bound-aries, and control of communications. The Third Meeting also created an Inter-American Defense Board to "recommend" to the American governments "the measures necessary for the defense of the Continent." Most of the wartime activity of this board was to plan and recommend action calculated to promote the unification of the defense of the hemisphere. In addition to planning for immedi-ate defense it has concerned itself with long-range security planning from a continental point of view. Though some of its functions have been assumed by the Advisory Defense Committee under the Char-ter of the Organization of American States, the board itself continues to operate independently under Resolution XXXIV of the Final Act of the Bogotá Conference.

The American regional organization is based upon the principle of equality of all member nations. Unlike the United Nations it does not contain any provision for the veto by any one member nor for weighted voting of any type. Nor does it condone the interven-tion of one American nation or group of nations in the affairs of another. At the Fifth Meeting of Foreign Ministers at Santiago in

August, 1959, the foreign ministers of several governments, including United States Secretary of State Christian Herter, reaffirmed their strong opposition to intervention, singly or collectively, by the American states in the affairs of their neighbors. Even in empowering the Inter-American Peace Committee to act to relieve threats to established governments in the hemisphere, the foreign ministers stipulated that the committee could act only with "the express consent of the states in the case of investigations that would have to be made in their respective territories." Under the Inter-American Treaty of Reciprocal Assistance, however, the Organ of Consultation, whether the Meeting of Ministers of Foreign Affairs or the Council of the Organization, reaches its decisions by a vote of two-thirds of the states which have ratified the Pact.

But apart from voting procedures, the role of the United States in the organization is bound to be large by any method of calculating influence—whether by population, by national income, or national wealth. "It always has been and will be the foreign policy of the United States which shapes the political attitude of the Organization of American States," Josef L. Kunz has written in the *American Journal of International Law*.[48] In the fiscal year 1949 the United States made a financial contribution to the organization which amounted to 72 per cent of the total contribution of all the member nations. This disproportionate financial support has been considered an element of weakness in the organization, exposing it to charges of domination by the wealthiest nation. Accordingly at the request of the United States the Council of the Organization agreed in 1950 that its percentage should be reduced to 66 per cent in equal steps over the next two years.[49] In pursuance of this decision the quota of the United States for the fiscal year 1952-1953, based on this new 66 per cent share, was limited to $1,877,402 out of a total budget of $2,859,699. As the budget of the organization has subsequently increased, the quota of the United States, remaining at 66 per cent of the total, has amounted to the following:

48. "Fourth Meeting of Consultation of Ministers of Foreign Affairs of American States," *Americal Journal of International Law*, XLV (October, 1951), 743-744.
49. Organization of American States, *Annual Report of the Secretary General for the Fiscal Year July 1, 1952-June 30, 1953* (Washington, 1953), Appendix V.

Fiscal Years	Total Budget	United States Quota
1953-1954	$3,459,796	$2,283,465
1954-1955	3,401,755	2,245,158
1955-1956	3,699,941	2,441,961
1956-1957	3,938,428	2,599,363
1957-1958	4,287,286	2,829,286
1958-1959	6,433,140	4,245,873
1959-1960 (est.)	7,235,544	4,775,459

The removal of cultural or psychological barriers to improved inter-American relations has long been a primary program of the inter-American system. This program, which has been carried out through the normal functioning of the various departments of the Pan American Union since 1890, has been interpreted as requiring not the superimposition of unwanted cultures but rather the mutual interchange of ideas and appreciation of cultural differences. The media which have been used have included lectures, concerts, publications, and moving pictures. These, along with the newer ones such as radio and television, offer almost limitless possibilities for promoting closer inter-American relations. The principal limiting factors are language differences, illiteracy, difficulties of communication and transportation, and lack of adequate financial support from member governments. Another is the intrinsic difficulty of giving mass appeal to this program. Exchange of rarefied or abstract ideas among intellectuals, particularly those who lack political influence, does not significantly advance, and indeed may actually retard the progress of inter-American relations. By reason of these difficulties, therefore, it is probable that the inter-American organizations remain unknown to tens of millions of persons throughout the Americas or are known only as a kind of mail-order house in Washington for distributing pamphlets and magazines. "Pan Americanism has existed for more than sixty years as a system and it still has not succeeded in penetrating the consciousness of the Latin American peoples," concludes the Mexican publicist Jorge Castañeda.[50] It has made even less impression on the people of the United States.

In order to remove some of these difficulties and at the same time to raise educational levels in the Americas, the Ninth International Conference of American States declared that "every person has the right to education" and that "the state has the duty to assist the indi-

50. Jorge Castañeda, *op. cit.*, 191.

vidual in the exercise of the right to education." The Inter-American Seminar on Literacy and Adult Education which met at Rio de Janeiro in 1949, impressed by the problems presented by the nineteen million children of school age who were not attending school and the seventy million illiterates in the Americas, recommended that the American nations provide facilities for a minimum of three years of primary education. A Seminar on Elementary Education held at Montevideo in the following year also emphasized the importance of reducing illiteracy through expanded programs and facilities for primary education.[51] But these recommendations have not been generally acted upon.

World War II stimulated an interest in the expansion of inter-American facilities in higher education and led to the establishment of an Inter-American University in Panama in 1943 and the signing of an inter-American convention for its operation at the First Conference of Ministers and Directors of Education of the American Republics at Panama later in that year.[52] Though this first inter-American university had an ill-starred career, the idea has been continued in the various technical centers which operate under inter-American auspices in many countries of Latin America and which provide technical instruction at the university level. But the plan for a unified inter-American university still has its sponsors. A resolution calling for a study of the possibility and desirability of establishing a university of the Americas to serve as a center of higher education for the people of the Americas has been under consideration in the United States Senate since 1956.[53] Such a broad program, necessitating new textbooks, new teacher-training facilities, new school buildings, and expansion of existing educational systems, presents possibilities for enriched inter-American cooperation. A broad program for such cooperation was endorsed by the Tenth

51. Pan American Union, *La Educación Universal en América y la Escuela Primaria Fundamental: El Plan de Montevideo* (Washington, 1950); and United Nations, Educational, Scientific and Cultural Organization, *Universal, Free and Compulsory Education: Conclusions of the Inter-American Seminar on Elementary Education, Montevideo, 1950* (Geneva, 1951).

52. Inter-American Conference of Ministers and Directors of Education of the American Republics, Panama, September 27 to October 4, 1943, *Final Act* (Washington, 1943), 46-57.

53. Senate Joint Resolution 174, 84th Congress, 2d Session, May 16, 1956; and Senate Joint Resolution 79, 86th Congress, 1st Session, March 16, 1959. See also Rafael L. Gómez Carrasco, "La Universidad Interamericana," *América* (Havana), XLIX (July-September, 1956), 58-66.

Inter-American Conference in March, 1954 (Resolutions II and XXI).

A further suggestion has been made that the organization set up branch offices in every capital city of the Americas to serve as true inter-American cultural centers. As a beginning the organization voted on July 1, 1953, to proceed with the establishment of four such national offices in Mexico, Peru, Brazil, and probably Argentina. By 1959 it had established fifteen such offices. For the guidance of programs of cultural *rapprochement*, as well as for those in the economic and political fields, it may well be that the Inter-American Conference ought to meet oftener than once every five years and that the restrictions upon the holding of specialized conferences, which allegedly tend to limit initiative in the formulation of new projects, ought to be removed. These are examples of the constructive action and imaginative planning which must be encouraged in order to achieve—not hemispheric solidarity, which implies a rigidity that is not conducive to progress in cooperative action, but an understanding cooperation among the governments and peoples of the Americas.[54]

Expansion of the services and increase in the effectiveness of the inter-American system have been the especial concern of the Inter-American Committee of Presidential Representatives, which was set up at the meeting of American Presidents and Presidents-Elect of the American nations at Panama in July, 1956, in pursuance of a suggestion made by President Eisenhower. In their final report, submitted to the chiefs of state of the American republics in May, 1957,

54. The following works have been found useful in the preparation of the foregoing account: 81st Congress, 2d Session, Senate Executive Report No. 15, *Charter of the Organization of American States*, Report of the Committee on Foreign Relations, August 24, 1950; Manuel S. Canyes, *The Organization of American States and the United Nations*, Pan American Union, 1949; Department of State, *Peace in the Americas*, Department of State Publication 3964, October, 1950; Organization of American States, *Annual Report of the Secretary General of the Organization of American States*, fiscal years ending June 30, 1950, June 30, 1951, and June 30, 1952; Alberto Lleras, Secretary General of the Organization of American States, *The Inter-American Way of Life*, (Washington, 1951); Arthur P. Whitaker, *Development of American Regionalism: The Organization of American States*, International Conciliation Pamphlet No. 469 (March, 1951), Carnegie Endowment for International Peace (New York); Walter F. Cronin, unpublished doctoral dissertation, "Some Basic Concepts of Inter-American Organization," Harvard University, 1949, 2 vols.; Enrique V. Corominas, *La Práctica del Hispanoamericanismo* (Madrid, 1952), 143-194; and Francisco Cuevas Cancino, *Del Congreso de Panamá a la Conferencia de Caracas 1826-1954*, 2 vols. (Caracas, 1955).

they recommended, among other things, that the Organization of American States take a more active role in improving agriculture, in helping the American nations to utilize the natural resources of the tropics, in developing technical research and training in transportation, in stimulating the flow of private capital into Latin America, in eliminating malaria from the hemisphere, in carrying out programs of social security, social welfare, and education in the American nations and educational exchange among them, and in expanding the inter-American program of technical cooperation. The ultimate objective, which, the committee declared, "is to make the Organization of American States a more effective organization," would be advanced by "the expansion and strengthening of the public relations activities of the Organization of American States and the establishment of local offices in all the American republics." The possibilities of inter-American cooperative effort to develop nuclear energy for peaceful uses were also explored by the committee. These recommendations, the committee estimated, would more than double the annual budget of the Organization of American States. In general they look toward the strengthening of the organization to make it truly the leading instrumentality of inter-American cooperation.[55]

A somewhat different conception of the future role of the Organization of American States was indicated by the proposal of President Manuel Prado of Peru in mid-December, 1957, that the Organization should establish ties with the North Atlantic Treaty Organization (NATO). The Foreign Minister of Brazil, José Carlos de Macedo Soares, had already announced that his country was disposed to apply for admission to NATO.[56] Soon afterward Secretary of State Dulles confirmed that NATO was interested in establishing "liaison with other collective defense organizations of a regional character, such as the Organization of American States."[57] This proposal, if implemented, would bring the inter-American regional organization into close alliance with "all the nations of the

55. Inter-American Committee of Presidential Representatives, *Summary of Proposals Made by Representatives at the First Meeting of the Committee,* Doc. 5 (Rev. 2), September 19, 1956, mimeographed, Washington; and Inter-American Committee of Presidential Representatives, *Report to the Chiefs of State of the American Republics,* Washington, May, 1957.
56. *La Prensa,* Buenos Aires, December 5, 1957.
57. John Foster Dulles, "Transcript of the Radio-Television Report to the Nation on NATO Conference at Paris by President Eisenhower and Secretary of State Dulles from the White House, Monday Evening, at 8:30 P.M. (EST), December 23, 1957," mimeographed.

free world" for more effective self-defense. But objections were raised by some Latin Americans that the nature of the Organization of American States is different from that of NATO, which is essentially a military alliance; that the OAS ought to limit itself to advancing the economic and political welfare of its twenty-one members and assuring their territorial integrity and political independence; and that such an alliance would invade a field that belonged to the United Nations. These views were voiced by President Ramón Villeda Morales of Honduras, by the foreign ministers of Mexico and the Dominican Republic, by Arturo Frondizi, who was soon to be elected president of Argentina, and by many nationalist political leaders in Brazil.[58] As the United States became increasingly committed to extracontinental objectives, these Latin American leaders feared that their countries would be dragged into political and military situations which had no direct relation to hemisphere defense.[59]

It is unrealistic to interpret relations among the American nations only or even mainly in the light of assumptions as to their common historical tradition with a common colonial experience and independence attained through revolutionary struggle, their common settlement by immigration from abroad, their common expansion into frontier wildernesses, their common ideology and basic attitudes, and their habits of cooperation in the meeting of common problems.[60] The peoples of the Americas North and South are not all conceived in the same image nor do they possess the same institutional concepts, nor do they share the same motives, nor are they moving in the same direction. In Latin America the idea of class, of economic and social group, of family, of collectivity is much more traditional and firmly established than in the United States.[61] Music, art, poetry, and oratory form the substratum of life. Literature has not yet been superseded by technology, nor religion by science. The things that count are the things that cannot be counted. The heart

58. *La Prensa*, Buenos Aires, December 30, 1957.
59. Jorge Castañeda, *op. cit.*, 187-188.
60. Pan American Union, Division of Intellectual Cooperation, "Is America a Continent? A Round Table Discussion," *Points of View*, No. 2, October, 1941; Edmundo O'Gorman, "Do the Americas Have a Common History?" Pan American Union, *Points of View*, No. 3, December, 1941; Helen Dwight Reid, "Regionalism under the United Nations Charter," in *The Americas and World Order*, International Conciliation Pamphlet No. 419 (March, 1946), Carnegie Endowment for International Peace (New York, 1946), 124-125; Jorge Basadre, "¿Tienen las Américas una Historia Común?" *Excelsior*, Lima, June-July, 1942, 7-9.   61. Alceu Amoroso Lima, *A Realidade Americana*, 90.

often overrules the head. The heritages and potentialities of the two Americas are markedly different. "North America is not Latin America," wrote Raúl Haya de la Torre in 1929. "Between the one and the other America there are abysmal differences."[62]

The people of the United States of the north in their experience of wrestling with forested and mountain wildernesses have developed an assertiveness commensurate with the forces of nature with which they were obliged to cope. Through reliance upon manual and mechanical power they have subdued their wildernesses, dotting them with farmhouses and cities and crisscrossing them with highways, railways, and airways. In this process they have become imbued with a functional, pragmatic, and assertive philosophy to which even their art has been obliged to accommodate itself. Their shibboleth was construction and more construction and their intellectualizing if it did not take the form of hand-mindedness had to justify itself as being demonstrably useful. But to Latin Americans the obstacles of nature were often to be enjoyed rather than conquered. They found it easier to bypass jungle and cordillera than to make frontal assaults upon them. Their life was complicated by the interlayering of Indian, Negro, European, and mestizo. Rivalry between the heritage of the past, the importations from abroad, the indigenous, and the new, seemed to make destruction necessary before the work of construction could begin. They have had to demolish before they could build.

Latin Americans have faced many of the same problems that the people of the United States have faced, but they have sought different solutions. The long lack of opportunities for self-government among the Latin Americans during their colonial experience, their affinity with the countries of southern Europe which largely peopled them and provided them with their political and cultural inclinations, the often wide disparity between their written and their unwritten constitutions, and, perhaps most important of all, their traditional class structure, almost approaching a caste system in some places —these are some of Latin America's basic dissimilarities from the United States. Latin Americans often resort to revolutions to effect governmental changes; they have a tendency to violence and political instability; they allow themselves to be ruled by dictators and by army chieftains. Less than half of the governments which

62. Letter dated Berlin, December, 1929, in *¿A Donde Va Indo-américa?*, 157.

have come to power in Latin America since World War II have done so through elections that can be called free in the North American sense of the word. The Western Hemisphere is not one world but two worlds—the Indo-Hispanic and the Anglo-Saxon.

Nevertheless the two worlds have many interests in common. The basic tenet of Pan-Americanism, or of what Professor Arthur P. Whitaker has called "the Western Hemisphere idea," is that "the peoples of the Western Hemisphere are united in a special relationship to one another that sets them apart from the rest of the world; above all, apart from Europe."[63] This conviction of both a common family stamp and a common separateness from the rest of the world underlay the doctrine which President James Monroe proclaimed in 1823. The basic pattern of United States policy toward Latin America has always been one form or another of the Monroe Doctrine. At times it has taken the form of a "romantic continentalism" which assumed that the American hemisphere is composed of democratically organized nations with common ideals and purposes.[64] However unrealistic may be the assumptions upon which this concept is based, panegyrics concerning Pan-Americanism must not be underestimated as factors making for unity. At times of intervention or threats of intervention from the Old World, Pan-Americanism has taken the form of a more tangible union superimposed upon the Americas, as it were, by the appearance of a non-American enemy.

Strong as this union appeared to be during World War II, Pan-Americanism was in fact weakened by the decision of the United States, made final at Pearl Harbor, to become involved in the war. At inter-American conferences before World War II the United States took the position that "among the foreign relations of the United States as they fall into categories the Pan-American policy takes first place in our diplomacy."[65] But with the involvement of the United States in World War II the primacy of Latin America in the policy and planning of the Roosevelt administration was abandoned. Thereafter the United States focused its main attention not on Latin America but on the theaters of war across the Atlantic and the Pacific. It allowed this area to recede into the background of its

63. "The Origin of the Western Hemisphere Idea," *Proceedings of the American Philosophical Society*, XCVIII (October 15, 1954), 323.
64. The stock arguments for this "romantic continentalism" are presented in Yepes, 76-88.
65. State Department's instructions to delegates to the Sixth International Conference of American States, Havana, January 16-February 20, 1928.

interest and concern. In its preoccupation with achieving total victory over its European and Asiatic enemies it appeared to have abandoned its faith in the New World. Moreover, when it succumbed to a policy of intervention in the non-American world, its own firm prewar commitment to the principles of nonintervention in the American hemisphere was weakened. As its will to win the war gathered momentum, its will to dominate uncooperative nations of the Western Hemisphere became stronger. Pan-Americanism has further declined by reason of the postwar division of the globe into Communist and non-Communist worlds rather than the traditional Eastern and Western Hemispheres. In the light of modern geopolitics the United States can no longer consider the Latin Americans to be its exclusive neighbors, as they were in the days of Monroe. The hemisphere of primary interest to the United States has been stretched horizontally, instead of north and south, to include western Europe and the shores of Asia. As the Western Hemisphere has thus lost its historic identity the Latin American peoples have come to play a diminished role in the foreign policy plans of the United States. At postwar inter-American conferences the United States has thrown Latin America into a secondary if not indeed a tertiary role by emphasizing its primary commitments in Europe and Asia. Only the imprecise and tenuous *mystique* of Pan-Americanism survives, reinforced by the lingering feeling of possible future need for a common defense against threats from abroad to the security of the American hemisphere.[66] The reciprocal value of close political relations between the nations of the Western Hemisphere has been lost sight of. Pan-Americanism conceived as a positive moral force in today's world remains only "the substance of things hoped for, the evidence of things not seen." The *simpatía* which existed between the people of Latin America and the United States before World War II is gone. Their relationship has swung back full circle to the kind of relationship that prevailed in the 1920's.

The Eisenhower administration has hoped that its Policy of the Good Partner would close the schism which opened up between the two Americas after World War II. But the only new features of its Latin American policy are its emphasis upon the Organization of American States as a multilateral instrument of inter-American cooperation and the suggestion of a technique—the Inter-American

66. Arthur P. Whitaker, *The Western Hemisphere Idea: Its Rise and Decline* (Ithaca, 1954).

Committee of Presidential Representatives—for improving the effectiveness of the organization. The United States under the Eisenhower administration seemed to be insisting perhaps more strenuously than at any time since the close of World War II that the Latin American nations must face their own responsibilities and not wait for the United States to solve their problems for them. They must not expect their economies when confronted with crisis to be bailed out by grants or stabilization loans. They must first put their own economies in order and look to private capital investment for new financial aid. To Latin America all this has a very familiar ring.

The United States was still living in the pre-World War II world. It was thinking in terms of a Latin America condemned to the production of agricultural and mineral raw materials and participating in world trade only on the classic triangular pattern. It seemed to be unaware of the emergent nationhood in the countries to the south. It was making no fundamental reappraisal or reorientation of its relations with its hemisphere neighbors. It was still taking them for granted and was giving its primary attention to areas of the world which seemed more important than Latin America in the Cold War. "In the last twelve years," the Brazilian ambassador in London, Assis de Chateaubriand, declared in July, 1958, "the Department of State has had only two patterns of action: the Marshall Plan dedicated to Europe and the John Foster Dulles Plan dedicated to Asia and the Middle East."[67] The expressions of friendship and goodwill which the United States directed to Latin America were effusive and sincere, but they fell short of constituting a vital policy. Even its vaunted International Finance Corporation was able to show only one loan at the end of its first year of operation—a $2 million investment in a German-owned electrical company in Brazil.[68]

Following a policy that had already been laid down by the Truman administration in the Economic Cooperation Act of 1948 and had had only limited success in Latin America, the Eisenhower administration pressed the investment guaranty program vigorously as a means of pressuring United States private capital into foreign countries. In the Mutual Defense Assistance Act in 1954 Congress allocated $200 million, and later an additional $300 million, of foreign aid funds to guarantee United States investors abroad against losses from inability to convert their investments or profits from a

67. Quoted in *La Prensa*, New York, July 6, 1958.
68. Washington *Evening Star*, July 30, 1957.

forcign currency into dollars and against losses from expropriation or confiscation of their property by a foreign government. It made this investment guaranty program applicable only to those investment projects which the President of the United States approved in advance and only in those foreign countries with which he chose to institute the program. This program was accepted by eight Latin American governments in 1955—Bolivia, Colombia, Costa Rica, Ecuador, Guatemala, Honduras, Paraguay, and Peru—and by Cuba in 1957. But in only five of these countries—Bolivia, Ecuador, Guatemala, Paraguay, and Peru—was the program implemented from its inception in 1948 through March, 1959, with actual investment guaranties. The total guaranties given in those five countries during that decade amounted to less than $16 million. By mid-1959 this program had not been accepted by other Latin American countries including Brazil, Chile, and Mexico. It seemed to imply that nations included in it had been judged by the President of the United States to have unstable economies.[69] Besides, the heavy emphasis which the United States was placing upon private investment in public statements and in lectures by United States ambassadors to foreign ministers gave the Latin Americans diplomatic leverage to use in negotiations with Washington. It gave the impression that the United States was glutted with capital desperately seeking outlets abroad. Countries with an absorptive capacity for it could therefore dictate their own terms.

Meanwhile the movement for bloc action by the Latin American nations, partly as a defensive maneuver, has continued to grow. It has been especially noteworthy in the economic field, in which Latin Americans feel the United States has shown least appreciation of their problems. Since their arguments for the creation of a common American market have not met with favorable action by the United States they are showing renewed interest in the creation of an exclusively Latin American market in order to stimulate their own national development, to provide outlets wider than national ones for their industrial production, to expand intra-Latin American trade, to pro-

69. Mutual Defense Assistance Act, Public Law 665, August 26, 1954, *United States Statutes at Large*, 83d Congress, 2d Session, 1954, LXVIII, 846-848; Public Law 726, July 18, 1956, *United States Statutes at Large*, 84th Congress, 2d Session, 1956, LXX, 558-559; and International Cooperation Administration, "Countries Participating in the Investment Guaranty Program," and "Quarterly Report of Investment Guaranties Issued since the Inception of the Program in 1948 through March 31, 1959," mimeographed leaflets.

mote the economic integration of their area, and to improve the living conditions of their peoples. But the method they are using to encourage the development of such a market is not the method of bilateral negotiation, through agreement between pairs of countries, which was commonly used in the years immediately after World War II. It is rather the method of regional agreement, inspired in part by the example of the European Coal and Steel Community.[70]

The establishment of a Latin American regional market was declared to be advisable by the representatives of all the American nations at their Economic Conference held in Buenos Aires in August and September, 1957.[71] At a subsequent meeting of Latin American experts on the regional market, which was held in Santiago in February, 1958, and which was presided over by former President Galo Plaza of Ecuador, certain specific bases of action were agreed upon. These declared that the market must be open to all Latin American countries, and the concessions which one member may grant to another must not be considered exclusive but must be automatically extended to all other member countries. The agreement for such a market should ultimately cover all goods produced in the Latin American region and should look toward the progressive reduction of all customs duties and other restrictions which hamper intra-Latin American trade. Under it the less advanced countries should receive special treatment which will help them to finance new industries and will enable them to find a decisive stimulus to their own industrialization in the growing consumption of the more advanced countries. The experts felt that a single customs tariff vis-à-vis the rest of the world should be eventually established and that a special system of multilateral payments should be worked out which will facilitate maximum trade among the Latin American nations. This latter system might conceivably be set up on other than a dollar basis. They also hinted at the need for Latin American price-fixing machinery by suggesting that export prices should be the same for any given commodity, irrespective of the market of destination.

Such a plan, if consummated, would increase the leverage of the Latin American nations in the modern world. It would, in the enthu-

70. United Nations, Department of Economic and Social Affairs, *Inter Latin American Trade: Current Problems*, 101.
71. Inter-American Conference, Economic Conference of the Organization of American States, Buenos Aires, August 15-September 4, 1957, *Final Act* (Washington, 1957), Resolution XL.

siastic words of *Excelsior* of Mexico City (January 11, 1958), enable them "to defend their economies, to regulate the exportation of both their raw and their processed materials, and to balance their finances." They would be able to deal on more nearly equal terms with foreign nations and blocs which are protecting their own agriculture, their industry, and their commerce with protective tariffs, import restrictions, and quotas. It might also, it has been optimistically suggested, lead to a common citizenship in a greater Latin American fatherland. As the economic recession in the United States deepened in early 1958, the project of a Latin American bloc was endorsed openly by both President Kubitschek of Brazil and President-elect Frondizi of Argentina.[72]

* * *

Latin America does not have the answer to all the world's problems. It itself is a problem area. But it can supply many of the answers to its own problems. The goal to be striven for is not Pan-Americanism as such but rather relations of good neighborliness among the American nations. The responsibility for achieving relations of this kind rests largely upon the United States, for, as Professor Rippy has observed, in inter-American relations the government and people of the United States "are the active agents, the role of the Latin Americans is largely passive."[73] But official attitudes of the United States toward Latin Americans during the decade after World War II were characterized by lack of warmth and considerateness, an absence of pleasantry and understanding, a failure to play the diplomatic game of give and take, an excess of straight-from-the-shoulder talk with threatening overtones. This Latin American policy has been essentially negative. It has been, as Dr. William Manger of the Organization of American States charged in an address in April, 1958, "a sort of hold-the-line attitude, characterized by a tendency to say 'no' to every proposal which they may advance, with no alternative solution coming from us."[74] All this has thrust them at

72. Associated Press dispatch in Washington *Evening Star,* April 10, 1958, and *Christian Science Monitor,* Boston, April 15, 1958.

73. *Latin America and the Industrial Age,* 260.

74. Statement of Dr. William Manger, Assistant Secretary General of the Organization of American States before the National Foreign Relations Commission of the American Legion, April 10, 1958, Press Release, Organization of American States.

arm's length from the United States. If these attitudes were motivated by the desire to diminish the dependence of the Latin American peoples upon the United States which many of them had acquired during the war, why did the United States oppose those Latin American governments which were working toward the same end? Under a good neighbor policy nationalism in Latin America is not necessarily inconsistent with the national interests of the United States.

Truly good neighbors refrain not only from taking advantage of each other but even from criticizing each other; they will see to it that good relations are cultivated at all times, not merely in war emergencies. The harmonious *convivencia* of the peoples of the American hemisphere should not be made dependent upon the conviction of a common family stamp, of a common separateness from the rest of the world, nor even of the need for mutual security against an outside enemy. It will not be advanced by insistence upon an inter-American solidarity which requires a similarity of governmental institutions, the establishment of a single Church-State relationship, or a uniform observance of civil liberties. Nor will it be advanced by any grading of the nations of the Americas as immature or mature, backward or advanced, inferior or superior. All methods of establishing categories of developed and undeveloped economies imply some pre-established theoretical standards. That such a grading—inevitably subjective and supercilious—often shades into intervention by the self-styled mature, advanced, and superior nations needs no demonstration here. In Theodore Roosevelt's characterization of Venezuela as "a corrupt pithecoid community" was implicit his corollary to the Monroe Doctrine authorizing intervention by the United States in Latin America to prevent "chronic wrongdoing." When differences among nations are even subtly regarded as evidences of inferiority, friendly international relations become difficult.[75] The people of the United States, President Kubitschek of Brazil has declared, "ought to accept us as we are."[76] If the United States carries out principles of good neighborliness only when it approves of the neighbors it is not laying a firm basis for cooperative international relations.

75. "Y", "On a Certain Impatience with Latin America," *Foreign Affairs,* XXVIII (July 1950), 565-580.
76. Address by President Juscelino Kubitschek before the Commercial Association of Santos, São Paulo, Brazil, January 29, 1957, *Diário Oficial,* Rio de Janeiro, January 30, 1957, 2189-2190.

The disparity between the constitutional system of most of the Latin American countries, which are republican and even, in some cases, democratic in form, and their political practices, in other words the "duplicity" in their political system, is often shocking to North Americans. The Latin American habit of constitution-making has produced a great many constitutions which do not correspond to existing realities. Many of them have been doctrinaire and fictional, spun out of futile argument as to the best forms of government and seeking to impose these forms upon societies to which they were not suited. Governments therefore have often been only imported experiments. They have not developed or even been allowed to develop as organic expressions of the life of the people. Their political institutions which appear on paper do not reflect their actual political habits. Latin Americans have, in Dr. Amoroso Lima's graphic phrase, tried on too many "wrong-sized shoes."[77] For this reason what is expected to work in Latin America does not work. And, on the other hand, systems that do not work elsewhere sometimes work well in Latin America. This is particularly true of the Latin American habit of changing or attempting to change government by revolutionary rather than by constitutional means. It must be considered not as evidence of immaturity, backwardness, or inferiority, but rather as a complex phenomenon growing out of the traditions and even the necessities of the Latin American situation. The people of Latin America, like those of other inadequately developed areas of the world, do not have the same aversion to revolution as do those of western Europe and the United States. Instead they often welcome radical change.

The revolutionary habit is destructive. A popular orgy of twenty-four hours with torch and machete may reduce to rubble the work of many years and even centuries. But it may be necessitated by the unredressed grievances of years and centuries against which the people madly and blindly strike back. In Alberdi's pregnant phrase, "things govern by means of men, not men by means of things."[78] The "things" that govern in Latin America are the perennial instabilities arising from land monopoly, economic inequality, and sub-marginal existence. These condition the underprivileged, inarticulate, and illiterate masses, who form the majority of the population

77. Alceu Amoroso Lima, "Men, Ideas, and Institutions," 121.
78. Juan Bautista Alberdi, *Escritos Póstumos* (16 vols., Buenos Aires, 1895-1901), I, *Estudios Económicos*, 325.

in most of the Latin American countries, to follow the leadership of a *caudillo* who will promise to establish social justice. Never does a *caudillo* come to power as an avowed dictator. His concern to represent the movement which he heads as an effort to curb abuses by incumbent officials and to give a "new deal" to the country attests the perennial devotion of the Latin American peoples to principles of self-government. Such a *caudillo,* once established in office, may try to retain popular support by redressing social and economic griev-ances. But if he attempts to do so he will run afoul of oligarchic groups who feel that he is jeopardizing their vested interests in the prevailing social and economic system and who will contrive his overthrow. The Arbenz government of Guatemala was thus over-thrown in June, 1954. A similar fate befell Perón in September, 1955, when he dared to challenge British commercial interests in Argentina and the Roman Catholic Church, which is a powerful political force in that country.

The successor to such a *caudillo* who must necessarily be accept-able to these oligarchic groups will govern by force. Under Arbenz' successor, Colonel Castillo Armas, only one political party, the *Movi-miento Nacional Democrático,* was permitted in Guatemala, and five secret police organizations were organized to maintain order and stamp out opposition and subversion. So emerges the dictator. Or, very often, because the leadership of the *caudillo* is intensely per-sonal, his impulses toward reform are frustrated and his program defeated by the palace clique who surround him. So it is that his attempts at social reform may result only in exploitation of the peo-ple by a new group of officeholders, and his attempts at constitutional reform may take the form of amendments confirming him in power or extending his term of office. Again he emerges as a dictator. "All the history of America, and the inheritance of the Spaniard and the Indian," wrote Francisco García Calderón, "has ended in the exalta-tion of the *caudillo.*"[79]

In most of the Latin American countries the presidency is an anxious seat. Its occupant must constantly cast apprehensive side-long glances over his shoulder for signs of disaffection. He walks a presidential tightrope. Even his closest friends and associates are suspect. It has been suggested facetiously that the test of the success of a president in Latin America is whether he can walk and not run to the nearest exit. For this reason the right of asylum, under which

79. *Latin America: Its Rise and Progress,* 365.

a discredited president may seek refuge in a foreign embassy or a foreign country, is a dearly cherished institution. It enables such a president to save his life if not his face and gives the new president a free hand to carry out his mandate until he too has lingered too long upon the stage of the presidency and must flee the country. But this method of changing presidents has the disadvantage of depriving the country of the advice of its ex-presidents—which would ordinarily serve as a stabilizing force. When they leave public office they find it difficult and often impossible to resume private life as residents of their own country. The number of elder statesmen left in most Latin American countries is therefore very small.

In these circumstances the prescription of a fixed constitutional term of four, five, or six years for the chief executive in accordance with the prevailing presidential system has only a fictional significance. By reason of the inflexibility of that system the process of transferring power from one *caudillo* to another, from one clique to another, or from the few to the many, has frequently been accomplished by revolutionary means because in the judgment of the political opposition it could not be accomplished otherwise. In those countries the temper of opposition parties, of those who mould public opinion in newspaper, press, and radio, and of mercurial underprivileged groups nursing long-endured frustrations, often changes suddenly. An administration which at the time of its installation in office may admirably accord with the general will, may in the course of a few months or some time before the expiration of its constitutional term of office commit such egregious errors or fail so completely to fulfill popular expectations that the people rise in fury against it. If a president who symbolizes the shortcomings of such an administration insists upon serving out his legal term of office he can be ousted only by revolutionary means, which appears to be the only means open to the opposition to exercise their reserved or natural right to choose the form of government under which they will live. Only in this way can the presidential system, which was taken over from the United States and embodied in the Latin American constitutions, be circumvented.

The long experience of this system during the last century and a quarter has conditioned Latin Americans to the necessity of revolution which provides them with a substitute for a needed but unscheduled election. The *cantinas* and *cafés* in Latin America are schools of democracy, for in their noisy and gesticulating discussions referenda on all the actions of government are taken. But they are also seedbeds of revolution. In them the impulse for popular, responsive government sometimes leads to violence. The tragedy of an ousted president is that he either did not know how to quit or was not able to quit when the quitting was good. The prevalent Latin American habit of revolution has the effect, therefore, of a parliamentary system, which in theory makes the executive continuously responsive to the legislature. Latin Americans by thus ignoring the specific tenure fixed in the constitution make it possible for the presidency to be responsive to popular pressures.[80] As an alternative to revolution the parliamentary system has been tried in several Latin American countries, specifically in Chile from 1891 to 1925 and in Cuba under its constitution of 1940, which continued in force until Batista was overthrown in early 1959. In Brazil a movement to establish a parliamentary-type government by constitutional amendment was narrowly defeated in the legislature in September, 1955.

* * *

A relationship of good neighborliness among the American nations does not require that all of them be replicas of each other or that what is good for one is necessarily good for all. Among them there may be disagreements—assertions and rebuttals—but always in the end a synthesis which will grow out of a realization of the value of richness in diversity and the need for continuous accommodation among dissimilar peoples; out of a desire to share and not to convert, to understand and not to correct; out of an inner-directed mutual appreciation of common interests and aims. That will come only through constructive cooperation in a hundred different ways, not necessarily involving self-sacrifice by either the United States or Latin America but rather exhibiting at all times the spirit of helpfulness which develops both the self-respect and the mutual respect of all. The best policy for the United States to follow toward Latin America is a middle course between neglect on the one hand and intervention on the other. Care must be taken also not to base policy upon the assumption that organizational improvements in the inter-American system represent the be-all and the end-all of inter-American cooperation. International machinery is not the sum total of international relations.

80. Dozer, "Roots of Revolution in Latin America," [274]-288.

In the relations between individuals north and south, therefore, high ethical standards should be maintained. Business men operating in Latin America will find it both good business and good sense to use persuasion rather than force to accomplish their will. If they insist upon being given a preferential position over nationals they only invite antiforeign resentment and render normal business operations difficult, perhaps impossible. While abstaining from participation in local politics they should cooperate with local governments to the fullest extent possible. They should use the largest possible number of local employees, should pay a high level of wages, should try to enlist the support of local capital, should invest their profits in the country in which they operate, and should obey its taxation laws. Sound business principles will suggest that the profits from business operations in Latin America should not be vastly greater than from similar operations in the United States and that the tested and proved system of a low margin of profit and a large turnover, developed in the United States but still unfamiliar to many Latin Americans, will prove to be most profitable in the long run. Business operations carried on in accordance with these principles will contribute materially to the welfare of the countries within which they operate without radically disturbing native cultures, living patterns, and locally cherished ideologies. Hit-and-run business operations, on the other hand, will not succeed nor will they advance the real interests of the United States in Latin America.

The business representatives of United States firms who are sent to work in Latin America should be carefully chosen on the basis of their characters, their knowledge of the area, and their sympathies with the Latin American peoples. Every such representative is, in effect, an ambassador from the United States, and he should exemplify the highest standards of United States conduct and morals. In those countries, where personality and sentiments are so highly esteemed, the success or failure of a United States company and public attitudes toward the United States are often determined by the character of its representatives from the north. Latin Americans still do not appreciate that the North American has endearing qualities of culture and gaiety harmonious with their own modes of life, quite apart from his financial canniness, technical know-how, and engineering skills. Too often the only characteristics which they discern in him are the urge to venture, to build, and to make money.

Our diplomatic officers have and should assume the duty to work in intimate cooperation with United States businessmen in Latin America, pointing out to them the effects of their policies upon Latin American sentiment and suggesting ways in which they can produce favorable psychological reactions to their business activities. The best efforts of United States diplomats in Latin America may be nullified by prejudicial activities of United States business concerns. The representatives of these concerns should understand that it is imperative in their own as well as in their country's interest that they should act toward the governments and peoples south of the Rio Grande in the same manner as they act toward their customers and patrons in the United States. Ignorance of the language of the country is a serious obstacle to cordial social contacts and productive business and professional relations. A knowledge of Spanish, French, or Portuguese, therefore, as well as some background of Latin American history and literature, is a valuable, even an essential asset in dealing with Latin Americans. In this respect the use of "community relations specialists" by certain United States business concerns overseas is heartening. These specialists are employed to keep the executives of their own company informed and abreast of the culture of the country in which they operate. All such efforts at cultural empathy by which citizens of the United States who live and work in Latin America may project themselves affirmatively into the culture and traditions of the country are needed to produce the closer and more productive cooperation among the nations of the Western Hemisphere, which is urgently important.

Current manifestations of national spirit in Latin America, rich with potentialities for self-government, economic development, and psychological uplift, must not be allowed to derogate from the wholesome cooperative undertakings of the inter-American community. We forget the travail that accompanied the actualization of the idea of the national state in western Europe and even in our own country. Nationalism in Latin America can be converted into a factor in our favor if we only apply the right method. The principles of national autonomy cannot be resisted by us unless we abandon our own basic belief in government by the consent of the governed. We who profess this belief cannot deny to other peoples the right to decide for themselves. Moreover the Western Hemisphere will be strengthened by having in Latin America governments which are strong in their own right, which represent their own true national values, and which reflect the majority will of their peoples. Breezy dismissals of nationalism as a "peculiar regional malady characterized by xenophobia or simply a mass inferiority complex" overlook the profound nature of this movement and its essentially constructive character. The stronger the nations of Latin America become, the greater will be the United States, *provided* we all remain good neighbors. The problem for each Latin American country that has an awakening sense of its own national destiny is, as former President Arévalo has succinctly expressed it, to extricate itself "from imperialist clutches without falling into those of venal and gangster-like adventurers, to withdraw itself from colonialism without succumbing to a chauvinistic arrogance."[81]

This nationalism is a conscious movement, but it is also a subconscious movement springing naturally out of the history, the folklore, the culture, the religion, the past victories and defeats, the feelings of superiority and inferiority of the Latin American peoples. When we resist the nationalist forces in Latin America, when we abhor them as something evil, when we treat them as a disease that needs to be quarantined and stamped out, when we equate all nationalist, reformist movements there with communism, we put ourselves in the position of undertaking to thwart the long-pent-up desires of the peoples of those countries for fuller development of their national resources, both human and material. We oppose some of the most dynamic leaders and effective morale builders in Latin America. We seek to undermine their leadership and to deprive them of their followings. If such an effort succeeds it destroys not only *their* but also *our* own best hope of better utilization of human effort and of increased production in Latin America. We defeat their attempts to achieve a new fullness of stature which we must believe is essential not only to a developing American program in world affairs but also to our own long-term interests in international peace and stability. We must reconcile ourselves to the fact that the responsibility of the United States for guaranteeing human rights, private property, and political stability in Latin America is quite limited. This must be the primary responsibilty of the Latin Americans. Anything that smacks of intervention in Latin American affairs, whether military, political, or cultural, will assuredly react against our own best interests there. Moreover, such action swells the very nationalism which it is intended to destroy and increases hostile feelings against us everywhere. If we persist in such action

81. Juan José Arévalo, January 16, 1958, quoted with permission.

we are likely to find ourselves eventually confronting the hostility of resurgent nations which feel they have become strong in spite of us. To set our faces against national self-determination in Latin America is to give substance to the charge of the Latin Americans that our aim is to keep them weak, disorganized, and unproductive.

Extraordinary diplomatic insights are required to deal successfully with such patriot governments. The qualities which a Latin American understands and values most in a foreigner or a foreign country are resoluteness, fairness, and friendliness. The skillful diplomacy of Dwight L. Morrow in Mexico in 1927-1930 demonstrated that the United States can quite readily cooperate in a mutually advantageous way with peoples who are undergoing nationalistic transformations and that even the business interests of the United States need not suffer in the process. To this end the United States should make sure that the diplomatic and consular representatives it sends to Latin America have not only a good knowledge of the main languages—Spanish, Portuguese, or French—but also a sympathetic appreciation of the racial sensibilities and cultural achievements of the countries to which they are sent. They will assuredly not promote the true interests of the United States if they ignore local traditions and feelings or adopt an attitude of "cool and correct" toward the government and people with whom they deal. Moreover, they must be masters of subtlety, for in Latin America everyone is a diplomat, skilled in finesse and political innuendo. Attention to protocol and social custom also is more important there than in many other countries, for life is socially stylized. But if the sympathy and interest of the diplomat is allowed to shine through these practices he will readily be accepted as a true ambassador of goodwill.

Conventional stereotypes still persist to poison relations. Latin America is too often typed in the United States as only a land of revolutions, disorder, instability, political and religious intolerance, backwardness, and disease—"a land inhabited by a docile, colorful, and shiftless people of an inferior mongrel race who sit around dreaming in an abstract, humanistic, and idealistic spiritual world with an olympic disregard for the better material things of life."[82] Of the peoples to the south North Americans have only a very limited and distorted picture. So grievous are these misconceptions that Dr. Eduardo Zuleta Angel, while serving as Colombian ambassador to the United States, reproached his fellow Latin Americans with

82. Galo Plaza, *Problems of Democracy in Latin America*, 16.

never having "seriously tried to make their countries known in the United States" and with never having "known how to 'sell' Latin America to American public opinion."[83] The Yankee on the other hand is condemned in Latin America as a grasping and insensitive materialist. He is viewed, declares former President Galo Plaza of Ecuador, as "a barbarian, well-intentioned, highly specialized, but immature mentally."[84] New York City is still represented as the loathsome epitome of North American capitalism, and upon Wall Street is vented the vitriol that debtors often direct toward their creditors.[85] The political experience of the Latin American countries in relation to the United States influences their current attitudes. The conquest of Mexico by the United States in 1846-1848, the seizure of Puerto Rico during the Spanish-American War, the later United States intervention in Cuba under the Platt Amendment, its involvement in Panama's secession from Colombia, the marine occupation of the Dominican Republic, Haiti, Nicaragua, and other Caribbean countries, the Veracruz expedition into Mexico in 1914, and the Department of State's "Blue Book" against the Argentine government in 1946 have cast long shadows. The phantom of William Walker still stalks through Central America.[86] The continuing strength of the latent and sometimes overt feelings of resentment at these incidents in Latin America can scarcely be overestimated. Nursed and fostered by powerful groups in these countries, this resentment is a never-to-be-forgotten element in the pattern of inter-American relations.

The normal state of Latin America is to be hostile to the United States. Various publications and recurring incidents betray the persistence of this hostility. In 1952 "Yanqui" imperialism in Latin America was reviewed vitriolically by a distinguished Argentine journalist, Ramón Oliveres, in a book of almost seven hundred pages.[87] The overthrow of the Arbenz government in Guatemala in

83. "A Program of Interamerican Public Relations" (Pan American Union, Washington, no date).   84. *Op. cit.*, 17.
85. See, for example, the book written by Communist-sympathizer Agustín Ferraris, assistant editor of the pro-Peronista afternoon newspaper *La Razón,* Buenos Aires, *Estados Unidos Cambia la Cara* (Buenos Aires, 1954), *passim;* and Juan José Arévalo, *Fábula del Tiburón y las Sardinas: América Latina Estrangulada* (Santiago de Chile, 1956), 153-274.
86. See, for example, Gregorio Selser, *Sandino, General de Hombres Libres* (Buenos Aires, 1955).
87. *El Imperialismo Yanqui en América: La Dominación Política y Económica del Continente* (Buenos Aires, 1952).

1954 stimulated a new outpouring of Latin American criticism of the United States as an imperialistic nation. For the overthrow of that government former Guatemalan President Arévalo immediately blamed the United States and the United Fruit Company in his book *Guatemala, La Democracia y el Imperio*.[88] In the following year he published a book-length diatribe against the United States, which in a pungent fable he compared to a shark lording it over the sardines.[89] A former foreign minister of Guatemala, Raúl Osegueda, bitterly chronicled the aggressions of the United States against Latin America in his *Operación Guatemala $$ OK $$*. Other volumes by Latin American authors critical of the United States published in 1953-1956 include two books by the founder of the Costan Rican Socialist Party, Vicente Sáenz, *Hispanoamérica contra el coloniaje* and *Auscultación Hispanoamericana*, Ezequiel Ramírez Novoa's *La Farsa del Panamericanismo y la Unidad Indoamericana*, and Oscar Waiss' *Nacionalismo y Socialismo en América Latina*.[90] As one phase of this renewed wave of literary resentment against the United States Sandino, the Nicaraguan leader who resisted the United States marine occupation of his country in the 1920's, is again being hailed as a hero and martyr in Latin America.[91] As a result the idea of a Latin American or at least a Spanish American union—a common front against foreign domination—still has its lyrical apostles.[92]

Many are the sources of discord and conflict between the United States and Latin America. The bilateral military agreements which the United States negotiated after 1950 with individual Latin American nations are criticized as derogating from the sovereignty of those nations and as aiming at the domination of the hemisphere by the United States.[93] When the Kubitschek government of Brazil co-

88. Juan José Arévalo, *Guatemala, La Democracia y el Imperio* (Montevideo, 1954).
89. Speech of Dr. Ernesto Castillero, Vice Minister of Foreign Relations of Panama, before the Second Congress of Students, Panama, December 16, 1957. See also Juan José Arévalo, *Fábula del Tiburón y las Sardinas*.
90. Vicente Sáenz, *Hispano América contra el Coloniaje, segunda edición* (Mexico, D. F., 1949), also published in English under the title *Latin America against the Colonial System* (Mexico, 1949), *Hispanoamérica contra el coloniaje*, 3d ed. (Mexico, 1956), and *Auscultación Hispanoamericana* (Mexico, 1954); Ezequiel Ramírez Novoa, *Las Farsa del Panamericanismo y la Unidad Indoamericana* (Buenos Aires, 1955); and Oscar Waiss, *Nacionalismo y Socialismo en América Latina* (Santiago de Chile, [1954]).
91. Gregorio Selser, *op. cit.*
92. Vicente Sáenz, *Auscultación Hispanoamericana*, 81-86.
93. Arévalo, *Fábula del Tiburón y las Sardinas*, 124-149.

operated with the United States by signing an agreement in January, 1957, permitting the latter to install a guided missile tracking station on the island of Fernando de Noronha, it stirred up so much anti-United States feeling that it refused to allow the agreement to be debated in the Brazilian Congress.[94] Panama's canal agreement with the United States which was concluded in 1955 and which raised Panama's annual receipts from the United States from $430,000 to $1,930,000 is not deemed to be satisfactory; agitation continues for a new treaty, a further increase in the annual payment, and an explicit acknowledgment of Panama's sovereignty over the Canal Zone.[95] The old *APRA* demand for the inter-Americanization of the canal is being circulated afresh—stimulated by the success of the Nasser government of Egypt in nationalizing the Suez Canal and by the counter-proposal of Secretary of State Dulles for the international-ization of that canal.[96] Latin American reaction to the incidents at Little Rock, Arkansas, showing the persistence of racial prejudice in the United States, has been uniformly critical. It has been strongest in Mexico, which sees a parallel between the treatment of Negroes and Mexicans in the United States, and in Brazil, which, choosing to overlook the subtle racial discriminations there, boasts of its congenial race relations. In this criticism of the United States the leftist press in the Latin American countries has been particularly outspoken.

The laments of the Latin Americans against the United States are long and loud. But, Latin Americans feel, their grievances go unredressed and often unnoticed. They bitterly object to our extrac-tive operations which, as they say, leave them with only holes in the ground. They circulate scathing denunciations of the exploitative

---

94. *Current History*, XXXII (April, 1957), 214, 239, 248.

95. *Department of State Bulletin*, XXXII (February 7, 1955), 237-243; and inaugural address by President Ernesto de la Guardia and address by re-tiring President Ricardo M. Arias Espinosa of Panama, October 1, 1956. See also *Panama American*, May 2, 1958, and *Star and Herald*, Panama, May 3, 6, 7, 1958.

96. *Christian Science Monitor*, May 31, 1958. Causes of Latin American hostility toward the United States are reviewed in three studies by S. Walter Washington, *A Study of the Causes of Hostility toward the United States in Latin America: Brazil*, Department of State, External Research Paper No. 126, February 24, 1956; *A Study of the Causes of Hostility toward the United States in Latin America: Chile*, Department of State, External Research Paper No. 126.1, August 28, 1956; and *A Study of the Causes of Hostility to-ward the United States in Latin America: Argentina*, Department of State, External Research Paper No. 126.2, May 27, 1957.

operations of United States business corporations in their countries. They fear the imposition of new tariff restrictions by the United States against their products, specifically petroleum and wool.[97] For the adverse effect of the international sugar quota system upon their economies some of them hold the United States responsible. Latin American markets for coffee in the United States since 1950 have been sharply reduced by the increasing popularity of African coffee.[98] The surplus cotton stocks in the United States have necessitated a cutback in cotton acreages in Brazil and Mexico and have caused an accumulation of unsold cotton supplies in Peru. Argentines charge that after we encouraged them to develop their tung oil production we imposed a quota upon it, and they resent our continuing "sanitary" restrictions upon their beef and other animal products. They still accuse the United States of unfair partiality to other areas of the world in its program of financial assistance to foreign countries. As a result "the feeling in South America is now stronger than ever," concluded the New York Times correspondent there, "that the United States, having helped Europe and Asia with massive loans and grants, must now come to the aid of the nations of this hemisphere that have always been loyal to it" (March 23, 1958).

These critical situations for Latin America have been exploited not only by Communists and other Marxists but also by political leaders who shrewdly know how to create a reaction of self-pity in the minds of Latin Americans, to play upon their feelings of inferiority, and to agitate them into a fever of rebellion against their North American "oppressors." Ambitious politicians in Latin America find it necessary to be anti-United States in order to win popular favor. They point to the policy which the United States followed after World War II, of carrying on its economic negotiations with the Latin American nations mainly on a bilateral rather than a collective basis as calculated to block the proper aspirations of those nations and as motivated by a desire to "divide and rule." This policy seemed inconsistent with the professed objective of the United States to create an inter-American bloc based upon common interests. Their feelings toward the United States were revealed by the assaults made upon Vice-President and Mrs. Richard Nixon in Lima and Caracas in

97. See statement by Dr. Silvio Gutiérrez, Venezuelan Minister of Development, in *Venezuela Up-to-Date,* Venezuelan Information Service, Washington, V, 10 (December, 1954), 9.
98. Gilberto Freyre, *New World in the Tropics* (New York, 1959), 271-276.

May, 1958—assaults which came as a complete surprise to the State Department! The condition of inter-American relations at that time, bluntly reported the chief formulator of Latin America policies for the Eisenhower administration, Dr. Milton Eisenhower, was "even more serious" than in 1953. To correct it, he declared, "heroic efforts are required."[99]

Colonialism in the Americas continues to be a disruptive issue, dividing the Latin American nations from the United States. Proposals advanced at several inter-American conferences after World War II by Latin American governments for an inter-American declaration against the continuance of foreign colonial systems in the Western Hemisphere have been viewed unsympathetically by the United States. Argentina and Guatemala have been especially assertive on this issue because of their respective claims to the Falkland (Malvinas) Islands and British Honduras (Belize), but they have been supported by several other nations, including generally the largest and most powerful—Brazil, Mexico, and Chile—which favor the termination of the American colonial regimes of Britain, France, the Netherlands, and, by implication at least, the United States. Over the opposition of the latter at the Bogotá conference in 1948 an American Committee on Dependent Territories was created by the vote of eighteen Latin American nations. Both at the Bogotá conference and at the conference at Caracas in 1954 the United States argued that action on this subject should not be taken because it involved the interests and responsibilities of foreign friendly governments not represented at the conferences and might jeopardize the solidarity of the anti-Soviet world. This argument has given rise to the charge in Latin America that an Anglo-American bloc has ranged itself against the Latin American bloc.[100] But this criticism has been allayed in part by the creation of the Commonwealth of Puerto Rico by the United States in 1952 and of the Federation of the Caribbean by the British government in 1957.[101] The hope has been expressed that at the

99. Dr. Milton S. Eisenhower, "Report to the President . . . on United States-Latin American Relations," December 27, 1958, The White House, mimeographed copy, 3-4.

100. Vicente Sáenz, *Hispano América contra el Coloniaje*, 149-150.

101. Department of State, *Ninth International Conference of American States, Bogotá, Colombia, March 30-May 2, 1948, Report of the Delegation of the United States of America with Related Documents* (Washington, 1948), 84-86; and Department of State, "Brief Report on the Tenth Inter-American Conference," mimeographed (Washington, undated), 2.

next inter-American meeting Puerto Rico should be represented by its own delegates.[102]

Related to the question of colonialism is the conflict over Antarctica in which both Argentina and Chile have advanced territorial claims based largely upon geographical contiguity. By an agreement concluded in 1947 these two nations joined in exchanging official observers in the Antarctic, thus establishing a measure of common action against all foreign claimants. While the United States itself has recognized no territorial claims in Antarctica, it has advanced none of its own, reserving, however, all its rights there based upon prior discovery and exploration. In 1947 it agreed with the other states signatory to the Inter-American Treaty of Reciprocal Assistance to include the American quadrant in the Antarctic in the mutual defense area and thus for the first time, in effect, brought it under the protection of the Monroe Doctrine.

Inter-American ill-feeling is sometimes whetted by the actions of tourists from the United States in Latin America. A well-dressed Costa Rican lady walking along a San José street was accosted by a woman tourist from the United States who reached for her silver necklace, fingered it, and brazenly asked her in bad Spanish how much she would take for it. The outraged Costa Rican lady slipped away from her and fled in amazement at such conduct. To cite another such incident, a Venezuelan lady, mistress of a beautiful and ancient estate set at the end of a double row of gigantic royal palm trees near Puerto Cabello, left her house unlocked one afternoon and in charge only of a native cook while she visited neighbors. When she returned to her home she found a party of tourists from the United States swarming through her rooms. Understanding English, she was shocked to hear the comments of the intruders as they prowled through the sleeping quarters of her home: "Why, they sleep in beds the same as we do!" "They even have indoor toilets here." When the cultured lady made known her displeasure at their intrusion she could hardly persuade her rude guests to leave.

Before tourists leave the United States they ought to be given instruction in the attitudes of the Latin American peoples and the

102. At the meeting of American Presidents in Panama in July, 1956, President José Figueres of Costa Rica expressed the wish that at the next meeting both Canada and Puerto Rico would be represented. República de Panamá, Ministerio de Relaciones Exteriores, *El Libro de Oro de la Reunión de Panamá* (Panama, 1956), 323-324.

amenities to be observed in meeting them. For providing such instruction the United States government has some responsibility. During World War II it provided useful guidebooks to the members of the armed forces as they embarked for service in Latin American countries. Dr. Milton Eisenhower included in his report to the President in November, 1953, a recommendation that "government departments should maintain information services" for United States citizens planning to travel in Latin America. A move in this direction was made in August, 1957, when the Eisenhower administration began to insert into passports letters from the President reminding United States travelers abroad that they represent their country on their travels. "As you travel abroad," the President's letter declared, "the respect you show for foreign laws and customs, your courteous regard for other ways of life and your speech and manner help to mold the reputation of our country."[103] Similar letters were distributed to members of the armed forces of the United States serving overseas. Such letters might well be expanded to offer suggestions of a specialized nature adapted particularly to travelers in the Latin American countries.

Greater, however, than the responsibility of the government to furnish such suggestions is the responsibility of business, religious, technical, and other organizations which send workers to Latin America. Steamship companies might be induced to provide insights and hints of this sort to their tourist passengers. It is not improbable that money and time devoted to the promotion of what Ambassador Rafael Heliodoro Valle has felicitously called "enlightened tourism" would yield greater returns in "goodwill and good neighborhood" than the more dramatic and overt propaganda activities. Little humble acts of appreciation and kindness often create the strongest ties among neighbors. The freedom that Latin Americans particularly desire is freedom from contempt. Having lived for centuries in the backwash of power and progress, they react bitterly to acts of condescending superiority by others. But they react warmly and spontaneously to acts of genuine understanding and respect.

* * *

103. Letter to "Dear Fellow Citizen," from the White House, signed Dwight D. Eisenhower, dated July 12, 1957.

Latin Americans are still, as Alexander von Humboldt described them a century and a quarter ago, *"mendigos harapientos sentados en bancos de oro"* (ragged beggars seated on benches of gold). Despite the wails of the prophets of doom, theirs is an area of enormous potentials.[104] It possesses abundant resources and labor, but it needs foreign capital and improved methods of production. In this area combined with other parts of the Western Hemisphere the United States can obtain all the materials which are essential to its own welfare and development.[105] As the late Dr. Carlos G. Dávila pointed out, "the Western Hemisphere is, or could be made, self-sufficient in practically every resource of raw material required either for the normal peaceful growth of the area, or, if need be, for the waging of a successful defensive war."[106] Efforts which the United States may expend therefore to develop the rich natural resources of Latin America may yield greater benefits than a similar effort anywhere else in the world. Here in the Latin American countries of the Western Hemisphere may be found the best possible area of future development for the United States. By means of Latin American resources, when properly exploited, the United States can become almost entirely free of dependence upon non-American countries, where distances are greater, transportation costs are correspondingly higher, and supply lines consequently are more susceptible of interruption in time of war.[107] Good relations with Latin America must be made a fundamental objective of the foreign policy of the United States. It behooves the people and government of the United States, while fully acknowledging all the differences which exist between Americans North and South, to strengthen all the possible ties with Latin America. Like the family that once had only one child and now has several more, we cannot afford to neglect the first child. Even though Latin

104. William Vogt, *Road to Survival* (New York, 1948); and Tannenbaum, *Mexico: The Struggle for Peace and Bread.* The Senate Banking and Currency Committee, headed by Senator Capehart, concluded in its report in March, 1954, that "The potential of this area [Latin America] for economic development is tremendous." 83d Congress, 2d Session, Senate Report No. 1082, *Study of Latin American Countries,* 641.

105. Details are provided in Senate Report No. 1627, 83d Congress, 2d Session, *Accessibility of Strategic and Critical Materials to the United States in Time of War and for Our Expanding Economy. Report of the Committee on Interior and Insular Affairs Made by its Minerals, Materials, and Fuels Economic Subcommittee,* July 9, 1954 (Washington, 1954).

106. "The Inter-American System," *World Affairs,* CXVII (Winter, 1954), 104.

107. Dávila, *We of the Americas, passim.*

Americans may no longer have first claim on our interest by reason of our new East-West orientation, they have not ceased to be our neighbors. "No aspect of our foreign policy," concluded the International Development Advisory Board in late 1954, "deserves more immediate or more serious consideration. None has more profound implications for our own security and growth."[108]

Our stakes in Latin America are high. Several of these countries, it should be repeated, are so situated as to be important to the protection of the Panama Canal and almost all of them produce materials vitally needed by the United States in war. From Latin America the United States receives 100 per cent of its imports of vanadium, more than 95 per cent of its imports of castor oil and quartz crystals, more than 80 per cent of its imports of crude petroleum and fuel oil, cordage sisal, and vegetable tannin materials, more than 60 per cent of its antimony, cadmium, and copper, more than 50 per cent of its beryl, bismuth, and lead, and a large proportion of its imports of chromite, manila fibers, fluorspar, manganese, tin, wool, and zinc.

These strategic interests of the United States in Latin America are supplemented by the economic. As noted above, United States private capital invested in Latin America totals approximately $6 billion and exceeds United States investment in every other major geographical area of the world. The commercial relations of the United States with Latin America were enormously expanded as a result of World War II. By 1952 Latin America ranked second only to Europe as a market for United States exports. In the first half of 1952 it took 24 per cent of this country's total exports, including about 50 per cent of its automobile exports, 40 per cent of its chemical shipments abroad, 40 per cent of its exports of electrical machinery, 35 per cent of its exports of industrial machinery, and a similar percentage of its agricultural machinery exports. Latin America is the principal source of United States imports. During the first half of 1952 it supplied 31 per cent of all shipments coming into the United States. The statistics of international trade show that Latin America is the principal area of commercial interest to the United States and that in turn the United States is the principal area of commercial interest to Latin America. They suggest also the large future commercial benefits which would accrue to the United States from an increase in the purchasing power, a rise in the standard of living, and the further

108. International Development Advisory Board, *An Economic Program for the Americas,* 14.

economic development of Latin America. It behooves the United States in its own interest to encourage rather than to dampen the explosion of aspirations in that area.

At the meetings of the Inter-American Committee of Presidential Representatives and at the first Economic Conference of the Organization of American States at Buenos Aires, United States representatives listened again to vigorous Latin American demands for the establishment of an inter-American bank as a means of providing additional financial backing for projects considered essential to Latin America's economic development and the improvement of standards of living.[109] But they turned deaf ears to these demands until the dramatic demonstrations against Vice-President and Mrs. Nixon occurred in Lima and Caracas. In 1958 the exports of the United States to Latin America declined by 10 per cent and its imports from Latin America by 5 per cent. The State Department accordingly took a new look at Latin American problems and concluded that the existing institutions of financial assistance were inadequate, as the Latin Americans had long insisted, to meet the urgent developmental needs of the hemisphere. Finally in August, 1958, the United States reversed its previous policy and offered to participate in the formation of a new billion-dollar Inter-American Bank organized to finance a wide variety of agricultural and industrial projects in Latin America. To the bank's capital the United States would contribute some $450 million over the first three years. When the United States made its share of the new Bank's capitalization available through Congressional appropriation in August, 1959, it was expected that the Bank would be able to receive applications for loans by the middle of 1960.

The relations of the United States with Latin America in the years ahead can be expected to be primarily economic. It is and has long been one of the objects of United States foreign policy to advance the commercial and financial interests of its citizens in Latin America, and accomplishments in this field have usually been viewed with pride and satisfaction as new sources of raw material and new markets for United States products have been opened up for development by United States enterprise. One of the principal objectives of United States policy toward Latin America is to cultivate friendly sentiments which will make possible further development along these lines.

But these financial and commercial activities of the United States in Latin America have not always served as a means of fostering

109. *New York Times,* January 11, 1959.

friendly sentiments. Sometimes United States companies operating there have pressed their government for protection against the consequences of their own poor business judgment, ill-considered investments, or over-zealous sales efforts. This pressure when successfully exerted has produced controversies with Latin American governments. The bonanza periods of United States commercial and financial activity in Latin America have not always coincided with periods of harmonious relations. Furthermore, as our experience has repeatedly shown, Latin American nations which need and receive help from the United States in times of financial distress sometimes do not continue as friends. We cannot buy their friendship. We can win them only by enlightened example, intelligent cooperation with them, and a decent respect for their rights and aspirations. It would be a profound mistake to believe that generous policies of technical assistance and capital investment are the answer to all inter-American problems. At least equally important are the political, cultural, and psychological relationships which combine with the economic to form the climate of opinion in the Americas. In all these areas of action the people of the United States can build up a reservoir of goodwill which will ensure continuing friendships with Latin America. In the end it is friends we want, not military allies nor obsequious suppliants nor political puppets. Friends will be won not by a high-powered advertising campaign, nor by anxious arrangements to make sure that our cartridges fit their guns, nor by dramatic efforts to "create respect for the power of the United States," nor even by insistence upon a common hostility to the Soviet Union. A pettifogging, routine policy will yield only bitter fruits. A harsh, strong-arm, and demanding policy will rebound against the United States for many future years. But a constructive, imaginative, and outreaching policy will yield us a greater number of enduring friends here than in perhaps any other area of the world. Such a policy will have to take the form of a revitalized Good Neighbor Policy. It would have validity even if Soviet Communism did not exist. Under such a policy all the peoples of the Americas can proceed together as friends on our common journey toward better destinies.

Bibliography

BOOKS, ARTICLES, AND DOCUMENTARY COLLECTIONS

ABELSON, MILTON. "Private United States Direct Investments Abroad," Department of Commerce, Bureau of Foreign and Domestic Commerce, *Survey of Current Business*, XXIX (November, 1949), 18-23.

AIKMAN, DUNCAN. *The All-American Front*, New York, 1940.

ALBERDI, JUAN BAUTISTA. *Escritos Póstumos*, 16 vols., Buenos Aires, 1895-1901, I, *Estudios Económicos*.

ALDUNATE PHILLIPS, ARTURO. *Estados Unidos, Gran Aventura del Hombre*, Santiago, 1943.

ALEXANDER, ROBERT J. *The Bolivian National Revolution*, New Brunswick, New Jersey, 1958.

———. *Communism in Latin America*, New Brunswick, New Jersey, 1957.

———. *The Perón Era*, New York, 1951.

AMERICAN COUNCIL ON EDUCATION. *Latin America in School and College Teaching Materials*, Washington, 1944.

American States Papers, Foreign Relations, 6 vols., Washington, 1832-1859.

ANAYA, RICARDO. *Nacionalización de las Minas de Bolivia*, Cochabamba, 1952.

ANDERSON, RICHMOND K., *et al.* "A Study of the Nutritional Status and Food Habits of Otomi Indians in the Mezquital Valley of Mexico," *American Journal of Public Health and the Nation's Health*, XXXVI (1946), 883-903.

ANGLO-AMERICAN CARIBBEAN COMMISSION. Meeting at Charlotte Amalie, St. Thomas, Virgin Islands of the United States, August 17-21, 1943. *Nutrition, Agriculture, Fisheries and Forestry*, no place or date of publication.

———. *Report of the Anglo-American Caribbean Commission to the Governments of the United States and Great Britain for the Years 1942-1943*, Washington, 1943.

ARBENZ GUZMÁN, JACOBO. *Informe del Ciudadano Presidente de la República, Coronel Jacobo Arbenz Guzmán al Congreso Nacional en su primer Período de sesiones ordinarias del año de 1953*, Guatemala, 1953.

ARCINIEGAS, GERMÁN. *The State of Latin America*, translated from the Spanish by Harriet de Onís, New York, 1952.

ARÉVALO, JUAN JOSÉ. *Discursos en la Presidencia (1945-1948)*, Guatemala, 1948.

———. *Escritos Políticos*, Guatemala, 1945.

———. *Escritos Políticos y Discursos*, Havana, 1953.

———. *Fábula del Tiburón y las Sardinas: América Latina Estrangulada*, Santiago de Chile, 1956.

———. *Guatemala, La Democracia y el Imperio*, Montevideo, 1954.

ARGÜELLO, AGENOR. *La Garra Yanqui*, Ahuachapán, El Salvador, 1934.

ARNOLD, GENERAL H. H. *Global Mission*, New York, 1949.

AROSEMENA, DR. JUAN DEMOSTENES. *Discurso pronunciado por el Presidente de la República de Panamá, Dr. Juan Demostenes Arosemena en la Sesión Inaugural de la Reunión Consultativa de los Ministros de Relaciones Exteriores de las Repúblicas Americanas*, Panama, 1939.

ASHER, ROBERT E. "The Economics of U.S. Foreign Policy," *Department of State Bulletin*, XXIX (July 6, 1953), 3-8.

BALCH, EMILY GREENE (ed.). *Occupied Haiti*, New York, 1927.

BALLIVIÁN C., RENÉ. *Hombres de Buena Voluntad*, La Paz, 1945.

BAMBILL, BENJAMÍN A. M. *Hacia la Realización de una Democracia Responsable: Homenaje al Libertador de la Nación Gral Juan Perón y a la Jefe Espiritual de la Nación, Eva Perón*, Buenos Aires, 1953.

BARREDA LAOS, FELIPE. *¿Hispano América en Guerra?* Buenos Aires, 1941.

BASADRE, JORGE. "¿Tienen las Américas una Historia Común?" *Excelsior*, Lima, June-July, 1942, 7-9.

BEALS, CARLETON, BRYCE OLIVER, HERSCHEL BRICKELL, SAMUEL GUY INMAN. *What the South Americans Think of Us: a Symposium*, New York, [1945].

BEALS, RALPH L. "Social Stratification in Latin America," *American Journal of Sociology*, LVIII (January, 1953), 327-339.

BEHRENDT, RICHARD F. "Economic Nationalism in Latin America," *Inter-Americana, Short Papers I*, The School of Inter-American Affairs, University of New Mexico, Albuquerque, 1941.

———. *Inter-American Economic Relations: Problems and Prospects*, New York, 1948.

BEMIS, SAMUEL FLAGG. *John Quincy Adams and the Foundations of American Foreign Policy*, New York, 1949.

———. *The Latin American Policy of the United States: An Historical Interpretation*, New York, 1943.

BERNSTEIN, HARRY. "Free Minds in the Americas," a paper prepared for the Latin American Conference "Responsible Freedom in the Americas," Bicentennial Celebration, Columbia University, New York, October 25-30, 1954, mimeographed.

———. *Modern and Contemporary Latin America*, New York, 1952.

———. "Power Politics on the Río de la Plata," *The Inter-American*, II (September, 1943), 11-13.

BLANKSTEN, GEORGE I. *Perón's Argentina*, Chicago, 1953.

BOLIVIA, REPÚBLICA DE, Ministerio de Relaciones Exteriores. *Boletín Oficial*, May-August, 1941, [La Paz, 1941].

BOLTON, HERBERT E. "The Epic of Greater America," *American Historical Review*, XXXVIII (April, 1933), 448-474.

BYRNES, JAMES F. *Speaking Frankly*, New York, 1947.

CABALLERO CALDERÓN, EDUARDO. "El Hombre y el Paisaje en América," *Continente*, Quito, II, 7 (April 1, 1944), 12-17.

———. *Latinoamérica: Un Mundo por Hacer*, Bogotá, 1944.

———. "Lo Que Hispanoamérica Representa en el Mundo Contemporáneo," *Cuadernos Americanos*, Madrid, III, 381-406.

———. *Suramérica, Tierra del Hombre*, Medellín, Colombia, 1944.

CAMPBELL, CAROLYN, AND OFELIA HOOPER. "The Middle Class of Panama," in *Materiales para el estudio de la clase media en la América Latina*, Publicaciones de la Oficina de Ciencias Sociales, Unión Panamericana, Washington, 1950, IV, 38-75.

CANYES, MANUEL S. *The Organization of American States and the United Nations,* Pan American Union, Washington, 1949.

CARDONA, D. ESTEBAN CHALBAUD. "Viaje al País de la Civilización y de la Justicia," *Revista Militar,* La Paz, Bolivia, September-October, 1945.

CARNEGIE ENDOWMENT FOR INTERNATIONAL PEACE, Division of International Law. *The International Conferences of American States: First Supplement, 1933-1940* . . . , Washington, 1940.

CASTAÑEDA, JORGE. *Mexico and the United Nations,* National Studies on International Organization, Prepared for El Colegio de México and the Carnegie Endowment for International Peace, New York, 1958.

CHAMBERLAIN, JOHN. "The Good Partner," *Barron's,* January 31, 1955.

CHAMBERS, EDWARD J. "Some Factors in the Deterioration of Argentina's External Position, 1946-1951," *Inter-American Economic Affairs,* VIII (Winter, 1954), 27-62.

CHASE, STUART. "Operation Bootstrap," in *Puerto Rico: Report of Progress, 1951,* National Planning Association, Planning Pamphlet No. 75, Washington, 1951.

CHRISTENSEN, ASHER N. *The Evolution of Latin American Government: A Book of Readings,* New York, 1951.

CLARK, J. REUBEN. *Memorandum on the Monroe Doctrine,* Washington, 1930.

COLÍN, JOSÉ R. *Requisitos Fundamentales para la Industrialización de México,* Mexico, 1945.

COLOMBIA, REPÚBLICA DE. *Diario Oficial,* Bogotá, 1939.

COORDINATOR OF INTER-AMERICAN AFFAIRS. *History of the Office of the Coordinator of Inter-American Affairs: Historical Reports on War Administration,* Washington, 1947.

COROMINAS, ENRIQUE V. *La Práctica del Hispanoamericanismo,* Madrid, 1952.

CORTINA, ALFONSO. "Latin America and United States Materials Policy," *Social Science,* XXVIII, Autumn Issue (October, 1955), 222-227.

COSÍO VILLEGAS, DANIEL. "Sobre Estados Unidos," *Revista de América,* Bogotá, I (March, 1945), [361]-365.

COUNCIL ON FOREIGN RELATIONS. *Political Handbook of the World: Parliaments, Parties and Press,* Walter H. Mallory, editor, 1930-1954, 25 vols., New York.

CRAVEN, WESLEY FRANK, AND JAMES LEE CATE (eds.). Air Historical Group, United States Air Force, *The Army Air Forces in World War II,* 2 vols., Chicago, 1949.

CRAVIOTO B., RENÉ, et al. "Composition of Typical Mexican Foods," *Journal of Nutrition,* XXIX (May, 1945), 317-329.

CRAWFORD, WILLIAM REX. *A Century of Latin-American Thought,* Cambridge, 1944.

CRONIN, WALTER F. "Some Basic Concepts of Inter-American Organization," unpublished doctoral dissertation, 2 vols., Harvard University, 1949.

CUBA, REPÚBLICA DE. *Diario de la Sexta Conferencia Internacional Americana,* Havana, 1928.

CUEVAS CANCINO, FRANCISCO, M. *Del Congreso de Panamá a la Conferencia de Caracas 1826-1954: el Genio de Bolívar a través de la Historia de las Relaciones Interamericanas,* 2 vols., Caracas, 1955.

Current History, "Report on Latin America," XXXII, April, 1957.

DÁVILA, CARLOS G. *North American Imperialism* (address delivered in Santiago, Chile, July, 1930), New York, 1930.

DÁVILA, CARLOS G. "The Inter-American System" (excerpts from a speech delivered at the University of Virginia, Charlottesville, Virginia, October 8, 1954), *World Affairs,* CXVII (Winter, 1954), 104-105.

————. *We of the Americas,* Chicago and New York, 1949.

DE CONDE, ALEXANDER. *Herbert Hoover's Latin American Policy,* Stanford, 1951.

DE ONÍS, JOSÉ. *The United States as Seen by Spanish American Writers (1776-1890),* New York, 1952.

DENNY, HAROLD N. *Dollars for Bullets, the Story of American Rule in Nicaragua,* New York, 1929.

DEPARTMENT OF COMMERCE. *American Direct Investments in Foreign Countries,* Washington, 1930.

————. *American Direct Investments in Foreign Countries, 1936,* Washington, 1938.

————. *American Direct Investments in Foreign Countries, 1940,* Washington, 1942.

————. *The Balance of International Payments of the United States, 1946-1948,* Washington, 1950.

————. *Foreign Aid by the United States Government,* Quarterly, 1952-1953, Washington.

————. *Foreign Commerce and Navigation of the United States for the Calendar Year 1937,* Washington, 1939.

————. *Foreign Commerce Weekly,* vols. 1-54 (1940-1955).

————, Bureau of Foreign and Domestic Commerce. *Foreign Transactions of the U.S. Government,* Quarterly, 1946-1951, Washington.

————. *Historical Statistics of the United States: A Supplement to the Statistical Abstract of the United States,* Washington, 1949.

————, International Economics Division. *International Transactions of the United States During the War, 1940-45,* Economic Series No. 65, Washington, 1948.

————. *Statistical Abstract of the United States,* annual volumes, Washington.

————, Office of Business Economics. *Foreign Grants and Credits by the United States Government,* Quarterly, September, 1953-March, 1956, Washington.

DEPARTMENT OF STATE. Archives, unclassified telegrams, despatches, and reports, 1930-1955.

————. "Brief Report on the Tenth Inter-American Conference," 8 pages mimeographed, Washington, undated.

————. *Bulletin,* vols. 1-33 (1939-1955), Washington.

————. *The Caribbean Islands and the War: A Record of Progress in Facing Stern Realities,* Washington, 1943.

————. *Consultation among the American Republics with Respect to the Argentine Situation: Memorandum of the United States Government,* Washington, February, 1946.

————. *Cooperation in the Americas,* Interdepartmental Committee on Scientific and Cultural Cooperation, Washington, January, 1948.

————. *Data Book, Latin America,* vol. I, *South America;* vol. II, *Middle America,* Washington, June, 1951.

————. *Executive Agreement Series 1-506,* Washington, 5 vols., 1930-1946.

————. *Final Act of the Third Meeting of Ministers of Foreign Affairs of the American Republics, Rio de Janeiro, January 28, 1942.* Press Release No. 47, February 1, 1942.

DEPARTMENT OF STATE. *Foreign Relations of the United States,* volumes on the American Republics, 1930-1938.

————. *Fourth Meeting of Consultation of Ministers of Foreign Affairs of American States, Washington, D. C., March 26-April 7, 1951, Report of the Secretary of State,* Department of State Publication 4928, Washington, 1953.

————. *Inter-American Conference for the Maintenance of Continental Peace and Security, Quitandinha, Brazil, August 15-September 2, 1947,* Washington, 1948.

————. "Korean Non-Military Assistance Program—Status of Offer as of January 2, 1951 (excluding personnel)," hectographed.

————. *Memorandum on the Monroe Doctrine, Prepared by J. Reuben Clark, Under Secretary of State, December 17, 1928,* Washington, 1930.

————. *Military Assistance to Latin America,* Department of State Publication 4917, Inter-American Series 44, Washington, 1953.

————. *Ninth International Conference of American States, Bogotá, March 30-May 2, 1948. Report of the Delegation of the United States of America with Related Documents,* Publication 3263, Washington, November, 1948.

————. *Peace in the Americas,* Publication 3964, Washington, October, 1950.

————. *Penetration of the Political Institutions of Guatemala by the International Communist Movement: Threat to the Peace and Security of America and to the Sovereignty and Political Independence of Guatemala: Information submitted by the Delegation of the United States of America to to the Fifth Meeting of Consultation of Ministers of Foreign Affairs of the American Republics, Serving as Organ of Consultation,* Washington, June, 1954.

————. *Point Four: Cooperative Program for Aid in the Development of Economically Underdeveloped Areas,* Publication 3719, Washington, January, 1950.

————. *Press Releases,* vols. 1-20 (1929-1939), Washington.

————. "Population Growth and Economic Development in Latin America," Intelligence Estimate Number 56, July 13, 1953.

————. *Report of the Delegate of the United States of America to the Seventh International Conference of American States, Montevideo, Uruguay, December 3-26, 1933,* Washington, 1934.

————. *Report of the Delegation of the United States of America to the Inter-American Conference for the Maintenance of Peace, Buenos Aires, Argentina, December 1-23, 1936,* Washington, 1937.

————. *Report of the Delegation of the United States of America to the Eighth International Conference of American States, Lima, Peru, December 9-27, 1938,* Washington, 1941.

————. *Report of the Delegate of the United States of America to the Meeting of the Foreign Ministers of the American Republics Held at Panama, September 23-October 3, 1939,* Washington, 1940.

————. *Report of the Delegation of the United States of America to the Inter-American Conference on Problems of War and Peace, Mexico City, Mexico, February 21-March 8, 1945,* Washington, 1946.

————. *Second Meeting of the Ministers of Foreign Affairs of the American Republics, Havana, July 21-30, 1940, Report of the Secretary of State,* Washington, 1941.

————. "Status of Offers of Military Assistance to the UN for Korea," January 8 and March 7, 1951, hectographed.

DEPARTMENT OF STATE. "Status of Offers to Unified Command for Korean Civilian Relief Program," March 22, 1951, hectographed.

————. "Summary of Offers of Assistance for Korea, 2 January 1951," mimeographed.

————. Treaties and Other International Acts Series.

————. The United States and Nicaragua: A Survey of the Relations from 1909 to 1932, Washington, 1932.

DESCARTES [pseudonym]. Artículos de Descartes: Política y Estrategia (no ataco, crítica) República Argentina, Buenos Aires, 1951.

DOZER, DONALD M. "Caribbean Relations with Non-American Countries," in The Caribbean: Contemporary International Relations, A. Curtis Wilgus, ed., Gainesville, Florida, 1957, 20-38.

————. "Certain Backgrounds and Results of the Havana Conference," World Affairs, CIII (September, 1940), 164-171.

————. "The New Social Pan-Americanism," The Catholic World, CLIII (July, 1941), [449]-453.

————. "Pan America Consults," World Affairs Interpreter, XI (Winter, 1941), 378-385.

————. "Roots of Revolution in Latin America," Foreign Affairs, XXVII (January, 1949), [274]-288, reprinted in Asher N. Christensen, The Evolution of Latin America Government: A Book of Readings, New York, 1951; and Olen E. Leonard and Charles P. Loomis, Readings in Latin American Social Organization and Institutions, East Lansing, Michigan, 1953.

DUGGAN, LAURENCE. The Americas: The Search for Hemisphere Security, New York, 1949.

DULLES, JOHN FOSTER. "Transcript of the Radio-Television Report to the Nation on NATO Conference at Paris by President Eisenhower and Secretary of State Dulles from the White House, Monday Evening, at 8:30 P.M. (EST), December 23, 1957," mimeographed.

DUQUENNE, LUCIEN, AND PIERRE BIONDINI. L'Argentine de Perón, Bordeaux, 1954.

ECUADOR, REPÚBLICA DEL. Registro Oficial, Quito, 1939.

Editor and Publisher: the Fourth Estate, International Year Book Number, 28 vols., New York, 1930-1957.

EGAÑA, JUAN. Escritos Inéditos y Dispersos, edited by Raúl Silva Castro, Santiago de Chile, 1949.

EISENHOWER, MILTON S. "Report to the President by Dr. Milton S. Eisenhower on United States-Latin American Relations," December 27, 1958, The White House, mimeographed copy.

————. "United States-Latin American Relations: Report to the President, November 18, 1953," Department of State Bulletin, XXIX (November 23, 1953), 695-717.

EMERGENCY ADVISORY COMMITTEE FOR POLITICAL DEFENSE. Second Annual Report Submitted to the Governments of the American Republics, July 15, 1943-October 15, 1944, Montevideo, 1944. English edition. Distributed by the Pan American Union, Washington, D. C.

EXPORT-IMPORT BANK OF WASHINGTON. Annual Report for 1942.

FABELA, ISIDRO. "Los Estados Unidos y la América Latina (1921-1929)," Cuadernos Americanos, Mexico, LXXIX, [7]-80.

FENWICK, CHARLES G. "Intervention: Individual and Collective," American Journal of International Law, XXXIX (October, 1945), 658-663.

FERRARIS, AGUSTÍN. *Estados Unidos Cambia la Cara*, Buenos Aires, 1954.
FINCH, GEORGE A. "The Inter-American Defense Treaty," *American Journal of International Law*, XLI (October, 1947), 863-866.
FOREIGN OPERATIONS ADMINISTRATION, Office of Research, Statistics and Reports. *Report on the Economic Situation in Latin America, Prepared for the International Development Advisory Board*, Washington, August, 1954.
FREYRE, GILBERTO. *Brazil: An Interpretation*, New York, 1945.
———. *New World in the Tropics*, New York, 1959.

GAEDECHENS, CARLOS. "Chile y la Conferencia Pan Americana," *Economía y Finanzas*, Santiago, Chile, February, 1939.
GAINES, THOMAS A. *Profits with Progress: Latin America's Bright Investment Future*, Latin American Investment Council, Stamford, Connecticut, 1954.
GANDÍA, ENRIQUE. *El Gigante del Norte: Una Visión de Estados Unidos*, Buenos Aires, 1942.
GARCÍA CALDERÓN, FRANCISCO. *Latin America: Its Rise and Progress*, translated by Bernard Miall, London, 1913.
GLICK, PHILIP M. *The Administration of Technical Assistance: Growth in the Americas*, Chicago, 1957.
GÓMEZ, EUGENIO. *Europa, Nuevo Mundo*, Montevideo, [1948].
GÓMEZ CARRASCO, RAFAEL L. "La Universidad Interamericana," *América*, Havana, XLIX (July-September, 1956), 58-66.
GONZÁLEZ-BLANCO, PEDRO. *Un Gobierno Popular sin Demogogia (la Argentina del General Perón)*, Mexico, 1951.
GRIFFIN, CHARLES C. (ed.). "Welles to Roosevelt: A Memorandum on Inter-American Relations, 1933," *Hispanic American Historical Review*, XXXIV (May, 1954), [190]-192.
GUATEMALA. Government Information Bureau, No. 17, Guatemala City, March 15, 1954 [4-page bulletin].
GUERRANT, EDWARD O. *Roosevelt's Good Neighbor Policy*, University of New Mexico Press, Albuquerque, 1950.
GUEVARA, TRISTÁN ENRIQUE. *Las Maestras Norteamericanas que Trajo Sarmiento. Conferencia pronunciada por Tristán E. Guevara en Buenos Aires . . . el 1 de Septiembre de 1954*. Publicado par el Servicio Cultural e Informativo de los Estados Unidos de América, [1954?].

HANKE, LEWIS. "The Americanization of America," in *Latin American Viewpoints, L. S. Rowe Lectures on Latin America delivered at the Wharton School, University of Pennsylvania, in the fall of 1941*, The American Academy of Political and Social Science, Philadelphia, 1942, 24-36.
HANSON, SIMON G. *Economic Development in Latin America: An Introduction to the Economic Problems of Latin America*, Washington, 1951.
———. *Utopia in Uruguay: Chapters in the Economic History of Uruguay*, New York, 1938.
HARING, CLARENCE H. *South America Looks at the United States*, New York, 1929.
HARRIS, SEYMOUR E. (ED.). *Economic Problems of Latin America*, New York, 1944.
HAYA DE LA TORRE, VÍCTOR RAÚL. *¿A Donde Va Indo-América?* Santiago de Chile, 1935.
———. *El Antimperialismo y el APRA*, 2d ed., Santiago de Chile, 1936.

HAYA DE LA TORRE, VÍCTOR RAÚL. *Impresiones de la Inglaterra Imperialista y la Rusia Soviética*, Buenos Aires, 1932.

HENDERSON, CHARLES B., Chairman, Reconstruction Finance Corporation and President, Metals Reserve Company. *Report on Activities of Metals Reserve Company from June 28, 1940, to November 1, 1944*, mimeographed.

HILTON, RONALD (ED.). *Hispanic American Report*, III-VI, 1950-1954, Stanford University.

———. *Hispanic World Report*, I-II, 1948-1950, Stanford University.

———. *Who's Who in Latin America: a Biographical Dictionary of Notable Living Men and Women of Latin America*, Parts I-VII, 3rd ed., Stanford, 1946-1951.

HOUSE COMMITTEE ON FOREIGN AFFAIRS, 81st Congress, 1st Session. *Hearings . . . on H.R. 5615, a Bill to Promote the Foreign Policy of the United States and to Authorize Participation in a Cooperative Endeavor for Assisting in the Development of Economically Underdeveloped Areas of the World, September 27-October 7, 1949. International Technical Cooperation Act of 1949 ("Point IV" Program)*, Washington, 1950.

HOUSE COMMITTEE ON FOREIGN AFFAIRS, 83d Congress, 2d Session. House Report No. 1454, *The Inter-American Study Mission: Report of the Inter-American Study Mission of the Committee on Foreign Affairs*, Washington, 1952.

HOUSE OF REPRESENTATIVES, 81st Congress, 2d Session. House Document No. 548, *Report on Audit of Export-Import Bank of Washington, 1949. Letter from Comptroller General of the United States Transmitting a Report on the Audit of Export-Import Bank of Washington for the Fiscal Year Ended June 30, 1949*, Washington, 1950.

HOUSE OF REPRESENTATIVES, 81st Congress, 2d Session. House Document No. 725, *Report on Audit of Export-Import Bank of Washington, 1950. Letter from the Comptroller General of the United States Transmitting Report on the Audit of Export-Import Bank of Washington for the Fiscal Year Ended June 30, 1950*, Washington, 1950.

HOUSTON, JOHN A. *Latin America in the United Nations*, Carnegie Endowment for International Peace, New York, 1956.

HULL, CORDELL. "Achievements of the Second Meeting of the Foreign Ministers of the American Republics," statement at the close of the meeting, Havana, July 30, 1940, Washington, 1940.

———. *The Memoirs of Cordell Hull*, 2 vols., New York, 1948.

HUMPHREYS, ROBIN A. *The Evolution of Modern Latin America*, Oxford, 1946.

IBARGUREN, CARLOS. *De Monroe a la Buena Vecindad: Trayectoria de un Imperialismo*, Buenos Aires, 1946.

INGENIEROS, JOSÉ. "Por la Unión Latina Americana," *Nosotros*, Buenos Aires, XLII (October, 1922), [145]-158.

"Inter-American Bank Convention," drafted by the Inter-American Financial and Economic Advisory Committee. *Department of State Bulletin*, II (May 11, 1940), 512-522.

INTER-AMERICAN COMMITTEE OF PRESIDENTIAL REPRESENTATIVES. *Report to the Chiefs of State of the American Republics*, Washington, May, 1957.

———. *Summary of Proposals Made by Representatives at the First Meeting of the Committee*, Doc. 5 (Rev. 2), September 19, 1956, mimeographed, Washington.

BIBLIOGRAPHY   423

INTER-AMERICAN CONFERENCE. Economic Conference of the Organization of American States, Buenos Aires, August 15-September 4, 1957, *Final Act,* Washington, 1957.

————. Seventh, Montevideo, 1933, *Minutes of the Second Committee, Problems of International Law, Minutes of the Fifth Session (December 19, 1933),* 109.

————. Eighth, Lima, 1938, *Director General of the Pan American Union, Report on the Results of the Conference Submitted to the Governing Board of the Pan American Union by the Director General,* Washington, 1939.

————. Ninth, Bogotá, 1948, Secretary General of the Organization of American States, *Report on the Ninth International Conference of American States,* Annals of the Organization of American States, vol. 1, no. 1, 1949.

————. Ninth, Bogotá, 1948, *Informe sobre los Resultados de la Conferencia,* Washington, 1948.

————. Ninth, Bogotá, 1948, *Chronological Collection of Documents* (Binder's title), Pan American Union, Washington, 1948.

————. Tenth, Caracas, 1954, *Some Problems of Economic Development in Latin America: Report Presented by the Pan American Union for the Information of the Delegates in Relation to Chapter II, Topic 7 of the Agenda,* Washington, 1953.

————. Tenth, Caracas, 1954, *Documents of the Plenary Sessions,* SP-1-SP-56, Caracas, 1954.

————. Tenth, Caracas, 1954, *Final Act,* Washington, 1954.

INTER-AMERICAN CONFERENCE of Ministers and Directors of Education of the American Republics, Panama, September 27 to October 4, 1943. *Final Act,* Washington, 1943.

INTER-AMERICAN CONFERENCE on Agriculture. Fourth, Montevideo, 1950, *Final Act,* Washington, 1951.

INTER-AMERICAN CONFERENCE on Problems of War and Peace. Mexico City, 1945, *Director General of the Pan American Union, Report Submitted to the Governing Board of the Pan American Union by the Director General,* Washington, 1945.

————. Mexico City, 1945, *Final Act,* Washington, 1945.

Inter-American Economic Affairs, Washington, 1947-1957, vols. I-X.

Inter-Continental Press Guide, 14 vols., 1944-1958, Havana.

INTERNATIONAL BANK FOR RECONSTRUCTION AND DEVELOPMENT. Annual reports 1-6, Washington, 1945-1951.

————. *The Basis of a Development Program for Colombia, Report of a Mission headed by Lauchlin Currie and sponsored by the International Bank for Reconstruction and Development in Collaboration with the Government of Colombia,* Washington, 1950.

————. *Report on the Proposal for an International Finance Corporation,* April, 1952.

————. *Report on the Status of the Proposal for an International Finance Corporation,* May, 1953.

————. *A Second Report on the Status of the Proposal for an International Finance Corporation,* June, 1954.

————. *Seventh Annual Meeting of the Board of Governors, Mexico City, D.F., September 3-12, 1952, Summary Proceedings,* Washington, December 15, 1952.

INTERNATIONAL COOPERATION ADMINISTRATION. "Countries Participating in the Investment Guaranty Program," mimeographed leaflet, January 6, 1959.

INTERNATIONAL COOPERATION ADMINISTRATION. "Quarterly Report of Investment Guaranties Issued since the Inception of the Program in 1948 through March 31, 1959," mimeographed leaflet.
INTERNATIONAL DEVELOPMENT ADVISORY BOARD. *An Economic Program for the Americas,* Washington, September, 1954.
———. *Guidelines for Point 4. Recommendations of the International Development Advisory Board,* Washington, June 5, 1952.
———. *Partners in Progress,* Washington, March, 1951.
INTERNATIONAL LABOUR OFFICE. *Labour Problems in Bolivia, Report of the Joint Bolivian-United States Labour Commission,* Montreal, 1943.
———. *Report of the Director-General to the Fifth Conference of American States Members of the International Labour Organization,* Rio de Janeiro, April, 1952, Geneva, 1952.
INTERNATIONAL MONETARY FUND. *International Financial Statistics,* vols. I-XI (1948-1958), Washington.
———. *Terms of Trade in Latin American Countries,* Washington, 1949.

JACKSON, HON. DONALD L., AND HON. MIKE MANSFIELD. *Report: The Bogotá Conference, A Summary of the Problems and Accomplishments of the Ninth International Conference of American States,* Washington, 1948.
JESSUP, PHILIP C. *Elihu Root,* 2 vols., New York, 1938.

KNIGHT, MELVIN M. *The Americans in Santo Domingo,* New York, 1928.
KUBITSCHEK, JUSCELINO. Address before the Commercial Association of Santos, São Paulo, Brazil, January 29, 1957, *Diário Oficial,* Rio de Janeiro, January 30, 1957, 2189-2190.
KUNZ, JOSEF L. "Fourth Meeting of Consultation of Ministers of Foreign Affairs of American States," *American Journal of International Law,* XLV (October, 1951), 743-744.

LABOUGLE, RICARDO DE. *Dos Mundos Frente a Frente,* Buenos Aires, 1953.
LANGER, WILLIAM L., AND S. EVERETT GLEASON. *The Undeclared War, 1940-1941,* New York, 1953.
———. *The Challenge to Isolation, 1937-1940,* New York, 1952.
LA RÉPUBLIQUE ARGENTINE, Ministére des Affaires Etrangéres. *Pacte de Non-Aggression et de Conciliation Argentin,* Buenos Aires, Imprenta del Gobierno, 1936.
LEPAWSKY, ALBERT. *The Bolivian Operation: New Trends in Technical Assistance,* International Conciliation Pamphlet No. 479, March, 1952, Carnegie Endowment for International Peace, New York, 1952.
LEWIS, CLEONA. *America's Stake in International Investments,* Washington, 1938.
LIBRARY OF CONGRESS, Legislative Reference Service. *Total Economic and Military Aid Extended by the United States Government to All Foreign Countries, July 1, 1940-December 31, 1951,* Washington, May 27, 1952.
———. *A Synopsis of Foreign Aid: 1940-1952,* Washington, May 1, 1952.
LIMA, ALCEU AMOROSO. *A Realidade Americana,* Rio de Janeiro, 1954.
———. "Men, Ideas, and Institutions: Humanism and Temperament of the People, " *Atlantic Monthly,* February, 1956, 117-121.
LLERAS CAMARGO, ALBERTO. "The Bogotá Conference," *Bulletin of the Pan American Union,* LXXXII (June, 1948), 308.
———. "The Government's Role in Latin American Business," *Mexican American Review,* XVI (October, 1948), 16-18.

LLERAS CAMORGO, ALBERTO. *The Inter-American Way of Life: Selections from the Recent Addresses and Writings of Alberto Lleras, Secretary General of the Organization of American States*, Pan American Union, Washington, 1951.

———. "The Two Americas," *The Lamp*, quarterly publication of the Standard Oil Company (New Jersey), XXXVI, 3 (September, 1954), 2-5.

MAFFRY, AUGUST. "Program for Increasing Private Investment in Foreign Countries: Report prepared for Technical Cooperation Administration, Department of State, Department of Commerce, Mutual Security Agency, December 18, 1952," mimeographed.

MANGER, WILLIAM. Statement before the National Foreign Relations Commission of the American Legion, April 10, 1958, Press Release, Organization of American States.

MANNING, WILLIAM R. (ed.). *Diplomatic Correspondence of the United States: Inter-American Affairs, 1831-1860*, 12 vols., Carnegie Endowment for International Peace, Washington, 1932-1939.

MARSH, MARGARET A. *The Bankers in Bolivia: A Study in American Foreign Investment*, New York, 1928.

MARTIN, PERCY ALVIN. *Latin America and the War*, Baltimore, 1925.

MEETING OF CONSULTATION OF MINISTERS OF FOREIGN AFFAIRS. *Program of the Meeting of Foreign Ministers of the American Republics for Consultation under the Inter-American Agreements of Buenos Aires and Lima, Panama, September 1939*, approved by the Governing Board of the Pan American Union at the Session of September 12, 1939. [Mimeographed, Washington, 1939.]

———. Director General of the Pan American Union, *Report on the Third Meeting of the Ministers of Foreign Affairs of the American Republics, Rio de Janeiro, January 15-28, 1942*, Washington, 1942.

———. *Final Act of the Fourth Meeting of Consultation of Ministers of Foreign Affairs*, Washington, March 26-April 7, 1951. Mimeographed, Washington, 1951.

MENDOZA LÓPEZ, ALBERTO. *La Soberanía de Bolivia Estrangulada*, La Paz, 1942.

MERLOS, SALVADOR R. *América Latina ante el Peligro*, San José, Costa Rica, 1914.

MÉXICO, SECRETARÍA DE GOBERNACIÓN. *Informe que Rinde al H. Congreso de la Unión el C. Presidente de la República, Lic. Miguel Alemán, Correspondiente a su gestión del 1° de Septiembre de 1951 al 31 de Agosto de 1952*, México, 1952.

MIKESELL, RAYMOND F. *Foreign Investments in Latin America*, Washington, 1955.

MISHKIN, BERNARD. " 'Good Neighbors'—Fact and Fancy," *The Nation*, CLXIX (November 26, 1949), 510-515.

MISTRAL, GABRIELA. "El Grito," *Boletín de la Sociedad Geográfica "Sucre,"* XXXVIII, 393-395 (August, 1943), [173]-175.

———. "Infantilidad del Norteamericano," *Atlántida*, Buenos Aires, May, 1944, 36.

MORENO QUINTANA, LUCIO M. "Pan Americanism and the Pan American Conferences," *Inter America: a Monthly that Links the Thought of the New World*, Carnegie Endowment for International Peace, New York, VIII (June, 1925), [429]-444.

MOSHER, ARTHUR T. *Case Study of the Agricultural Program of ACAR in Brazil* (National Planning Association, *Technical Cooperation in Latin America* [no. 4]), Washington, December, 1955.

MOSK, SANFORD A. *Industrial Revolution in Mexico*, Berkeley and Los Angeles, 1950.

MOYANO LLERENA, CARLOS, in collaboration with ROBERTO MARCENARO and EMILIO LLORENS. *Argentina, Social y Económica*, Buenos Aires, 1950.

MUMFORD, LEWIS. "Orozco in New England," *New Republic*, LXXX (October 10, 1934), 231-235.

MUNRO, DANA G. *The United States and the Caribbean Area*, Boston, 1934.

NATIONAL PLANNING ASSOCIATION. "Private Investment in Underdeveloped Countries: a statement of Principles by the Steering Committee of the National Planning Association," Special Report No. 30, October 16, 1951, Washington, 1951.

———. *Administration of Bilateral Technical Cooperation*, Washington, 1956.

———. *Technical Cooperation in Latin America: Recommendations for the Future by the NPA Special Policy Committee on Technical Cooperation*, Washington, 1956.

———. *Technical Cooperation in Latin America: The Role of Universities in Technical Cooperation*, Washington, 1955.

———. *Technical Cooperation in Latin America: Technical Cooperation— Sowing the Seeds of Progress*, Washington, 1955.

NEARING, SCOTT, AND JOSEPH FREEMAN. *Dollar Diplomacy; A Study in American Imperialism*, New York, 1925.

NEWMAN, PHILIP C., JOHN E. ELLMAN AND ROBERT S. ARIES. *Technical Cooperation with Underdeveloped Countries*, New York, 1952.

NORTHEASTERN COUNCIL FOR LATIN AMERICAN AND INTER-AMERICAN STUDIES, Clement G. Motten, Virgil Salera, Richard L. Davies, H. W. Balgooyen. *Latin America: Development Programming and United States Investments*, Philadelphia, [1956].

NUERMBERGER, GUSTAVE A. "The Continental Treaties of 1856: An American Union 'Exclusive of the United States,'" *The Hispanic American Historical Review*, XX (February, 1940), [32]-55.

NUÑEZ ARCA, P. *Perón, Man of America*, Buenos Aires, 1950.

O'GORMAN, EDMUNDO. "*Do the Americas Have a Common History?*" Pan American Union, *Points of View*, No. 3, December, 1941, Washington, 1941.

OLIVERES, RAMÓN. *El Imperialismo Yanqui en América: La Dominación Política y Económica del Continente*, Buenos Aires, 1952.

ORGANIZATION OF AMERICAN STATES. *Acta de la Sesión Conmemorativa del Congreso de Panamá de 1826, 18-22 de Julio de 1956*, Washington, 1956.

———. *Annual Report of the Secretary General*, fiscal years 1950-1954, Washington, 1950-1956.

———. *Provisional Final Act of the Fifth Meeting of Consultation of Ministers of Foreign Affairs Held in Santiago, Chile, August 12-18, 1959*, Santiago, 1959.

———. [Inter-American Economic and Social Council], *Resoluciones Aprobadas en la Reunión de Ministros de Hacienda o de Economía en IV Sesión Extraordinaria del Consejo Interamericano Económico y Social, 22 de noviembre-2 de diciembre de 1954*, Quitandinha, Petropolis, Brasil, 1954.

OSBORNE, HAROLD. *Bolivia, a Land Divided*, London, 1955.

OSEGUEDA, RAÚL. *Operación Guatemala $$ OK $$*, Mexico, D. F., 1955.
OSTRÍA GUITÉRREZ, ALBERTO. *The Tragedy of Bolivia: A People Crucified*, New York, [1959].

PADILLA, EZEQUIEL. *Free Men of America*, Chicago and New York, 1943.
PANAMÁ, REPÚBLICA DE. *Memoria que el Secretario de Estado en el Despacho de Relaciones Exteriores y Comunicaciones Presenta a la Asemblea Nacional en sus Sesiones Ordinarias de 1940*, Panama, 1942.
————. Ministerio de Relaciones Exteriores, *El Libro de Oro de la Reunión de Panamá*, Panamá, 1956.
PAN AMERICAN UNION. *Analfabetismo en América según los Ultimos Censos o Estimaciones*, Washington, Agosto, 1954. Cuadro 1.
————. Division of Education, *La Educación Fundamental del Adulto Americano, Seminarios Interamericanos de Educación*, No. 7, Rio de Janeiro, 1949, Washington 1951.
————. Division of Intellectual Cooperation, "Is America a Continent? A Round Table of Discussion," *Points of View*, No. 2, October, 1941, Washington, 1941.
————. *La Educación Universal en América y la Escuela Primaria Fundamental: El Plan de Montevideo*, Washington, 1950.
————. *Foreign Investments in Latin America: Measures for their Expansion*, Washington, September 15, 1954.
————. Governing Board, *Minutes*, 1947, 2 vols., Washington, 1947.
————. "Palabras pronunciadas por el Sr. Washington P. Bermudez el 18 de noviembre de 1957, al concluir su mandato como presidente del Consejo Interamericano Económico y Social," ES-RAE-Doc. 10/57, mimeographed.
————. *El Problema de la Vivienda Económica en la América Latina: Informe Preparado por el Secretariado Técnica para Uso de los Miembros de la Comisión Ad Hoc, Consejo Inter-Americano Económica y Social*, Washington, 1953.
————. *Selected Economic Data on the Latin American Republics*, Washington, 1954.
————. *Status of the Pan American Treaties and Conventions*, Law and Treaty Series, Washington, periodically revised.
Paz del Río, illustrated brochure, no author, Bogotá, 1954, 54 pages.
PAZ DEL RÍO. *Una Grande Realización Francesa en Colombia: Estudio presentado ante el Instituto de Estudios Americanos del Comité Francia-América, el 11 de junio de 1954, por Jacques Wetzel, Director General de los Establecimientos Delattre & Frouard Réunis*, Bogotá, [1954], 8 pages.
PENDLE, GEORGE. *Uruguay, South America's First Welfare State*, Royal Institute of International Affairs, London and New York, 1952.
PERÓN, JUAN DOMINGO. *Doctrina Peronista: Filosofica, Política, Social*, Buenos Aires, 1947.
————. *Doctrina Peronista: Perón Expone su Doctrina* [Buenos Aires], 1951.
————. *El Pueblo Quiere Saber de qué se Trata*, Buenos Aires, 1944.
PERÚ, REPÚBLICA DEL, Ministerio de Relaciones Exteriores. *Congresos y Conferencias Internacionales en que ha tomado parte el Perú*, edited by Ricardo Aranda, 4 vols., Lima, 1909-1913.
PINTO SANTA CRUZ, ANÍBAL. *Hacia Nuestra Independencia Económica*, Santiago de Chile, 1953.
PIZER, SAMUEL, AND FREDERICK CUTTER. "Private United States Direct Investments Abroad," Department of Commerce, *Survey of Current Business* (January, 1951), 20-23.

PIZER, SAMUEL AND FREDERICK CUTTER. "Growth in Private Foreign Investments," Department of Commerce, *Survey of Current Business* (January, 1954), 5-9.

PLAZA LASSO, GALO. "Latin America's Contribution to the United Nations Organization," *The Americas and World Order*, International Conciliation Pamphlet No. 419 (March, 1946), Carnegie Endowment for International Peace, New York, 150-157.

———. *Problems of Democracy in Latin America*, Chapel Hill, 1955.

POBLETE TRONCOSO, MOISÉS. *La Economía Agraria de América Latina y el Trabajador Campesino*, Santiago de Chile, 1953.

POOLE, BERNARD L. *The Caribbean Commission: Background of Cooperation in the West Indies*, Columbia, South Carolina, 1951.

PREBISCH, RAÚL. Address at the Informal Discussion on Economic Development During the Seventh Annual Meeting of Governors of the International Bank for Reconstruction and Development, September 10, 1952, International Bank for Reconstruction and Development, Seventh Annual Meeting, Board of Governors, Mexico, D. F., Document No. 19.

PRESIDENT'S MATERIALS POLICY COMMISSION, William S. Paley, Chairman. Report to the President, *Resources for Freedom*, 5 vols., Washington, June, 1952.

"Primer Congreso Nacional de la Industria de Transformación," proceedings in part, *Revista de Economía*, Mexico, X (May 31, 1947), 27-65.

QUINTANILLA, LUIS. *A Latin American Speaks*, New York, 1943.

RAMÍREZ NOVOA, EZEQUIEL. *La Farsa del Panamericanismo y la Unidad Indoamericana*, Buenos Aires, 1955.

REID, HELEN DWIGHT. "Regionalism under the United Nations Charter," in *The Americas and World Order*, International Conciliation Pamphlet No. 419 (March, 1946), Carnegie Endowment for International Peace, New York, 1946, 120-127.

REPETTO, NICOLÁS. *Impresiones de los Estados Unidos*, Buenos Aires, 1943.

REYES, ALFONSO. *Ultima Tule*, Mexico, 1942.

RIPPY, J. FRED. "Contributions of the U.S. Government to Latin America, Fiscal Year 1956," *Inter-American Economic Affairs*, IX (Autumn, 1955), 87-96.

———. *Globe and Hemisphere: Latin America's Place in the Postwar Foreign Relations of the United States*, Chicago, 1958.

———. "The Inter-American Highway," *Pacific Historical Review*, XXIV (August, 1955), 287-298.

———. *Latin America and the Industrial Age*, 2d. ed., New York, 1947.

———. *Latin America in World Politics: An Outline Survey*, New York, 1928.

———. "Literary Yankeephobia in Hispanic America," *Journal of International Relations*, XII (January, April, 1922), 350-371, 524-538.

———. "State Department Operations: The Rama Road," *Inter-American Economic Affairs*, IX (Summer, 1955), 17-32.

———. *The Capitalists and Colombia*, New York, 1931.

———. *The Caribbean Danger Zone*, New York, 1940.

———. "U.S. Government Assistance to the Underdeveloped Countries, 1945-1953," *Inter-American Economic Affairs*, VIII (Spring, 1955), 43-57.

RIVERA, DIEGO. *Portrait of America*, New York, 1934.

ROBERTSON, WILLIAM SPENCE. *Hispanic-American Relations with the United States*, Carnegie Endowment for International Peace, New York, 1923.

RODÓ, JOSÉ ENRIQUE. *Ariel,* 2d ed., Montevideo, 1900; and 4th ed. Barcelona, 1930.
ROJAS, RICARDO. *Eurindia (Obras,* Tomo V), Buenos Aires, 1924.
ROOSEVELT, FRANKLIN D. *The Cruise of President Franklin D. Roosevelt to South America* (Log of the U.S.S. "Indianapolis," November 18 to December 15, 1936), Washington, 1937.
———. "Our Foreign Policy," *Foreign Affairs,* VI (July, 1928), 573-586.
ROSENMAN, SAMUEL I. (compiler). *The Public Papers and Addresses of Franklin D. Roosevelt,* 13 vols., New York, 1938-1950.
RUIZ-GUIÑAZÚ, ENRIQUE. *La Política Argentina y el Futuro de América,* Buenos Aires, 1944.

SAAVEDRA LAMAS, CARLOS. "Monroismo Económico," *Desfile,* Buenos Aires, September 12, 1941.
SÁENZ, VICENTE. *Auscultación Hispanoamericana,* Mexico, 1954.
———. *Hispano América contra el Coloniaje,* segunda edición, Unión Democrática Centroamericana, Departamento Editorial, Mexico, 1949, also published in English under the title *Latin America against the Colonial System,* Mexico, 1949.
———. *Hispanoamérica contra el Coloniaje,* 3d ed., *con varias notas adicionales y un epílogo sobre Bolívar y el Congreso de Panamá,* Mexico, 1956.
SÁENZ PEÑA, ROQUE. *Escritos y Discursos,* 2 vols., Buenos Aires, 1914-1915.
SÁNCHEZ, GEORGE I. *Mexico: A Revolution by Education,* New York, 1936.
SÁNCHEZ, LUIS ALBERTO. *Un Sudamericano en Norteamérica: Ellos y Nosotros,* Santiago, Chile, 1942.
SARMIENTO, DOMINGO FAUSTINO. *Facundo,* 2d. ed., Buenos Aires, 1940.
SCHMECKEBIER, LAURENCE E. *Modern Mexican Art,* Minneapolis, 1939.
SCHNEIDER, RONALD M. *Communism in Guatemala, 1944-1954,* New York, 1958.
SCHURR, SAM H., AND JACOB MARSCHAK. *Economic Aspects of Atomic Power,* Princeton, 1950.
SCHURZ, WILLIAM LYTLE. *Latin America: A Descriptive Survey,* N. Y., 1949.
———. "The Southern Republics of South America: A Regional Economy," in *Political, Economic, and Social Problems of the Latin-American Nations of Southern South America,* University of Texas, Institute of Latin-American Studies, Latin American Studies VI, Austin, 1949, [58]-67.
SCOTT, JAMES BROWN (ed.). *The International Conferences of American States, 1889-1928,* New York, 1931.
SELSER, GREGORIO. *Sandino, General de Hombres Libres,* Buenos Aires, 1955.
SEMPRUM, JESÚS. "El Norte y el Sur," *Cultura Venezolana,* Caracas, I (November and December, 1918).
SENATE. Committee on Banking and Currency, Interim Report, *Study of Latin American Countries: A Study of the Operations in Latin American Countries of the Export-Import Bank and the International Bank and Their Relationship to the Expansion of International Trade,* 83d Congress, 2d Session, Senate Report No. 1082 (Capehart Report), Washington, 1954.
———. Committee on Foreign Relations, 81st Congress, 2d Session, Senate Executive Report No. 15, *Charter of the Organization of American States, Report of the Committee on Foreign Relations, August 24, 1950,* Washington, 1950.
———. Committee on Foreign Relations, 83rd Congress, 2d Session, Special Subcommittee on Security Affairs, *Strength of the International Communist Movement, October 15, 1953,* Washington, 1953.

SENATE, Committee on Foreign Relations, 83d Congress, 2d Session, Special Subcommittee on Security Affairs, *Strength of the International Communist Movement, May, 1954,* Washington, 1954.

———. Committee on Interior and Insular Affairs, Minerals, Materials, and Fuels Economic Subcommittee, 83d Congress, 2d Session, Report No. 1627, *Accessibility of Strategic and Critical Materials to the United States in Time of War and for Our Expanding Economy,* Washington, 1954.

SEOANE, MANUEL. *El Gran Vecino: América en la Encrucijada,* Santiago, 1942, and 2d ed., Santiago, 1944.

———. "If I Were Nelson Rockefeller," *Harper's Magazine,* CLXXXVI (February, 1943), [312]-318.

———. "Impressions of a Roving Peruvian," *Tomorrow,* New York, II (March, 1943), 29-30.

———. *Nuestra América y la Guerra,* Santiago de Chile, 1940.

———. "Where Do We Go from Here," *Inter-American,* V (March, 1946), 23-24.

SILVA, CARLOS ALBERTO. *La Política Internacional de la Nación Argentina,* Buenos Aires, 1946.

SILVA, J. FRANCISCO V. *Reparto de América Española y Pan-Hispanismo,* Madrid, [1918].

SIMPSON, EYLER N. *The Ejido: Mexico's Way Out,* Chapel Hill, 1937.

SINGER, H. W. "Economic Progress in Underdeveloped Countries," *Social Research,* XVI (March, 1949), [1]-11.

SMITH, O. EDMUND, JR. *Yankee Diplomacy: U.S. Intervention in Argentina,* Dallas, 1953.

SOULE, GEORGE, DAVID EFRON, AND NORMAN T. NESS. *Latin America in the Future World,* New York, 1945.

STARK, HARRY N. "War Bolsters Haiti's Economy," *Foreign Commerce Weekly,* December 12, 1942.

STEBBINS, RICHARD P. The Council on Foreign Relations, *The United States in World Affairs, 1951,* New York, 1952.

SUBERCASEAUX, BENJAMÍN. "Así Son Los Norteamericanos," *Continente,* Quito, II, 7 (April 1, 1944), 9-22.

———. "The Cloying Good Neighbor," *The Nation,* CLVII (September 11, 1943), 293-295.

———. *Retorno de U.S.A.,* Santiago de Chile, 1943.

TANNENBAUM, FRANK. *Mexico: The Struggle for Peace and Bread,* New York, 1950.

TANSILL, CHARLES C. *The Foreign Policy of Thomas F. Bayard, 1885-1897,* New York, 1940.

TAVARES DE SÁ, HERNANE. *The Brazilians: People of Tomorrow,* New York, 1947.

———. "Camouflage of Harmony," *Inter-American,* III (August, 1944), 10-13, 43.

TAYLOR, AMOS E. "The Impact of European Recovery on Inter-American Trade," in *Political, Economic, and Social Problems of the Latin American Nations of Southern South America,* University of Texas, Austin, 1949, [7]-16.

TORIELLO GARRIDO, GUILLERMO. Address in the Third Plenary Session, Tenth Inter-American Conference, Caracas, Venezuela, March 5, 1954, Doc. 95, English, Chronological Collection of Documents, Pan American Union.

TREASURY DEPARTMENT. *Census of American-Owned Assets in Foreign Countries,* Washington, 1947.
TRELLES, CARLOS M. *Estudio de la Bibliografía Cubana sobre la Doctrina de Monroe,* Havana, 1922.

UGARTE, MANUEL. *The Destiny of a Continent,* edited with an introduction and bibliography by J. Fred Rippy, translated from the Spanish by Catherine A. Phillips, New York, 1925.
UNITED NATIONS. Department of Economic Affairs, *Instability in Export Markets of Under-Developed Countries in Relation to their Ability to Obtain Foreign Exchange from Exports of Primary Commodities, 1901 to 1950,* New York, 1952.
――――. Department of Economic Affairs, *Relative Prices of Exports and Imports of Under-Developed Countries: A Study of post-war terms of trade between under-developed and industrialized countries,* New York, 1949.
――――. Department of Economic Affairs, *Study of Inter-Latin American Trade,* New York, 1957.
――――. Department of Economic Affairs, *Study of the Prospects of Inter-Latin-American Trade (Southern Zone of the Region),* New York, 1954.
――――. Department of Economic and Social Affairs, *Energy in Latin America,* Geneva, 1957.
――――. Department of Economic and Social Affairs, *Foreign Capital in Latin America,* New York, 1955.
――――. Department of Economic and Social Affairs, *Inter Latin American Trade: Current Problems,* New York, January, 1957.
――――. Department of Public Information, *The Economic Growth of Twenty Republics: The Work of the Economic Commission for Latin America,* 3d rev. ed., New York, 1956.
――――. Department of Social Affairs, *The Population of Central America (Including Mexico), 1950-1980,* New York, 1954.
――――. Department of Social Affairs, *The Population of South America, 1950-1980,* New York, 1955.
――――. *Documents of the United Nations Conference on International Organization, San Francisco, 1945* (London and New York, United Nations Information Organization, 1945), vol. III.
――――. Economic and Social Council, *Economic Development of Under-Developed Countries: Methods of Financing Economic Development of Under-Developed Countries. Survey of Policies Affecting Private Foreign Investment* (8 March 1950).
――――. Economic and Social Council, 6th Year, 13th Session, Geneva, 30 July-21 September 1951, Official Records.
――――. Economic and Social Council, *Taxation in Capital-Exporting and Capital-Importing Countries of Foreign Private Investment in Latin America* (December 5, 1952).
――――. Economic Commission for Latin America, *Analysis and Prospects of Inter-Central-American Trade,* Sixth Session, Bogotá, Colombia, 29 August 1955.
――――. Economic Commission for Latin America, *Economic Bulletin for Latin America,* vol. II, no. 2, October, 1957.
――――. Economic Commission for Latin America, *Economic Survey of Latin America,* annual volumes, 1948-1956, New York.

UNITED NATIONS. Economic Commission for Latin America, Fourth Session, Mexico, D.F., 28 May 1951, *Economic Survey of Latin America, 1950: Recent Facts and Trends in the Economy of Venezuela.*

————. Economic Commission for Latin America, Press Section, "Conclusion of the First Meeting of the Group of Latin American Experts on the Regional Market," Santiago, Chile, February 11, 1958, re-issued by the United Nations Washington Information Office on behalf of the Washington group of ECLA, typewritten, 6 pages.

————. Economic Commission for Latin America, *Progress Report on the Central American Economic Integration Programme* (17 October 1953-9 May 1955), Sixth Session, Bogotá, Colombia, 29 August 1955.

————. Economic Commission for Latin America, *Recent Developments and Trends in the Economy of El Salvador*, New York, 1951.

————. Economic Commission for Latin America, *A Study of Inter-Latin American Trade*, Sixth Session, 29 August 1955, Bogotá, Colombia.

————. Economic Commission for Latin America, *A Study of Trade between Latin America and Europe*. Prepared by the Secretariats of the Economic Commission for Latin America, the Economic Commission for Europe, and the Food and Agriculture Organization of the United Nations, Geneva, 1953.

————. Economic Commission for Latin America, Third Session, 5 June 1950, Montevideo, *Trade Trends and Policies of Latin American Countries.*

————. Economic Commission for Latin America, *United States Capacity to Absorb Latin American Products*, Mexico City, May 28, 1951.

————. Educational, Scientific and Cultural Organization, Inter-American Seminar on Elementary Education, *Universal, Free and Compulsory Education: Conclusions of the Inter-American Seminar on Elementary Education, Montevideo, 1950*, Geneva, 1951.

————. Food and Agriculture Organization, *The State of Food and Agriculture, 1955: Review of a Decade and Outlook*, Rome, Italy, September, 1955.

————. General Assembly, Tenth Session, *Official Records, Plenary Meetings*, New York, 1955.

————. *Report of the Agent General of the United Nations Korean Reconstruction Agency: Organization and work of the Agency from its activation in February 1951 to 15 September 1952*, General Assembly, Official Records: Seventh Session, Supplement No. 19, New York, 1952.

————. Statistical Office, International Monetary Fund, and International Bank for Reconstruction and Development, joint publication, *Direction of International Trade* (Statistical Papers, Series T), I-VI (1950-1956), no place of publication.

————. Statistical Office, *National Income and Its Distribution in Under-Developed Countries*, New York, 1951.

UNITED STATES SECTION, ANGLO-AMERICAN CARIBBEAN COMMISSION. *Sugar and the Caribbean Problem for 1942-43-44; A Report to the President of the United States*, Washington, 1942.

UNITED STATES MISSION TO THE UNITED NATIONS. "Status of Offers to Unified Command for Korean Civilian Relief Program," March 13, 1951, mimeographed.

URUGUAY, REPÚBLICA ORIENTAL DEL. Ministerio de Relaciones Exteriores, *Antecedentes Relativos al Hundimiento del Acorazado "Admiral Graf Spee" y a la Internación del Barco Mercante "Tacoma,"* Montevideo, 1940.

VANDENBERG, ARTHUR H., JR. *The Private Papers of Senator Vandenberg,* Boston, 1952.

VENEZUELAN INFORMATION SERVICE. *Venezuela Up-to-Date,* vols. I-VII, Venezuelan Embassy, Washington, 1949-1957.

VERISSIMO, ERICO. *Gato Preto en Campo de Neve,* Porto Alegre, 1941.

VOGT, WILLIAM. *Road to Survival,* New York, 1948.

WAISS, OSCAR. *Nacionalismo y Socialismo en América Latina,* Santiago de Chile, [1954].

WASHINGTON, S. WALTER. *A Study of the Causes of Hostility toward the United States in Latin America: Brazil,* Department of State, External Research Paper No. 126, Washington, February 24, 1956.

———. *A Study of the Causes of Hostility toward the United States in Latin America: Chile,* Department of State, External Research Paper No. 126.1, Washington, August 28, 1956.

———. *A Study of the Causes of Hostility toward the United States in Latin America: Argentina,* Department of State, External Research Paper No. 126.2, Washington, May 27, 1957.

WELLES, SUMNER. *Address before Institute of World Affairs,* New School of Social Research, May 29, 1944.

———. *Naboth's Vineyard: The Dominican Republic, 1844-1924,* 2 vols. New York, 1928.

———. *The Time for Decision,* New York, 1944.

———. *Where Are We Heading?* New York, 1946.

WHETTEN, NATHAN L. *Rural Mexico,* Chicago, 1948.

WHITAKER, ARTHUR P. *Argentine Upheaval,* New York, 1956.

———. *Development of American Regionalism: The Organization of American States,* International Conciliation Pamphlet No. 469, March, 1951, Carnegie Endowment for International Peace, New York, March, 1951.

———. "Guatemala, OAS and U.S.," *Foreign Policy Bulletin: An Analysis of Current International Events,* XXXIII (September 1, 1954), 4-7.

——— (ed.). *Inter-American Affairs,* 5 vols., 1941-1945, New York, 1942-1946.

———. "The Origin of the Western Hemisphere Idea," *Proceedings of the American Philosophical Society,* XCVIII, 323-326.

———. *The United States and Argentina,* Cambridge, 1954.

———. *The Western Hemisphere Idea: Its Rise and Decline,* Ithaca, 1954.

———. "What Should the New Administration Do About Latin America?" *Foreign Policy Bulletin,* XXXII (April 15, 1953), 5-6.

WHITE, HARRY DEXTER. Papers, Princeton University.

WILLIAMSON, RENE DE VISME. *Culture and Policy: The United States and the Hispanic World,* Knoxville, 1949.

WILLIS, ROBERT S., AND CLIFTON R. WHARTON, JR. "Flota Mercante Grancolombiana," *Inter-American Economic Affairs,* II (Summer, 1948), 25-40.

WOLFE, BERTRAM D. *Diego Rivera: His Life and Times,* New York, 1939.

WOOD, MARIE V. "Agricultural Development and Rural Life in Haiti, 1934-1950," unpublished doctoral dissertation, The American University, Washington, D. C.

WOOD, RICHARDSON, and VIRGINIA KEYSER. *United States Business Performance Abroad: The Case Study of Sears, Roebuck de México, S. A.,* National Planning Association [Washington], May, 1953.

WRIGHT, ALMON R. "Defense Sites Negotiations Between the United States and Panama, 1936-1948," *Department of State Bulletin,* XXVII (August 11, 1952), 212-217.

WYTHE, GEORGE. *Industry in Latin America,* 2d ed., New York, 1949.

"Y". "On a Certain Impatience with Latin America," *Foreign Affairs,* XXVIII (July, 1950), 565-580.

YEPES, J. M. *Philosophie du Panaméricanisme et Organisation de la Paix,* Neuchâtel, 1945.

ZEA, LEOPOLDO. *América como Consciencia,* Mexico, 1953.

ZULETA ANGEL, DR. EDUARDO, Ambassador of Colombia to the United States. "A Program of Interamerican Public Relations," Pan American Union, Washington, no date.

NEWSPAPERS AND PERIODICALS

The data about the newspapers and periodicals listed below have been compiled from *Inter-Continental Press Guide,* 14 vols., Havana, 1944-1958; *Editor and Publisher; The Fourth Estate, International Year Book Number,* 28 vols., New York, 1930-1957; Council on Foreign Relations, *Political Handbook of the World: Parliaments, Parties and Press,* Walter H. Mallory, ed., 25 vols., New York, 1930-1954; and various reports in Department of State Archives.

ARGENTINA

Buenos Aires Herald, Buenos Aires, daily English-language newspaper, established in 1876, reported a daily circulation of 30,000 in 1944. May 28, 1941.

Cabildo, Buenos Aires, Nazi-subsidized. July 21, 1944.

La Capital, Rosario, established in 1867, one of the most influential provincial newspapers of Argentina, reported a daily circulation of 100,000 in 1945. May 14, 1945.

Crisol, Buenos Aires, tabloid established in 1932, subsidiary of *El Pampero* and directed by its editor Enrique P. Oses, Axis-subsidized, outspokenly anti-United States, an estimated circulation of 5,000-10,000 in 1941, was placed on the Proclaimed List on July 30, 1943. December 5, 1941.

Crítica, Buenos Aires, established in 1913, prodemocratic, one of the principal afternoon newspapers of Buenos Aires, claimed a daily circulation of 315,000 in 1939, had a certified daily circulation of 300,000 in 1945 and 1950. June 23, 1930; Aug. 8, 1930; Jan. 16, 1941; May 20, 1941; Dec. 25, 1941.

Democracia, Buenos Aires, established in 1949, daily newspaper organ of the Perón government, reported a daily circulation of 250,000 in 1951. Oct. 11, 1951.

El Diario, Buenos Aires, established in 1881, reported a daily circulation of 150,000 in 1945. Nov. 4, 1936; June 1, 1937.

La Época, Buenos Aires, established in 1915, organ of the Perón government. March 17, 1946.

El Federal, Buenos Aires, established in Feb., 1944, succeeding *El Pampero,* Nazi-subsidized. May 22, 1944.

La Fronda, Buenos Aires, first published in 1929, Argentine nationalist, anti-United States, financed by Manuel Fresco, head of the *Unión Nacionalista Argentina* (Argentine Nationalist Union), had an estimated daily circulation of 15,000 in 1944. May 13, 1940; May 6, 1944; July 26, 1944.

La Hora, Buenos Aires, Communist newspaper, established in 1940. May 31, 1946.

El Líder, Buenos Aires, daily newspaper organ of the Perón government, claimed a circulation of 25,000 in 1950. Aug. 12, 1950.

El Mundo, Buenos Aires, established in 1928, had a certified daily circulation of 300,000 in 1939 and 1945. June 1, 1937; Nov. 7, 1940; May 29, 1941; Sept. 13, 1941.

El Municipio, Almirante Brown, weekly newspaper. Aug. 3, 1944.

La Nación, Buenos Aires, established in 1870, had a certified daily circulation of 220,000 in 1939, 1941, 1944, 1945, and 1947, appealing to upper-class pro-United States readers, reported a daily circulation of 320,000 in 1950. Mar. 8, 1930; June 1, 6, 19, 1931; July 3, 1931; July 12, 1934; Feb. 20, 1936; June 13, 1936; Aug. 16, 20, 1936; Dec. 2, 1936; June 1, 1937; Sept. 17, 1938; April 10, 13, 1940; Nov. 7, 1940; Dec. 15, 1940; Jan. 20, 22, 1941; Feb. 5, 1941; May 28, 29, 1941; Sept. 3, 13, 1941; Nov. 2, 1941; Nov. 5, 1942; Mar. 11, 1944; Mar. 4, 1945; Apr. 24, 1945; Jan. 20, 1946; June 28, 1949.

Noticias Gráficas, Buenos Aires, established in 1931, reported a daily circulation of 312,500 in 1939, 270,000 in 1941, 230,000-270,000 in 1945, 300,-000 in 1950. Nov. 3, 1936; June 19, 1940; July 17, 1940; Dec. 25, 1941; Feb. 15, 23, 1951.

El Orden, Buenos Aires. March 12, 1930.

El Pampero, Buenos Aires, established in 1939, pro-Nazi and subsidized by Hitler's government, with an estimated daily circulation of 100,000 in 1941, 20,000 in 1942 and 1943, edited by Enrique P. Oses in 1941-1942. Feb. 4, 1941; Dec. 1, 1941.

La Prensa, Buenos Aires, established in 1870, owned by the Paz family, had a certified daily circulation of 240,000 in 1939, 300,000 in 1945, 422,233 in 1950. Mar. 6, 1930; Apr. 25, 1931; May 3, 11, 13, 24, 1931; July 6, 1931; Nov. 10, 1932; June 17, 1934; July 13, 1934; Dec. 2, 1936; June 1, 1937; Aug. 1, 1937; Nov. 7, 17, 1940; Jan. 20, 1941; May 20, 1941; Sept. 13, 1941; Dec. 5, 30, 1957.

La Razón, Buenos Aires, daily newspaper established in 1905, reported a daily circulation of 192,000 in 1944. July 18, 1934; June 1, 1937.

Tribuna, Buenos Aires, established in 1945, daily newspaper organ of the Perón government. Mar. 15, 1947; June 23, 1947.

BOLIVIA

La Calle, La Paz, established in 1936, reported a daily circulation of 15,000 in 1946. Jan. 26, 1946.

El Diario, La Paz, established in 1905, claimed a daily circulation of 15,000 in 1939, 21,000 in 1945 and 1947. July 27, 1930; January 26, 1946.

La Noche, La Paz, established in 1936, had a certified circulation of 5,000 in 1939, and 7,000 in 1945, reported a daily circulation of 10,000 in 1947, owned by Mario Flores. Dec. 30, 1940; May 28, 1941; Feb. 26, 1946; Mar. 7, 1946; Apr. 6, 1946; Sept. 2, 1947.

Pregón, La Paz. Jan. 26, 1946.

El Pueblo, La Paz, Communist. Mar. 26, 1949.

La Razón, La Paz, established in 1917, had a certified daily circulation of 15,000 in 1939 and 1945, reported a daily circulation of 24,000 in 1947 and 25,000 in 1950. Nov. 11, 1932; Oct. 30, 1937; Dec. 31, 1940; Jan. 26, 1946; Mar. 29, 1947; Oct. 19, 1949; Apr. 9, 1950.

La República, La Paz, established in 1920, newspaper organ of the Genuine Republican Party, claimed a daily circulation of 3,000 in 1942, 25,000 in 1945. Nov. 16, 1932; June 24, 1942.

Tribuna, La Paz, established in 1944. Mar. 2, 1950.

Ultima Hora, La Paz, established in 1929, claimed a circulation of 5,000 in 1939, 10,000-14,000 in 1945 and 1950, and 3,700 in 1951. Oct. 7, 1937; Jan. 26, 1946; Jan. 10, 1951.

BRAZIL

Brasil-Portugal, Rio de Janeiro, established in 1944. Feb. 22, 1947.

Correio da Manhã, Rio de Janeiro, established in 1901, reported a daily circulation of 35,000 in 1939 and 1942, 40,000 in 1944 and 1945, and 60,000 in 1947 and 1950, appealing to middle-class readers, owned by Dr. Paulo de Bittencourt. Oct. 15, 1940; Apr. 27, 1941; Dec. 1, 1946; Feb. 1, 1947; Mar. 14, 27, 1947; Apr. 24, 1947; May 11, 1947; Nov. 6, 1948; Jan. 7, 9, 22, 25, 27, 1949; Mar. 9, 1949; May 10, 13, 1949; June 8, 1949; Jan. 9, 1954.

Diário Carioca, Rio de Janeiro, established in 1928, claimed a daily circulation of 15,000 in 1939, 25,000 in 1944, 4,650 in 1950, directed by Dante Jobim. Apr. 1, 1941; May 29, 1941; Oct. 29, 1941; Apr. 21, 1945; Nov. 8, 1948; May 15, 1949.

O Diário, Belo Horizonte, established in 1935, had a certified daily circulation of 20,000 in 1944, 22,000 in 1945. Mar. 11, 1944.

Diário da Noite, Rio de Janeiro, established in 1929, a member of the Assis Chateaubriand Associated Dailies, claimed a daily circulation of 95,000 in 1939, 75,000 in 1945, directed by A. de Athayde. July 29, 1937; Dec. 26, 1944; Oct. 12, 1946; Nov. 4, 1946.

Diário de Notícias, Rio de Janeiro, established in 1930, claimed a daily circulation of 30,000 in 1939, 46,000 in 1945, appealing to middle- and upper-class readers. July 20, 1940; Dec. 10, 1941; Dec. 12, 1943.

Diário de Pernambuco, Recife, established in 1825, considered the oldest existing newspaper in Latin America, a member of Assis Chateaubriand's newspaper chain *Diários Asociados,* claimed a daily circulation of 11,000 in 1943, 25,000 in 1945 and 1950, consistently supported the United States and the United Nations during World War II. Sept. 24, 1943.

Diário Latino, Rio de Janeiro. Aug. 20, 1938.

Diário Trabalhista, Rio de Janeiro. Oct. 5, 1946.

Folha Carioca, Rio de Janeiro. Feb. 22, 1947.

Folha da Manhã, Recife, established in 1938, reported a circulation of 8,000 in 1939, 1943, and 1944. July 1, 1943; Mar. 15, 1944.

Folha do Povo, Rio de Janeiro, daily newspaper of the Communist Party. Mar. 4, 1949.

A Gazeta, São Paulo, established in 1906, reported a daily circulation of 60,000 in 1939, 75,000 in 1943, had a certified daily circulation of 100,000 in 1945. Nov. 24, 1943.

Gazeta de Notícias, Rio de Janeiro, established in 1872, claimed a daily circulation of 5,000 in 1939 and 1944, 8,000 in 1945. July 12, 1944.

O Globo, Rio de Janeiro, established in 1925, reported a daily circulation of 90,000 in 1943 and 1944, 85,000 in 1945, directed by Roberto Marino. Sept. 21, 1943; July 8, 1944.

O Jornal, Rio de Janeiro, established in 1919, belongs to the Associated Dailies of Assis Chateaubriand, reported a daily circulation of 35,000 in 1939,

51,000 in 1943 and 1944, 48,000 in 1945, and had a certified daily circulation of 95,600 in 1950. Mar. 7, 1930; Nov. 11, 1932; Mar. 19, 1938; Aug. 20, 1938; Oct. 29, 1941; Sept. 2, 14, 1943; Dec. 19, 1943; Apr. 30, 1944; Oct. 4, 1944; Sept. 3, 1945; Oct. 6, 1945; Dec. 3, 1945; Oct. 5, 1946; Nov. 5, 1946; Jan. 27, 1949; Mar. 26, 1949.

Jornal do Brasil, Rio de Janeiro, established in 1891, reported a daily circulation of 55,000 in 1943, 32,000 in 1944, 30,000 in 1945, and 32,000 in 1947, directed by Barbosa L. Sobrinho. Aug. 21, 1935; Dec. 19, 1943; Nov. 25, 1945; Apr. 13, 1947; Jan. 7, 1949.

Jornal do Comércio, Rio de Janeiro, established in 1827, reported a daily circulation of 10,000 in 1939, 18,000 in 1945, and 32,000 in 1950, directed by Dr. Elmano Cardim. Nov. 11, 1932; Nov. 28, 1936; May 29, 1941; Apr. 18, 1945; Dec. 17, 1948.

A Manhã, Rio de Janeiro, established in 1941, conservative newspaper, reported a daily circulation of 5,000 in 1943, 12,000 in 1944, and 12,800 in 1947. Jan. 28, 1944; Nov. 19, 1944; Sept. 23, 1946.

O Mundo, Rio de Janeiro. July 10, 1948.

A Noite, Rio de Janeiro, established in 1911, had a certified circulation of 210,000 in 1939, 1944, and 1945, reported a daily circulation of 100,000 in 1947. Apr. 5, 1944; Feb. 6, 1945; Nov. 17, 1945; Dec. 18, 1945; Feb. 22, 1947; Sept. 19, 1947.

O Radical, Rio de Janeiro, established in 1932, claimed a daily circulation of 45,000 in 1939, 58,000 in 1944, 30,000 in 1945, appealing to the lower classes, owned by Rodolfo Carvalho. Feb. 1, 1944.

Tribuna da Imprensa, Rio de Janeiro, reported a daily circulation of 20,000 in 1952, directed by Carlos Lacerda. Aug. 15, 1950; July 6, 1952.

Tribuna Popular, Rio de Janeiro, founded in 1945, official organ of the Communist Party of Brazil, daily newspaper, published by Pedro Motta Lima, editor-in-chief Aydano do Conto Ferraz. Sept. 19, 1946; Mar. 17, 1947.

Vanguarda, Rio de Janeiro, reported a daily circulation of 32,000 in 1947. Feb. 22, 1947.

CHILE

La Crítica, Santiago. Nov. 9, 1940.

El Diario Ilustrado, Santiago, established in 1902, reported a daily circulation of 43,000 in 1944, 57,939 in 1945, and 57,039 in 1950, appealing to Catholic upper-class readers. June 26, 1930; May 29, 1941; Apr. 18, 1945; Apr. 4, 1947; Nov. 5, 1948; May 9, 10, 1949.

La Hora, Santiago, rightist, established in 1935, claimed a daily circulation of 25,000 in 1939, 42,000 in 1944, and 45,000 in 1945 and 1947, directed by M. Muirhead. Oct. 30, 1939; May 29, 1941; Oct. 29, 1942; Apr. 17, 1945; Oct. 24, 1946; Nov. 5, 1948.

Hoy, Santiago, weekly magazine friendly to the United States and the United Nations in World War II, claimed a weekly circulation of 30,000 in 1944. Oct. 29, 1942.

El Imparcial, Santiago, established in 1926, reported a daily circulation of 20,000 in 1939, 25,000 in 1945. Nov. 7, 1936; May 28, 1941; Sept. 13, 1941.

El Mercurio, Antofagasta, established in 1906, reported a daily circulation of 15,000-20,000 in 1943, had a certified daily circulation of 12,000 in 1945. Jan. 10, 1944.

El Mercurio, Santiago, established in 1900, pro-British, the so-called "Bible of the upper classes" in Chile, reported a daily circulation of 60,000 in

1939 and 1945, 75,000 in 1950, and 85,000 in 1954, owned by Agustín Edwards and heirs. Jan. 5, 1930; July 8, 1930; Aug. 17, 1930; Mar. 10, 1934; Mar. 4, 1935; Feb. 19, 1940; Nov. 7, 10, 15, 1940; May 29, 1941; Aug. 16, 1941; Sept. 13, 1941; Aug. 23, 1945; Apr. 2, 1949; July 5, 1953; June 30, 1954; Jan. 11, 1955.

La Nación, Santiago, established in 1917, claimed a daily circulation of 40,000 in 1939, 1945, and 1947, appealing to upper-class readers. June 2, 1937; Oct. 7, 1937; Apr. 22, 1938; May 20, 1939; June 17, 1939; May 29, 1941; Sept. 13, 1941; Apr. 17, 1945; Oct. 27, 1954.

La Opinión, Santiago, established in 1932, claimed a daily circulation of 20,000 in 1939, and 35,000 in 1945 and 1947. Mar. 16, 1941; May 29, 1941; Dec. 28, 1947.

La Patria, Concepción, established in 1924, claimed a daily circulation of 20,000 in 1939, 43,000 in 1944, 1945, and 1947. Mar. 8, 11, 1946.

El Siglo, Santiago, Communist daily newspaper, established in 1940. May 29, 1941; Sept. 13, 1941.

COLOMBIA

El Colombiano, Medellín, established in 1912, organ of the Conservative Party, had a daily circulation of 17,565, in 1944. July 16, 1945.

El Correo, Medellín, established in 1913, reported a daily circulation of 20,000 in 1947. Feb. 1, 1945.

Diario de la Costa, Cartagena, established in 1915, the largest daily newspaper in Cartagena, had a certified circulation of 9,500 in 1944 and 1945, owned and directed by Carlos Escallón. Mar. 4, 1945; Oct. 11, 1945.

Diario Popular, Bogotá, daily newspaper organ of the Social Democratic (Communist) Party, directed by Gilberto Viera. July 4, 1945; Jan. 16, 20, 1946; Nov. 14, 1946.

El Espectador, Bogotá, established in 1887, leftist Liberal in point of view, reported a daily circulation of 22,000 in 1939, 26,000 in 1945, and 59,000 in 1950, owned by Luis and Gabriel Cano. Mar. 5, 1930; July 11, 1934; Dec. 2, 1936; Aug. 10, 1945; Jan. 5, 1946; Jan. 16, 1948; Jan. 31, 1949; Apr. 25, 1949.

El Liberal, Bogotá, established in 1911, represents the left wing of the Liberal Party, reported a daily circulation of 15,000 in 1939, 33,600 in 1945, and 46,000 in 1948 and 1950, directed by Alberto Lleras Camargo. Oct. 14, 1938; Sept. 12, 1941; Sept. 5, 1945; Apr. 15, 1946; Apr. 13, 1947; June 10, 1947; Dec. 5, 1947; Jan. 17, 1948; Dec. 21, 1949.

Mundo al Día, Bogotá, established in 1924, proprietor Arturo Manrique, had the largest circulation of any newspaper in Colombia in 1930. Apr. 21, 1931.

El Nuevo Tiempo, Bogotá, established in 1902. July 6, 1931.

La Razón, Bogotá, established in 1936, reported a daily circulation of 15,300 in 1939, 29,770 in 1945 and 1948, directed by Juan Lozano y Lozano. Dec. 2, 1936; Oct. 7, 1937; May 16, 1940; Dec. 30, 1940; Jan. 15, 1946; June 10, 1947.

Relator, Cali, established in 1915, Liberal Party organ, reporting a daily circulation of 23,000 in 1939, 25,155 in 1945 and 1950, appealing to upper-class readers. Apr. 12, 1949.

El Siglo, Bogotá, established in 1935, organ of the Conservative Party, reported a daily circulation of 17,500 in 1939, had a certified daily circulation of 40,000 in 1945, claimed a daily circulation of 85,000 in 1947, owned and directed by Laureano Gómez. Dec. 27, 1939; June 23, 1940.

El Tiempo, Bogotá, established in 1911, organ of the right-wing of the Liberal party, had a certified daily circulation of 55,000 in 1939, 80,000 in 1944, 1945, and 1947, 140,841 in 1950, and 80,000 in 1954, owned by Dr. Eduardo Santos, ex-President of Colombia, edited by Roberto García Peña. Mar. 6, 1930; July 12, 1934; Dec. 1, 1936; May 16, 1940; Dec. 31, 1940; Sept. 13, 1941; Dec. 19, 1941; June 2, 1943; May 10, 1944; Mar. 1, 1945; Apr. 12, 14, 17, 1945; July 4, 16, 25, 1945; Jan. 15, 1946; Mar. 28, 1947; June 10, 16, 1947; Oct. 1, 1947; Dec. 5, 27, 1947; Jan. 15, 20, 1948; Feb. 15, 1948; June 19, 26, 29, 1954.

COSTA RICA

Diario de Costa Rica, San José, established in 1918, organ of the rightist Social Democratic Party, published by León Cortes Castro, who after his retirement from the presidency of Costa Rica, was considered the leader of the Costa Rican opposition to the United States, had a certified daily circulation of 8,850 in 1939, 15,000 in 1943, 1944, and 1945, and reported a daily circulation of 19,000 in 1950, taken over by ex-President Otilio Ulate. Nov. 4, 1936; Dec. 24, 1936; Jan. 5, 6, 1943; Nov. 7, 1946; Dec. 22, 1949.

La Nación, San José, reported a daily circulation of 10,000 in 1947. Oct. 25, 1946; Dec. 25, 1946; and Jan. 7, 1947.

La Nueva Prensa, San José. April 4, 1930.

La Prensa Libre, San José, established in 1889, reported a daily circulation of 7,500 in 1939 and 1944, 10,000 in 1945, and 12,000 in 1950. Jan. 7, 1949; June 8, 1949.

El Trabajo, San José, weekly newspaper organ of leftist *Vanguardia Popular.* Mar. 15, 1947; Aug. 21, 1947.

La Tribuna, San José, established in 1919, reported a daily circulation of 9,000 in 1942, 1944, and 1945, appealing to upper-class readers. Aug. 22, 1941; Oct. 20, 1942.

Ultima Hora, San José, daily newspaper owned by *La Tribuna.* Nov. 14, 1946.

CUBA

Alerta! Havana, established in 1932, conservative, affiliated with *Diario de la Marina,* reported a daily circulation of 36,000 in 1939, 33,000 in 1945. May 10, 1940; Oct. 29, 1945.

Avance (*El Avance Criollo*), Havana, established in 1934, reported a daily circulation of 18,000 in 1939, 14,500 in 1945, appealing to upper-class readers, directed by O. Zayas Portela. March 2, 1936; Nov. 4, 1936; May 13, 1940; Dec. 31, 1940; March 13, 24, 1941; Aug. 14, 1941.

El Crisol, Havana, established in 1934, had a certified daily circulation of 77,500 in 1939, and 80,000 in 1945 and 1947. June 21, 1940; Aug. 15, 1941; Dec. 11, 1947.

Cuba Nueva en Acción (*Acción*), Havana, established in 1934, had a daily circulation of 8,781 in 1944. June 25, 1941.

Diario de la Marina, Havana, established in 1832, pro-United States during World War II, and anti-Communist, appealing to upper-class readers, directed by Dr. José I. Rivero, reported a daily circulation of 34,000 in 1939, 27,950 in 1942, 28,900 in 1945, and 41,000 in 1950. May 14, 1931; Jan. 22, 1936; Nov. 5, 1936; Feb. 5, 1939; May 12, 30, 1940; June 9, 19, 21,

1940; Aug. 25, 1940; Oct. 26, 1940; Nov. 7, 1940; Dec. 31, 1940; Jan. 3, 1941; Apr. 15, 1941; May 23, 1941; June 21, 1941; Aug. 15, 1941; Apr. 19, 1942; Mar. 14, 1947; Jan. 22, 1949; Mar. 13, 1949.

The Havana Post, Havana, established in 1898, had a daily circulation of 5,150 in 1944. Jan. 12, 1941.

Heraldo de Cuba, Havana, established in 1913. May 12, 1931.

Hoy, Havana, established in 1937, Communist newspaper, reported a daily circulation of 18,000 in 1945 and 27,000 in 1950, directed by Aníbal Escalante. June 12, 1940; June 22, 26, 1941; Aug. 15, 1941; Mar. 29, 1946; Feb. 23, 1947; Mar. 5, 7, 14, 1947; May 25, 1947; Dec. 11, 1947; Mar. 13, 14, 1949.

Información, Havana, established in 1937, reported a daily circulation of 60,000 in 1939, had a certified daily circulation of 40,000 in 1944 and 1945, and reported a daily circulation of 35,000 in 1950, directed by Dr. Santiago Claret. June 21, 1940; Jan. 1, 1941; Mar. 19, 1941; Jan. 16, 1945; Nov. 7, 1947; Sept. 28, 1949.

Luz, Havana, established in 1933, had a certified daily circulation of 14,073 in 1944 and 25,000 in 1945. Sept. 3, 1940.

El Mundo, Havana, established in 1901, reported a daily circulation of 27,000 in 1939, 25,700 in 1945, and 28,000 in 1947, appealing to upper-class readers, directed by A. García Ruíz. Nov. 5, 1936; Feb. 20, 1938; June 21, 1940; May 28, 1941; May 19, 1946; Nov. 20, 1946.

El País, Havana, established in 1921, claimed a daily circulation of 51,555 in 1945. Mar. 29, 1930; Oct. 20, 1945.

Prensa Libre, Havana, established in 1941, had a certified daily circulation of 55,450 in 1945, directed by Sergio Carbó. June 23, 24, 1941; Aug. 15, 1941; Dec. 21, 1945.

Tiempo, Havana. Dec. 18, 1940.

DOMINICAN REPUBLIC

Listín Diario, Ciudad Trujillo, founded in 1889, reported a daily circulation of 7,500 in 1939 and 1941, organ of the Dominican Party of President Rafael Trujillo. June 2, 1933; Dec. 21, 1935; Mar. 25, 1936; Mar. 18, 1941; Sept. 9, 13, 1941; Oct. 30, 1941; Nov. 15, 1941.

La Nación, Ciudad Trujillo, established in 1940, owned by President Rafael Trujillo, reported a daily circulation of 10,000 in 1944 and 1945, and 20,000 in 1950. May 10, 1940; Aug. 23, 1941; Sept. 13, 1941; Oct. 29, 1941; May 18, 20, 21, 1946; Jan. 24, 1949.

La Opinión, Ciudad Trujillo, established in 1922, reported a daily circulation of 10,000 in 1939, and 9,000 in 1945, directed by José Ramón Estella. May 23, 1930; Dec. 4, 1930; Mar. 30, 1936.

ECUADOR

El Comercio, Quito, established in 1906, had a certified daily circulation of 16,000 in 1939, and 23,000 in 1944 and 1945. Dec. 31, 1940; Mar. 26, 1944; May 4, 5, 6, 10, 1944; Aug. 19, 1944.

La Patria, Quito, conservative-Catholic morning newspaper. Dec. 10, 1943; July 3, 1946.

Pica-Pica, Quito, popular tabloid newspaper. Aug. 20, 1944.

El Telégrafo, Guayaquil, established in 1884, had a certified daily circulation of 16,000 in 1939, reported a daily circulation of 18,500 in 1944 and 1945, directed by M. E. Castillo y Castillo. July 4, 1932; Dec. 8, 10, 1941; Mar. 16, 26, 1944; Aug. 19, 1944; Dec. 7, 1944.

El Universo, Guayaquil, Ecuador's largest newspaper, established in 1921, had a certified daily circulation of 21,000 in 1939, 22,500 in 1945, friendly to the United States during World War II, directed by Ismael Pérez Pezmiño. Dec. 9, 11, 1941; Aug. 19, 1944; Apr. 18, 1945; July 4, 1945.

GUATEMALA

Diario de Centro-América, Guatemala City, established in 1880, official organ of the Ubico government, reported a daily circulation of 5,000 in 1939 and 1945. Sept. 8, 1936.

El Imparcial, Guatemala City, established in 1922, had a certified daily circulation of 10,000 in 1939 and 14,000 in 1945, reported a daily circulation of 25,000 in 1947 and 30,000 in 1952, owned and edited by Alejandro Córdova. Aug. 3, 1937; Oct. 6, 1945; Feb. 25, 1947; Nov. 4, 1952.

El Liberal Progresista, Guatemala City, established in 1926, organ of the *Partido Liberal Progresista* (Liberal Progressive Party), reported a daily circulation of 7,800 in 1939, 10,000 in 1942, had a certified daily circulation of 18,000 in 1945. May 10, 1937; Aug. 2, 1937; June 14, 15, 1940; Apr. 17, 1942.

Mediodía, Guatemala City. Jan. 18, 1947.

Nuestro Diario, Guatemala City, established in 1922, semiofficial organ of the Ubico government, reported a daily circulation of 12,000 in 1947, and 12,500 in 1950, appealing to upper-class readers. Apr. 22 and May 24, 1932; July 9, 1934; Aug. 5, 1937; Oct. 6, 1937; July 5, 1941; Apr. 11, 1944; Mar. 4, 7, 1945; Apr. 3, 19, 1945; Aug. 31, 1949.

El Tiempo, Guatemala City. Mar. 29, 1930.

HAITI

La Nation, Port-au-Prince, a popular Socialist newspaper. Nov. 18, 1947.

Le Nouvelliste, Port-au-Prince, established in 1896, reported a daily circulation of 5,000 in 1939, 6,000 in 1944, 8,000 in 1947, and 3,200 in 1952, owned and edited by Ernest G. Chauvet. Jan. 10, 1945; Nov. 12, 1945; Apr. 16, 1946; Nov. 17, 1947; Dec. 18, 1953.

Le Soir, Port-au-Prince, established in 1941, reported a daily circulation of 5,000 in 1945, owned and edited by Gerard de Catalogue. July 4, 1945; Nov. 13, 1945; Dec. 5, 1945; July 4, 1949.

HONDURAS

El Cronista, Tegucigalpa, established in 1912, had a certified daily circulation of 4,500 in 1939, 5,500 in 1941, reported a daily circulation of 5,500-6,000 in 1945, owned and edited by Manuel M. Calderón. Apr. 6, 1930; Dec. 15, 1934; Jan. 16, 1936; Sept. 23, 1936; Aug. 7, 1939; Jan. 20, 1941.

Diario Comercial, San Pedro Sula, established in 1932. Dec. 14, 1936.

Diario Moderno, Tegucigalpa. May 5, 1930.

La Época, Tegucigalpa, established in 1933, owned by President Tiburcio Carías Andino, reported a daily circulation of 3,000 in 1939 and 4,600 in 1945. June 26, 1936; Nov. 6, 1940; Dec. 30, 1940.

El Norte, San Pedro Sula, established in 1921, claimed a daily circulation of 5,000 in 1944. Nov. 6, 1940; Mar. 18, 1941.

La Tribuna, Tegucigalpa, established in 1927. Aug. 4, 1948.

MEXICO

Acción, Nogales, Sonora, daily newspaper established in 1938. Nov. 12, 1942.

Así, Mexico City, weekly magazine, established in 1940, claimed a weekly circulation of 18,000 in 1944. Sept. 18, 1943; Apr. 1, 1944.

Boletín de Unidad, Mexico City, established in 1940. Nov. 7, 1940.

Correo de España, Mexico City, established in 1854. Sept. 27, 1854.

El Dictamen, Vera Cruz, established in 1898, reported a daily circulation of 14,000 in 1939 and 1945, appealing to upper-class readers. June 27, 1940; Feb. 4, 1941; June 1, 1941.

Excelsior, Mexico City, established in 1917, had a certified daily circulation of 71,000 in 1939, 84,000 in 1945, 94,458 in 1950, and 116,000 in 1953, appealing to upper-class readers, edited by R. de Llano. Aug. 24, 1931; Nov. 9, 10, 1932; Dec. 10, 1937; Apr. 1, 1938; Mar. 26, 29, 1941; Aug. 15, 1941; Sept. 13, 21, 1941; Oct. 29, 1941; Dec. 8, 1943; Aug. 17, 1945; Mar. 2, 1946; Apr. 28, 1953; Jan. 11, 1958.

El Hombre Libre, Mexico City. June 11, 1936.

Hoy, Mexico City, weekly magazine, established in 1937, reported a weekly circulation of 48,000 in 1944 and 55,000 in 1946, generally critical of the United States during World War II. June 4, 1938; June 29, 1940; Nov. 7, 1942; Aug. 28, 1943; Sept. 4, 1943; Nov. 11, 1944; Dec. 30, 1944; Aug. 31, 1946.

Mañana, Mexico City, weekly, established in 1943, reported a weekly circulation of 18,000 in 1945 and 24,000 in 1946. Nov. 3, 1945; Sept. 14, 1946.

El Mexicano, Ciudad Juárez, established in 1933, had a certified daily circulation of 4,000 in 1944 and 1945. Apr. 22, 29, 1941; June 30, 1941.

El Mundo, Tampico, established in 1918, reported a daily circulation of 15,500 in 1939, had a certified daily circulation of 25,000 in 1945. Oct. 30, 1939.

El Nacional, Mexico City, established in 1919, official newspaper organ of the *Partido Nacional Revolucionario,* or government party, reported a daily circulation of 42,000 in 1939, 50,000 in 1944, 1945, and 1947, and 25,000 in 1950. Aug. 25, 1935; Aug. 29, 1936; Oct. 8, 1937; Nov. 6, 7, 1940; Dec. 3, 1945; Nov. 11, 1946; Apr. 17, 1949; Feb. 23, 1950.

El Noroeste, Nogales, Sonora, established in 1926, reported a circulation of 1,000 in 1939. June 24, 1931.

Novedades, Mexico City, established in 1935, conservative, Catholic newspaper, had a certified daily circulation of 100,000 in 1944 and 1945, and reported a daily circulation of 104,000 in 1950 and 1952, edited by G. Herrerías. Dec. 7, 1943; May 9, 1944; Aug. 13, 1944; Sept. 8, 1944; Nov. 28, 1944; Mar. 26, 27, 1945; May 16, 1945; Nov. 7, 1945; June 20, 1946; Nov. 8, 1946; Feb. 22, 1951.

La Palabra, Mexico City. Feb. 26, 1935.

El Popular, Mexico City, established in 1938, newspaper organ of the Mexican Confederation of Labor *(CTM),* mainly directed by Vicente Lombardo Toledano, president of the *CTM* and the Confederation of Latin American Workers *(CTAL),* reported a daily circulation of 12,000 in 1944 and 1945. June 5, 1940; Oct. 7, 1941; Oct. 30, 1942.

Post, Mexico City, Nov. 2, 1940.

La Reacción, Mexico City. May 12, 1941.

Todo, Mexico City, reported a weekly circulation of 35,000 in 1944 and 52,000 in 1946, weekly illustrated magazine of conservative tone. May 4, 1939; Feb. 19, 1942; Aug. 29, 1946.

Ultimas Noticias, Mexico City, established in 1936, reported a daily circulation of 36,000 in 1939, had a certified circulation of 136,000 in 1944, 100,000 in 1945, and 124,000 in 1947, conservative in outlook, appealing to upper-class readers, owned by *Excelsior.* Aug. 15, 1936; Dec. 1, 1936; Apr. 1, 1938; Aug. 17, 1938; Sept. 13, 1938; Mar. 2, 1939; Oct. 5, 1939; Mar. 20, 1944; Sept. 10, 1946.

El Universal, Mexico City, established in 1916, had a certified daily circulation of 104,300 in 1939, 82,900 in 1945, and 70,831 in 1950, appealing to upper-class readers. Aug. 20, 1931; Nov. 10, 1932; Nov. 5, 1936; Nov. 18, 1938; June 5, 1940; Nov. 7, 1940; Oct. 3, 1941; Dec. 13, 1945; July 7, 1950.

El Universal Gráfico, Mexico City, established in 1922, had a certified daily circulation of 32,000 in 1939 and 64,630 in 1945. Nov. 25, 1936; July 6, 1939.

La Voz de México, Mexico City. May 5, 1946.

NICARAGUA

El Diario Nicaragüense, Granada, daily newspaper of the Conservative Party, established in 1884. Apr. 7, 1948.

Flecha, Managua, established in 1939, reported a daily circulation of 5,000 in 1947 and 7,000 in 1949. Sept. 23, 1943.

Novedades, Managua. Aug. 15, 1941.

La Prensa, Managua, established in 1926, had a daily circulation of 9,000 in 1944, 6,000 in 1947, and 4,000 in 1948, organ of the Conservative Party. Apr. 11, 1948.

PANAMA

Calle 6, Colón, a weekly newspaper. July 20, 1946.

Colón al Día, Colón. Apr. 5, 1946.

La Estrella de Panamá, Panama, established in 1849, with English-language *Star and Herald,* reported a daily circulation of 12,000 in 1939, 26,080 in 1945, and 31,000 in 1950, edited by José I. Fábrega. Nov. 6, 1936; Nov. 19, 1937; July 19, 1940; July 4, 1945; Dec. 4, 1945; Mar. 31, 1946; Apr. 1, 1946; July 4, 1946; July 22, 1947; Sept. 3, 1949; Feb. 21, 1950.

La Opinión, Panama. June 13, 1945.

El Panamá-América (The Panama American), established in 1925, both Spanish- and English-language editions, reported a daily circulation of 10,000 in 1939, 30,000 in 1944, 1945, and 1947, the newspaper organ of ex-President Harmodio Arias. Apr. 20, 1936; Oct. 7, 1937; July 19, 1940; Nov. 8, 1940; Dec. 30, 1940; June 3, 1941; Sept. 4, 6, 8, 1944; Apr. 6, 1945; May 21, 1945; Nov. 7, 1946; Jan. 27, 1947; Feb. 23, 1947; Mar. 4, 1947; May 2, 1958.

Panama Tribune, Panama, English-language weekly, established in 1928, had a weekly circulation of 6,000 in 1944 and 9,000 in 1947. July 18, 1940; May 28, 1941; June 1, 1941; Aug. 22, 1941; Feb. 2, 1947.

La Razón, David. Nov. 6, 1946.

Star and Herald, Panama, English-language newspaper, established in 1849, affiliate of *Estrella de Panamá,* had a certified daily circulation of over 26,000 in 1944 and 1945, and reported a daily circulation of 30,000 in 1948. Oct. 7, 1937; Apr. 21, 1938; Dec. 31, 1940; Nov. 9, 1942; Aug. 20, 1944; May 27, 1945; July 10, 18, 1945; Dec. 15, 1945; Jan. 17, 1946; Sept. 15, 1947; Dec. 23, 24, 1947; May 3, 6, 7, 1958.

PARAGUAY

El Orden, Asunción, established in 1923, estimated circulation of 6,000 in 1933, second largest in Paraguay, appealing to upper-class readers. May 31, 1933.

El País, Asunción, established in 1935, as successor to *El Orden,* reported a daily circulation of 6,000 in 1939, had a certified daily circulation of 10,000 in 1945, friendly to the United States, appealing to upper-class readers, owned by Artazo brothers, edited by Marcos Fuster. July 5, 1945; Oct. 31, 1945.

La Razón, Asunción, established in 1946, reported a daily circulation of 4,500 in 1948. Apr. 16, 1947; Nov. 5, 1948.

La Tribuna, Asunción, established in 1925, reported a daily circulation of 4,500 in 1939, had a certified daily circulation of 15,000 in 1945 and 18,000 in 1947, appealing to upper-class readers, directed by Dr. Raúl Paiva. Apr. 12, 1946.

La Unión, Asunción, daily newspaper organ of the Colorado Party, superseded *La Razón* in 1948, reported a daily circulation of 2,500 in 1950. Mar. 4, 1949.

PERU

El Callao, Callao, daily newspaper established in 1883, claimed a circulation of 4,500 in 1946. Oct. 29, 1946.

El Comercio, Lima, established in 1839, reported a daily circulation of 70,000 in 1939 and 1945, 90,000 in 1950, and 110,000 in 1954, owned by Miró Quesada family, appealing to upper-class readers. May 11, 1931; Oct. 18, 1937; Nov. 7, 8, 1940; Mar. 10, 1941; Dec. 8, 1941; June 29, 1954; Jan. 30, 1955.

La Crónica, Lima, established in 1914, reported a daily circulation of 25,000 in 1939, had a certified daily circulation of 42,000 in 1945, directed by Dr. Rafael Larco Herrera. Mar. 8, 1938; Dec. 31, 1940; Jan. 22, 1941; Mar. 18, 1941; Aug. 16, 1941; Sept. 13, 1941; June 15, 1945.

Jornada, Lima, established in 1944, progovernment newspaper, reported a daily circulation of 10,000 in 1947 and 1948, appealing to upper-class readers. June 7, 1947.

La Noche, Lima, established in 1932, claimed a daily circulation of 3,000 in 1942 and 1945. Jan. 22, 1941.

Nuevo Tiempo, Lima, progovernment newspaper, established in 1948. Jan. 3, 1949.

La Prensa, Lima, established in 1902, reported a daily circulation of 38,000 in 1939, had a certified daily circulation of 38,000 in 1945, reported a daily circulation of 40,000 in 1950, and 4,500 in 1952. Apr. 15, 1941; Dec. 9, 1941; July 4, 1945; June 16, 1952.

Universal, Lima, established in 1934, reported a daily circulation of 22,800 in 1945. Oct. 7, 1937; Aug. 18, 1938; May 31, 1941; Aug. 16, 1941.

Vanguardia, Lima, daily Communist newspaper. June 28, 1946; Mar. 18, 1947.

SALVADOR, EL

El Centroamérica, San Salvador. Nov. 9, 1940.

El Diario de Hoy, San Salvador, established in 1936, had a certified daily circulation of 10,200 in 1939 and 12,490 in 1945. Nov. 2, 7, 1936; Dec. 1, 1936; June 7, 1943; Oct. 8, 1945.

El Diario Latino, San Salvador, established in 1890, reported a daily circulation of 8,300 in 1939 and 8,900 in 1945, 1947, and 1948, owned by Miguel Pinto. Nov. 7, 1936; Nov. 8, 1940; Dec. 30, 1946; Jan. 2, 1947; Mar. 18, 1947; Dec. 30, 1947.

El Espectador, San Salvador. May 10, 1930.

El Gran Diario, San Salvador, reported a daily circulation of 9,700 in 1944. Nov. 9, 1940.

Lider, San Salvador, organ of the Student Democratic Front, a publication of the University students of San Salvador. Sept. 6, 1944.

La Prensa, San Salvador, established in 1915. Feb. 7, 1938.

La Prensa Gráfica, San Salvador, established in 1903, had a certified daily circulation of 11,500 in 1945 and 14,576 in 1947. Nov. 7, 1940; Dec. 5, 1946.

La República, San Salvador, established in 1910. Jan. 10, 1941.

La Tribuna, San Salvador, established in 1933, leftist and very critical of the propertied classes, reported a daily circulation of 6,500 in 1945. Mar. 8, 9, 1945; Apr. 20, 1945.

UNITED STATES

Business Week, New York. Sept. 10, 1955.

Christian Science Monitor, Boston. Apr. 15, 1958; May 31, 1958; June 7, 1958.

El Continental, El Paso, Texas. Sept. 24, 1943.

Evening Star and *Sunday Star,* Washington. Mar. 4, 1951; Apr. 10, 1958.

New York Herald Tribune, New York. Feb. 10, 1931; Mar. 25, 28, 1942; Apr. 1, 1942.

New York Times, New York. Sept. 14, 1930; Mar. 25, 28, 1942; Apr. 1, 1942; Oct. 9, 1942; Nov. 27, 28, 29, 1943; Sept. 4, 1944; Sept. 2, 1946; June 14, 1950; Dec. 21, 1950; May 29, 1951; June 4, 1951; Apr. 21, 27, 1953; May 20, 1953; Aug. 2, 1953; Nov. 14, 1953; June 19, 21, 22, 23, 24, 27, 1954; Aug. 26, 1954; Mar. 23, 1958.

La Prensa, New York. Oct. 25, 1941; June 12, 1958; July 6, 1958.

Washington Post, Washington, D. C. Mar. 23, 1958.

URUGUAY

Acción, Montevideo, daily newspaper organ of the Colorado-Batllista Party, claimed a daily circulation of 10,000 in 1950 and 1952, and 15,000 in 1954. Jan. 24, 1949; Feb. 10, 1955.

El Bien Público, Montevideo, established in 1878, Roman Catholic, reported a daily circulation of 4,000 in 1945. June 23, 1939; Oct. 29, 1941.

El Debate, Montevideo, established in 1931, anti-Communist, anti-United States newspaper organ of the Herrerista faction of the Blanco Party, reported a daily circulation of 30,000 in 1939, 1944, 1945, and 38,000 in 1948. Dec. 3, 1936; Nov. 23, 1938; Mar. 17, 1939; July 5, 9, 1940; July 29, 1944; Aug. 10, 1944; May 3, 1946; Mar. 16, 1947.

El Día, Montevideo, established in 1886, Uruguay's oldest newspaper, organ of the Colorado Party, reported a daily circulation of 50,000 in 1939 and 1945, directed by Rafael Batlle Pacheco. Aug. 27, 1936; Dec. 3, 4, 1936; June 4, 1937; Oct. 7, 1937; Mar. 22, 1938; Apr. 13, 1945.

El Diario, Montevideo, established in 1917, newspaper organ of the Riverista faction of the Colorado Party, reported a daily circulation of 65,000 in 1939 and 75,000 in 1945, appealing to upper-class readers. July 15, 1934; Nov. 9, 1934; Dec. 3, 1936; Mar. 14, 1939.

Diario del Plata, Montevideo. Mar. 9, 1930.

Diario Popular, Montevideo, established in 1941, representing Communist-dominated elements of Uruguayan labor, had a certified daily circulation of 12,000 in 1944, directed by Dr. Juan Francisco Pasos. Oct. 23, 24, 1946.

La Mañana, Montevideo, established in 1916, organ of the Riverista faction of the Colorado Party, conservative, favorable to the United States and the United Nations during World War II, reported a daily circulation of 40,000 in 1939, 53,000 in 1945 and 1947, and 18,000 in 1948, directed by Aníbal P. Gardares. Mar. 6, 1930; Dec. 3, 1936; Nov. 7, 1940; Mar. 19, 1945; Nov. 15, 1945; Nov. 7, 1946; Mar. 15, 1947; Mar. 19, 1948.

Marcha, weekly newspaper organ of the *Agrupación Demócrata Social,* critical of the United States. July 28, 1944; Sept. 8, 1944.

Montevideo, Montevideo. Jan. 2, 1941.

El País, Montevideo, established in 1918, organ of the Blanco Independiente Party, friendly to the United States and the United Nations, reported a daily circulation of 45,000 in 1939, a certified daily circulation of 60,000 in 1944 and 1945, reported a daily circulation of 50,000 in 1950 and 1952, and 60,000 in 1954, appealing to middle and upper classes, directed by Eduardo Rodríguez Larreta. Nov. 2, 4, 11, 1936; Oct. 7, 1937; Nov. 10, 1938; Nov. 4, 5, 9, 1940; May 2, 5, 25, 1941; June 7, 1944; Jan. 7, 1949; Apr. 12, 1949; May 16, 1952; May 29, 1954; June 29, 1954.

El Plata, Montevideo, established in 1916, organ of the Blanco Party, reported a daily circulation of 35,000 in 1939, 50,000 in 1945, and 75,000 in 1947, directed by Dr. Andrés Ramírez. Dec. 3, 4, 1936; Apr. 15, 1940; Mar. 19, 1947.

El Pueblo, Montevideo, established in 1932, had a certified daily circulation of 25,500 in 1945. Sept. 3, 5, 1936; Dec. 3, 1936; Mar. 11, 1939; May 11, 1940.

La Tribuna Popular, Montevideo, established in 1879, reported a daily circulation of 18,000-30,000 in 1945. Dec. 3, 1936; Apr. 16, 1945.

El Uruguay, Montevideo, a daily newspaper with a general appeal, circulation figures not available. June 7, 1936; Nov. 7, 1936.

VENEZUELA

Ahora, Caracas, established in 1936, had a certified daily circulation of 10,300 in 1939, reported a daily circulation of 15,000 in 1945, directed by Juan de Guruceaga. Nov. 10, 24, 1938.

Crítica, Caracas, daily newspaper, circulation figures unavailable. Nov. 6, 1940; Dec. 31, 1940.

La Esfera, Caracas, established in 1927, conservative newspaper, had a certified daily circulation of 27,000 in 1939, claimed a daily circulation of 27,000-30,000 in 1945 and 35,000-50,000 in 1950, directed by Ramón David León. Apr. 15, 1940; Dec. 31, 1940; Oct. 3, 1945; July 4, 1946; Sept. 21, 1946; Mar. 21, 1947; Nov. 4, 1948.

El Heraldo, Caracas, established in 1922, reported a circulation of 35,000 in 1939, 37,900 in 1944 and 1945, directed by Angel María Corao. June 17, 1931; Nov. 4, 1936; Feb. 19, 1944.

El Nacional, Caracas, established in 1943, reported a daily circulation of 21,000 in 1944 and 1945, directed by Antonio Arraiz. Jan. 13, 30, 1944.

El País, Caracas, established in 1943, the newspaper organ of the anti-Communist *Acción Democrática,* reported a daily circulation of 27,550 in 1945 and 40,000 in 1947, directed by V. Rodríguez. Apr. 12, 1944; Aug. 5, 7, 1945; Jan. 30, 1946; June 14, 1946; Aug. 8, 1946; Sept. 19, 21, 1946.

El Universal, Caracas, established in 1909, reported a daily circulation of 25,000 in 1944 and 1954. Dec. 14, 1938; Dec. 29, 1950.

ACCIÓN *Democrática,* Venezuela, 158, 287, 315, 338, 348
Acheson, Dean, 329
Acosta García, Julio, 125
Agrupación de Trabajadores Latino Americanos Sindicalistas (ATLAS), 272
Aikman, Duncan, 49
Alberdi, Juan Bautista, 276
Alemán, Miguel, 251, 265, 328
Alessandri, Arturo, 302
Alianza Popular Revolucionaria Americana (APRA), 8, 90, 110, 287, 288-289, 315, 338, 405
Alvarez del Real, Evelio, 97
Alvaro, Moacir, 155
American Association of University Women, 82
American Council on Education, 207
American Federation of Labor, 156
American Principles, Declaration of, Lima, 24, 39
Anderson, Marian, 181
Anglo-American Caribbean Commission, 119
Antarctica, 408
Aranha, Dr. Oswaldo, 218, 240, 251, 284, 373-374
Arbenz Guzmán, Jacobo, 263, 265, 283, 287, 289, 294, 299, 338, 340, 342, 343, 396, 403
Arciniegas, Germán, 150
Arévalo, Juan José, 147, 212, 265, 287, 289, 339, 348, 401, 404
Arévalo Martínez, Rafael, 166
Argentina: and United States, 137-143, 146, 195, 215-216, 219-220, 234

Argüello, Agenor, 21
Arias, Arnulfo, 80, 102, 285
Ariel, 1, 8, 45. *See also* Rodó, José Enrique
Arosemena, Juan, 83
Arze, José Antonio, 322
Arze, Walter Guevara, 357
Assis Chateaubriand, Francisco de, 121, 133, 143, 196, 314, 390
Atlantic Charter, 102-103, 136, 211, 221, 291
Auténtico Movement, 290, 338

BAHAMA Islands, 118
Baldomir, Alfredo, 66
Baldomir, Dr. José M., 158, 164, 170
Banco Nacional de Fomento, Ecuador, 281
Banco Nacional de Fomento, Honduras, 281
Barbados, 118
Barreda Laos, Dr. Felipe, 50, 98
Batista, Fulgencio, 94, 285, 398
Batlle Berres, Luis, 219
Batlle y Ordóñez, José, 288
Bauer Aviles, Carlos, 22
Bayard, Thomas F., 19
Belo, José María, 89, 169, 177, 184
Belt, Dr. Guillermo, 264
Berle, Adolf A., 215
Bermuda, 118
Berreta, Tomás, 241
Betancourt, Rómulo, 158, 160-161, 170, 182, 204, 214, 287; on race problem, 181, 220
Beteta, Ramón, 44
"Black List." *See* United States, Proclaimed List

447

Blaine, James G., 19
Blanco-Fombona, Rufino, 4
Blue Book on Argentina. *See* United
States, Blue Book
Board of Economic Warfare, 137
Boggino, Dr. Juan, 151, 166, 167
Bogotá, Economic Agreement of, 244,
245, 259, 264, 275, 356
Bohan, Merwin, 281
Bolívar, Simón, 46, 148, 304, 317
Braceros, 126, 183, 305
Braden, Spruille, 211-220 *passim*
Bramuglia, Juan Atilio, 316
Brasil Milano, Plinio, 168
Brazilian-United States Joint Defense
Board, 79
Bridges, Styles, 135
Brum, Baltasar, 380
Bunge, Alejandro, 281
Bustamante, José Luis, 285
Butler, Hugh, 148, 149

CABALLERO Calderón, Eduardo, 133,
205, 305, 322
Café Filho, João, 346
Calderón Guardia, Rafael Angel, 65,
94
Caliban, 1, 2, 4, 8, 19, 166, 210
California, 52, 53, 82, 132, 158, 179,
190
Calvo Doctrine, 259
Canada, 66, 358, 368
Canessa, Roberto, 356
Cantilo, José María, 49, 53
Capehart, Homer, 349
Carbó, Sergio, 51
Cárdenas, Lázaro, 33, 34, 42, 96
Carillo, Alejandro, 153
Carnevali, Dr. Gonzálo, 206
Carter, Albert E., 70
Casanova, José Manuel, 30, 264
Castañeda, Jorge, 382
Castellanos, Jorge, 345
Castillo, Ramón S., 108, 141
Castillo Armas, Colonel Carlos, 283,
343, 370, 396
Castro, Fidel, 300
Caudillo, 292-293, 300, 302, 396
Chaco War, 34
Chacón, Gustavo, 201, 216
Chacón, Roberto, 155
Chapultepec, Act of, 221, 332, 336
Chavez, Dennis, 97
Churchill, Winston, 102, 237

Clark, J. Reuben, "Memorandum on
the Monroe Doctrine," 9, 12, 15
Clay, Henry, 18, 147
Clayton, William L., 259
Clayton Plan, 259-260
Colín, José R., 303
Colonialism, 407-408
Commodity Credit Corporation, 123,
200
Communism: in Latin America, 16,
41, 62, 96, 101, 217, 220, 223-224,
225, 240, 261, 286, 288, 311-313,
336-347, 358, 362, 406; in Spain,
41; in United States, 17, 29, 101
Condor, 79
Confederación de Trabajadores de
América Latina (CTAL), 96, 272
Consultation, procedure and meetings
of, 39, 333, 377, 380; Panama,
1939, 55-57, 71, 83, 142, 231, 333,
377; Havana, 1940, 67-68, 72, 73,
80, 114, 142, 377; Rio de Janeiro,
1942, 113, 115, 127, 141, 144, 377,
380; Washington, 1951, 324, 327,
340, 377; Santiago, Chile, 1959,
378, 380-381
Cooke, Juan I., 215
Coolidge, Calvin, 9, 28
Coordinator of Inter-American Af-
fairs, 72, 81, 115, 116, 119, 133,
200, 232.
Cordero Amador, Raúl, 196
Corominas, Enrique V., 305
Corporación de Fomento de la Pro-
ducción, Chile, 232, 281, 307
Corporación Ecuatoriano de Fomento,
281
Corporación Venezolano de Fomento,
281
Corrêa e Castro, Pedro Luis, 226
Cortina, Alfonso, 301
Cosío Villegas, Daniel, 188, 197-199,
207, 220, 224
Costa, Dante, 173, 177
Cruz-Coke, Eduardo, 212, 213
Cultural Relations, Division of, State
Department, 81
Currie, Lauchlin, 283

DARÍO, Rubén, 4
Dávila, Carlos G., 13, 224, 288, 410
de Andrade, Theophilo, 211, 213, 217
de Castaing, Haydee, 185
Defense Supplies Corporation, 200

de la Guardia, Ricardo Adolfo, 80
de la Torriente, Cosme, 90
de Onís, Federico, 228
Dewey, Thomas E., 149
Dietrich, Marlene, 133
Don Quixote, 86, 188, 212, 376
Double taxation, 245
Duggan, Laurence, 109
Dulles, John Foster, 369, 385, 390, 405
Dumbarton Oaks meetings, 145, 335
Dutra, Eurico Gaspar, 339

Economic Charter of the Americas, 259
Edison, Thomas A., 3
Edwards, Agustín, 25
Edwards Bello, Joaquín, 169, 204, 296
Egaña, Juan, 46
Eisenhower, Dwight D., 355, 369, 372, 384, 389, 390, 407, 409; Policy of the Good Partner, 355, 369, 389
Eisenhower, Dr. Milton S., 269, 282, 407, 409
Eloy Blanco, Dr. Andrés, 168, 186
Emergency Advisory Committee for Political Defense, 138, 334, 380
Esquivel Obregón, Dr. Toribio, 132
European Recovery Program, 242
Export-Import Bank, 76, 129, 232, 247, 270, 331, 369

Fabela, Isidro, 4
Fábricas Militares, Argentina, 291
Fairbanks, Douglas, 133
Falkland Islands, 5, 407
Farm Security Administration, 183
Farrell, General Edelmiro, 139, 140
Federal Bureau of Investigation, 79
Fernández, Jorge, 152, 155, 156, 159, 160, 161, 163, 165, 168, 170, 172, 174, 176, 178, 180, 186-187, 189, 203, 206
Figueres, José, 287
Flores, Mario, 223
Flota Mercante Grancolombiana, 320-321
Fomento corporations, 200, 202, 281. See also Corporación de Fomento de la Producción, Chile; Corporación Ecuatoriano; Corporación Vene-zolano; and Instituto de Fomento de la Producción, Guatemala
Foreign Economic Administration, 200
Forsyth, John, 18
France, 9, 58, 59, 65, 66, 67, 68, 70, 74, 119, 163, 167, 172, 195, 230, 240, 314, 315, 353, 407
Franco, General Francisco, 40-44, 209-210, 348
Franklin, Benjamin, 148
Fresco, Manuel, 139
Freyre, Gilberto, 221
Frondizi, Arturo, 306, 386, 393

Gaitán, Jorge Eliecer, 287
Gajardo, Oscar, 165, 187
Galapágos Islands, 80, 114, 122, 134, 135, 202
Gallegos, Rómulo, 285
Gandía, Enrique, 173, 208
Gans y Martínez, Dr. Oscar, 130
García, Pedro Julio, 175
García Calderón, Francisco, 4, 396
García Peña, Roberto, 157, 169, 171, 184, 203, 206, 208, 223, 376
Georges, François, 221
Germany: mentioned, 9, 43, 46, 47, 49, 50, 51, 52, 53, 55, 58, 59, 60, 61, 62, 63, 65, 67, 68, 70, 73, 74, 78, 90, 95, 98, 99, 101, 104, 105, 107, 114, 115, 120, 139, 141, 144, 145, 146, 163, 172, 179, 195, 202, 230, 239, 261, 311, 344, 350, 358
Gómez, Alejandro, 333
Gómez, Dr. Federico, 278
Gómez, José F., 5
González Videla, Gabriel, 337, 339
Good Neighbor Policy. See Roosevelt, Franklin D.: Good Neighbor Policy; and United States: Good Neighbor Policy
Grable, Betty, 133
"Graf von Spee," 57
Grant, Ulysses, 67
Grau San Martín, Dr. Ramón, 90, 110
Great Britain: mentioned, 9, 49, 50, 55, 58, 61, 62, 65, 66, 70, 73, 74, 86, 91, 93, 94, 114, 119, 140, 146, 172, 195, 198, 230, 261, 314, 318, 351, 407
Guadalupe Hidalgo, Treaty of, 1, 18
Guerra, Angel, 240
Guerra, Dr. Ramiro, 92

HAGUE Conventions of 1907, 55, 58
Harriman, Averell, 244
Havana, Act of, 67, 68
Hawaiian Islands, 142. *See also* Pearl Harbor
Haya de la Torre, Víctor Raúl, 8, 22, 50, 287, 289, 387
Hearst, William Randolph, 30
Herter, Christian, 381
Hitler, Adolf, 40, 44, 61, 70, 75, 91, 96, 101, 102, 104, 105, 180, 188, 195, 196, 226, 239
Hollywood, 7, 133, 170, 207, 208
Hoover, Herbert, 9, 12, 15, 16, 19, 28, 372
Hudicourt, Pierre, 302
Huertematte, Julio E., 257
Hughes, Charles Evans, 28
Hull, Cordell, 19, 24, 25, 33, 35, 39, 42, 49, 53, 72, 77, 110, 126, 137, 138, 140, 208, 237, 260
Humphreys, Robin A., 303

IBÁÑEZ, Carlos, 265, 287, 294, 300, 320
Ingenieros, José, 5-6
Ingram, Admiral Jonas, 126
Institute of Inter-American Affairs, 124
Instituto Argentina de Promoción de Intercambio (IAPI), 291
Instituto de Fomento de la Producción, Guatemala, 281
Inter-American Bank, 232, 235, 272, 369-370, 412
Inter-American Coffee Board, 334
Inter-American Commercial Institute, 71
Inter-American Commission on Territorial Administration, 68
Inter-American Committee of Presidential Representatives, 357, 384-385, 389-390, 412
Inter-American Council of Jurists, 378
Inter-American Cultural Council, 378
Inter-American Defense Board, 122, 334, 340, 380
Inter-American Development Commission, 232
Inter-American Economic and Social Council, 257, 378

Inter-American Financial and Economic Advisory Committee, 71, 73, 231, 334
Inter-American highway, 75, 872
Inter-American Juridical Committee, 334
Inter-American Neutrality Committee, 56
Inter-American Treaty of Reciprocal Assistance, 332, 378, 381, 408
International Bank for Reconstruction and Development, 243, 248, 265, 270, 275, 367, 372
International Committee for the Application of the Agreement Regarding Non-Intervention in Spain, 43
International Conferences of American States: First, Washington, 1889-1890, 232; Second, Mexico City, 1902, 232; Third, Rio de Janeiro, 1906, 333; Fourth, Mexico City, 1910, 334; Fifth, Santiago, 1923, 333; Sixth, Havana, 1928, 7, 55, 333, 334; Seventh, Montevideo, 1933, 19, 20, 24, 25, 232, 333; Conference for the Maintenance of Peace, Buenos Aires, 1936, 24, 25, 31, 39, 377, 380; Eighth, Lima, 1938, 24, 25, 39, 44, 47, 53, 333, 377, 380; Conference on Problems of War and Peace, Mexico City, 1945, 146, 215, 259, 330, 332, 335; Conference for the Maintenance of Continental Peace and Security, Quitandinha, 1947, 242, 324, 332; Ninth, Bogotá, 1948, 244, 272, 275, 324, 336, 340, 380, 382, 407; Tenth, Caracas, 1954, 340, 341, 353, 356, 357, 369, 379, 383-384, 407; Fourth Inter-American Conference on Agriculture, 1950, 298; Meeting of Ministers of Finance or Economy, Quitandinha, 1954, 355, 357, 369
International Development Advisory Board, 250, 411
International Finance Corporation, 248, 370, 390
International Labour Organization, 297, 340, 379
International Monetary Fund, 237, 265, 367, 369

Intra-Latin American trade, 318-321
Italy: mentioned, 43, 47, 50, 61, 62, 65, 70, 74, 75, 105, 107, 114, 125, 141, 313, 314, 344
Ivanissevich, Dr. Oscar, 314

JAPAN: mentioned, 47, 50, 52, 61, 75, 95, 97, 105, 107, 113, 114, 115, 139, 141, 142, 144, 145, 146, 163, 166, 189, 196, 202, 247, 261, 344, 350
Jaramillo Alvarado, Dr. Pío, 149, 203, 212
Jefferson, Thomas, 1, 148
Jews, 159, 179
Jiménez, Enrique, 190
Johnson, Hallett, 222
Joint Military Board for the Northeast (Brazil), 79
Juárez, Benito, 148
Justicialismo (Justicialism), 274, 294, 296
Justo, Agustín P., 33

KENNAN, George F., 210
Knox, Philander C., 87
Korean War, 316, 326, 331, 348, 356, 359
Kubitschek, Juscelino, 287, 302, 393, 394, 404
Kunz, Josef L., 381

LACERDA, Carlos, 225, 272, 329, 332
Lane, Arthur Bliss, 110
Langsdorff, Captain Hans, 57
Latin America: anti-"Yanquismo," 5-8, 14-16, 21-22, 48, 50, 51-54, 95-99, 108, 131-136, 139-141, 196-200, 210-211, 216-218, 223-224, 321-323, 343-345, 403-407; bloc action, 2, 5, 6, 37, 144-145, 317-323, 391-393; dictatorships, 33, 50-51, 83, 211-213, 226; and Good Neighbor Policy, 35-37, 98, 193-196, 236; and Spain, 40-45, 209-210, 348; dependence upon United States, 46, 63, 64, 71, 83, 91, 94, 99, 103, 105-107, 112, 234-235, 268, 314; and Axis, 49, 53-54, 57-68, 70-71, 73-74, 89; Axis populations in, 74-75; trade with United States, 48-49, 128, 326-327, 349; neutrality, 48, 55, 60, 61, 62, 63, 64, 65, 69, 72, 95, 98, 99, 107, 115, 142, 145, 314-317, 322-323; and United States bases, 67, 95, 210; and "no-transfer" principle, 68; aid to United States, 79-80, 121-123, 125-127, 145, 194, 200, 210; nationalism, 3, 6, 132, 199, 219, 259, 263, 271, 294, 301-306, 310, 353, 359, 394, 400-402; measures relating to foreign private capital, 258-259, 373-374; nationalistic legislation, 260-261, 264-265, 289-291, 294; postwar expectations, 230-236, 241, 269-270, 275; postwar disillusionment, 236-241, 270-273, 325, 355; contrasted with Anglo-America, 203-209, 222, 280, 375, 386-388; authority of the state, 275-276, 287-290; civil liberties, 226, 300, 308-309; trade with E u r o p e, 127, 348-353; s o c i o-economic pressures, 226-228, 234, 239, 276-280, 287-297, 323-326, 339, 346, 356-357, 360-364, 364-365; food costs, 229, 277-278; decline in purchasing power, 237, 355, 359-360; land problem, 297-300; labor organization, 294-295, 307; export economy, 229-230, 262-263, 266-268, 325-327; investment climate in, 243, 247, 251-252, 261; investment in United States, 282-283; investment in, 243, 247, 252-254, 255-257, 265, 357-360, 373-374, 411; industrialization, 230-232, 233, 235, 261, 267-269, 275, 306-307, 345, 363-366, 368-376; living conditions in, 227-229, 239, 277-280, 327, 346, 360-361; national planning in, 280-281; sources of revenue, 283-284; "Third Position," 314-317, 323-324; and Soviet Union, 351-353; population, 358-359, 364-365; radioactive minerals, 369; regional market, 391-393
League of Nations, 6, 7, 14, 221
Lemke, William, 29
Lend-Lease. *See* United States
Leo XIII, Pope, 288
Library of Congress, Washington, 81
Lie, Trygve, 328
Lima, Dr. Alceu Amoroso, 375, 395
Lincoln, Abraham, 18, 148

Lleras Camargo, Dr. Alberto, 227, 335
Lloyd Aéreo Boliviano, 79
Lombardo Toledano, Vicente, 96, 272
London, Declaration of, 1909, 55
Lopes Cançado, Dr. Alvaro, 164, 172
López, Alfonso, 47, 144, 298, 318
López Videla, Jorge, 168
LUFTHANSA, 79
Luis Pereira de Souza, Washington, 158, 159, 166, 169, 173
Lutheran, 74

MacArthur, General Douglas, 126
Macedo Soares, José Carlos de, 385
Madariaga, Salvador de, 29
Madison, James, 1, 67
Maestri, Dr. Raúl, 91
Magalhaes Júnior, Raymundo, 154, 181
Manger, Dr. William, 393
Manrique, Ramón, 133, 147, 163, 167, 199, 204, 209, 220, 223, 274
Mariátegui, José Carlos, 4
Marques, Arnaldo Leão, 168, 174
Marshall, George C., 242, 390
Martí, Jorge, 235
Martí, José, 2
Martin, Joseph, 222
Martínez Báez, Antonio, 324
Maschke, Arturo, 369
McKellar, Kenneth, 136
Medina Angarita, Isaías, 149, 155, 168
Mendoza López, Alberto, 130
Merlos, Salvador R., 4
Merritt Report, 134
Metals Reserve Company, 126, 200
Mexican-American Commission for Economic Cooperation, 230, 233
Mexican-United States Joint Defense Commission, 78, 122
Miller, Edward G., Jr., 210, 329, 331
Miranda, Francisco de, 46
Mistral, Gabriela, 130, 318
Mixed companies, 250
Monroe Doctrine, 6, 9, 13, 15, 17, 32, 36, 39, 46, 47, 67, 68, 70, 83, 92, 109, 136, 336-337, 340, 367, 388, 394, 408
Monroe, James, 32, 332, 388
More, Federico, 323
Moreno Quintana, Lucio M., 4

Morinigo, Higinio, 289
Morrow, Dwight L., 9, 402
Movimiento Nacional Democrático, Guatemala, 396
Movimiento Nacional Revolucionario (MNR), Bolivia, 262, 287, 290
Movimiento Sindical Independiente de Trabajadores (MOSIT), Venezuela, 294
Múñoz-Marín, Luis, 287
Mussolini, Benito, 40, 44

Nacional Financiera, Mexico, 281
National Association of Commissioners, Secretaries, and Directors of Agriculture, 221
National Automobile Show, New York, 82
National Planning Association, 246
Netherlands, The (Holland), 59, 60, 96, 119
Neves da Fontoura, João, 329
New Mexico, 52, 82, 97
Nicholson, Meredith, 110
Nixon, Richard, 406-407, 412
Non-intervention, 19, 20, 28, 34, 36, 43, 102, 109, 110, 112, 194, 211, 213, 270, 333, 341-343, 357, 381, 389, 401, 403
Non-recognition, policy of. See Recognition.
North Atlantic Treaty Organization (NATO), 314, 385-386
Novoa, Carlos, 239

Office for Coordination of Commercial and Cultural Relations between the American Republics. See Coordinator of Inter-American Affairs
O'Higgins, Bernardo, 46
Oliveres, Ramón, 403
Organización Regional Interamericana de Trabajadores (ORIT), 272
Organization of American States, 332-336, 340, 341, 367, 372, 377-382, 385-386, 389, 393
Organization of Central American States (ODECA), 321
Orozco, José Clemente, 7
Ortiz, Roberto M., 60, 108
Ortiz Echagüe, Fernando, 105, 150
Osegueda, Raúl, 404

Oses, Enrique P., 95
Ospina Pérez, Dr. Mariano, 241
Ostría Gutiérrez, Alberto, 315
Oumansky, Constantin, 223, 311

PADILLA, Ezequiel, 23, 91, 95, 102, 106, 126, 186, 235
Padilla, Dr. Tiburcio, 163-164
Padilla Franco, Monica, 180
Panama Canal, 5, 52, 61, 80, 100, 104, 123, 127, 131, 205, 322, 405, 411
Panama, Declaration of, 56, 57, 58, 64, 106
Pan-American Airways, 79
Pan-Americanism, 2, 4, 37, 40, 57, 63, 67, 69, 74, 82, 96, 107, 112, 130, 139, 142, 143, 147, 148, 192, 193, 196, 197, 206, 213, 221, 240, 273, 314, 382, 388, 389
Pan American trade cartel, 72, 73
Pan American Union, 7, 111, 166, 206, 333-336, 372, 378, 382
Partido Acción Revolucionaria (PAR) Guatemala, 289
Partido de la Izquierda Revolucionaria (PIR), Bolivia, 287, 290, 313, 322
Partido Socialista Popular, Cuba, 338
Partido Trabalhista Brasileiro (PTB), 289
Paz Estenssoro, Víctor, 287, 290, 299
Pearl Harbor, 81, 97, 108, 112, 113, 114, 115, 116, 118, 120, 122, 123, 129, 142, 144, 153, 160, 163, 192, 380
Peñaranda, Enrique, 144
Pérez Jiménez, Marcos, 294
Pérez Lobo, Rafael, 207
Perón, Evita, 274, 295
Perón, Juan Domingo, 139, 193, 239, 264, 287-301 *passim,* 306, 307, 316, 317, 328, 337, 338, 351, 373; and Braden, 215-217, 220, 396
Pershing Expedition, 52, 113
Peyrera, Carlos, 4
Philippine Islands, 51, 94, 114, 126, 161, 190
Picado, Dr. Clodomiro, 130, 212
Picón-Salas, Mariano, 207-208, 305, 315
Pius XI, Pope, 288
Platt Amendment with Cuba, 20, 403
Plaza Lasso, Galo, 339, 392, 403

"Point Four." *See* United States, technical assistance
Poland, 55, 59, 351, 353
Prado, Antonio, 4
Prado, Manuel, 385
Prado Valladares, Dr. José Antonio do, 173
Prío Socarrás, Carlos, 265, 285
Protestants, 159, 209
Pueyrredón, Dr. Honorio, 78, 93
Puig Casauranc, José Manuel, 20

QUADROS DA SILVA, Atys, 182, 183, 189
Quintanilla, Luis, 166, 171, 172, 185, 196, 203, 206

RAMA Road, Nicaragua, 75
Ramírez Novoa, Ezequiel, 404
Rão, Vicente, 356
Recaurte, Gustavo Wills, 325
Recognition and non-recognition, policy of, 138, 140, 142, 219
Reconstruction Finance Corporation, 123, 124
Reis, Fernanda, 191
Repetto, Nicolás, 156, 160, 161, 165, 171, 175, 178, 186
Reyes, Alfonso, 99, 318
Reynolds, Robert, 135
Ríos, Juan Antonio, 129
Ríos Gallardo, Conrado, 218
Rippy, Professor J. Fred, 195, 393
Rivera, Diego, 7
Rivera Schreiber, Ricardo, 357
Rocha, Geraldo, 323
Rockefeller, John D., Jr., 85, 177
Rockefeller, Nelson, 200, 336. *See also* Coordinator of Inter-American Affairs
Rodó, José Enrique, 1, 2, 3, 4, 84, 155, 167, 203, 304
Rodríguez Larreta, Dr. Alberto, 214-215
Rojas, Ricardo, 304
Rojas Pinilla, Gustavo, 290, 350
Roman Catholicism, 21, 26, 53, 62, 82, 94, 105, 132, 159, 180, 209, 212, 288, 311, 316, 358, 396
Roosevelt, Franklin D.: elected president, 16-17; Good Neighbor Policy, 17-26, 35-37, 38-39, 47, 109, 110, 111, 112, 148 *passim,* 216, 221, 325, 345; visits Colombia, 19; New

Deal, 23, 27-30, 33, 51, 88, 89, 113, 126, 148, 177, 292, 314; re-elected president 1936, 27-31; visits Brazil, Argentina, Uruguay, 31-33; and democracy, 28-29, 32-33, 50, 51, 54, 88-89, 148, 150, 226; and Mexico, 33-34, 233; and Spain, 41-45; and Axis, 38-39, 60, 65, 93, 99, 100-106; Declaration of Panama, 56, 58; "quarantine speech," 45-46, 48, 52, 62, 64; aid to Latin America, 71, 72, 75, 76, 77, 78; re-elected president 1940, 1944, 87-88, 149, 176; popularity in Latin America, 27-29, 31-32, 35-37, 86-88, 92, 93, 94, 148-151, 192, 226, 234, 292; and Policy of Good Partner, 112-113, 115, 126, 132, 141, 193, 194, 223, 235, 258; death, 150-151, 188; mentioned, 9, 81, 82, 84, 86, 87, 88, 89, 90, 91, 95, 98, 122, 135, 136, 137, 139, 140, 145, 146, 149, 176, 177, 191, 192, 212, 221, 224, 260, 292, 325, 337, 345, 369, 388

Roosevelt, Theodore, 9, 87, 150, 221, 394

Root, Elihu, 19

Rowe, Dr. Leo S., 334

Rubber Development Corporation, 200

Rubber Reserve Company, 201, 202

Ruiz Guiñazú, Enrique, 108, 141-142

SAAVEDRA Lamas, Carlos, 7

Saboia de Medeiros, Roberto, 156, 159, 170

Sáenz, Vicente, 404

Sáenz Peña, Roque, 4

Saladrigas Zayas, Dr. Carlos, 90

Sánchez, Luis Alberto, 170, 176, 315

Sandino, Augusto César, 216, 404

Santos, Eduardo, 55

Santos, Enrique ("Caliban"), 154, 161, 194, 199, 203, 204, 208-209, 210, 223-224

Sarmiento, Domingo Faustino, 304, 362

Saude, Alimentação, Transporte, e Electrica (SALTE), 269, 281, 290

SCADTA (Sociedad Colombo-Alemana de Transportes Aéreos), 65, 79

Schmidt, Augusto Frederico, 254, 270, 274

SEDTA (Sociedad Ecuatoriana de Transportes Aéreos), 79

Semprúm, Jesús, 4

Seoane, Manuel, 90, 110, 148, 153, 184

Servicio Cooperativo Interamericano de Salud Pública, 116, 199

Silva, Francisco V., 5

Silva Herzog, Jesús, 254

Smoot-Hawley Act, 1930, 15

Socialism: in United States, 17, 29, 313-314; in Latin America, 288-290, 292

Société Haïtiano-Américaine de Développement Agricole (SHADA), 201

Somoza, Anastasio, 51, 70, 75, 89, 90

Soviet Union (Russia): mentioned, 2, 49, 51, 101, 102, 153, 154, 163, 218, 240, 271, 288, 290, 310-316, 317, 322-323, 332, 335, 337, 338, 342, 345, 351, 352, 358

Spain: mentioned, 2, 40, 41, 42, 43, 44, 75, 159, 172, 195, 209, 276, 313, 316, 348, 353

Stalin, Josef, 62, 96, 101, 237, 311

Stevenson, Coke R., 180, 183

Stimson, Henry L., 11, 12

Stockdale, Sir Frank, 119

Storni, Vice Admiral Segundo, 138

Subercaseaux, Benjamín, 160, 175

Sumner, Charles, 18

TABLADA, José Juan, 7

Taussig, Charles W., 119

Tavares de Sá, Hernane, 135, 157, 171-172, 182, 196, 205

Tello, Manuel, 324

Terra, Gabriel, 33, 50

Texas, 52, 82, 132, 161, 168, 180, 181, 183

Torriello, Guillermo, 340, 343

Trujillo, Rafael Leonidas, 290

Truman, Harry S., 151, 189, 191, 192, 209, 237, 240, 244, 245, 246, 248, 249, 250, 251, 253, 255, 311, 312, 313-314, 324, 325, 329, 331, 336, 345, 370, 390

Tyler, John, 18

Ubico, Jorge, 87
Ugarte, Manuel, 4, 5, 178-179, 203, 304
Ulloa, Dr. Alberto, 92
Unión Cívica Radical, Argentina, 290, 306, 307
Unión Nacional Sinarquista (Partido de la Fuerza Popular), 210
United Fruit Company, 263, 342, 404
United States: "a colossus," 1, 2, 3, 5, 8, 210, 375; policy of "big stick," 12, 20, 34, 35, 87, 98, 113, 217, 218, 222, 341, 345; "dollar diplomacy," 4, 14, 20, 30, 37, 87, 113, 130, 136, 193, 217, 222, 248, 258, 341; imperialism, 1-2, 4, 6, 8, 13-14, 19, 21, 22, 27, 32, 35, 36, 50, 51, 52, 54, 62, 87, 95, 96, 101, 114, 130, 135, 136, 139, 143, 148, 190, 196, 208, 217, 221, 223, 224, 254, 292, 313, 317, 344, 345, 403, 404; protectionism and tariff, 2, 15, 16, 18, 26, 33, 36, 406; interventions, 3-4, 6-7, 9-12, 13-15, 17, 20-22, 48, 52-53, 87, 138, 141, 214-218, 254, 341-343, cost of, 12; economic depression, 10, 15-16, 22; presidential election, 1932, 16; Good Neighbor Policy, 18-19, 26-28, 30, 33, 34, 35-38, 40, 51, 52, 75, 87, 88, 98, 105, 107, 109-113, 115, 125, 126, 130, 131, 136, 137, 139, 141, 143, 147, 148, 149, 150, 151, 152, 179, 183, 192-195, 197, 199, 216, 217, 223, 258, 270, 394, 401, 413, and Republican Party, 149, 221-222; Braden corollary, 211-221, abandoned, 222-224, 240-241 (See also Roosevelt, Franklin D., Good Neighbor Policy); commercial reciprocity, 20, 23-25, 28, 34, 49, 260; Democratic Party, 16-17, 26, 28, 35-36, 53, 221-222; Republican Party, 16, 26, 27, 28, 36, 87, 135-136, 149, 221, 222; Constitutional Union Party, 29; presidential election, 1936, 26, 27, 28, 29, 30; relations with Japan, 22, 50; relations with Mexico, 1, 33-34, 126, 183, 220, 305; defender of Latin America, 46, 63-64, 66-67, 79-80, 90-91, 100, 104, 106, 113-114, 122-123, 145; and Axis, 45-46, 48, 53, 67-68, 73-74, 90-92, 95, 100-107; investment in Latin America, 3, 6, 11-12, 243, 251-254, 257-258, 390-391; trade with Latin America, 9-12, 25-26, 48, 49, 73-74, 76-77, 411; neutrality, 40, 42, 55, 58, 62, 63, 105, 112; "no transfer" principle, 67, 68, 80; relations with Spain, 2, 41-45, 209-210, 348; presidential election, 1940, 87-88; cultural relations, 115-116, 125, 132-134; military preparedness, 48, 62, 63, 66, 92, 103; defense bases, 78, 79, 97, 98, 114, 125, 130, 134, 135, 162, 191, 194, 210; aid to Latin America, 71-72, 75-78, 116-124, 128, 129, 130, 147-148, 194, 235, 331, 367, 370-373, 412; Lend-Lease, 80, 81, 93, 94, 98, 123, 124, 129, 137, 142, 194; war production, 62, 106, 153, 156; dependence upon Latin America, 121, 122, 410-412; price ceilings, 155-156, 237; "Proclaimed List," 100, 101, 139, 142, 178, 196; presidential election, 1944, 149, 176; race situation in, 154, 158, 169, 178-183, 220-221, 387, 405; demobilization, 157, 189-190; and democracy in Latin America, 150, 211-213, 216, 218-219; "Blue Book" ("Memorandum on the Argentine Situation"), 215-216, 403; compared with Russia, 2, 218, 314-317; technical assistance, 245, 257, 325, 361-363, 370-372; bilateral investment agreements, 244, 247; investment guaranty program, 245-248, 257, 390-391; interim arms program, 330; bilateral military agreements, 330-331, 404
United Nations: in World War II, 114, 140, 143-146, 196, 202, 337; post-war organization, 146, 189, 200, 212, 214, 237, 252, 315, 316, 321, 327, 328, 332, 334, 336, 340, 343, 348, 352, 354, 367, 372, 379; mentioned, 302, 386
Urriologoitia, Mamerto, 261

Vaccaro L., Carlos Alfonso, 220
Valadés, José C., 109, 111, 179, 186

Valle, Rafael Heliodoro, 409
Vandenberg, Arthur H., 222, 336
Vargas, Getúlio, 31, 61, 115, 215, 255, 287, 289, 294, 299, 324, 329, 338
Vasconcelos, José, 4, 14, 36, 114, 172, 176, 177, 318
Velasco Ibarra, José María, 136, 148, 287, 339
Veloso, Leão, 214
Venezuelan Basic Economy Corporation, 250
Verissimo, Erico, 84, 85, 86, 159, 160, 176, 185
Vila-Lobos, Heitor, 82
Vildósola, Carlos Silva, 14
Villarroel, Major Gualberto, 138, 140
Villeda Morales, Ramón, 386
Virgin Islands, 117, 118, 120
von Humboldt, Alexander, 410

WACs, 154, 208
Wainer, Samuel, 257, 272
Waiss, Oscar, 404
Walker, William, 2, 150, 403
Wall Street, 7, 8, 15, 21, 23, 30, 52, 97, 315, 344, 403
Walt Disney Productions, Inc., 116
War Manpower Commission, 183
Washington, George, 3, 148
Welles, Sumner, 17, 21, 39, 43, 55, 71, 95, 103, 110, 111, 115, 126, 137, 195, 217
Western Hemisphere Trade Corporations Clause, 122, 243, 247
Whitaker, Professor Arthur P., 143, 388

White, Harry Dexter, 239
Wilson, Woodrow, 17, 19, 26, 221, 292, 318
Workmen's Revolutionary Party, 131
World Health Organization (WHO), 278, 379
World War I, 49, 56, 113, 126, 231, 306, 333, 350
World War II: effects on Latin America, 54-73, 117-120, 147, 195-196, 226, 229-230, 231, 242, 281, 289, 302, 315, 318, 323, 329, 333-334, 348, 364, 383, 388; effects on United States, 56, 58, 60, 62, 66-67, 86, 112, 117-120, 147, 177, 187, 192, 236, 310, 333-334, 348, 357, 383, 388; mentioned, 40, 43, 113, 126, 152, 158, 179, 222, 225, 243, 267, 272, 276, 280, 282, 285, 290, 292, 306, 321, 326, 350, 351, 352, 355, 356, 359, 360, 363, 367, 370, 371, 372, 375, 380, 389, 390, 392, 393, 406, 407, 409
World War III, 312-313, 322, 344

YACIMIENTOS Petrolíferos Fiscales (YPF), Argentina, 291
Yale University Glee Club, 116
Yankeephobia. See Latin America, Anti-"Yanquismo"
Yrigoyen, Hipólito, 302

ZEA, Leopoldo, 305
Zuleta Angel, Dr. Eduardo, 189, 241, 325, 402